The Power of Critical Thinking

The Power of Critical Thinking

SIXTH CANADIAN EDITION

Chris MacDonald
Lewis Vaughn

OXFORD
UNIVERSITY PRESS

Oxford University Press is a department of the University of Oxford.
It furthers the University's objective of excellence in research, scholarship,
and education by publishing worldwide. Oxford is a registered trade mark of
Oxford University Press in the UK and in certain other countries.

Published in Canada by Oxford University Press
8 Sampson Mews, Suite 204, Don Mills, Ontario M3C 0H5 Canada

First Canadian Edition published in 2008
Second Canadian Edition published in 2010
Third Canadian Edition published in 2013
Fourth Canadian Edition published in 2016
Fifth Canadian Edition published in 2019

Library and Archives Canada Cataloguing in Publication

Title: The power of critical thinking / Chris MacDonald, Lewis Vaughn.
Names: Vaughn, Lewis, author. | MacDonald, Chris, 1969- author.
Description: Sixth Canadian edition. | Includes bibliographical references and index.
Identifiers: Canadiana (print) 20230227953 | Canadiana (ebook) 20230228003 | ISBN 9780190163860 (softcover) | ISBN 9780190163877 (loose-leaf) | ISBN 9780190163815 (HTML) | ISBN 9780190163884 (EPUB)
Subjects: LCSH: Critical thinking—Textbooks. | LCGFT: Textbooks.
Classification: LCC BC177 .V38 2023 | DDC 160—dc23

Cover and interior art: © iStock/phototechno
Cover and interior design: Sherill Chapman

Oxford University Press is committed to our environment.
Wherever possible, our books are printed on paper that
comes from responsible sources.

Printed and bound by Marquis, Canada

Brief Contents

Contents

List of Boxes

Food for Thought

Everyday Problems and Decisions

Critical Thinking and the Media

Review Notes

From the Publisher

The sixth Canadian edition of *The Power of Critical Thinking* builds on the successful approach used in the previous Canadian editions that have served instructors and students so well. It gives first-time students a comprehensive, engaging, and step-by-step introduction to critical thinking, providing them with the tools they need to apply their critical thinking skills to the real world.

The sixth edition retains qualities that will be familiar to long-time users while adding new features to help students use their critical thinking skills in everyday life. Highlights include the following:

Student-friendly tone.
Without compromising rigour or oversimplifying material, this introductory text is written in an engaging tone that students will enjoy. The authors tackle tough topics with a casual approach, mixed with humour where appropriate, to enhance students' understanding and enjoyment.

1 | The Power of Critical Thinking 3

When you were born, you were completely without opinions or judg-
ments or values or viewpoints—and now your head is overflowing
with them. Opinions help you to make your way through the world.
They guide you to success (or failure), to understanding (or ignorance), to good
decisions (or bad), and to empowerment (or paralysis). Some of your beliefs truly
empower you, and some blind you. Some of your beliefs are true; some are not. But
the question is, *which ones are which?* **This kind of question—a question about the**
quality of your beliefs—is the fundamental concern of critical thinking.
Determining the quality or value of your beliefs requires thought, and the
kind of thinking that does this job best is critical thinking—a skill that a univer-
sity or college education seeks to foster. This means that critical thinking is not
directly about *what* you think but rather *how* you think.
The quality of beliefs is not about what factors *caused* you to have the beliefs
that you do. A sociologist might tell you how society has influenced some of your
moral views. A psychologist might describe how your emotions cause you to cling
to certain opinions. Your best friend might claim that you have unconsciously
absorbed most of your beliefs directly from your parents. But none of these speculations have much to do with the central task of critical thinking.
Critical thinking focuses not on what *causes* a belief but on *whether it is worth*
believing. A belief is worth believing, or accepting, if we have *good reasons* to accept it.

critical thinking
The systematic evaluation or formulation of beliefs or statements by rational standards.

"... **there is no shame in not** knowing. The problem arises when irrational thought and attendant behavior fill the vacuum left by ignorance."
—Neil deGrasse Tyson

Critical thinking helps us to assess our beliefs and core values. Consider some of your most valued beliefs. Are they supported by good reasoning?

Reasons for Belief and Doubt

Chapter Objectives

When Claims Conflict

You will be able to

- understand that when a claim conflicts with other claims we have good reason to accept, we have good grounds for doubting it.
- recognize that if a claim conflicts with our background information, we have good reason to doubt it.
- appreciate that when we are confronted with a claim that is neither completely dubious nor fully credible, we should proportion our belief to the evidence.
- realize that it is not reasonable to believe a claim when there is no good reason for doing so.

Experts and Evidence

You will be able to

- understand what makes someone an expert and what does not.
- understand that if a claim conflicts with expert opinion, we have good reason to doubt it.
- realize that when the experts disagree about a claim, we have good reason to suspend judgment.
- recognize fallacious appeals to authority.
- distinguish true experts from non-experts by using the four indicators of expertise.

Abundant exercises.

Hundreds of exercises, many of which are updated or new to this edition, draw from contemporary culture, politics, and media to provide students with the practice they need to become confident critical thinkers. Select answers are provided at the back of the book (Appendix B). Additional answers are available in the online student and instructor resources.

Emphasis on evaluation of evidence, authority, and credibility.

Students are encouraged to critically assess evidence and claims put forward by experts, news media, politicians, business leaders, and friends. In each case, the main principles and procedures are explained and illustrated.

An updated art program.

New photos and cartoons, along with thought-provoking captions, reinforce key concepts in each chapter. Most captions pose questions that will prepare students for in-class discussions and participation.

Rigorous attention to detail.

All exercises, philosophical facts, figures, and diagrams have been checked and validated by a panel of leading experts in the field.

6 | Deductive Reasoning: Categorical Logic 227

We'll diagram the first premise first ("All robots are machines")—but not just because it happens to be the first premise. In categorical syllogisms with both a universal and a particular premise, we should always diagram the universal premise first. The reason is that diagramming the particular premise first can lead to confusion. For example, in the argument in question, if we were to diagram the particular premise first ("Some professors are robots"), we would end up with an X in the area where the robots and professors circles overlap. That section, however, is split into two subsections by the machines circle:

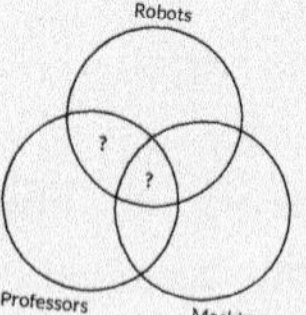

So then the question arises in which subsection we should place the X. (That's why there are question marks in the diagram above—to point out, just for now, the uncertainty.) Should we put the X in the area overlapping with the machines circle—or in the part not overlapping with the machines circle? Our choice *does* affect what the diagram says about the validity of the argument. But if we diagram the universal premise first, the decision of where to insert the X is made for us because there would be only one relevant subsection left (and we can't place an X in a shaded area, because shaded means *empty*):

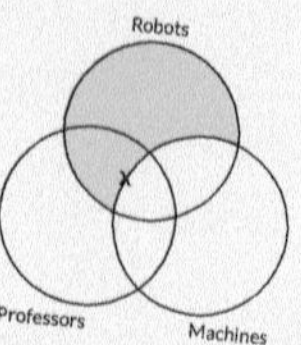

Enhanced Pedagogy

This edition of *The Power of Critical Thinking* builds on the pedagogical approach that has successfully helped students practise and refine their critical thinking skills.

Everyday Problems and Decisions

The Mechanic Says My Car Needs Repairs. But Does It?

When we think about relying on expert advice, we often focus on people with sophisticated scientific knowledge and multiple university degrees—people like heart surgeons and lawyers and structural engineers.

But many of the people we interact with more frequently for everyday household needs fit the definition of "expert" we use in this book. That is, they are more knowledgeable about a particular subject area or field than most other people are. The experienced plumber who fixes a leaky faucet, the electrician who replaces light switches and wiring in your aging house, and the master carpenter who installs new doors on your kitchen cabinet are all experts. They know things about the work they do that most of us simply do not. You might be able to look online to figure out how to replace a light fixture yourself, but an expert electrician can tell you whether, given the age of your house and the state of its wiring, it would be wise for you to attempt to do so. These sorts of experts have both knowledge and judgment that the rest of us

Consider auto mechanics. Fifty years ago, it was relatively common for car o basic maintenance themselves: changing oil, replacing worn brake pads, and even Today—in part because modern automobiles are so much more complex—we are car to a licensed mechanic for that sort of work. Of course, when we take our car to t maintenance, it's always possible that the mechanic will spot additional worries: a loos a wheel out of alignment, or even a transmission in need of replacement. These additional repairs can cost a lot! And when the mechanic gives you the bad news, a new issue arises: are they telling you the truth? It's likely that most mechanics are honest, and won't recommend unnecessary repairs. But the issue raises an important and interesting point about experts in general. We hire experts to do things we don't know how to do. But precisely because we lack their expertise, we often can't tell whether the work they have done for us is good work, or whether the advice they give us is good advice.

"Everyday Problems and Decisions" boxes allow students to apply their critical thinking skills to real-world issues.

1 | The Power of Critical Thinking 13

decide rationally. Generally, when that happens, good critical thinkers do not just randomly choose to accept or reject a statement. They suspend judgment until there is enough evidence to make an intelligent decision.

1.2.2 Reasons and Arguments

Reasons provide support for a statement. That is, they provide us with grounds for believing that a statement is true. Reasons are themselves expressed as statements. So a statement expressing a reason is used to show that another statement is true or likely to be true. This combination of statements—a statement (or statements) supposedly providing reasons for accepting another statement—is known as an **argument**. Arguments are the main focus of critical thinking; they are the most important tool we have for evaluating the truth of statements (our own and those of others) and for formulating statements that are truly worthy of acceptance. Arguments are, therefore, essential for the advancement of knowledge in all fields. In everyday conversation, people use the word *argument* to indicate a debate or an angry exchange. In critical thinking, however, *argument* refers to the process of providing reasons in support of a statement.

The statements (reasons) given in support of another statement are technically called the **premises**. The statement that the premises are intended to support is called the **conclusion**. We can define an argument, then, like this:

ARGUMENT: A group of statements in which some of them (the premises) are intended to support another of them (the conclusion).

The following are some simple arguments:

1. Because you want a job that will allow you to make a difference in the world, you should consider working for a charitable organization like Doctors Without Borders.
2. The *Globe and Mail's Report on Business* says that people should invest heavily in gold. Therefore, investing in gold is a smart move.
3. When Joseph takes the bus, he's always late. And he's taking the bus today, so I'm sure he's going to be late.
4. A lot of my friends have seen that Netflix movie, and literally none of them said it was any good. And my mom hated it. So it must be pretty bad.
5. No one should drink a beer brewed by a giant corporation. Labatt's Blue is brewed by a giant corporation. So no one should drink it.

Here are the same arguments where the parts are easily identified:

1. [Premise] Because you want a job that will allow you to make a difference in the world, [Conclusion] you should consider working for a charitable organization like Doctors Without Borders.
2. [Premise] *The Globe and Mail's Report on Business* says that people should invest heavily in gold. [Conclusion] Therefore, investing in gold is a smart move.

argument
A group of statements in which some of them (the premises) are intended to support another of them (the conclusion).

premise
In an argument, a statement or reason given in support of the conclusion.

conclusion
In an argument, the statement that the premises are intended to support.

A marginal glossary highlights key terms near their first mention in the text, reinforcing important concepts for students.

Review Notes

Why Critical Thinking Matters

- Our thinking guides our actions, so it should be of high quality.
- If you have never critically examined your beliefs, they are not truly yours.
- Critical thinking is one way of defending against the cognitive biases that tend to lead us to sions and bad decisions.
- To examine your beliefs is to examine your life. Socrates said: "The unexamined life is not v
- Critical thinking involves determining what we're justified in believing, being open to new p fairly assessing the views of others and ourselves.
- Critical thinking complements our emotions and can enhance our creativity.
- Critical thinking is thinking outside the box.

"Review Notes" boxes appear throughout each chapter to reiterate the main points of chapter sections, improving comprehension and making later review more efficient.

Food for Thought

Folk Psychology

A big part of our "background information" comes from folk psychology, the skill we all have for correctly attributing to other people (and sometimes animals) moods, beliefs, desires, intentions, memories, and so on. We use the fact that other people have those things as a way to explain and predict their behaviour.

Have you ever seen someone lifting cushions off a couch one at a time or lifting pieces of paper on a desk to look under them? If you have, you probably immediately knew what was going on: they were searching for something. You recognize the behaviour: that's what searching looks like. Or imagine you know that your friend John loves chocolate and hates vanilla. The waiter at lunch tells you that the dessert special today is chocolate or vanilla. What will John choose? Yes, you can quite easily predict the future here and without any magical powers. You know that John will choose chocolate. How do you know? Not just beca that John loves chocolate but because you know that people tend to choose things they love psychological principle, and you don't need a PhD in psychology to know it.

The term *folk psychology* was coined by the philosopher Daniel Dennett in 1981. Folk p sists, according to Dennett, of the stuff everyone knows about how other people's minds wor other people have hopes and dreams; that they love some things and hate other things; tha things that happen to them; that they can perceive the world around them using their sens hearing, touch, and so on.

Our capacity for folk psychology is essential; it's what allows us to live and work togethe psychology is what lets you know that punching someone will make them mad, that gossip will hurt their feelings, and that flirting with their girlfriend will make them jealous. And you ca

"Food for Thought" boxes provide additional, sometimes humorous, material on a topic and challenge students to apply the critical thinking skills they are learning. The material is purposely diverse in both subject matter and format, and has been extensively updated in this edition to cover fresh and contemporary topics.

Critical Thinking and the Media

Why Critical Thinking Matters in a Media-Rich World

The dominance of media—including old-fashioned media like TV and newspapers, as well as modern social media like Facebook and Instagram and Twitter—helps to make clear the relevance of critical thinking.

Picture first a very different context: imagine yourself on a moon base, working alone as a technician to maintain the base's systems until the next batch of astronauts arrive. This is clearly an important task, one that requires some critical thinking. Is that alarm a sign of real trouble, or just a faulty light? When Mission Control says, "There's a small problem, but it's under control," are they hiding something or telling you the truth? What's the best way to fix that leaky hose? These are all issues that require you to consider options, use your knowledge, and arrive at the best beliefs possible under the circumstances. But while the issues may be substantial, the critical thinking tasks are relatively straightforward. You have the and the only people you are in contact with—the staff at Mission Control—are very clearly on yc

Now consider the world you really live in. As you navigate your own life—school, family, wo many questions on which you may not have much expertise. What computer should you buy? you date? Which school should you attend? How much exercise do you need? And on many of you'll be getting input from a large range of sources, including friends, family, news reporters,

New "Critical Thinking and the Media" boxes apply the critical thinking skills discussed in each chapter to the topics of media, advertising, and news, helping students become more critical consumers of media.

1 | The Power of Critical Thinking 23

Exercise 1.3

Which of the following passages contain *arguments*? For each argument you find, specify what the conclusion is.

1. Nachos are delicious and easy to make. So they're the perfect study food.*
2. Nachos are delicious and easy to make, which is why I make them whenever I'm studying.
3. Don't do that—you'll break it!
4. This weather is perfect for going to the beach! There's also a discount on surfing lessons that's good today only!
5. Is Alexei planning on buying a new motorcycle this year?
6. If you light that cigarette in here, I will leave the room.
7. *Independence Day: Resurgence* was a terrible movie, and not even Liam Hemsworth could save it.*
8. I know that David Hume was the greatest philosopher of the last 500 years because my philosophy professor taught us that in class.
9. Iron Man is a cooler superhero than Thor because technology is just way cooler than mythology.
10. "Whether our argument concerns public affairs or some other subject, we must know some, if not all, of the facts about the subject on which we are to speak and argue. Otherwise, we can have no materials out of which to construct arguments." (Aristotle, *Rhetoric*)
11. If you hire Kaitlin, you'll have a first-rate editor. You should hire Kaitlin.*
12. Many believe that there is no soul and that the mind is simply a result of electrical and chemical signals interacting in the brain. So they think that consciousness is a purely physical phenomenon. I reject this notion!
13. "Canada's economy has been unambiguously strong for about a year, according to the high-frequency data Statistics Canada collects every month. Gross domestic product probably will expand by at least three per cent this year, something that some economists thought our aging and relatively unproductive economy might never do again. The unemployment rate (6.2 per cent in August) is about as low is it ever gets, and could push lower still. The median household income in Canada is about $70,000, roughly 10 per cent more than a decade ago, according to census figures released last month. That's an excellent number, considering household wealth in the United States barely grew over the same period." (Kevin Carmichael, in *Canadian Business*, 6 October 2017)
14. "Murtaza Haider, a professor of real estate management and the director of the Urban Institute at [Toronto Metropolitan University], said renting and buying can each make sense at different points in life. For those who are in their 20s or early 30s, renting might be a better option because it provides flexibility. 'When you're young, I would say that the better

Hundreds of exercises cover a wide range of topics. They are found throughout each chapter, presented progressively from simple to complex, elementary to more advanced, and familiar to unusual.

Contemporary Design

The design of the sixth Canadian edition reflects the vibrancy and excitement of learning how to think critically without sacrificing content or authoritativeness.

Aids to Student Learning

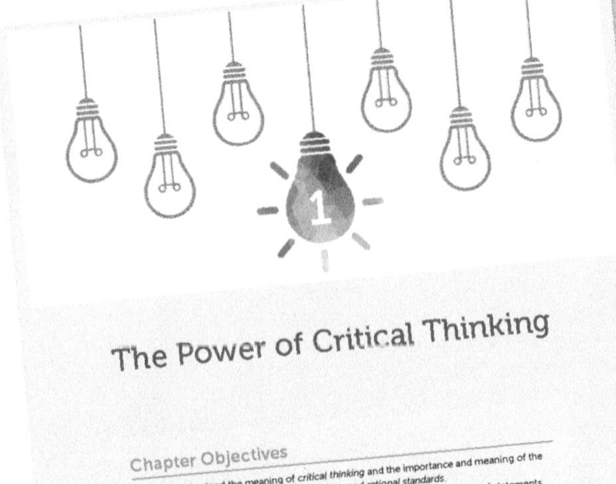

The Power of Critical Thinking

Chapter Objectives

- To understand the meaning of *critical thinking* and the importance and meaning of the terms *systematic*, *evaluation*, *formulation*, and *rational standards*.
- To understand how critical thinking is related to logic, the truth or falsity of statements, knowledge, and personal empowerment.

Why It Matters

You will be able to

- appreciate why critical thinking is better than the passive acceptance of beliefs.
- appreciate the relevance of the claim "The unexamined life is not worth living" to critical thinking.
- understand the flaws in the following claims: "Critical thinking makes people too critical or cynical," "Critical thinking makes people cold and unemotional," and "Critical thinking is the enemy of creativity."
- appreciate the usefulness of critical thinking in all human activities.

How It Works

You will be able to

- distinguish between statements and non-statements.
- understand the basic concepts of reasons, argument, inference, premise, and conclusion.
- use indicator words to help identify premises and conclusions.
- distinguish between passages that do and do not contain an argument.
- identify arguments in various contexts and distinguish between arguments and superfluous material, between arguments and explanations, and between premises and conclusions.

Chapter openers preview the contents of each chapter with chapter objectives that provide a concise overview of the key concepts to be covered.

Chapter summaries at the end of each chapter provide additional support to ensure that students have identified and understood key concepts.

Writing modules embedded within the end-of-chapter student activities in the first five chapters introduce the rudiments of argumentative essay-writing.

2 | The "Environment" of Critical Thinking 59

Critical Thinking and Writing Exercise

From Issue to Thesis

For many students, the biggest challenge in writing an argumentative essay is deciding on an appropriate thesis—the claim, or conclusion, that the essay is designed to support or prove. Very often, when an essay runs off track and crashes, the derailment can be traced to a thesis that was bad from the beginning.

Picking a thesis out of the air and beginning to write is usually a mistake. Any thesis statement that you craft without knowing anything about the subject is likely to be ill-formed or indefensible. It's better to begin by selecting an issue—a question that's controversial or in dispute—and then researching it to determine what arguments or viewpoints are involved. To research it, you can survey the views of people or organizations involved in the controversy. Read articles and books, talk to people, and do some research online. This process should not only inform you about various viewpoints but also tell you what arguments are used to support them. It should also help you to narrow the issue down to one that you can easily address in the space you have.

Suppose you begin with the question of whether Canada has serious industrial pollution problems. After investigating this issue, you would probably see that it is much too broad to be addressed in a short paper. You should then restrict the issue to something more manageable—for example, whether recent legislation to allow coal-burning power plants to emit more sulphur dioxide will harm people's health. With the scope of the issue narrowed, you can explore arguments on both sides. You cannot examine every single argument, but you should assess the strongest ones, including those that you devise yourself. You can then use what you've already learned about arguments to select one that you think provides good support for its conclusion. The premises and conclusion of this argument can then serve as the bare-bones outline of your essay. Your argument might look like this:

[Premise 1] High amounts of sulphur dioxide in the air have been linked to increases in the incidence of asthma and other respiratory illnesses.

[Premise 2] Many areas of the country already have high amounts of sulphur dioxide in the air.

[Premise 3] Most sulphur dioxide in the air comes from coal-burning power plants.

[Conclusion] Therefore, allowing coal-burning power plants to emit more sulphur dioxide will most likely increase the incidence of respiratory illnesses.

For the sake of the example, the premises of this argument are made up. But the argument of your essay must be real, with each premise that could be called into question supported by an additional argument. After all, your readers are not likely to accept the conclusion of your argument if they doubt your premises.

In some cases, your paper may contain more than one argument supporting a single conclusion, or it may offer a critique of someone else's argument. In either case, investigating an issue and the arguments involved will follow the pattern just suggested. In a critique of an argument (or arguments), you offer reasons why the argument fails and you thereby support the thesis that the conclusion is false or at least unsupported.

This process of devising a thesis statement and crafting an argument to back it up is not linear. You will probably have to experiment with several arguments before you find one that's suitable. Even after you decide on an argument, you may later discover that its premises are dubious or that they cannot be adequately supported. Then you will have to backtrack to investigate a better argument. Backtracking in this preliminary stage is relatively easy. But if you postpone this rethinking process until you are almost finished with your first draft, it will be harder—and more painful.

232 Part Three | Arguments

2. Doritos are delicious, because Doritos are salty and high in fat and all foods that are salty and high in fat are delicious.
3. All SUVs are evil vehicles because all SUVs are gas guzzlers and all gas guzzlers are evil vehicles.*
4. Anyone who thinks meat production is environmentally sustainable is ill-informed. Since a majority of people who eat meat think meat production is environmentally sustainable, a majority of people who eat meat are ill-informed.
5. Cancer patients are not allowed to donate their organs because the organs could contain cancer. And no doctor would allow the donation of organs that could contain cancer.
6. Some electric vehicles are "clean" vehicles, since all clean vehicles ultimately get their energy from renewable resources, and some electric vehicles do not ultimately get their energy from renewable resources.
7. Some arguments are valid, so some syllogisms must be valid since all syllogisms are arguments.
8. No wimps are social activists because no wimps are people of honest and strong convictions. And all social activists are people of honest and strong convictions.*
9. Most people who drive SUVs are road hogs who don't care about the environment or environmental issues. Road hogs who don't care about the environment or environmental issues are the true enemies of the planet. **Therefore, people who drive SUVs are the true enemies of the planet.**
10. Some useless gimmicks promoted as "sure cures" are placebos that can make people feel good. Vitamin pills are useless gimmicks promoted as sure cures for a variety of illnesses. So some vitamin pills are placebos that can make people feel good even if they don't cure anything.

Field Problems

1. Think of a piece of *ethical advice* you have received that was presented in syllogistic form. (Hint: this often happens when a speaker's first premise is a general ethical principle and his or her second premise relates that rule to your current situation. The conclusion will be advice aimed specifically at you.) Is the argument a good one? Did you take the advice?
2. Check recent news reports to find one categorical statement made by a prominent Canadian or American business leader. Translate the statement into standard form. (1) Construct a *valid* categorical syllogism using the statement as the conclusion and supplying whatever premises you deem appropriate. Assume that your premises are true. (2) Then construct an *invalid* syllogism using the same statement as the conclusion and supplying premises, also assumed to be true. In both arguments, try to keep the statements as realistic as possible (e.g., close to what you may actually read in a newsmagazine).
3. Go online and check the opinion or editorial section of your local newspaper or one of the national newspapers (the *Globe and Mail* or

6 | Deductive Reasoning: Categorical Logic 233

National Post). Within one of the editorials or letters to the editor, find a categorical syllogism that you suspect is invalid. Recall that, in many cases, arguers will leave a premise or conclusion unstated, so you might only see two of the three claims that make up the syllogism and have to infer what the third one is. Assess its validity using the Venn diagram method. If it is indeed invalid, write a 150- to 200-word explanation of how you would explain, to someone who doesn't know about categorical logic, what's wrong with the argument.

Self-Assessment Quiz

1. What are the two qualities that can be expressed in categorical statements?
2. What is a quantifier? What are the two quantities that can be used in categorical statements?

For each of the following statements, identify the subject and predicate terms, the quality, the quantity, and the name of the form (universal affirmative, universal negative, particular affirmative, or particular negative).

3. Every employee who works under Françoise quits within a month.
4. No excuse is a good enough excuse for breaking a promise to a friend.
5. Some animals are not good pets.

Translate each of the following statements into standard categorical form, and indicate whether the form is A, E, I, or O.

6. A man who sexually harasses women cannot truly be called a man.
7. Swimming is a good form of exercise.
8. Hasko is the finest scholar in the department.
9. Nobody who wants an A in this class would wait until the night before the exam to study.
10. A politician is someone who firmly believes that getting elected makes one right.

Construct Venn diagrams to test the validity of each of the following syllogisms.

11. No *S* are *M*. No *M* are *P*. Therefore, all *S* are *P*.
12. All *S* are *M*. Some *P* are not *M*. Therefore, some *S* are not *P*.
13. All *M* are *P*. All *M* are *S*. Therefore, all *S* are *P*.
14. All *M* are *P*. Some *S* are not *M*. Therefore, some *S* are not *P*.
15. No *S* are *M*. All *P* are *M*. Therefore, no *S* are *P*.

Integrative Exercises

These exercises pertain to material in Chapters 1–6.

1. What is critical thinking?
2. What is an argument?
3. Wh...

For each of the following arguments, specify the conclusion and premises, and indicate any argument indicator words.

234 Part Three | Arguments

anything bad, so she must be doing it for your own good.

6. I will go for a jog unless it's raining, and I will stay home if my kids are sick. The kids aren't sick; therefore, I will go for a jog.
7. Either Canada will eventually deal justly with Indigenous peoples or it will be satisfied to live with injustice for generations to come. But Canadians will not be satisfied to live with injustice. So Canada will eventually deal justly with Indigenous peoples.
8. Either Sareh is irresponsible, or something prevented her from being on time. She's never irresponsible, so something must have prevented her from being on time.

For each of the following arguments, determine whether it is deductive or inductive, valid or invalid, and strong or weak.

9. Kevin is either deluded or a fraud. If he actually believes in the healing power of herbal tea, he's deluded. If he's selling it without believing in it, he's a fraud. And he's too smart to be deluded. He's a fraud.
10. Assad currently works for Microsoft and was hired six months ago. Anyone who isn't fired within three months of being hired by Microsoft will probably stay at the company for the rest of their career. That's why Assad will most likely spend the rest of his career at Microsoft.
11. I read that book and thought it was boring. You're not going to like it.
12. The comet has appeared in the sky every 60 years for the past four centuries. It will appear in the sky again tonight. Tonight is precisely 60 years since its last appearance.

For each of the following arguments, identify the implicit premise that will make the argument valid.

13. Either you drank the last beer in the fridge or I did. So it must have been you!
14. My sister just ate sushi at a totally sketchy place in a bad part of town, and the raw tuna she ate smelled a bit funky. I'll just go ahead and dial 911 now!
15. The prime minister accepted a significant gift from someone who happened to be seeking special favours from the government. The prime minister should therefore resign.

Writing Assignments

1. Write a 600-word essay arguing either for or against making vaccination mandatory during a pandemic. Structure your argument as a categorical syllogism.
2. Write a 300-word criticism of your own argument from Question 1 above. Focus your criticism on whichever of your categorical premises you think an opponent is most likely to focus on.
3. Write a 600-word rebuttal to Essay 9 ("What If You Could Save 250 Lives by Feeling a Little Disgusted?") in Appendix A. Make sure to note Essay 9's premises and conclusion.

Student activities included at the end of each chapter reinforce concepts and ideas through a variety of formats, including the following:

- "Field Problems" that invite students to apply newly acquired and refined critical thinking skills to real-world problems.
- "Self-Assessment Quizzes" that allow students to test their understanding of the material.
- "Integrative Exercises" that help students to bring information and techniques from multiple chapters together, ensuring that their understanding of critical thinking is comprehensive.
- "Writing Assignments" that allow students to apply their knowledge and to practise working in longer formats such as essays.

Supplements

The Power of Critical Thinking also includes a comprehensive online ancillary package available at **www.oup.com/he/MacDonald-Vaughn6Ce**. An instructor's manual, a test bank, and a comprehensive set of PowerPoint slides are available to those teaching the course. (Please contact your OUP sales representative for login and password information.) A student study guide is also available online (no password required); this effective resource allows students to take advantage of study notes, practice quizzes, and additional exercises.

Preface

It is a pleasure to introduce the sixth edition of the Canadian version of *The Power of Critical Thinking*. It is, once again, about as Canadian as a beaver politely sipping a Tim Hortons coffee while watching a hockey game. Once again, all ten of the Essays for Evaluation at the back of the book are by Canadian authors, writing about things Canadians care about. Beyond continued frequent references to all things Canadian, though, we've updated many of the end-of-chapter exercises, expanded discussions of key concepts, and added several new textboxes, including a new textbox on critical thinking and the media in every single chapter. As in previous editions, we've worked hard to keep the book readable and informal yet rigorous. No one would believe us if we described a textbook as *fun*, but we like to think that this is as close to fun as a textbook can be expected to get.

Acknowledgements

Most of the key ideas in this book were found on a crystal tablet delivered to the authors by little green people from Mars. Just kidding! A book like this is the product of plenty of hard work by real Earth-people, including people other than those lucky enough to have their names on the front cover. Among those who deserve thanks, I'd like to begin at the very top of the list with my friends at Oxford University Press, including Jeff Marshall and *especially* Kelly Lewars and Emma Guttman-Moy, for their patience and support and for the very high quality of their work. Emma and Kelly, in particular, were patient and gracious beyond all reasonable expectations in dealing with a professor who always has too much going on, and who wasn't always as good as he should have been at answering emails quickly. I'd also like to thank my terrific research assistant, Priyanka Datta, for her very keen eye in going over the manuscript and helping me update it in numerous important ways. In addition, I would like to thank several anonymous reviewers for their excellent feedback and suggestions. I'd also *like* to blame the reviewers and editors for any mistakes that you may find. But of course, you're a critical thinker, so you won't believe that for a second. Naturally, I bear responsibility for whatever mistakes remain. If you spot a mistake—and if you're really sure it's a mistake!—please do let me know. Finally, as always, I would like to thank Professor Nancy Walton, who expands both my mind and my heart every day.

Reviewers

We gratefully acknowledge the contributions of the following reviewers as well as those who chose to remain anonymous, whose insightful comments and suggestions have helped to make this new edition better than it would otherwise have been:

Peter Denton, International College of Manitoba
Blake Freier, University of Waterloo
Thomas Land, University of Victoria/Toronto Metropolitan University
Brian Lefresne, Humber College

Chris MacDonald
Ted Rogers School of Management
Toronto Metropolitan University

The Power of Critical Thinking

PART ONE

Basics

The Power of Critical Thinking

Chapter Objectives

- To understand the meaning of *critical thinking* and the importance and meaning of the terms *systematic*, *evaluation*, *formulation*, and *rational standards*.
- To understand how critical thinking is related to logic, the truth or falsity of statements, knowledge, and personal empowerment.

Why It Matters

You will be able to

- appreciate why critical thinking is better than the passive acceptance of beliefs.
- appreciate the relevance of the claim "The unexamined life is not worth living" to critical thinking.
- understand the flaws in the following claims: "Critical thinking makes people too critical or cynical," "Critical thinking makes people cold and unemotional," and "Critical thinking is the enemy of creativity."
- appreciate the usefulness of critical thinking in all human activities.

How It Works

You will be able to

- distinguish between statements and non-statements.
- understand the basic concepts of reasons, argument, inference, premise, and conclusion.
- use indicator words to help identify premises and conclusions.
- distinguish between passages that do and do not contain an argument.
- identify arguments in various contexts and distinguish between arguments and superfluous material, between arguments and explanations, and between premises and conclusions.

When you were born, you were completely without opinions or judgments or values or viewpoints—and now your head is overflowing with them. Opinions help you to make your way through the world. They guide you to success (or failure), to understanding (or ignorance), to good decisions (or bad), and to empowerment (or paralysis). Some of your beliefs truly empower you, and some blind you. Some of your beliefs are true; some are not. But the question is, *which ones are which?* This kind of question—a question about the *quality* of your beliefs—is the fundamental concern of **critical thinking**.

critical thinking
The systematic evaluation or formulation of beliefs or statements by rational standards.

Determining the quality or value of your beliefs requires thought, and the kind of thinking that does this job best is critical thinking—a skill that a university or college education seeks to foster. This means that critical thinking is not directly about *what* you think but rather *how* you think.

The quality of beliefs is not about what factors *caused* you to have the beliefs that you do. A sociologist might tell you how society has influenced some of your moral views. A psychologist might describe how your emotions cause you to cling to certain opinions. Your best friend might claim that you have unconsciously absorbed most of your beliefs directly from your parents. But none of these speculations have much to do with the central task of critical thinking.

"... there is no shame in not knowing. The problem arises when irrational thought and attendant behavior fill the vacuum left by ignorance."
—Neil deGrasse Tyson

Critical thinking focuses not on what *causes* a belief but on *whether it is worth believing*. A belief is worth believing, or accepting, if we have *good reasons* to accept it.

Critical thinking helps us to assess our beliefs and core values. Consider some of your most valued beliefs. Are they supported by good reasoning?

The better the reasons, the more likely the belief is to be true. Critical thinking offers us a set of standards embodied in techniques, attitudes, and principles that we can use to assess beliefs and determine if they are supported by good reasons. After all, we want our beliefs to be true—to be good guides for dealing with the world—and critical thinking is the best tool we have for achieving this goal.

Here's one way to wrap up these points in a concise definition:

> **CRITICAL THINKING:** The systematic evaluation or formulation of beliefs or statements by rational standards.

Critical thinking is *systematic* because it involves distinct procedures and methods. It entails *evaluation* and *formulation* because it's used both to assess existing beliefs (yours or someone else's) and to arrive at new ones. And it operates according to *rational standards* because it involves beliefs that are judged by how well they are supported by reasons.

The effort involved in thinking critically is well worth it because it is one of the few tools we have to counteract the natural limitations of the human brain. Some of those limitations are pretty easy to spot, of course. All of us make mistakes of reasoning from time to time: we fail to give enough attention to key facts, we forget things, we jump to conclusions, and so on. But some errors of reasoning are more common than others. Some are so common that psychologists have studied them and given them names. These are called "cognitive biases," and evidence suggests that some of them are nearly universal—that is, they affect all of us. For example, we tend to judge facts differently depending on just how they are stated, or "framed." We might react quite positively to an announcement that a struggling company had been able to "save" 300 jobs (out of 1000) but quite negatively to an announcement that the company was "laying off" 700 people (out of 1000), even though the result is exactly the same. Framing the issue in terms of jobs saved—which sounds like a good thing—makes us think more positively about the whole scenario. Another example of cognitive bias: if you ask people to estimate how likely it is that the average Canadian will die in a car crash compared to how likely it is that they will die in a plane crash, they're likely to overestimate the relative likelihood of dying in a plane crash, just because they've seen scary images on TV of planes crashing and can readily call those images to mind. (In reality, even those who fly frequently are much less likely to die in a plane crash than in a car crash.) In general, we tend to overestimate how common dramatic events are and underestimate how common more boring events are. (Some more of these cognitive biases are touched upon in Chapter 4.) We know that mistakes of reasoning like these are common, and it's easy to see how they can lead to bad conclusions and bad decisions—bad decisions about how to invest our time, bad decisions about how to travel, bad decisions about what to eat, and so on. Our best defence is to look at the facts carefully and think critically.

logic
The study of good reasoning, or inference, and the rules that govern it.

Critical thinking, of course, involves **logic**. Logic is the study of good reasoning, or inference, and the rules that govern it. But critical thinking is broader than logic because it involves not only logic but also the examination of the truth or falsity of individual statements, the evaluation of arguments and evidence, the use of analysis and investigation, and the application of many other skills that help us to decide what to believe or do.

Ultimately, what critical thinking leads you to is knowledge, understanding, and—if you put these to work—empowerment. In Chapters 2 and 3, you'll get a more thorough grounding in critical thinking and logical argumentation as well as plenty of opportunities to practise your new skills. Consider this chapter an introduction to those important lessons. Focus on soaking up the big ideas. They will help you to prepare for the skills you'll learn in later chapters.

1.1 Why It Matters

In large part, who we are is defined by our actions and choices, and our actions and choices are guided by our thinking—so our thinking had better be good. Almost every day we are hit by a blizzard of opinions, assertions, arguments, and pronouncements from all directions. They all try to get us to believe, to agree, to accept, to follow, to submit. If we care whether our choices are right and our beliefs true, if we want to rise above blind acceptance and random choices, we need to use the tools provided by critical thinking.

Of course, we always have the option of taking the easy way out. We can simply grab whatever beliefs or statements come blowing by in the wind, adopting viewpoints either because others hold them or because they make us feel good. But then we give up control over our lives and let the wind take us in some random direction as if we had no more say in the outcome than a leaf in a storm.

A consequence of going with the wind is a loss of personal freedom. If you passively accept beliefs that have been handed to you by your parents, your culture, your teachers, or social media, then those beliefs are *not really yours*. You just happened to be in a certain place and time when they were handed out. If they are not really yours and if you still let them guide your choices and actions, then they—not you—are in charge of your life. Your beliefs are yours only if you critically examine them for yourself and decide that they are supported by good reasons.

Of course, thinking critically is not only important because of how it matters for ourselves. It is also important because of the impact that our decisions have on other people. If we are parents, then we ought to think critically about the health care choices we make on behalf of our children. If we are professionals, we have a duty to think critically about the advice and guidance we offer our clients or patients. And all of us have an obligation to think critically in order to make good choices about how we treat our shared environment—whether that means keeping our shared classroom environment tidy or preserving our natural environment for future generations.

Food for Thought

Were We Overconfident about Overconfidence?

When you're not very good at something, are you likely to know it? Are people who know little about a topic likely to realize how little they know? Several decades ago, two psychology professors, David Dunning and Justin Kruger, decided to find out. They gave student volunteers short tests on topics like logic and grammar. Then they asked each student how well each of them thought they had done. Some students thought they had done better than they really had, and some thought they had done worse. But what was most interesting is that Dunning and Kruger thought they detected a pattern: the students who had done badly tended to think they had done better than they really had, but students who had done well tended to believe they had done worse than they really had. This study, and others like it, soon became quite famous and led to what is now called "the Dunning–Kruger effect," according to which people who know little about a topic tend to have an exaggerated idea of how much they know, and people who know a lot about a topic tend more often to be too modest.

National Palace Museum/Wikipedia

"To know that you do not know is the best. To think you know when you do not is a disease. Recognizing this disease as a disease is to be free of it."

—Lao Tzu, Chinese Philosopher

However, there is more to the story. Many researchers accepted (and some seemed to verify) the work done by Dunning and Kruger, and its conclusions were thus accepted by psychologists for nearly two decades. But other researchers have since re-examined Dunning and Kruger's data, and have criticized their analysis. One group of researchers, led by Edward Nuhfer, demonstrated that the patterns Dunning and Kruger spotted can easily result from random data—that is, such patterns can appear (for complex mathematical reasons) even if there's no real pattern to how people over- and underestimate their own understanding. Other research suggested that overconfidence and underconfidence are in fact pretty evenly distributed.

So the existence of the Dunning–Kruger effect is today very much in doubt. But what remains much more certain is the danger that lies—for all of us!—in overestimating how much we know. Overconfidence is to be avoided wherever possible.

The story of the Dunning–Kruger effect is also a very good illustration of the power of science to self-correct through critical thinking. We'll discuss that further in Chapter 10.

Our choice to apply critical thinking skills is not an all-or-nothing decision. Each of us already uses critical thinking to some degree. We often evaluate reasons for (and against) believing that someone famous has committed a crime, that one candidate in an election is better than another, that regulation of biotechnology should be strengthened or weakened, that we should buy a particular kind of car, that a new friend is trustworthy, that one university is better than another, that the piece of legislation being considered in Parliament would be bad for the environment, or that buying stock in Apple is a good investment. But the more urgent consideration is not just whether we sometimes use critical thinking, but *how well* we use it.

"If I ever go to Japan, I'm sure the pilot will be able to find it, so why do I have to know where it is?"

We don't always have the option of leaving the hard thinking to others!

Many people, however, will reject all of this—and maybe you are one of them. Such people believe that critical thinking—or what they assume to be critical thinking—makes a person excessively critical or cynical, emotionally cold, and creatively constrained. For example, there are some who think that anything that sounds like logic and rationality must be negative—designed to attack someone else's thinking and score points by putting people in their place. A few of them take the word "critical" here to mean "negative" or "whiny" or "picky."

"By three methods we may learn wisdom: First, by reflection, which is noblest; second is by imitation, which is easiest; and third by experience, which is the bitterest."

—Confucius

Now, no doubt some people try to use critical thinking primarily for offensive purposes—for example, to score cheap points in a debate—but this approach goes against critical thinking principles. The *critical* in critical thinking is used in the sense of "exercising or involving careful judgment or judicious evaluation." Critical thinking is about determining what we are justified in believing, and that involves an openness to other points of view, a tolerance for opposing perspectives, a focus on the issue at hand, and fair assessments of arguments and evidence.

Some people fear that if they apply critical thinking to their lives, they will become cold and unemotional—like a computer that works strictly according to logic and mathematical functions. But this fear is misplaced. Critical thinking and feelings actually work best together. Certainly, part of thinking critically is ensuring that we don't let our emotions distort our judgments, but critical thinking can also help us to clarify our feelings and deal with them more effectively. Our emotions often need the guidance of reason. If you're angry at a friend because she broke a promise, *reason* might prompt you to look into the situation further, perhaps to find out whether your friend actually had a valid excuse for breaking that promise. Likewise, our reasoning needs our emotions. It is our feelings that motivate us to action, and without motivation our reasoning would never get off the ground.

Everyday Problems and Decisions

What Should I Believe?

Decisions about what to believe are some of the most important decisions we ever make. What we believe shapes who we are, and our beliefs guide us in what we decide to do. Decisions about what to believe, in other words, are the foundations for all of our *other* decisions. Consider the importance of each of the following decisions about what to believe:

Whether I believe. . .	**influences whether I. . .**
COVID-19 is a serious public health risk	get vaccinated.
that a particular politician is honest	vote for her.
I can afford mortgage payments	buy a house.
that my neighbour's dog is friendly	pat it on the head or stay clear.
that a particular country is safe to visit	take my vacation there.

Food for Thought

Passion and Reason

"Reason is, and ought only to be the slave of the passions." That's what Scottish philosopher David Hume wrote in his *Treatise on Human Nature* (1738). What did he mean by this? He meant roughly that reason, far from being at odds with emotion, is best thought of as serving it. Our emotions (or "passions" as Hume referred to them) tell us what we *want*; our reason tells us what to *do* about it, based in part on what we can reasonably believe will be effective in achieving our goals. Our passions, for example, may tell us that we want to become a lawyer—perhaps because we want to promote justice and defend the innocent. But it is *reason* that helps us to get there. Reason tells us that, in order to become a lawyer, we need to study hard during our undergraduate careers, get good grades, and go to law school.

Then there's the dubious assumption that critical thinking is the enemy of creativity. To some people, critical thinking is a cold and rigid mode of thought that limits the imagination, hinders artistic vision, and prevents "thinking outside the box." But critical thinking and creative thinking are not at all opposed to one another. Good critical thinkers can let their imaginations run free, just like anyone else. They can create and enjoy poetry, music, art, literature, and plain old fun in the same way and to the same degree as the rest of the world. Critical thinking can complement creative thinking because it is needed to assess and enhance whatever is created. Scientists, for example, often dream up some very far-fetched theories (an important part of doing science). These theories pop into their heads in the same way that the idea for a great work of art appears in the mind of a painter. But then scientists use all their critical thinking skills to evaluate what they have produced (as artists typically do)—and this critical examination enables them to select the most promising theories and to weed out those that are unworkable. (We'll return to the notion of testing theories in Chapter 10.)

In a very important sense, critical thinking simply *is* thinking outside the box. When we passively absorb the ideas we encounter, when we refuse to consider any alternative explanations or theories, when we conform our beliefs to the wishes of the group, and when we let our thinking be controlled by bias, stereotypes, superstition, and wishful thinking, that's when we are deep, deep in the box. But when we have the courage to think critically, we can rise above all that. When we are willing to put our beliefs on trial in the court of critical reason, we open ourselves up to new possibilities, the dormant seeds of creativity.

Critical thinking covers a lot of territory. It's used across the board in all disciplines, all areas of public life, all the sciences, all sectors of business, and all occupations. (You'll see some examples of this in Chapter 11.) It has played a major role in all the great endeavours of humankind—scientific discoveries, technological innovations, philosophical insights, social and political movements, literary creation and criticism, judicial and legal reasoning, democratic nation-building, and more. The *lack* of critical thinking has also left its mark. Many of the great tragedies of history—including wars, massacres, holocausts, tyrannies, bigotries, epidemics, and witch hunts—grew out of famines of the mind where clear, careful thinking was much too scarce.

Food for Thought

Architecture: Creativity through Critical Thinking

Creativity and critical thinking are inseparable in the field of architecture. Facing regulatory constraints (building codes, municipal bylaws), physical constraints (structural requirements, material limitations), and project-specific constraints (client desires and budget), an architect adds his or her personal experience, knowledge of precedent, and abstract problem-solving to develop a clear physical design solution. The most creative architectural designs result from a complex web of information, skillfully interpreted.

Eric Fruhauf

As you work your way through this book, think about the parallels between the field of architecture and the general task of critical thinking.

In architecture school, it is the design critique session or 'crit' that prepares architects for this design process. Each student's design is presented to a group of fellow students, professors, and practitioners; its merits are tested, difficult questions are asked, and alternatives suggested. This process of critical thinking, over time, hones the architect's creative skills.

—Eric Fruhauf, OAA. Professor of Architecture, Civil, and Building Science at Algonquin College, Ottawa.

Review Notes

Why Critical Thinking Matters

- Our thinking guides our actions, so it should be of high quality.
- If you have never critically examined your beliefs, they are not truly yours.
- Critical thinking is one way of defending against the cognitive biases that tend to lead us to false conclusions and bad decisions.
- To examine your beliefs is to examine your life. Socrates said: "The unexamined life is not worth living."
- Critical thinking involves determining what we're justified in believing, being open to new perspectives, and fairly assessing the views of others and ourselves.
- Critical thinking complements our emotions and can enhance our creativity.
- Critical thinking is thinking outside the box.

Critical Thinking and the Media

Why Critical Thinking Matters in a Media-Rich World

The dominance of media—including old-fashioned media like TV and newspapers, as well as modern social media like Facebook and Instagram and Twitter—helps to make clear the relevance of critical thinking.

Picture first a very different context: imagine yourself on a moon base, working alone as a technician to maintain the base's systems until the next batch of astronauts arrive. This is clearly an important task, one that requires some critical thinking. Is that alarm a sign of real trouble, or just a faulty light? When Mission Control says, "There's a small problem, but it's under control," are they hiding something or telling you the truth? What's the best way to fix that leaky hose? These are all issues that require you to consider options, use your knowledge, and arrive at the best beliefs possible under the circumstances. But while the technical issues may be substantial, the critical thinking tasks are relatively straightforward. You have the expertise, and the only people you are in contact with—the staff at Mission Control—are very clearly on your side!

Now consider the world you really live in. As you navigate your own life—school, family, work—you face many questions on which you may not have much expertise. What computer should you buy? Who should you date? Which school should you attend? How much exercise do you need? And on many of these topics, you'll be getting input from a large range of sources, including friends, family, news reporters, and advertisers. In fact, there is so much information, and so many voices, that some days you may wish you were on the moon!

The many voices coming to you through the media require special attention. Some of them are well-intentioned, but wrong about important things. Some are trying to influence your political and social views to match their own. Some of them are just trying to sell you things.

In this chapter, we've defined *critical thinking* as the systematic evaluation or formulation of beliefs or statements by rational standards. What does that imply for a context in which media plays such an important role?

In this book, we will attempt to provide you with tools you can use to evaluate the many messages coming at you every day from the media. And, importantly, we will attempt to instill in you a suitable attitude toward the media: one that lets you maintain an open mind, while at the same time proportioning your belief in what the media tells you to the strength of the reasons available.

1.2 How It Works

As you can see, critical thinking has extremely broad applications. Principles and procedures used to evaluate beliefs in one discipline can be used to assess beliefs in many other arenas (and we will examine some of those in detail in Chapter 11). But the basics of good critical thinking are the same everywhere. Here are the common threads that make them universal.

1.2.1 Claims and Reasons

Critical thinking is a rational, systematic process that we apply to beliefs of all kinds. Of course, we can really only evaluate beliefs that are made explicit; for obvious reasons, it's hard to evaluate beliefs that are kept hidden from us. We can only evaluate our *own* beliefs once we say (or maybe admit!) to ourselves, "This is what I believe." And we can evaluate other people's beliefs by looking at the things those people actually say or write—though sometimes we can *figure out* what it is that they think from the things that they *do*. So although we are interested in evaluating the quality of beliefs in general, we are mostly limited to evaluating beliefs that someone makes explicit by making some statement or claim. (We'll say something about the role unstated beliefs can play in arguments and about how to bring them to light and assess them in Chapter 3.)

statement (claim)
An assertion that something is or is not the case.

A **statement** is an assertion that something is or is not the case. The following are all statements:

- A triangle has three sides.
- I am cold.
- You are a liar.
- You are not a liar.
- I see blue spots before my eyes.
- 7 + 5 = 12
- 7 + 5 = 11
- You should never make fun of someone's disability.
- Canada is farther north than Mexico.
- The best explanation for his behaviour is that he was drunk.
- The capital of Canada is Winnipeg.
- Rap music is better than Celtic fiddle music.
- An electron is a subatomic particle.

Fly Logic

How can we reveal hidden beliefs in order to evaluate them?

So statements, or claims, are the kind of things that are either true or false. (Notice that at least three of the claims above are definitely false,

Food for Thought

Religious Faith and Critical Thinking

There are those who argue that faith and reason are incompatible. However, much theology and philosophy of religion are the result of thinking critically about religious ideas (often contrary to the preferences of religious authorities). Faith is not "believing something without proof." Rather, faith is sometimes described as "trusting without reservation," and thus the way we reason about matters of faith is more like the way we reason about relationships. That is to say, it's usually less about demonstrating the validity of a proposition than about describing the way the world appears to be from the position of faith. This requires the instruments of critical thought no less than any other area of human inquiry: it requires the use of evidence, it requires us to reason validly from premises to conclusions, and it requires the ability to respond to and account for objections. Critical reasoning thus comes into play whenever a faithful person experiences doubt and then has to make sense of that doubt. Or when a faithful person meets with objections and has to formulate a response. Within that context, critical reasoning is essential for understanding what communities of faith claim to believe and how they justify those beliefs.

—Scott Paeth, Professor, Religious Studies, Peace, Justice and Conflict Studies, DePaul University, Chicago

but that doesn't stop them from counting as statements!) They assert (rightly or wrongly) that some state of affairs is or is not actual. You may know that a specific statement is true, or you may know that it is false, or you may not know either way. There may be no way to find out at the time if the statement is true or false. There may be no one who believes the statement. But it would be a statement nonetheless.

Some of the thoughts we express, though, do *not* express statements:

- Does a triangle have three sides?
- How are you feeling?
- Turn that music off!
- Hey, dude.
- LOL!

The first two sentences are questions, the third is a command, the fourth is a greeting, and the fifth is an exclamation that is common in email and text messaging. None of them asserts that something is or is not the case. They are meaningful things to say, but they're not *statements. They are not the sorts of things that are capable of being either true or false.*

When you're engaged in critical thinking, you're mostly either evaluating statements or formulating them. In both cases your primary task is to figure out how strongly to believe them. The strength of your belief should depend on the quality of the reasons in favour of the statements. Statements backed by good reasons are worthy of strong acceptance. Statements that fall short of this standard deserve only weaker acceptance at best.

Sometimes you may not be able to assign any substantial weight at all to the reasons for or against a statement—there simply may not be enough evidence to decide rationally. Generally, when that happens, good critical thinkers do not just randomly choose to accept or reject a statement. They suspend judgment until there is enough evidence to make an intelligent decision.

1.2.2 Reasons and Arguments

Reasons provide support for a statement. That is, they provide us with grounds for believing that a statement is true. Reasons are themselves expressed as statements. So a statement expressing a reason is used to show that another statement is true or likely to be true. This combination of statements—a statement (or statements) supposedly providing reasons for accepting another statement—is known as an **argument**. Arguments are the main focus of critical thinking; they are the most important tool we have for evaluating the truth of statements (our own and those of others) and for formulating statements that are truly worthy of acceptance. Arguments are, therefore, essential for the advancement of knowledge in all fields. In everyday conversation, people use the word *argument* to indicate a debate or an angry exchange. In critical thinking, however, *argument* refers to the process of providing reasons in support of a statement.

argument
A group of statements in which some of them (the premises) are intended to support another of them (the conclusion).

The statements (reasons) given in support of another statement are technically called the **premises**. The statement that the premises are intended to support is called the **conclusion**. We can define an argument, then, like this:

premise
In an argument, a statement or reason given in support of the conclusion.

conclusion
In an argument, the statement that the premises are intended to support.

> **ARGUMENT:** A group of statements in which some of them (the premises) are intended to support another of them (the conclusion).

The following are some simple arguments:

1. Because you want a job that will allow you to make a difference in the world, you should consider working for a charitable organization like Doctors Without Borders.
2. The *Globe and Mail*'s *Report on Business* says that people should invest heavily in gold. Therefore, investing in gold is a smart move.
3. When Joseph takes the bus, he's always late. And he's taking the bus today, so I'm sure he's going to be late.
4. A lot of my friends have seen that Netflix movie, and literally none of them said it was any good. And my mom hated it. So it must be pretty bad.
5. No one should drink a beer brewed by a giant corporation. Labatt's Blue is brewed by a giant corporation. So no one should drink it.

Here are the same arguments where the parts are easily identified:

1. [Premise] Because you want a job that will allow you to make a difference in the world, [Conclusion] you should consider working for a charitable organization like Doctors Without Borders.
2. [Premise] *The Globe and Mail*'s *Report on Business* says that people should invest heavily in gold. [Conclusion] Therefore, investing in gold is a smart move.

3. [Premise] When Joseph takes the bus, he's always late. [Premise] And he's taking the bus today, [Conclusion] so I'm sure he's going to be late.
4. [Premise] A lot of my friends have seen that Netflix movie, [Premise]and literally none of them said it was any good. [Premise] And my mom hated it. [Conclusion] So it must be pretty bad.
5. [Premise] No one should drink a beer brewed by a giant corporation. [Premise] Labatt's Blue is brewed by a giant corporation. [Conclusion] So no one should drink it.

"Wisdom tends to grow in proportion to one's awareness of one's ignorance."

—Anthony de Mello, Indian Jesuit priest and psychotherapist

The arguments above are all quite different. They are all on very different topics. And some have just one premise, while others have two or three. Some are about what we should believe is true, while others are about what we believe should be *done*. But what all of these arguments have in common is that reasons (the premises) are offered to support or prove a claim (the conclusion). This logical link between premises and conclusion is what distinguishes arguments from all other kinds of discourse. This mental process of reasoning from a premise or premises to a conclusion based on those premises is called **inference**. We infer the conclusion of an argument from its premise or premises. Being able to identify arguments, to pick them out of a larger chunk of non-argumentative writing if need be, is an important skill on which many other critical thinking skills are based.

inference

The process of reasoning from a premise or premises to a conclusion based on those premises.

Next, consider this passage:

> Universal pharmacare (a government system for paying for prescription drugs) would cost the Canadian government about $20 billion, which would have to be paid for through taxes. The Canadian government has considered introducing such a plan. That $20 billion paid through taxes would be less than the total amount currently being paid by Canadians privately for their prescriptions.

Is there an argument here? No. This passage consists of several claims, but no reasons are presented to support any particular claim (conclusion). This passage can be turned into an argument, though, with some minor editing:

> Universal pharmacare would cost the Canadian government about $20 billion, which would have to be paid for through taxes. The Canadian government has considered introducing such a plan. The $20-billion plan would cost less than the total amount currently being paid by Canadians for their prescriptions. The Canadian government should go ahead and institute universal pharmacare.

Now we have an argument because *reasons* are given for accepting a conclusion, namely a conclusion about what the Canadian government *should* do. Here's another passage:

> Allisha used the online banking app on her iPhone to check the balance of her chequing account. It said that the balance was $125.

> Allisha was stunned that it was so low. She called her brother to see if he had been playing one of his stupid pranks. He said he hadn't. She wondered: was she the victim of bank fraud?

Where is the conclusion? Where are the reasons? There are none. This is a little story built out of descriptive claims, but it's not an argument. It's not trying to convince you, the reader, of anything. It could be turned into an argument if, say, some of the claims were restated as reasons for the conclusion that bank fraud had been committed.

Being able to distinguish between passages that do and do not contain arguments is a very basic skill—and an extremely important one. Many people think that if they have clearly stated their beliefs on a subject, they have presented an argument. But a mere declaration of beliefs never counts as an argument. Often such assertions of opinion are just a jumble of unsupported claims without an argument of any kind. A writer or speaker of these claims gives the readers or listeners no grounds for believing the claims. In writing courses, this kind of absence of supporting premises is sometimes called a "lack of development."

Here are two more examples of discussion without argument:

> Recently, a high school football game in New Brunswick was called off after one of the teams, Moncton's École l'Odysée Olympiens, saw nine players leave the field with head injuries.
>
> The words spoken afterward by an opposing coach laid bare an uncomfortable truth. "That's how football is," Scott O'Neal of Sackville's Tantramar Titans told CBC.
>
> The problem is not the way the game is played so much as it is the nature of the sport itself. (Editorial, *Globe and Mail*, 22 October 2017)

> These tax changes will make income taxes more fair for Canadians, particularly those of us who have income tax deducted from each of our paycheques. Those crying foul over proposed changes to federal tax laws say that they are concerned about how these changes will affect their ability to manage their lives, including repayment of their student loans, the cost of having and raising children, and the ability to save for retirement. (Carol Ogden [letter], *Vancouver Sun*, 4 September 2017)

The passage about football seems to be moving toward expressing an opinion (which may or may not be justified), but no reasons supporting a conclusion are offered. Note the contentious tone in the second passage, which is part of a letter to the editor. This passage sounds like part of an argument—it certainly expresses an opinion. But in the section that is shown, there is no argument. It's just a point of view presented without any support at all.

Sometimes people also confuse **explanations** with arguments. An argument gives us reasons for believing *that something is the case*—that a claim is true or at least probably true. An explanation, though, tells us *why or how something is the case.*

explanation
A statement or statements intended to tell why or how something is the case.

Arguments have something to prove; explanations do not. Look carefully at this pair of statements:

1. Adam obviously stole the money—he was the only one with access to it.
2. Yes, Adam stole the money, but he did it because he needed it to buy food.

Sentence 1 provides an argument. Sentence 2 provides an explanation. Sentence 1 tries to show that something is the case—that Adam stole the money—and the reason offered in support of this statement is that he alone had access to it. That's why we should believe that he did it. Sentence 2 does not try to prove that something is the case (that Adam stole the money). Instead, it attempts to explain why something is the case (why Adam stole the money). Sentence 2 takes for granted that Adam stole the money and then tries to explain *why* he did it. In a different context, of course, the fact that Adam had a motive—hunger—that might tend to make people steal could be offered as a reason to believe that he did, in fact, steal on this occasion. But in the absence of such a context, this sentence is most naturally read as an explanation rather than an argument. (Note that explanations can sometimes be used as *parts* of arguments. When they play that role, explanations are powerful intellectual and scientific tools that help us to understand the world; that is why this textbook has several chapters in Part 4 devoted to explanations used in this way.)

It's not always easy to recognize an argument and to locate both premises and a conclusion, but there are a few tricks that can make the job more manageable. For one, there are **indicator words** that are frequently included in arguments and signal that a premise or conclusion is present. For example, in argument 1, presented earlier in this chapter, the indicator word *because* tips us off to the presence of the premise "Because you want a job that will allow you to make a difference in the world." In argument 2, *therefore* points to the conclusion "Therefore, investing in gold is a smart move."

indicator words
Words that are frequently included in arguments and signal that a premise or conclusion is present.

Here are some common premise indicators:

because	due to the fact that	inasmuch as
in view of the fact	being that	as indicated by
given that	since	for
seeing that	assuming that	the reason being
as	for the reason that	

These words almost always introduce a premise—something given as a reason to believe some conclusion.

And here are some common conclusion indicators:

therefore	it follows that	it must be that
thus	we can conclude that	as a result
which implies that	so	which means that
consequently	hence	ergo

Using indicator words to spot premises and conclusions, however, is not foolproof. They're just good clues. You will find that some of the words just listed are used when no argument is present. For example,

- I am here *because* you asked me to come.
- I haven't seen you *since* Canada Day.
- He was *so* sleepy he fell off his chair.

The words "because," "since," and "so" are very often used as indicator words, but they are not being used that way in the sentences above.

Note also that arguments can be put forth without the use of *any* indicator words:

> We must each take steps to protect our environment. We can't rely on the government—federal and provincial regulators already have their hands full. Government can't be everywhere at once, and they usually get involved only after some environmental catastrophe has already happened. Individual responsibility is the key.

As you may have noticed from these examples, the basic structure of arguments can vary in several important ways. For one thing, arguments can have any number of premises. Arguments 1 and 2 (found earlier in the chapter) have one premise; arguments 3 and 5 each have two premises; and argument 4 has three premises. In extended arguments that often appear in essays, editorials, reports, blog postings, speeches, and other works, there can be many more premises. Also, the conclusion of an argument may not always appear after the premises. As in the above argument about the environment, the conclusion may be presented first.

Occasionally, the conclusion of an argument can be disguised as a question—even though a question is usually not a claim at all. (For purposes of examining such arguments, we may need to rewrite the conclusion as a statement; in some arguments, we may also need to do the same for the premises.) Most of the time readers have no difficulty discerning what the implied conclusion is, even when it is stated as a question. See for yourself:

> Do you think for one minute that backbench Liberals in Parliament will be happy about the prime minister's refusal to have a serious debate about electoral reform? A lot of Liberal Members of Parliament were elected by constituents who have very strong views about the need to change the way elections are currently run in this country.

The opening sentence of this passage is a question, but the answer is one that the writer assumes will be clear and obvious to the reader—namely, "no."

"Nothing in all the world is more dangerous than sincere ignorance and conscientious stupidity."

—Martin Luther King, Jr.

Probably the best advice for anyone trying to uncover or dissect arguments is this: *Find the conclusion first*. Once you figure out what claim someone is trying to prove, it becomes much easier to isolate the premises being offered in support of it. Ask yourself, "What claim is this writer or speaker trying to persuade me to

Review Notes

Claims, Reasons, and Arguments

- *Statement* (claim): An assertion that something is or is not the case.
- *Premise:* A statement given in support of another statement.
- *Conclusion:* A statement that premises are used to support.
- *Argument:* A group of statements in which some of them (the premises) are intended to support another of them (the conclusion).
- *Explanation:* A statement or statements asserting why or how something is the case.
- *Indicator words:* Words that are frequently found in arguments and signal that a premise or conclusion is present.

believe?" If the writer or speaker is not trying to convince you of anything at all, of course, then there is no argument to examine.

1.2.3 Arguments in the Rough

As you've probably guessed by now, in the real world arguments almost never appear neatly labelled as they are here. In everyday life, arguments usually come embedded in a tangle of other sentences that serve many other functions besides articulating an argument. They may be long and hard to follow. And sometimes a passage that sounds like an argument isn't one. Your main challenge is to identify the conclusion and premises without getting lost in all the "background noise."

Consider this passage:

> [1] A.L. Jones used flawed reasoning in his letter yesterday praising this newspaper's decision to publish announcements of same-sex unions. [2] Mr Jones asserts that same-sex unions are a fact of life and therefore should be acknowledged by the news media as a legitimate variation on social partnerships. [3] But the news media are not in the business of endorsing or validating lifestyles. [4] They're supposed to report on lifestyles, not bless them. [5] In addition, by validating same-sex unions or any other lifestyle, the media abandon their objectivity and become political partisans—which would destroy whatever respect people have for news outlets. [6] All of this shows that the news media—including this newspaper—should never endorse lifestyles by announcing those lifestyles to the world.

There's an argument here, but it's surrounded by additional, unnecessary material. The conclusion is sentence 6: "All of this shows that the news media—including this newspaper—should never endorse lifestyles by announcing those lifestyles to the world." Since we know what the conclusion is, we can identify the premises and separate them from other information. Sentences 1 and 2 are not premises; they're background information about the nature of the dispute. Sentence 3 presents the first premise, and sentence 4 is essentially a restatement of that premise. Sentence 5 is the second premise.

Stripped clean of non-argumentative material, the argument looks like this:

> [Premise] The news media are not in the business of endorsing or validating lifestyles. [Premise] In addition, by validating same-sex unions or any other lifestyle, the media abandon their objectivity and become political partisans—which would destroy whatever respect people have for news outlets. [Conclusion] All of this shows that the news media—including this newspaper—should never endorse lifestyles by announcing those lifestyles to the world.

Now see if you can spot the conclusion and premises in this one:

> [1] You have already said that you love me and that you can't imagine spending the rest of your life without me. [2] Once, you even tried to propose to me. [3] And now you claim that you need time to think about whether we should be married. [4] Well, everything that you've told me regarding our relationship has been a lie. [5] In some of your letters to a friend you admitted that you were misleading me. [6] You've been telling everyone that we are just friends, not lovers. [7] And worst of all, you've been secretly dating someone else. [8] Why are you doing this? [9] It's all been a farce!

And you thought that romance had nothing to do with critical thinking! In this passionate paragraph, an argument is alive and well. The conclusion is in sentence 4: "Everything that you've told me. . . has been a lie." Sentence 9, the concluding remark, is essentially a repetition of the conclusion. Sentences 1, 2, and 3 are background information on the current conflict. Sentences 5, 6, and 7 are the premises, the reasons that support the conclusion. And sentence 8 is an exasperated query that's not part of the argument.

You will discover that in most extended argumentative passages, the premises and conclusions make up only a small portion of the total number of words. A part of the text is background information and restatements of the premises or conclusion. Most of the rest consists of explanations, digressions, examples or illustrations, and descriptive passages.

"Ignorance, allied with power, is the most ferocious enemy justice can have."

—James Baldwin

As you can see, learning the principles of critical thinking or logic requires at least some prior knowledge and ability. But you may wonder (especially if this is your first course in critical or logical reasoning), "Where does this prior knowledge and ability come from?"—and do you have these necessary tools? Fortunately, the answer is yes. Since you are, as the ancient Greek philosopher Aristotle says, a rational animal, you already have the necessary equipment—namely, a logical sense that helps you to reason in everyday life and enables you to begin honing your critical reasoning.

Food for Thought

It's Not Personal

One benefit of the approach taught in this book is that it allows us to de-personalize arguments. An argument, after all, is a thing that exists independently of the person who put it forward. If I make a bad argument, but make it *clearly*, then you and I can both sit back and examine its parts and its logic. If the argument is weak, we can both identify its weaknesses, using the tools in this book. (Think of making a piece of art, and then *standing back* to examine it carefully.) And—importantly—if you find an error in my argument, that's a criticism of the argument, not a criticism of me. Of course, if I continue to believe the argument after the error has been pointed out to me, then I'm making an error and perhaps behaving badly. But in principle, we should both be able to separate the argument (a set of premises and a conclusion) from me (the human being who put it forward).

This is useful when dealing with difficult and controversial topics. In such circumstances, our egos often get tangled up with our points of view. Critical thinking means the ability to take an argument—whether it is yours or mine—and lay it out for careful analysis. If an argument you put forward contains errors, then I'm not going to accept it, but I can still accept *you* as a person, as a friend, and as a colleague. Likewise, if an argument I put forward contains errors, I can let you point that out to me without taking it as an attack on me as a person.

This approach can also help you make sure *your own* arguments are strong. The fact that you believe something doesn't make your favourite argument for that belief a good one. If we disentangle our arguments from our egos, we are likely to be better able to evaluate them honestly in order to come to more well-founded beliefs.

Summary

Critical thinking is the systematic evaluation or formulation of beliefs, or statements, by rational standards. Critical thinking is *systematic* because it involves distinct procedures and methods. It entails *evaluation* and *formulation* because it's used both to assess existing beliefs (yours or someone else's) and to devise new ones. And it operates according to *reasonable standards* in that beliefs are judged according to the reasons and reasoning that support them.

Critical thinking matters because our lives are defined by our actions and choices and our actions and choices are guided by our thinking. Critical thinking helps to guide us toward beliefs that are worthy of acceptance and that can help us to be successful in life, however we define success.

A consequence of not thinking critically is a loss of personal freedom. If you passively accept beliefs that have been handed to you by your family and your culture, then those beliefs are not really yours. If they are not really yours and you let them guide your choices and actions, then they—not you—are in charge of your life. Your beliefs are yours only if you examine them critically for yourself to see if they are supported by good reasons.

Some people believe that critical thinking will make them cynical, emotionally cold, and creatively constrained. But there is no good reason to believe that this is the case. Critical thinking does not necessarily lead to cynicism. It can complement our feelings by helping us sort them out. And it doesn't limit creativity—it helps to perfect it.

Critical thinking is a rational, systematic process that we apply to beliefs of all kinds. As we use the term here, *belief* is just another word for statement or claim. A *statement* is an assertion that something is or is not the case. When you're engaged in critical thinking, you are mostly either evaluating a statement or trying to formulate one. In both cases your primary task is to figure out how strongly to believe the statement (on the basis of how likely it is to be true). The strength of your belief will depend on the strength of the reasons in favour of the statement.

In critical thinking, an argument is not a fight but a set of statements—statements supposedly providing reasons for accepting another statement. The statements given in support of another statement are called the *premises*. The statement that the premises are used to support is called the *conclusion*. An argument, then, is a group of statements in which some of them (the premises) are intended to support another of them (the conclusion).

Being able to recognize an argument is an important skill on which many other critical thinking skills are based. The task is made easier by indicator words that are often found in arguments and signal that a premise or conclusion is present. Premise indicators include *for*, *since*, and *because*. Conclusion indicators include *so*, *therefore*, and *thus*.

Arguments almost never appear neatly labelled for identification. They usually come embedded in a lot of statements that are not part of the arguments. Arguments can be complex and long. Your main task is to identify the conclusion and premises without getting lost in the maze of words.

Exercise 1.1

Answers to exercises marked with an asterisk (*) may be found in Appendix B, Answers to Exercises.

Review Questions

1. What is critical thinking?*
2. In what sense is critical thinking *systematic*, and in what ways does it involve *evaluation* and *formulation*?
3. Is critical thinking primarily concerned with *what* you think or with *how* you think?
4. What does the term *critical* refer to in critical thinking?*
5. According to the text, what does it mean to say that critical thinking is done according to rational standards?*

6. According to the text, what is the relationship between critical thinking and personal freedom?
7. What is logic, and what vital role does it play in critical thinking?
8. What is a statement?*
9. Give an example of a statement. Then give an example of a sentence, on the same topic, that is not a statement.
10. According to the text, how should we go about deciding how *strongly* to believe a statement?
11. What is an argument?*
12. What is a premise?
13. What is a conclusion?*
14. Give an example of an argument with two premises.
15. Why can't an assertion or statement of beliefs by itself be an argument?
16. Do all expressions of disagreement contain an argument?
17. True or false? The following passage contains an argument. *Sample passage:* Jail sentences for criminals should be longer. I know I'm right!*
18. True or false? The following passage contains an argument. *Sample passage:* Some people say that herbal tea can cure a headache. But there's simply no real evidence that herbal tea can do that.
19. What role do indicator words play in arguments?*
20. List three conclusion indicator words.
21. List three premise indicator words.
22. Give an example of a sentence that uses the word *since* as something *other than* an indicator word.
23. What is probably the best strategy for trying to find an argument in a complex passage?*
24. Do all good arguments contain indicator words?

Exercise 1.2

Which of the following are *statements*? Which are not?

1. I should go to class today.*
2. Is the COVID-19 virus easy to kill by washing your hands thoroughly?
3. Do not allow your biases to distort your thinking.
4. Given that you believe in free speech, do you agree that racists have the right to express themselves freely on campus?*
5. Nachos are delicious!
6. Should our medical decisions be guided by reason, emotion, faith, or all three?
7. Was that new breakfast place any good?*
8. What have you done to make the world a better place?
9. The burgers at Burg-o-Rama made me sick.
10. Maybe you should study harder next time.*

Exercise 1.3

Which of the following passages contain *arguments*? For each argument you find, specify what the conclusion is.

1. Nachos are delicious and easy to make. So they're the perfect study food.*
2. Nachos are delicious and easy to make, which is why I make them whenever I'm studying.
3. Don't do that—you'll break it!
4. This weather is perfect for going to the beach! There's also a discount on surfing lessons that's good today only!
5. Is Alexei planning on buying a new motorcycle this year?
6. If you light that cigarette in here, I will leave the room.
7. *Independence Day: Resurgence* was a terrible movie, and not even Liam Hemsworth could save it.*
8. I know that David Hume was the greatest philosopher of the last 500 years because my philosophy professor taught us that in class.
9. Iron Man is a cooler superhero than Thor because technology is just way cooler than mythology.
10. "Whether our argument concerns public affairs or some other subject, we must know some, if not all, of the facts about the subject on which we are to speak and argue. Otherwise, we can have no materials out of which to construct arguments." (Aristotle, *Rhetoric*)
11. If you hire Kaitlin, you'll have a first-rate editor. You should hire Kaitlin.*
12. Many believe that there is no soul and that the mind is simply a result of electrical and chemical signals interacting in the brain. So they think that consciousness is a purely physical phenomenon. I reject this notion!
13. "Canada's economy has been unambiguously strong for about a year, according to the high-frequency data Statistics Canada collects every month. Gross domestic product probably will expand by at least three per cent this year, something that some economists thought our aging and relatively unproductive economy might never do again. The unemployment rate (6.2 per cent in August) is about as low is it ever gets, and could push lower still. The median household income in Canada is about $70,000, roughly 10 per cent more than a decade ago, according to census figures released last month. That's an excellent number, considering household wealth in the United States barely grew over the same period." (Kevin Carmichael, in *Canadian Business*, 6 October 2017)
14. "Murtaza Haider, a professor of real estate management and the director of the Urban Institute at [Toronto Metropolitan University], said renting and buying can each make sense at different points in life. For those who are in their 20s or early 30s, renting might be a better option because it provides flexibility. 'When you're young, I would say that the better

option is to rent until such time that you know that you are here for five to 10 years, and that's where you invest in ownership,' Haider said." (CBC.ca, 19 March 2022)

15. "U.S. President Donald Trump has been using the powers of his office to make grand gestures that reflect his election campaign promises of last year. Under close scrutiny, however, his grandest gestures have no effect beyond their publicity value. Canada should pursue its trade negotiations with the United States on the assumption that Mr. Trump is aiming for another grand, empty gesture." (Editorial, *Winnipeg Free Press*, 17 October 2017)*
16. "The Sony PlayStation 5 is the best gaming console around," said Omar. "No way," said Nadia. "The Nintendo Switch is better any day of the week."

Exercise 1.4

Which of the following contains an *argument?* For each argument, specify both the conclusion and the premise or premises.

1. When day comes we ask ourselves, where can we find light in this never-ending shade? (Amanda Gordon, *The Hill We Climb*)*
2. You have neglected your duty on several occasions, and you have been absent from work too many times. You are not fit to serve in your current position.
3. Racial profiling is not an issue for white people, but it is a serious issue for visible minorities.
4. The flu epidemic on the east coast is real. Government health officials say so. And I personally have read at least a dozen news stories that characterize the situation as a "flu epidemic."*
5. People who get their health information from bloggers are sadly misguided. If these bloggers were any good, they'd all be making a good living as doctors or something.
6. Investing in my new restaurant is a sure thing! A number of restaurant critics have said my poutine is the best in town. Also, my mom says my cooking is amazing.
7. "A question that often comes up is whether you can be both fat and fit. The short answer to that question is yes. You can be both fat and fit in the same way that you can be both blond and left handed." (Christopher Labos, *Montreal Gazette*, 1 November 2017)*
8. Cory's movie-review podcast is always interesting. The reviews are tough, but they're always fair. The podcast is definitely worth listening to!

9. Some people say the poor folks who have pitched tents in the park should be evicted. I bet those same people never give a dime to help anyone in need. People who don't sympathize with the poor make me sick.
10. It's a law of economics that if prices go up, demand will fall. So raising the price of our shoes is sure to hurt sales.*
11. "[N]one of the information gathered indicated that Mr. Wernick may have contravened any of his obligations under the Act . . . I therefore did not have reason to believe that Mr. Wernick had contravened the Act and did not pursue the matter further." (Federal Ethics Commissioner Mario Dion, quoted in *The Globe and Mail*, 10 March 2020)

Exercise 1.5

For each of the following conclusions, write at least two premises that could *reasonably* be offered in support of it. Your proposed premises can be entirely imaginary. To come up with premises, think of what kind of statement (if true) would persuade a reasonable person to believe the conclusion.

Example

Conclusion: Google would be a good company to work for.

Premise 1: Google has been consistently profitable for several years now.
Premise 2: Google has a casual and fun-loving workplace culture.

1. Life in small towns is better than life in big cities.
2. My mom is a very good boss.
3. Indigenous Peoples in Canada have the right to hunt and fish on their traditional lands.*
4. The president of our school is a good leader.
5. The president of our school is a bad leader.
6. When it comes to animals, MacDonald doesn't know what he's talking about.*
7. The mayor doesn't seem to understand the rules related to the ethics of "conflict of interest."
8. Life on earth is better overall than it was 25 years ago.
9. The internet is the best tool that law enforcement officials have against terrorists.*
10. Online pornography is bad for society.
11. Online pornography is good for society.
12. Schools should not have dress codes.*
13. Students are right to be protesting against rising tuition.
14. *Game of Thrones* is the greatest series in the history of television.

Exercise 1.6

For each of the following sets of premises, write a conclusion that would be supported by the premises (your conclusion should depend at least in part on all of the premises). Neither the conclusion nor the premises need actually to be true.

Example

Premise 1: The value of your shares in the company will continue to decline for at least a year.

Premise 2: Anyone with shares whose value will continue to decline for at least a year should sell now.

Conclusion: You should sell now.

1. Premise 1: You can't stand the sight of blood.
   Premise 2: You don't like science classes.
2. Premise 1: Most elderly Canadians in long-term care facilities have been vaccinated against COVID-19.
   Premise 2: All of the main vaccines against COVID-19 have been proven to be highly effective.*
3. Premise 1: The president of the university is very unhappy with the dean of the Faculty of Arts.
   Premise 2: The president has the power to remove deans from their positions.
4. Premise 1: All married people are happier than unmarried people.
   Premise 2: You are married.*
5. Premise 1: Thérèse will be happy if the government passes a law that will make it easier for her mom to immigrate to Canada.
   Premise 2: It looks like the government is indeed about to pass a new law that will make it easier for people like Thérèse's mom to immigrate.
6. Premise 1: If you don't believe in God, then there is nothing to make you act ethically.
   Premise 2: You don't believe in God.
7. Premise 1: Adding long-term bonds to an investment portfolio will lower its return.
   Premise 2: Priyanka just added long-term bonds to her investment portfolio.
8. Premise 1: There is a great deal of pornography of all kinds on the internet.
   Premise 2: Most people in Canada have access to the internet.
   Premise 3: A society that allows access to pornography doesn't care about its children.*
9. Premise 1: People who don't recycle their cans and bottles aren't serious about sustainability.
   Premise 2: People who aren't serious about sustainability don't care about the environment.
   Premise 3: Françoise doesn't recycle at all.

Exercise 1.7

For each of the following passages, determine whether or not there is an argument present. If so, identify the premises and the conclusion.

1. Advertising is not manipulative as some people seem to think. The main thing advertising does is to provide us with information about products. And ads that don't provide much information are really just trying to entertain us, not manipulate us.*
2. Ted Rogers, founder of Rogers Communications, turned the tiny media company he inherited from his father into a multi-billion-dollar corporation. He was renowned for his passion and energy. And he donated millions of dollars to worthy charities. Ted Rogers was a great leader.
3. "WhatsApp is now used by almost 60 million people in Germany and is by far the most widely used social media application, even ahead of Facebook," Johannes Caspar, the data commissioner, said in a statement Tuesday. "It is therefore all the more important to ensure that the high number of users, which makes the service attractive to many people, does not lead to an abusive exploitation of data power." (*Toronto Star*, 13 April 2021)*
4. It's wrong to treat corporations as if they're people. People—people like you and me—have the right to free speech, and corporations don't. Corporations also don't have a conscience. Corporate lawyers may try to convince you that corporations have rights, just like you and I do. But all rights are *human* rights, and one thing is for sure . . . there's nothing human about a corporation.
5. Although Canadians like to think that we are a fair and just society, this is a boldfaced lie. Indigenous Peoples in Canada have never, ever been treated fairly. Over hundreds of years, the Canadian government and non-Indigenous Canadians have treated them badly. Today, many people in Indigenous communities live in terrible conditions. People can talk about our fairness all they want, but there is no doubt that treatment of Indigenous Peoples is abhorrent.

Field Problems

1. Find a blog that interests you. Select an entry that contains at least one argument. Identify the conclusion and each premise.
2. From the same blog, find an entry that presents a point of view but that contains no argument at all. Rewrite the entry so that it contains at least one argument. Try to preserve as much of the original entry as possible and stay on the same topic.
3. Go to the website of a major newspaper (or your own town's main newspaper). Find a story that has reader comments posted below it. Find a comment that presents an argument—not just an opinion!—and identify the premise and conclusion.
4. Find an online advertisement that seems to present an argument in favour of the conclusion that "you should buy this product." What premises are offered?

Self-Assessment Quiz

1. What is an argument?
2. From the following sentences, indicate which ones are *not* statements:
   a. Critical thinking means acting like an emotionless robot.
   b. Give two examples of premise indicators.
   c. The Canadian Charter of Rights and Freedoms guarantees the rights and freedoms set out in it, subject only to such reasonable limits prescribed by law as can be demonstrably justified in a free and democratic society.
   d. Is the Blue Water Café the best restaurant in Vancouver?
3. Read the following argument, and then, from the list below it, select the conclusion that is supported by the premises contained in the argument:

   I spoke to a number of students on campus who see nothing wrong with plagiarism. I tried to explain the issue to them, but they just didn't get it. They didn't understand that using other people's work without giving them credit is just like stealing. And they didn't seem to think plagiarism hurts anyone, even though it means that other students who do their own work are at a disadvantage.

   a. University students are not intelligent.
   b. Plagiarism is illegal.
   c. Some university students should learn more about ethical arguments related to plagiarism.
   d. University students generally don't respect the law.
4. Does the following passage contain an argument? If it does, specify the conclusion.

   The time has come to abolish government, worldwide, and for all of us to live free lives. Anyone who doesn't understand why is a fool. The truth is there, if you care to look.
5. Does the following passage contain an argument? If it does, specify the conclusion.

   "The news" is an invaluable part of how we understand and relate to the world. But news is only one kind of storytelling, only one way to make sense of the world. There are other powerful and meaningful forms of storytelling practised by artists—by singers, poets, dancers, and more—that can help us to make a different kind of sense out of our shared experiences. In moments of crisis, the power of artists to heal, to unite, to challenge inequalities, and to reaffirm our faith in each other and in our community's values, is tangible. It is, in fact, essential. Without culture, as I wrote in my book, there is no future. (Simon Brault, *Ottawa Citizen*, 22 October 2014)

Which of the following sentences and sentence fragments are likely to be conclusions, and which are likely to be premises?

6. After all, the premiere of this province has made one mistake after another.
7. It follows that Nova Scotia's forests will need to be managed carefully if they are to be sustainable.
8. So, you should vote Conservative in the next election.

For questions 9–11, write at least two premises for each of the conclusions provided. You can make up the premises, but you must make sure that they provide reasonable support for the conclusion.

9. Eyewitness evidence is not always reliable.
10. Computers will very soon be able to play *Jeopardy* well enough to beat humans reliably.
11. Dean Brown, who for years was "the voice of the Ottawa Senators," is the best hockey announcer in sports broadcasting today!

Read the following argument. Then in questions 12–15, supply the information requested.

> [1] Is global warming a real threat? [2] Or is it a hoax dreamed up by the Chinese to put us at a competitive disadvantage? [3] Some politicians apparently think that the idea of global climate change is nonsense. [4] But a recent study showed them to be wrong. [5] Reputable government agencies have studied the issue and published convincing conclusions. [6] Such reports generally give no support to the idea that global warming isn't happening and that we should all go back to sleep. [7] Instead, they suggest that global warming is definitely real and that it could have catastrophic consequences if ignored. [8] For example, global climate change could cause heat waves, extreme weather, and water shortages in many parts of North America. [9] There are many such reports, including a very influential one from the United Nations. [10] Yes, our political leaders need to accept that global warming is real. [11] It is as real as hurricanes and ice storms.

Identify by number all the sentences in the argument that fulfill each of the following roles:

12. Conclusion
13. Premise or premises
14. Repetition of conclusion or premise
15. Background information

Critical Thinking and Writing Exercise

This is the first of five end-of-chapter lessons, or modules, designed to help you think about, plan, and write good argumentative essays. The modules are progressive, starting here with a few fundamentals of the writing process and then later covering basic guidelines and concepts that can help you to think critically and write intelligently about arguments and issues. Though each module is linked in some fashion to material in the corresponding chapters, modules are meant to serve as stand-alone (though cumulative) tutorials to be used as your instructor sees fit.

Arguments and Argumentative Essays

As we note in this chapter, an argument is a group of statements in which some of them (the premises) are intended to support another of them (the conclusion). This combination of statements-supporting-another-statement is not only the basic structure of an argument, it's the general design of an argumentative essay. An argumentative essay tries to support a particular conclusion or position on an issue by offering reasons to support that conclusion. Arguments (in the critical thinking sense) are not passionate exchanges of unsupported views or pointless contests of the is-too/is-not variety, and neither are argumentative essays. A mere sequence of statements expressing your views is not an argument. And several pages of such statements do not constitute an argumentative essay.

In an argumentative essay, your main task is to provide rational support for a claim. (In an English writing class, this claim might be called your "thesis statement.") If you are successful, you will have shown that there are good reasons to accept your view of things. Readers who think critically may well be persuaded by your arguments. If you write well, you may be able to make your essay even more persuasive through rhetorical or stylistic devices that add emphasis, depth, and vividness to your writing. No one wants to read a boring essay. What you should not do, however, is rely entirely on non-argumentative elements to persuade your audience. Strong emotional appeals, for example, can indeed persuade some people some of the time, but they really prove nothing. In truly effective argumentative essays, the primary persuasive device is the provision of good reasons.

Basic Essay Structure

Good argumentative essays generally contain the following elements, though not necessarily in the order shown here:

- Introduction (or opening)
- Statement of thesis (the claim to be supported)
- Argument supporting the thesis
- Assessment of objections
- Conclusion

In the *introduction*, you want to do at least two things: (1) grab the reader's attention and (2) provide background information for the thesis. Effective attention-grabbers include boldly stated conclusions, compelling quotations, interesting anecdotes, opinions of experts, shocking or unexpected claims, and vivid imagery. Whatever attention-grabbers you use, *they must be related to the topic of the essay*. There's no use telling a good story if it has nothing to do with your thesis. Providing background for your thesis often means explaining why your topic is important, telling how you became concerned, or showing that there is a problem to be solved or a question to be answered. Very often the introduction, sometimes consisting of no more than a sentence or two, is laid out in the first paragraph of the essay. In general, the shorter the introduction, the better.

The *thesis statement* also usually appears in the first paragraph. This is the statement that you hope to support or prove in your essay; it is the conclusion of the argument that you intend to present. You want to state the thesis in a single sentence and do so as early as possible in the essay. Your thesis statement is like a compass to your readers, guiding them through your essay from premise to premise, showing them a clear path. It also helps *you* stay on course by reminding you to keep every part of the essay related to your single unifying idea. Your thesis statement should be restricted to a claim that can be defended in the space allowed (often only 750 to 1000 words). Not restricted enough: "Tuition is too high." Better: "Tuition increases at Degrassi College are unacceptable." Better still: "The recent tuition increase at Degrassi College is unnecessary for financial reasons." (More on how to devise a properly restricted thesis statement in a moment.)

The main body of the essay is the fully developed *argument supporting the thesis*. This means that the basic essay structure consists of the thesis statement followed by each premise or reason that supports the thesis. Each premise in turn is stated clearly, explained and illustrated sufficiently, and supported by examples, statistics, expert opinion, and other evidence. Sometimes you can develop the essay very simply by devoting a single paragraph to each premise. At other times, each premise may demand several paragraphs. In any case, you should develop just one point per paragraph, and every paragraph should be clearly related to the thesis statement.

A sketch of the argument for the Degrassi College essay, then, might look like this:

- Premise: If the college has a budget surplus, then a tuition increase is unnecessary.
- Premise: The college has had a budget surplus for the last five years.
- Premise: If the college president says that the school is in good shape financially and therefore doesn't need a tuition increase, then it's probably true that the school doesn't need a tuition increase.
- Premise: In an unguarded moment, the president admitted that the school is in good shape

financially and therefore doesn't need a tuition increase.

- Thesis statement: Therefore, the recent tuition increase at Degrassi College is probably unnecessary for financial reasons.

Good argumentative essays also include an *assessment of objections*—an honest effort to take into account any objections that readers are likely to raise about the thesis statement or its premises. When you deal with such objections in your essay, you lend credibility to it because you're making an attempt to be fair and thorough. In addition, when you carefully examine objections, you can often see ways to make your argument or thesis statement stronger. It isn't necessary to consider every possible objection, just the strongest or the most common ones. Sometimes it's best to deal with objections when you discuss premises that are related to them. At other times it may be better to handle objections near the end of the essay after defending the premises.

Finally, your essay—unless it's very short—must have a *conclusion*. The conclusion usually appears in the last paragraph of the essay. Usually it reiterates the thesis statement (though usually not in exactly the same words). If the argument is complex or the essay is long, the conclusion may contain a summary of the argument. Good conclusions may reassert the importance of the thesis statement, challenge readers to do something about a problem, tell a story that emphasizes the relevance of the main argument, or bring out a disturbing or unexpected implication of a claim defended in the body of the essay.

Guidelines for Writing the Essay

1. *Determine your thesis statement.* Do *not* write on the first thesis idea that pops into your head. Select a topic you're interested in, and narrow its scope until you have a properly restricted thesis statement. Research the topic to find out what issues are being debated. When you think you have an idea for a thesis statement, stop. Dig deeper into the idea by examining the arguments associated with that claim. Choose a thesis statement that you think you can defend. If you come to a dead end, start the process over.
2. *Create an outline.* Establish the basic framework of your outline by writing out your thesis statement and all the premises that support it. Then fill in the framework by jotting down what points you will need to make in defence of each premise. Decide what objections to your argument you will consider and how you will respond to them. (Note: An argument diagram of the sort discussed in Chapter 3 can also serve as a kind of essay outline.)
3. *Write a first draft.* As you write, don't be afraid to revise your outline or even your thesis statement. Writing will force you to think carefully about the strengths and weaknesses of your argument.
4. *Stay on track.* Make sure that each sentence of your essay is clearly related somehow to your thesis statement and argument.
5. *Zero in on your audience.* Decide what audience your essay is intended for and *write to them*. Is it readers of the local paper? Fellow students? People who are likely to disagree with you?
6. *Support your premises.* Back up the premises of your argument with examples, expert opinion, statistics, analogies, and other kinds of evidence.
7. *Let your final draft sit.* If possible, when you've finished writing your paper, set it aside and read it the next day. You may be surprised how many mistakes this fresh look can reveal. If you can't set the essay aside, ask a friend to read it and give you some constructive criticism.
8. *Revise.* Your first effort will almost never be your very best work. Every good writer knows that editing and revising is the key to putting their best work forward. If need be, write a second draft and a third. Good writers aren't afraid of revisions; they depend on them.

Writing Assignments

1. Read Essay 7 in Appendix A ("Nurses, Social Media, and Whistleblowing"), and outline the argument presented. Specify the thesis statement or main conclusion and each supporting premise.
2. Write a 500-word paper in which you defend a claim that *contradicts* the thesis statement in Essay 1 ("Deterrence") in Appendix A. Pretend that all the evidence cited in Essay 1 actually supports your thesis statement. You may alter the details of the evidence accordingly.
3. Study the argument presented in Essay 3 ("Electronics in the Classroom") in Appendix A. Identify the conclusion and the premises and objections considered, then write a two-page rebuttal to the essay. That is, defend the claim that students should not be given a choice about whether to use laptops in the classroom.
4. Select an issue from the following list and write a 500-word paper defending a claim pertaining to the issue:
   - Should professors ban laptops from their classrooms?
   - Should Canadian households be legally required to recycle?
   - Should flu shots be mandatory for health care workers?
   - Should all Canadian provinces allow beer and wine to be sold in corner stores, like Quebec does?

The "Environment" of Critical Thinking

Chapter Objectives

- To appreciate that there are ways to (1) detect errors in our thinking, (2) restrain the attitudes and feelings that can distort our reasoning, and (3) achieve a level of objectivity that makes critical thinking effective.
- To understand that the most common barriers to critical thinking can be sorted into two categories: (1) those that arise because of *how* we think and (2) those that occur because of *what* we think.

Category 1: How We Think

You will be able to

- detect and overcome self-interested thinking by (1) watching out for instances when your deliberations get personal, (2) being alert to ways that critical thinking can be undermined, and (3) ensuring that no relevant evidence or ideas have been left out.
- appreciate how group thinking can distort critical thinking.
- understand the meaning of *peer pressure, appeal to popularity,* and *stereotyping* and be able to cite examples of each.

Category 2: What We Think

You will be able to

- understand what a world view is and how certain specific ideas in a world view can undermine critical thinking.
- critique the notion of subjective relativism.
- critique the notion of social relativism.
- define *philosophical skepticism* and explain how it relates to critical thinking.

Critical thinking does not happen in a vacuum but in an "environment" or context that is often hostile to it. It takes place in the minds of real people like you and me who almost always have thoughts, feelings, and experiences that, if we are not careful, would sabotage critical reasoning at every turn.

Recall our definition of critical thinking: *The systematic evaluation or formulation of beliefs or statements by rational standards.* This definition implies, of course, that several factors must be present for the process of critical thinking to be possible. If the process fails to be systematic, or falls short of being a true evaluation or rigorous formulation, or ignores rational standards, then critical thinking isn't happening. Because we are fallible (capable of making errors), there are thousands of ways that this failure of reason could occur. And there is no cure for our fallibility.

We should expect, then, that thinking critically will often be difficult, and indeed it sometimes is. But there are ways to (1) detect errors in our thinking, (2) restrain the attitudes and feelings that can distort our reasoning, and (3) achieve a level of objectivity that makes critical thinking possible.

Doing all this—and doing it consistently—requires *awareness*, *motivation*, and *practice*. If we are to think critically, we must be *aware* not only of what is involved in good critical thinking but also of what can result from sloppy thinking. Then we must *practise* avoiding the pitfalls and using the skills and techniques that critical thinking requires. And we must be *motivated* to do all of this because it is unlikely that we will use critical thinking very much if we can't appreciate its value—if we can't appreciate its value, we would have little motivation to make the extra effort.

We can sort the most common barriers to critical thinking into two main categories: (1) those hindrances that arise because of *how* we think and (2) those that occur because of *what* we think. There is some overlap in these categories, since how people think is often a result of what they think and vice versa. But in general, category 1 barriers are those that come into play because of psychological factors (our fears, attitudes, motivations, and desires), and category 2 barriers are those that arise because of certain philosophical ideas we have (our beliefs *about* beliefs). For example, a category 1 hindrance is the psychological tendency we all have to shape our opinions to match those of our peers. A common category 2 problem is the belief some people have that objectivity in thinking is impossible or that we really don't know anything or that we don't truly know what we think we know.

In this chapter we review the most common category 1 and 2 barriers to critical thinking and practise uncovering and neutralizing them. Finding the motivation to learn these lessons well and to watch for these barriers is up to you.

Critical Thinking and the Media

Advertising and Our Media Environment

In this book, we've said that critical thinking is an important mechanism in achieving and maintaining control over your own life. After all, you want the beliefs that guide your behaviour to be truly yours—beliefs that you understand and endorse. The media-rich environment in which we all live makes that a challenge. One particular problem has to do with advertising.

Most significant news and entertainment sources feature ads. The reason mainstream TV shows are "free" to you is that they are paid for by advertisers. Subscription services like Netflix tend not to have advertising, but they are the exception.

The same goes for most online news content: most of it is supported by advertising. A handful of news outlets that are non-profit or supported by government may be able to avoid advertising, but many of them also feature ads—even if they are not profit-oriented, they still need financial support in order to break even.

All of this means that if you want to access information and entertainment through normal media channels, you are going to be subject to advertising. And there is a lot of it, these days. The amount spent on trying to convince you to buy things is truly staggering. In 2021, a report by emarketer.com suggested that total spending worldwide on digital advertising reached $455.30 billion in that year.[1] In the face of such lavish spending on trying to get you to believe that you need particular products, the need for critical thinking skills becomes all the more evident.

2.1 Category 1: How We Think

No one is immune to category 1 barriers. We all have psychological tendencies and habits that affect our behaviour and shape our thinking. They tend to stick around, haunting our minds until we have the awareness and the will to break free of them.

2.1.1 Am I Really Special?

As humans we spend a great deal of time protecting and maintaining our own mental framework, our own *selves*—a perfectly natural urge that does no harm until we push our self-serving efforts too far. How far is too far? From the standpoint of critical thinking, we have taken things too far when we accept claims for no good reason—when our thinking is no longer systematic and rational. In effort to protect ourselves, we often distort our own judgment and thereby raise our risk of error, which is ironically a risk to ourselves.

Chris Wildt/CartoonStock

The instinct to seek out information that affirms our beliefs and our worldview is a natural one, but it can be dangerous if it blinds us to information we really need.

Self-interested thinking takes several forms. We may decide to accept a claim *solely because it advances, or coincides with, our interests.* You may think, "I believe the province should lower the sales tax on anything bought at a convenience store because I own a convenience store," or "I am against all forms of gun control because I am a hunter," or "This university should not raise tuition fees—because I am a student and I don't want to pay more tuition." There is nothing inherently wrong with accepting a claim that happens to advance your own interests. The problem arises when you accept a claim *solely because* it furthers your interests. Self-interest (or anyone's interests, for that matter) alone simply cannot establish the truth of a claim. If you base your beliefs on self-interest alone, you are abandoning critical thinking.

Here's a classic example of self-interested thinking inspired by the film *Twelve Angry Men:*

> Twelve jurors sit in a room deliberating over whether to find the defendant guilty of murder. The accused is a Puerto Rican teenager who has grown up in the rough and impoverished streets of the inner city. At first, all but one juror (the jury foreman) vote guilty. The foreman persuades the other jurors to examine the evidence once again. Their deliberations go on for hours, and as they do, the prosecution's case slowly falls apart. Apparently damning evidence that had seemed so strong earlier is now shown to be full of holes. They take another vote, but this time 11 jurors, including the foreman, vote not guilty, while one man (juror number 10) insists that the other jurors are deluded and that the boy is undoubtedly guilty. The jurors ask him to explain his reasons. He angrily insists again that the boy is guilty, but he can't provide any evidence or reasons that suggest the boy's guilt. He just rants at the other jurors, muttering something about his dead son and Puerto Ricans being "no good" and "against everything I believe in." Finally the other jurors think they understand what's behind the seemingly irrational stance of juror number 10: he wants to convict the boy for personal reasons—perhaps because he wants to avenge his son's death, because he feels threatened by ethnic minorities, because he had been wronged by another Puerto Rican boy, or because of some other bias that has nothing to do with the guilt or innocence of the defendant.

In this example, the other members of the jury eventually realize that the judgments of juror number 10 are self-serving and linked to his own emotional needs. What gave him away? An obvious clue is his emotional insistence on his own point of view. But an even more telling clue is his clear rejection of all relevant evidence. The reasons for acquitting are perfectly clear to the other jurors, but he won't (or can't) consider them. In everyday life, these two clues often signal the presence of powerful self-interest at work.

The influence of self on your thinking can take another form. You may be tempted to accept claims *for no other reason than that they help you save face.* We all like to think of ourselves as excelling in various ways. We may believe that we are above average in intelligence, integrity, talent, compassion, physical beauty, athletic ability, or other things. And we not only like to think such things about ourselves; we want to be seen that way by others as well. But sometimes things happen that should lead us to doubt whether we really are that way. The challenge comes when we accept or reject claims just to cover up the cracks in our image. You make a mistake, but you can't admit it's your fault because being at fault would require you to adjust your self-image in unflattering ways. You behave badly, and you try to justify your behaviour. You make a judgment or observation that turns out to be wrong, and you're too embarrassed or proud to admit it. In such circumstances, it may be tempting to let our beliefs be shaped by our wishes in order to "save face"—that is, in order to preserve our image of ourselves. But accepting, and then relying on, such false beliefs is unlikely to serve us well in the

Showtime/The Kobal Collection/Art Resource

In *Twelve Angry Men*, one juror, for personal reasons, holds out for a guilty verdict despite overwhelming evidence that the accused is innocent. How often do you think this kind of self-interested thinking occurs in real-life juries?

long run. (In Chapter 4 we'll learn that sometimes self-interested thinking can even alter our perceptions.)

The consequences of self-centred thinking can be self-destructive. In the realm of critical thinking, this devotion to yourself can prevent careful evaluation of claims, limit critical inquiry, blind you to the facts, provoke self-deception, encourage rationalizations, lead you to suppress or ignore evidence, and promote wishful thinking. And these mistakes can decrease your chances of success (however you define success) and limit your personal growth, maturity, and self-awareness. This tendency toward being self-centred can also leave you wide open to propaganda and to manipulation by people who want to appeal to your personal desires and prejudices. How easy would it be for people to control your choices and thoughts if they told you exactly what you wanted to hear? (There are in-depth discussions of these lapses in critical thinking in Chapters 4 and 5.)

"To be conscious that you are ignorant is a great step to knowledge."

—Benjamin Disraeli (Prime Minister of the United Kingdom, 1874–80)

When examining a claim or making a choice, how can you overcome the excessive influence of your own psychological needs? Sometimes you can do it only with great effort, and sometimes the task is much easier, especially if you remember these three guidelines:

- Watch out when things get personal.
- Be alert to ways that critical thinking can be undermined.
- Ensure that nothing has been left out.

2.1.1.1 Watch Out When Things Get Personal

You are most likely to let your self-interest get in the way of clear thinking when you have a big personal stake in the conclusions you reach. You may be deeply committed to a particular view or belief, or you may desperately want a particular claim to be false or unjustified, or you may be devoted not to particular claims but rather to *any* claims that contradict those of someone you dislike. Such excessive enthusiasm can wreck any attempt at a careful, fair evaluation of a claim.

The twentieth-century philosopher Bertrand Russell argued that the passionate holding of an opinion is a sure sign of a lack of reasons to support the opinion:

> When there are rational grounds for an opinion, people are content to set them forth and wait for them to operate. In such cases, people do not hold their opinions with passion; they hold them calmly, and set forth their reasons quietly. The opinions that are held with passion are always those for which no good ground exists; indeed the passion is the measure of the holder's lack of rational conviction.[2]

The dead giveaway that you are skewing your thinking is a surge of strong emotions (like the one that gripped juror number 10). If your evaluation or defence of a position evokes anger, passion, or fear, your thinking could be prejudiced or clouded. It is possible, of course, to be emotionally engaged in an issue and still think critically and carefully. But most of the time, getting worked up

Everyday Problems and Decisions

Self-Concept and Consumerism

It is always important to watch out when things get personal. One of the situations in which this is particularly important is when someone is trying to sell you something. Of course, there is a sense in which buying consumer goods *should* be personal—after all, more often than not you are buying things for *yourself*, and your own desires and values have a proper role to play. However, advertisers and salespeople may try to make purchases personal in another sense: they may try to convince you that having their product is essential to your self-concept, your own understanding of who you are. In such situations, it is worth taking a step back and asking:

- Is my sense of worth really tied to how expensive my jeans are?
- Does having a car with more horsepower make *me* more powerful?
- Will this shampoo really go beyond cleaning my hair to making me a happier person?

Consumer purchases can be important decisions: if they are going to be *personal*, they should be about what you want, not what someone else *wants* you to want!

over a claim or conclusion is reason enough to suspect that your thinking is not as clear as it should be.

The rule of thumb is this: if you sense a rush of emotions when you deal with a particular issue, pause for a moment. Think about what's happening and why. Then continue at a slower pace and with greater attention to the basics of critical reasoning, double-checking to ensure that you are not ignoring or suppressing evidence or getting sloppy in your evaluations.

2.1.1.2 Be Alert to Ways That Critical Thinking Can Be Undermined

If you understand the techniques and principles of critical thinking, and you have practised applying them in a variety of situations, you are more likely than not to detect your own one-sided, self-centred thinking when it occurs. An alarm should go off in your head: "Warning—faulty reasoning ahead!"

When your alarm sounds, double-check your thinking, look for lapses in arguments and claims, and weed them out.

2.1.1.3 Ensure That Nothing Has Been Left Out

A common flaw in reasoning is the failure to consider evidence or arguments that *do not support* your preferred claims or positions. For example, you may secretly want a particular claim to be true, so you knowingly or unknowingly look for evidence in its favour but ignore evidence against it. The chances of making this mistake increase substantially when you believe that things you value are at stake.

This kind of preferential treatment for some statements over others is part of a common phenomenon called *selective attention* (see Chapters 4 and 5). In selective

J. Bruce Walton, n8images, ©2021

Psychologists have long known that a lot of what we experience is subconsciously fabricated by our own brains. One example is the phenomenon known as *pareidolia*—the tendency for our brains to "see" things in abstract stimuli. Have you ever "seen" the shape of a bunny or whale in a cloud? Do you see faces in the knots in this tree? Can you think of other examples where your brain tells you something is there when it really isn't?

attention, we notice certain things and ignore others—usually without even being aware that we're doing it. We may ignore facts that contradict our beliefs and seek out facts that support them. Scientific research has repeatedly confirmed this behaviour. In a typical study, researchers showed subjects both *evidence for* and *evidence against* the reality of extrasensory perception (ESP). Subjects who already doubted the existence of ESP recalled both kinds of evidence accurately. But subjects who already believed in ESP remembered both kinds of evidence as *proving* ESP. They somehow recalled even the disconfirming evidence as supporting their belief in ESP!

The remedy for this problem is to *make a conscious effort to look for opposing evidence*. Don't consider your evaluation of a statement or argument finished until you've carefully considered *all the relevant reasons, including ones that don't support your own pet views*. Ask yourself, "What is the evidence or reasons against this statement?" Doing so is often psychologically difficult. Our natural tendency is to look for evidence that supports our views. But a willingness to look for opposing evidence is a key element of intellectual honesty.

This approach is at the heart of science. A basic principle of scientific work is not to accept a favoured theory until competing (alternative) theories are thoroughly examined (more on this in Chapter 10).

2.1.2 The Power of the Group

In the 2015 movie *The Force Awakens* (part of the Star Wars series), one of the central figures is a young man, a First Order stormtrooper whom we initially know only as "FN-2187." The young man (played by John Boyega) has a number, rather than a name, because he has been trained since childhood for one purpose: to be a soldier, loyal and dedicated to winning at all costs. A central theme of the drama in *The Force Awakens* lies in the young man's refusal to mindlessly follow his commander's cruel orders, his escape from the First Order, and his growing individualism. He even adopts a name—Finn—in place of his previous numerical designation. By the end of the movie, Finn is no longer a mere number; he is a *person*.

Although we frequently proclaim the importance of individualism, we humans spend a great deal of our time trying to conform to groups or be part of them. We want to belong, we want the safety and comfort of numbers, and we want the approval of our beloved tribe. All of that is perfectly normal. We are, after all, social creatures. Conformist tendencies are a fact of life and are in some

Food for Thought

Fake News

In the broadest sense, *fake news* is just false information masquerading as news. Writing and publishing fake news is an old practice, probably as old as journalism itself. Fake news takes many forms and is created for many reasons.

It is important to differentiate fake news from news stories that merely contain mistakes. For example, in April of 2020 (early in the COVID-19 pandemic) *National Public Radio* (NPR) in the US wrongly reported that a man had been arrested for refusing to wear a mask. NPR soon issued a correction: the man had been arrested for assaulting a police officer, after the officer asked him to put a mask on. That's not a fake story; that's just a mistake made by a reporter.

We can also distinguish fake news from the form of satire in which fictional news stories are presented for humorous purposes. In such stories, there is no intent to deceive the audience—indeed, the audience needs to realize that the news is "fake" in order to get the joke. The humour website *The Beaverton* features stories with headlines that sound just like news headlines, but all its news stories are 100 per cent fictional. The stories in *The Beaverton* aren't intended to deceive, though: they're successful as humour only because the audience knows they aren't true.

The term *fake news* became politicized during the 2016 presidential election in the US when Donald Trump began using the term in a very different way: Trump used the term *fake news* to refer, essentially, to news stories he didn't like, or that distracted from his key messages, even when those stories were factually accurate and were reported by highly reputable news organizations like the *New York Times*. Ironically, that very election saw a huge proliferation of genuine fake news (i.e., fictional stories written to look like news). Some of that fake news was politically motivated and involved scandalous fake stories about specific politicians. Some of it, on the other hand, was financially motivated, since—in a news environment powered by Facebook's newsfeed algorithm—online advertising revenue could be gained by writing stories that were popular online, even if they were false.

Review Notes

Avoiding Self-Interested Thinking

- Watch out when things get personal and you become emotionally invested in an issue.
- Beware of the urge to distort your thinking to save face.
- Be alert to ways that critical thinking can be undermined.
- Ensure that nothing has been left out of consideration.
- Avoid selective attention.
- Make a conscious effort to look for opposing evidence.

cases useful. But trouble appears when our conformism hampers—or obliterates—critical thinking.

We all belong to multiple groups—family, work groups, gender, church, clubs, professional societies, political parties, advocacy groups, you name it—and we can

catwalker/Shutterstock

You don't have to be a movie hero to learn to think for yourself.

be susceptible to pressure from all of them. Much of the time there is intense pressure to fit into groups and to adopt the ideas, attitudes, and goals endorsed by them. Sometimes the influence of the group is subtle but strong, and it can occur in the most casual, unofficial gatherings. The claims and positions adopted by the group can be implicit, never spoken, and yet still be well understood. The Facebook group, the cluster of Christians or Muslims or Jews who happen to meet on the bus, the collection of peers who support the same political cause—all these groups can exert a surprising influence on the beliefs of the members of those groups.

Group pressure to accept a statement or to act in a certain way has several different faces (some of which we cover in more detail in later chapters). When we're talking about the pressure to conform that comes from your peers, it's called—not surprisingly—**peer pressure**. When we're talking about an argument that tries to support a conclusion on the basis of the mere popularity of a belief, that's known, appropriately enough, as an **appeal to popularity** (also known as an *appeal to the masses*). In all cases, the lapse in critical thinking comes from the fact that the views or behaviour of the group *alone* is taken as reason to support a claim (see Chapter 5).

peer pressure
Group pressure to accept or reject a claim solely on the basis of what one's peers think or do.

appeal to popularity (or appeal to the masses)
The fallacy of arguing that a claim must be true merely because a substantial number of people believe it.

Group pressure can happen quickly. For example, if you're listening to a speech by a member of your own political party, you may immediately find yourself positively disposed toward the speaker—not because you agree with them but because they are a member of your group or because you see other people in the audience around you nodding their heads.

Group pressure can also take a while to have an effect. Consider this example:

"Believe nothing, no matter where you read it, or who said it, no matter if I said it, unless it agrees with your own reason and your own common sense."

—The Buddha

> Aimee has just become a new member of the Eco-Awareness Club on campus. She's been considering joining ever since Frosh Week. She's away from home for the first time and hasn't made very many new friends. She likes to feel that she belongs to something, and she shares most of the group's beliefs. And the club includes some of the smartest and most active students on campus, so being part of the club makes her feel like part of the "in" crowd. She soon finds out that she agrees with members of the club on every social and political issue—except one, and it's related to cannabis. Even though cannabis has been de-criminalized

in Canada, use of cannabis is still illegal in public spaces such as parks. Everyone else in the group is strongly in favour of an even more permissive policy with regard to cannabis. Aimee is against it because she's read a lot about it and the arguments *against* allowing cannabis use in public spaces seem to be stronger than the arguments in favour. But she doesn't want to jeopardize her membership in the club—or her new friendships—over this one issue. So when the topic comes up, she stays quiet. The arguments she hears from her new friends seem pretty weak. But as time goes on, she stops thinking about the arguments and tries not to think about the topic at all. Over time, her views on the subject start to change, until finally she finds herself being wholeheartedly in favour of allowing cannabis use in public spaces.

"A great many people think they are thinking when they are really rearranging their prejudices."

—William James (American philosopher and psychologist)

Here, the need to belong slowly overcomes critical reasoning in a specific subject area (regulation of cannabis use). On other topics, Aimee may be an astute critical thinker.

stereotyping
Drawing conclusions about people based merely on their membership in some group.

There's another kind of group influence that we have all fallen prey to: the pressure that comes from assuming that our own group is the best, the right one, the chosen one, and all other groups are, well, not as good. You can see this kind of ethnocentrism in religions, political parties, generations, social classes, and many other groups. The assumption that your group is better than others is at the heart of prejudice. If we are honest with ourselves, most of us recognize that we are susceptible to this force.

This we-are-better pressure is probably the most powerful of all. We all have certain beliefs, not because we have thought critically about them but because our parents raised us to believe them or, because of the flow of conversation, our social group has instilled them in us. That is, we may believe what we believe—and assume that our beliefs are better than anyone else's—because we were born into a family or society that maintains such views. Someone may be a Catholic or a Conservative or a racist primarily because they were born into a Catholic or Conservative or racist family or society. Like the influence of the self, this external pressure can lead to wishful thinking, rationalization, and self-deception. Group thinking can also easily generate narrow-mindedness, resistance to change, and **stereotyping**. (Again, more on these problems in Chapters 4 and 5.)

Peer pressure is pervasive in some settings, but it seldom serves as a good excuse.

Food for Thought

Critical Thinking and Racism

Some forms of racism may be inherited from one's environment: a particular individual may end up with racist attitudes just because their family or their community has such attitudes. We are not responsible for the groups we are born into, but *retaining* racist views generally requires one or more failures of critical thinking.

Racism typically involves prejudice. Prejudice in its broadest sense is a judgment or opinion—whether positive or negative—based on insufficient reasons. To be prejudiced literally means to pre-judge—to judge before we have the relevant information. Judging without relevant information is a clear mistake from the

Shingwauk Residential Schools Centre/Handout via REUTERS

For more than 100 years the Canadian government funded a network of residential schools for Indigenous children, administered by Christian churches, with the explicit goal of converting the children to Christianity and bringing them into mainstream culture. This system saw several generations of Indigenous children forcibly taken away from their families so that they could be "educated" at such schools, sometimes far from their own communities. Thousands of children died in these schools, mostly from a combination of disease and neglect, and many more suffered from abuse. The effects on survivors, and on their families and communities, have been tragic. The last residential school closed in 1997. The 2015 report of the Truth and Reconciliation Commission is an excellent source from which to learn more.

point of view of critical thinking. But usually the term *prejudice* is used in a narrower sense to mean a negative attitude or set of beliefs about members of a group of people. At the heart of prejudice, then, is a failure of critical thinking. And the use of critical thinking is an important part of ridding ourselves of such prejudiced views. If we act in a prejudiced way, our failures of critical thinking threaten to impose real injustices on others.

Bias is another word for prejudice, in both the general and the narrower sense. Sometimes the word is also used to mean a simple inclination of temperament or outlook—as in "My bias is in favour of tougher laws." But more often it refers to a reflexive negative attitude toward a group of people.

Racism is a lack of respect for the value and rights of people of different races or geographical origins. Usually this attitude is based on prejudice—specifically, an unjustified judgment that one group of people is somehow superior to another.

As comfortable as our inherited beliefs are, when we accept them without good reason we risk error, failure, and delusion. And as we discussed in Chapter 1, if we have certain beliefs solely because they were given to us, they are not really our beliefs. The sign of a maturing intellect is having the will and the courage to gradually eliminate those beliefs that we come to realize are groundless.

For critical thinkers, the best way to deal with the power of the group is to make a conscious effort to proportion your belief to the strength of reasons. We should only hold strongly to those beliefs for which there are strong reasons.

After thinking critically about claims favoured by groups, you may find that the claims are actually on solid ground and you really do have good reason to accept them. Or you may find that there is no good reason for believing them, and so you don't accept them. Either way, critical thinking will give you a clearer view of the group and yourself.

Critical thinking, then, is independent thinking. That's why, to many people, those who have most dramatically achieved independent thinking—people like Aristotle, or Einstein, or Elijah Harper, or Viola Desmond—are heroes.

Review Notes

Avoiding Group Pressure on Your Thinking

- Group pressure can come in the form of peer pressure, appeals to popularity, and appeals to common practice.
- Group-centred thinking can degenerate into narrow-mindedness, resistance to change, and stereotyping.
- The best way to defend yourself against group thinking is to always proportion your acceptance of a claim according to the strength of reasons.

2.2 Category 2: What We Think

world view
A philosophy of life; a set of fundamental ideas that helps us to make sense of a wide range of important issues in life. A world view defines for us what exists, what should be, and what we can know.

A **world view** is a philosophy of life, a set of fundamental ideas that helps us make sense of a wide range of important issues in life. The ideas are fundamental in that they help to guide us in the evaluation or acceptance of many other, less basic ideas. They are answers to the "big questions" of life, such as "What do I know?" "Is knowledge possible?" "What is real and what is not?" "How do I know which actions are morally right?" "Are people basically good or bad?"

The interesting thing about world views is that we all have one; all of us have adopted (or inherited) certain fundamental ideas about the world. You may have unknowingly absorbed the ideas from your family or society, and you may not have thought much about them, but you have a world view nonetheless. Even the rejection of all world views is a world view.

Elements of some world views—certain fundamental but problematic ideas—may undermine critical thinking. These notions can give rise to category 2 barriers to critical reason, for they may affect our thinking through the content of our beliefs.

2.2.1 Subjective Relativism

Like science, critical thinking is based on a number of propositions that few people would think to question. Science, for example, is based on the proposition that the world is publicly understandable—that the world has a certain structure (independent of what anyone thinks or prefers), that we can know the structure, and that this knowledge can, in principle, be acquired by anyone. Think, for example, of the idea that the Earth revolves around the sun. This is true independent of anyone's beliefs or preferences, and its truth can be verified by anyone who takes the time to check carefully. Critical thinking is based on similar ideas. Among the most basic is the notion that the truth of a claim does not depend on what a person thinks. That is, your believing that something is true *does not make it true.*

subjective relativism
The idea that truth depends on what someone believes.

subjectivist fallacy
Accepting the notion of subjective relativism or using it to try to support a claim.

The alternative idea that truth depends on what someone believes is called **subjective relativism**, and if you accept this notion or use it to try to support a claim, you are said to be committing an error of reasoning known as the **subjectivist fallacy**. This view says that truth depends not on the way things are but solely on what someone believes. It says that truth, in other words, is relative to individuals. Truth, in this view, is a matter of what a person believes—not a matter of how the world is. This means that a given proposition can be true for one person but not for another. If you believe that the Earth revolves around the sun, then it is true (for you) that the Earth revolves around the sun. If someone else believes the opposite—that the sun revolves around the Earth—then it is true (for her) that the sun revolves around the Earth.

You've probably encountered subjective relativism more often than you realize. You may have heard someone (maybe even yourself!) say, "This is *my* truth, and that's *your* truth" or "This statement is true *for me*."

Subjective relativism can undermine critical thinking in a fundamental way. In large part, critical thinking is about determining whether statements are true or false. But if we were able to make a statement true just by believing it to be true, then critical thinking would be unnecessary. The subjectivist fallacy, they say, may be an attempt to excuse avoiding the tough job of critical inquiry.

Most philosophers see the situation this way: We use critical thinking to find out whether a statement is most likely to be true or false. Objective truth is about the world, about the way the world is regardless of what we may believe about it. To put it differently, there is a way the world is, and our beliefs do not make it that way. The world is the way it is, regardless of how we feel about it.

These same philosophers would probably be quick to point out exceptions to the rule and to point out that some objective truths *are* about our subjective states or inner processes. It might be true—objectively true—for example, that you're feeling pain right now. But if so, the claim that you are feeling pain right now is an *objective* truth about your *subjective* state. I could be wrong about whether you are in pain, even if you could not be wrong about that yourself.

Also, they would readily admit that there are some things about ourselves that obviously *are* relative because they are one way for us and another way for someone else. You may prefer chocolate ice cream, and someone else may prefer vanilla. The deliciousness of chocolate ice cream is then relative to you. But the truth about these states of affairs—the fact that you prefer one while I prefer the other—is not itself relative.

Subjective relativism (as well as other forms of relativism) is controversial, and we needn't spend much time on it here. But you should know at least that philosophers have (through the use of critical thinking!) uncovered some odd implications of subjective relativism, ones that seem to render it implausible. First, they point out that if we could make a statement true just by believing it to be true, we would each be infallible. We could not possibly be in error about anything that we sincerely believed. We could never be mistaken about where we parked the car or what the capital of Nigeria is or which planet is the largest or the smallest. Personal infallibility is, of course, absurd, and this is a pretty compelling argument against subjective relativism.

But many critics think the biggest problem with subjective relativism is that it's self-defeating. It defeats itself because its truth implies its falsity. The relativist says, "All truth is relative." If this statement is objectively true, then it refutes itself because if it is objectively true that "All truth is relative," then the statement itself is an example of an objective truth, which is precisely the kind of truth that it denies exists! So if "All truth is relative" is objectively true, it is objectively false.

2.2.2 Social Relativism

To escape the difficulties of subjective relativism, some people posit **social relativism**, the view that truth is relative to societies. The idea here is that truth

social relativism
The view that truth is relative to societies.

Food for Thought

Constructing Your Own World—From the News

Many social commentators worry that the wild diversity of news sources that characterizes the modern world actually poses a problem: each of us can potentially choose news sources—TV news, websites, and so on—that only reinforce our own points of view. Once upon a time, our grandparents all watched the same handful of news broadcasts and read the same newspapers. On one hand, this meant they had to rely upon a relatively small number of sources, but it also meant that they were—literally!—all on the same page. TV news had to maintain a degree of neutrality and broadcast stories that were of interest to people from a wide range of political and social points of view. They couldn't cater to anybody and had to try to please everybody. Today, with hundreds of cable channels and thousands of news sources online, each of can exclusively rely on news sources whose editorial slant and story choices we find particularly interesting and comforting. Many see this as a problem.

While listening to views that correspond to our own may be enjoyable, listening *only* to such views can be dangerous. After all, we expand our world views and mature emotionally by listening to diverse views. We may not always agree with what we hear, but we can learn much from hearing what issues are important to people who differ from us.

depends not on your own beliefs but on your society's collective beliefs. So a claim can be true for the Chinese but false for Americans, true for college students but false for public officials, true for Protestants or Muslims but false for atheists. To many, this kind of relativism, like the subjective kind, also seems to render critical thinking pointless. After all, why bother to think critically when your own society's traditional beliefs are, by definition, always true?

Social relativism is attractive to many because it seems to imply an admirable egalitarianism—the notion that the beliefs of different societies are all in some important sense equal. And in general, respect for other cultures is a good thing. But we shouldn't confuse the idea that all societies are worthy of equal respect with the idea that all claims are worthy of equal respect. The former is an important moral principle; the latter is a failure of critical thinking and a recipe for disaster.

In fact, a lot of philosophers maintain that social relativism has most of the same defects that subjective relativism has. For example, according to social relativism, individuals may not be infallible but societies are. In other words, it implies that the beliefs of whole societies cannot possibly be mistaken. But this notion of societal infallibility is no more plausible than the idea of individual infallibility. Is it plausible that no society has ever been wrong about anything—never been wrong about the causes of disease, the best form of government, the number of planets in our solar system, the existence of witches, or the beliefs behind the Nazi policies that resulted in the killing of six million Jews?

Critics like to point out that just as subjective relativism is self-defeating, so is social relativism. The claim that "all truth is relative to societies" is self-defeating because if it is objectively true, it is an example of an objective truth—true for all people everywhere. And that means that the claim (that all truth is relative) must be objectively false.

In summary, if you accept relativism, you may be tempted to care very little about critical thinking, and that would be your loss. Fortunately, there is no good reason why you should neglect critical thinking in the name of relativism.[3]

"What we need is not the will to believe, but the will to find out."

—Bertrand Russell

2.2.3 Skepticism

If knowledge were impossible, then critical thinking—as a way of coming to know the truth or falsity of claims—would seem to be out of a job. Most of us, though, believe that we *can* acquire knowledge. We feel confident that we know a great many things—that we are alive, that our shoes are a certain colour, that there is a tree on the lawn, that the Earth is not flat, that rabbits cannot fly, that 2 + 2 = 4. But not everyone would agree that we can truly know such things. There are some who believe that we know much less than we think we do or perhaps even nothing at all. This view is known as **philosophical skepticism**, and thinkers who raise doubts about how much we know are known as **philosophical skeptics**.

philosophical skepticism
The view that we know much less than we think we do or that we know nothing at all.

philosophical skeptics
Those who embrace philosophical skepticism.

This is no place to dive into a debate on skepticism, but we can take a quick look at the most important type of philosophical skepticism and see what, if anything, it has to do with critical thinking. This form of skepticism says that knowledge requires certainty—if we are to know anything, we must be certain of it. This means that our knowledge isn't really knowledge unless it is beyond any *possibility* of doubt. If knowledge requires certainty, however, there is very little that we know because there are always considerations that can undermine our certainty. There is always, it seems, room for at least some doubt.

But a more reasonable approach is to say that our knowledge *does not* require absolute certainty. All of us can cite many situations in which it does seem reasonable to say we have knowledge—even though we do not have absolutely conclusive reasons. We might claim to know, for example, that it is raining, that our dog has spots, that we were born, and that the moon is not made of green cheese—even though we are perhaps not *absolutely certain* of any of these. These examples seem to be among many examples of things that we do know. It makes sense to say that we know them not because they are beyond all *possible* doubt but because they are beyond all *reasonable* doubt. For practical purposes, that is enough. Doubt is always possible, but it is not always reasonable or useful. Rejecting a reasonable claim to knowledge just because of the bare possibility that you may be wrong is neither reasonable nor necessary.

Critical thinking does have a job to do in our efforts to acquire knowledge. Its task, however, is not to help us find claims that we cannot possibly doubt but instead to help us evaluate claims that vary in degrees of reasonable doubt—that is, from claims that we have very little reason to doubt to claims that we have very strong reason to doubt.

Summary

Critical thinking takes place in a mental environment consisting of our experiences, thoughts, and feelings. Some elements in this inner environment can sabotage our efforts to think critically or can at least make critical thinking more difficult. Fortunately, we can exert some control over these elements. With practice, we can detect errors in our thinking, restrain attitudes and feelings that can disrupt our reasoning, and achieve enough objectivity to make critical thinking possible.

The most common of these hindrances to critical thinking fall into two main categories: (1) those barriers that crop up because of *how* we think and (2) those that occur because of *what* we think. The first category is composed of psychological factors such as our fears, attitudes, motivations, and desires. The second category is made up of certain troublesome philosophical beliefs, such as subjective relativism or social relativism.

None of us is immune to the psychological obstacles. Among them are the products of egocentric thinking. We may accept a claim solely because it advances our interests or just because it helps us save face. To overcome these pressures, we must (1) be aware of strong emotions that can warp our thinking, (2) be alert to ways that critical thinking can be undermined, and (3) ensure that we take into account *all* relevant factors when we evaluate a claim.

The first category of hindrances also includes those that arise because of group pressure. These obstacles include conformist pressures from groups that we belong to and ethnocentric urges to think that our own group is superior to others. The best defence against group pressure is to proportion our beliefs according to the strength of reasons.

We may also have certain beliefs that can undermine critical thinking (the second category of hindrances). Subjective relativism is the view that truth depends solely on what someone believes—a notion that may make critical thinking look pointless. But subjective relativism leads to some strange consequences. For example, if subjective relativism were true, each of us would be infallible. Also, subjective relativism has a logical problem—it's self-defeating. Its truth implies its falsity. There are no good reasons to accept this form of relativism.

Social relativism is the view that truth is relative to societies—a claim that would also seem to make critical thinking unnecessary. But this notion is undermined by the same kinds of problems that plague subjective relativism.

Philosophical skepticism is the doctrine that we know much less than we think we do. One form of philosophical skepticism says we cannot know anything unless the belief is beyond all possible doubt. But this is not a plausible criterion for knowledge. To count as knowledge, claims need not be beyond all possible doubt but beyond all *reasonable* doubt.

Exercise 2.1

Answers to exercises marked with an asterisk (*) may be found in Appendix B, Answers to Exercises.

Review Questions

1. What are the two main categories of common barriers to critical thinking?*
2. According to the text, what are the essential ingredients of critical thinking?
3. What is peer pressure?
4. What is fake news?
5. From the standpoint of critical thinking, what counts as a sign that that you have allowed your bias in favour of yourself to go too far?*
6. According to the text, what is the difference between self-interested thinking and face-saving thinking?
7. When are you most likely to let your self-interest get in the way of clear thinking?*
8. According to the text, what should you do if you sense a rush of emotion when you think about a particular issue?
9. What is selective attention? What is one remedy for this problem?
10. According to the text, how might selective attention affect your thinking when you are examining evidence for or against a claim?
11. How might the influence of a group that you belong to affect your attempts to think critically?*
12. What are some of the possible consequences of self-centred thinking?
13. What is the appeal to popularity?
14. What is a world view?*
15. What is social relativism?
16. According to the text, how could social relativism make critical thinking unnecessary?
17. Is critical thinking concerned with the *objective* or the *subjective* truth of claims?*
18. How is social relativism different from subjective relativism?
19. What is philosophical skepticism?
20. Why is it incorrect to say that knowledge requires certainty?
21. What kind of doubt is involved in acquiring knowledge?*

Exercise 2.2

Indicate whether each of the following passages most likely contains examples of self-interested thinking, face-saving, or group pressure—or none of the above.

1. Feng: Canada's healthcare system is the best in the world.

Tim: Why do you think Canada's is better than, say, Australia's? Do you agree that both countries have similar systems and that their health outcomes are similar?
Feng: Well, yes.
Tim: Do you agree that all the other indicators of quality are nearly identical?
Feng: Yes, but Canada's is still better.*

2. Ying: Corporate profits should be taxed at a lower rate than they are.
Priyanka: What makes you think that?
Ying: I've got money invested in several corporations, and if corporate profits are highly taxed, my investment won't be profitable!
3. Don't waste your inheritance by donating to feed the homeless. They're mostly just drug addicts anyway. But I'm involved with a great charity that would put that money to good use.
4. Yeah, she broke up with me. But the breakup had nothing to do with me. She's just too flaky to be in a relationship.*
5. I don't agree with immigrants' claims that they are being treated badly at the border. If I endorsed those claims, every friend I've got would turn their backs on me.
6. Amanda: The new Spider-Man movie was terrible. There was nothing good about it at all.
Ben: But it's #1 at the box office. When Dave and Theresa and I went to see it, we all loved it.
Amanda: Well, come to think of it, the movie did have some great action scenes. And Tom Holland, who played Spider-Man, is a very good actor.
7. Hinduism is superior to all other religions. I was raised Hindu, and all my relatives are Hindus. This is the only religion I've known, and everyone I know and trust tells me it's the one true religion.*
8. Don't tell me this class isn't useful! I've been teaching it for years, and I certainly know what I'm doing!
9. Moosehead is the best beer in the world. I've never tried any of those weird foreign beers, and I don't intend to.
10. Free speech should not extend to those who would deny human rights to transgendered Canadians. Right now transphobes are allowed to state their views on the internet and many university campuses. That's just not how I was raised.*
11. If my friend Professor Snyder is teaching the class, my daughter is guaranteed to get an "A." I think Professor Snyder is the ideal person to teach the class.

Exercise 2.3

Read each of the following claims. Then select from the list any statements that, if true, would constitute good reasons for accepting the claim. Be careful: in some questions, none of the choices are correct.

1. John: The newspaper accounts of the charges of pedophilia lodged against Father J. Miller, a Catholic priest in our town, are likely false.*
   a. The charges come from a single source who is a known liar.
   b. John is a Catholic.
   c. Important evidence that would exonerate Father Miller was not mentioned in the newspaper account.
   d. The town is predominately Catholic.
2. Petra: You should consider attending Twin Eagles Community College.
   a. Petra is a recruiter for Twin Eagles Community College.
   b. You've seen stats suggesting that graduates of Twin Eagles Community College are typically hired quite quickly after they graduate.
   c. You've seen on their website that Twin Eagles Community College has a number of programs that interest you.
   d. Petra has a degree in education.
3. Janette: The rate of violent crime among real Canadians is lower than it is among immigrants.*
   a. Janette's family has lived here in Canada for over 100 years.
   b. Janette's family immigrated to Canada in 2017.
   c. Janette is a member of her community's Neighbourhood Watch group.
   d. Janette has a degree in criminology.
4. Nanako: You should visit Japan for your next holiday.
   a. Nanako was born in Japan and knows how beautiful it is there.
   b. Nanako knows you well enough to know what kind of vacation you would enjoy.
   c. Nanako's brother owns a travel agency that specializes in trips to Japan.
   d. You've told Nanako before that you've always wanted to visit Asia.
5. ACME Inc. can supply us with the best materials at the lowest price.
   a. ACME has a good reputation in the industry.
   b. The person in charge of purchasing has a sister who works at ACME.
   c. ACME has a history of being accused of using shady business practices to drive down their costs.
   d. A report submitted by an independent third party suggests that ACME's prices are best.
6. Zaid: "This project is sure to be a failure."*
   a. Zaid wasn't included in the planning process.
   b. The project is far behind schedule.
   c. Zaid's boss, Jen, has doubts about this project.
   d. Everyone in the lunch room is making jokes about the project.
7. Angelo: Cannabis should be distributed only through government-run dispensaries.
   a. There is evidence that broadening distribution outlets for cannabis would result in reduced quality control and would not serve the needs of consumers well.

b. All of Angelo's friends smoke cannabis.
c. Angelo works at a government cannabis dispensary.
d. Angelo has already said on television that the government should strictly control the cannabis business.

Exercise 2.4

Read the following passages. Determine whether each one contains examples of the kind of group pressure that encourages people to conform (peer pressure or appeal to popularity) or the type that urges people to think that one's own group is better than others. For each example of group pressure, specify the possible negative consequences of such pressure. A couple of these are very difficult to classify.

1. Marie-Eve is straight, has an active dating life, and is strongly attracted to men. She has never considered any other path. She believes that there's nothing wrong with legally limiting marriage to unions between a man and a woman.*
2. Prathamesh is trying out for his university's varsity lacrosse team. Nearly everyone on the team is religious, although various team members adhere to different religions. Prathamesh hasn't ever really been religious, and he's not even sure that he believes in God. He notices that he hasn't been invited to many of the team events.
3. Yang Lei is a conservative blogger for one of Canada's most popular conservative news and commentary websites. But she yearns for bigger and better things—most especially, a regular column for a newsmagazine. She gets her dream job, though the magazine does have liberal leanings. The first few columns she writes for the magazine are a shock to her friends. Politically, her new columns are middle-of-the-road or even suspiciously left-leaning.
4. An Atlantic Canadian university has invited a famous writer to be a guest speaker in the campus-wide distinguished-speaker series. She is an accomplished poet and essayist. She is also a Marxist and believes Canada should move in a more socialist direction. During her speech, she is shouted down by a small group of conservative students and faculty.*
5. Adam is afraid of heights. At the local fair, his friends want to go on the Ferris wheel and really want him to go on it with them. They accuse him of being "a baby," and tell him he would join them if he were "a real man." They all laugh when they hear Adam screaming from the top of the wheel.
6. A prominent politician in Ottawa presents a carefully reasoned argument against the use of quotas to make sure that women have equal access to government jobs. He points to studies that show that women are relatively successful at getting such jobs, and he argues that there are strong moral reasons in favour of always hiring the most qualified candidate. That evening, his office receives dozens of angry emails from women and men who say his

statement was sexist and who threaten not to vote for him in the next election. The next day, he issues a press release apologizing for his comments. He states that he is a strong supporter of woman's rights and that his comments on hiring quotas were "taken out of context."

7. A friend of yours argues that recycling is the most important environmental issue and that he's never heard anyone deny it.*

Exercise 2.5

Read the following scenarios. Indicate whether each one contains examples of self-interested thinking or face-saving, and, for each instance, briefly outline the possible negative consequences.

1. Last year, Neera Co. operated at a loss for the first time since it was founded 60 years ago. The new CEO blamed poor market conditions for the loss. So far this year, Neera Co. has been losing even more money than last year, and its shareholders have started voicing their concerns. The CEO is planning to release a statement that blames the workers' union's unfair wage demands for driving up costs and hurting the company.*
2. City councillor Jackson is in a position to cast the deciding vote on two proposals for the development of a new city park. Proposal 1 involves a parcel of land near Jackson's own house, and would give him a beautiful view. Its drawbacks are that it would cost the city twice as much as proposal 2 and is not easily accessible to most of the public. Proposal 2 suggests a parcel of land near the centre of town. It is convenient to the public, has a more beautiful setting, and will raise property values in the area. Councillor Jackson says, without providing any evidence, that there's "too much traffic" around the second site and that the obvious best choice is proposal 1.*
3. Antonio is running in the municipal election for a position on his city council. On election night, he has two speeches prepared. If he wins, he plans on stating in his speech that he is glad that the people have spoken so clearly and given him this honourable task. If he loses, he plans to express his disappointment in how poorly the election was run and how poorly the volunteers running the polling stations were trained.
4. Louisa is an entrepreneur—she's started a business selling her own handmade ceramic coffee mugs with original artwork painted onto them. She has invested thousands of dollars in the equipment required, and has paid a web developer to build her a website to sell her coffee cups. During the first month that the website is operating, Louisa makes only a handful of sales, and gets two complaints from customers who say her mugs are low quality. When her friends ask her about how things are going, Louisa blames the web developer for having produced a low-quality website.

5. Simone and Justin are in a heated debate about anthropogenic global warming (AGW)—the idea that human activity is responsible for substantial warming of the Earth over the past hundred years or so. Simone rejects this idea, believing instead that the changes observed over the last hundred years have been part of a natural global cycle. Justin rejects that view in favour of the "anthropogenic" (human-caused) point of view. Simone cites a number of facts that seem to prove her case. In addition, she alleges that AGW is false because there have been a number of other substantial changes in global temperatures in the last thousand years that clearly have nothing to do with human activity. Justin has no answer for this argument and looks exasperated. Simone is about to declare victory when Justin suddenly begins to quote the research findings of reputable climate scientists showing that the current change in climate really is *uniquely* sudden and severe after all. After the debate, some of Justin's friends quietly congratulate him for being clever enough to "quote" research "findings" that are actually entirely fictitious.

Field Problems

1. Recall a situation in your past in which the beliefs of a member of your own family may have been skewed by self-interest, face-saving, or group pressure. Think about (1) how one or more of these three factors affected their beliefs, (2) what the consequences (negative or positive) of the event were, and (3) what beliefs they might have acquired instead if they had used critical thinking. Take notes to help you remember the facts, and be prepared to present your story in class.
2. Recall a situation in which your own beliefs were apparently skewed by self-interest, face-saving, or group pressure to conform. (This is tough! Be honest with yourself!) Identify the three factors mentioned in the preceding question.
3. Assess a speech by a Canadian politician—federal, provincial, or municipal. Examine the speech for evidence that the politician is making use of *peer pressure, appeal to popularity,* or *stereotyping.* Explain briefly what you found.

Self-Assessment Quiz

1. According to the definition of critical thinking given in the text, what factors must be present for critical thinking to take place?
2. What is subjective relativism?
3. According to the text, what is skepticism?
4. What degree of doubt do we attempt to surpass in the acquisition of knowledge?
5. According to the text, why is it important to look for opposing evidence when evaluating claims?

Read the following scenarios. State whether each one contains examples of self-interested thinking, face-saving, or both.

6. Trish predicted that the new *Saturday Night Live* spin-off show would be amazing. But in fact, TV critics almost all think the show stinks, and TV audiences—influenced perhaps by critics—generally stay away from it. Trish complains that the critics are all "biased" and that most TV viewers have lousy taste anyway.
7. Lois's parents tell her she's very good at poetry. And her friends say so too. Lois gets a C+ in her poetry class. Lois continues to believe that she's got a future as a poet.
8. One day Julie and Jill hear their instructor read a list of arguments for and against reforming the way that Canada screens immigrants. Half the arguments are in favour of reform, and half are against it. Julie is on the pro side, and Jill is on the con side. Later, when they discuss the immigration arguments, they recall the facts differently. Julie remembers that most of the arguments heard in class were in favour of reform. Jill remembers only the arguments against changes and recalls very few pro arguments.

Specify whether the following passages are examples of face-saving, self-serving, group pressure thinking, or a combination of these.

9. Everyone else in our group thinks that copying-and-pasting from Wikipedia is totally fine. That fact alone ought to persuade you that it's OK.
10. People should look for advice from experts when important health decisions need to be made.
11. In Canada about 90 per cent of the population has some kind of religious belief or affiliation with some religious organization. In light of this, how can you say you're an unbeliever? If you're an unbeliever, you're un-Canadian.
12. Why don't you download the Telegram app? We all use it, and group messaging you would be so much easier if you had it too.

Read each of the following passages, and state whether it is an example of the subjectivist fallacy or social relativism.

13. This may not be your truth, but it's *our* truth.
14. Chinese diplomat: "My country cannot be judged by some universal standard. It must be judged by its own unique values and norms."
15. It may not be true for you that children require strict discipline, including spanking, but it's true for my kids!

Integrative Exercises

These exercises pertain to material in Chapters 1 and 2.

1. What is an argument?
2. What is a statement or claim?
3. Give an example of a statement and an example of a sentence that is not a statement.
4. Name one way in which a world view can influence your evaluation of a claim.

For each of the following passages, indicate whether it contains an argument. For each argument, specify what the conclusion is and whether the passage contains an appeal to popularity, or peer pressure, or neither.

5. They say that money is the root of all evil. But money is only evil if you want more than your share of it. So greed is the real problem.
6. We all have an obligation to foster a working environment that is inclusive and that reflects the diversity of our community. Inclusion is ethically important, and diversity has been proven to improve group decision-making.
7. Women should not be allowed in combat roles in the military—that's just the way I was raised.
8. I look forward to the day when, with the help of new technology, the world is able to turn its back entirely on fossil fuels.

9. Your family loves you, and we all think you're wrong about Frank. That should be enough to convince you not to marry him.

Read each of the following claims. Then select from the list any statements that, if true, would constitute good reasons for accepting the claim. Some statements may have no good reasons listed.

10. There should be harsher punishments for sexual harassment in the workplace.
    a. Countries with the harshest punishments for sexual harassment have the lowest incident rates of sexual harassment.
    b. Polls show that Canadians think that, overall, companies don't do as much as they should to reduce rates of sexual harassment in the workplace.
    c. Someone you know was sexually assaulted in the workplace.
    d. Punishing workplace sexual harassment is the only way to ensure the integrity of our workplaces, and thus it is the only morally correct course of action.
11. It's getting harder and harder for young Canadians to find a decent job that pays a living wage.
    a. I haven't found a job despite graduating over three months ago.
    b. Surveys show that joblessness among Canadians aged 18–25 is higher than it was last year.
    c. Many Canadian companies are opening up branches in foreign countries.
    d. My cousin has a master's degree, but she has been working at Starbucks for over a year now.
12. Apple laptops are the best on the market.
    a. I use an Apple laptop and always tell people how great it is.
    b. Apple laptops are popular with students at the best universities.
    c. *Laptop World* magazine has ranked the Apple MacBook Pro in the top 3 every year for the last 5 years.
    d. My accountant uses an Apple laptop.

For each of the following passages, determine whether an argument is present and whether peer pressure or an appeal to popularity is being used. Some passages may not contain arguments, and some may not contain examples of either group pressure or appeal to popularity.

13. "Canada has a dog-dumping problem. Scrolling through headlines from the past year reveals stories, spanning from B.C. to New Brunswick, of dogs dumped like trash, in forests, in parks, on roadsides and in actual trash. The latest to make news: a little white dog found duct taped inside a box last week on the side of a Manitoba highway. The truth is that for every disturbing dog-dumping story deemed newsworthy, there is an even more disturbing number of abandoned and surrendered pets not making headlines, and this is a sign of a much greater problem. As a culture, Canadians lack respect for the duties of dog ownership, and throwing away animals like garbage is just par for the cruel course." (Jessica Scott-Reid, *Globe and Mail*, 26 November 2017)
14. The facts are plain. Everyone with a brain in their head knows it. If we don't act to slow global warming, we are dooming future generations.
15. You cannot seriously believe that Seattle is more beautiful than Vancouver. I don't know a single Vancouverite who believes that!

Critical Thinking and Writing Exercise

From Issue to Thesis

For many students, the biggest challenge in writing an argumentative essay is deciding on an appropriate thesis—the claim, or conclusion, that the essay is designed to support or prove. Very often, when an essay runs off track and crashes, the derailment can be traced to a thesis that was bad from the beginning.

Picking a thesis out of the air and beginning to write is usually a mistake. Any thesis statement that you craft without knowing anything about the subject is likely to be ill-formed or indefensible. It's better to begin by selecting an issue—a question that's controversial or in dispute—and then researching it to determine what arguments or viewpoints are involved. To research it, you can survey the views of people or organizations involved in the controversy. Read articles and books, talk to people, and do some research online. This process should not only inform you about various viewpoints but also tell you what arguments are used to support them. It should also help you to narrow the issue down to one that you can easily address in the space you have.

Suppose you begin with the question of whether Canada has serious industrial pollution problems. After investigating this issue, you would probably see that it is much too broad to be addressed in a short paper. You should then restrict the issue to something more manageable—for example, whether recent legislation to allow coal-burning power plants to emit more sulphur dioxide will harm people's health. With the scope of the issue narrowed, you can explore arguments on both sides. You cannot examine every single argument, but you should assess the strongest ones, including those that you devise yourself. You can then use what you've already learned about arguments to select one that you think provides good support for its conclusion. The premises and conclusion of this argument can then serve as the bare-bones outline of your essay. Your argument might look like this:

[Premise 1] High amounts of sulphur dioxide in the air have been linked to increases in the incidence of asthma and other respiratory illnesses.

[Premise 2] Many areas of the country already have high amounts of sulphur dioxide in the air.

[Premise 3] Most sulphur dioxide in the air comes from coal-burning power plants.

[Conclusion] Therefore, allowing coal-burning power plants to emit more sulphur dioxide will most likely increase the incidence of respiratory illnesses.

For the sake of the example, the premises of this argument are made up. But the argument of your essay must be real, with each premise that could be called into question supported by an additional argument. After all, your readers are not likely to accept the conclusion of your argument if they doubt your premises.

In some cases, your paper may contain more than one argument supporting a single conclusion, or it may offer a critique of someone else's argument. In either case, investigating an issue and the arguments involved will follow the pattern just suggested. In a critique of an argument (or arguments), you offer reasons why the argument fails and you thereby support the thesis that the conclusion is false or at least unsupported.

This process of devising a thesis statement and crafting an argument to back it up is not linear. You will probably have to experiment with several arguments before you find one that's suitable. Even after you decide on an argument, you may later discover that its premises are dubious or that they cannot be adequately supported. Then you will have to backtrack to investigate a better argument. Backtracking in this preliminary stage is relatively easy. But if you postpone this rethinking process until you are almost finished with your first draft, it will be harder—and more painful.

Argument and Emotion

As we saw earlier, the point of an argument is to provide rational support for a claim by supplying good reasons for accepting a conclusion. And argument, of course, is the main focus of a good argumentative essay. Nonetheless, experienced writers often enhance the persuasive power of their argumentative essays through the use of various emotional appeals. Inexperienced writers, though, sometimes get the argumentative and emotional elements confused or out of balance. To avoid such problems, try to stick to these rules of thumb:

- Be fair to the opposing view. Summarize or restate the opposing arguments clearly and accurately. Avoid sarcasm, ridicule, or loaded (emotive) words in describing other viewpoints. Don't say, for example, "this so-called argument," "that ridiculous view," or "this idiotic proposal."
- Be fair to your opponent. Avoid personal attacks, insults, stereotyping, and innuendo. Keep the main focus on the quality of your opponent's arguments, not on his or her character.
- Avoid appeals to your own self-interest or the wishes of your preferred group.
- If you have strong feelings about an issue, try to channel those feelings into creating the best arguments possible—not into emotional displays.

Writing Assignments

1. Read Essay 2 ("The Last Honourable Man") in Appendix A, and write a summary of the essay in 75–100 words. Mention the thesis statement and each supporting premise.
2. Study the argument presented in Essay 8 ("Unrepentant Homeopaths") in Appendix A. Identify the conclusion and the premises and objections considered. Then write a 500-word rebuttal to the essay. That is, defend the claim that it is morally right to promote homeopathy.
3. Select an issue from the following list and write a 600-word essay defending a statement pertaining to the issue. Follow the procedure discussed in the text for identifying a thesis and an appropriate argument to defend it.
   - Are the mainstream news media biased?
   - Should a single corporation be allowed to buy up as many media outlets (newspapers, radio and TV stations, book publishers, etc.) as it wants?
   - Should the Canadian government be allowed to arrest and indefinitely imprison, without trial, any Canadian citizen who is suspected of terrorism?
   - Should corporate taxes be raised or instead lowered?

Notes

1. "Worldwide Digital Ad Spending 2021," *eMarketer*, 29 April 2021. https://www.emarketer.com/content/worldwide-digital-ad-spending-2021
2. Bertrand Russell, *Let the People Think* (London: William Clowes, 1941), 2.
3. For a thorough review of various forms of relativism, see Theodore Schick and Lewis Vaughn, *How to Think about Weird Things*, 3rd ed. (Mountain View, CA: Mayfield, 1999), 68–92.

Making Sense of Arguments

Chapter Objectives

Argument Basics

You will be able to

- distinguish between deductive and inductive arguments.
- understand the terms *valid*, *invalid*, and *sound*.
- understand the terms *strong*, *weak*, and *cogent*.

Judging Arguments

You will be able to

- follow the four-step procedure for determining whether an argument is deductive or inductive, good or bad.
- obtain a familiarity with indicator words that suggest that an argument is deductive or inductive.

Finding Missing Parts

You will be able to

- use the three-step procedure for uncovering implicit premises.

Argument Patterns

You will be able to

- memorize and be able to recognize the argument patterns known as *modus ponens*, *modus tollens*, *hypothetical syllogism*, *denying the antecedent*, *affirming the consequent*, and *disjunctive syllogism*.
- use the counterexample method for determining if a deductive argument is valid or invalid.

Diagramming Arguments

You will be able to

- understand the definition of *dependent* and *independent premises.*
- follow the three-step procedure to diagram arguments, both simple and complex ones, including those embedded in extraneous material.

Assessing Long Arguments

You will be able to

- understand the challenges involved in assessing long arguments.
- follow the procedure for diagramming long arguments.

In this chapter we resume our discussion of arguments begun in Chapter 1, dig deeper into the dynamics and structure of different types of argument, and get a lot more practice identifying and critiquing simple (and not so simple) arguments in their "natural habitat."

Recall that in Chapter 1 we defined an argument as a group of statements in which some of them (the premises) are intended to support another of them (the conclusion). An essential skill is the ability to identify arguments in real-life contexts and to distinguish them from non-arguments. To recognize an argument you must be able to identify the premises and the conclusion. Indicator words such as *because* and *since* often signal the presence of premises, and words such as *therefore* and *thus* can point to a conclusion.

3.1 Argument Basics

The point of *devising* an argument is to try to show to your audience (or perhaps just to yourself) that a statement or claim (namely, your conclusion) is worthy of acceptance. The point of *evaluating* an argument is to see whether this task has been successful—whether the argument shows that the statement (the conclusion) really is worthy of acceptance. When the argument shows that the conclusion is worthy of acceptance, we say that the argument is *good*. When the argument fails to show that the conclusion is worthy of acceptance, we say that the argument is *bad*. There are different ways, however, that an argument can be good or bad. This is because there are different types of arguments.

deductive argument
An argument intended to provide logically conclusive support for its conclusion.

inductive argument
An argument in which the premises are intended to provide probable, not conclusive, support for its conclusion.

Arguments come in two main forms—**deductive** and **inductive**. A deductive argument is one that is intended to provide, and potentially capable of providing, logically *conclusive* support for its conclusion. An inductive argument is one that is intended to provide, and only capable of providing, *probable*—not conclusive—support for its conclusion.

Food for Thought

Changing Your Mind

People change their minds about all kinds of things, both trivial and important. One day you believe one thing, and then at some later date you realize, perhaps to your own surprise, that you now believe the exact opposite. And people change their minds for all kinds of reasons, both good and bad. Sometimes people change their minds because they have been presented with a compelling argument that their previous belief was mistaken. On the other hand (as discussed in Chapter 2), sometimes people change their minds for bad reasons, such as peer pressure or face-saving.

Of course, in some cases you don't *need* good reasons. If you open the freezer to grab some vanilla ice cream, but then decide instead to grab the chocolate ice cream, there's no harm in that! Even if you don't know *why* you now want chocolate, it doesn't really matter—all that matters is that you want what you want, and it's none of anyone else's business. But when the matter is an important one, such as what career to choose or whom to vote for, it is worth spending time thinking carefully about the forces that may have resulted in a mental about-face.

Torontonian/Alamy Stock Photo

Election campaigns typically focus on persuading citizens to vote for particular candidates. Sometimes that involves appeals to reason, but not always. What other persuasive strategies have you seen used by politicians during campaigns?

3.1.1 Deductive Arguments

A deductive argument that provides decisive logical support is said to be **valid**; a deductive argument that fails to provide such support is said to be **invalid**. A deductively valid argument is such that if its premises are true, its conclusion *must* be true. That is, if the premises are true, there is no way that the conclusion can be false. In logic, *valid* is a technical term; it is not a synonym for *true*. A deductively valid argument simply has the kind of logical structure that *guarantees* the truth of the conclusion *if* the premises are true. "Logical structure" refers not to the content of an argument but to its construction, that is, the way the premises and conclusion fit together. Because of the guarantee of truth in the conclusion, deductively valid arguments are said to be **truth-preserving**: in a valid deductive argument, if you start with true premises, the structure of the argument "preserves" that truth, all the way through into the conclusion.

valid argument
A deductive argument that succeeds in providing conclusive support for its conclusion.

invalid argument
A deductive argument that fails to provide conclusive support for its conclusion.

truth-preserving
A characteristic of a valid deductive argument in which the logical structure guarantees the truth of the conclusion if the premises are true.

Here's a simple deductively valid argument:

Sheldon is a physicist.
All physicists are good at math.
So Sheldon is good at math.

And here's a classic:

All men are mortal.
Socrates is a man.
Therefore, Socrates is mortal.

And here is one in regular paragraph form:

[Premise] All Canadian police officers carry a gun. [Premise] Alexandra is a Canadian police officer. [Conclusion] Therefore, Alexandra carries a gun.

In each of these arguments, if the premises are true, the conclusion must be absolutely, positively true. In the last argument, for example, if Alexandra is a Canadian police officer but doesn't carry a gun, then the first premise must actually be false, because there's at least one Canadian police officer—Alexandra—who doesn't carry a gun. So you may or may not agree with the premises, but it is impossible for the premises to be true and the conclusions false. The conclusion *follows logically* from the premises. And the order of the premises makes no difference. Indeed, it doesn't even matter whether the premises are stated before or after the conclusion. What matters is the logical relation between them.

A deductively *invalid* version of these arguments might look like this:

Sheldon is a physicist.
Sheldon is a man.
So all physicists are men.

If Socrates has horns, he is mortal.
Socrates is mortal.
Therefore, Socrates has horns.

In each of these, the conclusion does *not* follow logically from the premises. Each is an attempt at a deductively valid argument, but the attempt fails—even if the premises were true, they would not guarantee that their conclusions are true. And again, this would be the case

Sidney Harris/CartoonStock

Not everything that sounds like a logical argument is one.

regardless of the order of the premises. Note that even an argument with a conclusion that is obviously true can be invalid if that conclusion is not supported by the premises offered. Look at this argument, for example:

> All whales have tails.
> All whales have eyes.
> Therefore, all whales are mammals.

It's obviously a silly argument, but it demonstrates something important. The conclusion here is obviously true—whales really are mammals—but the argument is invalid: the conclusion doesn't *follow from* the premises offered. After all, lots of things have tails and eyes but are not mammals.

"The most perfidious way of harming a cause consists of defending it deliberately with faulty arguments."

—Friedrich Nietzsche

3.1.2 Inductive Arguments

An inductive argument that succeeds in providing probable—but not conclusive—logical support for its conclusion is said to be **strong**. An inductive argument that fails to provide such support is said to be **weak**. An inductively strong argument is such that if its premises are true, its conclusion is *probably* or *likely* to be true. The structure of an inductively strong argument cannot guarantee that the conclusion is true if the premises are true—but the conclusion can be rendered probable and worthy of acceptance. (Here again, the structure and content of an argument are separate issues.) Because the truth of the conclusion cannot be guaranteed by the truth of the premises, inductive arguments are not truth-preserving.

strong argument
An inductive argument that succeeds in providing probable—but not conclusive—support for its conclusion.

weak argument
An inductive argument that fails to provide strong support for its conclusion.

Let's turn our first two deductively valid arguments into inductively strong arguments:

> Most physicists are good at math.
> Therefore, Sheldon (a physicist) is probably good at math.

> Almost all humans are mortal.
> Socrates is a human.
> Therefore, Socrates is probably mortal.

Notice that in the first argument, it's entirely possible for the premise to be true and the conclusion false. After all, if only *most* physicists are good at math, there is no guarantee that Sheldon is good at math. Yet the premise, if true, makes the conclusion probably true. Likewise, in the second argument it is possible that even if 99.9 per cent of humans are mortal and Socrates is human, the conclusion that Socrates is mortal could be false. But the premises, if true, make it likely that the conclusion is true.

3.1.3 Good Arguments

Logical validity, or logical strength, is an essential characteristic of good arguments. But there is more to good arguments than having the proper structure. Good arguments also have *true premises*. A good argument is one that has the

Nick Kim/CartoonStock

How might focusing only on an argument's logic, without paying attention to the truth of its premises, be dangerous?

proper structure *and* true premises. Take a look at this argument:

All pigs can fly.
Michael is a pig.
Therefore, Michael can fly.

Both of the premises of this argument are false (assuming that "Michael" is in fact a human being or some other non-pig), but the conclusion follows logically from those premises. That is, if the premises were true—if pigs really could fly and if Michael were a pig—then it would also be true that Michael would be able to fly. But as it is, it's a deductively valid argument with all the parts in the right place—even though the premises and conclusion are false. But it is not a good argument because a good argument must also have true premises and this argument doesn't. A deductively valid argument that also has true premises is said to be **sound**. A sound argument is a good argument that gives you good reasons for accepting its conclusion. Such an argument, in other words, gives us everything that we could hope for in a deductive argument.

sound argument
A deductively valid argument that has true premises.

It is important to note, however, that even deductively valid arguments can have true or false premises and true or false conclusions. Validity is only about structure and what claims follow logically from what. So deductively valid arguments can have false premises and a false conclusion, false premises and a true conclusion, or true premises and a true conclusion. See for yourself:

False Premises, False Conclusion
All businesses are corporations.
All corporations are allowed to vote.
Therefore, all businesses are allowed to vote.

False Premises, True Conclusion
If something is lighter than helium, it must also be heavier than water.
Gold is lighter than helium.
Therefore, gold is heavier than water.

True Premises, True Conclusion
Abshir is a human.
All humans are mammals.
Therefore, Abshir is a mammal.

A valid argument, though, cannot have true premises and a false conclusion—that's impossible.

A good inductive argument must also have true premises. This example illustrates why:

> The first humans were roaming the earth just as the dinosaurs were dying out.
> So it's likely that we will find human fossils mixed in with dinosaur fossils.

This is an inductively strong argument (because its premise, if true, would make its conclusion quite likely), but it's not a good argument because its premise is false—the first humans appeared on earth about 65 million years after the last dinosaurs died out! When inductively strong arguments also have true premises, they are said to be **cogent**. Good inductive arguments are cogent; bad inductive arguments are not cogent. The argument above, about fossils, is inductively strong but not cogent. The word cogent represents the highest form of praise available for an inductive argument: a cogent inductive argument is one that we can rely upon. Here's an example of a cogent inductive argument:

cogent argument
A strong inductive argument with all true premises.

> Humans appeared on earth millions of years after the last dinosaurs died out. So it's very unlikely that we will find human fossils mixed in with dinosaur fossils.

You may have noticed another important difference between deductive and inductive arguments. The kind of support that a deductive argument can give a conclusion is *absolute*. Either the conclusion is shown to be true, or it is not shown to be true. There is no sliding scale of truth or falsity for deductive arguments. The support that an inductive argument can provide a conclusion, however, can range from very weak to extremely strong. An inductive argument, that is, might provide a little support, a moderate amount of support, or a lot of support for its conclusion.

Review Notes

Deductive and Inductive Arguments

A deductive argument

- is intended to provide conclusive support for its conclusion;
- is said to be *valid* if it succeeds in providing conclusive support for its premise. (A valid argument is such that if its premises are true, its conclusion must be true.); and
- is said to be *sound* if it is valid and has true premises.

An inductive argument

- is intended to provide probable support for its conclusion;
- is said to be *strong* if it succeeds in providing probable support for its conclusion. (A strong argument is such that if its premises are true, its conclusion is probably true.); and
- is said to be *cogent* if it is a strong argument and has true premises.

Both deductive and inductive arguments can be manipulated in various ways to yield new insights. For example, let's say that you have formulated a valid deductive argument and you know that the conclusion is false. From these facts you can infer (based on the definition of a valid deductive argument) that at least one of the premises must be false. Using this approach, you can demonstrate that a premise is false because in at least one valid argument that premise leads to a false conclusion. Or let's say that you've constructed a valid argument and you know that your premises are true. Then you can infer that the conclusion must be true—even if the conclusion is contrary to your expectations. Or maybe you put forth a strong inductive argument and you know that the premises are questionable. Then you know that the conclusion also can't be trusted—it might end up being true, but you can't assume so based on the weak premises of this argument.

Exercise 3.1

Answers to exercises marked with an asterisk (*) may be found in Appendix B, Answers to Exercises.

1. What is an inductive argument?
2. What is a deductive argument?
3. Are deductive arguments truth-preserving? Why or why not?
4. What type of arguments do the terms *valid* and *invalid* apply to?*
5. What kind of support does an inductive argument provide for its conclusion when the argument is strong?
6. Can an inductive argument guarantee the truth of the conclusion if the premises are true? Why or why not?
7. What is the difference between an inductively strong argument and a deductively valid one?
8. What is the term for valid arguments that have true premises?*
9. What is the term for strong arguments that have true premises?
10. Can a valid deductive argument have false premises and a true conclusion? Can it have false premises and a false conclusion?
11. What logical conclusion can you draw about an argument that is deductively valid but has a false conclusion?
12. Is it possible for a valid argument to have all true premises and a false conclusion?*
13. In what way are conclusions of deductive arguments absolute?

3.2 Judging Arguments

When it comes to deductive and inductive arguments, the most important skills you can learn are being able to identify both kinds of arguments and determining whether individual arguments you come across are good or bad. Much of the rest of this text is devoted to helping you get good at these skills. This chapter will serve as your first lesson and give you a chance to practise what you learn.

So the obvious questions here are the following: When you come face to face with an argument to evaluate, (1) how can you tell whether it's deductive or inductive and (2) how can you determine whether it gives you good reasons for accepting the conclusion (whether it's sound or cogent)? The following is a suggested four-step procedure for answering these questions, a procedure that will be elaborated on here and in later chapters.

Step 1. Find the conclusion of the argument, and then identify its premises. Use the techniques you learned in Chapter 1. You'll have plenty of chances to sharpen this skill in later chapters.

Step 2. Ask, "Is it the case that if the premises are true the conclusion *must* be true?" If the answer to that question is yes, you should treat the argument as *deductive*, for it is very likely meant to offer conclusive support for its conclusion. The argument, then, is deductively valid, and you should check to see if it's sound by checking whether all of the premises are true. If the answer is no, proceed to the next step.

Step 3. Ask, "Is it the case that if the premises were true, its conclusion would *probably be* true?" If the answer is yes, treat the argument as *inductive*, for it is very likely meant to offer probable support for its conclusion. The argument, then, is inductively strong, and you should check to see if it's cogent. If the answer is no, proceed to the next step.

Step 4. Ask, "Is the argument intended to offer conclusive or probable support for its conclusion but *fails* to do so?" If you reach this step, you will have already eliminated two possibilities: a valid argument and a strong one. The remaining options are an invalid argument or a weak one. So here you must discover what type of (failed) argument is intended. There are two guidelines that can help you do that.

> **GUIDELINE 1:** Generally, if an argument looks deductive or inductive because of its *form*, assume that it is intended to be so.

Bad arguments may sometimes look like good arguments because the arrangement of their premises and conclusion—their form—is similar to that found in reliable arguments. (You saw some of these reliable argument forms in the argument examples presented earlier in this chapter.) Such argument forms are an indication of what kind of argument is intended, and that fact gives you some guidance on determining argument type.

> **GUIDELINE 2:** Generally, if an argument looks deductive or inductive because of the types of *indicator words* used (and if its form yields no other clues), then assume that it is intended to be so.

Arguments are often accompanied by words or phrases that identify them as deductive or inductive. Terms that tend to signal a deductive argument include

"It necessarily follows that," "it logically follows that," "absolutely," "necessarily," and "certainly." Words signalling an inductive argument include "likely," "probably," "chances are," "odds are," and "it is plausible that." Such indicator words, though, are not foolproof clues to the type of argument because they are sometimes used in misleading ways. For example, someone might end an inductively strong argument with a conclusion prefaced with "it necessarily follows that," suggesting (incorrectly) that the argument is deductively valid. But argument-type indicators may still be useful, especially when the argument form provides no clues (i.e., when Guideline 1 doesn't apply).

In step 4, once you discover which kind of argument is intended, you will know that it is either invalid or weak (because in steps 2 and 3 we eliminated the possibility of a valid or strong argument).[1]

"He who strikes the first blow admits he's lost the argument."

—Chinese proverb

Let's try out the four-step procedure on a few arguments. Consider this one:

> [Premise] Unless we do something about the massive Ebola epidemic in Africa, the whole continent will be decimated within six months. [Premise] Unfortunately, we won't do anything about the Ebola epidemic in Africa. [Conclusion] It necessarily follows that the population of Africa will be decimated within six months.

Step 1 is already done for us; the premises and conclusion are clearly labelled. In step 2 we must ask, "Is it the case that if the premises are true, the conclusion must be true?" The answer is yes, if it's true that the Ebola epidemic in Africa will decimate the population in six months unless "we do something" and it's true that "we won't do anything," then the conclusion that the population of Africa will be decimated in six months *must* be true. So this argument is deductively valid. To determine if it's sound, we would need to check to see if the premises are true. In this case, the first premise is false because, under current conditions, it would take longer than six months for the epidemic to decimate the population of the whole continent. The other premise ("we won't do anything") is at least dubious, since we can't predict the future. So what we have here is a deductively valid argument that's unsound—a bad argument.

Now let's analyze this one:

> [Premise] The Quebec-based French-language group "l'impératif français" works diligently to make sure businesses in Quebec use French in their daily operations. [Premise] The Quebec government has affirmed its commitment to preserving the French language. [Premise] And most Canadians are in favour of official bilingualism. [Conclusion] Let's face it, the French language is guaranteed to survive in Quebec!

Again, step 1 is already done for us. At step 2 we can see that even if the three premises of this argument are all true, the conclusion can still be false. After all, even if everything described in the premises is true, the French language could

Food for Thought

When Reasoning Crashes. . . Leave the Scene of the Accident

Sometimes an argument goes off into a ditch, and you don't know why. Here's an example of a wrecked argument from the great American satirical writer Ambrose Bierce (1842–1914?). Can you figure out exactly what the problem is with this silly argument?

> Sixty men can do a piece of work sixty times as quickly as one man.
> One man can dig a posthole in sixty seconds.
> Therefore, sixty men can dig a posthole in one second.

still die out in Quebec (perhaps because new immigrants speak English or other languages or because of the influence of American TV, movies, and magazines). So the argument can't be deductively valid. But if we go through step 3, we can see that if all the premises are true, the conclusion is likely to be true, making the argument inductively strong. If the premises *are* true, the argument would be cogent.

See what you think of this one:

> [Premise] If you act like Bart Simpson, you will be respected by all your classmates. [Premise] But you don't act like Bart Simpson at all. [Conclusion] It follows that you will not be respected by all your classmates.

This argument fails the tests in steps 2 and 3: it is not deductively valid, and it is not inductively strong. But it does have features that suggest it is an attempt at a deductive argument. First, it displays a pattern of reasoning that can, at first glance, seem deductive. Actually, it uses an argument pattern that is always deductively *invalid* (called "denying the antecedent," an argument form we will look at shortly). This alone should be evidence enough that the argument is indeed deductive but invalid. But it also contains a phrase ("it follows that") that suggests an attempt at a deductive form.

You'll get a lot more exposure to argument forms and indicator words in the rest of this chapter (and the rest of this text). Ultimately, practice in distinguishing different types of arguments and their relative worth is the only way to gain competence (and confidence!) in making these judgments.

So far in this chapter, we've spent most of our time assessing the logical structure of arguments—that is, whether they are valid or invalid, or strong or weak. We haven't focused as much attention on evaluating the truth of premises because that's a big issue that's best considered separately—which is what we do in Part 2 of this book.

Exercise 3.2

Answers to exercises marked with an asterisk (*) may be found in Appendix B, Answers to Exercises.

For each of the following arguments, follow the four-step procedure to determine whether it is deductive or inductive, valid or invalid, and strong or weak. State the results of applying each step.

Example 1

Dexter did not commit the murder. After all, someone who had committed the murder would have dirt on his shoes and blood on his hands. Dexter's shoes and hands are clean.

Step 1: Conclusion: Dexter did not commit the murder. Premises: Someone who had committed the murder would have dirt on his shoes and blood on his hands. Dexter's shoes and hands are clean.
Step 2: Deductively valid.
Step 3: Does not apply.
Step 4: Does not apply.

Example 2

Most people who smoke cannabis are irresponsible and forgetful. Looks like you smoke cannabis all the time! Therefore, you're irresponsible and forgetful.

Step 1: Conclusion: Therefore, you're irresponsible and forgetful. Premises: Most people who smoke cannabis are irresponsible and forgetful. Looks like you smoke cannabis all the time.
Step 2: Not deductively valid.
Step 3: Inductively strong.
Step 4: Does not apply.

1. Ethel played hockey at Saint Mary's University. If she played for Saint Mary's, she's probably a very good athlete. So clearly she is a very good athlete.*
2. You've been dating Barry for months now. And you would have to have poor judgment to be dating Barry. So I think you clearly have poor judgment.
3. You're a finance major, and all finance majors are obsessed with bitcoin, so you must be obsessed with bitcoin!
4. "Good sense is of all things in the world the most equally distributed, for everybody thinks himself so abundantly provided with it, that even those most difficult to please in all other matters do not commonly desire more of it than they already possess." (René Descartes, *A Discourse on Method*)
5. People with racist tendencies also have low self-esteem. People who have benefited from racist systems—which is comparable to having racist tendencies—also probably have low self-esteem.

6. Every mechanic has had special training, and everyone with special training has a university degree. Thus, every mechanic has a university degree.*
7. All dogs are loyal. All dogs are good guard animals. It necessarily follows that all loyal animals are good guard animals.
8. Anyone who is not a bigot will agree that Chris is a good fellow. Some people in this neighbourhood think that he's definitely not a good fellow. Some people in this neighbourhood are bigots.
9. Some immigrants are from India, and some immigrants have degrees in engineering. So some immigrants from India also have degrees in engineering.*
10. If Indigenous groups are against the Keystone XL pipeline, then the pipeline must be a terrible risk to the environment. Indigenous groups are against the pipeline. Therefore, it must be a terrible risk to the environment.
11. Public protest has never accomplished anything. We shouldn't waste our time participating in the protest march.
12. One dresser drawer was open, some money had been taken out of the safe, and there were strange scratches on the wall. I think that someone must have burglarized the place.
13. All the evidence in this trial suggests that Robert Pickton is guilty of murder. Let's face it: he's definitely guilty.
14. "When we speak we are afraid our words will not be heard or welcomed. But when we are silent, we are still afraid. So it is better to speak."—Audre Lorde.
15. If minds are identical to brains—that is, if one's mind is nothing but a brain—androids could never have minds because they wouldn't have brains. Clearly, a mind is nothing but a brain, so it's impossible for androids to have minds.*
16. "From infancy, almost, the average girl is told that marriage is her ultimate goal; therefore her training and education must be directed towards that end." (Emma Goldman, "Marriage and Love")
17. If store windows are being broken all over town, the hockey riot has started. So the riot has begun. Dozens of windows have already been broken.
18. If you have a fever, headache, and unexplained bruising, then you have Ebola. And you do have a fever, headache, and unexplained bruising. So you most certainly have Ebola!

Exercise 3.3

For each of the following arguments, indicate whether it is valid or invalid, strong, or weak.

1. André says that the Raptors' new lineup is really good. So it must be really good!
2. Lottery corporations encourage people to make foolish wagers. Encouraging people to make foolish wagers is immoral. It follows that lottery corporations are immoral.

3. If the *Globe and Mail* reports that deaths due to COVID-19 are declining, then deaths due to COVID-19 are declining. The *Globe and Mail* has reported exactly that. Deaths due to COVID-19 must be declining.*
4. In any triangle, if $l = 5$ *and* $w = 4$, then $a = 10$. And in this triangle, $l = 5$ *and* $w = 4$; therefore, for this triangle $a = 10$.
5. Any show that tries to imitate *Schitt's Creek* probably sucks. And that new show is totally trying to imitate *Schitt's Creek*. It's gotta suck.
6. "Poetry is finer and more philosophical than history; for poetry expresses the universal and history only the particular." (Aristotle, *Poetics*)
7. Vaccinations save lives. It is unwise to skip your baby's scheduled vaccinations.
8. Either your thinking is logical or it is emotional. It's obviously not logical. It's emotional.*
9. Either you're lying or you're not telling the whole story. You're obviously not lying, so you're just telling part of the story.
10. A recent Gallup poll says that 69 per cent of Canadians believe in the existence of heaven but only 43 per cent say they believe in hell. People are just too willing to engage in wishful thinking.
11. Drug addicts often support their habits by shoplifting, and George has been caught shoplifting three times. He's an addict for sure.
12. "We say that a person behaves in a given way because he possesses a philosophy, but we infer the philosophy from the behavior and therefore cannot use it in any satisfactory way as an explanation, at least until it is in turn explained." (B.F. Skinner, *Beyond Freedom and Dignity*)
13. You failed your driver's test twice. You've had three traffic tickets in the last two years. And your own brother won't let you drive him to hockey practice. It's pretty clear you're not a very good driver.
14. Bachelors are unmarried. George is a bachelor. He is unmarried.*
15. We ought to ban the sale of tequila in campus pubs. Anything that makes people violent should be banned, and tequila makes people violent.
16. If there is a tax cut this year, the deficit will rise. There has already been a tax cut. The deficit is sure to rise.
17. Many diseases like COVID-19 are carried in small droplets of fluid, and masks can help stop those. And Canada's top doctors say they think masks are important. So it's pretty clear that wearing a mask during a pandemic is a good idea.
18. If the United States is willing to wage war in the Middle East, it can only be because it wants the oil supplies in the region. Obviously, the United States is willing to go to war there. The United States wants that oil.*
19. "Someone must have been telling lies about Joseph K., for without having done anything wrong he was arrested one fine morning." (Franz Kafka, *The Trial*)
20. If you had a disability like I do, then you would understand the barriers faced by people like me. But you're not disabled. You're never going to understand what I'm going through.

21. I like poetry. My English Poetry teacher likes me. So I'm going to pass my English Poetry course, no problem!*
22. Anyone willing to take the lives of innocent people for a cause is a terrorist. Many Christians, Jews, and Muslims have taken innocent lives in the name of their religious cause. Many Christians, Jews, and Muslims have been terrorists.
23. If the landlady is at the door, it's probably because she's looking for this month's rent. There she is. She must want the rent.

3.3 Finding Missing Parts

Sometimes arguments, especially informal ones, may seem to have a few pieces missing. Premises (and sometimes even conclusions) are often left unstated. These implicit premises, or assumptions, are essential to the argument. Of course, certain assumptions are frequently left unsaid for good reason: they are obvious and understood by all parties to the argument, and boredom would set in fast if you actually tried to mention them all. If you wish to prove that "Socrates is mortal," you normally wouldn't need to explain what *mortal* means and that the name "Socrates" refers to an ancient philosopher and not to your dog. But many arguments do have unstated premises that are necessary to the chain of reasoning and so must be made explicit to fully evaluate the arguments.

For instance:

> Handguns are rare in Canada, but the availability of shotguns and rifles poses a risk of death and injury. Therefore shotguns and rifles should be banned, too!

Notice that there is a kind of disconnect between the premise and the conclusion. The conclusion is about banning something, but the premises—the reasons given—don't say anything about banning anything. The conclusion follows from the premise *only* if we assume an additional premise, perhaps something like this: "Anything that poses any risk of death or injury should be banned." With this additional premise, the argument becomes:

> Handguns are rare in Canada, but the availability of shotguns and rifles poses a risk to public safety. Anything that poses any risk of death or injury should be banned. Therefore, shotguns and rifles should be banned, too!

Now that all the premises are spelled out, you can evaluate the *full* argument just as you would any other. Not only that, but you can see that the unstated premise is questionable, which is the case with many implicit premises. Not everyone would agree that absolutely anything raising the risk of death or injury should be banned, for if that were the case we would have to outlaw cars, airplanes, most prescription drugs, most occupations, and who knows how many kitchen appliances! Many unstated premises are like this one—they're controversial and hence unstated. But they're also important to evaluate and therefore should not be left unexamined.

Here's another argument with an unstated premise:

> Anyone who craves political power cannot be trusted to serve the public interest. So I say Premier Sakinofsky can't be trusted to serve the public interest.

As stated, this argument seems like a rush to judgment because the first premise concerns *anyone* who craves power and suddenly Premier Sakinofsky is denounced as untrustworthy. Something's missing. What we need is another premise connecting the first premise to the conclusion: "Premier Sakinofsky craves political power." Now let's plug the implicit premise into the argument:

> Anyone who craves political power cannot be trusted to serve the public interest. Premier Sakinofsky craves political power. So he can't be trusted to serve the public interest.

"The difficult part in an argument is not to defend one's opinion, but rather to know it."

—André Maurois

So exactly when should we try to find an unstated premise? The obvious answer is that we should do so when there appears to be something essential missing—an implied, logical link between premises and conclusion that is not a common-sense, generally accepted assumption. Such implicit premises should never be taken for granted because, among other things, they are often deliberately hidden or downplayed to make the argument seem stronger.

Be aware, though, that many times the problem with an argument is not unstated premises but invalid or weak structure. Consider this:

> If that potion contains arsenic, he will die. But it does not contain arsenic, so he will not die.

This argument is invalid; the conclusion does not follow from the premises. (After all, arsenic isn't the only poison that could be in that potion! So even if the premises are true, the conclusion need not be.) Like most invalid arguments, it can't be salvaged without altering it beyond what is clearly implied. It's just a bad argument. The same goes for weak arguments. They usually can't be fixed without adding or changing premises gratuitously. Remember, the point of articulating unstated premises is to make explicit what is already implicit. Your job as a critical thinker is not to make bad arguments good; that task belongs to the one who puts forward the argument in the first place.

To make sure that your investigation of implicit premises is thorough and reasonable, work through the following three-step process:[2]

Step 1. Search for a credible premise that would make the argument *valid*, one that would furnish the needed link between premise (or premises) and conclusion. Choose the supplied premise that

a. is most plausible

and

b. fits best with the author's intent.

The first requirement (a) means that you should look for premises that are either true or, at least, not obviously false. The second requirement (b) means that premises should fit—that is, at least not conflict—with what seems to be the author's point or purpose (which, of course, is often difficult to figure out).

principle of charity
The interpretive principle that says that whenever we find someone's meaning unclear, we should attempt to interpret it in a such a way as to make them make sense, rather than interpreting them as saying something silly or confused.

straw man
The fallacy of distorting, weakening, or oversimplifying someone's position so it can be more easily attacked or refuted.

These two requirements embody what is sometimes known as "the principle of charity in interpretation" or just "the principle of charity." The **principle of charity** says that whenever we find someone's meaning unclear, we should attempt to interpret it in such a way as to make them make sense, rather than interpreting them as saying something silly or confused. And what "makes sense" will often depend on context. Imagine if someone says to you, "this steak is not good." Just what does "good" mean here? "Good" can mean lots of things. If you're at a restaurant, and the person sitting across from you says, "This steak is not good," she probably means that the steak is tough or not very tasty. But if you're in your kitchen and your roommate takes a raw steak out of the fridge, sniffs it, and says, "This steak is not good," it's quite likely that she means that steak is spoiled. If you looked at your roommate and asked her just how bad the steak tasted, you would be guilty of interpreting her uncharitably: the context clearly indicates that she's not talking about the steak *tasting* good but about whether it is spoiled.

Interpreting charitably is the *fair* thing to do, and it's the thing that's most likely to aid in clear communication. And when it comes to *criticizing* someone else's argument, you want to be especially fair in stating what you think their argument is. Criticizing a version of their argument into which you've inserted a silly or irrelevant premise isn't very productive, and it isn't very fair. In fact, that amounts to a well-known fallacy known as the **straw man** fallacy, which we'll discuss in more detail in Chapter 5.

If the premise you supply is plausible and fitting (with the author's intent), use it to fill out the argument. If the premise you supplied is either not plausible or not fitting, go to step 2.

Step 2. Search for a credible premise that would make the argument as *strong* as possible. Choose the supplied

Betsy Streeter/CartoonStock

There's nothing wrong with arguing occasionally—in the sense of "having a debate"—but might you fare better by presenting actual arguments and avoiding fallacious ones?

premise that fulfills stipulations (a) and (b). If the premise you supply is plausible and fitting, use it to fill out the argument. If it is either not plausible or not fitting, consider the argument beyond repair and reject it.

Step 3. Evaluate the reconstituted argument. If you're able to identify a credible, implicit premise that makes the argument either valid or strong, assess this revised version of the argument, paying particular attention to the plausibility of the other premise or premises.

Now let's apply the procedure above to a few arguments:

> If the Bank of Canada lowers interest rates one more time, there will be a deep recession. So I'm telling you there's going to be a deep recession.

The first step is to see if there's a credible premise that would make the argument valid. We can see right away that one premise will do the trick: "The Bank of Canada is about to lower interest rates again." Adding it to the argument will supply the link needed between the existing premise and the conclusion. We also can see that our new premise is plausible (the Bank of Canada has in fact lowered interest rates many times in the past) and seems to fit with the point of the argument (to prove that there will be a recession). Our resulting argument, though, is probably not a good one because the premise about the effect of the Bank of Canada's lowering interest rates is questionable.

Now examine this one:

> Security officer Blart lied on her employment application about whether she had a criminal record. Security officer Blart will do a bad job of screening passengers for weapons.

The sentence "Security officer Blart will do a bad job of screening passengers for weapons" is the conclusion here. To try to make this argument valid, we would need a premise like "Any security officer at Vancouver International Airport who has lied on their employment application about having a criminal record will do a bad job of screening passengers for weapons." This premise fits the point of the argument, but it isn't plausible. Surely it can't be the case that *any* security officer who has lied will do a bad job of screening. A more plausible premise is "Most security officers at Vancouver International Airport who have lied on their employment applications about having a criminal record will do a bad job of screening passengers for weapons." This premise will do, and this is now a good argument—assuming that the other premise is true.

What about this one?

> The use of marijuana should be legal because it's an act that brings pleasure to people's lives.

To make this argument valid, we need a premise that connects the idea of something being legal with the idea of bringing pleasure. We would need to add this premise (or one like it): "Any act that brings pleasure to people's lives should be legal." But this premise is hard to accept since many heinous acts—such as murder and theft—may bring pleasure to some people, yet few of us would think those acts should be legal. To try to make the argument strong, we might add this premise instead: "Some acts should be legal simply because they bring pleasure to people's lives." This premise is actually controversial, but it at least is not obviously false. It also fits with the point of the argument. If we decide that the premise is neither plausible nor fitting, we would declare the argument beyond repair.

Identifying and filling in missing parts is an important skill. And it's a challenging one, so it's important to spend some time practising it. Finding missing parts is challenging in part because it requires interpreting what is seen—the parts of the argument that are right in front of you—in order to form a reasonable hypothesis about what is not seen. Adding to the challenge is that arguers are sometimes unclear and may not even be sure themselves of what they are trying to say. But if we value critical thinking, the challenge of figuring it out is worth the effort.

Critical Thinking and the Media

News vs Editorial Content

Mainstream news sources, including major newspapers like the *Globe and Mail*, TV news sources such as *Global News*, and online sources such as CNN.com, tend to include two very different kinds of content.

On one hand, there is the straightforward reporting of the day's news. News reporters—in theory—simply relay to the audience the facts of what happened. "The prime minister said such-and-such." "Five thousand people attended the rally." "Critics said the new law was unnecessary." Of course, reporters can be biased in various ways. But the general idea adhered to by serious journalists is that reporting the news is just that: reporting what is going on, rather than offering an opinion. It's fine to report the opinions of others—it is often useful, even crucial, to know what informed observers think of current events, or whether public opinion supports current government policy. In reporting the news, though, reporters are expected to do their best to keep their own opinions out of it.

On the other hand, there is opinion content, aimed at providing perspective and perhaps at convincing readers or viewers of some point of view. Sometimes, but not always, opinion content is clearly marked as such. Historically, major newspapers limited opinion content to the "Opinions" or "Editorial" section of the paper. In some cases, opinion content is written by, and reflects the opinions of, the outlet's editorial board or columnists hired to express their opinions. Some news outlets also publish "letters to the editor" from readers.

Being able to tell the one from the other—to tell news content from opinion content—is a crucial ability. The key skill is to look for a conclusion: a piece of writing in which the author presents a conclusion is an opinion piece, not just news. But be cautious: as this chapter points out, in some cases an author may be trying to convince you of a particular conclusion, even if that conclusion remains entirely unstated.

Exercise 3.4

For exercises marked with an asterisk (*), there are answers in Appendix B, Answers to Exercises.

I. For each of the following arguments, state the implicit premises that will make the argument valid.

Example

The engine is sputtering. It must be out of gas.
Implicit premise: Whenever the engine sputters, it's out of gas.

1. Any member of Parliament who is caught misusing campaign funds should resign their seat. The honourable member from Algoma-Manitoulin-Kapuskasing should resign.*
2. Avner prays every day, so he must be devoutly religious.
3. If you get a good grade on your essay, it's because I gave you excellent feedback on your first draft. I must have given excellent feedback on your first draft.
4. A major terrorist attack *will* happen in this country. The RCMP doesn't have a very serious focus on stopping terrorism.
5. The author of this new book on international peacekeeping is either biased or incompetent as a journalist. So she's biased.*
6. Ghazal is almost certain to get an A in critical thinking, because she's a very strong student overall.
7. The government of Saudi Arabia is bound to fall! After all, the Taliban regime in Afghanistan fell because it was deeply sexist.
8. The Canadian government should limit its military activities to the western hemisphere because it doesn't have the resources to cover the whole world.
9. Salmon has lots of vitamin D. So it must be healthy for you.
10. Taslima did not criticize US military action in the Gulf War or in the war in Afghanistan. She must be pro-American.*

II. For each of the following arguments, change a premise or add a premise to make the argument strong.

1. That dude with the beard was in the coffee shop when my laptop was stolen while I was in the bathroom. He was staring at me 20 minutes earlier. So he's probably the one who stole it.
2. Morgan has a habit of keeping junk that she really should throw out, so she is likely going to end up on one of those reality shows about "hoarders."
3. Six out of 10 of my teenage friends love rap music. So 60 per cent of all teens love rap music.*
4. Professor Niemi has published widely on the topic she teaches. She's probably a very good professor.

5. Seventy-one per cent of the faculty and staff at Spadina College are Conservatives. So most of the students are probably Conservatives.
6. If Assad's fingerprints are on the vase, then he's probably the one who broke it. He's probably the one who broke it.*
7. The owner of the team is almost certainly going to spend big on a star player. If he really wants to make the finals next year, he will do it by spending money on a star player.
8. Ninety per cent of students at the University of Northern Saskatchewan graduate with a BA degree. Li Fong will probably graduate from the University of Northern Saskatchewan with a BA degree.
9. The murder rates in the Atlantic provinces are very low. The murder rates in most large cities in the western provinces are very low. So the murder rate in Toronto must be very low.*
10. Shelagh is a typical Canadian. So she probably loves hockey.

3.4 Argument Patterns

Earlier we discussed the importance of being familiar with patterns, or forms, of argument—that is, the structures on which the content of an argument is laid. The point was that knowing some common argument forms makes it easier to determine whether an argument is deductive or inductive. But being familiar with argument forms is also helpful in many other aspects of argument evaluation. Let's take a closer look at some of these forms.

3.4.1 Affirming the Antecedent

Since argument forms are structures distinct from the content of an argument, we can easily signify different forms by using letters to represent statements in the arguments. Each letter represents a different statement in much the same way that letters are used to represent values in a mathematical equation. Consider this argument:

> If the job is worth doing, then it's worth doing well.
> The job is worth doing.
> Therefore, it's worth doing well.

We can represent this argument like this:

> If *p*, then *q*.
> *p*.
> Therefore, *q*.

Food for Thought

Arguments on the Net

The internet is fertile ground for all manner of arguments—good and bad, boring and silly. Here's one that has gone around the world a few times online:

> Adolf Hitler was evil.
> Adolf Hitler was a vegetarian.
> Therefore, vegetarianism is evil.

What's wrong with this argument? If you don't know, the following section on argument patterns will help you. An important clue that something is fishy here is that any argument of this form can be used to try to "frame" practically anybody. Consider:

> Dominic lives in Montreal.
> Dominic is tall.
> Therefore, everyone who lives in Montreal is tall.

The internet is also a terrific place to find bad political arguments. Consider this one:

> Donald Trump thinks limiting immigration is a good idea.
> I don't like Donald Trump.
> So limiting immigration must be a bad idea!

What's wrong with this one? If it's not obvious, try this argument that follows the same pattern:

> Donald Trump thinks 2 + 2 = 4.
> I don't like Donald Trump.
> So 2 + 2 must not equal 4!

The point, of course, is this: the simple fact that your least (or most!) favourite person supports a claim is not a good reason either to believe it or disbelieve it. But it's also useful to remember that even though the argument above about immigration is a bad argument, its conclusion might still be true, and we may well be able to provide strong support for that conclusion—with a different argument!

Notice that the first line in the argument is a compound statement. That means it's composed of at least two constituent statements—"the job is worth doing" and "it's worth doing well"—which are represented in this case by *p* and *q*. So we have two statements in this argument that are arranged into an argument form, one that is both very common and always valid. We can plug any statements we want into this form, and we will still get a valid argument. The premises may be true or false, but the form will be valid.

Some of the more common argument patterns that you encounter are like this pattern—they're deductive and **conditional**. They are conditional in that they contain at least one conditional, or "if–then," premise. We describe such premises as conditional because they state the *conditions under which* a certain state of affairs

conditional statement
An "if–then" statement; it consists of the antecedent (the part introduced by the word *if*) and the consequent (the part introduced by the word *then*).

will obtain. The first statement in a conditional premise (the *if* part) is known as the **antecedent**. The second statement (the *then* part) is known as the **consequent**.

The conditional pattern shown here is called **affirming the antecedent** or, to use the Latin term, ***modus ponens***. Any argument in the *modus ponens* form is valid—if the premises are true, the conclusion absolutely must be true. In the argument form shown here, this means that if "If *p*, then *q*" and "*p*" are both true, the conclusion has to be true also. (Try your own example, filling in any true statements you want for "If *p*, then *q*" and "*p*." If your premises are true, then your conclusion will also be true.) These facts, then, provide a way to quickly size up any conditional argument. If an argument is in the form of *modus ponens*, it's valid, regardless of the content of the statements. That's a very handy thing to know.

antecedent
The first part of a conditional statement (If *p*, then *q*), the component that begins with the word *if*.

consequent
The part of a conditional statement (If *p*, then *q*) introduced by the word *then*.

affirming the antecedent/ modus ponens
A valid argument form:

If *p*, then *q*.
p.
Therefore, *q*.

3.4.2 Denying the Consequent

Another common conditional argument form is called **denying the consequent** or ***modus tollens***:

If Austin is happy, then Barb is happy.
Barb is not happy.
Therefore, Austin is not happy.

denying the consequent/ modus tollens
A valid argument form:

If *p*, then *q*.
Not *q*.
Therefore, not *p*.

The form of *modus tollens* is:

If *p*, then *q*.
Not *q*.
Therefore, not *p*.

Like *modus ponens*, *modus tollens* is always valid. If the premises are true, the conclusion must be true. Make up your own example to see for yourself! So any argument that's in the *modus tollens* pattern is valid.

3.4.3 Hypothetical Syllogisms

A third common conditional argument form is called **hypothetical syllogism**. *Hypothetical* is just another term for conditional. A **syllogism** is an argument (usually deductive) made up of three statements—two premises and a conclusion. (*Modus ponens* and *modus tollens* are particular kinds of syllogisms. We'll discuss "categorical" syllogisms—deductive syllogisms that show the logical relationships between three categories of things—in Chapter 6, and we'll discuss inductive "statistical" syllogisms in Chapter 8.) In a hypothetical syllogism, all three statements are conditional, and the argument is always valid:

hypothetical syllogism
A valid argument made up of three hypothetical, or conditional, statements:

If *p*, then *q*.
If *q*, then *r*.
Therefore, if *p*, then *r*.

syllogism
A deductive argument made up of three statements—two premises and a conclusion.

If you leave the door open, the cat will get out.
If the cat gets out, it will get hit by a car.
Therefore, if you leave the door open, the cat will get hit by a car.

If *p*, then *q*.
If *q*, then *r*.
Therefore, if *p*, then *r*.

People often use hypothetical syllogisms to reason about causal chains of events. They try to show that one event will lead unavoidably to a sequence of events that will finally conclude in a single event that seems far removed from the first. This linkage has prompted some to label hypothetical syllogisms "chain arguments."

Here's another example of a hypothetical syllogism:

If the Habs lose this game, they're out of the playoffs.
If the Habs are out of the playoffs, there will be riots in Montreal.
Therefore, if the Habs lose this game, there will be riots in Montreal.

Because the *structure* of this argument is the same as the structure of the previous argument (that is, they're both hypothetical syllogisms), the symbolized version is exactly the same:

If *p*, then *q*.
If *q*, then *r*.
Therefore, if *p*, then *r*.

Review Notes

Valid Conditional Argument Forms

Affirming the Antecedent

(***Modus Ponens***)	**Example**
If *p*, then *q*.	If Champ barks, a burglar is in the house.
p.	Champ is barking.
Therefore, *q*.	Therefore, a burglar is in the house.

Denying the Consequent

(***Modus Tollens***)	**Example**
If *p*, then *q*.	If it's raining, the park is closed.
Not *q*.	The park is not closed.
Therefore, not *p*.	Therefore, it's not raining.

Hypothetical Syllogism

	Example
If *p*, then *q*.	If Tanvir steals the money, he will go to jail.
If *q*, then *r*.	If Tanvir goes to jail, his family will suffer.
Therefore, if *p*, then *r*.	Therefore, if Tanvir steals the money, his family will suffer.

3.4.4 Denying the Antecedent

There are also two common conditional argument forms that are *not* valid, though they superficially resemble valid forms. One is called **denying the antecedent.** For example:

denying the antecedent
An invalid argument form:

If *p*, then *q*.
Not *p*.
Therefore, not *q*.

If Einstein invented the steam engine, then he's a great scientist.
Einstein did not invent the steam engine.
Therefore, he is not a great scientist.

Denying the antecedent is represented like this:

If *p*, then *q*.
Not *p*.
Therefore, not *q*.

You can see the problem with this form in the preceding argument. Even if the antecedent, *p*, is false (if Einstein did not invent the steam engine), that doesn't show that he's not a great scientist because he could be a great scientist on account of some other great achievement. Thus, denying the antecedent is clearly an invalid pattern because it's possible for the premises to be true and the conclusion false.

"Mistakes are made on two counts: an argument is either based on error or incorrectly developed."

—Thomas Aquinas

Here's another example of this form:

If Alexander the Great jumped off the CN Tower without a parachute, then Alexander the Great would be dead.
Alexander the Great did not jump off the CN Tower without a parachute.
Therefore, Alexander the Great is not dead.

Even if Alexander the Great did not jump off the CN Tower without a parachute, that in itself does not show that he is not dead. After all, there are lots of ways to die. And in fact, we know that he died (of illness) more than 2300 years ago. In other words, it's possible for both premises in this argument to be true while the conclusion is nonetheless false. So the argument is invalid.

3.4.5 Affirming the Consequent

There's another common invalid form you should know about: **affirming the consequent.**

affirming the consequent
An invalid argument form:

If *p*, then *q*.
q.
Therefore, *p*.

Here's an instance of this form:

If Brandon is the capital of Manitoba, then Brandon is in Manitoba.
Brandon is in Manitoba.
Therefore, Brandon is the capital of Manitoba.

We represent this form like this:

If *p*, then *q*.
q.
Therefore, *p*.

Obviously, in this form it's possible for the premises to be true while the conclusion is false, as this example shows. This pattern, therefore, is invalid.

3.4.6 Disjunctive Syllogism

disjunctive syllogism
A valid argument form:

Either *p* or *q*.
Not *p*.
Therefore, *q*.
In the second premise of the syllogism, either disjunct (either of the parts separated by "or") can be denied.

The final pattern we will look at is a common non-conditional argument form called **disjunctive syllogism**. It's valid and extremely simple:

Either Ralph walked the dog, or he stayed home.
He didn't walk the dog.
Therefore, he stayed home.

It's called a disjunctive syllogism because it starts with a disjunction—a statement that says that one or another of two things is true. Each of those things (in this case "Ralph walked the dog" and "he stayed home") is called a disjunct. The symbolized form of the argument above is thus:

Either *p* or *q*.
Not *p*.
Therefore, *q*.

Keep in mind that in a disjunctive syllogism, either disjunct can be denied, not just the first one. Here's an example in which the second of the two disjuncts is denied:

Either Seth Meyers was joking or he is out of touch with current events.
But I *know* he's not out of touch with current events!
So he must have been joking.

These six deductive argument forms (four valid ones and two invalid ones) can help you to streamline the process of argument evaluation. If you want to find out quickly if a deductive argument is valid, you can compare it to these patterns to do that. (But remember, a good deductive argument has both a valid form and true premises.) You need only to see if the argument fits one of the forms. If it fits a valid form, it's valid. If it fits an invalid form, it's invalid. If it doesn't fit any of the forms, then you need to find another way to evaluate the argument. The easiest way to use this form-comparison technique is to memorize all six forms so that you can recognize them whenever they arise.

Review Notes

Invalid Conditional Argument Forms

Denying the Antecedent	**Example**
If *p*, then *q*.	If the cat is on the mat, she is asleep.
Not *p*.	She is not on the mat.
Therefore, not *q*.	Therefore, she is not asleep.
Affirming the Consequent	**Example**
If *p*, then *q*.	If the cat is on the mat, she is asleep.
q.	She is asleep.
Therefore, *p*.	Therefore, she is on the mat.

Disjunctive Syllogism (Valid)

Symbolized Version	**Example**
Either *p* or *q*.	Either we light the fire or we will freeze.
Not *p*.	We cannot light the fire.
Therefore, *q*.	Therefore, we will freeze.

Sometimes you can see right away that an argument has a valid or invalid form. At other times, you may need a little help figuring this out, or you may want to use a more explicit test of validity. In either case, the *counterexample method* can help. With this technique you check for validity by simply devising a parallel argument that has the same form as the argument you're evaluating (the test argument) but has obviously *true premises and a false conclusion*. Recall that any argument having true premises and a false conclusion cannot be valid. So if you can invent such an argument that also has the same pattern as the test argument, you've proved that the test argument is invalid.

For example, let's say that you are confronted with this argument:

> If old-fashioned values are lost, then young people will abandon marriage.
> Young people have abandoned marriage.
> Therefore, old-fashioned values have been lost!

And to check this test argument, you come up with this parallel argument, which has exactly the same form:

> If George is a dog, then he is warm-blooded.
> George is warm-blooded.
> Therefore, he is a dog.

This argument has the same pattern as the previous one—but the premises can easily be true and the conclusion false (assuming, for example, that George is your brother!). So the test argument too must be invalid. You may have already guessed that it is an instance of affirming the consequent. The counterexample method, though, works not just for the deductive forms we've discussed but for all deductive forms. (We will discuss other deductive forms in upcoming chapters.)

Exercise 3.5

Answers to exercises marked with an asterisk (*) may be found in Appendix B, Answers to Exercises.

For each of the following arguments, determine whether it is valid or invalid, and indicate the argument pattern.

1. If the Vikings had sailed up the St Lawrence, there would be archaeological evidence of that.
   But there is no such evidence.
   So the Vikings did not sail up the St Lawrence.*
2. Either Donovan just magically became a better dancer or he's been taking lessons.
   He hasn't magically became a better dancer.
   So he must have been taking lessons.
3. If it doesn't have the Forest Stewardship Council's mark on it, then it's not sustainably harvested paper.
   This paper doesn't have the Forest Stewardship Council's mark on it.
   So it's not sustainably harvested paper.
4. If traffic is bad, I'll get to campus late for class.
   But the traffic isn't bad.
   I won't get to campus late for class.
5. If my AirPods haven't been charging overnight, the batteries will be dead.
   The batteries aren't dead.
   Therefore, my AirPods must have been charging overnight.
6. If *CBC News* omits important news stories, then it is irresponsible.
   It is not irresponsible.
   So *CBC News* does not omit important news stories.*
7. If ESP (extrasensory perception) were real, psychic predictions would be completely reliable.
   Psychic predictions are completely reliable.
   Therefore, ESP is real.
8. If my iPhone has been plugged in, the battery must be OK.
   My iPhone has not been plugged in.
   Therefore, the battery must be dead.

9. If ESP (extrasensory perception) were real, psychic predictions would be completely reliable.
   ESP is real.
   Therefore, psychic predictions are completely reliable.*
10. If Tammy has a PhD, she will be hired.
    Tammy was not hired.
    Therefore, Tammy does not have a PhD.
11. If interest rates go up, bond prices must go down.
    Bond prices went down.
    Therefore, interest rates went up.
12. If our dog Dorothy goes out in the rain, she will get wet.
    If Dorothy gets wet, she will smell bad.
    Therefore, if Dorothy goes out in the rain, she will smell bad.

Exercise 3.6

For each of the following premises, add another premise and a conclusion to make it valid in two different ways—*modus ponens* and *modus tollens.*

1. If Bob and Doug are more than fifteen minutes late, we will need to start without them.
2. If Lino is telling the truth, he will admit to all charges.*
3. If China adopts North American patterns of consumption, then the environment is doomed.
4. If the new vaccine prevents the spread of Ebola, the researchers who developed the vaccine should get the Nobel Prize.
5. If religious conflict in Nigeria continues, thousands more will die.*
6. If people love Tim Hortons coffee, there will be long line-ups at every Tim Hortons every morning.
7. If you want to see a really good movie, check out that new one starring Steven Yeun.
8. If our politicians realize that they serve the people, and not the other way around, our laws would be much more reflective of our society's values and beliefs.
9. If solar power can supply six megawatts of power in Vancouver (which is certainly not the sunniest place in the world), then solar power can transform the energy systems in sunnier places like Edmonton and Calgary.*
10. If *x*, then *y*.

Exercise 3.7

Use the counterexample method to create a parallel argument for each of the invalid arguments in Exercise 3.5. Write out each parallel argument, and represent its form with letters as discussed earlier. Answers are provided for 4, 5, 7, 8, and 11.

Example

Test Argument

> If the government is corrupt, the media will be critical of them.
> The media have been very critical of the government.
> Therefore, the government is corrupt.

Parallel Argument

> If Beyoncé could fly, she sure would be famous.
> She is famous.
> Therefore, Beyoncé can fly.

> If *a*, then *b*.
> *b*.
> Therefore, *a*.

3.5 Diagramming Arguments

Most of the arguments we've looked at so far have been relatively simple. When arguments are more complex (and in real life they usually are!), you may find it increasingly difficult to sort out premises from conclusions and parts of an argument from non-argumentative background noise. If you can visualize the structure of an argument, though, the job gets much easier. That's where argument diagramming comes in.

Let's begin by diagramming the following very simple argument before moving on to more complicated ones.

> Justin Trudeau has great ideas for preserving the natural environment. That's for sure! Therefore, Trudeau being prime minister is good for Canada.

We must first underline any premise or conclusion indicator words (e.g., "since," "therefore," and "because"):

> Justin Trudeau has great ideas for preserving the natural environment. That's for sure! <u>Therefore</u>, Trudeau being prime minister is good for Canada.

Next we number all the statements (and *only* the statements, not questions, etc.) in the passage, in sequential order.

> (1) Justin Trudeau has great ideas for preserving the natural environment. (2) That's for sure! (3) <u>Therefore</u>, Trudeau being prime minister is good for Canada.

And then we cross out all extraneous statements—those that are neither premises nor conclusions, those that are redundant, and those that are nothing more than background information or other logically irrelevant material.

> (1) Justin Trudeau has great ideas for preserving the natural environment. (2) ~~That's for sure!~~ (3) Therefore, Trudeau being prime minister is good for Canada.

We've crossed out claim (2) because it is redundant—it just adds emphasis to what is said in claim (1).

Finally, we draw the diagram. Put the numbers associated with the premises inside squares, and place those squares above the number for the conclusion, which is itself put inside a circle. (In our diagramming method, squares will always represent premises, and circles will always represent conclusions.) Then draw arrows from the premises to the conclusion they support. Each arrow represents a logical relationship between premise and conclusion, a relationship that we might normally indicate with the word "therefore" or with the words "is a reason or premise for."

This diagram is very simple because the argument it represents is very simple. It has just one premise and one conclusion. And it has just one arrow, showing that premise (1) is being used here in support of conclusion (3).

Now we're ready to try a slightly more complicated example.

> What do I think of shopping at H&M? I'll tell you! They've got great prices, and they've got a good selection of men's clothes. So H&M is a great place to shop!

The first thing we do is underline any premise or conclusion indicator words (e.g., "therefore," "since," and "because"):

> What do I think of shopping at H&M? I'll tell you! They've got great prices, and they've got a good selection of men's clothes. So H&M is a great place to shop!

Next we number all the statements (and *only* the statements) in the passage in sequential order.

> What do I think of shopping at H&M? (1) I'll tell you! (2) They've got great prices, and (3) they've got a good selection of men's clothes. (4) So H&M is a great place to shop!

We haven't numbered that first sentence because it's a question, not a statement—it's merely there to introduce the topic.

And then we cross out all extraneous statements—those that are neither premises nor conclusions, those that are redundant, and so on.

> ~~What do I think of shopping at H&M?~~ (1) ~~I'll tell you!~~ (2) They've got great prices, and (3) they've got a good selection of men's clothes. (4) So H&M is a great place to shop!

We've crossed out the first two sentences because they're not essential to the structure of this argument. The first sentence isn't a statement at all. And the second one, though it *is* a statement, doesn't really have any content: it just announces that an argument is on its way.

Finally, we draw the diagram. Place the numbers of the premises inside squares, and put the number for the conclusion inside a circle. Put the premises above the conclusion on your page. Then draw arrows from the premises to the conclusion they support.

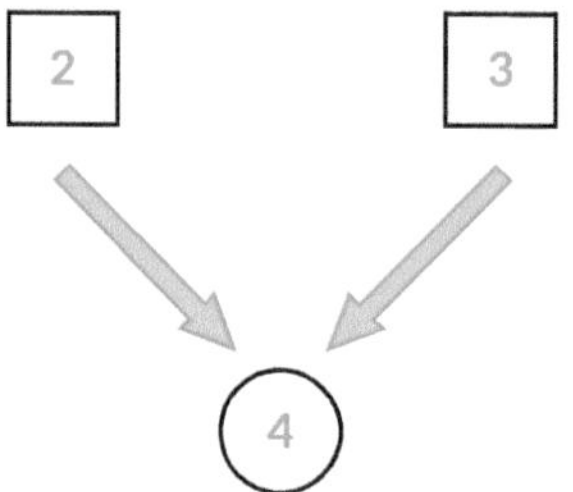

Here we see that our diagram—our argument—is one step more complicated than our previous example. This one has two premises, each lending some support to the conclusion. The logical "flow" from the two premises to the conclusion is represented by the two arrows.

Next, let's try something even more complicated.

> There is no question in my mind. I therefore maintain that Dexter is the murderer. Because if he did it, he would probably have bloodstains on the sleeve of his shirt. The bloodstains are tiny, but they are there. Any observant person could see them. Also, the murder weapon was within his reach for quite a while before the crime was committed. And since of all the people in the house at the time, he alone does not have an airtight alibi, he must be the killer.

Again, the first thing we do is underline any premise or conclusion indicator words (e.g., "therefore," "since," and "because"):

> There is no question in my mind. I therefore maintain that Dexter is the murderer. Because if he did it, he would probably have bloodstains on the sleeve of his shirt. The bloodstains are tiny, but they

> are there. Any observant person could see them. Also, the murder weapon was within his reach for quite a while before the crime was committed. And since of all the people in the house at the time, he alone does not have an airtight alibi, he must be the killer.

Next, we number all the statements (and *only* the statements) in the passage in sequential order. (For the purposes of diagramming, an if–then statement is considered one statement, and multiple statements in a single compound sentence are to be counted as separate statements. Such statements are usually joined by "and," "or," or "but.")

> (1) There is no question in my mind. (2) I therefore maintain that Dexter is the murderer. (3) Because if he did it, he would probably have bloodstains on the sleeve of his shirt. (4) The bloodstains are tiny, but they are there. (5) Any observant person could see them. (6) Also, the murder weapon was within his reach for quite a while before the crime was committed. (7) And since of all the people in the house at the time, he alone does not have an airtight alibi, (8) he must be the killer.

And then we cross out all extraneous statements, noise, redundancies, and anything else that is neither a premise nor a conclusion.

> (1) ~~There is no question in my mind.~~ (2) I therefore maintain that Dexter is the murderer. (3) Because if he did it, he would probably have bloodstains on the sleeve of his shirt. (4) The bloodstains are tiny, but they are there. (5) ~~Any observant person could see them.~~ (6) Also, the murder weapon was within his reach for quite a while before the crime was committed. (7) And since of all the people in the house at the time, he alone does not have an airtight alibi, ~~he must be the killer~~.

Finally, we draw the diagram. Again, place the numbers of the premises inside squares and above the number for the conclusion, which is itself placed inside a circle. Squares will represent premises, and circles will represent conclusions. Draw arrows from the premises to the conclusion they support.

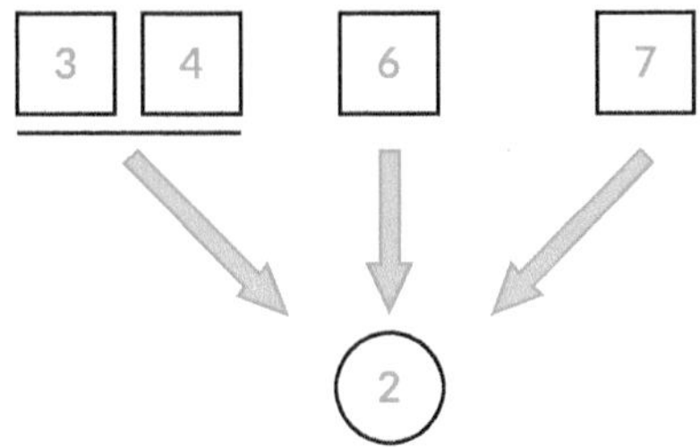

In this diagram, you can see that premises 3 and 4 are handled differently from premises 6 and 7. The reason is that some premises are **independent** and some are **dependent**.

independent premise
A premise that does not depend on other premises to provide support to a conclusion. If an independent premise is removed, the support that other premises supply to the conclusion is not affected.

dependent premise
A premise that depends on at least one other premise to provide joint support to a conclusion. If a dependent premise is removed, the support that its linked dependent premises supply to the conclusion is undermined or completely cancelled out.

An independent premise offers support to a conclusion *without the help of any other premises*. If other premises are omitted or undermined in an argument, the support supplied by an independent premise does not change. We represent this fact in the diagram by drawing separate arrows to the conclusion from premises 6 and 7, both of which give it independent support. If we delete one of these premises, the support that the other one gives does not change.

Premises 3 and 4 are dependent premises. They do depend on each other to jointly provide support to a conclusion. If either premise 3 or 4 is removed, the support that the remaining premise supplies is undermined or completely cancelled out. By itself, premise 3 ("Because if he did it, he would probably have bloodstains on the sleeve of his shirt") offers no support whatsoever to the conclusion ("Dexter is the murderer"). And by itself, premise 4 ("The bloodstains are tiny, but they are there") doesn't lend any support to the conclusion. But together, premises 3 and 4 offer a good reason to accept the conclusion. We represent dependent premises by underlining them *together*, as in our diagram. Since dependent premises together act as a single premise, or reason, we draw a single arrow from the combined premises (from the line between 3 and 4, each of which is inside its own square) to the conclusion. With the diagram complete, we can see clearly that two independent premises and one set of dependent premises provide support for the conclusion (statement 2).

Now, consider this argument:

> (1) The famous trial lawyer Clarence Darrow (1857–1938) made a name for himself by using the "determinism defence" to get his clients acquitted of serious crimes. (2) The crux of this approach is the idea that humans are not really responsible for anything they do because they cannot choose freely—they are "determined," predestined, if you will, by nature (or God) to be the way they are. (3) So in a sense, Darrow says, humans are like wind-up toys with no control over any action or decision. (4) They have no free will. (5) Remember that Darrow was a renowned agnostic who was skeptical of all religious claims. (6) But Darrow is wrong about human free will for two reasons. (7) First, in our moral life, our own common-sense experience suggests that sometimes people are free to make moral decisions. (8) We should not abandon what our common-sense experience tells us without good reason—and (9) Darrow has given us no good reason. (10) Second, Darrow's determinism is not confirmed by science, as he claims—but actually conflicts with science. (11) Modern science says that there are many things (at the subatomic level of matter) that are not determined at all: (12) they just happen.

Bettman/Getty Images

Clarence Darrow was skilled at argumentation, which he used to good effect in his most famous case, the so-called Scopes Monkey Trial of 1925, in which he defended a man (John Scopes) charged with teaching evolution in a public school. Give examples of other fields, beside law, in which good reasoning is essential.

Indicator words are scarce in this argument, unless you count the words *first* and *second* as signifying premises, but they're not reliable indicators. After we number the statements consecutively and cross out extraneous statements, the argument looks like this:

> ~~(1) The famous trial lawyer Clarence Darrow (1857–1938) made a name for himself by using the "determinism defence" to get his clients acquitted of serious crimes. (2) The crux of this approach is the idea that humans are not really responsible for anything they do because they cannot choose freely—they are "determined," predestined, if you will, by nature (or God) to be the way they are. (3) So in a sense, Darrow says, humans are like wind-up toys with no control over any action or decision. (4) They have no free will. (5) Remember that Darrow was a renowned agnostic who was skeptical of all religious claims.~~ (6) But Darrow is wrong about human free will for two reasons. (7) First, in our moral life, our own common-sense experience suggests that sometimes people are free to make moral decisions. (8) We should not abandon what our common-sense experience tells us without good reason—and (9) Darrow has given us no good reason. (10) Second, Darrow's determinism is not confirmed by science, as he claims—but actually conflicts with science. (11) Modern science says that there are many things (at the subatomic level of matter) that are not determined at all: (12) ~~they just happen~~.

To simplify things, we can eliminate several statements right away. Statements 1 through 4 are just background information on Darrow's views. Statement 5 is irrelevant to the argument; his agnosticism has no logical connection to the premises or conclusion. Statement 12 is a rewording of statement 11.

After this elimination process, only the following premises and conclusion (statement 6) remain:

> (6) But Darrow is wrong about human free will for two reasons.
> (7) First, in our moral life, our common-sense experience suggests that sometimes people are free to make moral decisions.
> (8) We should not abandon what our common-sense experience tells us without good reason.
> (9) Darrow has given us no good reason.
> (10) Second, Darrow's determinism is not confirmed by science, as he claims—but actually conflicts with science.
> (11) Modern science says that there are many things (mostly at the subatomic level of matter) that are not determined at all.

The question is, how are these premises related to the conclusion? Well, premises 7, 8, and 9 are dependent premises supporting the conclusion. Taken separately, these premises are weak, but together they constitute a plausible reason for accepting statement 6. Premise 10 directly supports the conclusion, and it in turn is supported by premise 11. These logical relationships can be diagrammed like this:

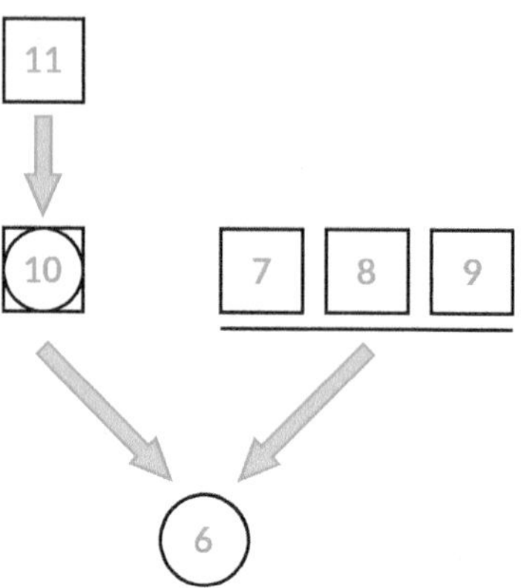

Notice how statement 10 is diagrammed. It is a premise leading to the conclusion (6), so it needs to be inside a square. But it is also a conclusion (supported by premise 11), so it also needs to be inside a circle. The circle–square combination indicates that the statement is a sub-conclusion, a statement that serves as both a premise *and* a conclusion.

Now read this passage:

> As a nervous world watches on, the Russian invasion of Ukraine continues. Everyone is wondering whether Ukraine can withstand the onslaught of Russia's military. In fact, Ukraine will almost certainly prevail. Ukraine is currently receiving substantial military aid from European countries, and such aid is very meaningful. Also, financial support from Europe and North America is a crucial issue, and such support has flowed in from Europe and North America. Finally, the effectiveness of Russia's own military is very much in doubt because recent evidence has shown substantial reliance on out-of-date equipment and technology.

Review Notes

Diagramming Arguments: Step by Step

1. Underline all premise or conclusion indicator words such as "since," "therefore," and "because." Then number the statements.
2. Cross out all extraneous material—redundancies, irrelevant sentences, questions, exclamations.
3. Draw the diagram using numbered squares to represent premises and numbered circles to represent conclusions. Connect premises and conclusions with arrows showing logical connections. Include both dependent and independent premises, and draw a line under dependent premises to connect them.

When we number the statements and underline the indicators, we get this:

> (1) As a nervous world watches on, the Russian invasion of Ukraine continues. (2) Everyone is wondering whether Ukraine can withstand the onslaught of Russia's military. (3) In fact, Ukraine will almost certainly prevail. (4) This is because Ukraine is currently receiving substantial military aid from European countries, (5) and such aid is very meaningful. (6) Also, financial support from Europe and North America is a crucial issue, (7) and such support has flowed in from Europe and North America. (8) Finally, the effectiveness of Russia's own military is very much in doubt, (9) because recent evidence has shown substantial reliance on out-of-date equipment and technology.

And here's the passage with the extraneous material crossed out:

> ~~(1) As a nervous world watches on, the Russian invasion of Ukraine continues. (2) Everyone is wondering whether Ukraine can withstand the onslaught of Russia's military.~~ (3) In fact, Ukraine will almost certainly prevail. (4) This is because Ukraine is currently receiving substantial military aid from European countries, (5) and such aid is very meaningful. (6) Also, financial support from Europe and North America is a crucial issue, (7) and such support has flowed in from Europe and North America. (8) Finally, the effectiveness of Russia's own military is very much in doubt, (9) because recent evidence has shown substantial reliance on out-of-date equipment and technology.

The conclusion is statement 3, and the premises are statements 4 through 9. The first two statements are extraneous. Statements 4 and 5 are dependent premises, and so are statements 6 and 7. Statements 8 and 9 constitute an argument that gives support to the conclusion of the passage. Statement 8 is the conclusion of that argument; statement 9 is the premise. The diagram of this argument is as follows:

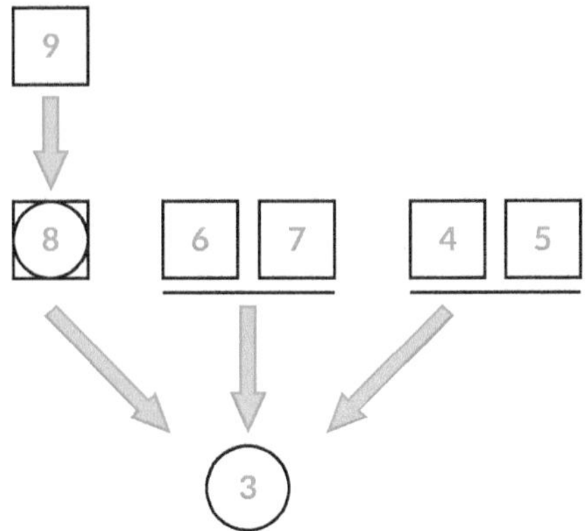

By the time you work through the diagramming exercises in this chapter, you will probably be fairly proficient in diagramming arguments of all kinds. Just as important, you will have a better appreciation of how arguments are built, how they are dissected, and how you can judge their value in a penetrating, systematic way.

Exercise 3.8

Answers to exercises marked with an asterisk (*) may be found in Appendix B, Answers to Exercises.

For each of the following diagrams, devise an argument whose premises and conclusion can be accurately depicted in the diagram. Write out the argument, number each statement, and insert the numbers into the diagram at the right places.

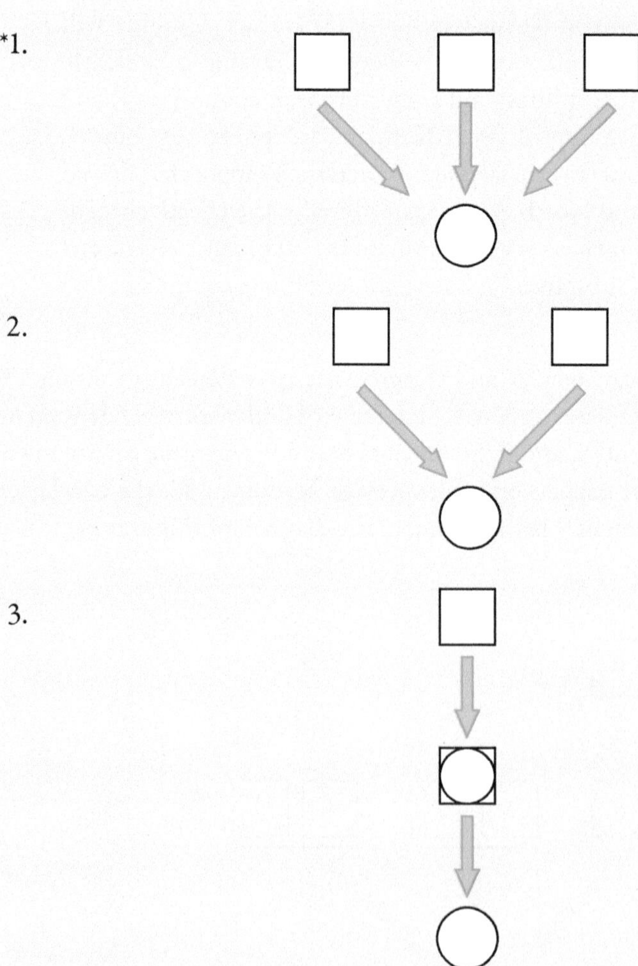

*4.

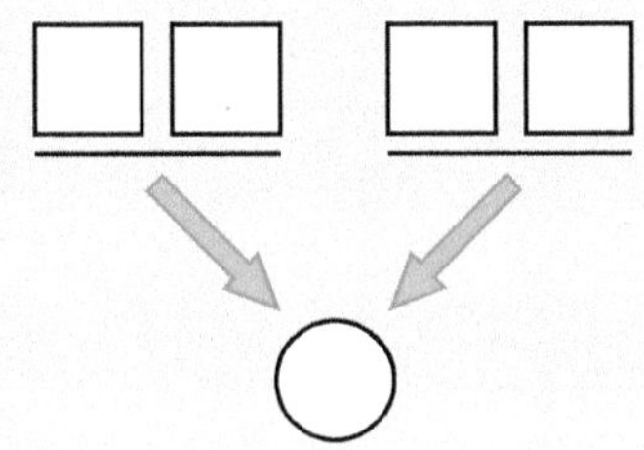

5.

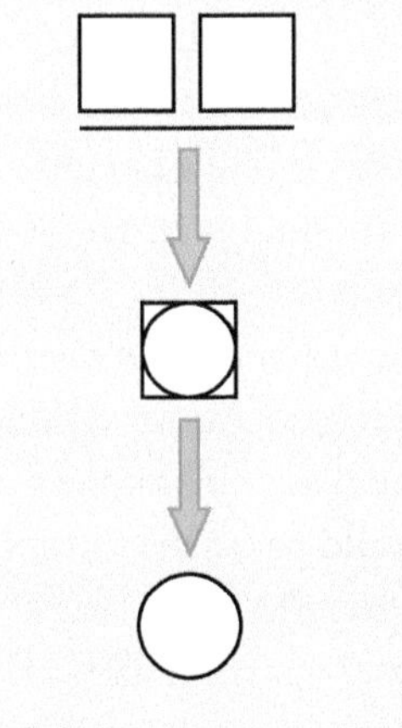

6.

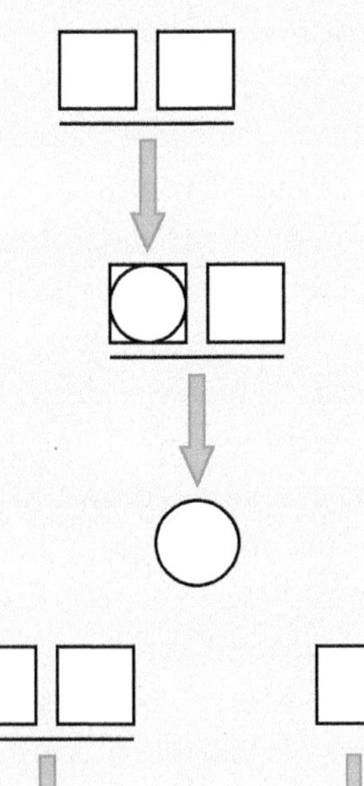

7.

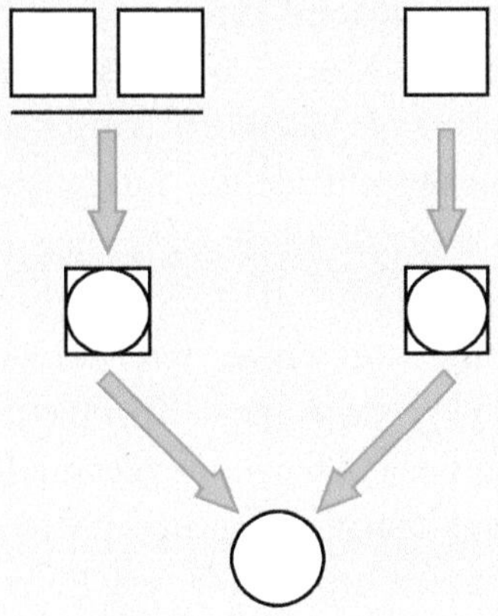

Exercise 3.9

Diagram the following arguments using the procedure discussed in the text.

1. Academic integrity violations are at an all-time low, and professors report that students are very focused on their studies. Our school's new associate dean seems to be doing a great job.
2. The dean of arts must be incompetent. Because the state of things around here suggests that he's either incompetent or lazy. He's not lazy, though, because he seems to be very good at finding ways to increase his own reputation.
3. If an individual in a coma is still a person, then giving him a drug to kill him is murder. Such an individual is in fact a person. Therefore, giving him the drug is murder.
4. I think that particular university is overrated. Their professors aren't very accomplished, and their students are a bunch of rich brats. They also try way too hard to get into the news by bragging about every minor success.
5. I think city council should pass a bylaw prohibiting smoking in all restaurants and bars. It won't be a popular move, but it's clearly the best thing from a public health point of view. By passing such a bylaw, city council would be setting a good example and reminding everyone what a serious risk smoking poses.
6. If Marla buys the house in the suburbs, she will be happier and healthier. She is buying the house in the suburbs. So she will be happier and healthier.*
7. If you don't set your alarm, you won't wake up in time. If you don't wake up in time, you'll miss the bus. If you miss the bus, you won't be able to write your final exam. If you miss one more final exam, you'll get kicked out of school. So if you don't set your alarm, you'll get kicked out of school.
8. "Grow accustomed to the belief that death is nothing to us, since every good and evil lie in sensation. However, death is the deprivation of sensation. Therefore... death is nothing to us." (Epicurus)
9. "A cause-and-effect relationship is drawn [by those opposed to pornography] between men viewing pornography and men attacking women, especially in the form of rape. But studies and experts disagree as to whether any relationship exists between pornography and violence, between images and behavior. Even the pro-censorship Meese Commission Report admitted that the data connecting pornography to violence was unreliable." (*Free Inquiry*, Fall 1997)
10. The existence of planets outside our solar system is a myth. There is no reliable empirical evidence at all showing that planets exist outside our solar system.*
11. If Li Yang gets a high score on her test, she will have a perfect grade point average. If she gets a low score, she will drop out of school. She will get a high score on the test, so she will have a perfect grade point average.
12. Richard is a registered nurse and most registered nurses are very knowledgeable. Therefore, Richard is probably very knowledgeable. Richard probably

studied very hard at school because most people who are very knowledgeable have studied very hard.

13. Jennifer is a 15-year-old. No 15-year-old has ever gained a PhD in nuclear physics. Therefore, Jennifer does not have a PhD in nuclear physics.
14. Gloria has to choose between chocolate and vanilla. But she hates vanilla. So she'll have chocolate.
15. It's very easy to tell whether bread is freshly baked or not. The aroma is unmistakable, and the inside will be soft and moist. Baker's Bakery says that their bread is freshly baked in their store every day, but they must be lying. There is no aroma, and the bread is hard and dry. I also saw a delivery guy from the local grocery store carrying bread into the bakery.
16. "It is clear that archaeologists have not yet come to terms with dowsing [the practice of searching for underground water or treasure by paranormal means]. Where it has been the subject of tests, the tests have been so poorly designed and executed that any conclusion whatsoever could have been drawn from them. The fact that such tests are usually carried out only by researchers with a prior positive view of dowsing means that the conclusions will likely also be positive. The normal processes of peer review and scholarly discussion have also failed to uncover the lack of properly controlled test conditions in such studies as those of Bailey et al. and Locock, causing a generation of students and general readers in the United Kingdom, at least, to remain under the impression that the reality of archaeological dowsing had been all but confirmed by science." (*Skeptical Inquirer*, March/April 1999)
17. There are at least two main views regarding the morality of war. Pacifism is the view that no war is ever justified because it involves the taking of human life. Just-war theory is the view that *some* wars are justified for various reasons—mostly because they help prevent great evils (such as massacres, "ethnic cleansing," or world domination by a madman like Hitler) or because they are a means of self-defence. I think our own moral sense tells us that occasionally (as in the case of World War II, for example), violence is morally justified. It would be hard for anyone to deny that a war to prevent something like the Holocaust is morally right.*
18. Some say that those without strong religious beliefs—non-believers in one form or another—cannot be moral. But millions upon millions of people have been non-believers or non-theists and yet have produced some of the most noble and most morally principled civilizations in history. Consider the Buddhists of Asia and the Confucianists of China. Consider also the great secular philosophers from the ancient Greeks to the likes of Bertrand Russell and John Searle of the twentieth century.
19. Glimglom is either a Jabberwocky or a Bugaboo or a Sceadugenga. But he's not a Jabberwocky because he doesn't have jaws that bite. And he's not a Bugaboo because he's not covered in goo. So he must be a Sceadugenga!

20. The picnic will probably be spoiled because there is a 90 per cent probability of rain.*
21. I'm pretty sure that café on Yonge Street we went to that one time will go out of business soon. Their coffee was nothing special, and their cakes tasted like they were baked a week ago. Some food critics have also criticized the café's poor service on several reputable review websites.
22. We should not reform Canada's Senate, because our current system of appointing senators works just fine and all senators do lots of good work by holding committee hearings that shed light on important issues.

3.6 Assessing Long Arguments

The general principles of diagramming can help you when you have to evaluate arguments that are much longer and more complicated than most of those in this chapter. Some arguments are embedded in extended passages, persuasive essays, long reports, and even whole books. In such cases, the kind of *detailed* argument diagramming we use to analyze short passages won't help you much. In very lengthy works, our three-step diagramming procedure would be tedious and time-consuming—if not maddening. But the *general approach* used in the procedure *is* relevant to longer arguments.

When you have to evaluate a very long passage, you are almost always faced with three obstacles:

1. Only a small part of the writing may contain statements that serve as the premises and conclusion. (The rest is background information, reiterations of ideas, descriptions, examples, illustrations, asides, irrelevancies, and more.)
2. The premises or conclusion may be implicit.
3. Many longer works purporting to be filled with arguments contain very few arguments or none at all. (It's common for many books—even bestsellers—to pretend to make a case for something but to be without any genuine arguments.)

Fortunately, you can usually overcome these impediments if you're willing to put in some extra effort. The following is a four-step procedure that can help:

Step 1. Study the text until you thoroughly understand it. You can't find the conclusion or premises until you know what you're looking for—and that requires having a clear idea of what the author is driving at. Don't try to find the conclusion or premises until you "get it." This understanding entails having an overview of a great deal of text, a bird's-eye view of the whole work.

Step 2. Find the conclusion. When you evaluate extended arguments, your first task, as in shorter writings, is to find the conclusion. There may be several main conclusions or one primary conclusion with several sub-conclusions (as depicted in some of the previous argument diagrams). Or the conclusion may be nowhere explicitly stated but embodied in metaphorical language or implied by large amounts of prose. In any case, your job is to come up with a single conclusion statement for each conclusion—even if you have to paraphrase large sections of text to do it.

Step 3. Identify the premises. Like the hunt for a conclusion, unearthing the premises may involve condensing large sections of text into a manageable form—namely, single premise statements. To do this you need to disregard extraneous material and keep your eye on the "big picture." Just as in shorter arguments, premises in longer pieces may be implicit. At this stage, you shouldn't try to incorporate the details of evidence into the premises, though you must take them into account to fully understand the argument.

Step 4. Diagram the argument. After you identify the premises and conclusion, diagram them just as you would a much shorter argument.

Let's see how this procedure works on the following selection:

> **No Place for Racial Profiling**
> In 2019, an Indigenous man—a member of the Heiltsuk Nation—and his teenage granddaughter were handcuffed in a Vancouver bank because of some apparent irregularities involving their identification. They were simply trying to open a bank account when the irregularities became apparent and bank employees called police. Would this sort of thing have happened to a white Canadian? Or did this man and his granddaughter end up in handcuffs simply because they were Indigenous? Racial profiling of this sort has never been shown to be effective in reducing the rate of actual financial crimes in any meaningful way. Everyone deserves the dignity of being treated with respect by Canadian financial institutions.

In this example, the author has given us a break by providing the conclusion in the title: discrimination by racial profiling is not justified. Notice that this conclusion is not explicitly stated in the text but is implied. Given this conclusion, we can see that the entire first half of the paragraph is background information—specifically, an example of racial profiling. The second half of the paragraph provides the supporting premises. Laid out in neat order, this argument looks like this:

(1) Racial profiling of this sort has never been shown to be effective in reducing the rate of actual financial crimes in any meaningful way.
(2) Everyone deserves the dignity of being treated with respect by Canadian financial institutions.
(3) Therefore, discrimination by racial profiling is unjustified.

The diagram of this argument looks like this:

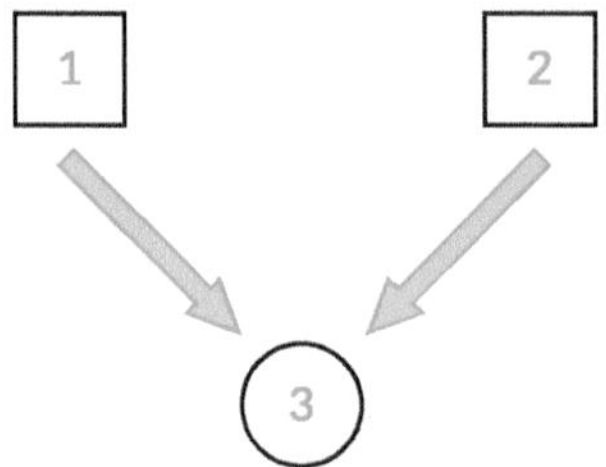

Food for Thought

No Arguments, Just Fluff

Once you get really good at spotting arguments in a variety of passages, you may be shocked to see that a massive amount of persuasive writing contains no arguments at all. Apparently, many people—including some very good writers—think that if they clearly express their opinions, they have given an argument. You could look at this state of affairs as evidence that people are irrational—or you could view it as a time-saver, since there's no need to waste your time on a bunch of unsupported opinions.

Unsupported opinions are everywhere, but they seem to permeate political writing, letters to the editor, and anything that's labelled "spiritual." Sometimes opinions are so weakly supported that they're almost indistinguishable from completely unsupported ones. Here's a taste:

> I am disgusted that [Toronto] Mayor John Tory is misusing my hard-earned tax dollars to hire private security guards to monitor our parks. The same dollars should, instead, be used to provide the services needed by people who are homeless. We need to build housing, not vermin-infested, disease-ridden "shelters." If homeless people are forced out of parks, where are they to go? Until the city provides the needed housing, Tory must not unleash the violence of police and "security" guards onto vulnerable people (many of whom, in other times, would have been given medical treatment for mental illness). Tory must show compassion. (Letter to the editor, *Toronto Star* website)

There's no argument there, just indignation.

> So after a decade of progress, we have our smog problem back (as if it ever left). Another problem overlooked? Couldn't be because of all the giant behemoths (SUVs) on the road, could it? Nah. Or letting all the trucks from south of the border into our country without safety and smog inspections, could it? Nah. It couldn't be because the government needs to have control of all it surveys? Nah. It must be something simpler, you think? Nah. (Letter to the editor, *Daily News* [Los Angeles] website)

There's no argument there either.

> How little is said or taught of the soul-life and its complete identification with the human being! To most men the soul is something apart from themselves that is only to be talked of and trusted in on special occasions: There is no real companionship, no intimate affiliation, between men's minds and souls in their everyday existence. Now there is in every man a divine power, and when that divinity, which is real self, is acknowledged and understood by the mind, it takes a very active part in man's life—indeed, it could fill at the very least one-half of his thought-life. (*Theosophy* website, www.theosophy-nw.org/theosnw/path/oc-kt.htm)

Nope.

A fact that can further complicate the argument structure of a long passage is that complex arguments can sometimes be made up of simpler arguments (sub-arguments). For example, the conclusion of a simple argument can serve as a premise in another simple argument, with the resulting chain of arguments constituting a larger complex argument. Such a chain can be long. The complex argument can also be a mix of both deductive and inductive arguments. Fortunately, all you need to successfully analyze these complex arguments is mastery of the elementary skills discussed earlier. (Recall that we used both a circle *and* a square to indicate that a particular statement is acting as both a premise of one sub-argument and the conclusion of another sub-argument.)

"Our minds anywhere, when left to themselves, are always thus busily drawing conclusions from false premises."

—Henry David Thoreau

The best way to learn how to assess long passages is to practise, which you can do in the following exercises. Be forewarned, however, that this skill depends heavily on your ability to understand the passage in question. If you can grasp the author's purpose, you can more easily paraphrase the premises and conclusion and uncover implicit statements. You will also be better at differentiating the extraneous stuff from the real meat of the argument. In the "Critical Thinking and Writing Exercise" for this chapter, we continue this discussion of evaluating long arguments.

Exercise 3.10

Answers to exercises marked with an asterisk (*) may be found in Appendix B, Answers to Exercises.

For each of the following passages, (1) list the conclusion and premises, and (2) diagram the argument.

1. "It could be that collagen supplements provide meaningful clinical benefit to arthritis and joint pain, but there's certainly no persuasive evidence yet to suggest that's the case. Based on what collagen is, how it's absorbed, and how we know collagen is actually synthesized in the body, it's highly implausible that a small supplement of amino acids consumed daily will have any meaningful therapeutic effects. While it appears to be safe to consume, Genacol, like other collagen supplements, appears to be little more than an expensive protein supplement. If you're seeking extra collagen, my suggestion is to skip the supplements, and go for a well-marbled steak. Enjoy it, but don't expect the steak, or a collagen supplement, to relieve your joint pain." (*Science-Based Pharmacy*, 11 November 2011)*
2. "[B]e smart about the shrimp you eat. Thankfully in Canada this is easier than in many places. Most of Canada's shrimp fisheries are considered to be ecologically sustainable with minimal bycatch, although some use

otter trawls which can severely damage sea floor habitats. Canada is home to one of the most sustainable prawn fisheries in the world—the B.C. spot prawn fishery. This fishery uses traps that do not result in as much bycatch or habitat damage. We also have programs like Oceans Wise that will tell you if the shrimp you want to buy for the barbecue or order in a restaurant won't harm the oceans they come from. Shrimp should be something special we eat in celebration of special events like World Oceans Day! Fortunately the timing coincides with the B.C. spot prawn season. Yes, you will pay more for the shrimp you eat but the oceans will pay less for your choices. Your long-term gain will be appreciating and eating other marine life for much longer." (Sarah Foster, InformedOpinions.org, 5 June 2014)

3. Corporations must continue to be treated as persons by courts in Canada, as they are in all other developed nations. "Personhood" in the legal sense merely means being treated by the courts as having rights and responsibilities. And without both legal rights and legal responsibilities, corporations would be very troubling figures within our communities. After all, if corporations did not have responsibilities, they would not have to honour warranties or fix defects in the products they make. That would clearly be bad for consumers. And if corporations had no legal rights, their property would never be secure. And if their property were never secure, it would be foolish to invest in them. And if no one invested in them, they would cease to exist. And if corporations ceased to exist, they would no longer produce goods and services and they would no longer provide jobs.
4. I just heard about another lawsuit accusing the Vatican of hiding instances of sexual abuse by priests in Canada and the United States. Sexual abuse is never OK, but I think such cases should be dismissed by courts in light of the community stature and function of priests and the benefits that accrue to society in the aftermath of the decision. Let's consider community stature first. The community stature of priests must always be taken into account in these abuse cases. A priest is not just anybody; he performs a special role in society—namely, to provide spiritual guidance and to remind people that there is both a moral order and a divine order in the world. The priest's role is special because it helps to underpin and secure society itself. Anything that could undermine this role must be neutralized as soon as possible. Among those things that can weaken the priestly role are publicity, public debate, and legal actions. Abuse cases are better handled in private by those who are keenly aware of the importance of a positive public image of priests. And what of the benefits of curtailing the legal proceedings? The benefits to society of dismissing the legal case outweigh all the alleged advantages of continuing with public hearings. The primary benefit is the continued nurturing of the community's faith, without which the community would cease to function effectively.

5. "The first thing that must occur to anyone studying moral subjectivism [the view that the rightness or wrongness of an action depends on the beliefs of an individual or group] seriously is that the view allows the possibility that an action can be both right and not right, or wrong and not wrong, etc. This possibility exists because, as we have seen, the subjectivist claims that the moral character of an action is determined by individual subjective states; and these states can vary from person to person, even when directed toward the same action on the same occasion. Hence one and the same action can evidently be determined to have—simultaneously—radically different moral characters. . . . [If] subjectivism . . . does generate such contradictory conclusions, the position is certainly untenable." (Phillip Montague, *Reason and Responsibility*).

Summary

Arguments come in two forms: deductive and inductive. A deductive argument is intended to provide logically conclusive support for a conclusion; an inductive one is intended to provide probable support for a conclusion. Deductive arguments can be valid or invalid, whereas inductive arguments are strong or weak. A valid argument with true premises is said to be sound. A strong argument with true premises is said to be cogent.

Evaluating an argument is the most important skill of critical thinking. It involves finding the conclusion and premises, checking to see if the argument is deductive or inductive, determining its validity or strength, and discovering if the premises are true or false. Sometimes you also have to ferret out implicit, or unstated, premises.

Arguments can come in certain common patterns, or forms. Two valid forms that you will often run into are *modus ponens* (affirming the antecedent) and *modus tollens* (denying the consequent). Two common invalid forms are denying the antecedent and affirming the consequent.

Analyzing the structure of arguments is easier if you diagram them. Argument diagrams can help you to visualize the function of premises and conclusions and the relationships among complex arguments with several sub-arguments.

Assessing very long arguments can be challenging because they may contain lots of verbiage but few or no arguments and many premises can be implicit. Evaluating long arguments, though, requires the same basic steps as assessing short ones: (1) ensure that you understand the argument, (2) find the conclusion, (3) find the premises, and (4) diagram the argument to clarify logical relationships.

Field Problems

1. Find a short passage online that claims to present an argument for a particular view but actually contains no real arguments at all. A good way to begin is by doing the following Google search: Google the phrase "I strongly believe" or something similar (in quotation marks), along with a word representing a controversial topic of your choosing—politics, religion, sports, animal rights, whatever. Such a search will almost certainly lead you to some strong statement of opinion presented without sufficient argumentation. Then rewrite the passage and include an argument for the original view.
2. Visit the Opinion section of the website of a major newspaper. Find an opinion that interests you. Write out the author's main premises and their conclusion. Now write out an argument on the same topic, but one that reaches the opposite conclusion. (It doesn't matter which "side" you agree with—the point is to explore the details of both sides of the issue!)
3. The next time you're watching television with commercials, or an ad before a YouTube video, find the argument in one ad (why you should buy this car or download that app, etc.). Write out its premises and conclusion. Are any of its premises hidden? Find another ad that contains no clear argument at all. If it contains no argument, does it still try to convince you of something? How?

Self-Assessment Quiz

1. What is a deductive argument? An inductive argument?
2. What distinguishes a valid argument from an invalid one?
3. What is an inductive argument? What is a *strong* inductive argument?
4. What is the difference between a cogent argument and a sound argument?

Say whether the following arguments are most likely intended to be deductive or inductive.

5. It's very likely that the provincial government will cut budgets across the board after the next election. And the party most likely to be elected has never been a big supporter of higher education. So our province will continue to provide inadequate funding to colleges and universities.
6. You're definitely going to enjoy this movie—it has great action sequences.
7. Professor Walton is an expert on health care resource allocation. And she says that they key factors in allocating vaccines during a pandemic are to protect the vulnerable and to make decisions in a way that is transparent. So vulnerability and transparency are important to keep in mind.

In each of the following arguments, identify the implicit premise that will make the argument either valid or strong.

8. KC Roberts and the Live Revolution is a funk band. So they're not likely to play any Drake tunes during their show Saturday night.
9. Given that so many people can't tell fake news from real news and can't even explain what counts as fake news, the future of the country does not look bright. Grades in university science courses will probably drop dramatically.
10. For each of the following, give an example of the argument pattern indicated.

    a. Denying the antecedent
    b. Affirming the consequent
    c. *Modus ponens*
    d. *Modus tollens*

Diagram the following arguments:

11. Bullock was rude to Al this morning, and Martha said Bullock didn't even apologize when he knocked over the milk at breakfast. He's in a bad mood!
12. The rule against lying is not a universal moral rule. If it were, then telling the truth should come naturally to everyone. But it does not come naturally to everyone because we all know lying is actually very common.
13. If dolphins have minds comparable to ours, then these creatures are self-conscious, intelligent, and creative. If they are self-conscious, then they should react appropriately when they see their reflections in a mirror. They do react appropriately. If they're intelligent, they should be able to solve complex problems. They can solve such problems. If they're creative, they should be able to create some form of art. In a rudimentary way, they do create art. They are definitely self-conscious, intelligent, and creative.
14. Someone left me a nice present after the party! But the only people who know that I like dark chocolate are Mark and his boyfriend Dave and also Francine. But Francine wasn't at the party. Oh wow—it must have been Mark and Dave!
15. Electric cars are typically better for the environment. And they're naturally quiet, so they don't contribute to noise pollution. Everyone should be buying electric cars!

Integrative Exercises

These exercises pertain to material in Chapters 1–3. For each of the following passages, state whether it contains an argument. If it does, specify the conclusion and premises, any argument indicator words, whether the argument is deductive or inductive, and whether it contains an example of face-saving or group-pressure thinking. Also identify any implicit premises, and diagram the argument.

1. Either the poison is in the glass on the left, or it's in the glass on the right. It can't be in the glass on the left, because I saw him appear to put it in the glass on the left, and I know he was trying to fool me. So it must be in the glass on the right. So I should drink the glass on the left.
2. If today's more potent marijuana were more dangerous than the marijuana of days gone by, then you would expect to see more drug-related deaths in Europe, where hashish—a more potent drug from the same plant as marijuana—is more common. But we do not, in fact, see higher rates of drug-related deaths in Europe. So marijuana that is more potent is not necessarily more dangerous.
3. "If it is to maintain the confidence of Canadians and their governments, which have generously bankrolled the company for decades, Bombardier must make public the results of its internal investigation into the Multiserv relationship and take appropriate action against any executives found to have acted contrary to the company's Code of Ethics and Business Conduct." (Konrad Yakabuski, *Globe and Mail*, 3 January 2018)
4. "The federal fiscal snapshot in July projects a pandemic-induced deficit of $343-billion in 2020–21 and a debt-to-GDP ratio jumping to 49 per cent from 30 per cent. Don't forget provincial debt, too. An Ontarian's combined government debt-to-GDP ratio will push toward 100 per cent of GDP and beyond. Such a high debt burden is an ailment that will become threatening when the economy returns to normal operations and interest rates rise. Just as we have done with the COVID-19 pandemic, we should address this ailment head-on." (Peter van Dijk and Glen Hodgson, *Globe and Mail*, 9 August 2020)
5. "A diverse workplace is a wonderful thing. First, it's a sign (although an imperfect one) that a company's hiring practices are fair. Second, it means that diverse viewpoints are brought to bear on

any problem the company faces." (*Business Ethics Highlights*, 6 December 2017)

6. Life on Earth today is better than it has ever been. We have technologies that our grandparents could only dream of. Life expectancies keep going up and up. And despite all the criticisms, I just don't think there's anything wrong with our modern consumer culture.
7. Fredo is going to get himself fired. He seems to think that acting like a bigshot all the time is going to impress people, but it's really just resulting in his co-workers getting very tired of him. And his sales numbers are nowhere near good enough to impress his boss, Karen.
8. Allow me to explain to you why I think that hockey is the greatest sport ever in the history of the entire world. It is incredibly fast-paced, since skating allows the players to move at great speeds. Also, a lot of skill is involved in controlling such a small puck with something like a hockey stick with so much precision. Finally, the checking and even the fighting make the sport very physical and exciting to watch.
9. People who have more than 10 pairs of shoes are not financially responsible. There's no reason to have that many pairs of shoes, since there wouldn't even be time to wear them all. And people who spend money on things they can't use are obviously irresponsible with their money. Also, my mom only has a couple of pairs of shoes, and she's the most financially responsible person I know.
10. If sex education in the schools can reduce the teen pregnancy rate or help delay the onset of teen sexual activity, I'm all for it. A recent study of several hundred teens showed that sex education in school lowered the incidence of teen pregnancy. We should have sex ed in all public schools.
11. The worst calamity that will befall the world in the next 20 years will be the use of small nuclear weapons by terrorists or rogue states. The death toll from such a state of affairs is likely to be higher than that of any other kind of human devastation. The United Nations just issued a report that comes to the same conclusion. We should act now to prevent the proliferation of nuclear weapons and nuclear-weapons-grade material from falling into the wrong hands.
12. "Dr. [Martin Luther] King was 26 when the Montgomery bus boycott began. He started small, rallying others who believed their efforts mattered, pressing on through challenges and doubts to change our world for the better. A permanent inspiration for the rest of us to keep pushing towards justice." (Barack Obama, Twitter, 15 January 2018)
13. Single-malt scotch is a beautiful drink. Five-and-a-half million Scots can't be wrong!
14. "*Coco* is one of the most beautiful movies I've ever watched. I laughed and cried and left the cinema smiling. Such a joy." (Trevor Noah, Twitter, 24 November 2017)
15. [O]n Thursday the Chinese envoy to Ottawa, Cong Peiwu, warned Canada against granting asylum to Hong Kong pro-democracy protesters. Cong said the "health and safety" of the 300,000 Canadian passport holders in Hong Kong could be jeopardized by these "violent criminals" and so Canada should not protect them. (*Reuters*, 16 October 2020)

Critical Thinking and Writing Exercise

From Thesis to Outline

In the "Critical Thinking and Writing Exercise" in Chapter 1, we saw that the second step in writing an argumentative essay (after determining your thesis statement, or conclusion) is to create an outline. Outlines are useful because, among other things, they help to avert disaster in the essay-writing phase.

Imagine writing two-thirds of your essay, then discovering that the second premise of your argument cannot be supported and is, in fact, false. You might have to throw out the whole argument and start over.

At the head of your outline, insert your thesis statement, expressing it as clearly and as precisely as possible. At every stage of outlining, you can then refer to the statement for guidance. The premises and conclusion of your argument (or arguments) will constitute the major points of your outline. The following, for example, is the preliminary outline for the essay discussed in the writing exercise at the end of Chapter 2:

> Thesis: Allowing coal-burning power plants to emit more sulphur dioxide will most likely increase the incidence of respiratory illnesses.
>
> I. High amounts of sulphur dioxide in the air have been linked to increases in the incidence of asthma and other respiratory illnesses.
> II. Many areas of the country already have high amounts of sulphur dioxide in the air.
> III. Most sulphur dioxide in the air comes from coal-burning power plants.
> IV. Therefore, allowing coal-burning power plants to emit more sulphur dioxide will most likely increase the incidence of respiratory illnesses.

After you clearly state the premises, ask yourself whether any of them need to be defended. As we discussed in Module 1, any premise likely to be questioned by your readers will need support. That is, the premise itself will need arguments to back it up, and the supporting arguments should be indicated in your outline. (Some premises, though, may not need support because they are obvious or generally accepted.) As discussed in this chapter, you can support a premise (claim) through deductive or inductive arguments with premises made up of examples, analogies, empirical evidence (such as scientific research or trustworthy observations), and authoritative judgments (such as those from reliable experts). Here's how the preceding outline might look with (fictional) supporting arguments clearly shown:

> **THESIS:** Allowing coal-burning power plants to emit more sulphur dioxide will most likely increase the incidence of respiratory illnesses.
>
> I. High amounts of sulphur dioxide in the air have been linked to increases in the incidence of asthma and other respiratory illnesses.
>   A. Environment Canada data show an association between high amounts of sulphur dioxide and increased respiratory illnesses.
>   B. Cities that monitor air pollution have noted increases in hospital admissions for asthma and other respiratory illnesses when sulphur dioxide emissions are high.
> II. Many areas of the country already have high amounts of sulphur dioxide in the air.
>   A. Scientists have reported high levels of sulphur dioxide in the air in fifteen major cities.
> III. Most sulphur dioxide in the air comes from coal-burning power plants.
>   A. Many environmental scientists assert that coal-burning power plants are the source of most sulphur dioxide.
>   B. A few owners of coal-burning power plants admit that their plants emit most of the sulphur dioxide in their region.
> IV. Therefore, allowing coal-burning power plants to emit more sulphur dioxide will most likely increase the incidence of respiratory illnesses.

You should expand your outline until you've indicated how you intend to provide support for each claim that requires it. This level of detail helps to ensure that you will not encounter any nasty surprises during the writing phase.

Your essay should somehow address objections or criticisms that your readers are likely to raise, and your outline should show how you intend to do this. Answering objections can make your case stronger and lend credibility to you as the writer. Sometimes it's best to address objections where they are likely to arise—in connection with specific premises or arguments. At other times, your essay may be more effective if you deal with objections at the end of it, near the conclusion.

As you work through your outline, don't be afraid to rework your thesis statement or to make changes in arguments. Satisfy yourself that the outline is complete and that it reflects a logical progression of points.

Argument and Ambiguity

Good writing is clear writing. Writing that isn't clear is ineffective—not to mention exasperating to its readers and sometimes embarrassing to its writer. An argument with unclear premises or conclusion is likewise ineffective. The lack of clarity undermines the argument, perhaps even rendering it useless.

Ambiguity is one of the many ways that a piece of writing can be unclear. A term or statement is ambiguous if it has more than one meaning and if the context doesn't reveal which meaning is intended. Consider these claims:

1. Morgan ate the ice cream with relish.
2. Kids make nutritious snacks.
3. It is impossible to live on water.
4. John met the girl that he married at a dance.
5. Helen saw the bird with powerful binoculars.
6. Luc hit the boy with the book.
7. The guy was all over the road; I had to swerve a number of times before I hit him.
8. Officers help dog bite victims.
9. Include your children when baking cookies.

All these claims are ambiguous, but they are ambiguous in different ways. Claims 1, 2, and 3 involve *semantic ambiguities*. Semantic ambiguities are due to possible multiple meanings of a word or phrase. In claim 1, the phrase "with relish" could mean "accompanied by a condiment made of chopped pickles" or "with pleasure or delight." In claim 2 the word "make" could mean either "prepare" or "constitute"—a difference between the kids' *making* food and *being* food. In claim 3 the phrase "live on water" could mean "subsist by drinking water" or "reside on water"—a distinction between the culinary and the sociological.

Semantic ambiguities often spark unnecessary and tedious debates. Disputants, for example, may disagree dramatically over whether a photo in a magazine is pornographic—but they disagree only because they have different ideas about what the term *pornographic* means. They may actually be in agreement about which photos they find offensive. But to one person, *pornographic* may describe any representation of nudity. To another person, *pornographic* may refer only to depictions of sexual acts. Another example: people might disagree over whether a particular politician counts as a *leader* simply because for some, the word merely names a role, while for others the word is reserved for people held in high regard.

Claims 4, 5, and 6 involve *syntactic ambiguities.* Syntactic ambiguities arise because of the sloppy way that words are combined. In claim 4, did John meet his bride-to-be at a dance, or did he marry her at a dance? In claim 5, did Helen use the binoculars, or did the bird use them? In claim 6, did Luc use a book to hit the boy, or did Luc hit a boy who was carrying a book?

Claims 7, 8, and 9 are not plainly either semantically or syntactically ambiguous, but they are unclear (and silly) just the same. In claim 7, was the writer deliberately trying to hit the guy or not? In claim 8, are the officers helping people who had been bitten, or are they using dogs to bite people? In claim 9, are we supposed to bake cookies alongside our children—or bake the children *into the cookies*? For each of these nine claims, there are two different, perfectly legitimate ways to understand the words that have been used—that is, different ways of understanding the meaning of those words if taken literally.

As a critical reader, your job is to be on alert for possible ambiguities, to understand the contexts that can help to clear up ambiguities, and to constantly ask, "What does this mean?" If the meaning of a claim is unclear, you are under no obligation to accept it. Likewise, if an argument contains ambiguous claims, you need not accept the argument. However, it may well be wise, and honourable, for you to make an effort to clear up the ambiguity by asking questions. Not all ambiguous claims are as silly as the ones listed above, and so it can be worthwhile to do your best to clear them up. For example, if someone said to you, "Jeff asked Akbar to give him his hat," there is genuine ambiguity there. Whose hat is it? Which "him" does the "his" in "his hat" refer to? Is it Jeff's hat (which he wants back) or Akbar's (which he wants to borrow)? The sympathetic listener here ought to do more than reject the claim: it is better simply to ask the question: *whose hat are you referring to?*

As a critical writer, your job is *not* to suppose that your readers will understand exactly what you mean but to strive to be perfectly clear about what you mean. Inexperienced writers too often assume that because they know what they mean, others will know too. The best corrective for unclear or ambiguous writing is the objective stance—the viewing of your writing from the standpoint of others. Good writers try hard to view their writing as others will, to step back mentally and try to imagine coming to their writing for the first time. In effect, they ask themselves, "Will my audience understand what I mean?" Achieving an objective attitude toward your writing is not easy. One thing that helps is to put your writing aside for a day or two after you complete it and then read it cold. Often after this "cooling down" period, passages that you thought were unambiguous turn out to be murky.

Another good tactic, of course, is to state explicitly what you intend your words to mean by offering a definition. But of course, you can't offer definitions for *every* word you use—not without ruining the "flow" of your essay. So definitions, while useful, must be used sparingly. (For more about definitions, see "Defining Terms" in Chapter 4's Critical Thinking and Writing Exercise.)

Writing Assignments

1. Create an outline for Essay 8 ("Unrepentant Homeopaths") in Appendix A. Specify the thesis statement, each premise, arguments supporting premises, any objections considered, and the conclusion.
2. Study the argument presented in Essay 7 ("Nurses, Social Media, and Whistleblowing") in Appendix A. Identify the conclusion and the premises and objections considered. Then write a two-page critique of the essay's argument.
3. Select an issue from the following list, and write a three-page paper defending a claim pertaining to the issue. Follow the procedure discussed in the text for outlining the essay and choosing a thesis and an appropriate argument to defend it. Where necessary, clarify terms.
   - Should Canada seek diplomatic ties with North Korea—a dictatorship with a terrible history of human rights violations?
   - In the fight against terrorism, should law enforcement agencies be allowed to spy on Canadian citizens by monitoring their email, wiretapping their phones, and checking records from public libraries—all without warrants?
   - Should university student governments have input into university curriculum?
   - Should youths between 14 and 17 be allowed to vote in Canadian elections?

Notes

1. This step-by-step procedure is inspired, in part, by Greg Bassham et al., *Critical Thinking: A Student's Introduction* (San Francisco: McGraw Hill, 2002), 56–62.
2. This procedure is inspired, in part, by Brooke Noel Moore and Richard Parker, *Critical Thinking*, 6th ed. (Mountain View, CA: Mayfield, 2001), 274–75.

PART TWO

Reasons

Reasons for Belief and Doubt

Chapter Objectives

When Claims Conflict

You will be able to

- understand that when a claim conflicts with other claims we have good reason to accept, we have good grounds for doubting it.
- recognize that if a claim conflicts with our background information, we have good reason to doubt it.
- appreciate that when we are confronted with a claim that is neither completely dubious nor fully credible, we should proportion our belief to the evidence.
- realize that it is not reasonable to believe a claim when there is no good reason for doing so.

Experts and Evidence

You will be able to

- understand what makes someone an expert and what does not.
- understand that if a claim conflicts with expert opinion, we have good reason to doubt it.
- realize that when the experts disagree about a claim, we have good reason to suspend judgment.
- recognize fallacious appeals to authority.
- distinguish true experts from non-experts by using the four indicators of expertise.

Personal Experience

You will be able to

- understand that it is reasonable to accept the evidence provided by personal experience only if there is no good reason to doubt it.
- appreciate the importance of the common factors that can give us good reason to doubt the reliability of personal experience—impairment, expectation, and innumeracy.

Fooling Ourselves

You will be able to

- appreciate why we need to resist the human tendency to resist contrary evidence.
- become sensitive to the possibility of confirmation bias.
- be alert to the possibility of the availability error.

Claims in the News

You will be able to

- gain a basic understanding of how the news media work and what factors influence the claims they generate.
- understand the skills involved in evaluating claims in the news.

Advertising and Persuasion

You will be able to

- understand and apply the guiding principle for thinking critically about advertising.
- exhibit familiarity with common tactics of persuasion used in advertising.

Let's remind ourselves once again what we are up to here. If we care whether our beliefs are true or reliable, and about whether we can safely use them to guide us and inform our choices, then we have to be careful about the reasons for accepting those beliefs. The better the reasons for acceptance, the more likely are the beliefs, or statements, to be true. Inadequate reasons, no reasons, or fake reasons (discussed in the next chapter) should lead us not to accept a statement but instead to doubt it.

As we saw in earlier chapters, the reasons for accepting a statement are often spelled out in the form of an argument, with the statement in question being the argument's conclusion. The reasons and conclusion together might constitute a deductive argument or an inductive argument. In such cases, the reasons for accepting the conclusion are normally there in plain sight. But in our daily lives, statements or claims very often appear on their own, without any accompanying stated reasons. An unsupported claim may be intended by the speaker, or writer, to act as the premise of an argument (and its truth value may then determine whether the argument is sound or cogent). Or the claim may simply be a stand-alone assertion of fact. Either way, if we care whether the claim is acceptable, we must try to evaluate the claim as it stands.

Of course, it helps to be knowledgeable about the subject matter of a claim. But it can be even more useful to understand and apply some critical thinking principles for assessing unsupported claims. Let's take a close look at these principles.

4.1 When Claims Conflict

Suppose you come across this claim on Twitter:

> *"The whole problem with the world is that fools and fanatics are always so certain of themselves, but wiser people so full of doubts."*
>
> —Bertrand Russell

> [Claim 1] The historic CHUM–CityTV building at the corner of Queen and John was demolished yesterday to make way for a new parking lot.

But imagine that the next tweet you see, from a different source, is this:

> [Claim 2] The historic CHUM–CityTV building at the corner of Queen and John was *not* demolished yesterday to make way for a new parking lot.

What do you make of such a conflict between claims? Well, as a good critical thinker, you can know at least that this conflict means that you have good reason to doubt claim 1 and therefore have no good grounds for immediately accepting it. You have good reason to doubt it because it conflicts with another claim you have just as much reason to believe (claim 2). When two claims conflict like this, they simply cannot both be true; at least one of them has to be false. So the following principle comes into play:

> *If a claim conflicts with other claims we have good reason to accept, we have good grounds for doubting it.*

With conflicting claims, you are not justified in believing either one of them fully until you resolve the conflict. Sometimes this job is easy. If, for example, the competing claims are reports of personal observations, you can often decide between them by making further observations. If the two tweets about the CHUM–CityTV building are from people who claim to have seen these things with their own eyes, then (if you live nearby) you can go to the corner of Queen and John streets to see with *your* own eyes whether the building really has been demolished. If a friend says your dog is sleeping on top of your car and you say your dog is not sleeping on top of your car (because you checked a short time ago), you can see who's right by simply looking again at the roof of your car. (Remember, though, that even personal observations can sometimes mislead us, as we'll soon see.)

Many times, however, sorting out conflicting claims requires a deeper inquiry. You may need to do some research to see what evidence exists for each of the conflicting claims. In the best-case scenario, you may quickly discover that one of the claims is not credible because it comes from an unreliable source (a subject discussed in the next few pages).

Now suppose that you're confronted with another type of conflict—this time a conflict between a claim and your **background information**. Background information is the huge collection of very well-supported beliefs that we all rely on to inform our actions and choices. A great deal of this knowledge consists of basic facts about everyday things, beliefs based on very good evidence (including our own personal observations and excellent authority), and justified claims that we would regard as "common sense" or "common knowledge." Suppose, then, that you're asked to accept this unsupported claim:

background information
The large collection of very well-supported beliefs that we all rely on to inform our actions and choices. It consists of basic facts about everyday things, beliefs based on very good evidence (including our own personal observations and excellent authority), and justified claims that we would regard as "common sense" or "common knowledge."

> I saw a baby lift a 500-kilogram weight.

You are not likely to believe this claim for the simple reason that it conflicts with an enormous number of your background beliefs concerning human physiology (and the physiology of babies in particular), gravity, weightlifting, and so on. Given what you already know about the world, the odds of that claim being true are very low.

Or how about this claim:

> The prime minister is entirely under the control of the chief justice of the Supreme Court of Canada.

This claim is not as clearly ridiculous as the previous one (it doesn't refer to something that is literally impossible), but it too conflicts with our background

Food for Thought

Fact and Opinion

When we evaluate claims, we are often concerned with making a distinction between facts and opinions. But just what is the difference? We normally use the word *fact* in two senses. First, we may use it to refer to a state of affairs—as in "We should examine the evidence and find out the facts." Second, we use the word *fact* to refer to true statements—as in "John smashed the dinnerware—that's a fact." Thus, we say that some claims, or statements, are facts and some are not. However (and here the English language is a bit tricky), a claim that is *about* some state of affairs is still referred to as a *factual claim*, as opposed to a *normative claim* about what should be done. A factual claim is a claim (right or wrong!) about the way something actually is. We use the word *opinion*, however, to refer to a belief—as in "It's John's opinion that he did not smash the dinnerware." Some opinions are true, so they are facts, whereas some opinions are not true, so they are not facts.

Sometimes we may hear somebody say, "That's a matter of opinion." What does this mean? Often it's equivalent to something like "Opinions differ on this issue" or "There are many different views on this." But it also frequently means that the issue is not a matter of objective fact at all but is instead entirely subjective—a matter of individual taste. Someone might say, for example, "The issue of which of Canada's provinces is the most beautiful is a matter of opinion." If I tell you "New Brunswick is the most beautiful province," I'm expressing an opinion. And statements expressing matters of opinion in this latter sense are not the kinds of things that people can really disagree on, just as two people cannot sensibly disagree about whether they like chocolate ice cream. When opinions differ in this sense, no amount of research will settle the dispute!

beliefs, specifically those having to do with the structure and workings of the Canadian government. If you know just a little about Canada's political system, you know that this claim is simply implausible. So we would have good reason to doubt this one also.

The principle we are using here is this:

> *If a claim conflicts with our background information, we have good reason to doubt it.*

Generally speaking, the more background information the claim conflicts with, the more reason we have to doubt it. We would normally—and rightfully—assign a low probability to any claim that conflicts with a great deal of our background information.

You would be entitled, for example, to have a *little* doubt about the claim that Joan is late for work if it conflicts with your background information that Joan has never been late for work in the 10 years you've known her. But you are entitled to have very *strong* doubts about, and to assign very low credibility to, the claim that André can turn a stone into gold just by touching it. You could even reasonably dismiss the claim without further investigation. Such a claim conflicts with too much of what we know about the physical world. Joan being late for work seems unlikely. But André turning a stone into gold is simply impossible.

It's always possible, of course, that a claim that conflicts with our background information is true and that some of our background information is actually wrong. So in many cases it's reasonable for us to examine a conflicting claim more closely. If we find that it has no good reasons in its favour and that it is not credible, we may reject it. If, on the other hand, we discover that there are strong reasons for accepting the new claim—say, a series of reliable scientific studies—then we may need to revise our background information. For example, we may be forced to accept the claim about André's golden touch (and to rethink some of our background information) if the claim is backed by strong supporting evidence. Our background information would be in need of some serious revision if André could produce this stone-to-gold transformation repeatedly under scientifically controlled conditions that ruled out error, fraud, and trickery.

So it is not reasonable to accept a claim if there is good reason to doubt it. And sometimes, if the claim is dubious enough, we may be justified in dismissing a claim out of hand. But what should we believe about a claim that is not quite dubious enough to discard immediately and yet not worthy of complete acceptance? We should measure out our belief according to the strength of reasons or evidence provided. That is,

> *We should proportion our belief to the evidence.*

The more evidence a claim has in its favour, the stronger our belief in it should be. Weak evidence for a claim warrants (that is, justifies) weak belief; strong evidence warrants strong belief. And the strength of our beliefs should vary across this spectrum according to the evidence.

Implicit in what we've said so far is a principle that deserves to be made explicit because it's so often ignored:

> *It's not reasonable to believe a claim when there is no good reason for doing so.*

"A belief which leaves no place for doubt is not a belief; it is a superstition."

—José Bergamin

Food for Thought

Folk Psychology

A big part of our "background information" comes from folk psychology, the skill we all have for correctly attributing to other people (and sometimes animals) moods, beliefs, desires, intentions, memories, and so on. We use the fact that other people have those things as a way to explain and predict their behaviour.

Have you ever seen someone lifting cushions off a couch one at a time or lifting pieces of paper on a desk to look under them? If you have, you probably immediately knew what was going on: they were searching for something. You recognize the behaviour: that's what searching looks like. Or imagine you know that your friend John loves chocolate and hates vanilla. The waiter at lunch tells you that the dessert special today is chocolate or vanilla. What will John choose? Yes, you can quite easily predict the future here and without any magical powers. You know that John will choose chocolate. How do you know? Not just because you know that John loves chocolate but because you know that people tend to choose things they love. That's a basic psychological principle, and you don't need a PhD in psychology to know it.

The term *folk psychology* was coined by the philosopher Daniel Dennett in 1981. Folk psychology consists, according to Dennett, of the stuff everyone knows about how other people's minds work. You know that other people have hopes and dreams; that they love some things and hate other things; that they remember things that happen to them; that they can perceive the world around them using their senses of sight, smell, hearing, touch, and so on.

Our capacity for folk psychology is essential; it's what allows us to live and work together in groups. Folk psychology is what lets you know that punching someone will make them mad, that gossiping about them will hurt their feelings, and that flirting with their girlfriend will make them jealous. And you can also typically predict how they might react in response. Folk psychology is also what allows you to motivate people to alter their behaviour: you know that they will tend to do more of something if you reward them for it, and to do less of something if you punish them for it.

For that matter, if it weren't for our command of folk psychology, how could we ever do something like drive on a highway? Think about it: hundreds of vehicles zooming all around us, each one of them a potentially lethal threat. How do we know that this is actually a pretty safe activity? Because we know that humans generally try to avoid getting killed, and so you can generally expect other drivers to behave in ways that will help them avoid an accident that might kill them as well as you.

Our capacity for folk psychology is, however, imperfect. Sometimes people behave in ways that make no sense to us: we see their behaviour but can't map it onto any particular understanding of what is on their mind. Sometimes it may simply reflect the fact that different people are different—we don't all think identically. So we may find ourselves truly puzzled and ask ourselves, "What on earth are they doing?" But the very fact that we sometimes ask this question just reinforces the fact that we generally do understand other people as creatures with minds, beings that have beliefs and act upon them in somewhat predictable ways. If we didn't see other people that way, if we didn't see them as doing things intentionally, we wouldn't bother to wonder why they do what they do.

The famous twentieth-century philosopher Bertrand Russell tried hard to drive this idea home. As he put it, "It is undesirable to believe a proposition when there is no ground whatever for supposing it true."[1] When you read this, it may seem pretty obvious, but it is amazing how many people do actually believe things without any good reason for doing so.

4.2 Experts and Evidence

expert
Someone who is more knowledgeable in a particular subject area or field than most others are.

When an unsupported claim—one for which no premises have been provided—doesn't conflict with what we already know, we are often justified in believing it simply because it comes to us from experts. An **expert** is someone who is more knowledgeable about a particular subject area or field than most other people are. Relevant expertise provides us with reasons for believing a claim because, in their specialty areas, experts are more likely to be right than we are. They are more likely to be right because (1) they have access to *more information* on the subject than we do and (2) they are *better at judging* that information than we are. Experts are familiar with the established facts and existing data in their field, and with the state of existing controversies in their field, and they know how to properly evaluate that information. Essentially, this means that they have a handle on the information and know how to assess the evidence and arguments for particular claims involving that information. They are true authorities on a specified subject. Someone who knows the basic information relevant to a particular field but who can't evaluate the reliability of a claim is no expert.

In a complex world where we can never be knowledgeable in every field, we must rely on experts—a perfectly reasonable thing to do. And as the world grows more complex, our need to rely on a range of experts keeps on growing. But good critical thinkers are careful about expert opinion, guiding their use of experts by some common-sense principles. One such principle is this:

> *If a claim conflicts with expert opinion, we have good reason to doubt it.*

This principle follows from our definition of experts. If they really are more likely to be right than non-experts about claims in their field, then any claim that conflicts with expert opinion is, at least initially, dubious—that is, it is subject to doubt.

Here's the companion principle to the first:

> *When there is disagreement about a claim among the relevant experts, we have good reason to doubt it.*

If a claim is subject to significant dispute among experts, then non-experts can have no good reason for accepting (or rejecting) it. Throwing up your hands and arbitrarily deciding to believe or disbelieve the claim is not a reasonable response. The claim must remain in doubt until the experts resolve the conflict or you resolve the conflict yourself by becoming informed enough to decide competently on the issues and evidence involved—a course that's possible but usually not feasible for non-experts.

Sometimes we may have good reason to be suspicious of unsupported claims, even when they are purportedly derived from expert opinion. Our doubt is justified when a claim comes from someone put forward as an expert who in fact is *not* an expert in the subject at hand. When we rely on such bogus expert opinion, we commit the fallacy known as the **appeal to authority**.

When experts disagree, critical thinkers begin to have doubts. In what other cases might it be reasonable to be suspicious of experts?

The fallacious appeal to authority usually happens in one of two ways. First, we may find ourselves disregarding this important rule of thumb: just because someone is an expert in one field, they are not necessarily an expert in another. The opinions of experts generally carry more weight than our own—but only in their own areas of expertise. Any opinions that they put forward outside their fields are no more authoritative than those of non-experts. Outside their fields, they are not experts.

appeal to authority
The fallacy of relying on the opinion of someone deemed to be an expert who in fact is *not* an expert.

We don't need to look far for real-life examples of such skewed appeals to authority. On any day of the week we may be urged to accept claims in one field that are based on the opinion of an expert from an unrelated field. An electrical engineer or Nobel Prize–winning chemist may assert that certain herbs can cure cancer. A radio talk-show host with a degree in physiology may give relationship advice. A geneticist expresses opinions about how to reform financial institutions. Sometimes the lack of relevant expertise is quite subtle: a scientist with expertise relevant to detecting global warming may not have the relevant expertise to tell us what we can or should *do* about global warming. The point is not that these experts can't be right—they might be unusually well-informed about a topic without being an actual expert on it. The point here is that their expertise in a particular field doesn't automatically give us reason to believe their pronouncements regarding another. There is no such thing as a general expert; there are only experts in specific subject areas.

Second, we may fall into a fallacious appeal to authority by regarding a non-expert as an expert. We forget that a non-expert—even one with prestige, status, or sex appeal—is still a non-expert. Movie stars, TV actors, famous athletes, politicians, and social media influencers endorse products of all kinds in TV, print, and digital advertising. Such people may be very good at what they

Everyday Problems and Decisions

The Mechanic Says My Car Needs Repairs. But Does It?

When we think about relying on expert advice, we often focus on people with sophisticated scientific knowledge and multiple university degrees—people like heart surgeons and lawyers and structural engineers.

But many of the people we interact with more frequently for everyday household needs fit the definition of "expert" we use in this book. That is, they are more knowledgeable about a particular subject area or field than most other people are. The experienced plumber who fixes a leaky faucet, the electrician who replaces light switches and wiring in your aging house, and the master carpenter who installs new doors on your kitchen cabinet are all experts. They know things about the work they do that most of us simply do not. You might be able to look online to figure out how to replace a light fixture yourself, but an expert electrician can tell you whether, given the age of your house and the state of its wiring, it would be wise for you to attempt to do so. These sorts of experts have both knowledge and judgment that the rest of us tend to lack.

Consider auto mechanics. Fifty years ago, it was relatively common for car owners to do at least basic maintenance themselves: changing oil, replacing worn brake pads, and even adjusting carburetors. Today—in part because modern automobiles are so much more complex—we are more likely to take our car to a licensed mechanic for that sort of work. Of course, when we take our car to the mechanic for basic maintenance, it's always possible that the mechanic will spot additional worries: a loose or missing clamp, a wheel out of alignment, or even a transmission in need of replacement. These additional repairs can cost a lot! And when the mechanic gives you the bad news, a new issue arises: are they telling you the truth? It's likely that most mechanics are honest, and won't recommend unnecessary repairs. But the issue raises an important and interesting point about experts in general. We hire experts to do things we don't know how to do. But precisely because we lack their expertise, we often can't tell whether the work they have done for us is good work, or whether the advice they give us is good advice.

Some tips from consumer advocates for dealing with car repair shops:

- Ask around! A mechanic or a shop with a good reputation among people you trust is more likely to be trustworthy.
- Ask to see licences and certifications: some repair shops proudly display their mechanics' credentials.
- Ask questions about pricing: does the repair shop charge a set fee, or an hourly fee? (Neither is necessarily better than the other, but asking such questions will help the shop identify you as a knowledgeable consumer!)
- Ask for a written quote or estimate: that makes it more likely that you'll understand what you're getting, and gives you a way of holding the shop accountable.

do, but they are not experts in the sense in which we are using the word here. Consider: award-winning actors may be extremely good at what they do but may be unable to give good advice on how other people should become good actors. The fact that they have talent doesn't mean that they have understanding. And when experts speak outside their areas of talent and experience (which is often the case), they give us no good reason for believing that the products are as advertised. Advertisers, of course, know this, but they hope that we will buy the products anyway because of the appeal or attractiveness of the celebrity endorsers. Matthew

McConaughey probably knows no more about cars than you do, but the makers of the Lincoln Navigator are betting that his star appeal will be a good substitute for actual expertise and persuade quite a few people to make a purchase.

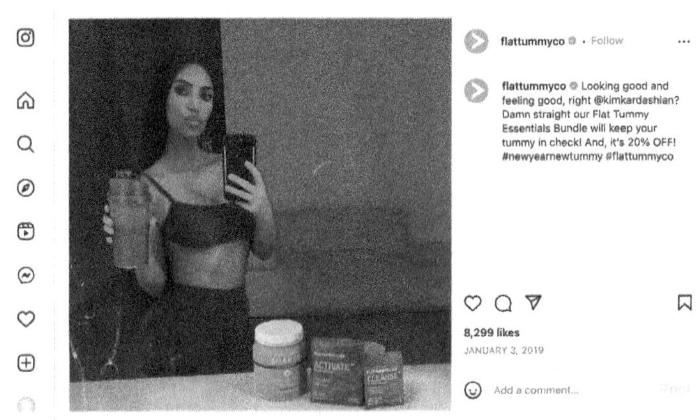

Instagram

Stars like Kim Kardashian have endorsed many products, without necessarily having the kind of expertise we can rely on. How should critical thinkers approach such endorsements?

Historically, regarding a non-expert as an expert has probably been the most prevalent form of the appeal to authority—with disastrous results. Political, religious, tribal, and cultural leaders have often been considered authorities, not because they knew the facts and could judge the evidence correctly but because culture, tradition, or whim dictated that they be regarded as authorities. When these "authorities" spoke, people listened and believed; some even went to war, persecuted unbelievers, or undertook countless other ill-conceived projects. If we are to avoid this trap, we must look beyond mere labels and titles and ask, "Does this person provide us with any good reasons or evidence?"

This question, of course, is just another way of asking if someone is a true expert. How can we tell? To be considered an expert, someone must have shown that they can assess relevant evidence and arguments and arrive at well-supported conclusions in a particular field. What are the indicators that someone has this essential kind of expertise? There are several that provide clues to someone's ability, but they do not guarantee true expertise.

In most fields, the following two indicators are considered minimal prerequisites for being considered an expert:

1. Education and training from reputable institutions or programs in the relevant field (usually evidenced by degrees or certificates)
2. Experience in making reliable judgments in the field (generally, the more years of experience, the better)

But, unfortunately, people can have the necessary education and experience and still not know what they're talking about in the field in question. Sadly, in the real world there are well-trained, experienced carpenters who do terrible work—and senior professors with PhDs whose professional judgment is unreliable. Two additional indicators of expertise, though, are more revealing:

3. Reputation among peers (as reflected in the opinions of others in the same field, relevant prestigious awards, and positions of authority)
4. Professional accomplishments

These two additional indicators are more helpful because they are likely to be correlated with the intellectual qualities expected in true experts. People with excellent reputations among their professional peers and with significant accomplishments to their credit are usually true experts, and their knowledge and judgment can generally be relied upon.

As we've seen, we are often justified in believing an otherwise unsupported claim because it's based on expert opinion. But if we have reason to doubt the opinion of the experts, we are not justified in believing the claim on the basis of that opinion. And chief among possible reasons for doubt (aside from conflicting expert opinion) is some sort of *bias*. When experts are biased, they are motivated by something other than the search for the truth—perhaps financial gain, loyalty to a cause, professional ambition, emotional needs, political outlook, sectarian dogma, personal ideology, or some other judgment-distorting factor. Therefore, if we have good reason to believe that an expert is biased, we are not justified in accepting the expert's opinion without further investigation.

But how can we tell when experts are biased? There are no hard-and-fast rules here. In the more obvious cases, we often suspect bias when an expert is being paid by special-interest groups or corporations to provide an opinion. We sometimes also suspect bias when the expert expresses very strong belief in a claim even though there is no evidence to support it or when the expert stands to gain financially from the actions or policies that they support. When an expert says, "My new discovery is great! Go out and buy some!" we have reason, at least, to worry that their professional judgment is being clouded by the prospect of profits.

"An expert is a man who has made all the mistakes which can be made in a very narrow field."

—Niels Bohr

An expert is in what we call a conflict of interest if they provide advice in a situation in which they have some "other" interest (often but not always financial) that may tend to skew or bias the advice they give. It's true that many experts can render unbiased opinions and do high-quality research even when they have a conflict of interest. Nevertheless, in such situations we have reasonable grounds to suspect bias—unless we have good reason to believe that the suspicion is unwarranted. These good reasons might include the fact that the expert's previous opinions in similar circumstances have been reliable or that he or she has a solid reputation for always offering unbiased assessments. In other words, there are things we can find out that may restore our trust, even in situations in which we might normally worry about bias.

Finally, keep in mind that there are certain kinds of issues that we probably don't want experts to settle for us. Indeed, in most of these cases the experts are just not capable of settling them for us. These issues usually involve matters of taste or moral, social, or political questions. If we're intellectually conscientious, we want to provide our own final answers to such questions, though we may draw heavily on the analyses and arguments provided by experts. We may study what the experts have to say and the conclusions they draw, and we may well find it useful to pay close attention to their reasoning. But we want ultimately to come to our own conclusions. We prefer this

Food for Thought

Evaluating Internet Sources

Can you trust the information you find on the internet? In many cases, no. In some cases, information presented is inaccurate merely because those presenting it lack the relevant expertise or are sloppy in doing their research. In other cases, material online is actually intended to mislead readers—perhaps to influence how the reader votes, or what they purchase. But if you understand how to judge the reliability of websites, and if you're willing to spend some time doing the judging, you can often find good and trustworthy information online. Finding reliable information online takes some effort because, unlike books and magazines, much of the information on the internet is not screened by editors, fact checkers, or anyone else before it hits cyberspace. Anyone can say anything on the internet. Thus, your online research should be guided by reasonable skepticism. If you want to know more about evaluating online sources, a good place to start is your college or university library. Many of them have, on their websites, excellent guides to internet research. Here is a checklist of questions to ask about online sources to help you assess their credibility. Some points to consider:

Authority

- Who is the author of the material, and how credible are they? (Note that in some cases, the author may be an organization, rather than an individual.)
- Is the author merely reporting what someone else said, or are they making claims that represent their own opinion? If they are merely reporting, are they a reporter for a credible news organization or other reliable source? If they are presenting their own point of view, does the author have relevant expertise?
- Does the author or organization provide contact information? In most cases, reputable authors and organizations provide some form of contact information so that readers can respond or ask for corrections where there are clear errors.

Publisher

- Who is the publisher of the material, and how credible are they? Is this just someone's amateur blog, for instance, or the website of a reputable news organization or government agency?
- Your goal should be to figure out who is ultimately responsible for this information being online, and whether they do anything to ensure its quality.

Audience and Goal

- Who is the information aimed at? Is it aimed at the general public, or at members of a particular industry or profession?
- Is it clearly aiming to convince its audience of something, or merely to inform them? (Be cautious! Sometimes items that aim to convince can be disguised as "merely informative.")
- Note that reputable news sources tend to mark clearly whether a given bit of content they publish is "news" as opposed to "commentary."

Currency

- Is the information presented up to date? Look carefully for a date of publication. Undated material obviously cannot be relied upon to be current. Beyond that, a lack of a date sometimes suggests that the publisher simply isn't very careful or concerned about accuracy.
- Within a given article, broken outbound links are often a warning sign that the story is old and may be out of date.

continued

Point of View

- If the information represents a point of view, does the publication make that clear? (It's perfectly fine for a website to present a particular political point of view or ideology, but it is best for them to say so explicitly. Check out the "About" link that you will often find at the top or bottom of the page.)
- If the material is presenting a point of view—that is, trying to convince readers of some conclusion—look carefully to see whether support is given. That is, is the writer presenting an argument (one you can evaluate using the tools in this book!), or are they merely presenting a point of view without support?

Support

- The internet is a big place, and so anything true and informative is likely to show up in more than one place. If some celebrity really did appear in public with, say, toothpaste on their shirt, it will likely be reported in more than one place. A website with "unique" information is one to be cautious of.[2]

Food for Thought

What Good Are Experts?

One of the things that frustrates many people about experts is that experts are sometimes wrong. This makes some people skeptical about whether experts have any value at all. If experts really are people who know more than the rest of us, then how is it that they are wrong as often as they sometimes seem to be?

One reason is that experts are, well, human. They make mistakes. And when experts make mistakes, they sometimes do it in full view of the public. If your great-grandfather had predicted back in 1943 that there would only ever be a need for about five computers in the entire world, no one would remember that terribly inaccurate prediction. But when Thomas Watson, who was then chairman of IBM, said precisely that, he said it in a public way that later made him look very foolish. That doesn't mean that Watson wasn't an expert. It just means he made an error in prediction, among what were likely a great many more accurate ones that no one recalls. Experts may make fewer mistakes than the rest of us, but they tend to make them in a very public way!

And sometimes the things experts are asked to do—such as to predict the course of a pandemic, or to predict how complex political situations will unfold—simply are things that no one is very good at. Such matters are simply too complicated and are influenced by too many variables for any one individual to predict them reliably.

Of course, sometimes experts are wrong in more blameworthy ways. Sometimes they make off-the-cuff comments without thinking the question through. Sometimes they express views outside their own areas of expertise without acknowledging that they are doing so. And sometimes they express their views with greater confidence than the evidence available really justifies: sometimes this is the result of ego, and sometimes it's the result of being nudged in that direction by the "pro versus con" format often preferred by news media.

But the fact that experts make mistakes doesn't mean they aren't useful. It just means we have to listen carefully to what they say and use our critical thinking skills. Journalist and author David Freedman wrote an entire book—called *Wrong*—about how and when experts go wrong. He concludes: "While it's clearly true that you should never trust experts blindly, there are many situations in which you should and even must trust them, and in which to do otherwise is nothing other than reckless."[3]

approach in large part because the questions are so important and because the answers we give help to define who we are. What's more, the experts usually disagree on these issues. So even if we wanted the experts to settle one of these questions for us, they probably couldn't.

Food for Thought

Anti-Expert Sentiments

During the 2016 debate over "Brexit" (the proposed departure of the UK from the European Union), the British justice secretary, Michael Grove, who was in favour of Brexit, was asked whether he could name any economists who were in favour of it. He responded by saying that "people in this country have had enough of experts." That might, of course, have been true, but Grove provided no evidence to support his claim. What other reason might Grove have had for making this assertion?

Anthony Collins/Alamy Stock Photo

When major political changes are afoot, how should we balance passion with appeal to the knowledge of credible experts?

Review Notes

Conflicting Claims

- If a claim conflicts with other claims that we have good reason to accept, we have good grounds for doubting it.
- If a claim conflicts with our background information, we have good reason to doubt it.
- We should proportion our belief to the evidence.
- It's not reasonable to believe a claim when there is no good reason for doing so.
- If a claim conflicts with expert opinion, we have good reason to doubt it.
- When the experts disagree about a claim, we have good reason to suspend judgment.

4.3 Personal Experience

We accept a great many claims because they are based on personal experience—our own or someone else's. Personal experience, broadly defined, arises from our senses, memory, and the judgment involved in those faculties. In countless cases, personal experience is just our evidence (or part of the evidence) that something is or is not the case. You believe that Jack caused the traffic accident because you, or someone else, witnessed it. You think that the herbal tea cured your headache because the pain went away after you drank it. You believe that PJ's Oyster Bar has great food because you had a wonderful meal there one time. You're sure that it was the other guy, not your friend Padraig, who threw the first punch because that's how you remember the incident. Or, as a member of a jury, you vote to convict the defendant because eyewitness testimony puts him at the scene of the crime with a gun in his hand. But can you trust personal experience to reveal the truth?

The answer is a qualified and cautious "yes." And here's the qualification in the form of an important principle:

> *It's reasonable to accept the evidence provided by personal experience only if there's no good reason to doubt it.*

If we have no good reason to doubt what our personal experience reveals to us, then we're justified in believing it. This means that if our faculties are working properly and our use of them is unimpeded by our environment, we're entitled to accept what our personal experience tells us. If we seem to see a cat on the mat under good viewing conditions—that is, we have no reason to believe that our observations are impaired by, say, poor lighting, cracked glasses, or too many beers—then we're justified in believing that there's a cat on the mat.

The problem is that personal experience, though generally reliable, is not infallible. Under certain circumstances, our senses, memory, and judgment just can't be trusted. It's easy enough to identify these circumstances in an abstract way, as you'll see later. The harder job is to (1) determine when they actually occur in real-life situations and (2) avoid them or take them into account in the process of proportioning belief.

The rest of this section is a rundown of some of the more common factors that can give us good reason to doubt the reliability of personal experience.

4.3.1 Impairment

This one should be obvious: if our perceptual powers are somehow impaired or impeded, we have reason to doubt them. The clear cases are those in which our senses are debilitated because we are seriously ill, injured, tired, stressed out, excited, drugged, drunk, distracted, dizzy, or disoriented. And just as clear are the situations that interfere with sensory input—when our environment is, say, too dark, too bright, too noisy, too hazy, or when the thing we are observing is too far away. If any one or more of these factors are in play, the risk of misperception is high, which gives us reason to doubt the trustworthiness of what we experience.

Memories can be affected by many of the same factors that interfere with accurate perception. They are especially susceptible to distortion if they are formed during times of stress—which helps to explain why the memories of people

"Besides learning to see, there is another art to be learned—not to see what is not."

—Maria Mitchell, nineteenth-century American astronomer

Food for Thought

How Reliable Is Eyewitness Testimony in Court? An Interview with Dr John Turtle*

What, in general, does the expert literature say about the reliability of eyewitness reports?

Research shows that people's memory for events they see for relatively short periods of time is susceptible to a number of factors that limit its accuracy and completeness. One way to gauge these limitations is to analyze cases in which people have been exonerated of crimes they were thought to have committed, usually on the basis of DNA testing of evidence retained from a crime scene. Out of hundreds of such cases of error reviewed over decades of research, mistaken eyewitness identification was involved about 70 per cent of the time. So we know people make mistakes, and that criminal investigation procedures and the court system often don't catch these mistakes.

What are some of the main factors thought to account for the low reliability of eyewitness reports?

A helpful way to organize the factors that affect eyewitness memory is to think of two categories. Estimator factors are ones whose effect on memory we can only estimate, such as exposure time, viewing conditions, stress, age, retention interval, and others. These are especially difficult to work with, because something like exposure time is often estimated to begin with, plus its effect on memory can only be estimated because so many other factors are involved. Nobody can answer the question of whether or not a particular 15-year-old female witness who saw a 40-year-old male stranger for 15 seconds at night from 6m away is likely to be accurate in her description or identification of the offender 3 weeks after the event.

The other category of factors that affect eyewitness memory are system variables—factors over which the legal system has at least some degree of control, such as how witnesses will be interviewed, how photos for a police lineup will be selected, how those photos will be presented, who conducts the lineup, and how the information will be used in an investigation or trial.

What's the best way for us to deal with what we know about the low reliability of eyewitness reports?

Police officers are making decisions every day about how to collect eyewitness evidence, so the recommendation from eyewitness researchers is to use the optimal procedures. For example, it is generally better practice to use a lineup of photos with one suspect and a number of known-innocent distractors instead of showing a single photo of the suspect to a witness. It's important to point out that the purpose of a lineup is not to test the witness for their accuracy at recognizing the perpetrator, because the suspect might not be the perpetrator; rather, the process is to test the investigator's hypothesis that the suspect is the perpetrator of the crime.

* Dr John Turtle, now retired, taught in Toronto Metropolitan University's Department of Psychology and is an acknowledged expert on eyewitness testimony.

who witness violent crimes or people who think they've seen ghosts are so often unreliable. These situations are understandably stressful.

The impairment of our faculties is complicated by the peculiar way they operate. Contrary to what many believe, our faculties are not like recording devices that make exact mental copies of objects and events in the world. Research suggests that they are more like artists who use bits of sensory data or memory fragments to concoct creative representations of things, not exact replicas. Our perception and memory are constructive, which means that what we perceive and remember is to some degree fabricated by our minds, and so perceptions and memories can sometimes be prone to error. For example, you see a man standing in the shadows by the road—then discover when you get closer that the "man" is a tree stump. Or you are anxiously awaiting a phone call from your elderly aunt Mary, and when a call comes and you hear the person's voice, you're sure it's her—then realize that it's a much younger woman asking for a charitable donation. Or while you're in the shower you hear the phone ring—but no one is calling and the ringing is something your mind is making up.

The constructive workings of our minds help us to solve problems and deal effectively with our environment. But they can also hinder us by manufacturing too much of our experiences from too little data. Unfortunately, the constructive tendency is most likely to lead us astray precisely when our powers of perception and memory are impaired or impeded. Juries, for example, are expected to be suspicious of the testimony of eyewitnesses who swear they plainly saw the dirty deed committed but were frightened, enraged, or a little tipsy at the time.

4.3.2 Expectation

A tricky thing about perception is that we often perceive exactly what we expect to perceive—regardless of whether there's anything there to detect. Have you ever watched the second hand on an electric clock move—then suddenly realize that the clock is not running at all? You "see" it moving because that's what you expect to see; after all, *moving* is what second hands *do*! Ever been walking through a crowd looking for a friend and hear her call your name—then find out later that she was actually 10 blocks away at the time? Such experiences—again the result of the constructive tendencies of mind—are common examples of how expectation can distort your perceptions.

Scientific research shows that expectation can have a more powerful effect on our experiences than most people think. In numerous studies, subjects who expected to see a flash of light, smell a certain odour, or feel an electric shock did indeed experience these things—even though suitable stimuli were never present. The mere suggestion that the stimuli would occur was enough to cause the subjects to report perceiving things that did not in fact exist.

Social psychologist John Ruscio gives another example:

> Aside from a close miss by what was reported to be a falling airplane part early in *The Truman Show* [the 1998 movie starring Jim Carrey], I cannot personally recall ever having heard of such an accident, fictitious or real. Students over the years have told me that they recall stories of people having found fallen airplane parts, but not of an actual fatality resulting from such falling parts. Shark attacks, on the other hand, are easily imagined and widely reported. Moreover, in the first movie that comes to my mind, the shark in *Jaws* actually did cause several fatalities. It may come as some surprise, then, to learn that in an average year in the United States thirty times more people are killed by falling airplane parts than by shark attacks.[9]

The availability error is likely at work in many controversies regarding environmental hazards. Because the alleged hazard and its effects can be easily and vividly imagined and the scientific data on the issue are not so concrete or memorable, the imagined danger can provoke a public scare even though the fear is completely unwarranted. Brain cancer from the use of cellphones and autism from childhood vaccines—both of these supposed hazards have provoked fear and public demands for action. But scientific studies have shown these concerns to be groundless.[10] Many environmental hazards are real, of course. But to conclude that they exist solely on the basis of scary thoughts is to fall prey to the availability error.

On the other hand, some environmental hazards are very hard to imagine vividly. Most of us have never lived through a catastrophic rise in sea level—even a brief one—and so it is hard for us to imagine in a clear way just what a dramatic rise in sea level globally would look like. This may make us underestimate the risks posed by global warming and the rise in sea level that may result from such warming. But we can all imagine vividly the inconvenience of driving less, of changing our diets so that we rely less on energy-intensive animal agriculture, and other lifestyle changes that collectively might help to combat global warming. If we think only of evidence that is easily available to us, we may severely misjudge this issue.

If we're in the habit of basing our judgments on evidence that's merely psychologically available, we will also frequently commit the error known as *hasty generalization*, a mistake discussed in detail in Chapter 8. We're guilty of hasty generalization when we draw a conclusion about a whole group (of things, people, or events) on the basis of an inadequate sample of the group. We fall into this trap when we assert something like this: "Honda Civics are pieces of junk. I owned one for three months, and it gave me nothing but trouble." Since our experience with a car is immediate and personal, for many of us it can be a short step from this psychologically available evidence to a hasty conclusion. If we give in to the availability error and stick to our guns about Civics being no good in the face of evidence to the contrary (say, automobile reliability research done by the Consumers Union or similar organizations), we should get an F in critical thinking.

Food for Thought

The Dangers of Fooling Ourselves

In many regards, we are our own worst enemies when it comes to thinking critically. In part, this reflects the fact that we are the ones who have the most *opportunity* to affect our thinking, for better or for worse. Occasionally, *other* people have the opportunity to affect our thinking. But we ourselves are the only ones who play a constant role in our own thinking. Whenever we are trying to figure out what to believe, our own thought patterns—including assumptions and biases—are sure to have an effect.

In this chapter, we outline three specific mechanisms by which we tend to fool ourselves—namely, resisting contrary evidence, looking for confirming evidence, and preferring available evidence. In reality, that is just a very small sample of the wide range of ways in which we have the tendency to fool ourselves.

In theory, a rational person wants to try to make sure that the ideas inside her head match reality out in the world. For example, imagine that I currently think that the capital of India is Kolkata, but I find out that it is actually New Delhi. In theory, I should change what I think. I should change my thinking so that it matches reality. But in practice, we often behave as if the world should change to match what we currently think about it. Our prior beliefs are "sticky" in a way that makes them persist even in the face of evidence to the contrary. Of course, in most cases it is impossible for the world literally to change to match our beliefs. But our behaviour often suggests a kind of denial of that fact: we try our best—mostly subconsciously—to try to bend reality so that it fits our prior understanding of it. And so we ignore evidence that the world is different from the way we believe it to be.

This is a common human tendency, one that is very difficult to escape. But the implication is that to be a critical thinker means to at least attempt to be honest with oneself about the tendency we all have—each and every one of us—to fool ourselves. We must all work hard to develop the habit of questioning ourselves. In particular, we need to work hard to seek evidence about how the world really is, especially when such evidence could challenge our own prior assumptions.

4.5 Claims in the News

In the Information Age, we are drenched with, well, information. And the news media are a major source of the information that confronts us every day. Through websites, blogs, social media, newspapers, magazines, television, and radio, information about what's happening in the world hits us like rain almost every waking hour. The claims—supported and unsupported—just keep coming at us. How can we cope with such an onslaught?

Once again, critical thinking must play a big role. Remember that information is just pieces of data, bundles of claims—not necessarily true, not always useful, and not the same thing as knowledge. Knowledge is true belief supported by good reasons; mere information doesn't have this lofty status. And to transform information into knowledge—our most useful commodity—we need critical thinking. Through critical thinking we can make sense of a great deal of the information coming from the news media. As you will see, most of the rest is not relevant and not worth our time.

Most of the news that reaches us, even when it gets to us through social media outlets such as Facebook or Twitter, has its origins with reporting done by traditional media outlets—namely, TV, newspapers, and radio. So let's begin by looking at how the traditional news media work—how and why they generate the claims that they do. Then we'll discuss how to critically examine the claims embedded in news reports, broadcasts, and multimedia presentations.

4.5.1 Inside the News

The news media include hundreds of newspapers (among the biggest and the best are the *Globe and Mail*, the *Washington Post*, the *New York Times*, and the *Los Angeles Times*), network news organizations (CTV, CBC, Global), cable news networks (CBC News Network, CTV News Channel, CNN), local and national radio broadcasts, local television news, American public television and radio, and newsmagazines (notably *Maclean's* and *L'actualité*). Most of these sources now have websites, which represent the important extension of their reach. In addition, there are an increasing number of news-containing and news-generating websites, such as TechCrunch, Mashable, BuzzFeed, and the Huffington Post. Most news can be found in newspapers (including their online versions), where news stories are generally longer, more comprehensive, and more in-depth than those of any other news source. Newspapers, especially the good ones, devote far more resources to gathering and reporting news than the electronic and internet media do, usually employing many more reporters and producing many more news stories. A large daily newspaper may contain 100,000 words, while a nightly television news broadcast may contain fewer than 4000. Other kinds of news sources (especially television stations and websites) are far more numerous than newspapers and are the primary news sources for millions of people even though they provide less news.

But not all news is created equal. Some news stories or reports are good, some are bad; some are reliable and informative, some are not. Most probably lie somewhere in between. The quality of news reporting depends on many factors, probably most of which are not under the control of the reporters.

Foremost among such factors is money. After all, news outlets—whether print, electronic, or online—are businesses with profit margins to maintain, salaries to pay, and shareholders to please. A news organization makes most of its money not from selling its product (news) through subscriptions or direct sales but from selling opportunities for other companies to advertise to the news outlet's audience. The organization wants a big audience because big audiences bring in big advertising dollars.

"What a newspaper needs in its news, in its headlines, and on its editorial page is terseness, humor, descriptive power, satire, originality, good literary style, clever condensation, and accuracy, accuracy, accuracy!"

—Joseph Pulitzer

The pressure on news organizations to turn an acceptable profit is immense and has been growing in the past two decades. Indeed, today many traditional news outlets (especially print outlets such as newspapers) are struggling to survive in the face of competition from online outlets, which tend to be cheaper to run

Food for Thought

Fake News Revisited

We examined *fake news* briefly in Chapter 2 of this book. We said that *fake news* is just false information masquerading as news, and that fake news happens for a variety of reasons: sometimes the goal is humour, and sometimes the goal is to mislead. It is worth thinking seriously about what it means to be a consumer of news in a world in which fake news—of both kinds—is relatively common. Fake news, after all, is designed to fool you: the writers want you to believe, even if briefly, that what you're reading is real.

Research suggests that people are generally bad at spotting fake news, and that, at the same time, they tend to overestimate their own ability to do so. A 2021 study showed research participants headlines formatted to look the way news headlines do when shown on Facebook. The results showed that about 90 per cent of participants thought that they were "better than average" at spotting fake news, and that those who most overrated their own abilities were also the most likely to fall for fake headlines.[11]

What can we do as individual consumers of news? Since most of us get our news via the internet these days, we can start by reviewing the tips presented in the box earlier in this chapter called Evaluating Internet Sources. Beyond that, we need to be *aware* that the environment of internet news consists of a combination of real news from reputable organizations, funny stories made up to look like news, and items that look like news but are designed to deceive.

and quicker to update as news unfolds. The old ideal of journalism as primarily a public service and not a cash cow has seldom been able to withstand the corporate push for profits. The effects of this trend on the nature and quality of the news have been profound. Two veteran reporters from the *Washington Post* explain some of the changes this way:

> Most newspapers have shrunk their reporting staffs, along with the space they devote to news, to increase their owners' profits. Most owners and publishers have forced their editors to focus more on the bottom line than on good journalism. Papers have tried to attract readers and advertisers with light features and stories that please advertisers—shopping is a favorite—and by de-emphasizing serious reporting on business, government, the country, and the world.
>
> If most newspapers have done poorly, local television stations have been worse. Typically, local stations provide little real news, no matter how many hours they devote to "news" programs. Their reporting staffs are dramatically smaller than even the staffs of shrunken newspapers in the same cities. The television stations have attracted viewers—and the advertising that rewards their owners with extraordinary profits—with the melodrama, violence, and entertainment of "action news" formulas, the frivolity of "happy talk" among their anchors, and the technological gimmicks of computer graphics and "live" remote broadcasting.

> The national television networks have trimmed their reporting staffs and closed foreign reporting bureaus to cut their owners' costs. They have tried to attract viewers by diluting their expensive newscasts with lifestyle, celebrity and entertainment features, and by filling their low-budget, high-profit, prime-time "newsmagazines" with sensational sex, crime, and court stories.
>
> All-news cable television channels and radio stations—to which the networks have ceded much of the routine coverage of serious national and foreign news—fill many of their hours as cheaply as possible with repetitive, bare-bones news summaries and talk shows that present biased opinions and argument as though they were news.[12]

Deliberately or unconsciously, editors and reporters may skew their reporting so as not to offend their advertisers, their audience, or their shareholders. They may also moderate their reporting to keep their sources of information open. Reporters get a great deal of their news from sources such as government officials, corporate public relations people, and advocacy-group spokespersons. A reporter who irritates these sources by writing stories that they don't like could end up being shunned by the sources. A key informant may simply stop taking a reporter's calls or answering emails. There is always the temptation, then, to craft inoffensive or watered-down stories to please the source. Not all news people give in to the temptation, but many do.

Editors and reporters are the ones who decide what's newsworthy and what isn't. And these decisions can help to give us a clearer picture of the world or a more distorted one. The distortion can happen in several ways. First, it can arise when reporters do what we might call passive reporting. Most reporters aren't investigative reporters, going off into the world and digging up the hard facts. Often, the news is simply handed to them by spokespersons and public relations experts hired by governments, corporations, and others who want to get their own version of the facts into the news media. In these situations, reporters may report only what they're told at press conferences or in press releases. The result is canned news that's slanted toward the views of the people who supply it.

Second, for a variety of reasons publishers, editors, producers, and reporters may decide not to cover certain stories or specific aspects of a story. With so much going on in the world, some selectivity is necessary and inevitable: it's literally impossible to report on every possible story and cover every possible angle. Too often, though, decisions not to cover something can lead the public to conclude that there is nothing happening when in fact something very important is happening. During the run-up to the war in Iraq, some massive anti-war protests occurred in the United States and Europe. But at least at first, the mainstream American news media didn't cover them, leading some observers to accuse the news media of bias in favour of the war. Likewise, some observers complain that the Canadian news media do not cover many international stories that news organizations in other countries cover in depth, such as famines and human rights violations in developing nations. The result, the complaint goes, is that Canadians may be blithely ignorant of what's really happening in the world. Also, many times the news media forgo covering a story because they deem it too complex or too unexciting for an audience hungry for titillation, scandal, and entertainment. The RCMP chasing a car thief on Highway 102 may get a full hour of TV coverage, but a debate over the role of the monarchy in Canada may get two minutes or less.

Third, editors, reporters, and producers can dramatically alter our perception of the news by playing certain aspects up or down. Television and radio news broadcasts can make a trivial news item seem momentous just by making it the lead story in the broadcast. Or they can make an important story seem inconsequential by devoting only 15 seconds to it near the end of the broadcast. Newspapers can play the same game by putting a story on the front page with a big headline and compelling photo—or embedding it on page 22 with a tiny headline. Parts of a story can also be arranged for the same effect, with the most telling information mentioned last.

Every piece of news is filtered through a reporter (as well as an editor or producer), most of whom try hard to get the story right. But reporters are subject to many pressures—internal and external—to push the story this way or that, to stray far from the laudable ideal of objective reporting based on professional journalistic standards. Reporters can slant the news by using loaded language and manipulating the tone of the writing, leaving out (or leaving in) certain details, putting facts in conspicuous (or inconspicuous) positions, inserting arguments and personal opinions, dramatizing parts of the story, and appealing to the reader's prejudices. In some cases, an entire media outlet (a magazine, TV news channel, or website) may have its own political leaning, a leaning that may quite consciously affect the way the outlet's reporters report the news.

Unfortunately, there is a trend these days for reporters to deliberately make themselves part of the story—to editorialize as they report the story, to try to exhibit attitudes common in the community, to offer subtle value judgments that the audience is likely to approve of. Here's an extreme example. On the nightly news, a film clip shows the arrest of activists who have chained themselves to some logging machines in a forest in British Columbia, and the reporter on the scene tells the TV audience, "Once again, the police are jailing those who interfere with the loggers' right to feed their families." Or maybe the reporter takes the opposite tack: "Once again, the police are jailing citizens fighting to protect our shared natural heritage."

All of this suggests that we should not assume without good reason that a news report is giving us an entirely accurate representation of events. And deciding whether in fact we have good reason is a job for critical thinking.

Food for Thought

Facebook and the News

It is a fact of life today that many people get their news online—typically from Facebook or another social media outlet. The problem is that the stuff that shows up in your Facebook "News Feed" is determined by something called "The Algorithm," a fancy equation that Facebook uses to individualize content for each and every user based on the preferences they've previously demonstrated through their clicking behaviour. Based on its understanding of your preferences, the algorithm decides just what mix of stuff to show you, including pictures posted by your friends, news items from mainstream media posted by your friends, items posted in Facebook groups you belong to, and pages that you've "liked." Most people only ever see a small fraction of the stuff posted by their friends: Facebook's secret algorithm decides for us which stuff we see. Keep in mind that Facebook is free to users but makes money from advertising: the algorithm is aimed at keeping you on the page as long as possible in order to maximize advertising revenue.

Naturally, this power to choose for us brings with it a lot of influence. It means that Facebook can effectively shape your reading habits, determining what you read and what you don't. From the point of view of traditional news media, this implies a tremendous threat. If someone at Facebook simply doesn't want a particular news story to be widely read, then a simple adjustment of the algorithm could—in principle—mean that very few people would actually see it, no matter how many times it was posted. For example, your friends might post a story from CBC or CNN about an issue you really care about. But if Facebook's algorithm says you won't see it, then you won't—not without making a special effort to find it. Worries of this kind don't rely on cynical assumptions about the human beings who work at Facebook. There's no need to imagine them hatching evil plans to stop you from finding out about specific stories or specific kinds of news. All that needs to happen is for the self-adjusting algorithm—adapting itself continuously in response to your behaviour and that of others—to decide, on your behalf, what stories are of interest to you.

4.5.2 Sorting Out the News

"In essence, I see the value of journalism as resting in a twofold mission: informing the public of accurate and vital information, and its unique ability to provide a truly adversarial check on those in power."

—Glenn Greenwald

Sometimes you won't be able to tell whether a news report is trustworthy, no matter how carefully you scrutinize it. Your only recourse then is reasonable skepticism. But most times you can at least get a few clues about the reliability of the report by taking the following critical approach.

4.5.2.1 Consider Whether the Report Conflicts with What You Have Good Reason to Believe

A report that conflicts with other reports that you believe are reliable or with facts you already know is not trustworthy. Likewise, a report that conflicts with expert opinion should not be accepted.

4.5.2.2 Look for Reporter Slanting

Look for slanting in news accounts just as you would look for it in any set of claims. Check for loaded or biased language; arguments or unsupported opinion; emotional appeals; appeals to authority, popularity, and tradition; and biased or subjective tone.

Harley Schwadron/CartoonStock

When someone tries to convince you that something really is newsworthy, what steps can you take to critically analyze their claim?

4.5.2.3 Consider the Source

Ask what the source is of the information presented in the story. Did the reporter uncover the facts herself—or does the information come directly from the government, corporations, or interest groups? How does the reporter know that the information is accurate? Does the information seem to be a simple statement of facts—or a pack of assertions designed to put someone in the best possible light?

4.5.2.4 Check for Missing Information

Be suspicious if essential facts are not presented in the story or if it seems so heavily edited that the context of remarks is mysterious. Sound bites, for example, are easy to misinterpret when they are presented without sufficient context.

4.5.2.5 Look for False Emphasis

The size of headlines, the position of stories, the order in which facts are presented—all these things can give unmerited emphasis to a story or some of its claims. To counteract this tactic, ask if the emphasis is really deserved—or, more broadly, if the story or story part is really as significant as the reporter would have you believe.

4.5.2.6 Check Alternative News Sources

How can you tell if the news you're getting is incomplete—if there's important news you're not seeing? You can't, unless you check alternative news sources for any missing stories. Reading a variety of newspapers, newsmagazines, journals of opinion, and websites is the best way to ensure that you're getting the big picture. To avoid confirmation bias, and to ensure that you're fully informed, you should read not only those sources that agree with you but also those that don't.

4.6 Advertising and Persuasion

Advertising is like air. It is everywhere, so pervasive and so natural that we forget it's there, sinking into and changing us every day. Advertising messages hit us rapid-fire and nonstop from television, radio, email, websites, blogs, podcasts, movie theatres, magazines, newsletters, newspapers, book covers, junk mail, telephones, fax machines, product labels, billboards, vehicle signs, T-shirts, wall posters, flyers, and who knows what else. Ads permeate all media—print, film, video, television, radio, and online. Most of us barely even notice (or at least *think* we barely notice) the hundreds of ads we see every day in the margins of our Facebook pages, our Google searches, our favourite online news sources. Caught in this whirl of words and sounds and images, we can easily overlook the obvious and disconcerting facts behind them: (1) all advertising is designed to influence, persuade, or manipulate us; (2) to an impressive degree and in many ways, it *does* successfully influence, persuade, or manipulate us; and (3) we are often oblivious to—or in outright denial about—how effectively advertising influences, persuades, or manipulates us.

The purpose of advertising is to sell products and services, promote causes or candidates, or alter attitudes and opinions. How well advertising does these jobs can be measured in money. Advertising in most media costs a great deal. A single full-page magazine ad can cost tens of thousands of dollars; a 30-second TV ad can run into the millions (especially on Super Bowl Sunday). But companies are willing to pay the price because advertising works. The revenues garnered from advertising can outweigh its costs by wide margins; in the case of a magazine ad or a TV spot, the gain could easily be hundreds of thousands or millions of dollars. In addition, advertisers and advertising agencies invest heavily each year in scientific consumer research to determine how to configure ads precisely to elicit the desired response from people. Again, they make these investments because there is a sure payoff. Consumers usually respond just as the research says they will. How do your eyes track across a newspaper ad when you are looking at it? Would you respond better to a TV commercial if the voiceover came from a CBC news anchor or from Taylor Swift? Would the magazine ad be more likely to sell you the cottage cheese if the headline used the word *creamy* instead of *smooth*? Would the ad copy on the junk-mail envelope increase sales if it were red instead of blue? You may not care about any of this, but advertisers do because such seemingly trivial bits of information can help them to influence you in ways you barely suspect.

However averse we are (or think we are) to advertising or to its aims, we cannot deny its appeal. We like advertising, at least some of it. We can easily point to ads that annoy us or insult our intelligence, but most of us can also recall ones that are entertaining, funny, inspiring, even informative. How, then, should good critical thinkers think about advertising? Our guiding principle should be this:

> *We generally have good reason to doubt advertising claims and to be wary of advertising's persuasive powers.*

This means that usually the most reasonable response to advertising is a degree of suspicion. If we prefer truth over falsehood, if we would rather not be mistaken or bamboozled, if we want to make informed choices involving our time and money, then a general wariness toward advertising ploys is justified. This principle does not assume that all ad claims are false or that advertising cannot be genuinely informative or useful. It simply says that we should not accept uncritically an ad's message or impact on us.

There are several reasons for this cautious approach. First, recall the purpose of advertising—to *sell or promote something*, whether a product, service, person, or idea. To put the point bluntly, though advertising can be both truthful and helpful, its primary function is *not* to provide objective and accurate information to consumers. Advertisers will tell you many good things about their products but are unlikely to mention all the bad. Their main job is *not* to help consumers make fully informed, rational choices about available options. Advertising is advertising—it is not intended to be an impartial search for facts or a program of consumer protection. We are therefore justified in maintaining the same attitude toward advertising that we would toward a complete stranger who wants to sell us something. His motives are obviously financial while his commitment to honesty is unknown, so we should beware.

Second, advertising has a reputation for—and a history of—misleading messages. The world is filled with ads that make dubious or false claims, use fallacious arguments (stated or implied), and employ psychological tricks to manipulate consumer responses.

A "beware of dog" sign isn't literally advertising, but it sure can be a false message, and in some cases is clearly intended to deceive. In what ways does advertising fall victim to fallacious appeals?

Some of these methods fit neatly in our rundown of fallacies in this chapter and the next. Ads frequently employ fallacious appeals to authority ("As an Olympic gold medal winner, I can tell you that PowerVitamin 2000 really works!"), appeals to emotion ("Enjoy the goodness and warmth of Big Brand Soup, just like Mother used to make"), appeals to popularity ("*The Globe and Mail*: Canada's Most Trusted News Source"), hasty generalizations ("Mothers everywhere will love Softie Diapers—our test mothers sure did!"), and faulty analogies ("As a businessman, I got a major corporation out of debt. As premier, I can get this province out of debt!"). But advertisers also use an array of other persuasive techniques, most of which do not involve making explicit claims or providing good reasons for acting or choosing. The following are some of the more common ones.

4.6.1 Identification

Many ads persuade by simply inviting the consumer to identify with attractive individuals (real or imagined) or groups. Most ads featuring celebrity endorsements use this tactic. The idea is to get you to identify so strongly with a celebrity that you feel his or her product choices are *your* preferred choices. Without providing a single good reason or argument, endorsement ads say, in effect, that if Kendall Jenner prefers Pepsi, if Gigi Hadid likes Tommy Hilfiger, if LeBron James loves Nike, maybe you should too. At least that's the implicit suggestion.

4.6.2 Slogans

Catchy, memorable phrases are the stock-in-trade of advertising. How could we forget such gems as "Just do it" (Nike), "I'm Lovin' It" (McDonald's), "Like a rock" (Chevrolet), "Don't leave home without it" (American Express), or "Time for Tims" (Tim Hortons)? Such catchphrases may not say much, but they do get our attention, engender appealing emotions or concepts, and get us to associate them with products or companies—again and again and again. Through repetition that seems to embed them in our brains, slogans surreptitiously get us to feel that one product or brand is better than another.

4.6.3 Misleading Comparisons

In advertising, comparisons can mislead in many ways. Consider these examples:

1. BeClean Paper Towels are 30 per cent more absorbent.
2. Big sale! The SuperX Gaming System for less than the suggested retail price!
3. Simply better-tasting tacos. No question.
4. Our mobile phone plan beats the competition. Long-distance calling is just 5 cents per minute, compared with our competitors who charge up to 10 cents a minute.

The problem with example 1 is its vagueness, which is of course deliberate. What does "30 per cent more absorbent" mean? Thirty per cent more absorbent than they used to be? Thirty per cent more absorbent than similar products are? If the latter, what similar products are we talking about? Are BeClean Paper Towels being compared to the *least* absorbent paper towels on the market? The *30 per cent* may seem impressive—until we know what it actually refers to. (Another relevant question is how absorbency was determined. As you might imagine, there are many ways to perform such tests, some of them likely to yield more impressive numbers than others.)

The claim in example 2 may or may not be telling us about a true bargain. We would probably view the "big sale" in a different light if we knew whether the store's *regular* prices are below the suggested retail prices or if *all* stores sell the gaming system below the *suggested* retail price.

Example 3 contains the same sort of vagueness we find in example 1 plus an additional sort of emptiness. The phrase "better-tasting tacos" is a claim about a subjective state of affairs—a claim that *anyone* could make about his or her own eating experience. You and a thousand other people might try the tacos and think they taste terrible. So the claim tells you nothing about whether you will like the tacos. The claim would be empty even if it were stretched to "The best-tasting tacos on Earth!" In the ad world, such exaggerations are known as *puffery*, which is regarded in advertising law as hype that few people take seriously.

Example 4 is misleading because it tries to compare apples and oranges. Maybe the service offered by one phone company is not like that offered by the others. Maybe the former gives you bare-bones service for five cents a minute; the latter gives you the same plus caller ID, call waiting, and free long distance on weekends. So comparing the two according to the per-minute charge alone may be deceptive.

4.6.4 Weasel Words

When advertisers want to *appear* to make a strong claim but avoid blatant lying or deception, they use what are known as *weasel words*. Weasel words water down a claim in subtle ways—just enough to ensure that it is technically true but superficially misleading. Consider:

1. You may have already won a new 2022 Ford pickup truck!
2. Some doctors recommend ginseng for sexual dysfunction.
3. When used properly, this product relieves up to 60 per cent of headaches in chronic headache sufferers.

Example 1 is typical junk-mail hype that seems to promise a valuable prize. But the weasel word *may* weakens the claim. Technically, you *may* have actually won since your winning is at least (remotely) possible. But in the typical sweepstakes, the odds of your winning anything are millions to one. Yes, you *may* have already won—and you *may* get hit by an asteroid tomorrow. Example 2 plays on the weasel word *some*. It is probably true that *some* (meaning at least one) doctors recommend ginseng for sexual dysfunction, but a huge majority of them do not. Using *some*, we could craft an infinite number of technically true but misleading (and ridiculous) claims about what doctors do and don't do. In Example 3 the weasel words are *up to*. Notice that many states of affairs would be consistent with this (vague) statement. It would be true even if just 1 per cent of headaches were relieved in almost all headache sufferers, and that would be pretty weak evidence that the product is likely to work for you.

Other weasels include *as many as*, *reportedly*, *possibly*, *virtually*, *many*, *seems*, and *perhaps*. Such words, of course, can have perfectly respectable uses as necessary qualifiers. But when you spot them in ads, watch out.

Summary

Many times we need to be able to evaluate an unsupported claim—a claim that isn't backed by an argument. There are several critical thinking principles that can help us to do this. An important one is this: if a claim conflicts with other claims we have good reason to accept, we have good grounds for doubting it. Sometimes the conflict is between a claim and your background information. Background information is the large collection of very well-supported beliefs that we rely on to inform our actions and choices. The relevant principle then is this: if a claim conflicts with our background information, we have good reason to doubt the claim.

It's not reasonable to accept a claim if there is good reason to doubt it. In the case of claims that we can neither accept nor reject outright, we should proportion our belief to the evidence. We should also do what we can to find out more.

An expert is someone who is more knowledgeable than most people in a particular subject area. The important principle here is this: if a claim conflicts with expert opinion, we have good reason to doubt it. We must couple this principle with another one: when the experts disagree about a claim, we have good reason to suspend judgment. When we rely on bogus expert opinion (opinion from a fake "expert" or someone who is an expert on the wrong topic) or on the opinion of an expert not backed up by the consensus of his or her peers, we commit the fallacy known as the appeal to authority.

Many claims are based on nothing more than personal experience, ours or someone else's. We can trust our personal experience—to a point. The guiding principle is that it's reasonable to accept the evidence provided by personal experience only if there's no reason to doubt it. Some common factors that can raise such doubts are impairment (stress, injury, distraction, emotional upset, and the like), expectation, and our limited abilities in judging probabilities.

Some of the common mistakes we make in evaluating claims are resisting contrary evidence, looking for confirming evidence, and preferring available evidence. To counteract these tendencies, we need to take deliberate steps to examine even our most cherished claims critically, to search for disconfirming evidence as well as confirming, and to look beyond evidence that is merely the most striking or memorable.

Many of the unsupported claims we encounter are in news reports. Reporters, editors, and producers are under many pressures that can lead to biased or misleading reporting. The biggest factor is money—the drive for profits in news organizations, especially those owned by large corporations or conglomerates. Reporters themselves may introduce inaccuracies, biases, and personal opinions. And the people who produce the news may decide not to cover certain stories (or aspects of stories), thereby sometimes giving a skewed or erroneous picture of an issue or event. Some things that look like news reports may even be entirely fake, though not everything that someone calls "fake" news necessarily is.

The best defence against being misled by news reports is a reasonable skepticism and a critical approach that involves, among other things, looking for slanting, examining sources, checking for missing facts, and being on the lookout for false emphasis.

Advertising is another possible source of unsupported or misleading claims. We should realize that we generally have good reason to doubt advertising claims and to be wary of the persuasive powers of advertising.

Exercise 4.1

Answers to exercises marked with an asterisk (*) may be found in Appendix B, Answers to Exercises.

Review Questions

1. What does the term *background information* refer to?
2. What is the appropriate next step when faced with a claim that conflicts with several other claims you have good reason to believe?
3. Is background information always reliable?
4. What should we do when we are confronted with a claim that is neither completely dubious nor fully credible?*
5. How can we identify someone as an expert?
6. What should our attitude be toward a claim that conflicts with expert opinion? Should we generally accept claims made by experts?
7. What should our attitude be toward a claim when experts disagree with each other about it?
8. What are the two versions of the fallacy of appeal to authority?
9. What, in most fields, are the two minimum requirements for being considered an expert?
10. Beyond the minimal prerequisites, what are two more telling indicators that someone is an expert?*
11. Name one of the three circumstances in which we should suspect that an expert might be biased.
12. What are some questions you can ask to determine whether the information you find online is accurate?
13. What are two factors that can give us good reason to doubt the reliability of personal experience?
14. According to the text, what are the two different ways in which we use the word "fact"?
15. What are some ways that people resist contrary evidence?
16. What is confirmation bias?
17. How can critical thinkers counteract confirmation bias?*

18. What is the availability error?
19. What is the connection between the hasty generalization and availability error?
20. What are some strategies you can use to help determine whether or not a news report is trustworthy?
21. According to the text, what is the guiding principle that we should use to in order to think critically about advertisements?
22. What are some of the strategies that advertisers use to try and make us buy into their claims regarding their products?

Exercise 4.2

On the basis of claims you already have good reason to believe, your background information, and your assessment of the credibility of any cited experts, indicate for each of the following claims whether you would accept it, reject it, or proportion your belief to the evidence. Give reasons for your answers. If you decide to proportion your belief to the evidence, state generally what degree of plausibility you would assign to the claim.

1. COVID-19 is a contagious respiratory disease caused by the SARS-CoV-2 virus.
2. The coronavirus pandemic was a plot hatched by the government of Canada.
3. Handwashing plays an important role in reducing the transmission of COVID-19.
4. According to Dr Feelgood, the spokesperson for Acme Mattresses, the EasyRest 2000 from Acme is the best mattress in the world for those suffering from back pain.*
5. Most Canadians have very low levels of credit card debt.
6. Lewis Harris, a physics professor at a major university, claims that the government is wrong to subsidize solar energy projects.*
7. All major Western government powers are monitoring and collecting private information on their citizens, even those suspected of no crime, and then sharing the collected information with each other.
8. Agnes Macphail, the first Canadian woman elected to Parliament (in 1921) died last year.
9. The New Democratic Party has held a majority of seats in Parliament more than a dozen times in Canada's history.
10. Fifteen women have died this year after smelling a free sample of perfume that they received in the mail.*
11. A chain letter describing the struggles of a nine-year-old girl with incurable cancer is circulating on the internet. The more people who receive the letter, the better the little girl's chances of survival.

12. A report from Health Canada says there is no evidence that high doses of the herb ephedra can cure cancer. Ephedra must be a bogus treatment.
13. According to Professor Heath, an expert on the work of Jurgen Habermas and a former student of his, Habermas was critical of Michel Foucault's tendency to smuggle normative claims into arguments that were supposedly only about facts.
14. The Egyptian pyramids were built by space aliens.*
15. The "fairy photos" produced by two girls early in the twentieth century were fakes.
16. Canada is likely to lead the world in medals at the Summer Olympics in Lost Angeles in 2028.
17. Your astrological "sign" plays a major role in determining your character and personality.*
18. Eleanor Morgan, a Nobel Prize–winning medical scientist, says that modern democratic systems (including developed nations) are not viable.
19. If the price of GM trucks goes up, people are more likely to buy Ford trucks instead.
20. The highway speed limit in Alberta is 160 km/h.

Exercise 4.3

For each of the following claims, decide whether you currently agree or disagree with it. If you currently agree with a claim, say what evidence would persuade you to reject the statement. If you currently disagree with a claim, say what evidence would persuade you to accept the statement. In each case, ask yourself if you would really change your mind if presented with the evidence you suggested.

1. Canada's system of universal, free health care results in a significantly higher quality of service and much shorter wait times compared to the system in the United States.
2. Canada needs to promote higher levels of immigration, since immigrants have always been the most productive elements of Canadian society.
3. An alien spacecraft crashed in Roswell, New Mexico, in 1947.*
4. Eating two eggs a day is good for you.
5. Eating two eggs a day is bad for you.
6. My yoga teacher is able to slow his heart rate down to two beats per minute.
7. The US president is a mere puppet, and the British government is "pulling the strings."
8. Meditation and controlled breathing can shrink cancerous tumours.*
9. The pyramids in Egypt are the most ancient structures on Earth.
10. Continually consuming information in very small doses—tweets and short online news stories—is reducing people's ability to focus when reading longer, more detailed stories.

Exercise 4.4

Examine the following newspaper story, and answer the questions that follow. Your local newspaper reports on Page 1:

> In a shocking decision, a provincial court judge sentenced a local thug to a mere six months in prison for sexually assaulting an innocent young girl. The girl, who cannot be identified due to her tender age, testified by video recording at trial. Her silky blonde hair hung down over her sweet face as she tearfully recounted the brutal assault. The accused sat smugly in the defendant's box, his beady eyes rolling toward the ceiling time and time again during the Crown prosecutor's eloquent summation. The defendant's lawyer, while mopping a sweaty brow, spoke after the decision was handed down, rambling about his client's own supposedly difficult childhood. A legal expert unconnected to the case, but who is renowned for his legal expertise, said that the short sentence handed out was utterly bizarre.

1. Is the story slanted toward or against a particular participant? How?
2. Are there instances of loaded or biased language or emotional appeals in the story? If so, give examples of each.
3. What significant person or persons did the reporter who wrote this story apparently fail to talk to? What effect might that have had on the reporting?
4. Assume the story was found on the internet. What information would you look for in order to determine whether the website is a credible one?
5. Rewrite just the first sentence of this story to reflect the same basic facts in a more neutral manner.

Field Problems

1. Find a controversial news story on the internet, and answer the questions in Exercise 4.4 about it.
2. Write down a claim in which you strongly believe—perhaps one that pertains to an important social, religious, or political issue. Then state what evidence would persuade you to change your mind about the claim. How easy or difficult would it be to conduct a sufficiently thorough search for such evidence?
3. Write down a claim that a member of your own family strongly believes but that you do not believe. Then state what evidence you think it would take to persuade that person to change their mind about the claim. Do you think they would change their mind if you provided the right evidence? If not, why not?
4. Think of the range of *experts* whose advice you rely on, either directly or indirectly, in your own

life. They may or may not be people you know by name. Try to think of at least five, and make a list. For each, name the source of their expertise. Is it extensive education, extensive experience, or something else that makes them reliable? If all of them gained their reliability in similar ways, try expanding your list by thinking up experts that gained their expertise in quite different ways.

Self-Assessment Quiz

1. How should a critical thinker regard an unsupported claim that conflicts partly with his or her background information?
2. What is "folk psychology," and how is it useful?
3. Why might the memory of an eyewitness be unreliable? Name at least two possible reasons.

For each of the following situations and the claim associated with it, indicate whether there may be good reasons to doubt the claim, and, if so, specify the reasons.

4. Hilary is about to leave a party and drive home. The host warns her that the evening's rain has turned to freezing rain, and that it may not be safe to drive. Hilary assures the host that she is an excellent driver, and so she will get home safely.
5. While walking through the woods on a windy day, Connor thinks he hears a voice whispering his name. It's almost too quiet to hear, but he thinks it says, "Connnnnnorrrrrr . . . come home!"
6. Constable Jones views the videotape of the robbery at the Tim Hortons that occurred last night. He sees the robber look into the camera. "I know that guy," he says. "I put him away last year on a similar charge."

For each of the following claims, say whether it is (a) almost certainly false, (b) probably false, (c) probably true, (d) almost certainly true, or (e) none of the above.

7. Canada experiences more rainfall than the United States.
8. A claim on Health Canada's website: about 100 children a year die as a result of their mothers smoking during pregnancy or from exposure to smoke at home.
9. When traditions break down, communities fall apart.
10. "The world shadow government behind the US government is at it again, destroying US buildings and killing people with staged acts of terrorism [on 11 September 2001], the intent of which being—among other things—to start WW III." (Website devoted to 9/11 theories)
11. Vaccination against infectious diseases is not necessary, because the body has a natural ability to heal itself.
12. The reason that funding for research into renewable energy sources is so scarce is that the big oil companies are trying their best to continue being the dominant players in the energy sector. They are constantly lobbying for the government to ignore alternative energy.

Read the following introduction to a magazine article (about commercial plasma donation), and then answer questions 13–15.

> **The Twisted Business of Donating Plasma**
> I needed the cash.
> That was how I found myself laying [sic] in a plasma "donation" room filled with about 40 couches, each equipped with a blood pressure cuff and a centrifuge. A white-coated attendant (workers aren't required to have medical or

nursing degrees) pricked my arm. He separated my plasma from my whole blood into a large bottle, and returned my protein-depleted blood, which flowed back into my arm to rebuild my nutrient supply.

"My house is so noisy with four kids so I come here for my relaxation," said a middle-aged, haggard-looking woman on the next couch, the plasmapheresis machine at her side whirring. A clinician instructed us both to pump and relax our fists, like cows milking our own udders.[13]

13. Is the story slanted in a way that seems to encourage readers to believe that the plasma donation industry is bad? How?
14. Are there instances of loaded or biased language or emotional appeals that make the industry seem especially bad?
15. What do you think the author's intention is in using the phrase "like cows milking our own udders"?

Integrative Exercises

These exercises pertain to material in Chapters 1–4.

1. What is a deductive argument? What is an inductive argument?
2. Can our background information help us to determine whether an argument is valid? If so, how? If not, why not?
3. What is the difference between appeal to authority and a reasonable reliance on expertise?

For each of the following arguments, specify the conclusion and premises, and say whether it is deductive or inductive. If it's inductive, say whether it is strong or weak; if deductive, say whether it is valid or invalid. If necessary, fill in any implicit premises and conclusions.

4. "[Paid d]onors [of blood plasma] receive, on average, $25–50 per donation. In Manitoba, where this practice has existed since 1984, donations are compensated at greater-than-minimum-wage levels. Canadian Plasma Resources pays between $30 and $50, while in the United States, donors receive between $25 and $50 per donation. Compensation is therefore not low, but it is not, on the other hand, so high as to unduly induce a potential donor into a donation. Given that the risks are not undue, and that payment, although not low, is not too high, there is no particularly good reason to worry about wrongful exploitation based on undue inducement." (https://www.donationethics.com/)
5. "The people of PEI have a voice and it deserves to be heard in return for a vote. Too many times people have voted for the Liberals and PCs and too many times those people have been let down by the party they voted for because the party has their own hidden agendas." (Online comment, 4 February 2011, *The Guardian*, Charlottetown, PEI)
6. If Canada truly cares about justice for Indigenous communities, it will make sure every community has access to clean water. But Canada has not ensured access to clean water, so Canada doesn't really care about justice for Indigenous communities.
7. The prime minister's popularity in BC will not go up if he goes ahead and approves the Trans Mountain pipeline. And it looks as if he's going to approve it. Thus, his popularity in BC is not going to rise.
8. Yes, the monarchy is part of our heritage. But Canada is a modern democracy, and in a modern democracy there is simply no room for the remnants of an outdated form of authoritarian rule. The people deserve a say. Our head of state should be elected.

9. If you cared about social justice, you would be down there with your friends at the protest in support of providing more resources for the homeless. If you were down at the protest, you wouldn't be sitting on the couch. But there you are, sitting on the couch eating Doritos. You don't care about social justice at all!
10. "Cold-FX is an undeniable Canadian sales success, but this seems to be due more to marketing, rather than science. The data published to date suggest that it may have some sort of a biological effect—but it's a small one, and for many people that take it, the data suggest it will not be effective in preventing colds or the flu." (*Science-Based Pharmacy*, 27 February 2009)
11. I did well on my chemistry exam, and my physics exam, and my biology exam. Even if I don't study, I'm sure I'm going to do well on my French exam too.
12. Nancy is serving lasagna and spaghetti at dinner tonight. Since Hendricus can't stand lasagna, you can bet he'll have the spaghetti.

For each of the following unsupported claims, specify whether it seems worthy of acceptance, rejection, or a degree of belief in between.

13. The heads of Canada's three biggest mobile phone companies agree that there's no need to reform the regulations regarding the pricing of telecom services in Canada.
14. I saw Ling last night. I know she moved back to China, but I woke up in the middle of the night and saw a shadow in the corner of my room and heard her voice saying she missed me.
15. COVID-19 is unlikely to be the last pandemic we experience during the coming decade. It is likely that there will be other pandemics in the "coronavirus category."

Critical Thinking and Writing Exercise

From Outline to First Draft

If you have developed a detailed outline for your essay, then you have a path to follow as you write. And while you're writing an argumentative essay, having a path is much better than searching for one. Your outline should make the writing much easier.

However, no outline is a finished work; the structure of your essay is likely to evolve as you write it. As you write, you may discover that your arguments are not as strong as you thought, or that other arguments would be better, or that changing a point here and there would make an argument more effective. If so, you should amend your outline to help you keep track and then continue writing. The act of writing is often an act of discovery, and good writers are not afraid of revisions or multiple drafts.

Recall from the exercise in Chapter 1 that good argumentative essays generally consist of these elements:

- Introduction (or opening)
- Statement of thesis (the claim to be supported)
- Argument supporting the thesis
- Assessment of objections
- Conclusion

Start your draft with a solid opening that draws your readers into your essay and prepares the way for your arguments. Good openings are interesting, informative, and short. Grab the attention of your readers with a bold statement of your thesis, a provocative quotation, a compelling story, or interesting facts. Prepare the way for your arguments by explaining why the question you're addressing is important, why you're concerned about it, or why it involves a pressing problem. Don't assume that your readers will see immediately that the issue you're dealing with is worth their time.

Include a clear statement of your thesis in your opening (in the first paragraph or very close by). In many cases, you will want to tell the reader how you plan to develop your argument or how the rest of the essay will unfold (without going into lengthy detail). In any case, by the time your audience reads through your opening, they should know exactly what you intend to prove and why.

Consider this opening for our imaginary essay on air pollution from Module 3:

> Respiratory experts at Health Canada say that sulphur dioxide in the air is a poison that we should avoid. Yet the provincial government wants to loosen environmental rules to allow coal-burning power plants to emit more sulphur dioxide than they already do. That's a bad idea. The latest evidence shows that letting the plants emit more of this poison will most likely increase the incidence of respiratory illnesses in hundreds of communities.

This opening gets the reader's attention by sounding the alarm about a serious health hazard. It provides enough background information to help us understand the seriousness of the problem. And the thesis statement in the last sentence announces what the essay will try to prove.

The body of your essay should fully develop the arguments for your thesis statement, or conclusion. You should devote at least one paragraph to each premise, though several paragraphs may be necessary. You may opt to deal with objections to your argument as you go along, perhaps as you put forth each premise or at the end of the essay just before the conclusion. Each paragraph should develop and explain just one idea, which is usually expressed in a topic sentence. Each sentence in each paragraph should relate to the paragraph's main idea. Any sentence that has no clear connection to the main idea should be deleted or revised. Be sure to link paragraphs together in a logical sequence using transitional words and phrases or direct references to material in preceding paragraphs.

Here are two paragraphs that might follow the air pollution opening:

> Scientists used to wonder whether there is a connection between airborne sulphur dioxide and respiratory illness—but no more. Research has repeatedly shown a strong link between high levels of sulphur dioxide in the air and diseases that affect the lungs. For example, data from studies conducted by Health Canada show that when levels of airborne sulphur dioxide in urban areas reach what the agency calls the "high normal" range, the incidence of respiratory illnesses increases dramatically. According to several Health Canada surveys of air quality, many major cities (not just Toronto) often have high normal levels of sulphur dioxide in the air. In addition, data from health departments in large cities show that when levels of airborne sulphur dioxide are at their highest, hospital admissions for asthma and other respiratory illnesses also increase.
>
> These findings, however, tell only half the story. Many parts of the country have more than just occasional surges in levels of airborne sulphur dioxide. They must endure unsafe levels continuously. New studies from Health Canada demonstrate that in at least 10 major cities, the amount of sulphur dioxide in the air is excessive all the time.

In this passage, a single paragraph is devoted to each premise. Each paragraph develops a single idea, which is stated in a topic sentence. (The topic sentence for the first paragraph is "Research has repeatedly shown a strong link between high levels of sulphur dioxide in the air and diseases that affect the lungs." For the second paragraph, the topic sentence is "Many parts of the country must endure unsafe levels continuously.") Each sentence in each paragraph relates to the topic sentence, and the relationships among the sentences are clear. Likewise, the connection between the discussion in the first paragraph and that of the second is apparent. The transitional sentence in the second paragraph ("These findings, however, tell only half the story.") helps to bridge the gap between the paragraphs. Both of them help to support the thesis statement.

How you end your essay is often as important as how you start it. In short or simple essays, there may be no need for a conclusion. The thesis may be clear and emphatic without a conclusion. In many cases, however, an essay is strengthened by a conclusion, and sometimes a conclusion is absolutely essential. Often, without an effective conclusion, an essay may seem to end pointlessly or to be incomplete. The typical conclusion reiterates or reaffirms the thesis statement without being repetitious. Or the conclusion of the essay's argument serves as the conclusion for the whole essay. In long or complex essays, the conclusion often includes a summary of the main points discussed.

Sometimes a conclusion is a call to action, an invitation to the reader to do something about a problem. Sometimes it relates a story that underscores the importance of the essay's argument. Sometimes it highlights a provocative aspect of a claim defended earlier. In all cases it serves to increase the impact of the essay.

The conclusion, however, is not the place to launch into a completely different issue, make entirely unsubstantiated claims, malign those who disagree with you, or pretend that your argument is stronger than it really is. These tactics will not strengthen your essay but weaken it.

Defining Terms

Your essay will do its job only if it is understood, and it will be understood only if the meaning of its terms is clear. As noted in the Module 3 exercise, sometimes a dispute can hang on the meaning of a single term. Clarify the meaning, and the disagreement dissolves. In an argumentative essay, clarifying terms often comes down to offering precise definitions of words that are crucial to your argument.

There are several different kinds of definitions. A lexical definition reports the meaning that a term has among those who use the language. For example, among English-speaking people, the word *rain* is used to refer to condensed atmospheric moisture falling in drops, which is the lexical definition. A stipulative definition reports a meaning that a term is deliberately assigned, often for the sake of convenience or economy of expression. If you assign a meaning to a familiar term or to a term that you invent, you give a stipulative definition. A precising definition reports a meaning designed to decrease ambiguity or vagueness. It qualifies an existing term by giving it a more precise definition. Someone, for example, might offer a precising definition for the word *old* (as it applies to the age of humans) by specifying that *old* refers to anyone over 80. A persuasive definition reports a meaning designed to influence attitudes or beliefs. It is usually not meant to be purely informative but is calculated to appeal to someone's emotions. Someone who opposes taxation, for example, might define *taxation* as "a form of state-run extortion." Someone who thinks that taxation is generally a good thing might define *taxation* as "a way for individuals to contribute financially to important social programs."

In general, any definition you offer should decrease vagueness or ambiguity and thereby increase the effectiveness of your writing. Your definitions should also be consistent. If you provide a definition for a term in your essay, then you should stick to that definition throughout. Altering the meaning of a term mid-essay or using more than one term to refer to the same thing can be confusing to the reader—and might even subvert your essay's argument.

Good writers are also very much aware of another kind of meaning—the meaning that comes from a word's connotations. Connotations are the feelings, attitudes, or images associated with a word beyond the literal meaning of the term. Consider these words: *food*, *sustenance*, *cuisine*, and *grub*. These terms have nearly the same literal meaning, but they differ in the emotions or attitudes they convey. Or what about these terms: *tavern*, *saloon*, *bar*, *watering hole*, and *dive*. They refer to the same kind of establishment, but the images or emotions conveyed are diverse, ranging from the respectable and pleasant (tavern) to the lowly and odious (dive).

Good writers make use of both the literal meaning of words and their connotations. Connotations, however, can sometimes mislead by obscuring or minimizing the facts. In debates about, for example, Quebec independence, those who want greater independence for Quebec may characterize their position as favouring "sovereignty and self-determination." Those opposed to it might label it as "seeking to break up Canada." Both these labels are meant to provoke certain attitudes toward the subject matter—attitudes that may not be supported by any evidence or argument. Words used to convey positive or neutral attitudes or emotions in place of more negative ones are known as euphemisms. Words used to convey negative attitudes or emotions in place of neutral or positive ones are called dysphemisms. Consider the disparate impact on the reader of each of the words within these pairs of terms, both of which refer to the same thing:

downsized	fired
revenue enhancements	tax increases
full-figured	fat
guerrillas	freedom fighters
resolute	pigheaded
emphatic	pushy
sweat	perspire
crippled	disabled
lied to	misled
passed away	died

Keep in mind that euphemisms often perform a useful social purpose by allowing us to discuss sensitive subjects in an inoffensive way. We may spare people's feelings by saying that their loved ones "have passed on" rather than that they "have died" or that their dog was "put to sleep" rather than "killed." Nevertheless, as critical thinkers, we should be on guard against the deceptive use of connotations. As critical writers, we should rely primarily on argument and evidence to make our case.

Writing Assignments

1. Write an alternative opening for Essay 4 ("What's Wrong with 'Body Mass Index'") in Appendix A. If you want, you may invent quotations or stories.
2. Write an outline for Essay 7 ("Nurses, Social Media, and Whistleblowing") in Appendix A. Include a thesis statement, each premise, and points supporting each premise.
3. Study Essay 9 ("What If You Could Save 250 Lives by Feeling a Little Disgusted?") in Appendix A. Identify the role that emotion plays in making arguments on both sides of the issue discussed in the essay.
4. Select one of the following topics, and extract an issue from it that you can write about. Investigate arguments on both sides of the issue, and write a three-page paper defending your chosen thesis.
   - supervised injection sites for drug addicts
   - drug-testing in the workplace
   - veganism
   - the #MeToo movement
   - diversity in the workplace
   - government censorship of media coverage of military activities
   - commercial whaling

- religion as a source of ethics
- endangered species
- animal rights
- the dangers of too much "screen time" for kids
- Indigenous land claims
- sexual harassment
- medical assistance in dying
- an oil pipeline from northern Alberta to Texas

5. Write a two-page rebuttal to Essay 8 ("Unrepentant Homeopaths") in Appendix A. Use the testimony of experts to help defend your view.

Notes

1. Russell, *Let the People Think*, 1.
2. Adapted from Duke University Libraries, "Evaluating Web Pages," formerly at http://library.duke.edu/services/instruction/library guide/evalwebpages.html (accessed 8 September 2009). Note that this resource is no longer available.
3. David Freedman, *Wrong: Why Experts Keep Failing Us—And How to Know When Not to Trust Them* (New York: Little, Brown and Company, 2010), 216.
4. This example was inspired by L.W. Alvarez, letter to the editors, *Science* (18 June 1965): 1541.
5. Terence Hines, *Pseudoscience and the Paranormal* (Buffalo, NY: Prometheus Books, 1988), 4–5.
6. Thomas Gilovich, *How We Know What Isn't So* (New York: Free Press, 1991), 54.
7. J. Cocker, "Biased Questions in Judgment of Covariation Studies," *Personality and Social Psychology Bulletin* 8 (June 1982): 214–20.
8. Dave Crenshaw, "How to Test the Cost of Switchtasking for Yourself." https://davecrenshaw.com/test-switchtasking/. Accessed June 22, 2021.
9. John Ruscio, "Risky Business," *Skeptical Inquirer* (March 2000), 22–26.
10. Peter Kan, Sara E. Simonsen, Joseph L. Lyon, and John R.W. Kestle, "Cellular Phone Use and Brain Tumor: A Meta-Analysis," *Journal of Neurooncology* 86 (2008): 71–8; Institute of Medicine, *Immunization Safety Review: Vaccines and Autism* (National Academies Press, 2004).
11. "Overconfidence in News Judgement." https://www.eurekalert.org/pub_releases/2021-05/uou-oin052621.php. Accessed June 21, 2021.
12. Leonard Downie Jr. and Robert G. Kaiser, *The News about the News* (New York: Vintage Books, 2003), 9–10.
13. Wellington, Darryl Lorenzo, "The Twisted Business of Donating Plasma," *TheAtlantic.com.* (28 May 2014). https://www.theatlantic.com/health/archive/2014/05/blood-money-the-twisted-business-of-donating-plasma/362012

Faulty Reasoning

Chapter Objectives

Irrelevant Premises

You will be able to

- recognize fallacies of irrelevant premises (genetic fallacy, composition, division, appeal to the person, equivocation, appeal to popularity, appeal to tradition, appeal to ignorance, appeal to emotion, red herring, and straw man).
- understand the concept of burden of proof and when it applies.

Unacceptable Premises

You will be able to

- recognize fallacies of unacceptable premises (begging the question, false dilemma, slippery slope, hasty generalization, and faulty analogy).

An argument is meant to prove a point—to provide good reasons for accepting a claim. As you know by now, sometimes an argument succeeds, and sometimes it doesn't. When it doesn't succeed, the problem is that the premises are false, or the reasoning is faulty, or both. If the premises are false—or at least cannot reasonably be accepted—then the argument has no foundation at all. And if the reasoning is faulty, then whatever support we would be tempted to attribute to reasonable-looking premises is undermined by a flimsy connection (or no connection at all) to the conclusion being aimed at. In either case, the argument is defective, bad, or bogus—call it what you will. The argument has failed in its attempt to provide you with reason for the particular belief embodied in its conclusion. This does not mean that the conclusion is false, but merely that it is (so far!) unsupported.

There are countless ways that an argument can be defective. But there are certain types of defective arguments that occur so frequently that they have names (given to them, in many cases, by ancient philosophers or medieval scholars) and are usually gathered into critical thinking texts so students can become aware of them. Such common, flawed arguments are known as **fallacies**, and they are therefore said to be fallacious.

fallacy
An argument form that is both common and defective; a recurring mistake in reasoning.

"Graph A is verified by Graph B. Graph B is verified by Graph C. Graph C is verified by Graph A. So you see...it's all verified."

Douglas Blackwell/CartoonStock

Sometimes fallacies are merely funny. What fallacy is being put to humorous use in the cartoon above?

Fallacies are often convincing; they can *seem* plausible. Time and again they are *psychologically* persuasive though *logically* impotent. The fact that they tend to be persuasive explains why they are so common. The primary reason for studying fallacies, then, is to be able to detect them so that you're not fooled by them.

We can divide fallacies into two broad categories: (1) those that have *irrelevant* premises and (2) those that have *unacceptable* premises.[1] Irrelevant premises simply have no bearing on the truth of the conclusion they are supposed to support. An argument may seem to offer reasons for accepting the conclusion, but the "reasons" have nothing to do with the conclusion. Such premises make it no more reasonable (or unreasonable) to believe the argument's conclusion than it was before you heard them. Unacceptable premises, on the other hand, are relevant to the conclusion but are nonetheless dubious in some way. An argument may have premises that pertain to the conclusion, but that do not adequately support it. Premises can be unacceptable because they are as dubious as the claim they're intended to support, either because the evidence they offer is too weak to support the conclusion adequately, or because they're otherwise so defective that they provide no support at all.

So, in good arguments, premises must be both relevant and acceptable. In fallacious arguments, at least one of these requirements is not met.

In this chapter we examine numerous fallacies of both types. We won't be able to discuss all known fallacies—there are just too many—but we will take a look at the most common ones. By the time you have finished this chapter, you should be able to spot these fallacies a mile away and have some sense of how to respond to them.

5.1 Irrelevant Premises

5.1.1 Genetic Fallacy

Despite its name, the genetic fallacy has nothing to do with genes in the biological sense. The **genetic fallacy** consists of arguing that a claim is true or false solely because of its origin. (The word "genetic" is related to the word "genesis," which means "origin" or "beginning.") Some examples of this fallacy:

genetic fallacy
The fallacy of arguing that a claim is true or false solely because of its origin.

> Selena's argument regarding Indigenous rights can't be right because she's of European descent.
>
> We should reject that proposal for solving the current welfare mess. It comes straight from an economist with known conservative leanings.
>
> We can't take this design seriously: it came from Pinterest, where literally anybody can post their ideas, even if they have no expertise in design.

These arguments fail because they reject a claim solely on the basis of where that claim comes from, not on its merits. In most cases, the source of an idea is irrelevant to its truth. Good ideas can come from questionable sources; bad ideas can come from sources that are usually reliable. Generally, judging a claim only by its source is a recipe for error.

"One must accept the truth from whatever source it comes."
—Moses Maimonides

There are times, however, when the origins of a claim can be a relevant factor. In court cases, when an eyewitness account comes from someone known to be a pathological liar, the jury is entitled to doubt the account. Or when a claim comes from someone who says they are an expert but who is in fact not an expert, then we should recognize that the claim deserves no more respect than it would if it came from any other non-expert. (See the discussion of "Appeal to Authority" in Chapter 4.)

5.1.2 Appeal to the Person

To commit the fallacy of **appeal to the person** (or ad hominem, meaning "to the man") is to reject a claim by criticizing the person who makes it rather than by examining the claim itself. For example:

appeal to the person/ad hominem
The fallacy of rejecting a claim by criticizing the person who makes it rather than the claim itself. *Ad hominem* means "to the man."

> Watanabe has argued for an increase in the tax on cigarettes. But he once ran as the NDP candidate in a provincial election, so he's a

> raving socialist who thinks all taxes are good. Anything he has to say on this issue is sure to be loony.
>
> We should reject Chen's argument for life on other planets. He relies on fortune-tellers for financial advice!
>
> You can't believe anything Beauchemin says about the benefits of federalism. She's a known separatist.
>
> Priya can't possibly have a reasonable view of politics. She reads horoscopes, so we know she is unreasonable and childish.

Such arguments are fallacious because they attempt to discredit a claim by appealing to something that's almost always irrelevant to it, such as a person's character, motives, or personal circumstances. Claims must be judged on their own merits—they are not guilty by association. We are never justified in rejecting a claim because of a person's faults unless we can show how a person's faults translate into faults in the claim—and this is almost never the case. Even when a person's character *is* relevant to the truth of claims (for example, when we must consider the merits of testimonial evidence), we are not justified in believing a claim false just because the person's character is dubious. If the person's character is dubious, we are left with no reason to think the claim is either true *or* false.

The fallacy of appeal to the person is usually regarded as a special case of the genetic fallacy. What distinguishes an appeal to the person is that it not only *mentions* a person as the origin of an argument, but it also *attacks* the person (usually their character) and usually ignores the argument altogether. To reject a claim simply because "it was made by Barry" is to commit the genetic fallacy; to reject a claim because "it was made by that moron Barry" is to commit the fallacy of appeal to the person.

The fallacy of appeal to the person comes in several varieties. One is the personal attack (just mentioned), which often simply consists of insults. The gist of these arguments is familiar enough. The arguer suggests that X's claims, ideas, or theories should be rejected because X is a radical, reactionary, extremist, right-winger, left-winger, fool, bonehead, moron, nutbar, or scum of the earth. Whatever psychological impact such terms of abuse may have, logically they carry no weight at all.

Another form of this fallacy emphasizes not a person's character but his or her circumstances. Here, for instance, someone making a claim might be accused of inconsistency—specifically, of maintaining a view that is inconsistent with his or her previous views or social or political commitments. For example:

> Edgar asserts that global warming is real, but he's a card-carrying member of a political party that is officially skeptical about climate change. So he can't believe in global warming; he's got to deny it.
>
> Madison *says* she's in favour of higher levels of immigration, but you can't take her seriously. That view goes against everything her whole family believes in.

These arguments are fallacious if they're implying that a claim must be true (or false) just because it's inconsistent with some aspect of the claimant's circumstances. The circumstances are irrelevant to the truth of the claim.

When such arguments are put forth as charges of hypocrisy, we get another ad hominem fallacy known as ***tu quoque*** (Latin for "you're another"). The fallacious reasoning goes like this: Ellen claims that X, but Ellen doesn't practise/live by/condone X herself—so X is false. Look:

tu quoque ("you're another") A type of ad hominem fallacy that argues that a claim must be true (or false) just because the claimant is hypocritical.

> West coast granola crunchers tell us we shouldn't drive SUVs because they use too much gas and are bad for the environment. But they drive SUVs themselves.
>
> What hypocrites! I think we can safely reject their stupid pronouncements.

But whether someone is hypocritical about their claims can have no bearing on the truth of those claims. We may, of course, condemn someone for hypocrisy, but we logically cannot use that hypocrisy as a justification for rejecting their views. Their views must stand or fall on their own merits.

In another variation of circumstantial ad hominem reasoning, someone might deduce that a claim is false because the person making it, given their circumstances, would be *expected* to make it. For example:

> Wilson claims that the political system in Cuba is terrific. But he *has* to say that. He's a card-carrying communist. So forget what he says.

Food for Thought

Hypocrisy in Politics

The version of *ad hominem* attack known as *tu quoque* plays an important—and typically unfortunate—role in political debate. Often it occurs in response to a critic who offers an argument against a decision or policy by a sitting politician. For example, imagine that the mayor of your city has proposed a hike in property taxes in order to support a new road repair initiative. A critic might point out that taxes are already high and that other sources of revenue would be preferable. It is common in such instances for a defender of the new policy to point out that the critic herself (or her own favourite political candidate or politician) has advocated raising property taxes in the past.

The accusation is essentially that the critic is being hypocritical: if you supported raising taxes in the past, why aren't you supporting that now? The implication is that the critic's stance is merely political, that she is criticizing the move now merely because a politician she opposes is proposing it. Of course, whether that's true or not will depend on the details. Perhaps there's a difference in the proposed size of the tax hike—perhaps the critic has supported a 1 per cent tax hike in the past but thinks that the mayor's proposed 5 per cent hike is excessive. Whether the charge of hypocrisy is fair, or is instead an illegitimate *tu quoque*, will depend on the situation.

But whether Wilson is a communist, and whether he would be expected or required to have certain views because of his connection to communism, is irrelevant to the truth of his claim.

Finally, we have the ad hominem tactic known as "poisoning the well." In this one, someone argues like this: X has no regard for the truth or has non-rational motives for espousing a claim, so nothing that X says should be believed—including the claim in question or possibly any claim made in the future! The idea is that just as you can't get safe water out of a poisoned well, you can't get reliable claims out of a discredited claimant. This tactic is fallacious because the fact that someone might have dubious reasons for making a claim does not show that the claim is false, nor does it mean that everything that comes out of the "poisoned well" can be automatically dismissed.

5.1.3 Composition

composition

The fallacy of arguing that what is true of the parts must be true of the whole. The error is thinking that the characteristics of the parts are somehow transferred to the whole, something that is not always the case.

The fallacy of **composition** involves arguing that what is true of the parts must be true of the whole. The error here is to think that the characteristics of the parts of a thing are somehow transferred to the thing as a whole, which is certainly not always the case. Likewise, the error is committed whenever we assume that what's true of a member of a group is true of the group as a whole. For example:

> The atoms that make up the human body are invisible. Therefore, the human body is invisible.
>
> Each member of the club is productive and effective. So the club will be productive and effective.
>
> Each note in the song sounds great. Therefore, the whole song will sound great.
>
> A piece of metal cannot do math, so a machine made out of pieces of metal cannot do math.

Sometimes, of course, the parts do in fact share the same characteristics as the whole. We may safely conclude that since all the parts of the house are made of wood, the house itself is made of wood. We commit the fallacy of composition, though, when we assume that a particular case must necessarily be like this.

The fallacy of composition often shows up in statistical arguments. Consider the following:

> The average small investor puts $2000 into the stock market every year. The average large investor puts $100,000 into stocks each year. Therefore, large investors (as a group) invest more money in the stock market than the small investor group does.

The fact that the average small investor invests less than the average large investor does not mean that small investors as a group invest less than large investors as a group. After all, there may be many more small investors than large investors.

5.1.4 Division

The flip side of the fallacy of composition is the fallacy of **division**—arguing that what is true of the whole must be true of the parts. This fallacy is also committed when we assume that what is true of a group is true of individuals within the group.

> This machine is heavy. Therefore, all the parts of this machine are heavy.
>
> The building Dimitri lives in is huge, so his apartment must be huge.
>
> A university degree is a valuable thing to have! So how can you possibly think that this course in underwater basket-weaving isn't valuable?

division
The fallacy of arguing that what is true of the whole must be true of the parts. The error is thinking that characteristics of the whole must transfer to the parts or that traits of the group must be the same as traits of individuals in the group.

These arguments are fallacious because they assume that characteristics of the whole are transferred to the parts or that traits of the group must be the same as traits of individuals within the group.

Like the fallacy of composition, the fallacy of division is frequently used in statistical arguments:

> Don't tell me you've had trouble finding a job. Unemployment in this entire province is at an all-time low!

Just because people *in general* have had good luck finding jobs, this doesn't mean that any specific job-seeker must necessarily have an easy time. The talents and opportunities of individuals, who make up the total workforce, may vary greatly.

5.1.5 Equivocation

The fallacy of **equivocation** is the use of a word in two different senses in an argument. For example:

equivocation
The fallacy of using a word in two different senses in an argument.

> The end of everything is its perfection.
> The end of life is death.
> Therefore, death is the perfection of life.
>
> Only man is rational.
> No woman is a man.
> Therefore, no woman is rational.
>
> Laws can only be created by law-givers.
> There are many laws of nature.
> Therefore, there must be a law-giver, namely, God.

In the first argument, *end* is used in two different senses. In the first premise it means *purpose*, but in the second it means *termination*. Because of this flip-flop in meanings, the conclusion doesn't follow from the premises—but it looks as if it should.

"The exact contrary of what is generally believed is often the truth."

—Jean de la Bruyère

In the second argument, *man* is the equivocal term. In the first premise it means humankind, but in the second it means male. So the conclusion doesn't follow because a claim about what makes humans different from animals can't support a conclusion about how women are (supposedly) different from men.

In the third argument, *laws* is used in two senses—rules of human behaviour in the first premise, and regularities of nature (as in "law of gravity") in the second. Consequently, the conclusion that tries to establish the existence of God doesn't follow.

The fallacy of equivocation occurs whenever a word has one meaning in one premise and another meaning in another premise or the conclusion. This shift in meaning always invalidates the argument.

Equivocation has historically played a central part in arguments over abortion because so much depends on the meaning of the terms used to refer to the unborn. Consider the following:

> Everyone agrees that a fetus is a human.
> All human beings have a right to life.
> Therefore, a fetus has a right to life.

Food for Thought

When Is a Church Not a Church?

In the wake of the discovery, in May of 2021, of the bodies of 215 Indigenous children in unmarked graves at the Kamloops Indian Residential School in British Columbia, there were calls for the Catholic Church to take responsibility in a variety of ways.

One response by some senior Catholic leaders was one that surprised many. They claimed that there *is no such thing* as the Catholic Church of Canada. Many Canadians, including many Catholic Canadians, might well have been surprised by this.

Archbishop Richard Gagnon of Winnipeg was one of the leaders within the Catholic Church who made this claim. He said:

> So it sounds kind of strange really for many people when I say and have said that there is no Catholic Church of Canada. There's the Catholic faith, but there's no Catholic Church of Canada. And so that may sound strange to our ears but not really when you think about it. There's no head office of the Catholic Church in Canada as such. Rather there are a series of churches, a series of Catholic churches which are autonomous. . ."[2]

Is Gagnon guilty of *equivocation* here? He is technically right that there is no legal entity *called* "the Catholic Church of Canada." Each individual Catholic church is its own legal entity. But on the other hand, the activities of those various Catholic churches receive at least informal leadership from the Canadian Conference of Catholic Bishops, and the bishops and archbishops from various parts of Canada all ultimately answer to the Pope, who is head of the Catholic Church globally. So to say that there "is no Catholic Church of Canada" might—or might not—count as equivocation, depending in part on whether we take the speaker to be referring to legal technicalities or to collective moral responsibility.

In the first premise, *human* is used in the sense of something having human physical characteristics such as human DNA. In the second premise, the word is used with *beings* in the sense of a person with moral rights. Because of this shift in meaning, the argument fails. The conclusion might be either true or false, but this argument cannot possibly support it.

5.1.6 Appeal to Popularity

The fallacy of the **appeal to popularity** (or to the masses) involves arguing that a claim must be true merely because a substantial number of people believe it.

appeal to popularity (or to the masses)
The fallacy of arguing that a claim must be true merely because a substantial number of people believe it.

The basic pattern of this fallacy is "Everyone (or almost everyone, most people, many people) believes X, so X must be true." For example:

> Most people approve of the provincial government's decision not to pay for in vitro fertilization treatments. So I guess that decision must be a good one.
>
> Of course Nova Scotia's rules for new drivers are justified. Everyone believes that they're justified.
>
> The vast majority of Canadians believe that the monarchy is a good thing. So how can you disagree?

These arguments are fallacious because they assume that a proposition is true merely because a great number of people believe it. But as far as the truth of a claim is concerned, what many people believe is typically irrelevant. Many people used to believe that certain women were witches and should be burned, that slavery was perfectly acceptable, that the Earth was the centre of the universe, and that blood-letting and purging were cures for just about every illness. In each of these cases, those people were absolutely mistaken. A large group's belief in a proposition, by itself, is no indication of truth.

What many people believe, however, can be an indication of truth if those people are experts or have expert knowledge in the issue at hand. If almost all ecologists say that a particular ecosystem is being threatened, ordinarily we should believe them.

Guy & Rodd/CartoonStock

The fact that someone else is doing something foolish, or even that a lot of people are, isn't a good argument in favour of you doing it too! How have appeals to popularity affected your own decision-making?

appeal to common practice
The fallacy of accepting or rejecting a claim solely on the basis of what groups of people generally do or how they behave (when the action or behaviour is irrelevant to the truth of the claim).

When the argument at hand is not about what many people *believe* but rather about what many people *do*, we may have a case of **appeal to common practice**. For example:

> Of course it's OK to speed! Everybody does it.
>
> But Mom, why can't I get a tattoo? All the other girls in my class already have one!
>
> There's nothing wrong with cheating a bit on your taxes. I read somewhere that nearly half of all taxpayers lie about *something* on their tax returns.

The problem here is very similar to the problem with appeal to popularity. The fact that a lot of people *do* something is generally not an indication that it's ethical, polite, or wise for you to do it too.

5.1.7 Appeal to Tradition

appeal to tradition
The fallacy of arguing that a claim must be true just because it's part of a tradition.

The **appeal to tradition** involves arguing that a claim must be true just because it's part of a tradition. For example:

> Acupuncture has been used for a thousand years in China. So it must work.
>
> Of course publishing pornography is wrong. In this community there's a tradition of condemning it that goes back to the early days of photography.
>
> Of course it's OK to have the company's CEO approve her own expense claims. We've always done it that way.

Such appeals are fallacious because tradition, like the masses, can be wrong. Remember that established traditions barred women from voting, stripped Indigenous peoples of their land, promoted the vengeful policy of "an eye for an eye," and sanctioned the sacrifice of innocents to the gods. These may have been traditions, but they were bad ones.

Be careful, though. It is also unreasonable to automatically *reject* a claim on the grounds that it's traditional. The point really is that a tradition should be neither accepted nor rejected without good reason. Knee-jerk acceptance of a tradition is just as bad as knee-jerk rejection of one.

5.1.8 Appeal to Ignorance

appeal to ignorance
The fallacy of arguing that a lack of evidence proves something. In one type of this fallacy, the problem arises from thinking that a claim must be true because it hasn't been shown to be false. In another type, the breakdown in logic comes when you argue that a claim must be false because it hasn't been proven to be true.

The **appeal to ignorance** consists of arguing that a lack of evidence proves something. In one variation of this fallacy, the problem arises from thinking that a claim must be true because it hasn't been shown to be false. For example:

> No one has shown that ghosts aren't real, so they must be real.
>
> It's clear that God exists because science hasn't proved that he doesn't exist.

> You can't show me one bit of evidence to disprove my theory that the current "Stanley Cup" is a fake and that the real one is hidden in Wayne Gretzky's basement. Therefore, my theory is correct.

The problem here is that a lack of evidence is supposed to prove something—but it logically can't do that. A lack of evidence alone can neither prove nor disprove a proposition. A lack of evidence simply reveals our ignorance about something.

In another variation of this fallacy, the breakdown in logic comes when you argue that a claim must be false because it hasn't been proved to be true. Look at these examples:

> No one has shown that ghosts are real, so they must not exist.
>
> It's clear that God doesn't exist because science hasn't proved that he does.
>
> You can't provide clear evidence for your theory that the current "Stanley Cup" is a fake and that the real one is hidden in Wayne Gretzky's basement. Therefore, your theory is false.

Again, the key lesson is: lack of evidence proves nothing. It does not give us a reason for believing a claim.

But what if our lesson here were wrong? If we could prove something with a lack of evidence, then we could prove almost anything. You can't prove that invisible men *aren't* having a keg party on Mars—does this mean that it's true that invisible men are having a keg party on Mars? You can't prove that Gandhi liked Uber (since he died more than 60 years before the ride-sharing service was launched)—does this prove that he didn't like Uber?

There are cases, however, that may seem like appeals to ignorance but actually are not. Sometimes when we carefully search for something, and when such a thorough search is likely to uncover it if there is anything to uncover, the failure to find what we're looking for can in fact show that it probably isn't there. A botanist, for example, may search a forest looking for a rare plant that used to grow only there but not find it even though she looks in all the likely places. In this case, her lack of evidence—her not finding the plant after a thorough search—may be considered good evidence that the plant has gone extinct. This conclusion would not rest on ignorance but on the knowledge that in these circumstances any thorough search would probably reveal the sought-after object if it were there at all. In such cases, an accusation that the botanist is making an appeal to ignorance would be off-target: she is instead accurately reporting the results of her diligent search.

This kind of inductive reasoning is widespread in science. Drugs, for example, are tested for toxicity on rodents or other animals before they are given to humans. If after extensive testing no toxic effects are observed in the animals (which are supposed to be relatively similar to humans in relevant ways), then the lack of toxicity—the fact that we haven't found negative effects—is considered evidence that the drug will probably not cause toxic effects in humans. Likewise, in the realm of "alternative" health care, most scientists regard the failure to find, after decades of testing, any evidence that homeopathic remedies have any physical effect as strong evidence that such remedies do not in fact work.

burden of proof
The weight of evidence or argument required by one side in a debate or disagreement.

In order to understand the significance of appeals to ignorance it is important to understand the notion of **burden of proof**. Burden of proof is the weight of evidence or argument required by one side in a debate or disagreement. Problems arise when the burden of proof is placed on the wrong side. For example, if Louise declares that "no one has shown that zombies aren't real, so they must be real," she implicitly puts the burden of proof on those who don't agree with her. She's asserting, in effect, "I say that zombies are real, and it's up to you to prove I'm wrong." Or to put it another way, "I'm entitled to believe that zombies are real unless you prove that they're not." But as we saw earlier, this line is just an appeal to ignorance, and the burden of proof for showing that zombies are real rests with *her*—not with those who don't share her belief. If her claim is unsupported, you need not accept it. If you take the bait and try to prove that zombies don't exist, you are accepting a burden of proof that should fall on Louise's shoulders, not yours.

Usually, the burden of proof rests on the side that makes a positive claim—an assertion that something exists or is the case rather than that something does not exist or is not the case. So in general, if a person (the claimant) makes an unsupported positive claim, he or she must provide evidence for it if the claim is to be accepted. If you doubt the claim, you are under no obligation to prove it wrong. You need not—and should not—accept it without good reasons (which the claimant should provide). Of course, you also should not reject the claim without good reasons. If the claimant does give you reasons for accepting the claim, you can either accept those reasons or reject them. If you reject them, you are obligated to explain the reasons for your rejection.

Everyday Problems and Decisions

Fallacies Can Be Deadly

Did you know that fallacies can be deadly? This is especially true when we are trying to sort out what to believe about health and health care. Take a look at this conversation:

YOU: Oh no—experts say we're seeing the start of another coronavirus pandemic. We need to wear masks for safety when we're around other people.

FRIEND: No, I don't think so. I don't see any reason to do that.

YOU: But public health experts are telling us that it's the wise thing to do.

FRIEND: But we really don't know, do we? This is a new pandemic, so there's no direct evidence that masks are going to be useful *this* time, just because they helped last time.

Don't let appeal to ignorance jeopardize your health!

5.1.9 Appeal to Emotion

The fallacy of the **appeal to emotion** is the use of emotions as premises (or as stand-ins for premises) in an argument. That is, it consists of trying to persuade someone of a conclusion solely by arousing his or her feelings rather than by presenting relevant reasons. When you use this fallacy, you appeal to people's guilt, anger, pity, fear, compassion, resentment, or pride—but not to good reasons that could actually give logical support to your case. Take a look:

appeal to emotion
The fallacy of using emotions in place of relevant reasons as premises in an argument.

> You should hire me for this network analyst position. I'm the best person for the job. If I don't get a job soon, my wife will leave me, and I won't have enough money to pay for my mother's heart medication. Come on, give me a break.
>
> Political ad: If school music programs are cut as part of the school board's new budget, we will save money—and lose our children to a world without music, a landscape without song. Let the children sing. Write to your member of the school board now and let them know what you think!

As arguments, these passages are fallacious not just because they *appeal* to strong emotions, but because they appeal to almost *nothing but* strong emotions. They urge us to accept a conclusion but offer no good reasons for doing so. We may feel compassion for the job hunter and his mother, but those feelings have no bearing on whether he is truly the best person for the job. We may recoil from the idea of children in a stark, tuneless world, but that overblown image and the emotions it evokes in us provide no logical support for the conclusion.

This kind of wielding of emotion in discourse is an example of *rhetoric*, the use of non-argumentative, emotive words and phrases to persuade or influence an audience. Arguments try to persuade by providing reasons logically connected to the point the arguer is trying to make. Rhetoric tries to persuade primarily through the artful use of language. There's nothing inherently wrong with using rhetoric, but its use becomes fallacious when there's an attempt to support a conclusion by rhetoric alone.

But in such cases the fallacy is easily avoided. Good writers often combine arguments with appeals to emotion in the same piece of writing, and no fallacy need enter the picture. A strong argument is presented, and

UNICEF Ireland

Many charities make well-intentioned use of appeals to emotion to raise awareness and stimulate interest. What difference do you see between charities using appeals to emotion, and companies using such appeals to sell music or clothing or gadgets?

it's reinforced by strong feelings. A Canadian marketing expert, quoted in the *Toronto Star*, made this point with regard to the controversial issue of road tolls:

> When it comes to making the case for tolls or new taxes to fight gridlock and expand transit, decision makers need to use an "aspirational" message, says a marketing expert.
>
> "We shop rationally, but we buy emotionally," said Chantel Broten, managing director of Jan Kelley Marketing, during a roundtable discussion on Wednesday organized by the Toronto City Summit Alliance. "You need to appeal to the head and the heart.
>
> "While drivers might vehemently object to paying more to drive, whether it is registration fees, higher gas taxes or new highway tolls, they might be willing to do so, for other reasons, such as "making things better for our children's children.
>
> . . .
>
> "It's not impossible," Broten said. "I don't want to pay more taxes or more tolls, but if I buy into the dream, I will."[3]

It's important to note that Broten isn't claiming that emotion is *enough*—but rather that an emotional appeal can draw people's attention to an argument that already makes sense.

5.1.10 Red Herring

red herring
The fallacy of deliberately raising an irrelevant issue during an argument. The basic pattern is to put forth a claim and then couple it with additional claims that may seem to support it but, in fact, are mere distractions.

Perhaps the most blatant fallacy of irrelevance is the **red herring**, the deliberate raising of an irrelevant issue during an argument. This fallacy gets its name from the practice of dragging a smelly fish across a trail to throw a tracking dog off the scent. The basic pattern is to put forth a claim and then couple it with additional claims that may seem to support it but in fact are mere distractions. For instance:

> Canada needs tougher immigration policies. I've got a neighbour who says we should let in *more* immigrants. The sixties . . . boy, what a great time that was for druggies and wackos! You should see the way that hippie dresses. . . . He hasn't figured out that the nineteen-sixties are over!
>
> The federal government should bring in mandatory minimum sentences for a greater range of serious crimes. I'm telling you, crime is a terrible thing when it happens to you. It causes death, pain, and fear. And I wouldn't want to wish these things on anyone.

Notice what's happening here. In the first example, the issue is whether Canada should have tougher immigration policies. But the arguer shifts the subject to the intelligence and dress of one particular person who favours more immigration. That person's intelligence and way of dressing, of course, have nothing to do with the main issue. The argument is bogus. In the second example, the issue is whether the federal government should institute more mandatory minimum sentences. But the subject gets changed to the terrible costs of crime, which is only remotely related to the main issue. (There's also an appeal to fear, here.) We can agree that crime can have awful consequences, but this fact has little to do with the merits and demerits of instituting mandatory minimum sentences.

"It's very easy to have slogans and rhetoric that people will follow, but eventually the slogans fall away."

—Saad Hariri, Prime Minister of Lebanon

5.1.11 Straw Man

Related to red herring is the fallacy of the **straw man**—the distorting, weakening, or oversimplifying of someone else's position so it can be more easily attacked or criticized. A straw man argument distracts the listener by focusing on a distorted version of the target argument rather than focusing on that argument itself. A straw man argument works like this: Reinterpret claim X so that it becomes the weak or absurd claim Y. Attack claim Y. Conclude that X is unfounded. For example:

straw man
The fallacy of distorting, weakening, or oversimplifying someone's position so it can be more easily attacked or refuted.

> David says he's in favour of equal marriage rights for gays. Obviously, he thinks gay relationships deserve special treatment and that the gay lifestyle should be celebrated and promoted. Do you really want your kids being taught that the gay lifestyle is best? David does, and he's dead wrong.
>
> The Official Opposition is opposed to the government's plan to increase spending on Canada's military. Why does the Opposition always want to leave Canada defenceless? Why do they want the military's budget slashed? They want Canada to be stuck with a military that can't defend our borders, let alone participate in our proud tradition of peacekeeping overseas.
>
> The premier says that the federal government ought to correct the "fiscal imbalance" by transferring more money to the provinces and territories. I think if he had his way, the federal government would give up all its powers and eventually waste away to nothing at all. Then there'd be nothing left to hold this country together. We can't let that happen! Oppose the premier's plan!

In the first passage, the speaker states that David is in favour of equal marriage rights for gays. His opponent, however, distorts his view, claiming that David is actually in favour of teaching children that the so-called gay lifestyle is *best*. David, of course, is not asserting this. This *distorted version* of David's position is easy to ridicule and reject, seemingly allowing his actual view to be dismissed without a further thought.

In the second passage, the arguer says that Official Opposition is against increasing military spending. Their position, though, is twisted into the claim that the military's budget should actually be *reduced* to such an extent that the military becomes useless. But it is unlikely that that is what the Opposition really wants. They simply don't want the military's budget *increased*.

The third passage is typical of the kind of fallacious arguments that crop up in debates over federal–provincial relations. Here, the speaker says that the premier wants the federal government to transfer more money to the provinces to help correct what some people see as the "fiscal imbalance" (i.e., the supposed mismatch between the responsibility the provinces have for major expenditures such as health care and education and their relative lack of financial resources compared to the federal government). But the premier's view gets characterized as implying that the federal government should eventually waste away to nothing. But wanting to make *some* change in the balance of power (and financial ability) between the two levels of government is not at all the same thing as wanting the federal government to have no role at all. Characterizing the premier's point of view as so extreme, however, is a way to generate strong opposition to it. After all, if the premier really did want to get rid of the federal government, that would indeed be an alarming proposition. Note that in debates over federal–provincial relations, the straw man tactic is also taken to bolster the other side of the dispute. Those who favour *greater* powers for the federal government are sometimes characterized as wanting to reduce the provinces to mere administrators of federal decisions and policies. But, of course, from the fact that someone wants to increase the powers of the federal government, it does not follow that they want to render the provinces entirely powerless.

Review Notes

Fallacies with Irrelevant Premises

- *Genetic fallacy:* Arguing that a claim is true or false solely because of its origin.
- *Appeal to the person:* Rejecting a claim by criticizing the person who makes it rather than the claim itself.
- *Composition:* Arguing that what is true of the parts must be true of the whole.
- *Division:* Arguing that what is true of the whole must be true of the parts or that what is true of a group is true of individuals in the group.
- *Equivocation:* The use of a word in two different senses in an argument.
- *Appeal to popularity:* Arguing that a claim must be true merely because a substantial number of people believe it.
- *Appeal to common practice:* Arguing that a practice is ethical or wise merely because a substantial number of people do it.
- *Appeal to tradition:* Arguing that a claim must be true or good just because it's part of a tradition.
- *Appeal to ignorance:* Arguing that a lack of evidence proves something.
- *Appeal to emotion:* The use of emotions as premises in an argument.
- *Red herring:* An irrelevant issue raised during an argument.
- *Straw man:* A distorted, weakened, or oversimplified representation of someone's position that can be more easily attacked or refuted than their true position.

5.2 Unacceptable Premises

5.2.1 Begging the Question

The fallacy of **begging the question** (or arguing in a circle) is the attempt to establish the conclusion of an argument by using that conclusion as a premise. To beg the question is to argue that a proposition is true because the very same proposition supports it:

begging the question The fallacy of attempting to establish the conclusion of an argument by using that conclusion as a premise. Also called arguing in a circle.

> *p*
>
> Therefore, *p*.

The classic question-begging argument goes like this:

> God exists. We know that God exists because the Bible says so and we should believe what the Bible says because God wrote it.

Or, more formally:

> The Bible says that God exists.
>
> The Bible is true because God wrote it.
>
> Therefore, God exists.

This argument assumes at the outset the very proposition ("God exists") that it is trying to prove. That is, it uses its own conclusion as a premise. Any argument that does this is fallacious.

Unfortunately, most question-begging arguments are not as obviously fallacious as "*p* is true because *p* is true." They may be hard to recognize because they are intricate or confusing. Consider this argument:

> It is in every case immoral to lie to someone, even if the lie could save a life. Even in extreme circumstances a lie is still a lie. All lies are immoral because the very act of prevarication in all circumstances is contrary to ethical principles.

At first glance, this argument may seem reasonable, but it's not. It reduces to this circular reasoning: "Lying is always immoral because lying is always immoral."

Food for Thought

Are We Begging the Question Yet?

In everyday usage, the phrase "beg the question" often refers to this famous fallacy; however, many times it does not. It is sometimes used (some would say misused) to mean something like "prompts the question" or "raises the question," as in "The rise in the crime rate begs the question of whether we have enough police officers on the job." As a critical thinker, you need to make sure you don't get these two uses confused.

Among the more subtle examples of question-begging is this famous one, a favourite of critical thinking textbooks:

> To allow every man unbounded freedom of speech must always be, on the whole, advantageous to the state; for it is highly conducive to the interests of the community that each individual should enjoy a liberty, perfectly unlimited, of expressing his sentiments.[4]

This argument, as well as the one preceding it, demonstrates the easiest way to subtly beg the question: just repeat the conclusion as a premise, but use different words.

5.2.2 False Dilemma

false dilemma
The fallacy of asserting that there are only two alternatives to consider when there are actually more than two, or asserting that there are two distinct alternatives that may in fact not be mutually exclusive.

The fallacy of **false dilemma** consists of either:

- asserting that there are only two alternatives to consider when there are actually more than two,

or

- asserting that there are two distinct alternatives that may in fact not be mutually exclusive.

Let's start with the first kind. Here's an example:

> Look, either you're in favour of government support for the arts or you're an uncultured thug. You're not in favour of government support for the arts. So you're an uncultured thug.

This argument contends that there are only two alternatives to choose from: either you're in favour of the government spending money to support the arts (painters, musicians, etc.) or you're an uncultured thug. And the arguer hopes that since you don't want to be seen as a thug, you'll change your mind and choose the other option—namely, to favour government support for the arts. But this argument works only if there really are just two alternatives. (A "dilemma" is a situation in which there are two equally undesirable possibilities.) But here there are actually other plausible possibilities. Maybe you like art but don't want to see the government spending tax dollars on it. Maybe you spend a lot of money on art and just don't think it's necessary for the arts to be supported by government. Because these possibilities are excluded, the argument is fallacious.

"I'm for truth, no matter who tells it. I'm for justice, no matter who it's for or against."
—Malcolm X

Here's another example:

> Either I saw you at the party, kissing Mark, or I was too drunk to see straight. But I wasn't drunk. So I saw you at the party, kissing Mark!

This argument says that there are only two possibilities: your friend was at the party, kissing Mark, or you were too drunk to see straight. And so your friend must have been there, kissing Mark, because you weren't drunk. But clearly in a situation like this there are more possible explanations than the ones being offered. You might have seen someone (at a distance) who was kissing Mark and who merely looked like your friend. You might not have been wearing your glasses. You might be misremembering and confusing that night with another night. Since the argument ignores these reasonable possibilities, it's fallacious.

Finally:

> We must legalize drugs. We either legalize them or pay a heavy toll in lives and the taxpayers' money to continue the war on drugs. And we cannot afford to pay such a high price.

At first glance, these two alternatives may seem to exhaust the possibilities. But there is at least one other option—to launch a massive effort to prevent drug use and thereby reduce the demand for illegal drugs. The argument does not work because it fails to consider this very reasonable possibility.

Note that these three arguments are expressed in disjunctive (either–or) form. But they can just as easily be expressed in a conditional (if–then) form, which says the same thing:

> Look, if you aren't in favour of government support for the arts, then you're an uncultured thug. You're not in favour of government support for the arts. So you're an uncultured thug.
>
> If I wasn't too drunk to see straight, then I saw you at the party, kissing Mark. I wasn't drunk. So I saw you at the party, kissing Mark!
>
> We must legalize drugs. If we don't legalize them, then we will pay a heavy toll in lives and the taxpayers' money to continue the war on drugs. And we cannot afford to pay such a high price.

Sometimes we encounter stand-alone disjunctive phrases rather than full-blown false dilemma arguments. These are false choices often presented as one-liners or headlines in tabloid newspapers, TV news programs, and social media. For example:

> Canada's Oil Sands: Economic Boon or Environmental Disaster?
>
> Apple: Innovator or Evil Giant?
>
> Is the Government Incompetent or Just Evil?

By limiting the possibilities, these headlines can imply that almost any outlandish imaginary state of affairs is actual occurring—without even directly asserting anything.

People are often taken in by false dilemmas because they don't think beyond the alternatives laid before them. Out of fear, the need for simple answers, or

The fallacy known as "false dilemma" is sometimes referred to as a false dichotomy. Someone who presents a dichotomy asserts a distinction between two things. A false dilemma takes this a step further and says we must choose one of two alternatives.

a failure of imagination, they don't ask, "Is there another possibility?" To ask this is to think outside the box and reduce the likelihood of falling for simplistic answers.

False dilemmas also arise when the arguer asserts that there are two distinct alternatives when in fact the two options offered may not be mutually exclusive. For example:

She's either delusional or a liar, but I can't figure out which!

This counts as a false dilemma because these two possibilities—being delusional and being a liar—are not in fact mutually exclusive. It is possible to be both, and some people *are* both.

Here's another example:

> Why are you so concerned about the rights of the *accused*? Are you interested in protecting the rights of accused criminals or protecting the rights of their victims?

Again, this is a false dilemma because the two options being offered are not necessarily in opposition to each other. We can be concerned with protecting the rights of those accused of crimes (e.g., presuming them "innocent until proven guilty") while at the same time wanting to work to assist and protect the victims of crime. In the face of a false dilemma of this kind, we should reply, "Why can't I be concerned with both?"

5.2.3 Slippery Slope

slippery slope
The fallacy of arguing, without good reasons, that taking a particular step will inevitably lead to further, undesirable steps.

The fallacy of **slippery slope** is to argue, without good reasons, that taking a particular step will inevitably lead to a further, undesirable step (or steps). The idea behind the metaphor, of course, is that if you take the first step onto a slippery slope, you will have to take others because, well, the slope is slippery. A familiar slippery slope pattern is "Doing action A will lead to action B, which will lead to action C, which will result in calamitous action D. Therefore, you should not do action A." It's fallacious when there is no good reason to think that doing action A will actually inevitably result in undesirable action D. Take a look at this example:

> Canada must not legalize Medical Assistance in Dying (MAiD). Even if access to MAiD is initially limited to those with "grievous and irremediable medical conditions," availability of the process is sure to broaden. Before long, medical definitions will be

> broadened, families will start pressuring the elderly to request MAiD, and ultimately anyone with a disability will be seen as a valid target for MAiD.

This argument was commonplace in the time leading up to the legalization of MAiD in Canada in 2016. It was fallacious because there was no good evidence that elders and those living with disabilities would be targeted or pressured into undergoing MAiD. According to Stuart Chambers, who teaches a course on the topic at the University of Ottawa, the years since (in addition to the experiences of other countries) have demonstrated that fears of abuse simply haven't been borne out.[5]

Sometimes a step that looks like progress can be the first step on a slippery slope. But then again, sometimes progress is just progress. When is the slippery slope argument fallacious?

Here are some more examples:

> If supporters of the federal government's firearms registry get their way, all recreational and hunting weapons will have to be registered with the federal government. Next thing you know, it'll be illegal to own a gun for target practice or to go hunting for rabbits, like my dad and I did when I was a boy. Eventually, the government will want to know if you own *any* weapon, whether it's a pocket knife or a baseball bat. So if you support the firearms registry, you're inviting the government to invade your privacy and interfere with your basic freedoms.

> We must ban pornography in all forms. Otherwise, rape and other sex crimes will be as common as jaywalking.

> All Canadians should oppose gay marriage. If gay marriage is allowed, before you know it anything goes—polygamy, incest, marrying animals . . . who knows!

These arguments follow the basic slippery slope pattern. They are fallacies, not because they assert that one event or state of affairs can inevitably lead to others but because there is no good reason to believe the assertions. Some arguments may look like slippery slope fallacies but are not because there is good reason to think that the steps are connected as described. Observe:

> If you have Lyme disease, you definitely should get medical treatment. Without treatment, you could develop life-threatening complications. Man, you could die. You should see your doctor now.

This one is not a fallacious slippery slope argument. There are good reasons to believe that the series of events mentioned would actually happen.

Food for Thought

Fallacious Vote-Seeking

On October 13, 2020, then-President Donald Trump gave a speech at a rally in Johnstown, Pennsylvania. During that speech, Trump made a number of questionable claims, and made use of a number of fallacies. Take, for example, this short bit from the first paragraph of his speech:

> This election is a simple choice. If Biden wins, China wins, all these other countries win. We get ripped off by everybody. If we win, you win, Pennsylvania wins and America wins, very simple.

There are at least two potentially fallacious arguments here. One is a slippery slope: if you let Biden win, then terrible things will happen. The other is a false dilemma: voters would have to choose either Biden-and-losing or Trump-and-winning. There were, Trump suggested, no other possibilities.

Of course, Canadian politicians can be prone to fallacious reasoning, too. In a televised exchange in 2017, conservative politician Doug Ford (who was at that time about to become premier of Ontario) made use of a classic red herring: when asked whether right-wing economic policies (the kind Ford advocated) were hurtful to working-class voters, Ford dodged the issue, saying that what really hurts people are high taxes. Of course, the point here is not the accuracy of Ford's claim, but that he inserted a point of his own rather than sticking to the question that was asked.

As we note in this chapter, sometimes people use fallacious arguments by accident, and sometimes they use them intentionally. Which do you think was the case in the examples above? Why might Trump genuinely have believed that voters faced this dilemma (that is, believed that the dilemma was not a *false* dilemma)? Why might Ford have thought that high taxes were the "real" issue? If Trump knew his statement created a false dilemma, or if Ford knew that his words were a red herring, why might each of them have said what they did anyway?

5.2.4 Hasty Generalization

hasty generalization
The fallacy of drawing a conclusion about a target group on the basis of a sample that is too small.

In Chapter 4, we pointed out the connection between the availability error and the fallacy known as **hasty generalization**. In Chapter 8, we will examine hasty generalizations at length. For now we need only recall that we are guilty of hasty generalization when we draw a conclusion about a whole group based on an inadequate sample of the group. This mistake is a genuine fallacy of unacceptable premises because the premises stating the sample size are relevant to the conclusion but they provide inadequate evidence. There is always an additional premise implied—namely, that the sample provided is adequate to justify the conclusion given. And that premise is unacceptable. For example:

> You should buy a Dell computer. They're great. I bought one last year, and it has given me nothing but perfect performance.
>
> The only male professor I've had this year was a sexist pig. All the male professors at this school must be sexist pigs.

> Psychology majors are incredibly ignorant about human psychology. Believe me, I know what I'm talking about: My best friend is a psych major. What an ignoramus!
>
> Americans are snobby and rude. Remember those two loud guys with really bad manners? They're American. I rest my case.
>
> The food at Pappie's Restaurant is awful. I had a sandwich there once, and the bread was stale.

Note that in each of these cases, the evidence given may be true and relevant, but the assumption that that evidence is *sufficient* is faulty—it is an unstated and false premise.

"One cool judgment is worth a thousand hasty counsels."

—Woodrow Wilson

5.2.5 Faulty Analogy

We will also discuss **arguments by analogy** in Chapter 8. Like hasty generalizations, defective arguments by analogy, or **faulty analogies**, are also fallacies involving unacceptable premises. An analogy is a comparison of two or more things that are alike in specific respects. An argument by analogy reasons this way: Because two or more things are similar in several respects, they must be similar in some further respect. For example:

argument by analogy (analogical induction)
An argument making use of analogy, reasoning that because two or more things are similar in several respects, they must be similar in some further respect.

faulty analogy
A defective argument by analogy.

> The last time we went on vacation and left you in charge of the house, you said you wanted to have "a few friends" over for a party, and the house was a mess when we got home. Likewise, this time you say you want to have "a few friends" over. So if we let you, I'm sure the house will be a disaster area when we get home!
>
> A watch is a mechanism of exquisite complexity with numerous parts precisely arranged and accurately adjusted to achieve a purpose—a purpose imposed by the watch's designer. Likewise, the universe has exquisite complexity with countless parts—from atoms to asteroids—that fit together precisely and accurately to produce certain effects as though arranged by plan. Therefore, the universe must also have a designer.

In a faulty analogy, the things being compared are not sufficiently similar in relevant ways. Such analogical arguments are said to be weak. For instance, you could argue that:

> Dogs are warm-blooded, nurse their young, and give birth to puppies. Humans are warm-blooded and nurse their young. Therefore, humans give birth to puppies too.

This argument by analogy is about as weak as they come—and a little silly. Dogs and humans are not sufficiently similar in relevant ways (in physiology, for one thing) to justify such a strange conclusion.

Review Notes

Fallacies with Unacceptable Premises

- *Begging the question:* The attempt to establish the conclusion of an argument by using that conclusion as a premise.
- *False dilemma:* Asserting that there are only two alternatives to consider when there are actually more than two.
- *Slippery slope:* Arguing, without good reasons, that taking a particular step will inevitably lead to a further, undesirable step (or steps).
- *Hasty generalization:* The drawing of a conclusion about a target group based on an inadequate sample size.
- *Faulty analogy:* An argument in which the things being compared are not sufficiently similar in relevant ways.

Critical Thinking and the Media

Fallacies in Advertising

As noted in this chapter, fallacies are argument forms that are both common and—from a logical point of view—defective. But as we also noted in this chapter, fallacies are often persuasive. They can be effective at persuading, even though they should not be.

The fact that fallacies can be persuasive makes them a tempting tool for advertisers. In Chapter 4, for instance, we pointed out that some ads make use of a fallacious *appeal to authority* by using a non-expert (like a movie star) to promote a product they have no authority to promote. But other fallacies, too, can show up in advertising.

Consider, for example, a tire company that implies that *either* you're willing to spend "a bit more" on better snow tires, or that you just don't care that much about your family's safety. Such an ad is making use of a *false dilemma*. An ad that simply tries to make you smile, without telling you anything at all about their product, is engaging in a kind of *appeal to emotion*. A commercial that tells you how popular a product is, without telling you why it is popular, is using an *appeal to popularity*. And a commercial that tells you that a famous athlete wore a particular brand of shoes while winning the championship is engaging in *hasty generalization*—implying, perhaps without saying it, that you too will excel at your favourite sport if you too wear that brand of shoes.

Most such arguments sound pretty silly if you say them out loud. Do you *really* believe that wearing Nikes will make you a star athlete? Surely not. And yet advertisers continue to use such arguments. Perhaps this means they doubt the audience's ability to think critically. Are they wrong about that?

Summary

Certain types of defective arguments that occur frequently are known as fallacies. Fallacies are often psychologically persuasive but logically flawed. We can divide fallacies into two broad categories: (1) those that have *irrelevant* premises and (2) those that have *unacceptable* premises.

Fallacies with irrelevant premises include the genetic fallacy (arguing that a claim is true or false solely because of its origin), composition (arguing that what is true of the parts must be true of the whole), division (arguing that what is true of the whole must be true of the parts or that what is true of a group is true of individuals in the group), appeal to the person (rejecting a claim by criticizing the person who makes it rather than the claim itself), equivocation (the use of a word in two different senses in an argument), appeal to popularity (arguing that a claim must be true merely because a substantial number of people believe it), appeal to ignorance (arguing that a lack of evidence proves something), appeal to tradition (arguing that a claim must be true or good just because it's part of a tradition), appeal to emotion (the use of emotions as premises in an argument), red herring (the deliberate raising of an irrelevant issue during an argument), and straw man (the distorting, weakening, or oversimplifying of someone's position so it can be more easily attacked or refuted).

Fallacies with unacceptable premises include begging the question (the attempt to establish the conclusion of an argument by using that conclusion as a premise), slippery slope (arguing, without good reasons, that taking a particular step will inevitably lead to a further, undesirable step or steps), hasty generalization (the drawing of a conclusion about a group based on an inadequate sample of the group), and faulty analogy (an argument in which the things being compared are not sufficiently similar in relevant ways).

Exercise 5.1

Answers to exercises marked with an asterisk (*) may be found in Appendix B, Answers to Exercises.

Review Questions

1. According to the text, what are the two broad categories of fallacies?
2. What is appeal to tradition?
3. Can the origin of a claim ever be relevant to deciding its truth or falsity?
4. What is the fallacy of division? How is it different from the fallacy of composition?*
5. What is the genetic fallacy?
6. Why is the fallacy of division fallacious?
7. What type of ad hominem argument is put forth as a charge of hypocrisy?
8. Which fallacy is poisoning the well a subtype of?
9. What is the fallacy of equivocation?
10. Why are appeals to popularity fallacious?*
11. What is the appeal to the person?

12. What are the two forms of the appeal to ignorance?
13. What is the proper response to an appeal to ignorance?
14. What is rhetoric? When does it become problematic?
15. According to the text, is it ever legitimate to use rhetoric and argument together?*
16. What is a red herring? How is it different from the straw man fallacy?
17. What is the basic pattern of argument of the straw man fallacy?
18. What is the fallacy of hasty generalization?
19. What are two types of false dilemma? Why are people often taken in by this fallacy?*
20. With whom does the burden of proof typically lie in a disagreement?
21. What is the fallacy of slippery slope?

Exercise 5.2

In the following passages, identify any fallacies of irrelevance (genetic fallacy, composition, division, appeal to the person, equivocation, appeal to popularity, appeal to ignorance, appeal to tradition, appeal to emotion, red herring, and straw man). Some passages may contain more than one fallacy, and a few may contain no fallacies at all.

1. "Seeing that the eye and hand and foot and every one of our members [i.e., body parts] has some obvious function, must we not believe that, likewise, a human being has a function over and above these particular functions?" (Aristotle)*
2. There has never been a more dangerous time to raise a child. Every parent I know has been talking about it!
3. The lobbyists who visited Parliament Hill yesterday said they're defenders of free markets. But they're really just a bunch of whiny rich guys trying to get handouts from the government.
4. It was a bad idea for all the countries of Europe to give up their old currencies and adopt the euro. Just ask any German how he feels about linking his country's economic fate to that of Greece!
5. The *National Post* says that a proposal to force companies to embrace corporate social responsibility amounts to a denial of the basic principles of the market economy. But you know that's false—after all, it's from the *National Post*!*
6. I think that students who cheat on exams should automatically be expelled from school. But Geraldo says he thinks that's harsh. I can't believe he thinks cheating is such a trivial thing!
7. Of course there is a God. Almost every civilization in history has believed in a deity of some kind.
8. Does acupuncture work? Can it cure disease? Of course it can. It has been used in China by folk practitioners for at least 3000 years.

9. The prime minister has misled the country about whether he was behind that decision. Surveys show that almost everyone in Canada thinks so.
10. Kelly says that many women who live in predominantly Muslim countries are discriminated against. But how the heck would she know? She knows nothing about the world's religions!*
11. From a politician: "Crime rates? Great question. But first, let me tell you about some of the great things our government has been doing for the environment."
12. That car you just bought was pretty expensive! I didn't realize that car parts are so expensive!
13. The study found that 80 per cent of women who took the drug daily had no recurrence of breast cancer. But that doesn't mean anything. The study was funded in part by the company that makes the drug.
14. "The only proof capable of being given that an object is visible, is that people actually see it. The only proof that a sound is audible, is that people hear it: and so of the other sources of our experience. In like manner, I apprehend, the sole evidence it is possible to produce that anything is desirable, is that people actually desire it." (John Stuart Mill, *Utilitarianism*, 1863)*
15. Imagine your friends looking admiringly at the brand-new Ram 1500 parked in your driveway. Imagine the joy you'll feel.
16. How do you know that everything you see around you is real and that we aren't actually in a simulation, similar to the world in *The Matrix*? Famous philosophers have accepted this scenario as a very real possibility. Besides, you can't actually know whether or not it's true because it would be impossible to find any evidence that disproves this idea. Any "evidence" you find might just be part of the illusion!
17. "The most blatant occurrence of recent years is all these knuckleheads running around protesting nuclear power—all these stupid people who do not research at all and who go out and march, pretending they care about the human race, and then go off in their automobiles and kill one another." (Ray Bradbury)
18. Every member of the all-star team is one of the best players on her home team. This team will never be beat!
19. Of course I believe in miracles. Every Christian does! I defy you to show me one bit of proof that miracles aren't possible.
20. The former mayor was convicted of drug possession, and he spent time in jail. So you can safely ignore anything he has to say about legalizing drugs.*
21. Yes, I copied another student's paper, but I don't deserve to be punished. I was under a lot of pressure, and if I'm punished I'll lose my scholarship.
22. Is the holy book the true word of God? There can be no doubt that it is, for it has inspired millions of believers for centuries.
23. We know that at its most basic level, matter is not alive. Clearly a bunch of non-living things can't just come together and make one living thing, so God must have created life.

Exercise 5.3

In the following passages, identify any fallacies of unacceptable premises (begging the question, false dilemma, slippery slope, hasty generalization, and faulty analogy). Some passages may contain more than one fallacy, and a few may contain no fallacies at all.

1. J.J. drives a big SUV! I can't believe he cares so little for the environment. He might as well be taking a chainsaw to the park and cutting down all the trees! I'm sure the police would arrest him in a heartbeat if he started doing that, so why aren't they taking his littering more seriously? I tell you, there'll be anarchy in the streets soon if people find out you can get away with committing crimes like littering!
2. If we don't allow professional athletes to use steroids, then how can we justify them taking cold medication when they've got a cold? And if cold medications get counted as "performance enhancing," shouldn't we just go all the way and say "no health care at all for professional athletes"?
3. Three thieves are dividing up the $7000 they just stole from the local bank. Robber number one gives $2000 to robber number two, $2000 to robber number three, and $3000 to himself. Robber number two says, "How come you get $3000?" Robber number one says, "Because I am the leader." "How come you're the leader?" "Because I have more money."
4. Either you are rich or you are poor. If you're rich, you don't have to worry about money. And if you're poor, you don't have any money to worry about. Either way, you've got no worries!*
5. That website wrongly reported that four people had been killed, when really it was only three. That site is nothing but a big pile of fake news.
6. I used to work with this engineering major, and, man, they are totally geeky.*
7. Fear is the path to the dark side. Fear leads to anger. Anger leads to hate. Hate leads to suffering. (Master Yoda in *Star Wars: Episode I—The Phantom Menace*)
8. Managing a country's budget is just like managing your family budget. You've got income, you've got expenses. And so it shouldn't take a PhD in economics to balance our federal budget!
9. A recent study conducted by PETA has shown that meat-eaters are significantly more likely to engage in violent behaviour than are vegetarians and vegans. Their study involved handing out questionnaires to 20 meat-eaters and 20 non–meat-eaters and scoring their answers on a behavioural scale.
10. Either we fire this guy or we send a message to other employees that it's OK to engage in sexual harassment in the workplace. Clearly, we need to fire him.*

Exercise 5.4

For each of the following claims, devise an argument using the fallacy shown in parentheses. Make the argument as persuasive as possible.

1. Hard drugs should be legalized. (slippery slope)
2. *Black Panther* is the best superhero movie ever made. (appeal to popularity)
3. Mrs Anan does not deserve the Nobel Prize. (appeal to the person)*
4. Zombies—just like in the *Walking Dead*—are real. (appeal to ignorance)
5. Every student who commits plagiarism should be kicked out of school. (slippery slope)
6. It's great that Scouts Canada welcomes LGBTQ kids as members. (begging the question)*
7. Quebec should remain a part of Canada. (false dilemma)
8. That sociology department is absolutely the worst department in the entire university. (hasty generalization)
9. We should reject the American suggestion that NAFTA is unfair and that Canada gains more from it than the US. (genetic fallacy)
10. The Nigerian court was right to sentence that woman to be stoned to death for adultery. (appeal to tradition)
11. Newfoundland's fisheries are a mess because the Department of Fisheries and Oceans—a federal department—has too much power over them. (red herring)*
12. The Canadian government needs to do more to support our most elderly citizens. (appeal to emotion)

Field Problems

1. Find a piece of writing on a popular blog that contains at least one fallacy. Point out the fallacious part, name the fallacy involved, and then rewrite the passage to eliminate the fallacy and strengthen the argument. (To rework the argument effectively, you may have to make up some facts.)
2. Print out at least two pages of comments posted under an online news story. Look through them all, circling and labelling any examples of fallacies. Find at least three examples.
3. What is one of the major political topics discussed in your city right now? Find a quote from one of your city politicians (mayor or councillor) on the subject. Can you find any fallacies being used? Do you think the fallacious argument will be psychologically persuasive for at least some voters?

Self-Assessment Quiz

Name the fallacy or fallacies in the following passages:

1. You want to know about this car's gas mileage? We can talk about that in a minute, and I think you'll be pleasantly surprised. But first, get in behind the wheel, and tell me how that leather seat feels!

2. I keep hearing stories about how masks keep disease from spreading. But where's the real proof? Show me the evidence, or stop complaining because you happened to vote for the government that's telling us to wear masks.
3. Legislation to officially recognize gay marriage was opposed by crazy religious groups across the country—which proves that the legislation is on the right track!
4. The mayor is a racist! At a city council meeting last night, he said that he won't support our proposal to name Main Street after Nelson Mandela. How can we tolerate elected officials who say that great black leaders don't deserve to be recognized?
5. Don't even tell me what Charlie thinks about protecting our oceans. She's a granola-eating vegan, and they all spout the same nonsense.
6. Our deputy prime minister is a woman, so don't tell me women still have a tough time in politics!
7. You advocate long jail terms for drug dealers because you don't understand how awful jail is. People in jail have almost no freedom, they seldom see their families, and they spend their days and nights in continual fear of violence and sexual assault.
8. It would appear that human cloning is inevitable. Either we push forward with ground-breaking technology or we admit that we have no scientific curiosity at all. And we do not lack scientific curiosity!
9. That must have been a terrible book. I don't know anyone who read it.
10. Atheistic philosophers have been trying for thousands of years to prove that there is no God, and they haven't succeeded yet. So God is real!
11. How can you, with a straight face, tell me that I should be a vegetarian? You're wearing a leather jacket!
12. Judges should not hand down anything but maximum sentences for all convicted criminals. If you start making exceptions, prosecutors will start asking for lighter sentences. Next thing you know, every criminal will be getting off with mere warnings.
13. If the professor really appreciated my hard work, he would have given me an A+ on my essay. But he only gave me a B+, so he obviously doesn't care about the time and effort I put into it.
14. When I was in elementary school, we were supposed to stand and recite "The Lord's Prayer" every day before class. That was dead wrong. No child should have to submit to such brainwashing.
15. Sure, Dilraj was caught stealing office supplies from the supply cabinet. But why should they fire him? After all, lots of people steal stuff from that cabinet.

Integrative Exercises

These exercises pertain to material in Chapters 1–5.

For each of the following passages, say whether it contains an argument. If it does, specify the conclusion and premises, whether the argument is deductive or inductive, whether it is a good argument (sound or cogent), and whether it is a fallacy. Some passages may contain no argument.

1. Are you seriously trying to tell me that there is no such thing as psychic abilities when in actual fact you have no proof at all that there isn't?
2. Dwayne always blushes when Carlito walks into the room, so he *must* have a crush on him!

3. "The large number of female voters for Arnold Schwarzenegger in California announces one thing: the death of feminism. That so many women would ignore his sexual misconduct and vote for him bespeaks the re-emergence of the reckless phallus." (Letter to the editor, *Newsday*)
4. Are we seriously supposed to listen to sermons on saving the planet from a movie star who flies all over the world in a private jet?
5. Elliot Page and Miley Cyrus are vegetarians. And guess what? Nazi leader Adolf Hitler was also a vegetarian. So it's obvious that Cyrus and Page are Nazis!
6. If you park illegally, you're breaking the law. And if you break one law, you'll break another. Soon, you'll be shoplifting. Next thing you know, you'll be committing major crimes and ending up in jail.
7. Either you turn off that TV right now and do your homework or you admit that you just don't care about succeeding in school at all.
8. Thinking is like swimming. Just as in swimming, it's easy to float on the top but hard to dive deep; it's easy in thinking to float along on the surface of an issue but difficult to use your brain to dive down into the deeper layers.
9. "If a cell, under appropriate conditions, becomes a person in the space of a few years, there can surely be no difficulty in understanding how, under appropriate conditions, a cell may, in the course of untold millions of years, give origin to the human race." (Herbert Spencer)
10. Pets should never be allowed to jump up on your furniture, and I simply will not listen to anyone who tries to tell me otherwise!
11. You should avoid carbs. I've talked to two different doctors, and they both pretty much told me carbs are evil.
12. Ripped jeans are totally in fashion this season. Just look around, and you'll see everyone is wearing them.
13. My professor says that telling a lie is never morally permissible. But that's ridiculous. The other day I heard him tell a boldfaced lie to one of his students.
14. There are those on campus who would defend a professor's right to question the teachings of Islam. But there is no such right. Racism is wrong and will always be wrong.
15. It's true! The British explorers of the seventeenth century saved the First Nations people from their backward ways. That's what my grandpa taught my dad, and what my dad taught me. If it weren't true, it wouldn't be in my grandpa's history textbook!

Critical Thinking and Writing Exercise

An Annotated Sample Paper

Let's see how the lessons of the four previous modules might be applied in a student-level essay. The essay on the following pages incorporates the main elements of good argumentative papers and, as even the best essays do, exhibits both strengths and weaknesses—some of which are noted in the margins. Read the paper carefully, taking in the annotations as you go and making sure you understand each point before moving on to the next. (Note that while the debate described in the essay is real, the sources cited in the essay are fictional, and are just there to illustrate the citation process.)

The Ethics of Consumer Risk

Thesis statement

Here the author clarifies the scope of their discussion.

Sometimes companies produce products that pose clear risks. In this essay, I will argue that it is ethically permissible to sell a product that has a known risk of causing fatal injuries, as long as the risk posed by the product is more or less the same as the risk posed by competitors' products. To be clear, the discussion here will not be about the everyday risks posed by products during everyday use, such as the risk of cutting yourself with a kitchen knife. Instead, I will discuss *unusual* risks that most consumers would not know about and consent to, such as risk of car crash or fire resulting in death. That is, I will argue that it is ethically permissible to sell a product that has non-obvious risks, as long as those risks are not unusual within a given industry.

This lets the reader know how many distinct arguments will support the thesis.

In this essay I will provide two arguments. First, I will argue that when a given risk is shared across products within an industry, it would be *unfair* to single out a particular manufacturer for blame. Second, I will argue that when a particular risk is common within an industry, it is more likely that consumers will already know about that risk, and effectively consent to it. I will also consider one counter-argument, namely Jonas's (2014) argument that selling products known to be very risky constitutes a conscious intention to kill.

First argument for thesis

Let us consider the fairness argument. Here I will argue that it is unfair, in two different ways, to hold a single company responsible without at the same time holding other companies responsible for acting in the same ways.

First part of first argument

Note the use of indicator words in this paragraph.

First, note that it is a fundamental ethical principle that like cases should be treated alike. This applies to ethical judgements, as well. So if two people for example have done the same thing, they should be judged the same way. It would be unfair to call one person unethical for doing a certain action, without also calling others who do the same thing unethical as well. This rule should be taken to apply to corporations as well: it would be wrong to hold a given company ethically responsible or criticize them when others in the same industry do the same things without being held responsible or facing criticism. Thus blaming a single company for selling a risky product without also (and equally) blaming all other companies in its industry is a form of basic ethical inconsistency. And such inconsistency is clearly to be avoided. On this basis, Finyas (2017) argues that entire industries should, collectively, be held responsible for unsafe products, and that it is unfair to single out particular companies for risks that are shared across an industry.

Second part of first argument

Second, consider the ethical importance of knowing in advance what you will be held responsible for or criticized for. It would generally be considered unfair to criticize someone for something that they could not have known, in advance, would be considered wrong. For example, if I throw out my roommate's old sweater that I sincerely believed she no longer wanted, it would be wrong for her to blame me, even if she loved the sweater. We should only be held responsible for *knowingly* doing wrong. Finyas argues (2017, p. 24) that the same rule should apply to companies. And one way in which companies come to know that they will be held responsible for particular behaviours is by seeing *other* companies in their industry being held responsible for those same behaviours. So, Finyas (2017, p. 30) argues that if a given company does not see other companies being blamed for the risks posed by their products, it is reasonable for them to think that they, too, will be free of blame for selling products with similar risks.

Cites sources

Second argument for thesis

Next, let us consider the question of consumer knowledge. In some cases, as Finyas (2017, p. 25) points out, consumers effectively consent to the risks posed by products. Some risks are obvious, such as the risk of cutting yourself with a kitchen knife. And some risks are subject to specific warnings, as when the instruction manual accompanying an electrical appliance warns that shock may result from getting the appliance wet. In those cases, most people will agree that the consumer effectively consents to the risk by buying the product, and if the consumer ends up getting hurt, the manufacturer is not to blame. If you cut yourself with a kitchen knife, you would not dream of suing the company that made the knife. Finyas (2017, p. 26) argues that this argument should be extended to risks that are widespread within an industry. When risks are widespread within an industry, Finyas argues, it is much more likely that consumers will have heard of those risks: they may have read stories about the risks online, and they might even know someone who was injured. In such cases, a company has the right to assume that consumers understand the risks involved, says Finyas, and so it would be unfair to blame such a company when injuries do in fact occur.

Provides an objection, or counter-argument

Contrary to the view provided by Finyas (2017), Jonas (2014) has provided a bold argument for stricter standards with regard to product safety. In particular, he argues (p. 110) that where a product poses a known risk of death, then selling that product can amount to *intending* those deaths—something that is clearly unethical.

Jonas provides (pp. 111–112) a mathematical example: If a product has a 100 per cent chance of killing the customer, and if you sell one to someone, then you are effectively intending to kill that person. And if the product has a 50/50 chance of killing the customer, and if you sell two of them, you effectively intend to kill (probabilistically) one of those two customers. Likewise, if a product has a one-in-one-thousand risk of death, and if you sell ten thousand of them, you know that ten people are likely to die. And if you sold your product to those 10 people without warning them, then you have effectively wrongfully killed them.

Responds to counter-argument

However, Jonas's argument is flawed. All products pose risks, and it would be unreasonable to hold all manufacturers responsible in all cases. Following Jonas's logic, imagine a company knows that one-in-one-million users of a given drug will die from it, but the drug will also greatly ease the suffering of almost all other users. Following Jonas's argument would mean accusing the company of intentionally killing one person, and that would be unreasonable, and unfair. And if Jonas's reasoning does not apply to the one-in-a-million case, there is no reason to think it applies in the other cases he describes.

All products carry risks, and some carry very serious risks. In many cases, manufacturers can and should reduce those risks. But some risks cannot be eliminated, and some can only be eliminated by making products so costly that consumers cannot afford them. When risks cannot be eliminated, then it is only fair to treat all companies the same with regard to those risks. Thus it must be considered ethically permissible to sell a product that has a known risk of causing even fatal injuries, as long

Restates thesis

as the risk posed by the product is more or less the same as the risk posed by competitors' products.

References:*

Finyas, T. (2017). "Shared Responsibility for Product Safety," *Canadian Journal of Business Ethics*, 6(3), 22–31.

Jonas, V.K. (2014). "Unsafe at Any Greed: Corporate Responsibility for Known Risks," *Australian Business Ethics Journal*, 22(4), 109–16.

*Note: These are fictional sources invented for illustrative purposes.

Writing Assignments

1. In a 300-word essay, argue that Canada should take bold action to improve the lives of Indigenous people living in some of Canada's poorest communities. Avoid fallacies. Then exchange essays with a classmate, and write a one-page critique of each other's paper, paying special attention to any fallacies you uncover. Be polite but honest!
2. Write a 500-word response to Essay 10 ("Christmas Is a Secular Holiday") in Appendix A, pointing out any fallacies you find—if any. If you find fewer than three fallacious arguments, describe fallacious arguments that the author could have resorted to in defence of his point of view if he weren't careful.
3. Write a 300-word paper arguing that the legal age for voting in provincial elections in Canada should be lowered to 16. Include at least two fallacies in the paper, but try to make them as convincing as you can. Exchange your paper with a classmate who has done the same assignment. Point out the fallacies in each other's papers.
4. Write a one-page essay criticizing the view that Canada should continue extracting oil from northern Alberta's oil sands. Make use of at least the genetic fallacy and the slippery slope fallacy. Then write a one-page critique of your own paper, making sure to point out the fallacies and explaining why they are problematic.

Notes

1. The inspiration for this unconventional categorization comes primarily from Ludwig F. Schlecht, "Classifying Fallacies Logically," *Teaching Philosophy* 14, no. 1 (1991): 53–64, and Gregory Bassham et al., *Critical Thinking: A Student's Introduction* (San Francisco: McGraw Hill, 2002).
2. Archbishop Richard Gagnon, *Friday Report*, 18 June 2021. https://m.facebook.com/watch/?v=786,508,648,662,312&_rdr. Accessed 23 June 2021.
3. Vanessa Lu, "How to Sell Toll Message: Appeal to Emotion, Youth," *Toronto Star*, 14 July 2010.
4. Reported in Richard Whately, *Elements of Logic* (London: Longmans, Green, and Co., 1826).
5. Stuart Chambers, "No Evidence of a 'Slippery Slope' on Medically Assisted Death," *Ottawa Citizen*, 3 February 2020. https://ottawacitizen.com/opinion/columnists/chambers-no-evidence-of-a-slippery-slope-on-medically-assisted-death. Accessed 4 June 2022.

PART THREE

Arguments

Deductive Reasoning: Categorical Logic

Chapter Objectives

Statements and Classes

You will be able to

- define subject term, predicate term, copula, quantifier, quantity, and quality.
- memorize the four standard-form categorical statements.

Translations and Standard Form

You will be able to

- translate ordinary statements into standard categorical form.
- translate singular statements into standard form.

Diagramming Categorical Statements

You will be able to

- construct a Venn diagram for any categorical statement.
- memorize the Venn diagrams for the four standard-form categorical statements.
- use Venn diagrams to tell if two statements are, or are not, equivalent.

Assessing Categorical Syllogisms

You will be able to

- understand the structure of categorical syllogisms.
- check the validity of a categorical argument by drawing Venn diagrams.

For centuries, philosophers, monks, scientists, linguists, and students have been enthralled by logic. Yes, *logic*. For many people, including some great thinkers such as Aristotle, Medhatithi Gautama, and the Chinese scholar known as Mozi (in ancient times) and Gottfried Leibniz and Ada Lovelace (in the last two centuries), logic has been, ironically, a *passion*—something deemed worthy of deep study and long devotion. For hundreds of years, logic (along with philosophy) was a required course in universities and was regarded as one of the grand pillars upon which a liberal arts education was based (the others were grammar, rhetoric, arithmetic, music, astronomy, and geometry). Even today scholars continue to be drawn into the depths of logic, never seeming to tire of exploration and application.

"Logic is the owner's manual for your brain. If you want your brain to serve you well rather than poorly, you owe it to yourself to learn—and apply—logic."

—Alexei Marcoux

But why do they bother? Why do they seem to think that logic is anything other than the dry and dusty preoccupation of dry and dusty philosophers? Well, maybe they bother because the study and use of logic, like the study and use of mathematics, is an exercise in exactitude, precision, clarity, and—above all—definite answers. All of which can be very satisfying. Or perhaps they bother because logic is the study of good reasoning or thinking and therefore should be part of every decision and every judgment we make.

"Bad reasoning as well as good reasoning is possible; and this fact is the foundation of the practical side of logic."

—Charles Sanders Peirce

Logic also produces real results for us. Out of the study of logic have come discoveries now used in electronic engineering, set theory, linguistics, mathematics, and, of course, philosophy. Investigations in logic have yielded insights that made the invention of computers possible. (See the box "Logic and Computers" in Chapter 7.)

We begin our study of formal logic by looking, in this chapter, at **categorical logic**. The basic unit of concern in categorical logic is the *statement component*. In categorical logic, we study the relationships not between entire statements but between components known as the subject and predicate of a statement. In Chapter 7, we will look at formal methods for assessing the relationships between entire statements, or propositions, when we study propositional logic.

categorical logic
A form of logic whose focus is categorical statements, which make assertions about categories, or classes, of things.

Both types of reasoning—categorical and propositional—are deductive, and in both our ultimate goal is the evaluation of arguments. In propositional logic, which is discussed in Chapter 7, this task is made easier with "truth tables." In categorical logic the primary tools are diagrams and calculation rules.

In categorical reasoning the statements or claims of interest are **categorical statements**—those that make simple assertions about categories, or classes, of things. They say how certain classes of things are, or are not, included in other classes of things. For example: "All cows are vegetarians," "No gardeners are plumbers," or "Some businesspeople are cheats."

categorical statement
A statement or claim that makes a simple assertion about categories, or classes, of things.

Categorical logic is unavoidable in daily life. Without thinking much about the process, we often use arguments composed of categorical statements.

We may reason, for example, that no pocket knives—no things that would be included in that category—are among the things that are permitted on a commercial airplane, because no sharp instruments are things allowed

Learning to master categorical logic is a big part of childhood!

on a commercial airplane and, after all, pocket knives definitely are sharp instruments. In a real-life conversation, we wouldn't state the argument so formally (and awkwardly), and we would probably make one of these premises implicit because it's too obvious to mention. Also, this whole process of reasoning would likely happen in seconds, with the argument zipping through our heads in a flash while we pack for the trip.

There are several good reasons why categorical logic—first formulated by Aristotle over 2000 years ago—is still around. Chief among these reasons are that (1) it is part of everyday reasoning and (2) understanding its rules leads to better, clearer thinking. If that is so, then learning how to use it well can only help us.

6.1 Statements and Classes

The words in categorical statements that name classes, or categories, of things are called *terms*. Each categorical statement has both a **subject term** and a **predicate term**. Look, for example, at this claim:

subject term
The first class, or group, named in a standard-form categorical statement.

predicate term
The second class, or group, named in a standard-form categorical statement.

All bears are omnivores.

The subject term here is *bears*, and the predicate term is *omnivores*. The statement says that the class of *bears—that is, of all animals that are within that large and varied group*—is included within the class of *omnivores*. We can express the *form* of the statement like this:

All *S* are *P*.

By convention, *S* stands for the subject term in a categorical statement; *P* stands for the predicate term.

This kind of statement—All *S* are *P*—is one of four **standard forms of categorical statements**. Here are all four forms together:

standard-form categorical statement
In categorical logic, a categorical statement that takes one of these four forms:

1. All *S* are *P*. (All bears are omnivores.)
2. No *S* are *P*. (No bears are omnivores.)
3. Some *S* are *P*. (Some bears are omnivores.)
4. Some *S* are not *P*. (Some bears are not omnivores.)

1. All *S* are *P*. (All bears are omnivores.)
2. No *S* are *P*. (No bears are omnivores.)
3. Some *S* are *P*. (Some bears are omnivores.)
4. Some *S* are not *P*. (Some bears are not omnivores.)

At this point, do not worry about whether you think these statements are true or false. What we are concerned with for the time being is the *structure* of these statements.

Standard-form statement 2, "No *S* are *P*," asserts that no member of the *S* class is included in the *P* class (no members of the class of bears are part of the class of omnivores). Statement 3, "Some *S* are *P*," asserts that some members of the *S* class are also members of the *P* class (some members of the class of bears are also members of the class of omnivores). Statement 4, "Some *S* are not *P*," asserts that some members of the *S* class are not members of the *P* class (some members of the class of bears are not members of the class of omnivores).

For the sake of simplicity, the terms in these statements about bears are single words, just nouns naming classes of things. But subject and predicate terms can also consist of noun phrases and pronouns. Noun phrases are used because several words may be needed to specify a class. Depending on the topic at hand, a simple noun like *bears* won't do to describe the category we are talking about, but a noun phrase like "bears that occur naturally in North America" will work well.

In standard-form categorical statements, subject and predicate terms can't be *anything but* nouns, pronouns, and noun phrases. Only nouns, pronouns, and noun phrases can properly designate classes. So the statement "All bears are omnivores" is in standard form because *bears* and *omnivores* are nouns; however, "All bears are omnivorous" is not in standard form, because "omnivorous" is an adjective, not a noun that designates a category.

As you might guess, many categorical statements you'll run into in everyday communications don't strictly fit any of these four patterns. But they eventually must be made to fit if you want to easily evaluate the validity of arguments containing these statements. So part of the job of assessing such arguments is to translate the categorical statements found "in the wild" into the tamer and clearer configurations of the standard forms. The challenge is to do these translations while being faithful to the meaning of the original statement.

To translate categorical statements accurately, you need to know more about how they're put together. Categorical statements have four parts and several characteristics expressed in these parts. You already know about two of these parts, the subject term and the predicate term. They are joined together by a third part called the **copula**, a linking verb—either *are* or *are not*.

The fourth part is the **quantifier**, a word that expresses the **quantity**, or number, of a categorical statement. The acceptable quantifiers are *all*, *no*, or *some*. The quantifiers *all* and *no* in front of a categorical statement tell us that it's *universal*. A categorical statement that begins with either *all* or *no* applies to every member of the class being discussed. The quantifier *some* at the beginning of a categorical statement says that the statement is *particular*—it applies to at least one member of a class.

Categorical statements can vary not only in quantity but also in the characteristic of **quality**, being either *affirmative* or *negative*. A categorical statement that *affirms* that a class is entirely or partly included in another class is said to be affirmative in quality, whereas a categorical statement that *denies* that a class is entirely or partly included in another class is said to be negative in quality.

copula
One of four components of a standard-form categorical statement; a linking verb—either *are* or *are not*—that joins the subject term and the predicate term.

quantifier
In categorical statements, a word used to indicate the number of things with specified characteristics. The acceptable quantifiers are *all*, *no*, or *some*. The quantifiers *all* or *no* in front of a categorical statement tell us that it's *universal*—it applies to every member of a class. The quantifier *some* at the beginning of a categorical statement says that the statement is *particular*—it applies to some but not necessarily all members of a class.

quantity
In categorical statements, the attribute of number, specified by the words *all*, *no*, or *some*.

quality
A characteristic of a categorical statement, determined by whether the statement affirms or denies that a class is entirely or partly included in another class. A categorical statement that affirms is said to be affirmative in quality; one that denies is said to be negative in quality.

The statement, "All diamonds are hard," for example, is affirmative, while the statement "No diamond is edible" is negative.

With this technical vocabulary, we can describe each of the standard forms of statements noted earlier.

1. All *S* are *P*. (All bears are omnivores.)
   This standard-form statement has a universal quantity and an affirmative quality. It *affirms* that *all* bears are included in the class of omnivores. So we characterize it as a *universal affirmative* statement, or claim.
2. No *S* are *P*. (No bears are omnivores.)
   This one *denies* that *all* bears are included in the class of omnivores. Put another way, the whole class of bears is *excluded* from the class of omnivores. It's a *universal negative* statement.
3. Some *S* are *P*. (Some bears are omnivores.)
   This one *affirms* that only *some* bears are included in the class of omnivores. It's a *particular affirmative* statement.
4. Some *S* are not *P*. (Some bears are not omnivores.)
   This one is referring to some bears—some particular subset of bears—and denies that *those* bears are included in the class of omnivores. It doesn't refer to the whole class of bears, just as statement 3 doesn't refer to the whole class. But in this case the statement denies, instead of affirms, that the partial class of bears is included in the class of omnivores. It's a *particular negative* statement.

Here are the four standard forms of categorical statements again with their quality and quantity listed:

A: All *S* are *P*. (universal affirmative)
E: No *S* are *P*. (universal negative)
I: Some *S* are *P*. (particular affirmative)
O: Some *S* are not *P*. (particular negative)

Notice that, in the way we've listed them this time, the statements are preceded not by numbers but by the letters A, E, I, and O. These letters are the traditional designations for the four standard forms of categorical statements and have been used this way by logicians for hundreds of years. We can say then, for example, that this or that statement is an A-statement or an O-statement, indicating the pattern of the arguments with an easy shorthand.

Something important to remember, even if it's obvious, is that all categorical statements should fit into one of these four standard forms and all statements that do fit into one of these have the *same* form. For example, "All bears are omnivores" and "All computers are electronic devices" are statements that share the same form—specifically, they are both A-statements.

Critical Thinking and the Media

Categorically You

Half a century ago, an ad for L'Oréal hair products invited women into a category everyone wants to be in, namely the category of worthy people. The slogan the company used? "L'Oréal. Because You're Worth It."

One of the ways advertisers attempt to persuade is by putting people into categories. In particular, they do so by trying to tell you what categories you are in, and what sorts of products people "like you" buy.

Think of the Home Depot slogan that says, "Home Depot: How Doers Get More Done." Taken literally, it's just a statement about a certain kind of people, namely doers—people who get things done. But the implication is evident: you want to see yourself as a doer, don't you? You're action-oriented, aren't you? The syllogism them becomes clear:

P1. Home Depot is for doers.
P2. You are a doer.
C. Therefore you should shop at Home Depot.

When made explicit, this might feel like a compelling argument. After all, that's what good deductive arguments do—they compel us to believe. But of course, a critical thinker will want to ask some question, such as "Even if Home Depot is for doers, is it the best place for doers to shop?" and "Is Home Depot the place to buy the stuff for doing the sort of stuff I really value doing?"

Exercise 6.1

Answers to exercises marked with an asterisk (*) may be found in Appendix B, Answers to Exercises.

For each of the following statements, identify the subject and predicate terms and the name of the form (universal affirmative, universal negative, particular affirmative, or particular negative). Also, state the traditional letter designation for each form (A, E, I, O).

1. Most dogs do not like mushrooms.*
2. No scientists are atheists.
3. No cats that have lived over 15 years in a domestic setting are pets free of health problems.
4. All urbanites who wear lumberjack jackets and big bushy beards are hipsters.
5. All theologians who have studied arguments for the existence of God are scholars with serious misgivings about the traditional notion of omnipotence.*
6. No professors lack education.
7. Some dogs are German Shepherds.
8. Some people who play the stock market are not millionaires.*

9. No taxpayers from the 2022 tax year are tax cheats.
10. No Canadian banks that had dealings with Enron are institutions that deserve our business!
11. Some of the protestors at the anti-mask rally were not well informed.
12. The Loch Ness Monster is fictional.*
13. No Indigenous groups have voluntarily given up their land.
14. Some terrorists are Canadian citizens.
15. Anyone who sells homeopathic treatments is either delusional or a fraudster.
16. No "new Canadians" are supporters of changes in the immigration rules.*
17. All child-abuse caseworkers are overburdened civil servants.

6.2 Translations and Standard Form

This is worth repeating: we translate ordinary statements into standard-form categorical statements so that we can handle them more efficiently. We want to handle them efficiently so that we can more easily evaluate the validity of arguments

Food for Thought

Categorically Musical

Believe it or not, categorical claims show up in the titles of many popular songs, throughout the years. Take a look at these, and see if you can figure out what each would look like if put into standard form. (And no, "No People Are People Who Have to Know" is not exactly a catchy title!)

- "Everybody Wants to Rule the World" (Tears for Fears, 1985)
- "All My Ex's Live in Texas" (George Strait, 1987)
- "I Wanna Dance With Somebody (Who Loves Me)" (Whitney Houston, 1987)
- "You Gotta Love Someone" (Elton John, 1990)
- "All I Want For Christmas Is You" (Mariah Carey, 1994)
- "No One Else Comes Close" (the Backstreet Boys, 1999)
- "Everybody's Got a Story" (Amanda Marshall, 2001)
- "Somebody That I Used to Know" (Gotye, feat. Kembra, 2011)
- "Nobody Has To Know" (Kranium, 2013)
- "Some People Are Worth Melting For" (Christophe Beck, from *Frozen*, 2013)
- "Beer Never Broke My Heart" (Luke Combs, 2019)

Each of the above titles has something in them hinting that a categorical claim is being made. The following are even less obviously categorical, but they really can be transformed into logically identical categorical statements. Can you see how?

- "You Need To Calm Down" (Taylor Swift, 2017)
- "It Ain't Me" (Kygo & Selena Gomez, 2017)
- "God Is a Woman" (Ariana Grande, 2018)
- "Truth Hurts" (Lizzo, 2019)

composed of categorical statements. Translation is necessary to bring out the underlying structure of statements. It is also important because ordinary language is too imprecise and ambiguous to use in the analysis of statements and arguments. You will appreciate this fact more as you work with categorical statements.

Translating statements into standard form is a straightforward process consisting of a few simple steps and some rules of thumb. Knowing the steps and the rules is important, but getting some *practice* translating statements is vital if you want to know how to translate fast and accurately. If you don't understand a particular point, you'll have an easier time if you go over it until you do rather than skipping it and looking at it later.

Just as a reminder, here's the pattern of all standard-form categorical statements:

Quantifier . . . Subject Term . . . Copula . . . Predicate Term

You need to know how to handle each of these parts. Since the copula must always be either *are* or *are not*, you don't have to spend a lot time trying to determine the correct verb. But pinning down the terms and quantifiers is a little more challenging.

6.2.1 Terms

In translating statements, your first order of business is usually to identify the terms and ensure that they designate proper classes. Once you identify the terms and distinguish the subject term from the predicate term, you'll know in what order the terms must appear in the statement because the subject term must always precede the predicate term. Identifying the terms, though, often involves rewording them so they actually name classes. Consider these translations, which we have done for you:

[Original] All dogs are loyal.
[Translation] All dogs *are* loyal animals.

Review Notes

The Four Standard-Form Categorical Statements

A: All *S* are *P*. (universal affirmative)	"All cars are Hondas."
E: No *S* are *P*. (universal negative)	"No cars are Hondas."
I: Some *S* are *P*. (particular affirmative)	"Some cars are Hondas."
O: Some *S* are not *P*. (particular negative)	"Some cars are not Hondas."

[Original] Some guys have all the luck.
[Translation] Some guys *are* people who have all the luck.

[Original] No nations can thrive without fair immigration policies.
[Translation] No nations *are* things that can thrive without fair immigration policies.

Sometimes it's easy to locate statement terms but not as easy to tell which is the subject term and which is the predicate term. This can happen when the order of the subject and predicate is reversed:

Beyond the mountains stood the redwood trees.

Here the subject is "the redwood trees." The sentence has a normal variation of subject–predicate order, common in English. If you understand the structure of such grammatical reversals, you should be able to identify the true subject and predicate terms. To see this, ask yourself: what is the sentence *about*? Notice that the key verb is *stood*. Who or what is doing the standing? It's the redwood trees, and so they are the subject of the sentence.

Difficulty distinguishing subject and predicate terms can also arise when the word *only* is in a statement. For example, which is the subject term and which is the predicate in these A-statements?

1. Only good listeners are wise advisers.
2. Only if something is a music file is it an. m4a file.
3. Hamburgers are the only real junk food.
4. The only crimes prosecuted are murders.

We can figure out statements 1 and 2 by using this formula: *The words "only" and "only if" precede the predicate term in an A-statement.* So the correct translations are:

1. All wise advisers are good listeners.
2. All. m4a files are music files.

The translations of statements 3 and 4 follow this formula: *The words "the only" precede the subject term in an A-statement.* Therefore the correct translations are:

3. All real junk food is hamburgers.
4. All prosecuted crimes are murders.

Now, what are the terms in these statements?

5. 2021 is not a year that will be remembered happily.
6. Lake Louise is Canada's happiest city.
7. Tuesday is the most depressing day of the week.
8. *Come from Away* is an amazing movie.
9. Elvira Kurt is a Toronto-based comedian.

"Intuition is a suspension of logic due to impatience."

—Rita Mae Brown (activist and feminist, 1944–)

Food for Thought

The Categorical Logic of Biology

Humans, as we all know, are mammals. And mammals are a category of animals characterized chiefly by the fact that they have fur or hair and that they produce milk for their young. But humans are also in other important biological categories: we are primates (like monkeys and gorillas); we are vertebrates (we have backbones, just as do sharks and eagles); and most fundamentally we are animals (just like jellyfish and mosquitoes). The system according to which all species of life on earth are sorted into categories is something we owe to eighteenth-century Swedish scientist Carl Linnaeus. Linnaeus is considered the father of taxonomy, the science of sorting things—including biological organisms, but other things too—into categories according to their characteristics. In some cases, the categorizations proposed by Linnaeus caused controversy: he argued, for example, that humans and monkeys were both part of a larger category, because humans and monkeys are anatomically very, very similar. Generations of scientists—now aided by DNA tests—have confirmed that humans and monkeys (as well as chimpanzees and baboons) are all part of the same branch of the great tree of life.

National Portrait Gallery of Sweden/Wikipedia

Carl Linnaeus (1707–1778) is considered the father of taxonomy, the science of sorting things. Linnaeus's focus was on sorting biological organisms, but taxonomy has many other uses.

These are known as **singular statements**. Each one asserts something about a single person or thing, including objects, places, and times. Each subject term is a noun (including names), pronoun, or noun phrase referring to an individual, particular item. In a way, the predicate terms specify classes but, alas, the subject terms don't. We can transform such statements, though, into universal statements (A-statements or E-statements). The trick is to think of each subject term as naming a class in which there's just one member. We can, for example, treat the subject term in statement 5 ("2021") as designating a class with 2021 as one member of that class, like this:

singular statements
In categorical logic, statements that assert something about a single person or thing, including objects, places, and times.

5. No years identical to 2021 are years that will be remembered happily.

We can translate our other singular statements in similar fashion:

6. All places identical to Lake Louise are places that are Canada's happiest city.
7. All days identical to Tuesday are the most depressing days of the week.

8. All things identical to the film *Come from Away* are amazing movies.
9. All persons identical to Elvira Kurt are Toronto-based comedians.

Now we can see more clearly that statements 6–9 are A-statements and that statement 5 is an E-statement.

Granted, translations of ordinary statements into standard-form categorical statements can sometimes sound awkward, as the preceding translations surely do. But when we translate statements in this way, we put them into a form that makes their logical connections transparent—which is handy when we're trying to check the validity of complex arguments.

6.2.2 Quantifiers

Some quantifiers may be in non-standard form, and some may be unexpressed. Consider these statements:

1. Every field-hockey player is an athlete.
2. Whoever is an artist is a genius.
3. Sharks are really good swimmers.
4. Nothing for sale is truly valuable.
5. Comets are ice balls.

Each is a universal statement with a non-standard or unexpressed quantifier. Here are the translations with the proper quantifiers:

1. All field-hockey players are athletes.
2. All artists are geniuses.
3. All sharks are really good swimmers.
4. No items for sale are truly valuable.
5. All comets are ice balls.

Statements 1, 2, and 4 have non-standard quantifiers; statements 3 and 5 have unexpressed quantifiers. Fortunately, most non-standard quantifiers are fairly easy to decipher. "Every professor," for example, obviously means all the professors. "Nothing" and "none" mean not any, which refers to all of them, whatever they are. Usually, unexpressed quantifiers are readily understood because of the nature of the terms. The statement "Sharks are really good swimmers" clearly refers to all sharks, not just some of them—any speaker who meant to say this only about some sharks likely would have been careful to say so. In some statements, though, the unexpressed quantifier is not obvious, as, for example, in "Trent University students are radicals." Is it "*All* Trent students" or "*Some* Trent students"? When in doubt, be charitable: assume that the speaker intends the quantifier that you think would make the statement most likely to be true. In this case, "All Trent students . . ." is a sweeping generalization that's unlikely to apply to every single student at Trent University. The claim more likely to be true is "Some Trent students . . ."

Food for Thought

Categorical Logic in Disguise . . .

Plenty of non-standard statements are equivalents of categorical statements in standard form.

A-Statement: "All *S* Are *P*."

Any weakness can be used against you.
Something is a real meal only if it includes meat.
Whatever is a capybara is a rodent.
Every dentist is university trained.
If something does not have wheels, then it is not a car.
Only professors are experts.
Good logicians make good mathematicians.
Every CEO is a good leader.
Only if a species produces milk for its young is it a mammal.

E-Statement: "No *S* Are *P*."

Nothing blue is an orange.
None of the meats contains fibre.
It is false that some vegetables are fruits.
If anyone is a baker, then she is not a banker.
All reptiles are non-birds.
Provinces are not territories.
Nothing that is a mind is a body.

I-Statement: "Some *S* Are *P*."

At least one astronaut is a hero.
A few carnival games are scams.
Many Nova Scotians are Haligonians.
There are doctors who are painters.
Most petty thieves are morons.
Several countries are landlocked.

O-Statement: "Some *S* Are Not *P*."

Most Scots are not highlanders.
There are non-atheist philosophers.
Canadian soldiers are not always peacekeepers.
A few rock stars are not attention-seekers.
Some philosophers are non-believers.
Some non-believers are philosophers.
Not all skiers are Canadian.
Many evergreen trees are not suitable Christmas trees.

Now consider these statements:

6. There are government workers who are spies.
7. Most social media influencers are snobs.
8. Several politicians are space aliens.

These are all particular categorical statements. Their translations are:

6. Some government workers are spies.
7. Some social media influencers are snobs.
8. Some politicians are space aliens.

The quantifier *some* is appropriate in all these statements because in logic it means "at least one." We therefore have only two options for expressing quantity in categorical statements: *all* and *fewer than all*. "Most," "a few," "several," "almost all," and similar terms are all translated as "some." Part of the reason for logic's restrictive definition of "some" is that, in everyday language, "some" is extremely vague. The word could mean "most," "two or three," "10 or more," or "many." Who knows? Logic, though, needs precision—more precision than is found in ordinary discourse.

Exercise 6.2

Answers to exercises marked with an asterisk (*) may be found in Appendix B, Answers to Exercises.

Translate each of the following statements into standard categorical form, and say whether the form is A, E, I, or O.

1. All Montreal Canadiens fans are loyal to their team.*
2. The only players who didn't suit up for the opening game were the ones injured in training.
3. Not every professor is an engaging speaker.
4. Most sharks will try to bite you if they get the chance.
5. Only cellphone companies that keep up with the latest technology are good investments.*
6. If it doesn't have DNA, then it can't be a life-form found on earth.
7. "People with pinched faces often have poisonous hearts." (Chinese proverb)
8. It's impossible for any mammal to also have gills.
9. "All intelligent thoughts have already been thought." (Johann Wolfgang von Goethe)*
10. "If it's worth doing, it's worth doing right."

11. All people who have not already been vaccinated should be found and convinced to get vaccinated.
12. "Brave are the hearts that beat beneath Scottish skies." ("Scotland the Brave")
13. Some things are meant to be forgotten.*
14. Very few senior citizens like rap music.
15. "There is no excellence without difficulty." (Ovid)
16. "All's well that ends well." (Shakespeare)

Exercise 6.3

Follow the instructions given for Exercise 6.2.

1. Only a fool tests the depth of the water with both feet. (African proverb)*
2. Any political party that gets less than 10 per cent of the vote in a general election should be considered a minor player in Canadian politics.
3. "People who wish to salute the free and independent side of their evolutionary character acquire cats." (Anna Quindlen)
4. All digital assistants like Apple's Siri are non-persons.*
5. Nothing that satisfies the heart is a material thing.*
6. It's not often that you see CEOs who aren't overpaid.
7. Work hard, and you'll soon have a good command of categorical logic.
8. Most treatments said to be part of "alternative medicine" are unproven.*
9. There are people among us here today who will one day rise to greatness.
10. "Anyone who has ever struggled with poverty knows how extremely expensive it is to be poor." (James Baldwin)
11. Some Acadians settled on what is called the "French Shore" of Nova Scotia.
12. Friday is the only day that gives her any joy.*
13. Many critical thinking textbooks make good bedtime reading.
14. "As long as poverty, injustice, and gross inequality persist in our world, none of us can truly rest." (Nelson Mandela)
15. The picture hanging on the wall is crooked.*
16. "[P]eople I really trust, none of them were cool in their younger years." (Taylor Swift)
17. "He who is being carried does not realize how far the town is." (African proverb)
18. Only you can prevent forest fires!
19. It is not the case that all birds are non-flightless birds.
20. "All great achievements require time." (Maya Angelou)*

6.3 Diagramming Categorical Statements

Venn diagrams
Diagrams consisting of overlapping circles that graphically represent the relationships between subject and predicate terms in categorical statements.

If you want more help in understanding the relationships between subject and predicate terms, you're in luck. You can represent such relationships visually with the use of **Venn diagrams** (named after the nineteenth-century British logician and mathematician John Venn). The diagrams consist of overlapping circles, each one representing a class specified by a term in a categorical statement. Here's an example:

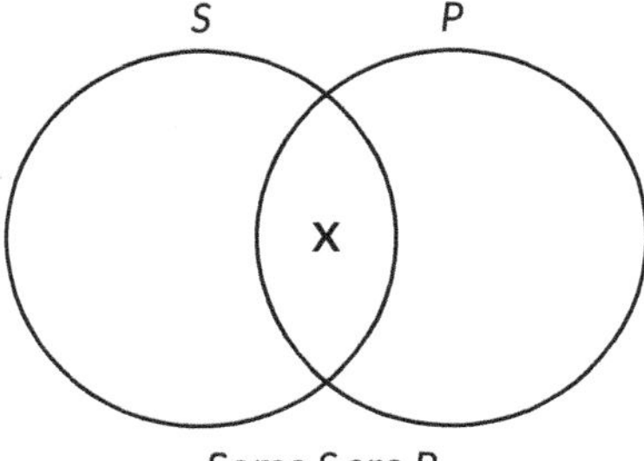

Some *S* are *P*.

This is the diagram for an I-statement: "Some *S* are *P*." The circle on the left represents the class of *S*, the circle on the right, the class of *P*. The area on the left contains only members of the *S* class; the area on the right contains only members of the *P* class. The area where the circles overlap is where any individuals that are both *S* members and *P* members would be, if they exist. The X in the overlapped area, however, gives more specific information. It shows that *at least one S* member is a *P* member. That is, there is at least one *S* that also is a *P*. This diagram, of course, represents *any* statement of the form "Some *S* are *P*"—like, for instance, "Some plants are cacti." The X on the diagram where the circles overlap, then, would mean that *at least one* plant is a cactus. The area of overlap between those two categories is not empty.

Now here's the diagram for an O-statement—"Some *S* are not *P*":

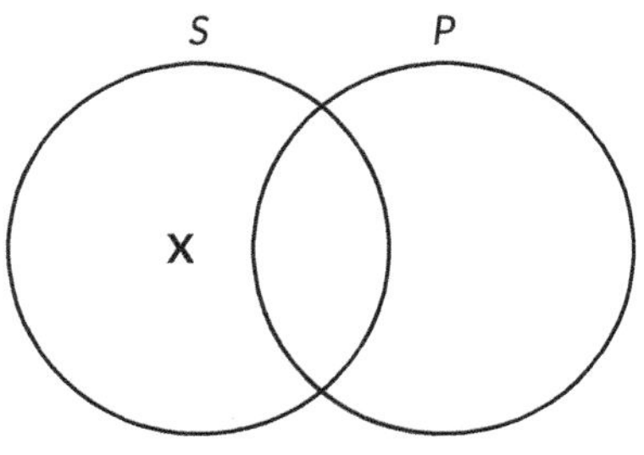

Some *S* are not *P*.

Here the X is in the *S* circle but outside the *P* circle, indicating that at least one *S* is not a *P*. In our plant example (in which the *S* circle represents the class of plants and the *P* circle represents the class of cacti), this diagram would show that at least one plant is not a cactus.

Here's the diagram for an A-statement—"All *S* are *P*":

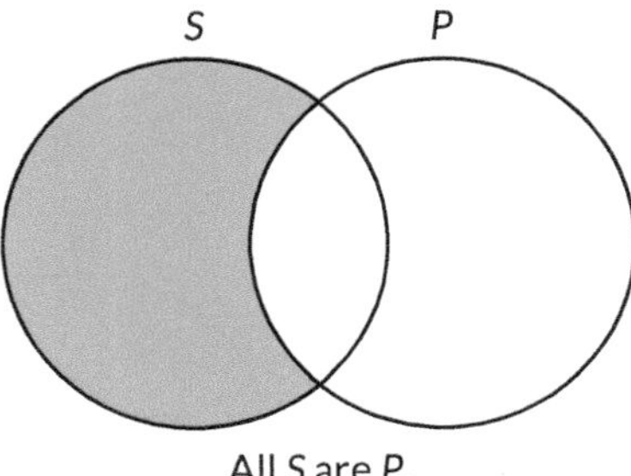

All *S* are *P*.

This diagram asserts that all members of the *S* class are also members of the *P* class ("All plants are cacti"). Notice that the part of the diagram where the *S* circle does not overlap the *P* circle is shaded, or "blacked out," showing that that area is "empty," or without any members. (If you want, think of it this way: in the shaded area, the lights are out because no one is home!) And this means that there are no members of *S* that are not also members of *P*. The remaining part of the *S* circle overlaps with the *P* circle, showing that *S* members—all of them—are also *P* members.

Finally, here is the diagram for an E-statement—"No *S* are *P*":

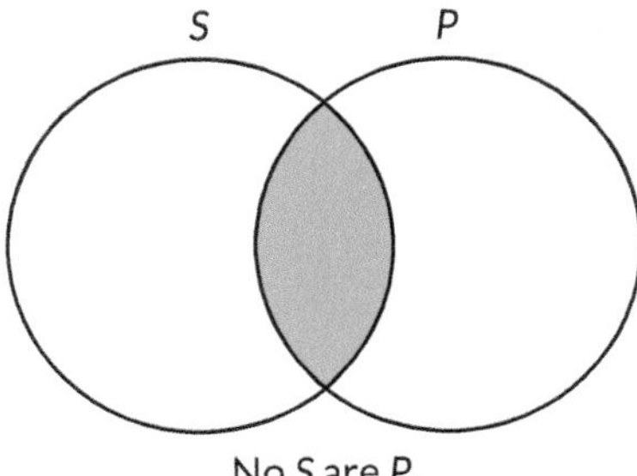

No *S* are *P*.

Here the area where the *S* circle and the *P* circle overlap is shaded (empty), meaning that there is no situation in which *S* overlaps with *P* (in which members of *S* are also members of *P*). So no members of *S* are also members of *P* ("No plants are cacti").

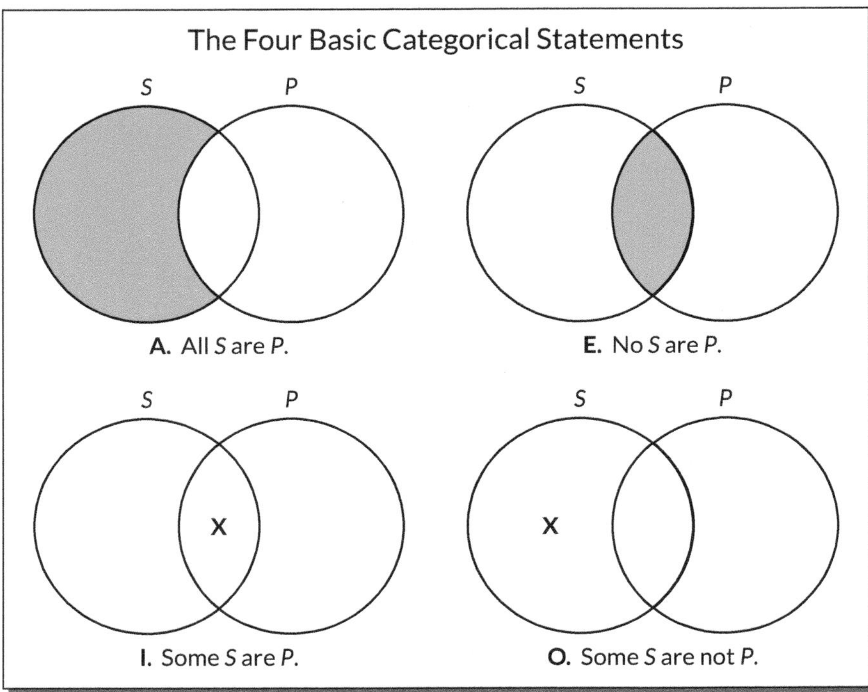

Venn diagrams can come in handy when you want to know whether two categorical statements are equivalent—that is, whether they say exactly the same thing—because sometimes we can say the same thing—make the identical logical claim—in two different ways. If the diagrams for the statements are identical, then the statements are logically equivalent.

Let's say that you want to know whether the following two statements say the same thing:

No *S* are *P*.
No *P* are *S*.

Review Notes

Three Steps to Diagramming a Categorical Statement

1. Draw two overlapping circles, each one representing a term in the statement.
2. Label the circles with the letters representing the terms.
3. Shade an area of a circle to show that an area is empty; insert an X to show that at least one member of a class is also a member of another class or that at least one member of a class is outside of another class.

On the surface, they look different. But are they really? If you diagram them both, you get your answer:

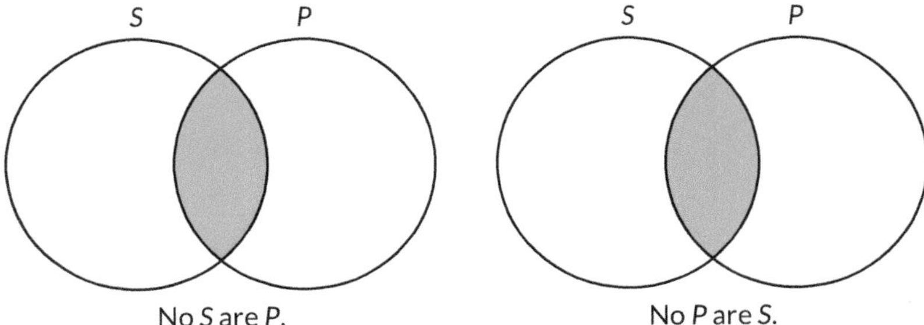

You can see that the diagrams are identical—they both show the area of overlap between the two circles as shaded, signifying that there are no members of *S* that are also members of *P* and vice versa. So the first statement ("No *S* are *P*," an E-statement) says the same thing as the second statement ("No *P* are *S*").

Likewise, if we compare the diagrams for "Some *S* are *P*" (I-statement) and "Some *P* are *S*," we can see that these statements are also equivalent:

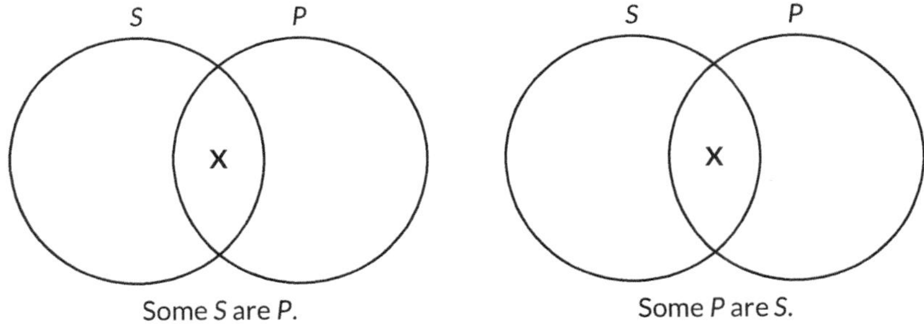

On the other hand, by comparing diagrams we can see that A-statements and E-statements are *not* equivalent (something you knew already, of course):

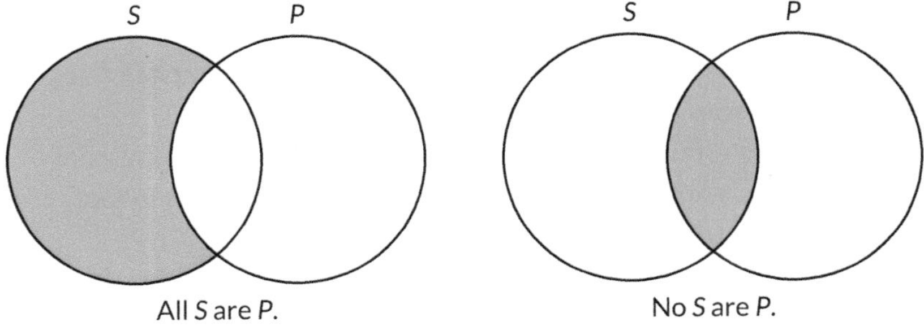

Let's examine one final pair of statements:

All *S* are *P*.
No *S* are non-*P*.

The diagrams clearly show that these are equivalent:

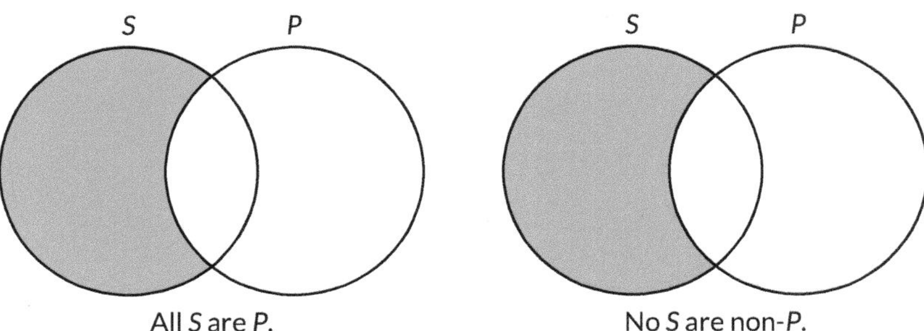

Exercise 6.4

Answers to exercises marked with an asterisk (*) may be found in Appendix B, Answers to Exercises.

Construct Venn diagrams for each of the following statements. Specify both the subject and predicate terms. If necessary, translate the statement into standard form before diagramming (A, E, I, or O).

1. No one is exempt from federal income tax.*
2. "No person has the right to rain on your dreams." (Marian Wright Edelman, children's rights activist)
3. Not in any country on Earth is bribery legal.
4. Some mammals live most of their lives in the water.
5. "Nothing is more useless in a developing nation's economy than a gun." (King Hussein I of Jordan)*
6. One of the few philosophers whose ideas have truly shaped the modern world is Adam Smith.
7. Some books are not written by either J.K. Rowling or Stephen King.
8. Some news stories are written by computers.*
9. "Into each life some rain must fall." (Henry Wadsworth Longfellow)
10. Some people with excellent reputations are not persons of excellent character.
11. The man who invented matches didn't get rich from his invention.
12. Every corporation has social obligations.*
13. No stone was left unturned.
14. You can always rely on Acme knives because they never break and never get dull.
15. "Few friendships could survive the moodiness of love affairs." (Mason Cooley)

Exercise 6.5

Construct Venn diagrams for each statement in the following pairs, and then say whether the statements are equivalent.

1. No *S* are *P*; No *P* are *S*.*
2. Some *S* are *P*; Some *P* are *S*.
3. All *S* are *P*; All *P* are *S*.*
4. All *S* are *P*; Some *P* are non-*S*.
5. All *P* are non-*S*; No *S* are *P*.
6. All *S* are non-*P*; All *P* are non-*S*.*
7. No non-*S* are *P*; No non-*P* are *S*.
8. No *S* are *P*; No *P* are *S*.
9. Some *S* are not *P*; Some *P* are not *S*.*
10. All *S* are non-*P*; No *P* are *S*.

6.4 Assessing Categorical Syllogisms

Once you understand the workings of categorical statements, you're ready to explore the dynamics of categorical arguments, or—more precisely—categorical syllogisms. As we saw in Chapter 3, a syllogism is a deductive argument made up of three statements: two premises and a conclusion. A **categorical syllogism** is one consisting of three categorical statements (A, E, I, or O) interlinked in a specific way. You can see the interlinking structure in this categorical syllogism:

categorical syllogism
A deductive argument consisting of three categorical statements.

"Logical consequences are the scarecrows of fools and the beacons of wise men."

—Thomas Henry Huxley

1. All elected officials are civil servants.
2. All politicians are elected officials.
3. Therefore, all politicians are civil servants.

If we diagram this argument as we did in Chapter 3, we come up with this structure:

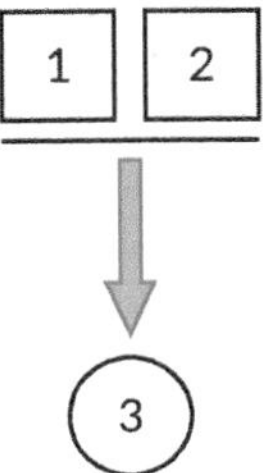

But this kind of diagram, though handy for understanding the overall structure of the argument, isn't much help here because it doesn't reveal the internal components and interlinking structure of the statements. Notice that each categorical statement has, as usual, two terms. But there are a total of only three terms in a categorical syllogism, each term being mentioned twice but in different

Everyday Problems and Decisions

Logical Errors and Racism

Being bad at categorical logic is at the heart of an awful lot of racism and general prejudice against various ethnic, racial, and religious groups. For example, in late 2020 an act of terrorism—a mass shooting—took place in Vienna, Austria. The killer was Muslim. Four people were killed, and twenty-two more were injured. Such incidents are terrible tragedies. And the tragedy of such events is only amplified by the unthinking racism that often follows. Many people, unfortunately, may have leapt hastily from the fact that the killer was Muslim to a general hatred or mistrust of Muslims. Consider what the relevant categorical syllogism would look like.

(1) Some killers (namely, the Vienna shooter) are Muslims.
(2) All killers are terrorists.
(3) Therefore, all Muslims are terrorists.

You can easily construct a Venn diagram to demonstrate that this is a flawed syllogism. That is, the premises, even if they are true, are incapable of providing support for the conclusion. This is particularly important to see, given that the conclusion of this argument has led so many people to act badly toward their fellow human beings.

A good command of categorical logic can save you from being wrong about—and then acting unethically toward—entire groups of people.

statements. So in the preceding argument, *politicians* appears in statements 2 and 3, *elected officials* in 1 and 2, and *civil servants* in 1 and 3.

In a categorical syllogism, we refer to the predicate term in the conclusion (*civil servants*, in this case) as the *predicate term* for the whole argument. The predicate term always also appears in one of the premises (premise 1, in the example above). The subject term in the conclusion is treated as the *subject term* for the whole argument. The subject term always also occurs in one of the premises (premise 2, in the argument above). The other term, the one that appears once in each premise but not in the conclusion, is referred to as the *middle term*. If we map out the argument with the terms labelled in this way, here's what we get:

Premise (1) [Middle term] [Predicate term].
Premise (2) [Subject term] [Middle term].
Conclusion (3) Therefore, [Subject term] [Predicate term].

We can symbolize this argument form with letters:

(1) All *M* are *P*.
(2) All *S* are *M*.
(3) Therefore, all *S* are *P*.

Here, *M* stands for the middle term, *P* for the predicate term, and *S* for the subject term.

So, summarizing, a categorical syllogism is one that has:

1. Three categorical statements—two premises and a conclusion.
2. Exactly three terms, with each term appearing precisely twice in the argument.
3. One of the terms (the middle term) appearing in each premise but not in the conclusion.
4. Another term (the predicate term) appearing as the predicate term in the conclusion and also in one of the premises.
5. Another term (the subject term) appearing as the subject term in the conclusion and in one of the premises.

A valid categorical syllogism, like a valid deductive argument of any other sort, is such that if its premises are true, its conclusion *must* be true. (That is, if the premises are true, the conclusion cannot possibly be false.) This fact, of course, you already know. Of more interest now is how we can *check the validity* of categorical syllogisms. Fortunately, there are several ways to do this, the simplest of which is

Food for Thought

Rules to Live By

Drawing Venn diagrams is a good way to both visualize what a syllogism is saying and test it for validity. But you can also check validity without diagrams. One technique is to assess the validity of a syllogism by determining if the argument follows certain rules. Some of these rules involve the fine points of syllogistic structure. But others are drawn from simple facts about syllogisms that you probably already know—or have suspected. Here are three such rules:

1. A valid categorical syllogism must possess precisely three terms.
2. A valid categorical syllogism cannot have two negative premises.
3. A valid categorical syllogism with at least one negative premise must have a negative conclusion.

Any standard-form categorical syllogism that breaks even one of these rules must be invalid. (On the other hand, a categorical syllogism that does not violate any of these rules is not necessarily valid. It may still be defective for other reasons.)

Here are some syllogisms that violate at least one rule:

All parrots are birds.
All birds are cold-blooded creatures.
Therefore, all pigeons are cold-blooded creatures.
(Violates rule 1)

No ebooks are paperbacks.
Some paperbacks are not thrillers.
Therefore, some thrillers are not ebooks.
(Violates rule 2)

No puppies are kittens.
Some dogs are puppies.
Therefore, some dogs are kittens.
(Violates rule 3)

the Venn diagramming method. This technique involves drawing a circle for each term (the subject, predicate, and middle term) in the argument (giving us three overlapping circles), then diagramming the premises on these circles (using shading and Xs, as discussed in the previous section). If the resulting diagram reflects the assertion in the conclusion, the argument is valid.

If you know how to diagram categorical statements, you can diagram an entire categorical argument. Remember that since a categorical statement has two terms, we need two circles to diagram it—one circle for each term.

And since a categorical syllogism has three terms, we need three circles, overlapping like this:

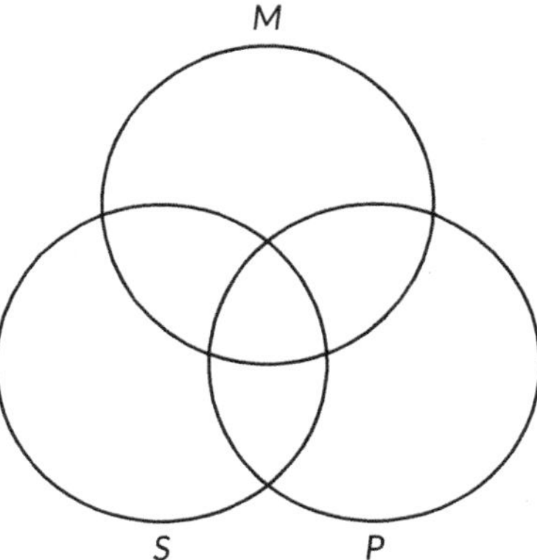

The top circle represents the class designated by the middle term (*M*); the bottom left circle, the subject term (*S*); and the bottom right circle, the predicate term (*P*). For clarity and consistency, it is best always to label the circles in this order. The two lower circles together represent the conclusion, since they stand for the relationship between the subject and predicate terms (*S* and *P*).

Let's diagram our syllogism about politicians and civil servants, diagramming one premise at a time. We can start by labelling the diagram like this, with three empty, overlapping circles:

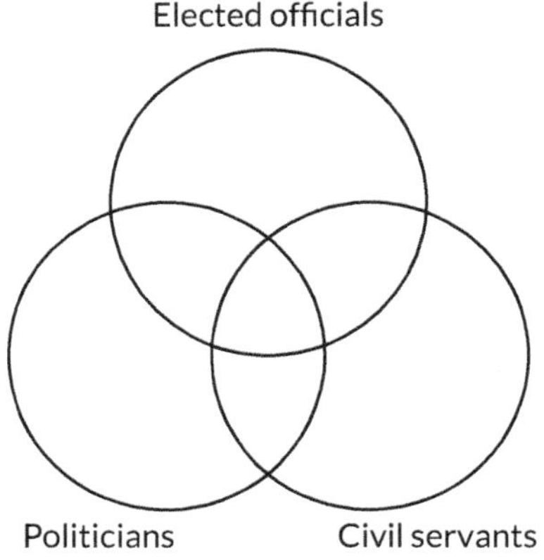

Now, we diagram the first premise ("All elected officials are civil servants"). To do this, we look *only* at the two circles involved in premise 1—namely the "elected officials" circle and the "civil servants" circle. For now, *ignore the other circle entirely*. You should literally pretend that it is not there at all. Premise 1 is an A-statement. So, to represent premise 1, we shade the part of the elected officials circle that does *not* overlap with the civil servants circle. This signifies that all the existing elected officials are also civil servants:

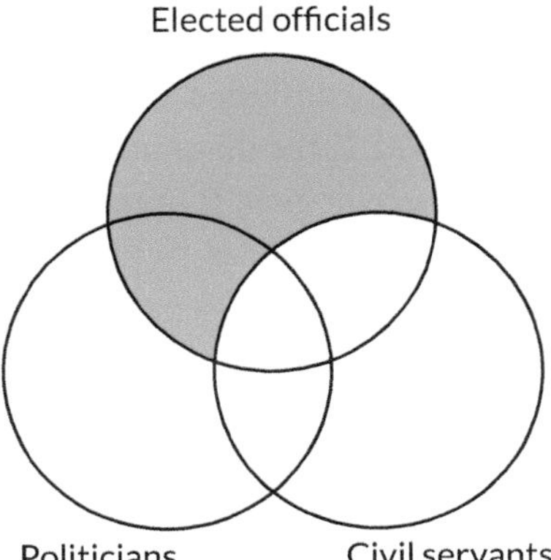

Notice that, if you just look at the two circles we're working with here, the diagram looks exactly like our original A-statement diagram above. Diagrams of A-statements *always* look like that!

Next, we diagram premise 2 ("All politicians are elected officials"). Again, we look only at the two circles that are relevant to that premise, ignoring the *P* circle entirely. Premise 2 is another A-statement, so we diagram it by shading the part of the politicians circle that does not overlap with the elected officials circle:

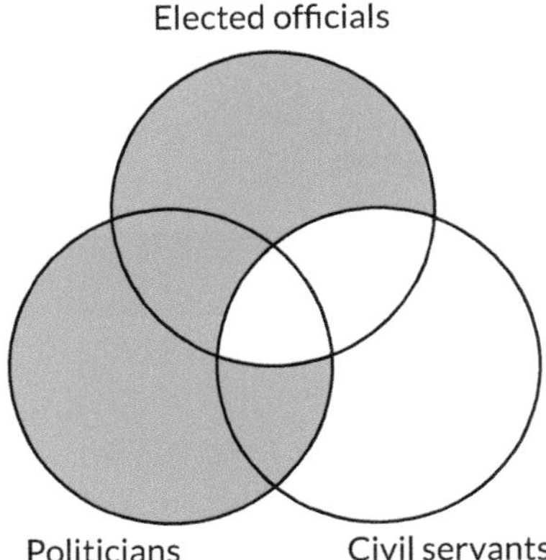

Now—and this is very important—we *stop drawing*. We diagram *only* the premises. We never, ever diagram the conclusion.

Why is that? Why not diagram the conclusion too? Recall that in a valid deductive argument, the premises imply the conclusion. So once we diagram the premises, the resulting combined diagram is already supposed to represent the information in the conclusion ("Therefore, all politicians are civil servants"). We can see that the politicians circle is shaded everywhere—except in the area that overlaps the civil servants circle. And this is how the diagram of the bottom two circles *should* be shaded if it were to depict the statement "All politicians are civil servants." (Look at the diagram, and ask yourself: where are the politicians? One part of the politician circle is shaded—empty. The only place you can find any politicians is in an area that overlaps with the civil servant circle. Hence, all politicians are civil servants.)

So the diagram does express what's asserted in the conclusion of our argument. The argument is therefore valid. If you diagram the premises of a categorical syllogism and the resulting combined diagram says the same thing as the conclusion, the syllogism is valid. If the diagram does not "contain" the conclusion (if information is missing), the syllogism is invalid.

This syllogism we just examined has two universal ("All") premises (both A-statements). Let's diagram one that has a particular ("Some") premise:

> All robots are machines.
> Some professors are robots.
> Therefore, some professors are machines.

Here's the diagram properly labelled:

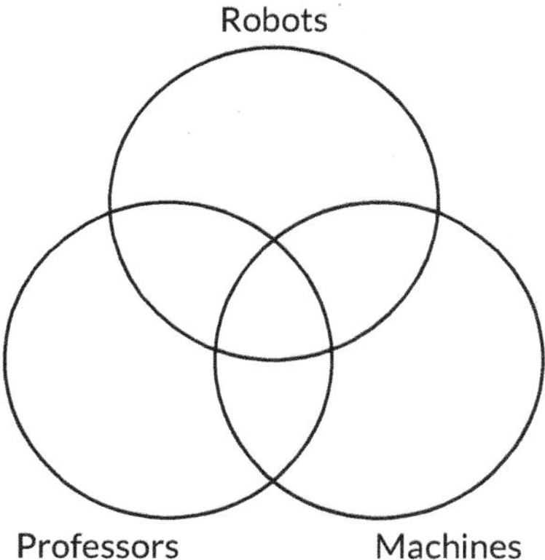

Review Notes

Five Steps to Checking Validity with Venn Diagrams

1. Draw three overlapping circles, each circle representing a term in the syllogism, with the two circles representing the subject and predicate terms placed on the bottom left and bottom right.
2. Label the circles with the letters representing the terms (*S*, *P*, and *M*).
3. Diagram the first premise. (But always diagram universal premises first. When diagramming a particular premise, if it's unclear where to place an X in a circle section, place it on the dividing line between subsections.)
4. Diagram the other premise.

NOW STOP. PUT DOWN YOUR PEN OR PENCIL.
OK, now finally . . .

5. Check to see if the two circles at the bottom of the diagram represent what is asserted in the conclusion. If it does, the argument is valid; if not, it's invalid.

We'll diagram the first premise first ("All robots are machines")—but not just because it happens to be the first premise. In categorical syllogisms with both a universal and a particular premise, we should always diagram the universal premise first. The reason is that diagramming the particular premise first can lead to confusion. For example, in the argument in question, if we were to diagram the particular premise first ("Some professors are robots"), we would end up with an X in the area where the robots and professors circles overlap. That section, however, is split into two subsections by the machines circle:

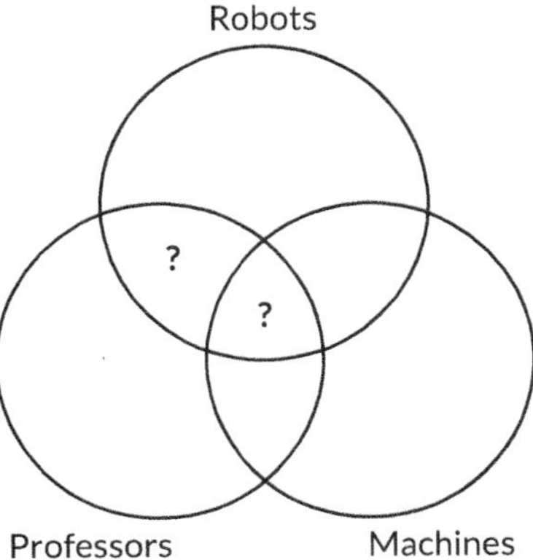

So then the question arises in which subsection we should place the X. (That's why there are question marks in the diagram above—to point out, just for now, the uncertainty.) Should we put the X in the area overlapping with the machines circle—or in the part not overlapping with the machines circle? Our choice *does* affect what the diagram says about the validity of the argument. But if we diagram the universal premise first, the decision of where to insert the X is made for us because there would be only one relevant subsection left (and we can't place an X in a shaded area, because shaded means *empty*):

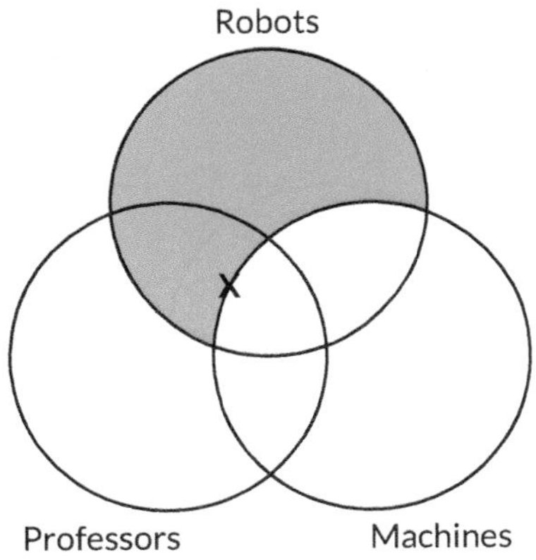

The resulting diagram represents the statement that some professors are machines, which is what the conclusion asserts. The syllogism, then, is valid.

But sometimes, diagramming the universal premise first still leaves us with a question about where the X should go. Consider this syllogism:

All barbers are singers.
Some Italians are singers.
Therefore, some Italians are barbers.

When we diagram the universal premise first, we see that the section where the Italians and singers circles overlap is divided between a subsection including barbers and a subsection excluding barbers. So the X could go in either subsection, and we have no way of knowing which:

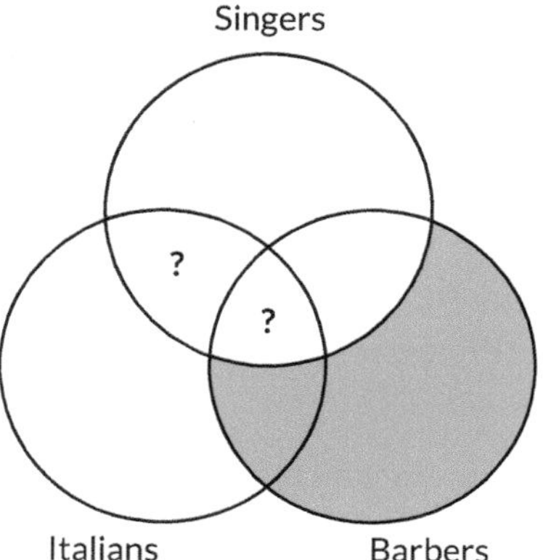

The question marks in the diagram above again suggest (again, just temporarily) our uncertainty. But question marks aren't really part of our diagramming method. So we eventually need to decide where to put the X! In situations like this one, the best approach is to be honest and indicate our uncertainty about where the X should go by placing it on the border between the two subsections, like this:

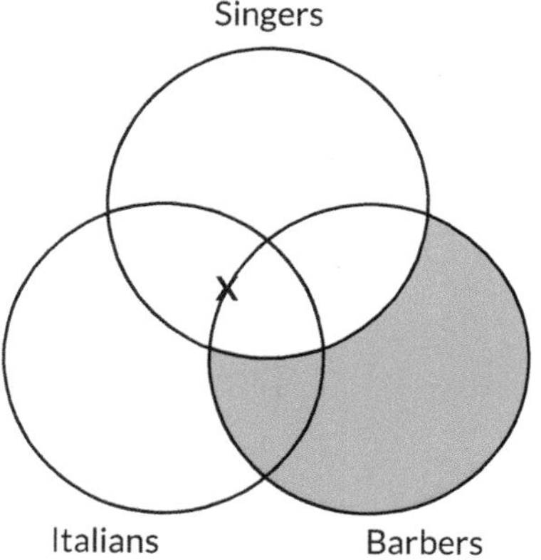

Food for Thought

The Limits of the Venn Diagram Method

A hard problem in the study of logic is the question of whether a universal statement (like "All *S* are *M*" or "No *S* are *M*") has what is called "existential import." (The word "import" here means importance, or significance.) That is, does such a statement actually imply that something exists? Does it imply that members of the class *S* exist? Or does it simply mean, for example, that if there are any *S*s in the world, they are all also *M*s?

Consider this example. If you say that "None of the rides at the theme park are roller coasters," are you necessarily implying that there *are some* rides at the theme park? You probably are; otherwise, it would be an odd thing to say in the first place. On the other hand, if you say that "No unicorns are dragons," are you necessarily implying that there *are some* unicorns in the world and that those unicorns happen to not be dragons? Hopefully not! So the "existential import" of a universal statement—that is, whether or not it implies that some members of the predicate term actually exist—depends on the context. But formal logic is, well, formal, and so the systems we use to test logical statements look only at the formal structure of an argument, independent of context.

But because of this problem, the Venn diagram method used in this textbook is not entirely foolproof. Consider the following syllogism:

All *S* are *M*.
All *M* are *P*.
Therefore some *S* are *P*.

Here's the Venn diagram for it:

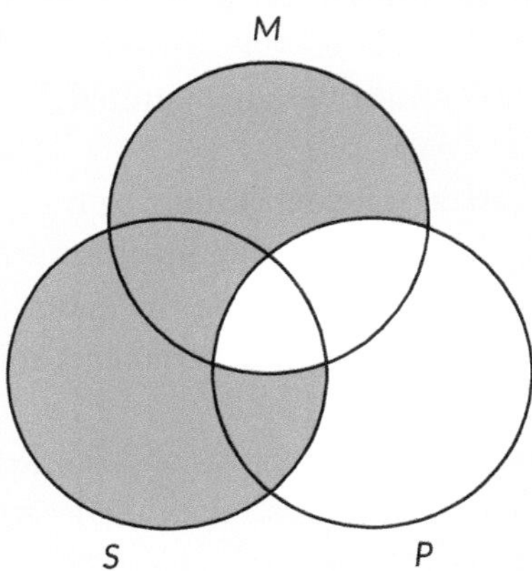

According to our method, the syllogism is invalid because you can't look at the above diagram and *see* that "Some *S* are *P*." But is it *really* invalid? Unfortunately, that depends on what we're talking about.

What if the argument represented above is the following: "All cats are mammals. And all mammals are fur-bearing animals. So some cats are fur-bearing." That certainly seems valid. If the premises are true, how could it be false that some cats are fur-bearing? After all, *some* in logic means "at least one."

The problem lies in the fact that *both* of this syllogism's premises are universal statements and the conclusion is a particular statement.

continued

The result is that the Venn diagram method used in this book will work for *nearly all* syllogisms you run across, and it will work for all the examples given in this book and in the exercises throughout this chapter. But it won't work reliably for syllogisms that have two universal premises and a particular conclusion. Those are relatively rare, but keep your eyes open, and when you spot them, ask yourself, "Does the person putting this argument forward actually believe that members of all those categories actually exist?"

An X placed in this position means that among things that are both Italians and singers, something is either a barber or not a barber—but we don't know which. Now, the conclusion says that some Italians are barbers. This conclusion is represented in the diagram only if there is an X *unquestionably* in the area where the barbers and Italians circles overlap. But we don't have an X unquestionably in that region; we have only an X that *may or may not be there*. That is, there's a question of just where the X is. Therefore, the diagram does not assert what the conclusion does, and so the argument is ruled invalid.

Summary

Every categorical statement has a subject term and a predicate term. There are four standard forms of categorical statements: (1) universal affirmative ("All dogs are mammals"), (2) universal negative ("No dogs are mammals"), (3) particular affirmative ("Some dogs are mammals"), and (4) particular negative ("Some dogs are not mammals").

Categorical statements must be translated into standard form before you can work with them. Translating involves identifying terms, ensuring that they designate classes, and determining the quantifiers. Drawing Venn diagrams is a good way to visualize categorical statements and to tell whether one statement is equivalent to another.

A categorical syllogism is an argument consisting of three categorical statements (two categorical premises and a categorical conclusion) that are interlinked in a structured way. The syllogism consists of a subject term, predicate term, and middle term. The middle term appears once in each premise. The subject term appears in one premise and the conclusion, and the predicate term appears in the other premise and the conclusion. You can use Venn diagrams to represent categorical statements, showing how the terms are related.

The easiest way to check the validity of a categorical syllogism is to draw a three-circle Venn diagram—three overlapping circles with the relationship between terms depicted graphically. If, after diagramming each premise, the diagram reflects what is asserted in the conclusion, the argument is valid. If it does not, the argument is invalid.

Exercise 6.6

Answers to exercises marked with an asterisk (*) may be found in Appendix B, Answers to Exercises.

For each of the following arguments, label the subject term, predicate term, and middle term. Then translate each syllogism into symbolic form using *S*, *P*, and *M* to represent the terms.

1. No essays are poems. Some blog entries are poems. So some blog entries are not essays.
2. All horses are mammals, and no mammals are lizards. Therefore, no lizards are horses.*
3. Some birds are parrots. All parrots make great pets. So some birds make great pets.
4. All corporations are structured such that their owners have limited liability, but some businesses are not structured such that their owners have limited liability. That's why some businesses are not corporations.
5. All horses are animals. All mammals are animals. Therefore, all horses are mammals.
6. Some DVDs are not film classics, but all black-and-white movies are film classics. Therefore, some black-and-white movies are not DVDs.*
7. All banks are financial services companies. All financial services companies are highly regulated. So all banks are highly regulated.
8. All roads are highways to Rome, but no mere paths are roads. So no mere paths are highways to Rome.
9. No elm trees are cacti. Some tall plants are elm trees. So some tall plants are not cacti.*
10. All thieves are criminals. All thieves are dangers to society. Therefore, all dangers to society are criminals.

Exercise 6.7

Draw Venn diagrams to test the validity of each of the arguments in Exercise 6.6. Answers are given for 2, 6, and 9.

Exercise 6.8

Translate each of the following arguments into categorical syllogistic form (premise, premise, conclusion), symbolize the argument (by using the conventional *S*, *P*, *M* variables), and draw a Venn diagram to test its validity.

1. Some "alternative" healers claim to cure cancer, for all herbalists are "alternative" healers and some herbalists claim to cure cancer.*

2. Doritos are delicious, because Doritos are salty and high in fat and all foods that are salty and high in fat are delicious.
3. All SUVs are evil vehicles because all SUVs are gas guzzlers and all gas guzzlers are evil vehicles.*
4. Anyone who thinks meat production is environmentally sustainable is ill-informed. Since a majority of people who eat meat think meat production is environmentally sustainable, a majority of people who eat meat are ill-informed.
5. Cancer patients are not allowed to donate their organs because the organs could contain cancer. And no doctor would allow the donation of organs that could contain cancer.
6. Some electric vehicles are "clean" vehicles, since all clean vehicles ultimately get their energy from renewable resources, and some electric vehicles do not ultimately get their energy from renewable resources.
7. Some arguments are valid, so some syllogisms must be valid since all syllogisms are arguments.
8. No wimps are social activists because no wimps are people of honest and strong convictions. And all social activists are people of honest and strong convictions.*
9. Most people who drive SUVs are road hogs who don't care about the environment or environmental issues. Road hogs who don't care about the environment or environmental issues are the true enemies of the planet. Therefore, people who drive SUVs are the true enemies of the planet.
10. Some useless gimmicks promoted as "sure cures" are placebos that can make people feel good. Vitamin pills are useless gimmicks promoted as sure cures for a variety of illnesses. So some vitamin pills are placebos that can make people feel good even if they don't cure anything.

Field Problems

1. Think of a piece of *ethical advice* you have received that was presented in syllogistic form. (Hint: this often happens when a speaker's first premise is a general ethical principle and his or her second premise relates that rule to your current situation. The conclusion will be advice aimed specifically at you.) Is the argument a good one? Did you take the advice?
2. Check recent news reports to find one categorical statement made by a prominent Canadian or American business leader. Translate the statement into standard form. (1) Construct a *valid* categorical syllogism using the statement as the conclusion and supplying whatever premises you deem appropriate. Assume that your premises are true. (2) Then construct an *invalid* syllogism using the same statement as the conclusion and supplying premises, also assumed to be true. In both arguments, try to keep the statements as realistic as possible (e.g., close to what you may actually read in a newsmagazine).
3. Go online and check the opinion or editorial section of your local newspaper or one of the national newspapers (the *Globe and Mail* or

National Post). Within one of the editorials or letters to the editor, find a categorical syllogism that you suspect is invalid. Recall that, in many cases, arguers will leave a premise or conclusion unstated, so you might only see two of the three claims that make up the syllogism and have to infer what the third one is. Assess its validity using the Venn diagram method. If it is indeed invalid, write a 150- to 200-word explanation of how you would explain, to someone who doesn't know about categorical logic, what's wrong with the argument.

Self-Assessment Quiz

1. What are the two qualities that can be expressed in categorical statements?
2. What is a quantifier? What are the two quantities that can be used in categorical statements?

For each of the following statements, identify the subject and predicate terms, the quality, the quantity, and the name of the form (universal affirmative, universal negative, particular affirmative, or particular negative).

3. Every employee who works under Françoise quits within a month.
4. No excuse is a good enough excuse for breaking a promise to a friend.
5. Some animals are not good pets.

Translate each of the following statements into standard categorical form, and indicate whether the form is A, E, I, or O.

6. A man who sexually harasses women cannot truly be called a man.
7. Swimming is a good form of exercise.
8. Hasko is the finest scholar in the department.
9. Nobody who wants an A in this class would wait until the night before the exam to study.
10. A politician is someone who firmly believes that getting elected makes one right.

Construct Venn diagrams to test the validity of each of the following syllogisms.

11. No *S* are *M*. No *M* are *P*. Therefore, all *S* are *P*.
12. All *S* are *M*. Some *P* are not *M*. Therefore, some *S* are not *P*.
13. All *M* are *P*. All *M* are *S*. Therefore, all *S* are *P*.
14. All *M* are *P*. Some *S* are not *M*. Therefore, some *S* are not *P*.
15. No *S* are *M*. All *P* are *M*. Therefore, no *S* are *P*.

Integrative Exercises

These exercises pertain to material in Chapters 1–6.

1. What is critical thinking?
2. What is an argument?
3. Why must every argument include at least two assertions or claims?
4. Can an inductive argument guarantee the truth of its conclusion?

For each of the following arguments, specify the conclusion and premises, and indicate any argument indicator words.

5. I've known the professor for a long time, and the only reason she'd get angry at you like that is if you did something really bad, or if she thinks it's for your own good. But I know you didn't do

anything bad, so she must be doing it for your own good.

6. I will go for a jog unless it's raining, and I will stay home if my kids are sick. The kids aren't sick; therefore, I will go for a jog.
7. Either Canada will eventually deal justly with Indigenous peoples or it will be satisfied to live with injustice for generations to come. But Canadians will not be satisfied to live with injustice. So Canada will eventually deal justly with Indigenous peoples.
8. Either Sareh is irresponsible, or something prevented her from being on time. She's never irresponsible, so something must have prevented her from being on time.

For each of the following arguments, determine whether it is deductive or inductive, valid or invalid, and strong or weak.

9. Kevin is either deluded or a fraud. If he actually believes in the healing power of herbal tea, he's deluded. If he's selling it without believing in it, he's a fraud. And he's too smart to be deluded. He's a fraud.
10. Assad currently works for Microsoft and was hired six months ago. Anyone who isn't fired within three months of being hired by Microsoft will probably stay at the company for the rest of their career. That's why Assad will most likely spend the rest of his career at Microsoft.
11. I read that book and thought it was boring. You're not going to like it.
12. The comet has appeared in the sky every 60 years for the past four centuries. It will appear in the sky again tonight. Tonight is precisely 60 years since its last appearance.

For each of the following arguments, identify the implicit premise that will make the argument valid.

13. Either you drank the last beer in the fridge or I did. So it must have been you!
14. My sister just ate sushi at a totally sketchy place in a bad part of town, and the raw tuna she ate smelled a bit funky. I'll just go ahead and dial 911 now!
15. The prime minister accepted a significant gift from someone who happened to be seeking special favours from the government. The prime minister should therefore resign.

Writing Assignments

1. Write a 600-word essay arguing either for or against making vaccination mandatory during a pandemic. Structure your argument as a categorical syllogism.
2. Write a 300-word criticism of your own argument from Question 1 above. Focus your criticism on whichever of your categorical premises you think an opponent is most likely to focus on.
3. Write a 600-word rebuttal to Essay 9 ("What If You Could Save 250 Lives by Feeling a Little Disgusted?") in Appendix A. Make sure to note Essay 9's premises and conclusion.

Deductive Reasoning: Propositional Logic

Chapter Objectives

Connectives and Truth Values

You will be able to

- understand the purpose and uses of propositional logic.
- understand the meaning, symbols, and uses of the four logical connectives—conjunction, disjunction, negation, and conditional.
- define *statement* and explain the distinction between simple and compound statements.
- translate simple statements into symbolic form.
- construct a truth table and use it to test the validity of arguments.
- identify the situations in which conjunctions, disjunctions, negations, and conditionals are true or false.
- understand the structure of conditional statements and the various ways in which they can be expressed.

Checking for Validity

You will be able to

- determine the validity of very simple arguments using truth tables.
- use parentheses effectively in expressing statements in symbolic form.
- use the short method to evaluate complex arguments.

We began our exploration of formal logic by studying categorical logic. In categorical logic the basic unit of our concern was the *statement component*; that is, we were interested in the logical relationships between the subject and predicate of various statements.

propositional logic
The branch of deductive reasoning that deals with the logical relationships among statements.

Here we take up an exploration of **propositional logic** (or truth-functional logic)—the branch of deductive reasoning that deals with the logical relationships among entire statements. In propositional logic, we use symbols to represent and clarify these relationships. If you master this material, you should reap at least two rewards right away. The first is a more thorough understanding of the power, precision, and dynamics of deductive reasoning. The second is the ability to evaluate the validity of very complex arguments.

How complex? Take a look at this deductive argument. Can you tell if it's valid?

1. Canada will be a just society only if it improves the situation of Indigenous peoples.
2. Canada will improve the situation of Indigenous peoples only if doing so will not significantly reduce the standard of living of middle-class Canadians.
3. If the standard of living of middle-class Canadians is reduced, then either Canada will not be a just society or it will not improve the situation of Indigenous peoples.
4. Canada will not improve the situation of Indigenous peoples.
5. Therefore, Canada will not be a just society.

If you don't know anything about propositional logic, the only way you can check this argument for validity is to rely on intuition, which is not a very reliable method. You just have to think it through, and the thinking it through will not be easy. But with a grounding in propositional logic, you can figure this one out in straightforward fashion with a high degree of certainty. By the end of this chapter, you will have the relevant tools.

7.1 Connectives and Truth Values

As we've seen, arguments are composed of statements. In Chapter 3, we used geometric shapes (circles, squares, and arrows) to represent the statements in the diagrams we drew. Each shape stood not for a logical relationship between statements but for a single statement. Propositional logic takes this symbolization to another level by using symbols to replace not just statements but also the *relationships between statements*—relationships that we specify with logical connective words, or connectives, such as "if . . . then" and "or." Propositional logic gets this work done by using the symbol language of **symbolic logic**, a branch of logic in its own right.

symbolic logic
Modern deductive logic that uses symbolic language to do its work.

Because these logical connectives specify the relationships between statements, they shape the *form* of the argument. Recall that the validity of an argument is a matter of the argument's form; that's why we can judge the validity of an argument apart from any consideration of the truth of its premises. So propositional logic helps us to assess the validity of an argument without being distracted by non-formal elements, such as the particular words used to express content.

So the symbols used to express an argument are of two types. You're already familiar with the first type; they're the lower-case letters, or **variables**, you use to represent propositions. For example, if *p*, then *q*. (There's no particular reason for using the letters *p* and *q* specifically; any letters will do, as long as you use them consistently. That is, once you've chosen *p* to represent, say, "Priya rode her bike," *p* must consistently be used to represent this same statement if it appears elsewhere in the argument.) The second type of symbols used to express an argument is the symbols for the logical connectives that indicate relationships between statements.

variables
In modern logic, the symbols, or letters, used to express a statement.

The following table presents the symbols for, and the meaning of, four logical connectives:

Symbol	Meaning	Example
&	Conjunction (and)	*p* & *q* Priya rode her bike, **and** John walked.
∨	Disjunction (or)	*p* ∨ *q* Either Priya rode her bike **or** John walked.
~	Negation (not)	~*p* Priya did **not** ride her bike. It is **not** the case that Priya rode her bike.
→	Conditional (if–then)	*p* → *q* **If** Priya rode her bike, **then** John walked.

These connectives are used in compound statements such as "The air is clean, and the sky is blue" or "If you stay up late, you will sleep in tomorrow." Remember that a **statement** (or **claim**) is an assertion that something is or is not the case. In other words, it is the kind of thing that can be either true or false. A **simple statement** is one that does not contain any other statements as constituents; a **compound statement** is composed of at least two simple statements.

statement (claim)
An assertion that something is or is not the case.

simple statement
A statement that doesn't contain any other statements as constituents.

compound statement
A statement composed of at least two constituent, or simple, statements.

Every statement has a truth value. That is, a statement is either true or false. Or, to be more precise, a true statement has a truth value of *true*, and a false statement has a truth value of *false*. In contrast, questions and exclamations don't have truth values: they are neither true nor false. Since statements can be put into symbolic form, and since arguments are made up of statements, we are able to express entire arguments symbolically.

Now let's say that we have converted an argument into its symbolic form, and we list all the *possible* truth values of the argument's variables (statements). In other words, we list under what circumstances a statement is true or false because of the influence of the logical connectives. How would this information help us?

It could help us quickly uncover the validity or invalidity of the whole argument. Given the possible truth values of some statements in the argument, and given the relationships of the statements with one another as governed by the logical connectives, we could infer the possible truth values of all the other statements. Then we would have to answer just one question: *Is there a combination of truth values in the argument such that the premises could be true and the conclusion false?* If the answer is yes, then the argument is invalid. If there is no such circumstance, the argument is valid.

If this is a little confusing so far, don't worry. It will become clearer as you digest the following examples and learn more about the dance between connectives and truth values. Let's look next at each of the four logical connectives introduced above.

7.1.1 Conjunction

conjunction
Two simple statements joined by a connective to form a compound statement.

conjunct
One of two simple statements joined by a connective to form a compound statement.

truth table
A table that specifies the truth values for claim variables and combinations of claim variables in symbolized statements or arguments.

Two simple statements joined by a connective to form a compound statement are known as a **conjunction**. Each of the component statements is called a **conjunct**. For example:

Julio is here, and Juan is here.

This compound claim is the conjunction of two simple claims. It claims that Julio is here, and it also claims that Juan is here. We symbolize it like this:

$p \,\&\, q$

The grammatical conjunction *and* is one of several terms that can express logical conjunction. Some others are *but*, *yet*, *nevertheless*, *while*, *also*, and *moreover*. In propositional logic, all these are logically equivalent; they are therefore properly symbolized by the ampersand (&). *Caution:* Make sure the connective really is conjoining two distinct statements and not a set of compound nouns as in "We went to Jack's bar *and* grill" or "Céline *and* Marie were a couple."

The truth value of a conjunction is determined by the truth value of its parts—that is, by the truth value of its conjuncts. For example, look at this conjunction:

Last night I had a Coke, and I also had an order of French fries.

That conjunction is true if, and *only* if, it's true *both* that you had a Coke last night and that you had French fries last night. Maybe you did have Coke last night, and maybe you didn't. Maybe you had French fries last night, and maybe you didn't. But if you indeed had both of them, then the conjunction—the whole statement—is true.

To identify and keep track of all the possible truth values of a conjunction, we can create a **truth table**, which is just a graphic way of displaying all the possibilities. Here's the truth table for the conjunction $p \,\&\, q$:

p	q	p & q
T	T	T
T	F	F
F	T	F
F	F	F

At the top of the table, you see a column heading for each of the component statements (in this case, one for p and one for q) and one for the conjunction (p & q) as a whole. The Ts and Fs below the line are abbreviations for *true* and *false*. The first two columns of Ts and Fs represent the four possible sets of truth values for the variables. Either p is true and q is true, or p is true and q is false, or p is false and q is true, or p is false and q is also false. Those are the only four combinations that are possible. The table shows, in other words, that there are only four combinations of truth values for the pair of variables p and q. Reading down the table, they are: T T, T F, F T, and F F. These are the only combinations possible for *any* conjunction (or any other two-variable compound).

The last column of Ts and Fs (under p & q) shows the possible truth values for the conjunction as a whole, given the four possible combinations of truth values of the pair of variables. This means that if you plug into the conjunction every possible pair of truth values, the conjunction will yield only these four truth values: T, F, F, and F.

In ordinary language, this is what each of the rows is saying:

Row 1: When p is true and q is true, p & q is true.
Row 2: When p is true and q is false, p & q is false.
Row 3: When p is false and q is true, p & q is false.
Row 4: When p is false and q is false, p & q is false.

(Think this through for yourself, using the example given above. If it's true that I had Coke last night and also true that I had French fries last night, then the statement "I had Coke and also had French fries last night" is clearly true. But if it's true that I had Coke last night but false that I had French fries last night, then "I had Coke and also had French fries last night" is, as a whole, false. And so on.)

Alan Turing (1912–1954) was a mathematician and logician and is considered the father of modern computer science. (Turing was played by Benedict Cumberbatch in the 2014 movie *The Imitation Game*.) How do computers use propositional logic?

Considering this truth table, maybe you've already guessed an important fact about the truth value of a conjunction: If just one statement in the conjunction is false, the whole conjunction is false; only if both conjuncts are true is the whole conjunction true. The truth table reflects this state of affairs. In the table, we see that p & q is true only within the row in which p is true and q is true (in the first row)—and that p & q is false whenever even one of

Food for Thought

Logic and Computers

It is no exaggeration to say that without logic, there would be no computers of any kind—no laptops, no iPads, no game consoles. In fact, without logic we would have to do without all devices that run on microchips (or "integrated circuits"), including mobile phones, calculators, and even microwave ovens.

The ability to formalize statements in the way that propositional logic does is what allows computers to do their work. In fact, the basic operations of all computers are based on roughly the same set of logical operators that you are learning about in this chapter. In computers, "logic gates" are the basis for all circuitry. A logic gate is a physical device that implements a logical function such as negation (a "NOT gate") or conjunction (an "AND gate") or disjunction (an "OR gate").

As you may already know, the fundamental language of all computers is called "binary," a language that translates everything into 1s and 0s. In logical terms, the 1s and 0s of binary code work exactly like the Ts and Fs in our truth tables. In fact, look at how similar a computer scientist's "AND gate" (on the left, below) is to the truth table for conjunction!

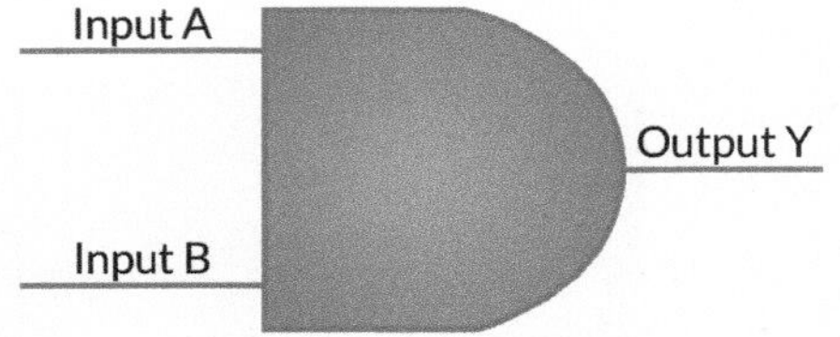

A	B	Y
0	0	0
0	1	0
1	0	0
1	1	1

the component statements is false (that is, in the other three rows). This should make perfect sense to you because in everyday speech, if one-half of a conjunction is false, we would normally regard the whole conjunction as false. For example, if someone says that they went to a movie with Sareh and bumped into Federica but you know for a fact that Federica was home alone all night, it makes perfect sense for you to say, "No, your story isn't true," even though one *half* of the story *is* true.

It's a good idea to remember the exact sequence of Ts and Fs in the first two columns of the previous truth table. That way you won't have to guess to make sure you include every possible combination of truth values. The first few columns in any truth table are usually entered automatically as guides.

disjunction
A compound statement of the form "Either *p* or *q*." A disjunction is true even if only one disjunct is true and false only if both disjuncts are false.

disjunct
A simple statement that is a component of a disjunction.

7.1.2 Disjunction

We saw earlier that in a conjunction, we assert that *p* and *q* are both true and that if just one conjunct is false, the whole conjunction is false. But in a **disjunction**, we assert that either *p* or *q* is true (though both might be) and that even if one of the statements is false, the whole disjunction is still true. Each statement in a disjunction is called a **disjunct**. For example:

Either Joan is home or Ann is lonely.

which we symbolize as

$p \vee q$

or

Either Laura or Matthew will row the boat.

which we also symbolize as

$p \vee q$

The symbol for disjunction (∨) is called a "wedge," which is roughly equivalent to the word *or*. The word *unless* is also sometimes used in place of *or* to form a disjunction, as in "I will go to the movies unless I stay home." This means the same thing, logically, as saying, "I will go to the movies, or I will stay home." The words *either* and *neither* usually signal the beginning of a disjunction.

The truth table for a disjunction looks like this:

p	q	$p \vee q$
T	T	T
T	F	T
F	T	T
F	F	F

The table shows us that $p \vee q$ is true in every possible combination of Ts and Fs *except one*, where both p and q are false (in the last row). This situation just reflects the fact that for a disjunction to be true, only one of the disjuncts must be true. The disjunction here, for example, is true if (1) Joan is home or (2) Ann is lonely or (3) Joan is home and Ann is lonely.

An important point to keep in mind is that, in English, the word *or* has two meanings. It can mean "one or the other, or both," which is called the *inclusive* sense. In this sense, $p \vee q$ means "p or q or both" ("If he's sick or tired, he won't go jogging"). But *or* can also mean "either but not both," which is called the *exclusive* sense. In the exclusive sense, $p \vee q$ means "p or q but not both" ("You can have either the chicken or the fish as your in-flight meal"). Standard practice in logic is to assume the inclusive sense when dealing with disjunctions. This approach is reflected in the truth table for a disjunction, and it simplifies the evaluation of disjunctive arguments. It has no effect on our evaluation of disjunctive syllogisms (discussed in Chapter 3); they would be valid forms regardless of whether the disjunction was construed as inclusive or exclusive. Look:

Either p or q.
Not p.
Therefore, q.

"Logic is not a body of doctrine, but a mirror-image of the world. Logic is transcendental."

—Ludwig Wittgenstein (philosopher, 1889–1951)

Food for Thought

Arguments We Have Known and Loved

Virtually every field has its share of well-worn arguments that are used to establish this theory or that proposition. But the discipline of philosophy—because it is, well, philosophy—is studded from end to end with influential arguments, including some especially famous ones.

> If something you can do will reduce suffering in the world, without causing you similar suffering, you should do it.
> Giving substantially to charities will reduce suffering in the world, without causing you any real suffering.
> Therefore, you should give substantially to charity.

> If lack of intelligence and lack of ability to communicate were sufficient to justify treating animals badly, it would also be sufficient to justify treating infants badly.
> But no one believes that it is OK to treat infants badly.
> Therefore, lack of intelligence and lack of ability to communicate is not sufficient to justify treating animals badly.

> If it's true that all our actions are determined by an indefinitely long chain of prior events, then people cannot perform free actions.
> It's true that all our actions are determined by an indefinitely long chain of prior events.
> Therefore, people cannot perform free actions.

> We can't be certain that we are not dreaming.
> If we can't be certain that we are not dreaming, we cannot be certain that what we sense is real.
> If we cannot be certain that what we sense is real, we cannot acquire knowledge through sense experience.
> Therefore, we cannot acquire knowledge through sense experience.

In the disjunctive syllogism, one of the disjuncts is denied, so the argument is valid in any case. But if one of the disjuncts is affirmed, the argument is invalid when the disjunction is inclusive:

> Either *p* or *q*.
> *p*.
> Therefore, not *q*.

Obviously, if the disjunction means "*p* or *q* or both," then by affirming *p* we cannot conclude not *q*.

If we know that the disjuncts in a disjunctive premise really are exclusive options ("either a bird or a fish"), then we can safely assume the exclusive meaning of *or* and examine the argument accordingly. Otherwise it's safest to stick to the inclusive sense.

7.1.3 Negation

A negation is the denial of a statement, which we indicate with the word *not* or some other term that means the same thing. For example, the negation of the statement "The price of eggs in China is very high" is as follows:

> The price of eggs in China is not very high.
>
> or
>
> It is not the case that the price of eggs in China is very high.
>
> or
>
> It is false that the price of eggs in China is very high.

Assuming we use p to represent the foregoing statement, here's how we would symbolize its negation:

$$\sim p$$

The symbol ~ is called a "tilde," and when we state $\sim p$ aloud, we say "not p." When a tilde appears in front of a statement, it indicates the reversal of the statement's truth value. A true statement becomes false; a false statement becomes true. One interesting consequence of this reversal is that a *double negation* is the same thing as *no* negation. For example, take the foregoing negation ("The price of eggs in China is not very high"). If you negate this negation ("It is not the case that the price of eggs in China is not very high"), you end up with something logically equivalent to the positive statement, "The price of eggs in China is very high." The truth table for a negation explains why such reversals can happen:

p	$\sim p$
T	F
F	T

7.1.4 Conditional

Remember conditional statements? We looked at them in Chapter 3 when we discussed valid and invalid argument forms (*modus ponens*, denying the antecedent, etc.). The basic form of a conditional is "if . . . then . . ." For example: "If the cat is on the mat, then the rat will stay home." Symbolized, a conditional looks like this: $p \rightarrow q$, where an arrow represents the connective. Recall also that in a conditional, the first part (p) is the antecedent and the second part (q) is the consequent.

Crowden Satz/CartoonStock

"Before I consent to being your Valentine you'll have to agree to these terms and conditions."

In a contract, the "terms and conditions" are part of what is often called the "fine print," but they can represent very important details in terms of who has to do what, and when.

Notice that a conditional asserts only that if the antecedent is true, then the consequent must be true. It does not assert either that the antecedent is actually true or that the consequent is actually true—but only that under specified conditions, a certain state of affairs will be true.

At first, you may find that the truth table for conditionals seems a little odd. But it makes good sense when you think about it:

p	q	$p \rightarrow q$
T	T	T
T	F	F
F	T	T
F	F	T

The table shows that a conditional is known to be false in only one situation—when the antecedent is true and the consequent is false. Put more precisely, a conditional statement is false if and only if its antecedent is true and its consequent is false. In all other possible combinations of truth values, a conditional is true—and this is the part that may strike you as odd.

Let's take each of the four combinations in turn and see how they work in this conditional statement: "If Mark is paid a dollar, then he'll eat a bug." The question we can ask is this: "Under what circumstances is the conditional statement (the whole statement, antecedent, and consequent together) true?" Well, it should be clear that if Mark is indeed paid a dollar, and if he does eat a bug, then the whole conditional would be true. This is the situation in the first row of the truth table.

What about the last row—what if the antecedent is false and the consequent is false? If it is false that Mark is paid a dollar, and it's false that he eats a bug, there is no reason to think that the conditional itself is false. Mark could reasonably assert that the conditional statement isn't false if he isn't paid a dollar and doesn't eat a bug.

"The art of reasoning becomes of first importance. In this line antiquity has left us the finest models for imitation."

—Thomas Jefferson (US president, 1801–9, praising the understanding of logic passed down to us from the ancient Greek philosophers)

Mark could also reasonably assert that the conditional isn't false even when the antecedent is false and the consequent is true (the situation in the third row). If Mark isn't paid a dollar and he still eats a bug, that doesn't prove that the conditional is false—it just proves that there are other conditions under which Mark will eat a bug!

This path brings us back to the fact that a conditional statement is false *only* when the antecedent is true and the consequent is false. That's the situation implied by the second row of our table above.

Conditional statements can be expressed in ways other than the if–then configuration, the standard form. Here are some conditionals in various patterns, with each one paired with the standard-form version:

1. You will fall off that ladder if you're not careful.
   If you're not careful, you will fall off that ladder.
2. Gregory will excel in school provided that he studies hard.
   If Gregory studies hard, then he will excel in school.

Everyday Problems and Decisions

Propositional Logic and Bad Choices

A poor command of propositional logic can lead to bad choices in life! Consider the following argument about a very important life decision:

> If finishing a university degree were generally as useless as I think it is, then surely a genius like Bill Gates would know that and would not bother finishing university. And guess what? Bill Gates didn't bother to finish university. So university is generally a bad idea. I might as well drop out now.

You should recognize this as an example of *affirming the consequent*, a fallacy first discussed in Chapter 3. In symbolic form, a simplified version of this argument would look like this:

$p \rightarrow {\sim}q$
${\sim}q$
$\therefore p$

You don't have to use symbolic logic every time you need to make a major life decision. But developing the relevant skills will help to train your brain to recognize errors like this when you see them. The result is almost certain to be better decisions, including ones that matter a lot!

3. Jenna would not have wrecked the car if she had not tried to beat that light.
   If Jenna had not tried to beat that light, she would not have wrecked the car.
4. I'll ride the bus only if I'm late.
   If I ride the bus, then I'm late.
5. Whenever I think, I get a headache.
   If I think, I get a headache.
6. I will walk the dog unless it's raining.
   If it's not raining, I will walk the dog.

Among these patterns, pair 4 and pair 6 are likely to cause you the most trouble. In pair 4, *only if* is the troublesome term. Just remember that whereas *if* introduces the antecedent of a conditional, *only if* introduces the *consequent* of a conditional. So in "I'll ride the bus only if I'm late," "only if" indicates that the consequent is "I'm late." So the antecedent is "If I ride the bus." You have to move *if* to the front of the antecedent to put the statement in standard form. In pair 6, the word *unless* is the sticking point. You need to understand that *unless* introduces the antecedent and means "if not." So here "unless it's raining" becomes "if it's not raining" in the antecedent position.

Because of such variations in conditional statements, it's important to translate conditionals into standard form (using variables and symbols) before you try to assess their validity. To do that, you must identify the antecedent and consequent and put them in the proper order (antecedent before consequent).

Review Notes

Statements and Connectives

- A simple statement, or claim, is one that does not contain any other statements as constituents. A compound statement is one composed of at least two simple statements.
- Logical connectives:
  - Conjunction (and): & If just one statement in a conjunction is false, the whole conjunction is false.
  - Disjunction (or): $\vee$ A disjunction is true even if one of the disjuncts is false.
  - Negation (not): ~ A negation "reverses" the truth value of any statement.
  - Conditional (if–then): $\rightarrow$ A conditional is false if and only if its antecedent is true and its consequent is false.
- Words used in conditionals:
  - *if*—introduces the antecedent; If p, then $q = p \rightarrow q$
  - *only if*—introduces the consequent; p only if $q = p \rightarrow q$
  - *provided*—introduces the antecedent; p provided $q = q \rightarrow p$
  - *unless*—introduces the antecedent; p unless $q = {\sim}q \rightarrow p$
  - *whenever*—introduces the antecedent; whenever p, $q = p \rightarrow q$

Critical Thinking and the Media

Propositional Logic in Ads

As we've made clear throughout this chapter, propositional logic is a common part of our everyday thinking, and of how we express ourselves. That's true for advertising, too. Advertisers frequently use the four logical connectives we discuss in this chapter—though sometimes they use different words that have the same meaning. Imagine, for example, the following hypothetical, but very plausible, advertising claims:

- "If you like burgers, you're going to love ours!" (conditional)
- "Either you buy the best, or you are settling for less." (disjunction)
- "He has the best of everything, and this is the watch he wears." (conjunction)
- "It's not just another pizza joint." (negation)

Understanding a bit about propositional logic—and how to evaluate propositional claims—can help you understand what claims are being made in the ads you see, and whether you should believe them. This is more important when the conditionals used get more complex. Look for example at the old advertising slogan for M & M candies: "Melts in your mouth, not in your hands." This compound claim is actually a conjunction (they've left out the word "and" in the middle) between a positive claim (our candy melts in your mouth) and a negation (our candy doesn't melt in your hand). Think, too, of the classic ad for Reese's Peanut Butter Cups that featured two people arguing over who was to blame for mixing two flavours. "You got peanut butter in my chocolate!" says the first person. "No," says the other, "you got chocolate in my peanut butter!" Causation aside, we can see that what each is saying is that the new mixture is a mixture of peanut butter and chocolate. It is a case of A & B. And as you know from reading this chapter, if "A & B" is true, then "B & A" is also equally true!

Exercise 7.1

Answers to exercises marked with an asterisk (*) may be found in Appendix B, Answers to Exercises.

Identify each of the following statements as a conjunction, disjunction, or conditional; identify its component statements; and indicate the symbol used to represent the connective.

1. The Liberals raised taxes, and the Conservatives cut programs.*
2. "If one is lucky, a solitary fantasy can totally transform one million realities." (Maya Angelou)
3. Either he didn't get my message or he's ignoring me.
4. There's no way I'm going to eat a bug!
5. If Taslima can read your mind, then you're in trouble.*
6. The Canucks will be in the playoffs if they win this game.
7. If God is all-powerful, then he can prevent evil in the world.*
8. The chief executive officer of the company recently resigned; there had been rumours of "financial irregularities" at the company.

Exercise 7.2

Translate each of the following statements into symbolic form. Use the letters in parentheses to represent each component statement. (Assume that the letters stand for positive statements so that a negated statement is indicated by putting a tilde [~] in front of a letter.)

1. Either we leave the house now or we're going to miss our flight. (*p*, *q*)*
2. You will eventually master propositional logic if you work systematically. (*x*, *y*)
3. Our opponents either got incredibly lucky, or cheated. (*p*, *q*)
4. People die, but ideas live forever. (*e*, *f*)*
5. Ronald will do fine on the exam, as long as he studies hard. (*x*, *y*)
6. Crossing the street without looking is not a good idea. (*r*)
7. "I've seen your daily routine. You are not busy." (Rey, in *Star Wars: The Last Jedi*) (*p*, *q*)
8. He will not benefit from instruction, and he will not learn on his own. (*g*, *h*)*
9. The Zika outbreak will soon spread to Canada unless we start extensive quarantine measures for people who are entering the country from infected areas. (*j*, *k*)
10. "I did not yield! And as you can see, I am not dead!" (T'Challa, in *Black Panther*) (y, *z*)
11. Many of the species that live in the rain forest will not survive, if we don't start preserving those forests. (*p*, *q*)

12. Unless we start preserving the rainforests soon, many species will go extinct. (x, y)
13. If Socrates is a man, he is mortal. (d, e)
14. It is not the case that the zoo won't accept any more mammals. (p)*
15. There really isn't enough snow, but I really wanted to go skiing this weekend. (a, b)
16. Either terrorists are hiding in every shadow or someone is trying to convince us that they are! (p, q)

Exercise 7.3

Say which of the following compound statements are true and which are false on the basis of what you happen to know personally about the truth value of their components. Rely on your own background knowledge to determine the truth value of those components!

1. Ostriches have wings → Ostriches can fly
2. Alligators are mammals & Dogs are mammals*
3. The Earth revolves around the sun & ~ The moon revolves around the Earth
4. The surface area of a cube increases → The volume increases
5. It is currently 6 p.m. ∨ It is currently not 6 p.m.
6. ~ Dogs are mammals ∨ Snakes are reptiles*
7. ~ Alligators are reptiles → Alligators are mammals
8. ~ Dogs are reptiles & Alligators have fur*
9. ~ ~ Dogs are reptiles → ~ ~ Snakes are mammals
10. ~ ~ Dogs are mammals ∨ Snakes are reptiles

Exercise 7.4

Indicate which of the following symbolized statements are true and which are false. Assume that the statements represented by the variables a, b, and c are true and that the statements represented by p, q, and r are false.

1. $p \rightarrow a$
2. $\sim a \vee \sim b$*
3. $\sim c \vee \sim b$
4. $b \,\&\, r$
5. $q \rightarrow b$*
6. $\sim a \,\&\, \sim q$
7. $b \,\&\, \sim q$
8. $\sim b \vee \sim p$
9. $b \rightarrow \sim c$*
10. $p \rightarrow \sim r$

Exercise 7.5

Translate each of the symbolic statements in Exercise 7.4 into a logically equivalent statement in English. Assume that the letters stand for positive statements. Possible answers are provided in Appendix B for 2, 5, and 9.

Exercise 7.6

Translate each of the following statements into symbolic form. Make sure that the letters you use stand for positive statements.

1. I'll explain how I wrote my essay, but I'm not going to write yours for you.
2. Either Canada will become more European or Canada will become more American.*
3. "You either die a hero, or you live long enough to see yourself become the villain." (Harvey Dent, *The Dark Knight*)
4. If you saw orcas in Canada, then you must have been on the coast of BC!
5. Science will never triumph over religion unless science can offer answers to the really big questions of human existence.*
6. If you cared about Indigenous rights, you wouldn't cheer for a team with an offensive name.
7. I'm not a fool, and I'm not going to take this abuse any longer.
8. Most Canadians don't seem too concerned, but Canada's oil sands are a very "dirty" source of oil.
9. Provided I pass my logic course, I will be able to organize my thinking better when I write essays.*
10. Canadians say they support human rights, but they certainly aren't above buying cheap products produced by foreign companies with inhumane working environments.

7.2 Checking for Validity

Now you're ready to put what you've learned about truth tables to use in determining the validity of arguments. The truth table test of validity is based on a basic, but very important, fact about validity that you've already encountered: *It's impossible for a valid argument to have true premises and a false conclusion.* So any procedure that allows us to easily check if the premises are true and the conclusion is false will help us to test an argument for validity. Truth tables can do this. Devising truth tables for arguments, then, can reveal the underlying structure—the form—of the arguments, even those that are fairly complex.

7.2.1 Simple Arguments

Let's start by analyzing a very simple, silly argument involving a conjunction:

> Ducks have webbed feet.
> Ducks have feathers.
> Therefore, ducks have webbed feet and ducks have feathers.

We symbolize the argument like this:

p
q
$\therefore p \,\&\, q$

Here we have each premise and the conclusion represented by variables, giving us a good look at the logical form of the argument. The symbol ∴ indicates that a conclusion follows (it's often translated as "therefore"). The argument is, of course, valid—a fact that you can likely see without the aid of a truth table. But it makes for a simple illustration:

p	q	$p \,\&\, q$
T	T	T
T	F	F
F	T	F
F	F	F

This truth table is a repeat of the one we looked at in the section on conjunctions. The top line of the table shows the two premises of the argument and its conclusion with their possible truth values listed below. Like all truth tables, this one shows every possible combination of truth values for the premises and conclusion.

When dealing with simple arguments, the first two columns of a truth table are reference columns in which the variables, or letters, of the argument are listed, followed by a column for each premise and then a column for the conclusion. In this case, though, the reference columns happen to be identical to the premise columns (since the premises just are p and q), so we won't repeat them.

Now we can ask the big question: "Does the truth table show (in any row) a state of affairs in which the premises of the argument are true and the conclusion false?" If we can find even *one* instance of this arrangement, we will have shown that that arrangement is possible, which it never is for a valid argument, and so we will have shown that the argument is invalid. Remember that we are trying to judge the *validity* of an argument, which is a matter of argument *form*. So if we can discover that it's *possible* for a particular argument form to have true premises and a false conclusion, we will know without further investigation that the argument is invalid. Not only that but we will know that *any* argument of the same pattern is invalid. The truth table can tell us definitively whether an argument is invalid because the table includes every possible combination of truth values. If the truth table doesn't reveal a situation in which the argument has true premises and a false conclusion, then the argument is valid.

As you can see in the previous table, there is no row in which the premises are true (T T) and the conclusion false (F). Therefore, the argument is valid.

"Logic takes care of itself; all we have to do is to look and see how it does it."

—Ludwig Wittgenstein

Review Notes

Common Argument Forms Symbolized

Modus Ponens, Affirming the Antecedent (Valid)

$p \rightarrow q$
p
$\therefore q$

Hypothetical Syllogism (Valid)

$p \rightarrow q$
$q \rightarrow r$
$\therefore p \rightarrow r$

Denying the Antecedent (Invalid)

$p \rightarrow q$
$\sim p$
$\therefore \sim q$

Modus Tollens, Denying the Consequent (Valid)

$p \rightarrow q$
$\sim q$
$\therefore \sim p$

Disjunctive Syllogism (Valid)

$p \vee q$
$\sim p$
$\therefore q$

Affirming the Consequent (Invalid)

$p \rightarrow q$
q
$\therefore p$

Here's a slightly more complex argument:

> If global warming continues, coastal regions will be permanently flooded.
> Global warming will not continue.
> Therefore, coastal regions will not be permanently flooded.

You should recognize this argument as an instance of denying the antecedent. Here it is symbolized, with negation and conditional connectives:

$p \rightarrow q$
$\sim p$
$\therefore \sim q$

Let's construct a truth table for this argument together. We will begin by figuring out what columns we need. Generally, we need at least one column for each variable, a column for each premise, and a column for the conclusion. For a two-variable argument, we need four rows to account for the four possible combinations of T and F: T T, T F, F T, and F F. We place those values in the first two columns immediately, since they are the same for every two-variable truth table:

p	q	$p \rightarrow q$ *Premise*	$\sim p$ *Premise*	$\sim q$ *Conclusion*
T	T			
T	F			
F	T			
F	F			

That's the easy part. The hard part begins when we start filling in the rest of the columns. As we saw earlier, the truth value of a compound statement (like $p \rightarrow q$) depends on the truth value of its components. That's why it's a good idea to start out with guide columns in a truth table. The truth value of these variables (letters) determines the truth value of statements that are composed of the variables. The truth value of these compound units in turn determines the truth value of any larger compound units.

For example, to figure out the content for the third column in the table, we need to use our knowledge of how conditional claims work. So, to fill in the first blank in the third column, we look to the left. There, we see that p is True and q is also True. And we know, from the truth table for conditionals, that when p is True and q is also True, the conditional $p \rightarrow q$ is also True. So we know to write "T" in that first position of the third column.

We can now reason our way through the rest of the column.

p	q	$p \rightarrow q$ *Premise*	$\sim p$ *Premise*	$\sim q$ *Conclusion*
T	T	T		
T	F	F		
F	T	T		
F	F	T		

Now, we use the same method (but with our knowledge of negation) to fill in the fourth and fifth columns. In the truth table, the truth value of $\sim p$ is the contradictory of p, and the truth value of $\sim q$ is the contradictory of q. So whatever the truth value of a statement, the tilde (~) reverses it, from true to false or false to true. (Adding the labels "premise" and "conclusion" is optional. We won't always do that here in the text. But it may prove helpful in your own work.)

p	q	$p \rightarrow q$ *Premise*	$\sim p$ *Premise*	$\sim q$ *Conclusion*
T	T	T	F	F
T	F	F	F	T
F	T	T	T	F
F	F	T	T	T

You can begin checking the argument's validity in two different ways. You can first inspect all rows that have a false conclusion and then see if the premises in that row are true, indicating an invalid argument. Or you can zero in on rows showing all true premises and then check to see if any of them have false conclusions. In this case, the third row is the key: in that row, both premises are true, and the conclusion is false. So the argument is invalid, and we don't need to check any other rows.

Now let's try this one:

Either we fight for freedom, or we give in to tyranny.
We won't give in to tyranny.
Therefore, we will fight for freedom.

Symbolized, it looks like this:

$p \vee q$
$\sim p$
$\therefore q$

And here is its truth table:

p	q	$p \vee q$ *Premise*	$\sim p$ *Premise*	q *Conclusion*
T	T	T	F	T
T	F	T	F	F
F	T	T	T	T
F	F	F	T	F

(Again, we've labelled the premises and conclusion in this truth table just to help you out, though it's not strictly part of the method.)

Is this argument valid? To find out, we need to check the table for any row that shows true premises and a false conclusion. The third row is the only one in which both premises are true—but the conclusion is also true. So this argument is valid.

7.2.2 Tricky Arguments

Arguments can get more complicated when variables and connectives are intricately combined into larger compounds and when the number of variables increases. In both these situations, truth tables can help you to unravel the complexities. Let's examine an argument that has both of these wrinkles. We'll go right to the symbolized form:

$p \rightarrow \sim(q \,\&\, r)$
p
$\therefore \sim(q \,\&\, r)$

Notice in these premises the use of parentheses to group variables. The parentheses enable us to symbolize arguments more precisely and to avoid confusion. In math, there is an obvious difference between $2 \times (3 + 4)$, which equals 14, and $(2 \times 3) + 4$, which equals 10. Likewise, there is a crucial difference between $p \rightarrow \sim(q \,\&\, r)$ and $(p \rightarrow \sim q) \,\&\, r$. The former symbolization would express a conditional such as "If it rains tomorrow, then we won't go to the fair and ride the roller coaster." But the latter symbolization would represent a very different conditional, such as "If it rains tomorrow, then we won't go to the fair, and we will ride the roller coaster." Such differences, of course, can affect the truth values of a statement and require a different truth table.

Here's a distinction involving parentheses that's worth committing to memory. Consider these two statements:

$\sim(q \,\&\, r)$
It is not the case that Leo sings the blues and Fats sings the blues.

$\sim q \,\&\, \sim r$
Leo does not sing the blues, and Fats does not sing the blues.

The first statement asserts that it is not the case that *both* Leo and Fats sing the blues. That is, it's not true that Leo and Fats are concurrently in the habit of singing the blues. Maybe Leo sings the blues, and Fats doesn't, or vice versa. On the other hand, the second statement says that Leo doesn't sing the blues and neither does Fats. If we hope that at least one of these guys sings the blues, we're out of luck.

Here's another distinction worth knowing. Look at these two statements:

> $\sim(q \vee r)$
> It is not the case that either Leo sings the blues or Fats sings the blues.
>
> $\sim q \vee \sim r$
> Either Leo does not sing the blues or Fats does not sing the blues.

The first statement says that neither Leo nor Fats sings the blues; it could also be symbolized as $\sim q$ & $\sim r$. The second statement says that it is not the case that *both* Leo *and* Fats sing the blues, which could also be expressed $\sim(q \,\&\, r)$.

Correctly symbolizing statements with parentheses is a straightforward business, but it requires close attention to what's being said. Your best clues to where to insert parentheses come from the words *either* and *neither*, conjunction and disjunction words such as *and* and *or*, and the punctuation in the sentences. Notice how the sentence clues in the following statements inform how the statements are symbolized:

> If the next prime minister is from Ontario, then neither the west nor Atlantic Canada will be happy.

We can symbolize the statements with the following variables:

> p—The next prime minister is from Ontario.
> q—The west will be happy.
> r—Atlantic Canada will be happy.
> $p \rightarrow \sim(q \vee r)$

And:

> Either John Oliver is funny, or the show is rigged, or the network has made a bad investment.
>
> p—John Oliver is funny.
> q—The show is rigged.
> r—The network has made a bad investment.
> $(p \vee q) \vee r$

Arguments like these that have three variables instead of two may look scary, but they're not. The steps you use to check the validity of a three-variable argument are the same ones you apply in two-variable arguments. You devise a truth table, calculate truth values, and check for true premises with a false conclusion. The truth table, of course, has an additional guide column for the third variable, and there are more rows to accommodate the larger number of possible true–false combinations. In a two-variable table there are four rows; in a three-variable table there are eight rows and thus eight combinations of truth values. Notice how the guide columns are laid out:

p	*q*	*r*
T	T	T
T	T	F
T	F	T
T	F	F
F	T	T
F	T	F
F	F	T
F	F	F

"Reason in man is rather like God in the world."

—Thomas Aquinas (philosopher and theologian, 1225–74)

To remember the truth values in each guide column, think of it this way: the first column is four Ts, then four Fs; the second column is alternating pairs of truth values beginning with T T; and the third column is alternating Ts and Fs starting with T.

Now let's test this argument for validity:

> If the Flames won game one but didn't win game two, then they've only won one game. But it's not true that they won game one but didn't win game two. Therefore, it's not the case that they've only won one game.
>
> *p*—The Flames won game one.
> *q*—The Flames won game two.
> *r*—The Flames have only won one game.
> $(p \& \sim q) \rightarrow r$
> $\sim(p \& \sim q)$
> $\therefore \sim r$

And here's the truth table for the argument:

	1	2	3	4	5	6	7
	p	*q*	*r*	*p* & ~*q*	(*p* & ~*q*) → *r*	~(*p* & ~*q*)	~*r*
1	T	T	T	F	T	T	F
2	T	T	F	F	T	T	T
3	T	F	T	T	T	F	F
4	T	F	F	T	F	F	T
5	F	T	T	F	T	T	F
6	F	T	F	F	T	T	T
7	F	F	T	F	T	T	F
8	F	F	F	F	T	T	T

This truth table has seven columns, and you can guess why six of them are there. The first three are the guide columns, and the last three are for the two premises and the conclusion. Column 4 is there because it simplifies the assigning of truth values to columns 5, 6, and 7—it is a component of the two premises. If we wanted, we could add more columns for other components such as $\sim r$ if the additions would make it easier to create the truth table.

The truth values for $(p \,\&\, \sim q)$ are, of course, determined by the truth values of its conjuncts. If just one conjunct is false, the conjunction is false (as it is in rows 1, 2, and 5 through 8). Only in rows 3 and 4 is the conjunction true. The truth value of the conditional $(p \,\&\, \sim q) \rightarrow r$ is based on the truth values of $(p \,\&\, \sim q)$ and r, with the conditional being false only when $(p \,\&\, \sim q)$ is true and r is false (row 4). In all other rows the conditional is true. The truth value of the premise $\sim(p \,\&\, \sim q)$ is the contradictory of the truth value for $(p \,\&\, \sim q)$. Likewise, the truth value of $\sim r$ is the contradictory of r.

Is there any row in which the premises are true and the conclusion false? Yes, that's the situation in rows 1, 5, and 7, so the argument is invalid. Of course, you may have figured that out already, since this argument is an example of denying the antecedent.

7.2.3 Streamlined Evaluation

With truth tables, you can accurately assess the validity of any propositional argument, even some fairly complicated ones. But as the arguments get more complicated (when they have more than two or three variables, for example), you may want a more efficient technique for calculating validity. Here's a good alternative method—one that just happens to be easier to master if you already know the ins and outs of truth tables.

In this approach—which we'll call the *short method*—we don't bother to produce a whole truth table, but we do try to construct some truth table rows (maybe only one if we're lucky). The basic strategy is based on the same fact we relied on in the truth table test: it's impossible for a valid argument to have true premises and a false conclusion. So we try to discover if there's a way to make the conclusion false and the premises true by assigning various truth values to the argument's components. That is, we try to prove that the argument is *invalid*. If we can do this, then we'll have the proof we need.

Let's try the short method on this argument:

$\sim q$
$p \rightarrow (q \vee r)$
r
$\therefore p$

First we write out the argument so that the premises and conclusion are in a single row:

$\sim q \qquad p \rightarrow (q \vee r) \quad r \qquad p$

Now we examine the conclusion. What truth value must we assign to it to ensure that it's false? Obviously, the answer is *false*—because there is only one variable in the conclusion and the conclusion must be false. So we label p with an F in the conclusion and everywhere else in the argument. Then our row looks like this:

$$\begin{array}{cccccccc} \sim q & \quad p & \rightarrow & (q & \vee & r) & r & \quad p \\ & \quad \text{F} & & & & & & \quad \text{F} \end{array}$$

Just one caution: as you work through the short method, you must remember that the truth values you mark under the argument row *apply to the variables (letters) only, not the premises.* To avoid any confusion, if you want you can write the truth values for the premises *above* the argument row. In this way you can indicate either (1) the premise truth values that you're trying for or (2) the premise truth values that result from your truth value assignments.

In this argument we can also tell right away that r must be true because it is a premise in the argument and we're trying to see if we can make all the premises true (and the conclusion false). Then we have:

$$\begin{array}{cccccccc} \sim q & \quad p & \rightarrow & (q & \vee & r) & r & \quad p \\ & \quad \text{F} & & & & \text{T} & \text{T} & \quad \text{F} \end{array}$$

Now we look at the first column because it will be easy to determine its truth value. Since the first premise must be true and it's a negation, q must be false. This fills out the whole argument with truth values:

$$\begin{array}{cccccccc} \sim q & \quad p & \rightarrow & (q & \vee & r) & r & \quad p \\ \text{F} & \quad \text{F} & & \text{F} & & \text{T} & \text{T} & \quad \text{F} \end{array}$$

We've shown then that the first and third premises are true. And we can now see that the second premise must also be true: the disjunction $(q \vee r)$ is true because one of the disjuncts is true (r). And the conditional (made up of p and the disjunction) is true because a false antecedent (p) and a true consequent $(q \vee r)$ yield a true conditional.

We have thus shown that this argument can have a false conclusion and true premises—the sign of an invalid argument.

Now let's try the short method on this argument:

$p \rightarrow q$
$q \rightarrow r$
$\sim r$
$\therefore \sim p$

Again, we write out the argument so that the premises and conclusion are in a single row:

$$p \rightarrow q \qquad q \rightarrow r \quad \sim r \qquad \sim p$$

Review Notes

The Short Method: Step by Step

1. Write out the symbolized argument in a single row.
2. Assign truth values to the variables in the conclusion to make the conclusion false. (Write the appropriate Ts or Fs below the row.) Assign these truth values to the same variables elsewhere.
3. Consistently assign truth values to variables in the premises. Assign truth values first to premises where specific truth values are "locked in."
4. Try to make assignments that yield a false conclusion and true premises. If you can, the argument is invalid. If you can't, the argument is valid.

Again, we start with the conclusion. Since the conclusion is a negation ($\sim p$), we know that there is only one way that the conclusion could be false—if p is true. We then must make p true everywhere else in the argument:

$$\begin{array}{cccccccc} p & \rightarrow & q & q & \rightarrow & r & \sim r & \sim p \\ \text{T} & & & & & & & \text{T} \end{array}$$

We now turn to the first premise, a simple conditional. The antecedent (p) is true, which means that if the conditional is to be true, its consequent (q) cannot be false (a true antecedent and a false consequent yields a false conditional). So we're forced to assign these truth values:

$$\begin{array}{cccccccc} p & \rightarrow & q & q & \rightarrow & r & \sim r & \sim p \\ \text{T} & & \text{T} & \text{T} & & & & \text{T} \end{array}$$

That leaves just r to deal with. Again, we are forced to assign a truth value to it. Because the premise is a negation and it must be true, r has to be false. But if r is false, the second premise (another simple conditional) must be false (truth values for the premises are shown *above* the argument row):

$$\begin{array}{cccccccc} & \text{T} & & & \text{F} & & \text{T} & \text{F} \\ p & \rightarrow & q & q & \rightarrow & r & \sim r & \sim p \\ \text{T} & & \text{T} & \text{T} & & \text{F} & \text{F} & \text{T} \end{array}$$

So we see that since there is only one way for the conclusion to be false, we are locked into truth values that prevent us from having all true premises. We simply cannot consistently assign truth values to this argument that will give us a false conclusion and true premises. Therefore, this argument is valid.

In using the short method like this, your overall goal is to see if you can prove invalidity in the most efficient way possible. You want to get the job done without a lot of unnecessary steps. The best strategy for doing this is to look for truth value assignments *that cannot be any other way* given the truth value assignments in the conclusion. That is, focus on premises with assignments that are "locked into" the argument by the truth values you've given the conclusion. Make assignments in those premises first, regardless of which premise you start with.

In the foregoing arguments, the conclusions could be made false in only one way, and that made the rest of the work easier. But sometimes a conclusion can be made false in more than one way. In such cases, your strategy should be to try each possibility—each way that the conclusion can be false—until you get what you're after: an argument with true premises and a false conclusion. As soon as you get it, stop. You've proven that the argument form is invalid, and there's no reason to continue making assignments. If you try all the possibilities and still can't prove invalidity, the argument is valid.

Let's take a look at one of these multiple-possibility arguments:

$p \rightarrow q$
$q \vee r$
$\sim q$
$\therefore p \,\&\, r$

$p \rightarrow q \qquad q \vee r \qquad \sim q \qquad p \,\&\, r$

In this argument, the conclusion is a conjunction, and that means it can be made false by any one of these combinations of truth values: F–T, T–F, and F–F. If we make separate rows for each of these possibilities, they look like this:

	p	$\rightarrow$	q	q	$\vee$	r	$\sim$	q	p	&	r
1	F					T			F		T
2	T					F			T		F
3	F					F			F		F

So can we consistently assign truth values to make the premises true and the conclusion false in any of these rows? We can forget about row 2 because in the first premise, q must be true (to avoid making the conditional false). And if q is true, the third premise would be false. Likewise, we must throw out row 3 because q again must be true (to ensure that the disjunction is true). And if q is true, we run into the same problem we have in row 2—the third premise must be false. Row 1, though, works. To make the third premise true, we must make q false. And when we assign a truth value of false to q in the rest of the argument, we make the premises true and the conclusion false. Therefore, the argument is invalid.

Food for Thought

Propositional Logic and Essay-Writing

Clarity of structure is an important element of any essay. This is especially true for argumentative essays, essays that are designed to convince the reader of some point of view. And believe it or not, a command of the basics of propositional logic can be a big help in this regard. In many cases, argumentative essays have an underlying structure that can be expressed in terms of propositional logic. Recognizing the structure of your own essay and writing it out using the methods explained in this chapter can help you to organize your thoughts and can help to ensure that the argument you are putting forward is a valid (and, you hope, sound) one.

For example, imagine an essay that basically argues this: "You need to either get vaccinated or subject your family to unnecessary risk. But you cannot ethically subject your family to extra risk. Therefore, you must get vaccinated." You probably recognize that as a simple disjunctive argument, which when translated into symbols would look like this:

$p \vee q$
$\sim q$
$\therefore p$

It would be easy to demonstrate using a simple truth table that this is a valid argument. And eventually you may have such an excellent command of logic that you will recognize instinctively that this argument is valid.

A short essay putting forward such a disjunctive argument would likely focus on the second premise and explain in some detail why putting your family at risk is such a bad thing. It would also have to explain why *those* are the two key options facing you, in order to avoid being accused of having put forward a false dilemma! If the dilemma is a false one (that is, if there are actually more than just the two options presented), then this argument is valid but not sound.

An essay might instead have a simple *conditional* structure. Imagine an argument that says, "If the tar sands were a sustainable economic resource, Alberta would be a prosperous place right now. But Alberta is not a prosperous place right now. Therefore, the tar sands are not a sustainable economic resource."

$p \rightarrow q$
$\sim q$
$\therefore \sim p$

You may well recognize this argument structure as denying the consequent (*modus tollens*), a valid conditional argument structure. A full essay putting forward this argument about the tar sands would have to justify in detail the initial conditional claim about the significance of long-term economic sustainability. Is long-term economic sustainability really essential to justifying exploiting the tar sands? If that conditional could be well supported, the argument would be a strong one, since the second premise (which states that Alberta is not a prosperous place right now) is (depending on when you read this!) a simple matter of fact that is widely agreed upon.

An essay of any substance is likely to have an underlying logical structure that is somewhat more complex than the two examples above. For example, an essay might have this slightly more complex version of a conditional structure:

$p \rightarrow (q \vee r \vee s)$
$\sim q$
$\sim r$
$\sim s$
$\therefore \sim p$

continued

An example of an essay with that type of structure might read like this: "If government intervention in that industry is warranted, then it must be either because its product is dangerous, or its ads are dishonest, or its financial reports are incomplete. But its product is not dangerous. And its ads are not dishonest. And its financial reports are not incomplete. Therefore, government intervention is not warranted." In an essay of any length, there would of course be a sub-argument establishing the truth of each of the premises. What is it, for example, that leads us to believe that the industry's products are not dangerous? If the argument for that is a propositional one, we could write it, too, in symbolic form.

What is the advantage of writing out the underlying logical structure of your essay's argument? There are at least three advantages. First, if you can write the structure of your argument using the tools of propositional logic, then you thereby reassure yourself that your essay does, in fact, have a logical structure. That is, you reassure yourself that you are putting forward a structured argument rather than just subjecting your reader to a string of loosely connected ideas. Second, once you see the logical structure of your own argument, you can use the tools presented in this chapter to verify that your argument is valid. Finally, if you are able to represent your argument in terms of propositional logic, it is all the more likely that your readers, too, will be able to see that there is an underlying logic to your essay.

Summary

In propositional logic we use symbols to stand for the relationships between statements—that is, to indicate the form of an argument. These relationships are made possible by logical connectives such as conjunction (and), disjunction (or), negation (not), and conditional (If . . . then . . .). Connectives are used in compound statements, each of which is composed of at least two simple statements. A statement is a sentence that can be either true or false.

To indicate the possible truth values of statements and arguments, we can construct truth tables, a graphic way of displaying all the truth value possibilities. A conjunction is false if at least one of its statement components (conjuncts) is false. A disjunction is still true even if one of its component statements (disjuncts) is false. A negation is the denial of a statement. The negation of any statement changes the statement's truth value to its contradictory (false to true and true to false). A conditional statement is false in only one situation—when the antecedent is true and the consequent is false.

The use of truth tables to determine the validity of an argument is based on the fact that it's impossible for a valid argument to have true premises and a false conclusion. A basic truth table consists of two or more guide columns listing all the truth value possibilities, followed by a column for each premise and the conclusion. We can add other columns to help us determine the truth values of components of the argument.

Some arguments are complex when variables and connectives are combined into larger compounds and when the number of variables increases. To prevent confusion, we can use parentheses in symbolized arguments to show how statement or premise components go together.

You can check the validity of arguments not only with truth tables but also with the short method. In this procedure we try to discover if there is a way to make the conclusion false and the premises true by assigning various truth values to the argument's components.

Exercise 7.7

Answers to exercises marked with an asterisk (*) may be found in Appendix B, Answers to Exercises.

Construct a truth table for each of the statements in Exercise 7.3. Answers are provided in Appendix B for 2, 6, and 8.

Exercise 7.8

Construct a truth table for each of the following arguments, and show whether the argument is valid or invalid.

1. $p \rightarrow q$
   p
   $\therefore q$ *
2. $p \vee q$
   q
   $\therefore {\sim}p$
3. $a \,\&\, b$
   $\therefore a$
4. $a \,\&\, b$
   ${\sim}a$
   $\therefore b$
5. $p \rightarrow q$
   ${\sim}p$
   $\therefore q$
6. $q \rightarrow r$
   $p \rightarrow q$
   $\therefore q$
7. $p \rightarrow q$
   ${\sim}q \,\&\, r$
   $\therefore r$ *
8. $a \vee (b \,\&\, c)$
   ${\sim}(b \,\&\, c)$
   $\therefore a$
9. $p \rightarrow q$
   $\therefore p \rightarrow (p \,\&\, q)$
10. $x \rightarrow y$
    $y \rightarrow z$
    $\therefore x \rightarrow z$
11. $(a \,\&\, b) \rightarrow (b \rightarrow c)$
    $(a \,\&\, b)$
    $\therefore a \,\&\, (b \,\&\, c)$
12. $(a \rightarrow {\sim}b) \vee {\sim}c$
    c
    $\therefore {\sim}b$
13. $(p \vee q) \rightarrow (p \,\&\, q)$
    $p \,\&\, q$
    $\therefore p \vee q$
14. $p \rightarrow q$
    ${\sim}(q \vee r)$
    $\therefore {\sim}p$ *

15. $(d \vee e) \rightarrow (d \,\&\, e)$
$\sim(d \vee e)$
$\therefore \sim(d \,\&\, e)$

16. $(p \rightarrow q) \rightarrow (p \rightarrow r)$
$\sim(p \rightarrow q)$
$\sim r$
$\therefore p$

17. $(d \vee e) \rightarrow f$
$f \rightarrow (d \,\&\, e)$
$\therefore d \rightarrow e$

18. $\sim(d \,\&\, e)$
$e \vee f$
$\therefore \sim d \,\&\, f$

19. $a \,\&\, \sim b$
$c \vee (a \rightarrow b)$
$\therefore a \,\&\, c$

20. $d \vee \sim e$
$f \rightarrow e$
$\therefore d \rightarrow \sim f$

Exercise 7.9

For each of the following arguments, translate it into symbols, construct a truth table, and determine the argument's validity.

1. If we give the union the raise they are demanding, then further work stoppages will be encouraged in future. If we do not give the union the raise that they demand, the work stoppage will bankrupt the company. We will not give the union the raise that they demand. Therefore, the work stoppage will bankrupt the company.
2. If there's a trade war between the United States and Mexico, then Canada will be drawn into it. But Canada and Mexico have a long history of prosperous trade relations, so Canada will not be drawn into the trade war. So there won't be a trade war between the United States and Mexico.
3. This is either olive oil or canola oil. And it's not olive oil, so it must be canola oil.*
4. "Men, it is assumed, act in economic matters only in response to pecuniary compensation or to force. Force in the modern society is largely, although by no means completely, obsolete. So only pecuniary compensation remains of importance." (John Kenneth Galbraith, *The New Industrial State*)
5. Joanne will go to the concert with Emilio, but only if Heather goes too. But Heather will only go to the concert if it's just her and Emilio. Joanne has stated that she'll only go if neither Emilio nor Heather do, since they're both being so annoying. Therefore, Joanne will go to the concert alone.
6. If I drink too much coffee, I won't sleep well tonight. And if I don't sleep well tonight, I'm not going to do well on tomorrow's test. I'm not going to do well on tomorrow's test!
7. Vice President Kamala Harris once said, "If you are fortunate to have opportunity, it is your duty to make sure other people have those opportunities as well." And I've clearly had lots of opportunity. So it follows that it's my duty to help others find opportunities as well.
8. If this government department lacks qualified staff, or talented leadership, it will fail. But it lacks neither, so it won't.

9. With true adulthood comes true responsibility. Until you are ready for both, you can have neither. I have seen that you are irresponsible, so you will not be treated like an adult.
10. Either there is evidence that crystals have healing powers or there is no such evidence. If there is no such evidence, then we have no reason to believe that crystals can heal the sick. If there is evidence, we do have reason to believe that crystals can heal the sick. There is no such evidence. Therefore, we have no reason to believe that crystals can heal the sick.
11. Either the herbal remedy alleviated the symptoms or the placebo effect alleviated the symptoms. If the placebo effect is responsible for easing the symptoms, then the herbal remedy is worthless. The herbal remedy alleviated the symptoms. So the herbal remedy is not worthless.*

Exercise 7.10

Use the short method to check the validity of the following arguments in Exercise 7.8: 1, 2, 5, 9, 10, 15, 16, and 18. Write the symbolized argument in one row, and assign truth values to each variable. Then, above the argument row, assign truth values to the premises and conclusion. Answers are provided in Appendix B for 2, 9, and 15.

Field Problems

1. Find two deductive arguments online or in your student newspaper. Aim for variety: make sure one is a conditional argument and the other makes use of disjunction. Symbolize the arguments, and determine the validity of each one by using the truth-table method.
2. Find an inductive argument in an advertisement. (Tip: the conclusion—sometimes hidden—of an ad is almost always "You should buy this!") Explain why you think the argument is strong, or cogent, or neither.
3. Think of a non-competitive activity that you enjoy participating in or watching—for example, cooking or playing solitaire or playing an instrument. Can you think of a "standard" bit of wisdom related to that activity that takes the form of a conditional statement? (For example, "If you're in situation X, you should always do Y.") Write out both valid and invalid arguments that use a conditional statement as their first premise.

Self-Assessment Quiz

1. What are the four logical connectives used in this chapter? How is each one symbolized?
2. Construct the truth table for each logical connective.
3. Under what circumstances is a disjunction false?
4. Which of the following symbolized statements are true and which are false? Assume that *a*, *b*, and *c* are true and *p*, *q*, and *r* are false.

$q \to c$
$c \to q$
$a \mathbin{\&} {\sim}q$
$a \vee {\sim}q$

5. Put the following statement into symbolic form: "Either I'm seeing things, or I just saw Professor Walton being interviewed on TV!"
6. Construct a truth table for each of the following arguments, and indicate whether the argument is valid or invalid.

   $p \to q$
   $r \to q$
   $\therefore q$

   $p \vee (q \mathbin{\&} r)$
   ${\sim}p$
   $\therefore q \mathbin{\&} r$
7. Translate this argument into symbols, construct its truth table, and indicate whether the argument is valid.

   If the construction company wants to make more money, it will build the office building too high. If the office building is built too high, it will have a high probability of collapsing. Either the construction company wants to make more money or it wants to go bankrupt. Since no company wants to go bankrupt, the office building will have a high probability of collapsing.
8. Translate this argument into symbols, construct its truth table, and indicate whether the argument is valid.

   Either Joe will go to the movie or Julia will not go to the movie. If the movie is *The Imitation Game*, then Julia will go to the movie. So if Joe goes to the movie, the movie is not *The Imitation Game*.

Construct arguments in English for each of the following symbolized arguments.

9. $x \to y$
   $y \to z$
   $\therefore x \to z$
10. $a \mathbin{\&} b$
   ${\sim}a$
   $\therefore b$
11. $(p \vee q) \to {\sim}(p \mathbin{\&} q)$
   $p \mathbin{\&} q$
   $\therefore {\sim}(p \vee q)$
12. $p \to q$
   ${\sim}p$
   $\therefore q$

Use the short method to check the validity of the following arguments. Write out the argument in a single row, and assign truth values to each variable.

13. $p \to q$
   q
   $\therefore p$
14. $p \vee (q \mathbin{\&} r)$
   ${\sim}p$
   ${\sim}q$
   $\therefore r$
15. $a \vee b$
   $b \vee c$
   $\therefore (b \mathbin{\&} c) \vee (a \mathbin{\&} b)$

Integrative Exercises

These exercises pertain to material in Chapters 3–7. For each of the following arguments, determine whether it is deductive or inductive, valid or invalid, strong or weak. Then diagram it using the shapes-and-arrows method we learned in Chapter 3. Also state whether the argument contains any appeals to popularity or common practice.

1. "[T]he fact remains that "superfood" is a marketing term, not a scientific one. It is possible to have a healthy diet without including any of the claimed superfoods, and an unhealthy one despite guzzling chaga coffee, maqui berries or tiger nuts. The only food that can legitimately be called a superfood is

whatever Superman eats." (*Montreal Gazette*, 3 June, 2022)

2. Homeopathy—the alternative "medicine" that uses infinitesimally small quantities of a substance diluted in water—is entirely bogus. If homeopathy worked, it would violate everything we know about how the human body works. In most cases, the effects people believe they experience can be chalked up to the placebo effect. And finally, scientists who have evaluated the clinical evidence agree that no one has ever proven any homeopathic remedy effective, despite many attempts to do so.
3. It is ridiculous for city council to pass a bylaw that bans smoking in all public places, including bars and private clubs. Many people enjoy smoking cigarettes and cigars, and in many cultures smoking has cultural and religious significance. A bylaw outlawing all forms of smoking is morally and legally unjustifiable.

For each of the following arguments, name the argument pattern—*modus ponens*, *modus tollens*, affirming the consequent, denying the antecedent, or none of these.

4. For you to have failed on the test, you must not have studied sufficiently. And from what you said, your studying was nowhere near adequate. I won't be surprised if it turns out you've failed.
5. Whenever there's an earthquake, houses shake. And we didn't feel our house shake, so there must not have been an earthquake.
6. If there were structures in nature that were so complex that they could not possibly have evolved through natural selection, the theory of evolution must be false. There are such structures, however—like the human eye. Consequently, evolution cannot be the right explanation for the existence of the peculiar life forms found on Earth.

Say which of the following symbolized statements are true and which are false. Assume that the statements represented by the variables *a*, *b*, and *c* are true and *p*, *q*, and *r* are false.

7. $b \vee \sim b$
8. $p \rightarrow a$
9. $b \rightarrow \sim r$

For each of the following arguments, specify the conclusion and premises (including any implied premises). Symbolize the argument, and construct a truth table to determine the validity of the argument.

10. Either *Hamlet* was written by Shakespeare or Shakespeare simply claimed credit for someone else's work. But if experts say he wrote it, then he wrote it. And almost every top expert agrees that he wrote it. So it is highly unlikely that Shakespeare simply claimed credit for someone else's work.
11. If the solar power industry can increase the efficiency of solar cells significantly, it will become the number one source of energy in the world. But it will never be able to increase efficiency very much. So the solar power industry will not become the primary source of the world's energy.
12. The surgery will be a success if the bullet is extracted and blood loss is controlled. The surgery is a success, and the patient has spoken to the press. So blood loss must have been controlled.

Translate each of the following arguments into categorical syllogistic form (premise, premise, conclusion), symbolize the argument (using the conventional *S*, *P*, *M* variables), and draw a Venn diagram to test its validity.

13. Professor Bertolini will not deviate from the course outline. He's a legal scholar, and legal scholars never deviate from their course outlines.
14. Some shoes are inexpensive, and all shoes that are expensive are fancy. Therefore, not all shoes are fancy.
15. Some contagious diseases are diseases caused by the influenza virus, and diseases caused by the influenza virus are always dangerous diseases. So some contagious diseases are dangerous diseases.

Writing Assignments

1. Write a 300-word essay that gives a deductive argument for why corporations should take their social responsibilities more seriously.
2. Select an issue from the following list, and write a 500-word paper defending a conclusion pertaining to the issue. Use one or more deductive arguments to make your case.

    - Should Canadian federal elections ever be held during national emergencies, like pandemics, or should they be delayed until the emergency has passed?
    - Should universities ban speeches by speakers who make certain people uncomfortable?
    - Should Canada increase funding for amateur sports?
    - Should there be an international court capable of charging entire countries with crimes?

3. Outline the argument in Essay 3 ("Electronics in the Classroom") in Appendix A, indicating the premises and the conclusion. Determine whether the argument is deductive or inductive.

Inductive Reasoning

Chapter Objectives

Enumerative Induction

You will be able to

- define *enumerative induction* and explain how it's used.
- define *target population*, *sample*, and *relevant property*.
- understand the two ways in which an enumerative induction can fail to be strong.
- understand the error known as *hasty generalization* and know how to avoid it.
- understand the basics of opinion polls and know the definitions of *random sampling*, *self-selecting sample*, *margin of error*, and *confidence level*.

Statistical Syllogisms

You will be able to

- explain what a *statistical syllogism* is.
- define *individual*, *group*, *characteristic*, and *proportion*.
- understand three ways in which statistical syllogisms can fail to be strong.

Analogical Induction

You will be able to

- formulate and evaluate an *argument by analogy*.
- use the following criteria to evaluate arguments by analogy: relevant similarities, relevant dissimilarities, the number of instances compared, and diversity among cases.

Causal Arguments

You will be able to

- define *causal claims* and *arguments.*
- apply Mill's methods to the evaluation of causal arguments.
- recognize the ways in which people can make errors in causal reasoning.
- define necessary and sufficient conditions.
- distinguish between necessary and sufficient conditions in everyday contexts.

Mixed Arguments

You will be able to

- explain what a *mixed argument* is and what its key components are.
- evaluate a mixed argument.

We now pass from an exploration of deductive arguments to a close examination of inductive ones—a relatively small step, since both these argument types are common features of our everyday lives. Recall from Chapter 3 that a deductive argument is intended to provide logically *conclusive* support for its conclusion; such an argument is either valid or invalid, sound or unsound. An inductive argument, on the other hand, is intended to supply only *probable* support for its conclusion, earning the label of "strong" if it succeeds in providing such support and "weak" if it fails. The conclusion of an inductively strong argument is simply more likely to be true than not. If the argument's premises are true, the argument is said to be cogent. Unlike valid deductive arguments, an inductively strong argument can never guarantee that the conclusion is true—but it can render the conclusion probably true, even highly likely to be true. Inductive arguments, then, cannot give us certainty, but they can give us high levels of probability—high enough at least to help us make useful discoveries in everything from physics to birdwatching.

Deductive logic is the invisible framework on which much of our reasoning hangs and is the solid bond that holds together the logical frameworks of mathematics, computer science, and other theoretical or abstract disciplines. Inductive reasoning, though, gives us most of what we know about the empirical workings of the world, allowing us—in science and in everyday life—to soar reliably from what we know to what we don't. It allows us to reason "beyond the evidence," from bits of what is already known to conclusions about what those bits suggest is probably true.

"The rules of probable inference are the most difficult part of logic, but also the most useful."

—Bertrand Russell

Inductive arguments come in several forms. In this chapter, we will examine four of these forms, and, as in previous chapters, we will focus on how to evaluate their merits in real-life contexts.

8.1 Enumerative Induction

As you may have noticed in Chapter 3, sometimes an inductive argument reasons from premises about a group, or class, of things to a conclusion about a single member of the group (that is, from general to particular). For example:

> Almost all of the students majoring in business say they're committed to environmental sustainability.
> Wei-en is majoring in business.
> Therefore, Wei-en probably is committed to environmental sustainability.

> More than three-quarters of residents in this neighbourhood buy Girl Guide cookies.
> Sam is a resident of this neighbourhood.
> Therefore, Sam will probably buy Girl Guide cookies.

Far more inductive arguments, however, reason from premises about individual members of a group to conclusions about the group as a whole (from particular to general). In such cases we begin with observations about some members of the group and end with a generalization about all of them. This argument pattern is called **enumerative induction**, and it's a way of reasoning that we all find both natural and useful.

enumerative induction
An inductive argument pattern in which we reason from premises about individual members of a group to conclusions about the group as a whole.

> Most peace activists I know are kind-hearted. So probably all peace activists are kind-hearted.

> Every Xphon smartphone I've bought in the last five years has had a faulty screen. Therefore, all Xphon smartphones probably have faulty screens.

> Forty out of the one hundred pickles that you've sampled from the barrel are rotten, so 40 per cent of all the pickles in the barrel are probably rotten.

More formally, enumerative induction has this form:

> X per cent of the observed members of group A have property P. Therefore, X per cent of all members of group A probably have property P.

Translated into this format, our pickle argument looks like this:

> Forty per cent of the observed pickles from the barrel are rotten. Therefore, 40 per cent of all the pickles in the barrel are probably rotten.

Enumerative induction comes with some useful terminology. The group as a whole—the whole collection of individuals in question—is called the **target population** or **target group**. The observed members of the target group are

target group (target population)
In enumerative induction, the whole collection of individuals under study.

sample (sample member)
In enumerative induction, the observed members of the target group.

relevant property (property in question)
In enumerative induction, a property, or characteristic, that is of interest in the target group.

called the **sample members** or **sample**. And the property we're interested in is called the **relevant property** or **property in question**. In the foregoing example, the target group is the pickles in the barrel, the sample is the observed pickles, and the property is the quality of being rotten.

Now, using this terminology we can study arguments by enumeration a little more closely. Remember that an inductive argument cannot only be strong or weak; it can also *vary* in its strength—in the degree of support that the premises give to the conclusion. So the strength of the argument depends on the premises as well as on how much is claimed in the conclusion. Let's look at some examples.

> **Argument 1**
> All the corporate executives Jacques has worked for have been corrupt.
> Therefore, all corporate executives are probably corrupt.

The target group is corporate executives: that's who the conclusion is about. The sample is the corporate executives Jacques has worked for (they are the examples he looked at). And the relevant property—the characteristic he's interested in—is being corrupt. We don't know how many corporate executives Jacques has worked for, but we must assume from what we know about employment patterns in corporate Canada that the number is small, probably no more than a dozen. Neither do we know exactly how many corporate executives there are, but we can safely guess that there are thousands or tens of thousands. It should be obvious, then, that this enumerative inductive falls short on at least one score: the sample is just too small. We simply cannot draw reliable conclusions about all corporate executives on the basis of a mere handful of them. The argument is therefore pretty weak.

With such a small sample of the target group, we can't even conclude that *most* corporate executives are corrupt. But we can make argument 1 strong by revising the conclusion to read, "*Some* corporate executives are probably corrupt." This is a much more limited generalization that requires a more limited supporting premise.

We can fault this argument on another count: the sample is not representative of the target group. With thousands of corporate executives working for thousands of corporations, we must assume that corporate executives—in temperament, morality, demographics, and many other factors—are a diverse lot. It is therefore highly unlikely that Jacques's former bosses are representative of all corporate executives in their corruptness (the relevant property). Consider also that it is highly likely that most of Jacques's work experience has been within just one or two industries in one or two places, and even if there are a lot of corrupt executives in those industries or in those places, those might not be representative of the Canadian business world more generally. If the sample is not representative of the whole, we cannot use it to draw accurate conclusions about the whole. Argument 1 is weak for that additional reason.

Consider this one:

> **Argument 2**
> Almost all the blue herons that we've examined at many different sites in the nature preserve (about 200 birds) have had birth defects. Therefore, most of the blue herons in the nature preserve probably have birth defects.

In this argument, the target group is the blue herons in the nature preserve, the sample is the 200 blue herons examined, and the relevant property is having birth defects. We would normally consider this a very strong enumerative induction. Assuming that the premise is true—that *almost all* of the 200 birds really did have birth defects—we would probably be surprised to discover that only a tiny minority of the target group as a whole had birth defects. Since the sample was drawn from many parts of the preserve, we would consider it representative of the target group. And because of the general uniformity of characteristics among birds in the wild, we would assume that a sample of 200 birds would be large enough to strongly support the conclusion. As it stands, argument 2 is strong.

On the other hand, a conclusion asserting that literally *all* of the target group had birth defects would normally go beyond what the evidence in the premise would support. There could easily be at least some blue herons in the preserve (assuming it were large enough) that don't have birth defects, even if most do.

So you can see that an enumerative inductive argument can fail to be strong in two major ways: its sample can be (1) too small or (2) not representative. Of course, it's possible for an enumerative induction to be perfectly strong but to have false premises, in which case the argument isn't cogent. That is, the data (or evidence) stated in the premises could have been misinterpreted, misstated, or simply mistaken.

"The deductive method is the mode of using knowledge, and the inductive method the mode of acquiring it."

—Henry Mayhew

8.1.1 Sample Size

Let's say that you decide to conduct a survey of university students to determine their attitude toward premarital sex. So you stand around in the student centre and query the first five students who pass by. Four out of the five say that premarital sex is immoral. You conclude that 80 per cent (four-fifths) of the student body are against premarital sex. Should you send your findings to the school newspaper—or maybe even to the CBC?

No way. This survey is a joke—the sample is much too small to yield any reliable information about the attitudes of the students as a whole. That verdict may seem obvious, but just about everyone at one time or another probably makes this kind of mistake, which is known as **hasty generalization**. We're guilty of hasty generalization whenever we draw a conclusion about a target group on the basis of a sample that is too small. People regularly make this mistake when dealing with all sorts of enumerative inductive evidence—political polls, consumer opinion

hasty generalization
The fallacy of drawing a conclusion about a target group on the basis of a sample that is too small.

surveys, scientific studies (especially medical research), quality control checks, anecdotal reports, and many others.

In our everyday experience, we may casually make, hear, or read hasty generalizations like these:

> You're looking for a pet? Don't get a Jack Russell terrier! My aunt had one, and it tore up her couch.
>
> One of the city councillors in my town was arrested and charged with fraud. I guess politicians really are all just crooks.
>
> Engineers are incredibly ignorant about current events. Believe me, I know what I'm talking about. My best friend is an engineering major. What an ignorant dude!
>
> Americans are snobby and rude. Remember those two arrogant guys with really bad manners at the party? They're American. I rest my case.
>
> The food at Pappie's Restaurant is awful. I had a sandwich there once, and the bread was stale.

In general, the larger the sample, the more likely it is to reliably reflect the nature of the larger group. In many cases, our common sense tells us when a sample is or is not large enough to draw reliable conclusions about a particular target group. A good rule of thumb is this: *The more homogeneous a target group is in traits relevant to the property in question, the smaller the sample can be while still being reliable; the less homogeneous, the larger the sample should be.*

For example, if we want to determine whether cottontail rabbits have teeth, we need to survey only a tiny handful of cottontail rabbits (maybe even just one) because cottontail rabbits are fairly uniform in their physical characteristics. In this sense, if you've seen one cottontail rabbit, you've seen them all: generally, all members of an animal species are very similar with regard to significant bits of anatomy. On the other hand, if we want to know the music preferences of South Asian Canadians who live in suburbs, surveying just a few won't do. Questioning a sample of 2 or 20 or even 200 suburban South Asian Canadians will not give us a reliable read on the music preferences of the target group. In social, psychological, and cultural properties, people are too diverse to judge a large target group by just a few of its members. In biological properties, however, *homo sapiens* is relatively uniform. We would need to survey only one normal member of the species to find out if humans have ears.

representative sample
In enumerative induction, a sample that resembles the target group in all relevant ways.

biased sample
A sample that does not properly represent the target group.

8.1.2 Representativeness

In addition to being big enough, a sample must be a **representative sample**—it must resemble the target group in all the ways that matter. If it does not properly represent the target group, it's a **biased sample**. An enumerative inductive argument is strong only if the sample is representative of the whole.

Many arguments using unrepresentative samples are ludicrous; others are more subtle:

> University students are glad that the Liberal Party is in power in Ottawa. Surveys of the members of the Young Liberals club on several university campuses prove this.
>
> Most nurses in this hospital are burned out, stressed out, and overworked. My brother is a nurse who works in the emergency department. He'll tell you his co-workers are absolutely miserable.
>
> No one is happy. Almost everyone is complaining about something. Just look at the letters to the editor in any big-city newspaper. Complaints, complaints, complaints!

To be truly representative, the sample must be like the target group by (1) having all the same relevant characteristics and (2) having them in the same proportions that the target group does. The "relevant characteristics" are features that could influence the property in question. For example, let's say that you want to survey adult residents of Winnipeg to determine whether they favour distributing condoms in high schools. Features of the residents that could influence whether they favour condom distribution include political party affiliation, ethnic background, and religion. So the sample of residents should have all of these features and have them in the same proportions as the target group (residents of Winnipeg). If half the adult residents of Winnipeg are Catholic, for example, then half the sample should consist of residents who are Catholic.

Say that we want to determine how the 10,000 eligible voters in a small town intend to vote in an upcoming federal election. We survey 1000 of them, which should be more than enough for our purposes. But the voters we poll are almost all over 70 years old and live in nursing homes. (Perhaps we surveyed people in nursing homes just because that's an easy place to find people willing to answer our questions.) Our sample is biased because it does not reflect the makeup of the target group, most of whom are people under 45 who live in their own homes, work in factories or offices, and have school-age children. Any enumerative argument based on this survey would be weak.

Inductive arguments often work by bringing many individual pieces of evidence to bear in order to support a conclusion. Of course, the source of all that evidence matters a lot. How does a representative sample improve a finding or argument?

We are often guilty of biased sampling in everyday situations. One way this happens is through a phenomenon called *selective attention* (see Chapters 2 and 4)—that is, the tendency to observe and remember things that reinforce our beliefs and to gloss over and dismiss things that undercut those beliefs. We may tell our friends that *Brooklyn Nine-Nine* is a lousy TV series because we remember that three episodes weren't very funny—but we conveniently forget the four other episodes that we thought were pretty good. Or we may be convinced that Dr. Jones is one of the legendary "absent-minded professors" you've heard about. But this generalization seems plausible to us only because we're on the lookout for instances in which the professor's behaviour seems to fit the stereotype and we don't notice instances that contradict the stereotype.

"You have to remember one thing about the will of the people: it wasn't that long ago that we were swept away by the Macarena."

—Jon Stewart

8.1.3 Opinion Polls

Enumerative inductions reach a high level of sophistication in the form of opinion polls conducted by professional polling organizations. Opinion polls are used to arrive at generalizations about everything from the outcome of federal elections to public sentiments about immigration reform to the consumer's appetite for tacos. But as complex as they are, opinion polls are still essentially inductive arguments (or the basis of inductive arguments) and must be judged accordingly.

So as inductive arguments, opinion polls should be conducted so that they (1) are strong and (2) have true premises. More precisely, any opinion poll worth believing must (1) use a sample that is large enough to represent the target population accurately in all the relevant population features and (2) generate accurate data (that is, the results must correctly reflect what they purport to be about). A poll can fail to meet this latter requirement through data-processing errors, botched polling interviews, poorly phrased questions, and the like. (See the box "How Survey Questions Go Wrong.")

In national polling, samples need not be enormous to be accurate reflections of the larger target population. Modern sampling procedures used in national polls can produce representative samples that are surprisingly small. Polling organizations such as Environics and Ipsos-Reid regularly conduct polls in which the target group is Canadian adults (more than 25 million), and the representative sample consists of only 1000 to 1500 individuals.

How can a sample of 1000 be representative of more than 25 million people? By using **random sampling**. To ensure that a sample is truly representative of the target group, the sample must be selected *randomly* from the target group. In a simple random selection, every member of the target group has an equal chance of being selected for the sample. Imagine that you want to select a representative sample from, say, 1000 people at a football game and you know very little about the characteristics of this target population. Your best bet for getting a representative sample of this group is to choose the sample members at random. Any non-random selection, based on preconceived notions about what characteristics are representative, will likely result in a biased sample.

random sample

A sample that is selected randomly from a target group in such a way as to ensure that the sample is representative. In a simple random selection, every member of the target group has an equal chance of being selected for the sample.

Food for Thought

How Survey Questions Go Wrong

Sometimes opinion polls are untrustworthy because of flaws in the way the questions are asked. The sample may be large enough and representative in all the right ways, but overall the poll is still dubious. Here are a few of the most common problems.

Phrasing of Questions

Poll results can be dramatically skewed simply by the way the questions are worded. A poll might ask, for example, "Are you in favour of the government limiting freedom by forcing people to wear masks during a pandemic?" The question is apparently about public health. But the wording of the question practically guarantees that a pretty large percentage of respondents will answer "no." The politically and emotionally charged characterization of mask mandates as "limiting freedom" and the government "forcing" people to do things would likely persuade many respondents to avoid answering "yes." More neutral wording of the question would probably elicit a very different set of responses.

Biased wording is often the result of simple sloppiness on the part of pollsters. But other times it's a deliberate attempt to manipulate the poll results. The crucial test of polling questions is whether they're likely to bias responses in one direction or another. Fair questions aren't skewed this way—or are skewed as little as possible.

Order of Questions

The order in which questions are asked in a poll can also affect the poll results. Pollsters know that if the economy is in bad shape and they ask people about the economic mess first and then ask them how they like the prime minister, the respondents are likely to give the prime minister lower marks than if the order of the questions were reversed. Likewise, if you're asked specific questions about crimes that have been committed in your hometown, then you're asked if you feel safe from crime, you're more likely to say no than if you're asked the questions in reverse order.

Restricted Choices

Opinion polls frequently condense broad spectrums of opinions on issues into a few convenient choices. Some of this simplification is necessary to make the polling process manageable. But some of it is both unnecessary and manipulative and therefore seriously distorts the opinions of those polled. Years ago, Daniel Goleman of the *New York Times* offered this nice example: "In one survey . . . people were asked if they felt 'the courts deal too harshly or not harshly enough with criminals.' When offered just the two options, 6 per cent said 'too harshly' and 78 per cent answered 'not harshly enough.' But when a third alternative was added—'don't have enough information about the courts to say'—29 per cent took that option, and 60 per cent answered 'not harshly enough.'"[1]

Selecting a sample in truly random fashion is easier said than done; humans have a difficult time selecting anything in a genuinely random way. Even a simple process, such as trying to pick names arbitrarily off a list of registered voters, is not likely to be truly random. Your choices may be skewed, for example, by unconscious preferences for certain names or by boredom and fatigue. Researchers and pollsters use various techniques to help them get close to true randomization.

They may, for instance, assign a number to each member of a population, then use a random-number generator to make the selections.

One approach that definitely does *not* yield a random sample is allowing survey subjects to choose themselves—that is, to choose to make themselves part of your sample. The result of this process is called a *self-selecting sample*—a type of sample that usually tells you very little about the target population. We would get a self-selecting sample if we published a questionnaire in a magazine and asked readers to fill it out and mail it in or if during a TV or radio news broadcast, we asked people to cast their vote on a particular issue by clicking options on a website or emailing their responses. In such cases, the sample is likely to be biased in favour of subjects who, for example, just happen to be especially opinionated or passionate, who may have strong views about the topic of the survey and are eager to spout off, or who may simply like to fill out questionnaires. Magazines, newspapers, talk shows, and news programs sometimes acknowledge the use of self-selecting samples by labelling the survey in question as "unscientific." But whether or not that term is used, the media frequently tout the results of such distorted surveys as though the numbers actually proved something.

So a well-conducted poll using a random sample of 1000 to 1500 people can reliably reflect the opinions of the whole adult population. Even so, if a second

Food for Thought

Mean, Median, and Mode

If you read enough opinion polls, you will surely encounter one of these terms: mean, median, or mode. These concepts are invaluable in expressing statistical facts, but they can be confusing. A mean is simply an average. The mean of these four numbers—6, 7, 4, and 3—is 5 (6 + 7 + 4 + 3 = 20 divided by 4 = 5). The median is the middle point of a series of values, meaning that half the values are above the point and half the values are below the point. The median of these 11 values—3, 5, 7, 13, 14, 17, 21, 23, 24, 27, 30—is 17 (the number in the middle). The mode is the most common value. The mode in this series of values—7, 13, 13, 13, 14, 17, 21, 21, 27, 30, 30—is 13 (the most frequently appearing value).

The notions of mean, median, and mode are often manipulated to mislead people. For example, imagine that the owner of a company announces that every employee (over 5000 of them) is getting a raise. And imagine further that she announces that the mean increase in income is going to be $5000. Front-line employees would begin to dream about how they would spend the extra $5000. But then they learn that the mean figure has been skewed higher because a few senior executives will be getting very large raises—maybe tens of thousands of dollars each—while front-line employees each get a measly raise of $300 to $500. The $5000 figure that the owner tossed out is the true mean, but it is painfully misleading. To the employees, what is much more revealing is the *median* raise, which is just $450. The mode, the most common figure, is $350. When they get all the facts, the workers stage a strike—the first one in the company's history caused by a better understanding of statistics.

well-conducted poll is done in exactly the same way, the results will not be identical to that of the first poll. The reason is that every instance of sampling is only an approximation of the results that you would get if you polled every single individual in a target group. And, by chance, each attempt at sampling will yield slightly different results. If you dipped a bucket into a pond to get a one litre sample of water, each bucketful would be slightly different in its biological and chemical content—even if the pond's content was very uniform.

"It is the mark of a truly intelligent person to be moved by statistics."

—George Bernard Shaw

Such differences are referred to as the **margin of error** for a particular sampling or poll. Competently executed opinion polls will state their results along with a margin of error. A poll, for example, might say that Candidate X will receive 62 per cent of the popular vote, plus or minus 3 percentage points (a common margin of error for polls). The usual way of expressing this number is 62 per cent ±3. This means that the percentage of people in the target population who will likely vote for Candidate X is between 59 and 65 per cent.

margin of error
The variation between the values derived from a sample and the true values of the whole target group.

Connected to the concept of margin of error is the notion of **confidence level**. In statistical theory, the confidence level is the probability that the sample will accurately represent the target group within the margin of error. A confidence level of 95 per cent (the usual value) means that there is a 95 per cent chance that the results from polling the sample (taking into account the margin of error) will accurately reflect the results that we would get if we polled the entire target population. So if our aforementioned poll has a 95 per cent confidence level, we know that there's a 95 per cent chance that the sampling results of 62 per cent ±3 points will accurately reflect the situation in the whole target group. Of course, this confidence level also means that there's a 5 per cent chance that the poll results will *not* be accurate.

confidence level
In statistical theory, the probability that the sample will accurately represent the target group within the margin of error.

Note that "confidence level" refers only to sampling error—that is, the probability that the sample does not accurately reflect the true values in the target population. It doesn't tell you anything about any other kinds of polling errors, such as bias, that can occur because of poorly worded questions or researchers who may consciously or unconsciously influence the kind of answers received.

Sample size, margin of error, and confidence level are all related in interesting ways.

This cartoon makes humorous use of a very serious failure to achieve a random sample. What population would the speaker's casual sample represent well?

- Up to a point, the larger the sample, the smaller the margin of error because the larger the sample, the more representative it is likely to be. Generally, for national polls, a sample size of 600 yields a margin of error of 4 per cent; a sample of 1000, 3 per cent;

Food for Thought

Polling: What We Don't Know about Residential Schools

In most cases, surveys are intended to help researchers understand what the public *thinks* on some issue. But in some cases, surveys can also tell us about how much—or how little—the public *knows*.

A 2020 survey, for example, revealed how little education most Canadians have received with regard to the residential schools—the schools that were part of the system that separated about 150,000 Indigenous children from their families, and at which many students were subjected to very serious abuse. According to the study (which surveyed 805 adults who attended school in Canada), nearly half of Canadians were taught nothing about residential schools during either elementary school or high school. For older Canadians, the deficit was even more dramatic. This is a sobering result, given that Canadians are among the most educated people in the world, overall.[2]

Of course, the survey reveals only what Canadians *remember* learning. And they could easily be remembering wrongly—in either direction! And it's at least *possible* (the survey doesn't tell us) that Canadians may nonetheless have a thorough understanding of what went on at residential schools. Perhaps there are many Canadians who have done substantial reading on their own, for example. But we have no specific reason to think that's the case.[3]

and a sample of 1500, 2.5 per cent. But enlarging the sample substantially, to well beyond 1500, does not substantially decrease the margin of error. Enlarging the sample from 1500 to 10,000, for example, pushes the margin of error down to only 1 per cent.

- The lower the confidence level, the smaller the sample size can be. If you're willing to have less confidence in your polling results, a smaller sample will do. If you can accept a confidence level of only 90 per cent (meaning there is a 10 per cent chance of getting inaccurate results), you don't need a sample size of 1500 to poll the adult population of an entire country.
- The larger the margin of error, the higher the confidence level can be. With a large margin of error (20 per cent, for example), you will naturally have more confidence that your survey results will fall within this wide range. This idea is the statistical equivalent of a point made earlier: you can have more confidence in your enumerative inductive argument if you qualify, or decrease the precision of, the conclusion.
- Here's a table showing roughly the relationship between sample size and margin of error for large populations (assuming a 95 per cent confidence level):

Survey Sample Size	Margin of Error
10,000	1.0%
2000	2.0%
1500	2.5%
1000	3.0%
500	4.5%
100	10.0%

Review Notes

Enumerative Induction

- *Target group:* The class of individuals about which an inductive generalization is made.
- *Sample:* The observed members of a target group.
- *Relevant property:* The property under study in a target group.
- *Hasty generalization:* The drawing of a conclusion about a target group on the basis of a sample that's too small.
- *Biased sample:* A sample that is not representative of its target group.
- *Simple random sampling:* The selecting of a sample to ensure that each member of the target group has an equal chance of being chosen.
- *Margin of error:* The variation between the values derived from a sample and the true values of the whole target group.
- *Confidence level:* The probability that the sample will accurately represent the target group within the margin of error.

To sum up, an enumerative induction, like any other inductive argument, must be strong and have true premises for us to be justified in accepting the conclusion. A strong enumerative induction must be based on a sample that is both large enough and representative. An opinion poll, as a sophisticated enumerative induction, must use a sufficiently large and representative sample and ensure that the data gathered reflect accurately what's being measured.

"There are two ways of lying. One, not telling the truth and the other, making up statistics."

—Josefina Vazquez Mota

Exercise 8.1

Answers to exercises marked with an asterisk (*) may be found in Appendix B, Answers to Exercises.

For each of the following enumerative inductions, (1) identify the target group, sample, and relevant property; (2) indicate whether the argument is strong or weak; and (3) if it's weak, say whether the problem is a sample that's too small, not representative, or both. Assume that the information provided in the premises of each argument is true.

1. A random, nationwide poll of several thousand readers of *Horse & Harness* magazine shows that 80 per cent of readers are against raising horses for their meat. Thus, most Canadian adults think Canada should ban the consumption of horse meat.*
2. One hundred and fifty samples of water taken from different sites all along the shoreline of Lake Winnipeg show unsafe concentrations of toxic chemicals. Obviously, the water in Lake Winnipeg is unsafe.

3. Most people agree that injecting hormones into livestock to make them grow faster is a fine idea. A national newspaper recently went to an agricultural fair and interviewed many of the exhibitors there. They all stated that injecting hormones into livestock is harmless to the animal and improves the efficiency of the food-production system.
4. For as long as records have been kept, Vancouver has received over 150 millimetres of rain in the month of December alone. Therefore, Vancouver is likely to get at least that much this December too.*
5. Over two-thirds of the adults in Toronto say they are in favour of banning the construction of new oil pipelines. And almost 70 per cent of Montrealers are, too. This makes it perfectly clear that a large majority of people in this country are in favour of banning the construction of new oil pipelines.
6. I asked several of my university professors about free speech on campus, and all of them said that it's very important. Clearly, anyone with a decent intellect will agree that protecting freedom of speech on campus is essential.
7. Most Canadians agree that allowing the slaughter of dogs for food, although common in some countries, is unethical. A national newspaper recently surveyed 900 randomly selected pet owners. 94 per cent of respondents said that it is unethical to kill dogs to eat.
8. Eighty-five per cent of dentists who suggest that their patients chew gum recommend Brand X gum. Therefore, 85 per cent of dentists recommend Brand X gum.*
9. Most newspaper reports of deaths at beaches involve sharks. Therefore, sharks must be a real worry for swimmers at beaches everywhere.
10. I would say there is an epidemic of child abductions in this country. In the past year alone, major network news organizations have reported five separate cases of children who were abducted by strangers.
11. The cloud is definitely not a secure way to store your data. Case in point: Apple's iCloud service was hacked in 2014, and many private photos of famous celebrities were leaked to the public. A few other cloud servers have also occasionally reported security issues that allowed unauthorized access to their stored data.
12. Most Canadians are happy with their jobs and derive a great deal of satisfaction from them. A survey of 1500 adults with an annual income of $48,000 to $60,000, employed in various occupations, supports this assertion. When these subjects were asked if they were happy and satisfied with their jobs, 82 per cent said yes.*

Exercise 8.2

For each of the enumerative inductions in Exercise 8.1, indicate whether the argument is strong or weak. If it's strong, explain how the sample could be modified to make the argument weak. If it's weak, explain how the sample could be modified to make the argument strong. Keep the modifications as realistic as possible. Answers are supplied in Appendix B for 1, 4, 8, and 12.

Exercise 8.3

For each of the following opinion polls, (1) determine whether the poll results offer strong support for the pollster's conclusion, and if they don't, (2) specify the source of the problem (sample too small, unrepresentative sample, or non-random sampling). Assume that the conducting of each survey is free of technical errors, such as mistakes in data processing or improper polling interviews.

1. Lisa carries out a survey to determine if Canadians are willing to support the arts by contributing money directly to local theatre groups. One night she and her assistants interview 200 people who are attending an exhibition of sculpture at the city's biggest art gallery. To help ensure random selection, they purposely select every third patron they encounter for interviewing. There is only one interview question: "Are you willing to support the arts by giving money to local theatre groups?" Seventy-six per cent of the interviewees answer yes. Anita later reports that a majority of Canadians are willing to support the arts by giving money to local theatre groups.*
2. A national polling organization surveys 1500 nurses chosen randomly from a national registry of this profession. The survey question is whether nurses are paid well enough for the difficult work they do. Ninety-four per cent of those surveyed say no. The pollsters conclude that there is a serious problem with how health care is funded in this country because most nurses are underpaid.
3. As part of the #MeToo movement, a national women's magazine publishes a questionnaire on sexual harassment in the workplace. Respondents are asked to complete the questionnaire and mail it in to the magazine. The magazine receives over 20,000 completed questionnaires in the mail. Sixty-two per cent of the respondents say that they've been sexually harassed at work. The magazine reports that most women have been sexually harassed at work.
4. The *Winnipeg Free Press* website invites visitors to "speak out" by participating in "Today's Poll." One day, the question is "Should Canada be willing to negotiate with terrorists, as one Liberal MP has suggested?" That day, 3201 people visit the website and give their answers. Of those, 2204 answer "no." I therefore conclude that 69 per cent of Winnipeggers oppose the idea of Canada negotiating with terrorists.
5. The local public health authority wants to find out how prevalent cannabis use is within the high schools in their region. They send counsellors to a number of classrooms and engage students in a group discussion about the topic. When asked, almost no students raised their hands to indicate that they had used cannabis products. Using this information, the health authority concluded that cannabis use is not common among high school students in their community.

Exercise 8.4

For each of the following arguments, state which conclusions from the accompanying list would be strongly supported by the premise given. Assume that all premises are true.

1. Five out of six vegetarians admit that they don't really like tofu.*
   a. Eighty-three percent of vegetarians don't really like tofu.
   b. Most vegetarians don't like tofu.
   c. Most vegetarians and vegans don't like tofu.
   d. Vegetarians actually hate tofu.
2. 84 (about 68 per cent) of the 124 university students who responded to a questionnaire published in the campus newspaper are opposed to the federal government's support for oil pipeline construction.
   a. Sixty-eight per cent of the readers of the campus newspaper are opposed to the federal government's support for pipeline construction.
   b. Sixty-eight per cent of the students attending this school are opposed to the federal government's energy policies.
   c. Some students attending this school are opposed to the federal government's support for pipeline construction.
   d. Most readers of the campus newspaper are opposed to the federal government's support for pipeline construction.
   e. Some students don't understand why pipeline construction is environmentally dangerous.
3. Nearly all (98 per cent) of clients at a wellness clinic owned by movie star Tim Timmins reported lower blood pressure after spending a week at the clinic doing yoga.
   a. By doing yoga, 98 per cent of people can reduce their blood pressure.
   b. By doing yoga, some people can experience a decrease in blood pressure.
   c. By doing yoga, some people at the Tim Timmins Clinic can experience a decrease in blood pressure.
   d. Yoga reduces blood pressure.
4. Nayaab told me that most of her friends—all visible minorities—have been selected (supposedly "randomly") for extra searches while going through security at Canadian airports.
   a. Visible minorities are being singled out for additional scrutiny at Canadian airports.
   b. Visible minorities are always singled out for additional scrutiny at Canadian airports.
   c. Some visible minorities are being singled out for additional scrutiny at Canadian airports.
   d. Some Canada Border Services agents are racist.
   e. The Canada Border Services Agency is racist.
5. Seventy-seven per cent of adults interviewed in three Edmonton shopping malls (650 people) say they will vote Conservative in the next federal election.

a. Most people will vote Conservative in the next federal election.
b. Seventy-seven per cent of adult residents of Edmonton will vote Conservative in the next federal election.
c. Many people in Edmonton will vote Conservative in the next federal election.
d. A substantial percentage of people who shop at malls in Edmonton will vote Conservative in the next federal election.

Exercise 8.5

The following statements suggest modifications to each of the opinion polls in Exercise 8.3. In each case, determine whether the modification (and any associated change in poll results) would make the pollster's conclusion more likely to be true or not more likely to be true.

1. Lisa supplements her research by conducting phone interviews of a random sample of 700 adult residents of her city (population 2 million), asking a slightly modified question: "Are you willing to support the arts by giving money to local theatre groups?" She conducts a similar poll in another large Canadian city. In both polls, at least 65 per cent of respondents say yes.*
2. The national polling organization surveys 1500 health professionals (physicians, nurses, pharmacists, and others) randomly from various national registries. Ninety-five per cent of the respondents say that nurses are underpaid.
3. The magazine receives over 25,000 completed questionnaires in the mail (instead of 20,000). Fifty-five per cent of the respondents say that they've been sexually harassed at work.
4. Seven thousand people visit the website on the day that the poll is posted (instead of 3201), and of those, 6000 answer "no" to the question (instead of 2204).
5. The health counsellors visiting the schools interviewed a large number of students privately, with parents' permission, and assured the students that whatever they said would be kept confidential. Only a tiny proportion of students—fewer than 3 per cent—said that they had consumed cannabis products.

8.2 Statistical Syllogisms

Very often we have incomplete, but reasonably reliable, information about a group or category of things, and on the basis of that knowledge, we can reach conclusions about particular members of that group or category. Will it be cold in Winnipeg on 12 January of next year? We don't know for sure, but we know that *most* January days in Winnipeg are cold, so we can reason inductively to a pretty firm conclusion. Will my flight from St. John's, Newfoundland, to

St. John, New Brunswick, get there safely? Well, *virtually all* commercial air flights in Canada—hundreds of them every day—land perfectly safely. So we can assert pretty confidently that, yes, your flight will get to St. John just fine. Is that conclusion a *deductive certainty*? No, but it's still very, very reliable.

In Chapter 6, we dealt with categorical syllogisms, which were deductive arguments consisting of three elements: two categorical premises and a categorical conclusion. But there are also *statistical syllogisms*, which are *inductive* arguments that apply a statistical generalization—a claim about what is true of *most* members of a group or category—to a specific member of that group or category. Here are a few examples:

Argument 1
Premise 1: Nearly 85 per cent of Canadians live in cities.
Premise 2: You're a Canadian.
Conclusion: So you live in a city.

Argument 2
Premise 1: Most professional basketball players are well over six feet tall.
Premise 2: Paul plays for the Raptors.
Conclusion: Paul is over six feet tall.

Argument 3
Premise 1: Almost all countries in Africa are very poor.
Premise 2: Zimbabwe is in Africa.
Conclusion: Zimbabwe is very poor.

Here is the pattern that all statistical syllogisms follow, when spelled out fully:

Premise 1: A proportion X of the group M has characteristic P.
Premise 2: Individual S is member of group M.
Conclusion: Individual S has characteristic P.

It is important, in analyzing a statistical syllogism, to be able to identify:

- The *individual* being examined.
- The *group* to which that individual is said to belong.
- The *characteristic* being attributed.
- The *proportion* of the group said to have that characteristic.

Sometimes the proportion will take the form of an actual statistic—that's where the term *statistical* syllogism comes from. It might be stated as a percentage (as in argument 1, above) or it could also be a fraction (such as 9/10). Sometimes specific numbers aren't available, and an arguer will use a word like "most" or "almost all" or "most of the time." The point is that the first premise is a *generalization*—a statement (usually rooted in some evidence) about the members of a group or class. (In fact, very often the first premise of a statistical syllogism will be arrived at by—that is, it will be the *conclusion* of—an argument using enumerative induction. We'll return to this point shortly.)

Because they are a type of inductive argument, statistical syllogisms—even good ones, with acceptable premises—cannot guarantee their conclusions. So sometimes they can lead us astray. For example, imagine you're in southern Ontario and a friend points out a scary-looking spider in a woodpile. "It's OK," you say. "Spiders in Canada are generally harmless. So I'm sure it can't hurt you." That's a statistical syllogism. But is the conclusion true?

Here's that same argument with its premises and conclusion spelled out:

> Premise 1: In general, the spiders that live in Canada are harmless.
> Premise 2 (unstated): That spider there is in Canada.
> Conclusion: That spider is harmless.

If the spider in question is a black widow spider (a spider whose natural habitat includes parts of southern Ontario and whose bite is relatively dangerous), your conclusion would be false—reasonable, but false!

8.2.1 Evaluating Statistical Syllogisms

Since statistical syllogisms, though very useful, are never airtight, we need a method for evaluating them.

8.2.1.1 Acceptable Premises

The first thing to consider, of course, is whether we have good reason to believe the premises. How is it that the generalization expressed in the first premise was arrived at? Is it common knowledge (such as "Most birds can fly" or "Most water on Earth is saltwater")? Is it based on a careful survey, one with a large enough, randomly selected sample? Here we can apply all the tools learned in the previous section on enumerative induction. If the grounding of the generalization is weak, then the argument is weak.

8.2.1.2 Statistical Strength

Second, and perhaps most obviously, we should ask ourselves: just how strong is the generalization being offered? Clearly, if our argument (about some member of the class M) is based on the claim that, say, "65 per cent of M are P," that's not nearly as strong as if that same argument were based on the claim that "99 per cent of M are P." We should clearly ask questions, then, when vague words such as *most* or *lots of* are used in statistical syllogisms. *Most* might just mean "more than half" or even "51 per cent of," and that's a pretty weak basis for a conclusion about any particular member of that group.

8.2.1.3 Typical or Randomly Selected

Statistical syllogisms take a generalization about a group or class and apply that generalization to a specific, individual member of that group or class. This will make most sense for members that we have reason to believe are typical of that group or class. It is most reasonable to assume that the individual is typical when he, she, or it is selected randomly from the population. If you know, for example, that "85 per cent of Canadians don't know CPR," then it's reasonable to suspect, of any randomly selected Canadian, that he or she doesn't know CPR. But if you're talking to someone wearing a white coat at a hospital or working at a fire station, it's much less reasonable to assume that *that* person is part of the 85 per cent of Canadians who don't know CPR. That person, in fact, is highly likely to be part of the other 15 per cent. Or how about this: if I ask you, "How much do you think this stamp is worth?" you might respond, "Well, most stamps are worth the value printed on them, and that one says '42 cents,' so it's worth 42 cents." In most circumstances, that might be a strong argument. But what if you have reason to believe that this particular stamp isn't a typical stamp? What if you happen to know that I'm a collector of rare and valuable stamps? In that situation, it's much more likely that the stamp I'm showing you is *not* a random or typical stamp, and so it would be unwise to jump too quickly to the conclusion that it's not worth much. Thus, we should always consider whether the individual person or item under consideration is likely to be a typical member of the group or whether you have reason to believe that they or it constitute an exception to the rule.

Exercise 8.6

Answers to exercises marked with an asterisk (*) may be found in Appendix B, Answers to Exercises.

For each of the following statistical syllogisms, identify (1) the individual being examined; (2) the group to which that individual is said to belong; (3) the characteristic being attributed to that group and individual; and (4) the proportion of the group that is said to have that characteristic. You may need to supply missing parts.

1. Barb rides recklessly. She rides her bike to work, and almost all people who ride their bikes to work ride recklessly.*
2. There is only a one-in-one-million chance of any given person winning that lottery. So even though you chose a ticket with your "lucky" numbers, it's very unlikely that you won.
3. Darlene has recently read a financial report that stated that only 1 per cent of Canada's population makes an annual net income of more than $191,000. For this reason, she doubts her friend Jessica's claim that she makes more than $191,000.
4. Almost every meal I've eaten at the Poolhouse Café has been wonderful. I'm sure the next one will be too.*
5. That car of yours will never make it to Saskatoon. Most Fords are pieces of junk!*

Exercise 8.7

Determine the most likely source of weakness for the following statistical syllogisms. (State whether the most likely problem is an unacceptable premise, a statistical weakness, or a non-typical individual. Give a few words of explanation for why you think the argument is weak in that particular way.)

1. I've met plenty of professional hockey players, and they all have inflated egos. Your boyfriend is a hockey player, eh? He must have a huge ego, too!*
2. Professor Norman grew up in a small mining town. Most people who grow up in small mining towns have never read Plato. So Professor Norman has never read Plato.*
3. Only 2 per cent of businesses owned by women ever exceed $1 million in annual revenue. So it's highly unlikely that Oprah Winfrey's business makes more than $1 million per year as you claim it does.
4. Most people in this town who voted—53 per cent of voters—voted for Mayor Doran. You voted. So you supported Mayor Doran.*
5. The odds of shark attack while at the beach are very high. So you should stay out of the water when you're at the beach.

8.3 Analogical Induction

An **analogy** is a comparison of two or more things alike in specific respects. In literature, science, and everyday life, analogies are used to explain or describe something. Analogies (often in the form of similes) can be powerful literary devices, both unforgettable and moving:

analogy
A comparison of two or more things alike in specific respects.

> It has been well said that an author who expects results from a first novel is in a position similar to that of a man who drops a rose petal down the Grand Canyon of Arizona and listens for the echo.
> (P.G. Wodehouse)

> Confiding a secret to an unworthy person is like carrying grain in a bag with a hole.
> (African proverb)

> . . . Out, out brief candle!
> Life's but a walking shadow, a poor player
> That struts and frets his hour upon the stage
> And then is heard no more. It is a tale
> Told by an idiot, full of sound and fury,
> Signifying nothing.
> (*Macbeth*, Act V)

argument by analogy (analogical induction)
An argument making use of analogy by reasoning that because two or more things are similar in several respects, they must be similar in some further respect.

But an analogy can also be used to *argue inductively for a conclusion*. Such an argument is known as an **analogical induction**, or simply an **argument by analogy**. An analogical induction reasons this way: because two or more things are similar in several respects, they must be similar in some further respect. For example:

> Humans can move about, solve mathematical equations, win chess games, and feel pain.
> Robots are like humans in that they can move about, solve mathematical equations, and win chess games.
> Therefore, it's probable that robots can also feel pain.

This argument says that because robots are like humans in several ways (ways that are already known or agreed on), they must be like humans in yet another way (a way that the argument is meant to establish). So analogical induction has this pattern:

> Thing A has properties P_1, P_2, and P_3 plus the property P_4.
> Thing B has properties P_1, P_2, and P_3.
> Therefore, thing B probably has property P_4.

"All perception of truth is the detection of an analogy."
—Henry David Thoreau

Argument by analogy, like all inductive reasoning, can establish conclusions only with a degree of probability. The greater the degree of similarity between the two things being compared, the more probable the conclusion is.

Recall that enumerative inductive has this form:

> X per cent of the observed members of group A have property P.
> Therefore, X per cent of all members of group A probably have property P.

Thus, the most blatant difference between these two forms of induction is that enumerative induction argues from some members of a group to the group as a whole, but analogical induction reasons from some (one or more) individuals to one further individual. In other words, enumerative induction argues from the properties of a sample to the properties of the whole group; analogical induction reasons from the properties of one or more individuals to the properties of another individual.

Arguments by analogy are probably used (and misused) in every area of human endeavour—but especially in law, science, medicine, ethics, archaeology, and forensics. Here are a few examples:

> **Argument 4: Medical Science**
> Mice are mammals, have a mammalian circulatory system, have typical mammalian biochemical reactions, respond readily to high-blood-pressure drugs, and experience a reduction in blood cholesterol when given our new experimental drug. Humans are mammals, have a mammalian circulatory system, have typical mammalian biochemical reactions, and respond readily to high-blood-pressure drugs. Therefore, humans will also experience a reduction in blood cholesterol when given our new experimental drug.

Argument 5: Religion
A watch is a mechanism of exquisite complexity with numerous parts precisely arranged and accurately adjusted to achieve a purpose—a purpose imposed by the watch's designer. Likewise, the universe has exquisite complexity with countless parts—from atoms to asteroids—that fit together precisely and accurately to produce certain effects as though arranged by plan. Therefore, the universe must also have a designer.

Argument 6: Law
The case before the court involves a search by the city police of a homeless man's cardboard shelter. At issue is whether it was improper for the police to enter the man's shelter without either permission or a warrant to search for evidence of a crime. A similar case—a relevant precedent—involved a search by the RCMP of an equipment trailer in which a man was living. In that case, the court ruled that the RCMP had violated section 8 of the Canadian Charter of Rights and Freedoms (the section that says, "Everyone has the right to be secure against unreasonable search or seizure"). Therefore, the court should also rule that the search by the city police of the homeless man's shelter violated section 8 of the Charter.

Argument 7: Forensics
Whenever we have observed this pattern in the spatter of blood, we have subsequently learned that the gunshot victim was about four feet from the gun when it was fired and was facing away from the assailant. In this crime scene, we have exactly the same pattern of blood spatter. Therefore, the victim was about four feet from the gun when it was fired and was facing away from the assailant.

Arguments by analogy are easy to formulate—perhaps too easy. To use an analogy to support a particular conclusion, all you have to do is find two things with some similarities and then reason that the two things are similar in yet another way. You could easily reach some very silly conclusions. You could argue this, for instance: ducks have two legs, two eyes, breathe air, and fly; humans have two legs, two eyes, and breathe air; therefore, humans can also fly. So the question is, how do we sort out the good analogical inductions from the bad (or really wacky)? How do we judge which ones have conclusions worth accepting and which ones don't?

Fortunately, there are some criteria we can use to judge the strength of arguments by analogy:

1. Relevant similarities
2. Relevant dissimilarities
3. The number of instances compared
4. Diversity among cases

If you find yourself thinking that they make perfect sense, that's probably because you already use these criteria in your own arguments by analogy.

Food for Thought

Analogical Induction in Ethical Reasoning

In Chapter 11, you will study in detail the uses of argument and critical thinking in ethical reasoning. For now, it's sufficient to know this: when we try to show that a particular action is right or wrong, we often rely on argument by analogy. We argue that, since an action is relevantly similar to another action, and the former action is clearly right (or wrong), then we should regard the latter action in the same way. For example, we might propose an argument like this:

> Premise 1: If I own an apple tree, it is ethically permissible for me to eat all the apples, or to sell them to others for a profit.
>
> Premise 2: Owning an apple tree is relevantly similar to owning a corporation.
>
> Conclusion: Therefore, it is ethically permissible for the owners of a corporation to be the sole beneficiaries of the corporation's activities.

Here, as in any argument by analogy, the conclusion can be established only with a degree of probability. And we would evaluate its strength in the same way we would any other analogical argument.

8.3.1 Relevant Similarities

The more relevant similarities there are between the things being compared, the more probable the conclusion. Consider this argument comparing the war in Afghanistan (2001–2021) to the war in Vietnam (1955–1975):

> In the Vietnam War, the United States had not articulated a clear rationale for fighting there, and the United States lost. Likewise, in the war in Afghanistan the United States has not articulated a clear rationale for fighting. Therefore, the United States will lose this war too.

There is just one relevant similarity noted here (the lack of rationale). As it stands, this argument is weak; the two wars are only dimly analogous. A single similarity between two wars in different eras is not enough to strongly support the conclusion. But watch what happens when we add more similarities:

> In the Vietnam War, the United States had not articulated a clear rationale for fighting, there was no plan for ending the involvement of US forces (no exit strategy), US military tactics were inconsistent, and the military's view of enemy strength was unrealistic. The United States lost the Vietnam War. Likewise, in the war in Afghanistan, the United States has not articulated a clear rationale for fighting, there is no exit strategy, US tactics are inconsistent, and the military's view of enemy strength is naive. Therefore, the United States will also lose this war.

With these additional similarities between the Vietnam War and the war in Afghanistan, the argument is considerably stronger. (The premises, of course, may be false, rendering the argument not cogent, even if the inference were strong.) Arguments 4–7 (medical science, religion, law, and forensics) can also be strengthened by citing additional relevant similarities between the things compared.

Notice that this first criterion involves *relevant* similarities. The similarities cited in an analogical induction can't strengthen the argument at all if they have nothing to do with the conclusion. A similarity (or dissimilarity) is relevant to an argument by analogy if it has an effect on whether the conclusion is probably true. The argument on war that was just given mentions four different similarities between the Vietnam War and the war in Afghanistan, and each similarity is relevant because it has some bearing on the probability of the conclusion. But what if we added these similarities?

1. In both wars, some combatants have green eyes.
2. In both wars, some soldiers were left-handed.
3. During both wars, ticket sales to movies in the United States increased.

These factors would make no difference to the probability of the conclusion. They're irrelevant and can neither strengthen nor weaken the argument.

Of course, it's not always obvious what counts as a *relevant* similarity. To be relevant, a similarity cited as part of an analogical argument clearly has to be connected in some significant way to the conclusion being argued for. There's no plausible connection, for example, between the colour of soldiers' eyes and their success in war. So that factor isn't relevant. In some cases, an explanation may be required to show *why* a particular similarity is actually relevant. In this regard, the burden of proof (as discussed in Chapter 5) is on the person putting forward the argument.

Well, that's one explanation. But it's probably not the best one. When does an observation count as a relevant similarity?

8.3.2 Relevant Dissimilarities

Generally, the more relevant dissimilarities—or disanalogies—there are between the things being compared, the less probable the conclusion is. Dissimilarities weaken arguments by analogy. Consider argument 4 (regarding the new experimental drug). What if we discover that blood pressure–lowering drugs that work in mice almost *never* work in humans? This one dissimilarity would severely weaken the argument and make the conclusion much less probable.

Pointing out dissimilarities in an analogical induction is a common way to undermine the argument. Sometimes finding one relevant dissimilarity is enough to show that the argument should be rejected. A familiar response to argument 5 (the watch argument) is to point out a crucial dissimilarity between a watch and the universe: the universe may resemble a watch (or mechanism) in some ways, but it also resembles a living thing, which a watch does not.

8.3.3 The Number of Instances Compared

The greater the number of instances, or cases, that show relevant similarities, the stronger the argument. In the war argument, for example, there is only one instance that has all the relevant similarities: the Vietnam War. But what if there were five additional instances—five different wars that had the relevant similarities to the war in Afghanistan? The argument would be strengthened. The Vietnam War, though it is relevantly similar to the war in Afghanistan, may be an anomaly, a war with a unique set of properties. But citing other cases that are relevantly similar to the war in Afghanistan shows that the relevant set of similarities is no fluke.

Argument 7 (the forensics induction) is an especially strong argument, in part because it cites numerous cases. It implies the existence of such instances when it says "Whenever we have observed this pattern. . . ."

8.3.4 Diversity among Cases

As we've seen, dissimilarities between the things being compared weaken an argument by analogy. Such dissimilarities suggest that the things being compared are not strongly analogous. And we've noted that several cases (instead of just one) that exhibit the similarities can strengthen the argument. In applying this criterion, however, we focus on a very different point: the greater the diversity among the cases that exhibit the relevant similarities, the stronger the argument.

Take a look at the following argument:

1. In my first year of university, one of my courses was taught by a young philosophy professor who handed out a very clear syllabus, explained his expectations, and demonstrated early on that he was always willing to answer any question, and the course ended up being a very good course.
2. In my second year of university, one of my courses was taught by a middle-aged sociology professor who handed out a very clear syllabus, explained his expectations, and demonstrated early on that he was always willing to answer any question, and the course ended up being a very good course.
3. In my third year of university, one of my courses was taught by a very old English professor who handed out a very clear syllabus, explained his expectations, and demonstrated early on that he was always willing to answer any question, and the course ended up being a very good course.
4. Now I'm in my fourth year, and I've got a middle-aged philosophy professor who has handed out a very clear syllabus, has explained his expectations, and has demonstrated early on that he is willing to answer any question.
5. Therefore, this new course will be a good course, too.

Review Notes

Analogical Induction

Analogical Argument Pattern

Thing A has properties P_1, P_2, and P_3, plus the property P_4.
Thing B has properties P_1, P_2, and P_3.
Therefore, thing B probably has property P_4.

Criteria for Judging Arguments by Analogy

1. The number of relevant similarities.
2. The number of relevant dissimilarities.
3. The number of instances compared.
4. The diversity among cases.

Here we have several similarities in question, and they exist between the new professor situation (described in premise 4) and three other professors (detailed in premises 1–3). But what makes this argument especially strong is that the cases are diverse despite the handful of similarities—one case involves a young philosophy professor, another a middle-aged sociology professor, and finally a very old English professor. This state of affairs suggests that the similarities are not coincidental or made up but are strongly linked even in a variety of situations.

As you know, an inductive argument cannot guarantee the truth of the conclusion, and analogical inductions are no exception. But by carefully applying the foregoing criteria, we can increase our chances of arriving at well-supported conclusions (or of identifying those conclusions that are not). This is a good thing—even though there is no magic formula for using the criteria in real-life situations.

Exercise 8.8

Answers to exercises marked with an asterisk (*) may be found in Appendix B, Answers to Exercises.

Evaluate each of the following passages, and indicate whether it contains (1) an argument by analogy, (2) a literary analogy, or (3) an enumerative induction. If the passage contains an argument by analogy, indicate the total number of things (instances) being compared, the relevant similarities mentioned or implied, the conclusion, and whether the argument is strong or weak.

1. "People are like stained-glass windows. They sparkle and shine when the sun is out, but when the darkness sets in, their true beauty is revealed only if there is a light from within." (Elisabeth Kübler-Ross)
2. "Duct tape is like the force. It has a light side, a dark side, and it holds the universe together." (Carl Zwanzig)*

3. Dan, Raj, and Bob all loved that movie, so Willow is going to love it too.
4. "People are like cities: We all have alleys and gardens and secret rooftops and places where daisies sprout between the sidewalk cracks, but most of the time all we let each other see is a postcard glimpse of a skyline or a polished square. Love lets you find those hidden places in another person, even the ones they didn't know were there, even the ones they wouldn't have thought to call beautiful themselves." (Hilary T. Smith, *Wild Awake*)
5. My brother was always good at arithmetic, so he'll be a whiz at algebra.*
6. Tolerating a vicious dictator is like tolerating a bully on the block. If you let the bully push you around, sooner or later he will beat you up and take everything you have. If you let a dictator have his way, he will abuse his people and rob them of life and liberty. If you stand up to the bully just once or—better yet—knock him senseless with a stick, he will never bother you again. Likewise, if you refuse to be coerced by a dictator or if you attack him, his reign will be over. Therefore, the best course of action for people oppressed by a dictator is to resist and attack.
7. I like hamburger, and I like steak, and I like roast beef. So I will like tongue.*
8. "Virtue is like a rich stone, best plain set." (Francis Bacon)
9. John S. Chen, the CEO of BlackBerry, has been in the tech business for over 30 years. Referred to by some as "a doctor for businesses," he has a proven track record of helping failing tech companies get back on track. He'll be able to drag BlackBerry back to the top of the industry in no time.
10. "Cutting the deficit by gutting our investments in innovation and education is like lightening an overloaded airplane by removing its engine. It may make you feel like you're flying high at first, but it won't take long before you feel the impact." (Barack Obama)
11. "Character is the foundation stone upon which one must build to win respect. Just as no worthy building can be erected on a weak foundation, so no lasting reputation worthy of respect can be built on a weak character." (R.C. Samsel)*

Exercise 8.9

Evaluate each of the following arguments by analogy, indicating (1) the things (instances) being compared, (2) the relevant similarities mentioned or implied, (3) whether diversity among multiple cases is a significant factor, (4) the conclusion, and (5) whether the argument is strong or weak.

1. Like two newlyweds, the countries of Europe have linked their economies together. Like newlyweds, they started out starry-eyed and optimistic about it all. And like newlyweds, the countries of Europe see clearly the benefits of this linking. But also like newlyweds, they are almost guaranteed to go

through some tough times together. And eventually, like so many newlyweds, they may well end up regretting the whole idea.*

2. I tried that Bolivian restaurant you recommended, and didn't like it. I also went to an Argentinian restaurant with Martin, and didn't like it at all. And last year, I ate fish at a Peruvian restaurant in the east end of town, and thought it was too salty. So I don't think I'm likely to like any other South American restaurants you might suggest.
3. "If a single cell, under appropriate conditions, becomes a person in the space of a few years, there can surely be no difficulty in understanding how, under appropriate conditions, a cell may, in the course of untold millions of years, give origin to the human race." (Herbert Spencer)
4. A manufacturing plant built in Halifax will provide huge economic benefits, without significant disadvantages. Several new, modern manufacturing plants in the Toronto area have brought jobs to that area as well as improving the city's tax base, without causing significant amounts of pollution or noise or disrupting traffic. The same can be said for two new plants that have opened up on the outskirts of Montreal as well as plants in Calgary and Vancouver.
5. Some people think suicide is immoral. But a well-established moral principle is that one is morally justified in using deadly force in self-defence when one is threatened with death or great pain from an assailant. A disease, such as terminal cancer, can also threaten one with death or great pain. So suicide—a use of deadly force—must sometimes be morally justified when it is an act of self-defence against an assailant (terminal disease) that threatens death or great pain. We are justified in using deadly force to avoid great pain, even when that deadly force is used against *ourselves*.*
6. "If we survey the universe, so far as it falls under our knowledge, it bears a great resemblance to an animal or organized body, and seems actuated with a like principle of life and motion. A continual circulation of matter in it produces no disorder: a continual waste in every part is incessantly repaired: The closest sympathy is perceived throughout the whole system. And each part or member, in performing its proper offices, operates both to its own preservation and to that of the whole. The world, therefore, I infer, is an animal, and the Deity is the soul of the world, activating it and activated by it." (Philo, in David Hume's *Dialogues Concerning Natural Religion*)
7. In her moral philosophy paper "A Defense of Abortion," Judith Jarvis Thomson writes, "[Imagine] you wake up in the morning and find yourself back to back in bed with an unconscious violinist. A famous unconscious violinist. He has been found to have a fatal kidney ailment, and the Society of Music Lovers has canvassed all the available medical records and found that you alone have the right blood type to help. They have therefore kidnapped you, and last night the violinist's circulatory system was plugged into yours, so

that your kidneys can be used to extract poisons from his blood as well as your own. [If he is unplugged from you now, he will die, but] in nine months he will have recovered from his ailment, and can safely be unplugged from you." Since most people would agree that you would be morally justified in unplugging yourself from the violinist, it also follows that it would be morally justified for a woman to abort (i.e., unplug herself from) her baby.

8.4 Causal Arguments

Our world is a shifting, multi-stranded, complicated web of causes and effects—and that's an oversimplification. Incredibly, the normal human response to the apparent causal chaos is to jump in and ask what causes what. What causes breast cancer? What made Malcolm steal the car? What produced that rash on Norah's arm? What brought the universe into existence? Why have the New Democrats never won a federal election? When we answer such questions (or try to), we make a **causal claim**—a statement about the causes of things. And when we try to prove or support a causal claim, we make a **causal argument**—an inductive argument whose conclusion contains a causal claim.

causal claim
A statement about the causes of things.

causal argument
An inductive argument whose conclusion contains a causal claim.

Causal arguments, being inductive, can give us only probable conclusions. If the premises of a strong causal argument are true, then the conclusion is only probably true, with the probability varying from merely likely to highly probable. The probabilistic nature of causal arguments, however, should not be thought of as a failing or weakness. Causal reasoning is simply different from deductive reasoning, and it is our primary method of acquiring knowledge about the workings of the world. The great human enterprise known as science is concerned mainly with causal processes and causal arguments, and few people would consider this work inferior or unreliable because it is not deductively unshakable. We now have very strong inductive arguments, for example, in favour of the claim that cigarettes cause cancer, that the HIV virus causes AIDS, and that chlorofluorocarbons contribute to the depletion of Earth's ozone layer. Each of these causal conclusions is very reliable and constitutes a firm basis for guiding individual and collective behaviour.

Causal arguments can come in several inductive forms, some of which you already know about. For example, we sometimes reason about cause and effect by using enumerative induction:

> One time, when I made an aluminum rod come in contact with the rotating circular-saw blade, sparks flew.
> Another time, when I made a steel nail come in contact with the rotating circular-saw blade, sparks flew.
> Many other times, when I made a brass key come in contact with the rotating circular-saw blade, sparks flew.
> Therefore, making a metal object come in contact with the rotating circular-saw blade always causes sparks to fly.

Occasionally, we may argue to a causal conclusion by using analogical induction:

> Ten years ago, a massive surge in worldwide oil prices caused a recession.
> Five years ago, a massive surge in worldwide oil prices caused a recession.
> Therefore, the current massive surge in worldwide oil prices will cause a recession.

"I would rather discover a single causal connection than win the throne of Persia."

—Democritus

Most often, though, we use another type of induction in which we reason to a causal conclusion by pinpointing the best explanation for a particular effect. Let's say that, after a hail storm, you discover that the roof of your car, which you had left parked outside in the driveway, has a hundred tiny dents in it. You might reason like this: the dents could have been caused by the mischievous kids next door, by a flock of deranged woodpeckers, or by the hail storm. After considering these options (and a few others), you decide that the best explanation (or hypothesis) for the dents is the hail storm. So you conclude that the hail storm caused the dents in your car's roof.

This is a very powerful and versatile form of inductive reasoning called **inference to the best explanation**. It's the essence of scientific thinking and a key part of our everyday problem-solving and knowledge acquisition (whether causal or non-causal). Because of the importance and usefulness of such reasoning, this book devotes three chapters to it in Part 4. So we won't try to cover the same ground here. Instead, we'll concentrate on some other inductive patterns of reasoning that have traditionally been used to assess causal connections.

inference to the best explanation
A form of inductive reasoning in which we reason from premises about a state of affairs to an explanation for that state of affairs:

> Phenomenon Q
> E provides the best explanation for Q.
> Therefore, it is probable that E is true.

8.4.1 Testing for Causes

The English philosopher John Stuart Mill (1806–73) noted several ways of evaluating causal arguments and formulated them into what are now known as "Mill's methods" of inductive inference. Despite their fancy name, however, the methods are basically common sense and are used by just about everyone. They also happen to be the basis of a great deal of scientific testing. Let's look at a few of the more important ones.

8.4.1.1 Agreement or Difference

A modified version of Mill's Method of Agreement says that if two or more occurrences of a phenomenon have only one relevant factor in common, that factor must be the cause.

Imagine that dozens of people stop into Elmo's corner bar after work as they usually do and that 10 of them come down with an intestinal illness one hour after leaving the premises. What caused them to become ill? There are a lot of possibilities. Maybe a waiter who had a flu-like illness sneezed into their drinks,

Food for Thought

Semmelweis, Clean Hands, and Childbed Fever

One of the most famous cases of successful causal reasoning in the history of science is the case of nineteenth-century Hungarian physician Ignaz Semmelweis. Semmelweis worked in the maternity section of the Vienna General Hospital in Austria. During that time period, childbirth was quite dangerous; in fact, many women died in the process. Semmelweis noticed a pattern, however. He noticed that women in one of the hospital's two maternity wards were several times more likely to die of a disease now known as "puerperal fever" (also known as "childbed fever") than were women in the other. He also noticed that women in the safer ward were cared for by midwives; women in the more dangerous ward were cared for by physicians, who often examined their patients directly after performing autopsies. Could there be a connection? Could the physicians be transferring something from the cadavers to their pregnant patients? Semmelweis believed so (even though scientists had not yet discovered the role of germs in producing disease). He instituted a policy under which all medical personnel were required to wash their hands with a chlorine solution after performing autopsies. In the months that followed, the death rate among women in the previously dangerous ward dropped from 10 per cent to about 3 per cent. Semmelweis's careful causal reasoning saved lives.

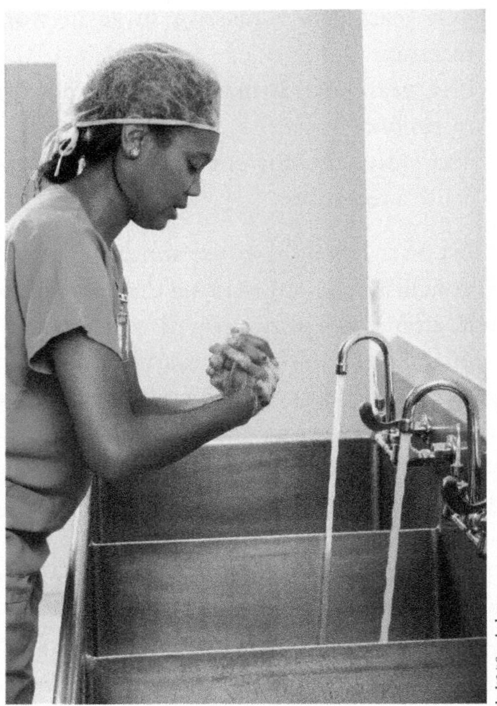
kali9/iStockphoto

Causal reasoning saves lives every day. Can you think of some other important, real-world applications for causal reasoning?

or the free tacos had gone bad, or another patron had a viral infection and passed it along via a handshake. But let's say that there is only one relevant factor that's common to all 10 people who got sick: they all had a drink from the same beer tap. We could then plausibly conclude that something in the beer probably caused the illness.

Public health officials often use the Method of Agreement, especially when they're trying to determine the cause of an unusual illness in a population of several thousand people. They might be puzzled, say, by an unusually large number of cases of rare liver disease in a city. If they discover that all the people affected have the same toxin in their bloodstreams—and this is the only common relevant factor—they have reason to believe that the toxin is the cause of the liver disease. In such situations, the poison may turn out to have an industrial or agricultural source.

Here's a schematic of an argument based on the Method of Agreement:

Instance 1: Factors *a*, *b*, and *c* are followed by *E*.
Instance 2: Factors *a*, *c*, and *d* are followed by *E*.
Instance 3: Factors *b* and *c* are followed by *E*.
Instance 4: Factors *c* and *d* are followed by *E*.
Therefore, factor *c* is probably the cause of *E*.

There's only one factor—factor *c*—that consistently accompanies effect *E*. The other factors are sometimes present and sometimes not. We conclude, then, that factor *c* brings about *E*.

Mill's (modified) Method of Difference says that the relevant factor that is present when a phenomenon occurs and that is absent when the phenomenon does not occur must be the cause. Here we look not for factors that the instances of the phenomenon have in common but for factors that are points of difference among the instances.

Suppose that the performance of football players on a CFL team has been consistently excellent except for six players who have recently been playing the worst games of their careers. The only relevant difference between the high- and low-performing players is that the latter have been taking daily doses of Brand X herbal supplements. If the supplement dosing is really the *only* relevant difference, we could plausibly conclude that the supplements are causing the lousy performance. (Finding out if the supplements are indeed the only relevant difference, of course, is easier said than done.)

So arguments based on the Method of Difference have this form:

Instance 1: Factors *a*, *b*, and *c* are followed by *E*.
Instance 2: Factors *a* and *b* are not followed by *E*.
Therefore, factor *c* is probably the cause of *E*.

8.4.1.2 Both Agreement and Difference

If we combine these two reasoning patterns, we get a modified version of what Mill called the "Joint Method of Agreement and Difference." Using this joint method is, obviously, just a matter of applying both methods simultaneously—a procedure that generally increases the probability that the conclusion is true. This combined method, then, says that the likely cause is the one isolated when you (1) identify the relevant factors common to occurrences of the phenomenon (the Method of Agreement) and (2) discard any of these that are present even when there are no occurrences (the Method of Difference).

Let's apply this combined method to the mystery illness at Elmo's bar. Say that among the 10 patrons who become ill, the common factors are that they all drank from the same beer tap and they all had the free tacos. So we reason that the likely cause is either the beer or the tacos. After further investigation, though, we find that other patrons who ate the tacos did not become ill. We conclude that the beer is the culprit.

The schematic for arguments based on the Joint Method of Agreement and Difference is:

> Instance 1: Factors *a*, *b*, and *c* are followed by *E*.
> Instance 2: Factors *a*, *b*, and *d* are followed by *E*.
> Instance 3: Factors *b* and *c* are not followed by *E*.
> Instance 4: Factors *b* and *d* are not followed by *E*.
> Therefore, factor *a* is probably the cause of *E*.

Factors *a* and *b* are the only relevant factors that are accompanied by *E*. But we can eliminate *b* as a possibility because when it's present, *E* doesn't occur. So *b* can't be the cause of *E*; *a* is most likely the cause.

You can see the Joint Method of Agreement and Difference at work in modern "controlled trials" used to test the effectiveness of medical treatments. In these experiments, there are two groups of subjects—one known as the experimental group, the other the control group. The experimental group receives the treatment being tested, usually a new drug. The control group receives a bogus, or inactive, treatment (referred to as a placebo). This setup helps to ensure that the two groups are as similar as possible and that they differ in only one respect—the use of the genuine treatment. A controlled trial, then, reveals the relevant factor *common* to the occurrence of the effect, which is the subjects' response to the treatment (Method of Agreement). And it shows the only important difference between the occurrence and non-occurrence of the effect: the use of the treatment being tested.

8.4.1.3 Correlation

In many cases, relevant factors aren't merely entirely present or entirely absent during occurrences of the phenomenon—they are closely *correlated* with the occurrences. The cause of an occurrence varies as the occurrence (effect) does. For such situations, Mill formulated the Method of Concomitant Variation. This method says that when two events are correlated—when one varies in close connection with the other—they are probably causally related. For instance, if you observe that the longer you boil eggs, the harder they get (and no other relevant factors complicate this relationship), you can safely conclude that this correlation between boiling and hardening is a causal connection. You have good evidence that the boiling causes the hardening.

In medical science, such correlations are highly prized because direct evidence of cause and effect is so hard to come by. We don't *see* causation directly. Correlations are often indirect evidence of one thing causing another. In exploring the link between cigarette smoking and lung cancer, for example, researchers discovered first that people who smoke cigarettes are more likely to get lung cancer than those who don't smoke. But later research also showed that the more cigarettes people smoke, the higher their risk of lung cancer. Medical scientists call such a correlation a *dose–response relationship*. The higher the dose of the element in question (smoking), the higher the response (the more cases of lung cancer).

Good statistical reasoning—and good critical thinking—might be correlated with taking stats. But is it *caused* by it?

This dose–response relationship between cigarette smoking and lung cancer is, when combined with other data, strong evidence that smoking causes lung cancer.

We can represent arguments based on the Method of Concomitant Variation like this:

> Instance 1: Factors *a*, *b*, and *c* are correlated with *E* being present.
> Instance 2: Factors *a*, *b*, and increased-*c* are correlated with increased *E*.
> Instance 3: Factors *a*, *b*, and decreased-*c* are correlated with decreased *E*.
> Therefore, factor *c* is causally connected with *E*.

An important cautionary note must accompany this discussion of correlation: correlation, of course, does not always mean that a causal relationship is present. A correlation could just be a coincidence (as we will discuss in the next section of this chapter). From 2000 to 2009, consumption of cheese in the US was strongly correlated with the number of people who died by falling down the stairs, but this doesn't mean that one was in any way causally linked with the other.[4]

8.4.2 Causal Confusions

Mill's methods and other forms of causal reasoning may be common sense, and useful, but they're not foolproof. No inductive procedure can guarantee the truth of the conclusion. More to the point, it's easy to commit errors in cause-and-effect reasoning—regardless of the method used—by failing to take into account pertinent aspects of the situation. This section describes some of the more common causal blunders to which we're all prey.

8.4.2.1 Misidentifying Relevant Factors

A key issue in any type of causal reasoning is whether the factors preceding an effect are truly relevant to that effect. In using the Method of Agreement, for example, it's easy to find a preceding factor common to all occurrences of a phenomenon. But that factor may actually be irrelevant. In the case of Elmo's bar, what

Food for Thought

Causal Confusion about Vaccine Side Effects

Causal confusions are especially challenging when it comes to health. Most of us are rightly vigilant about our health, and we keep our eyes open for things that might affect our well-being. We want to learn about what things can help us and what things might hurt us. If you get stung by a bee and your arm swells up, you've likely learned something new and important: you may be allergic to bee stings and need to consult a doctor. In other cases, your doctor may put you on a medication and specifically tell you to watch out for side effects. They might tell you that some percentage of people taking this drug develop severe headaches; therefore, if that happens to you, you'll want to notify your doctor, because they may want to prescribe a different drug. In the context of a public health emergency, like a pandemic, this pattern poses challenges. When a vaccine is given to millions of people, those millions of people are likely going to be paying special attention to their health afterwards. Sometimes they'll experience genuine side effects, and sometimes they'll be fooled by faulty causal reasoning. Scientist and science writer Derek Lowe explained the problem this way:

> [I]f you take 10 million people and *just wave your hand back and forth over their upper arms*, in the next two months you would expect to see [within that population] about 4,000 heart attacks. About 4,000 strokes. Over 9,000 new diagnoses of cancer. And about 14,000 of that ten million will die, out of usual all-causes mortality. No one would notice. That's how many people die and get sick anyway.
>
> But if you took those ten million people and gave them a new vaccine instead, there's a real danger that those heart attacks, cancer diagnoses, and deaths will be attributed to the vaccine. I mean, if you reach a large enough population, you are literally going to have cases where someone gets the vaccine and drops dead the next day (just as they would have if they *didn't* get the vaccine). It could prove difficult to convince that person's friends and relatives of that lack of connection, though. *Post hoc ergo propter hoc* is one of the most powerful fallacies of human logic, and we're not going to get rid of it any time soon. Especially when it comes to vaccines. The best we can do, I think, is to try to get the word out in advance. Let people know that such things are going to happen, because people get sick and die constantly in this world. The key will be whether they are getting sick or dying at a noticeably higher rate once they have been vaccinated.[5]

if all those who became ill had black hair? So what? We know that hair colour is very unlikely to be related to intestinal illness. *Relevant* factors include only those things that could possibly be causally connected to the occurrence of the phenomenon being studied. We could reasonably judge that factors relevant to the intestinal illness would include all the conditions that might help transmit bacteria or viruses.

Your ability to identify relevant factors depends mostly on your background knowledge—what you know about the kinds of conditions that could produce the occurrences in which you're interested. Lack of background knowledge might lead you to dismiss or ignore relevant factors or to assume that irrelevant factors must play a role. The only cure for this inadequacy is deeper study of the causal possibilities in question.

8.4.2.2 Mishandling Multiple Factors

Most of the time, the biggest difficulty in evaluating causal connections is not that there are so few relevant factors to consider—but that there are so many. Too often, the Method of Agreement and the Method of Difference are rendered useless because they cannot, by themselves, narrow the possibilities to just one.

At the same time, ordinary causal reasoning is often flawed because of the failure to consider *all* the relevant antecedent factors. (Later chapters will refer to this problem as the failure to consider alternative explanations.) Sometimes this kind of oversight happens because we simply don't look hard enough for possible causes. At other times, we miss relevant factors because we don't know enough about the causal processes involved. This again is a function of skimpy background knowledge. Either way, there is no countermeasure better than your own determination to dig out the whole truth.

8.4.2.3 Being Misled by Coincidence

Sometimes ordinary events are paired in unusual or interesting ways. You think of Quebec, then suddenly a TV ad announces low-cost train fares to Montreal; you receive some email just as your doorbell and the phone both ring; or you stand in the lobby of a hotel thinking of an old friend and then see her walk in. Plenty of interesting pairings can also show up in scientific research. Scientists might find, for example, that men with the highest rates of heart disease may also have a higher daily intake of water. Or women with the lowest risk of breast cancer may own Toyotas. Such pairings are very probably just coincidence, merely surprising correlations of events. A problem arises, though, when we think that there nevertheless *must be* a causal connection involved.

For several reasons, we may very much *want* a coincidence to be the result of a cause-and-effect relationship, so we come to believe that the pairing *is* causal. Just as often, we may mistake causes for coincidences because we're impressed or excited about the conjunction of events. Since the pairing of events may seem "too much of a coincidence" to be coincidence, we conclude that one event must have caused the other. You may be thinking about how nice it would be for your sister to call you from her home in Nunavut—then the phone rings, and it's her! You're tempted to conclude that your wishing *caused* her to call. But such an event, though intriguing and seemingly improbable, is not really so extraordinary. Given the ordinary laws of statistics, seemingly incredible coincidences are common and must occur. Any event, even one that seems shockingly improbable, is actually very probable over the long haul. Given enough opportunities to occur, events like this surprising phone call are virtually certain to happen to *someone*.

People are especially prone to think, "it can't be just coincidence" because, for several psychological reasons, they misjudge the probabilities involved. They may think, for example, that a phone call from someone at the moment they're

Food for Thought

Spurious Correlations

If you look at enough data, about enough topics, you're bound to find something correlated with something. To illustrate this point, author and data nerd Tyler Vigen put together an entire website dedicated to graphs of "spurious correlations"—correlations that are almost certainly entirely coincidental and empty of causal meaning. See for yourself!

Number of people who drowned by falling into a pool

correlates with

Films Nicolas Cage appeared in

Correlation: 66.6% (r=0.666004)

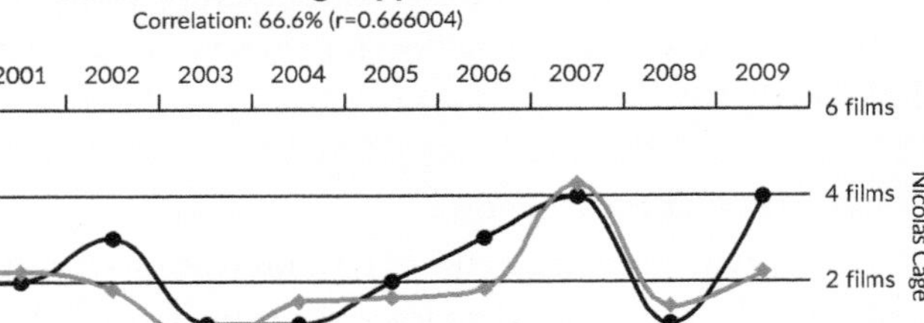

Per capita cheese consumption

correlates with

Number of people who died by becoming tangled in their bedsheets

Correlation: 94.71% (r=0.947091)

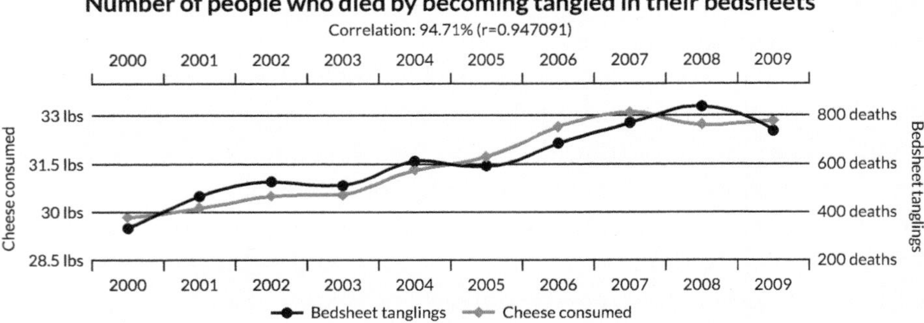

Graphs like these serve as a warning: when you spot a correlation, you need to think carefully (perhaps using the skills you've learned in this chapter) about whether the correlation is a meaningful one.

thinking of that person is incredible—but only because they've forgotten about all the times they've thought of that person and the phone *didn't* ring. Such probability misjudgments are a major source of beliefs about the paranormal or supernatural, topics that we address in Chapter 10.

Unfortunately, there is no foolproof way to distinguish coincidence from cause and effect. But this rule of thumb can help:

> *Don't assume that a causal connection exists unless you have good reason for doing so.*

Generally, you have a good reason for suspecting that a causal connection exists if the connection passes one or more standard causal tests (such as the ones we've been discussing)—and if you can rule out any relevant factors that might undermine the verdict of those tests. Usually, when a cause-and-effect connection is uncertain, only further evaluation or research can clear things up.

8.4.2.4 Confusing Cause with Temporal Order

A particularly common type of misjudgment about coincidences is the logical fallacy known as ***post hoc, ergo propter hoc*** ("after that, therefore because of that"). It is true that a cause must precede its effect. But the fact that one event precedes another doesn't mean that the earlier one *caused* the later. To think so is to be taken in by this fallacy. Outrageous examples of post hoc arguments include "The rooster crowed, then the sun came up, so the rooster's crowing caused the sunrise!" and "Jasmine left her umbrella at home on Monday, and that caused it to rain." You can clearly see the error in such cases, but consider these arguments:

post hoc, ergo propter hoc *("after that, therefore because of that")*
The fallacy of reasoning that just because B followed A, A must have caused B.

> **Argument 8**
> After the training for police officers was enhanced, violent crime in the city decreased by 10 per cent. So enhanced training caused the decline in violent crime.
>
> **Argument 9**
> An hour after Julio drank the cola, his headache went away. The cola cured his headache.
>
> **Argument 10**
> As soon as Smith took office and implemented policies that reflected his conservative theory of economics, the economy went into a downward slide characterized by slow growth and high unemployment. Therefore, the Smith policies caused the current economic doldrums.
>
> **Argument 11**
> I wore my black shirt on Tuesday and got an F on a math quiz. I wore the same shirt the next day and flunked my psych exam. That shirt's bad luck.

The conclusion of argument 8 is based on nothing more than the fact that the enhanced training preceded the reduction in violent crime. But crime rates can decrease for many reasons, and the enhanced training may have had nothing to do with the decline in crime. For the argument to be strong, other considerations besides temporal order would have to apply—for example, that other possible causes or antecedent factors had been ruled out; that there was a close correlation between amount of training and decline in crime rates; or that in previous years (or in comparable cities) enhanced training was always followed by a decline in violent crime (or no change in training was always followed by steady crime rates).

Argument 9 is also purely post hoc. Such reasoning is extremely common and underlies almost all folk remedies and a great deal of quackery and bogus self-cures. You take a vitamin E capsule, and four hours later your headache is gone. But was it really the vitamin E that did the trick? Or was it some other overlooked factor, such as something you ate, the medication you took (or didn't take), the nap you had, the change in environment (from, say, indoors to outdoors), or the stress reduction you felt when you had pleasant thoughts? Would your headache have gone away on its own anyway? Was it the *placebo effect*—the tendency for people to feel better when treated even when the treatment is fake or inactive? A chief function of controlled medical testing is to evaluate cause-and-effect relationships by systematically ruling out post hoc thinking and irrelevant factors.

Argument 10 is typical post hoc reasoning from the political sphere. Unless there are other good reasons for thinking that the economic policy is causally connected to specific economic events, the argument is weak and the conclusion unreliable.

Argument 11 is 100 per cent post hoc and undiluted superstition. There is no difference in kind between this argument and much of the notorious post hoc reasoning of centuries ago: "That woman gave me the evil eye. The next day I broke my leg. That proves she's a witch, and the Elders of Salem should have her put to death!"

Everett Collection/Shutterstock

What role did the post hoc fallacy play in Salem during the witch trials of the 1690s?

8.4.2.5 Ignoring the Common Causal Factor

Sometimes A and B are correlated with each other, and genuinely causally connected, but A doesn't cause B and B doesn't cause A. Rather, both A and B are caused by some third factor, C, that they share in common. One often-cited example is this: there is a correlation between sales of ice cream and deaths due to drowning across the months of the year. Does ice cream cause people to drown? No. Does drowning somehow cause a rise in ice cream sales? Highly unlikely! The truth is that both of those things are more common during a particular season—namely, summer. In the heat of summer, more people go swimming, and therefore, the rate of drownings goes up. And sales of ice cream likewise go up in summer. So summertime is the *common causal factor* shared by those two variables. (Note: *common* here means "shared," not "frequent." It refers to the factor they have in common.) Another example: imagine reading about a survey that suggests that Canadians with access to high-speed internet tend to go out to see bands play live more frequently than people with poor internet access do. Is there a causal connection between the two? Well, there might be: maybe people use the internet

Everyday Problems and Decisions

Causal Reasoning and Voting

Causal reasoning arguably plays an important role in electoral politics—that is, in how we vote. After all, we want to vote for people who are going to cause (or at least try to cause) outcomes that we approve of. And when sitting politicians cause outcomes that we like, we want to vote for them again. But figuring out whether a given politician or government policy really *caused* the outcome you liked (or disliked!) isn't always easy.

One example: in April of 2020, Canada's national unemployment rate and various provincial unemployment rates soared to roughly double what they had been a year earlier. Was government to blame? After all, government has the power to enact a range of policies related to employment, and governments typically are happy to take credit when unemployment is *low*. So why not blame them for the *high* unemployment in April of 2020? The answer will be obvious to most of you. April of 2020 is when the COVID-19 pandemic really hit, and the pandemic had an enormous effect on employment: many companies laid off workers, and others cancelled plans to hire new employees.

This is a dramatic example, a case in which government policies very likely had little or no causal connection to the outcome we are all concerned with. But in other cases, government is much more likely to be causally responsible. Indeed, sometimes the causal connection is quite clear: if the number of regulations aimed at a particular industry jumps dramatically while a particular political party is in power, it's safe to assume that that party *caused* the jump, because in Canada's political system, being able to pass regulations goes along with being in power.

In other situations, the connection is much less clear, even if plausible. When crime rates go down, is it because the government passed new laws that increased jail terms for certain crimes? Or because they passed new anti-poverty laws, reducing the number of people desperate enough to turn to crime? Or was it something else entirely? When pollution levels are up, is it because government relaxed anti-pollution laws, or because economic production levels are up, or because dirty water or dirty air is flowing into our region from some other province or country?

Engaging in questionable causal reasoning is, of course, sometimes also a political tactic. When your political opponent is in power, you naturally want to say that *everything* is their fault. Stock market down? *Their fault!* Unemployment up? *Their fault!* Rainy during the long weekend? You'll find some way to claim that it's *their fault!* But the temptation to make such claims shouldn't stop you from thinking critically about them.

to find out when good bands are playing, and Canadians without good internet access are left out. But it's more likely that there's a common causal factor connecting the two: people who live in the city are much more likely to have high-speed internet than people who live in rural areas. People who live in the city also tend to live near lots of clubs and bars where they can hear live music. More evidence would be needed before we could be certain what the real causal story is.

8.4.2.6 Confusing Cause and Effect

Sometimes we may realize that there's a causal relationship between two factors but we may not know which factor is the cause and which is the effect. We may be confused, in other words, about the answers to questions like these:

> Does your coffee drinking cause you to feel stressed out—or do your feelings of being stressed out cause you to drink coffee?
>
> Does participation in high school sports produce desirable virtues, such as discipline and self-reliance—or do the virtues of discipline and self-reliance lead students to participate in high school sports?
>
> Does regular exercise make people healthy—or are healthy people naturally prone to regular exercise?

As you can see, it's not always a simple matter to discern what the nature of a causal link is. Again, we must rely on our rule of thumb: *don't assume that a causal connection exists unless you have good reason for doing so.* This tenet applies not only to our ordinary experience but also to all states of affairs involving cause and effect, including scientific investigations.

In everyday life, sorting cause from effect is often easy because the situations we confront are frequently simple and familiar—as when we're trying to discover what caused the kettle to boil over. Here, we naturally rely on Mill's methods or other types of causal reasoning. But as we've seen, in many other common circumstances, things aren't so simple. We often cannot be sure that we've identified all the relevant factors or ruled out the influence of coincidence or correctly distinguished cause and effect. Our rule of thumb, then, should be our guide in all the doubtful cases.

Science faces all the same kinds of challenges in its pursuit of causal explanations. And despite its sophisticated methods and investigative tools, it must expend a great deal of effort to pin down causal connections. Identifying the cause of a disease, for example, usually requires not one study or experiment but many. The main reason is that it's always tough to uncover relevant factors and exclude irrelevant or misleading factors. That's why we should apply our rule of thumb even to scientific research that purports to identify a causal link. In Chapters 9 and 10, we'll explore procedures for evaluating scientific research and for applying our rule of thumb with more precision.

"Luck has nothing to do with it, because I have spent many, many hours, countless hours, on the court working for my one moment in time, not knowing when it would come."

—Serena Williams

Review Notes

Causal Confusions

- Misidentifying relevant factors
- Overlooking relevant factors
- Confusing coincidence with cause
- Confusing cause with temporal order (post hoc fallacy)
- Ignoring the common causal factor
- Confusing cause and effect

8.4.3 Necessary and Sufficient Conditions

To fully appreciate the dynamics of cause and effect and to be able to skilfully assess causal arguments, you must understand two other important concepts: **necessary condition** and **sufficient condition**. Causal processes always occur under specific conditions. So we often speak of cause and effect in terms of *the conditions for the occurrence of an event*. Scientists, philosophers, and others go a step further and emphasize a distinction between necessary and sufficient conditions for the occurrence of an event:

> *A necessary condition for the occurrence of an event is one without which the event cannot occur.*
>
> *A sufficient condition for the occurrence of an event is one that guarantees that the event occurs.*

necessary condition
A condition for the occurrence of an event without which the event cannot occur.

sufficient condition
A condition for the occurrence of an event that guarantees that the event occurs.

Suppose you drop a water-filled balloon from the top of a building (aiming it at your least favourite professor, of course) and it breaks on the pavement. What are the *necessary* conditions for the breaking of the balloon (the effect)? There are several, including (1) your releasing the balloon, (2) the force of gravity acting on the water, (3) the weakness of the material that the balloon is made of (its breakability), and (4) the hardness of the pavement. If any one of these conditions is not present, the water balloon will not break. To state the obvious, if you don't release the balloon, it won't drop. If gravity is not in force, the balloon won't fall. If the balloon material isn't breakable, it won't break. If the pavement isn't hard enough, even a breakable balloon won't rupture. (For the sake of illustration, this list of necessary conditions is incomplete. Many, if not most, events in nature actually have large numbers of necessary conditions.)

What are the *sufficient* conditions for the balloon's breaking? Not one of the four conditions by itself is sufficient to cause the balloon to break. None *guarantees* the occurrence of the effect; none suffices to produce the event. But all the necessary conditions combined (these four and others) are sufficient to guarantee the balloon's breaking.

Failing to feed a healthy goldfish for a few weeks is a sure way to kill it. So this deprivation is a sufficient condition for its death, as is removing the water from its fishbowl. But neither taking away the fish's food nor draining its bowl is a *necessary* condition for a goldfish's death, because its death can be caused without resorting to either of these methods. On the other hand, necessary conditions for *sustaining* the fish's life include feeding it, providing it with water to live in, ensuring that the water is properly oxygenated, and so on. Again, in this instance, the whole set of the necessary conditions would constitute a sufficient condition for sustaining the fish's life.

In cases in which a complete set of necessary conditions constitutes a sufficient condition for an event, we say that the conditions are *individually necessary and jointly sufficient* for an event to occur. As the previous examples suggest, however, it's possible to have a set of conditions that are individually necessary but *not* jointly sufficient. Say some of the conditions necessary for sustaining the goldfish's life are present but not all of them are. Because some necessary conditions are missing, the sufficient condition for keeping the fish alive would not exist. On the other hand, it is also possible to have a set of conditions that are jointly sufficient but not individually necessary. By not feeding a goldfish for weeks, we would create a set of conditions sufficient for the death of the fish. But these conditions are not necessary for the death of a goldfish because we could ensure its death in other ways.

So there are conditions that are necessary but not sufficient for the occurrence of an event, and conditions that are sufficient but not necessary. There are also conditions that are *both* necessary and sufficient for an event. The Earth's being more massive than the moon is both a necessary and sufficient condition for the moon's being less massive than the Earth. A piece of paper's being heated to a sufficiently high temperature in the presence of oxygen is both a necessary and sufficient condition for the combustion of the paper.

In some situations, depending on our interests or practical concerns, we may focus on necessary causal conditions and in other situations on sufficient causal conditions. When we're interested in *preventing or eliminating* a state of affairs, we often zero in on necessary causal conditions. If you were a scientist trying to discover how to prevent mosquito infestations, you would try to determine the necessary conditions for the occurrence of mosquito infestations. Uncovering and understanding just one necessary condition could give you everything you need to control the problem. If you found out, for example, that a necessary condition for mosquito breeding is standing water, you would need to look no further for an answer. Eliminating the standing water would prevent infestations.

When we're interested in *bringing about* a state of affairs, we're likely to focus on sufficient causal conditions. If you were a doctor devoted to treating clogged arteries in your patients, you would seek out treatments scientifically proven to be sufficient for alleviating the condition. The treatments might include surgery to remove the blockage or a procedure called balloon angioplasty to widen artery passageways.

Your success in appraising causal arguments often depends heavily on your ability to distinguish between statements expressing causes as necessary conditions and statements expressing causes as sufficient conditions. Consider:

> In the current situation, the prime minister will call an election if Parliament doesn't vote in favour of his proposal to cut taxes.

This statement says that the condition required for the prime minister to call an election is Parliament not supporting his proposal to cut taxes. But is this a necessary or sufficient condition? The use of the word *if* by itself signals a sufficient condition. If sufficient condition is what's meant, then the statement says that Parliament's refusal to support the tax cuts will automatically trigger an election call. This outcome is assured if Parliament doesn't cooperate.

But if the statement is meant to express the idea that Parliament's refusal to support the tax cut is a necessary condition, then we're talking about a very different situation. If Parliament's refusal is a necessary condition, then it *will not* unavoidably trigger an election call because the refusal may not be the *only* necessary condition. The idea of a necessary condition is expressed by the phrase "only if" before the stipulated condition. To express necessary condition, the statement should read:

> In the current situation, the prime minister will call an election only if Parliament doesn't vote in favour of his proposal to cut taxes.

So, depending on the kind of causal condition meant, the statement could describe an election that's sure to happen if the condition obtains—or an election that may not occur even if the condition obtains.

As you might expect, conditions that are *both* necessary and sufficient are indicated by the phrase "if and only if." For example:

> The paper will combust if and only if it's heated to a sufficiently high temperature in the presence of oxygen.

None of this discussion, however, should lead you to think that a causal condition must be *either* necessary or sufficient. It could be neither:

> Late delivery of the package caused John to miss his deadline.
> Ricardo's stubbornness caused the negotiations to break down.

Critical Thinking and the Media

Advertising Necessary and Sufficient Conditions

One of the most popular ways in which companies promote foods, vitamins, and dietary supplements is by pointing out the role that key nutrients play in good health.

For example, a brand of cereal may advertise that it is high in dietary fibre, and that dietary fibre has been shown to play a role in lowering the risk of heart disease. A brand of green tea aimed at men may claim that it contains a nutrient that "supports good prostate health." A brand of milk may point out that milk contains calcium, and that calcium promotes healthy bones.

All of these claims may be true . . . depending, at least, on how you interpret words and phrases like "promotes" and "supports" and "plays a role in." Each of those is much more modest—less impressive—than words and phrases like "causes" or "gives you" or "creates."

In this chapter, you've learned the difference between necessary and sufficient conditions. How does that distinction apply to a claim about, for example, the role that calcium plays in "promoting" healthy bones? Well, it's certainly true that calcium plays a role in maintaining strong bones. And so dietary calcium is a necessary condition for good bone health. But that's different from saying that milk in particular is necessary for bone health, because there are many sources of dietary calcium (including leafy green vegetables). And it's also quite different from saying that calcium in general, or milk in particular, is going to be sufficient to ensure strong bones—especially among people with medical conditions such as osteoporosis.

Why do advertisers use such weak language, rather than making stronger claims? In some cases, it may be because they know that stronger claims would be dishonest and would open them up to legal liability. And they hope that consumers won't apply their critical thinking skills to the weaker claims they make involving "supporting" and "promoting."

Exercise 8.10

Answers to exercises marked with an asterisk (*) may be found in Appendix B, Answers to Exercises.

Analyze each of the following causal arguments. Identify the conclusion, and say whether the argument appeals to the Method of Agreement, the Method of Difference, the Joint Method of Agreement and Difference, or correlation. In some cases, the conclusion may be implied but not stated. State whether the argument is strong or weak.

1. If we look at Instance 1, when factors A, B, and C were present, we see that E happened. In Instance 2, when factors A, B, and D were present, E happened. In Instance 3, when factors A and C were present, E did not happen. In Instance 4, when C and D were present, E did not happen. And in Instance 5, when A, C, and D were present, E did not happen. Therefore, B caused E.
2. Research suggests that eating lots of fruits and vegetables may provide some protection against several types of cancer. Studies have revealed that the risk of getting cancer associated with the lowest intakes of fruits and vegetables

is twice as high as that associated with the highest intakes. This association holds for several types of cancer, including cancers of the breast, colon, pancreas, and bladder.*

3. Whenever a murder happens in a predominantly White neighbourhood, the police are quick to respond. But when a murder happens in a Black neighbourhood, the cops take forever just to show up. It's clear that police just don't care about Black lives the way they care about White lives.
4. We tested 20 samples of ground beef from six different processing plants across Canada. All samples were subjected to the standard test for *E. coli* O157:H7. Test results showed that 17 of them were free of *E. coli* and hence, in this regard, safe for human consumption. The other three, however, showed significant levels of *E. coli*. The only relevant factor common to these three samples is that they all came from processing plants owned by a single company, JBR Meats, Inc. (and none of the 17 uncontaminated samples came from a plant owned by JBR). We conclude that there are significant deficiencies in JBR's food-safety procedures.
5. Three students in this class attended a party while they were unvaccinated. They also happen to be the only three who refused to wear masks during their in-person class. And guess what? Those are the only students who caught COVID-19.
6. A new survey conducted by a Christian think-tank indicated that 20 per cent *more* people were now praying regularly at home, compared to ten years ago. Most of the people who reported having started praying at home since the last survey also stated that they had started following religious leaders on social media.
7. Educators have frequently noted the connection between education level and salary. The higher a person's education level is, the higher their annual salary is likely to be. Education increases people's earning power.*
8. "On 20 May 1747, I took twelve patients [with] scurvy on board the *Salisbury* at sea. Their cases were as similar as I could have them. They all in general had putrid gums, the spots and lassitude, with weakness of their knees. They lay together in one place, being a proper apartment for the sick in the fore-hold; and had one diet in common to all. . . . Two of these were ordered each a quart of cider a day. Two others took [25 drops of] vitriol three times a day. . . . Two others took two spoonfuls of vinegar three times a day. . . . Two of the worst patients [were given a half pint of seawater daily]. . . . Two others had each two oranges and one lemon given them every day. . . . The two remaining patients took [small doses of nutmeg, garlic, mustard seed, and a few other ingredients]. The consequence was that the most sudden and visible good effects were perceived from the use of the oranges and lemons; one of those who had taken them being at the end of six days fit for duty. . . . The other was the best recovered of any in his condition, and being now deemed pretty well was appointed nurse to the rest of the sick. As I shall have occasion elsewhere to take notice of the effects of other medicines in this disease,

I shall here only observe that the result of all my experiments was that oranges and lemons were the most effectual remedies for this distemper at sea." (James Lind, *Of the Prevention of the Scurvy*, 1753)

9. A professor wanted to figure out which of two teaching methods was superior: having students read the relevant chapter before her lecture, or after it. So she taught two sections of the same course, each with between fifty and sixty students. The classes were taught at 10 a.m. on different days, and the students in both classes were similar in terms of major, GPA, and other academic factors. For one section of the course, students were instructed to read the relevant chapter before class, and then the professor lectured on it. For the other section, students received a lecture to prepare them before being instructed to read the relevant chapter. At the end of the term, the students in the second section (the "lecture first, read later" section) had a class average that was 2.5 per cent higher than students in the other section. The professor concluded that the "lecture first, read later" method resulted in better learning.
10. Kristyn is the owner of a small chain of beauty shops called simply "Kristyn's." Six months ago, the manager of the chain, Fey, quit to start her own shop, and Kristyn hired Daniella to replace her. Last week, while looking over the chain's payroll, Kristyn noticed a lot of unfamiliar names. After talking to Daniella about it, Kristyn figures out that turnover among estheticians has gone up a lot since Fey left. In addition, Kristyn finds out that Daniella has been taking a very active and direct role in managing the estheticians at each of the five shops. Kristyn concludes that Daniella is not an effective manager.
11. The risk of atherosclerosis (hardening of the arteries) is linked to the amount of "bad" cholesterol (low-density lipoproteins) in the bloodstream. The higher those cholesterol levels, the greater the risk of atherosclerosis. There's a causal connection between levels of "bad" cholesterol and risk of atherosclerosis.
12. As a grocery stocker at Loblaw, Garrett has noticed that whenever sales of hot dogs go up, so do sales of ketchup.
13. Investigators tested the performance of four gasoline-powered lawnmowers before and after a tune-up. The machines differed in age, manufacturer, engine type, and controls. The performance of every mower was better after the tune-up, leading the testers to conclude that tune-ups can improve the performance of lawnmowers.*
14. Minhiriath, Enedwaith, and Rohan are geographical regions that have similar climates year-round. They are renowned for a unique flower that only grows within their borders, the lissuin. Last year, Minhiriath experienced an unusual amount of rainfall, much more than Enedwaith and Rohan. Their lissuin didn't grow properly, whereas those in the other two locations grew like they did every year. Therefore, growth of the lissuin depends very heavily on the amount of rain the flowers receive.
15. Sometimes reception on my phone is excellent, and sometimes it's terrible. There's only one important factor that seems to make a difference. When

I'm out on the street, the reception is excellent. When it's terrible, I'm usually at school. For some reason, being in this building interferes with my phone reception.

16. The price of a barrel of oil on the world market has hit $40 only 12 times in the last 30 years. Sometimes major world economies were in recession, and sometimes they weren't. Sometimes there was an increase in the average fuel consumption of cars, sometimes not. War has been the only constant.*
17. I think Charlie is upset because he got a rejection letter from art school on Friday. He was pretty happy all week, but then he started acting really bummed out just before the weekend.
18. In our test, after people washed their hands with Lather-Up germicidal soap, no germs whatsoever could be detected on their hands. But under exactly the same conditions, after they washed their hands with Brand X germicidal soap, plenty of germs were found on their hands. Lather-Up is better.
19. For years now, violent crimes in the downtown core of this city have consistently averaged three to four per month. After the police doubled foot patrols there, the rate has been one or two violent crimes every three months. That police presence has made a huge difference.*
20. The cause of Barry's criminal behaviour—his involvement in pickpocketing and purse-snatching—is no mystery. Barry commits most of his criminal acts when the outdoor temperatures are highest. When it's very cold out, he behaves himself. In fact, the incidence of his criminal behaviour rises as the temperature rises. Barry's problem is that he has a heat-sensitive personality.

Exercise 8.11

For each argument in Exercise 8.10, identify errors in causal reasoning that are most likely to occur in the circumstances indicated. The possibilities include (a) misidentifying or overlooking relevant factors, (b) being misled by coincidence, (c) falling for the post hoc fallacy, and (d) confusing cause and effect. Answers for 2, 7, 13, 16, and 19 are provided in Appendix B.

Exercise 8.12

For each of the following causal statements, indicate whether the specified cause is (a) a necessary condition, (b) a sufficient condition, (c) a necessary and sufficient condition, or (d) neither a necessary nor a sufficient condition.

1. Sylvia's exposure to the influenza virus caused her to get the flu.*
2. The trees along the river were cut down, and then we sprayed pesticides on the remaining vegetation; next thing you know, soil along the banks of the river started to erode quickly.

3. The game was tied, until Fred VanVleet hit a three-pointer at the buzzer, winning the game for the Raptors.
4. Chopping off the head of the king put an end to him.*
5. Carla was sipping her latte, and so she ended up driving right through a red light.
6. I won't tolerate your cheating! I want you to move out right now!
7. Taz yelled at the customer just because it was his last day at work, so he knew he couldn't be fired for it.
8. BUS22 is a required course for all accounting majors, which is why Kaitlin was allowed to register in the class.
9. A single spark started the internal combustion engine.*
10. When carbon atoms are organized in the proper crystalline arrangement, they make a diamond.

8.5 Mixed Arguments

We noted in Chapter 3 the distinction between deductive and inductive arguments. We said that a deductive argument is intended to provide logically *conclusive* support for its conclusion and that an inductive argument is intended to provide *probable*—not conclusive—support for its conclusion. In Chapters 6 and 7, we discussed deductive reasoning in more detail and ways of evaluating deductive arguments. And here in Chapter 8, we've discussed several forms of inductive reasoning and ways of evaluating them. Since the processes for evaluating deductive and inductive arguments are so different, it makes sense to learn about them separately. But in real life, arguers will very often combine inductive and deductive elements within a single, compound argument. Let's look briefly at the notion of **mixed arguments** and how to evaluate them.

mixed argument
An argument that includes both inductive and deductive elements.

There are no limits to the ways in which arguers may try to combine deductive and inductive elements within a single, mixed argument. One of the simplest ways in which deductive and inductive elements may be combined is seen when one of the *premises* of a categorical syllogism is actually the *conclusion* of an inductive argument—say, an argument that uses enumerative induction. Here's an example:

> In our study, we gave 100 average Canadian consumers a simple quiz about basic science. None of them passed it. It seems average Canadian consumers just don't have an understanding of basic science. Only people who understand science should get to have a say on scientific issues like the safety of genetically modified wheat. So average Canadians consumers should not have a say on genetically modified wheat.

The first part of that argument is an example of enumerative induction: it's a kind of survey, one that reaches a dramatic conclusion based on a rather small sample:

- *Target population:* Canadian consumers
- *Sample:* 100 Canadian consumers
- *Relevant property:* understanding of basic science
- *Conclusion:* 0 per cent of Canadian consumers understand basic science.

The second part of the argument is a categorical syllogism:

> Premise 1: No Canadian consumers understand basic science.
> Premise 2: All people who should get a say on the safety of genetically modified wheat are people who understand basic science.
> Conclusion: No Canadian consumers are people who should get a say on the safety of genetically modified wheat.

Let's look at those two components of the argument, beginning with the inductive part. How strong is the argument that "no Canadian consumers understand basic science?" The first thing to note, of course, is that the sample is very small: a sample of just 100 people leaves a very large margin of error. We also need more information about whether the sample was random or representative. We would also, ideally, want to ask questions about just what kind of quiz was administered and what the quiz-givers count as "basic" science. But even with the minimal information available here, and especially given the small sample, it looks as if this inductive part of the argument is pretty weak. But let's accept it for now, for the sake of argument, and move on to assess the deductive component of the argument.

Since the conclusion is about Canadian consumers and whether they're the sort who should have a say, we'll assign *S* and *P* (subject and predicate) this way:

> *S* = Canadian consumers
> *P* = people who should get a say on the safety of genetically modified wheat

We'll assign *M* (for middle term) to the term that's left—namely, the bit about understanding basic science:

> *M* = people who understand basic science

Next, let's take the categorical syllogism expressed above and put it into standard form, using the letters we just assigned:

> No *S* are *M*.
> All *P* are *M*.
> Therefore, no *S* are *P*.

Now we can ask, is this a valid argument? Let's do a Venn diagram to figure it out. Diagramming the two premises produces a diagram like this:

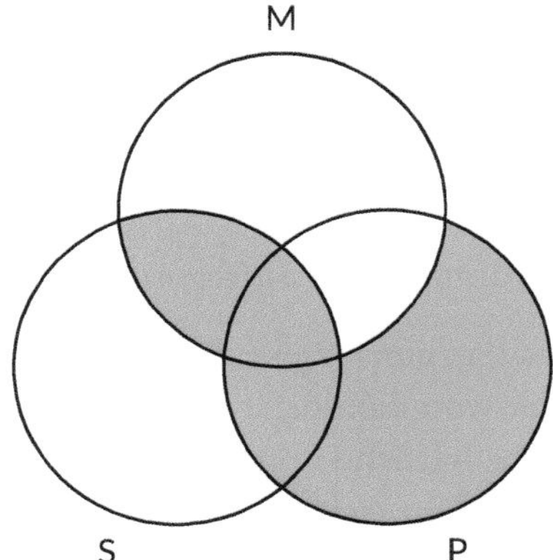

Does this diagram—with the premises drawn in—show the thing that is stated in the conclusion—namely, that "No *S* are *P*"? Yes, you can clearly see that the area of overlap between the *S* circle and the *P* circle is entirely shaded out. It's empty, just as it should be to show that "no *S* are *P*." The deductive part of our overall argument, then, is valid.

So what about our mixed argument as a whole? Well, the deductive part is fine. But since the inductive argument offered in support of one of the premises for the deductive part is quite weak, we should consider this mixed argument, as a whole, to be weak.

Summary

An inductive argument is intended to provide only probable support for its conclusion, being considered strong if it succeeds in providing such support and weak if it does not.

Inductive arguments come in several forms, including enumerative, analogical, and causal. In enumerative induction, we argue from premises about some members of a group to a generalization about the entire group. The entire group is called the *target group*; the observed members of the group, the sample; and the group characteristics we're interested in, the relevant property. An enumerative induction can fail to be strong by having a sample that's too small or not representative. When we draw a conclusion about a target group on the basis of too small a sample, we are said to commit the error of hasty generalization. Opinion polls are enumerative inductive arguments, or the basis of enumerative inductive arguments, and must be judged by the same general criteria used to judge any other enumerative induction.

In analogical induction, or argument by analogy, we reason that since two or more things are similar in several respects, they must be similar in some further respect. We evaluate arguments by analogy according to several criteria: (1) the number of relevant similarities between things being compared; (2) the number of relevant dissimilarities; (3) the number of instances (or cases) of similarities or dissimilarities; and (4) the diversity among the cases.

A causal argument is an inductive argument whose conclusion contains a causal claim. There are several inductive patterns of reasoning used to assess causal connections. These include the Method of Agreement, the Method of Difference, the Method of Agreement and Difference, and the Method of Concomitant Variation. Errors in cause-and-effect reasoning are common. They include misidentifying relevant factors in a causal process, overlooking relevant factors, confusing cause with coincidence, confusing cause with temporal order, ignoring the common causal factor, and mixing up cause and effect.

Crucial to an understanding of cause-and-effect relationships are the notions of necessary and sufficient conditions. A necessary condition for the occurrence of an event is one without which the event cannot occur. A sufficient condition for the occurrence of an event is one that guarantees that the event occurs.

Mixed arguments are ones that include both deductive and inductive elements within a single argument. They are quite common, as when the conclusion of an inductive argument is used as a premise for a deductive argument, such as a syllogism. In such cases, you will need to use the tools for evaluating both inductive and deductive arguments to determine the quality of the argument as a whole.

Field Problems

1. Devise an extended argument by analogy (200–250 words) to support the idea that a business giving $10,000 to a government official as a thank-you for helping win a government contract is just like giving a waiter or waitress a tip. Use several relevant similarities in your argument. Then write a short *critique* of your own argument (100–150 words), focusing especially on relevant dissimilarities and the number of relevant similarities.
2. Design an opinion poll to determine the percentage of people in the community where you live who believe that people who use municipal parks should be charged a user fee. Specify all of the following parameters: (1) the target group; (2) the makeup and size of the sample; (3) the methods for ensuring a random sample; (4) the methods for ensuring a representative sample; (5) the exact phrasing of the polling question(s); (6) the method for gathering the responses (telephone survey, "man on the street" poll, email questionnaire, etc.); and (7) the acceptable margin of error. Explain the reasons for your choices.
3. Visit a health-related website and find a causal argument on a matter of health. Then critique it, explaining why it's strong or weak, specifically noting whether it misidentifies or overlooks relevant factors, confuses cause with coincidence, commits the post hoc fallacy, ignores the common causal factor, confuses cause and effect, or mishandles or misunderstands necessary and sufficient conditions.
4. Think of a causal claim that you recall being put forward by someone you know—perhaps a claim about what caused their cold, or an accident they saw happen, or their bad grade on a particular test at school. Did they put forward a causal argument or merely a causal claim? Do you see any evidence of any of the "usual" errors that affect causal reasoning?

Self-Assessment Quiz

1. What is the logical form of enumerative induction, described schematically?
2. In enumerative induction, what do we mean by the terms "target group," "sample," and "relevant property"?
3. What are the two major ways in which an enumerative induction can fail to be strong?
4. In statistical syllogism, what do we mean by the terms *individual*, *group*, *characteristic*, and *proportion*?

For each of the following enumerative inductions, state whether the argument is strong or weak. If it's weak, indicate whether the problem is a sample that's too small, not representative, or both.

5. David Milgaard was wrongly convicted of murder in Saskatchewan in 1970. Donald Marshall Jr. was wrongfully convicted of murder in Nova Scotia in 1971. And Guy Paul Morin was wrongfully convicted, in 1994, of the 1984 murder of Christine Jessop in Ontario. Look at the evidence! People whose last names begin with an *M* get a raw deal from the Canadian justice system!
6. Over 90 per cent of the members of a national women's amateur hockey league (2500 members) are in favour of additional funding for amateur sports. Everyone in my running club is in favour of such funding. And all my pals from the gym are in favour of more funding for amateur sports. The fact is, almost all Canadians who are concerned with their fitness are in favour of additional funding for amateur sport.
7. Canadians are still fond of their first prime minister, Sir John A. Macdonald. A poll showed that the largest group of respondents—44 per cent—disapprove of removing Macdonald's name from buildings and landmarks, even though some of his policies caused harm to Indigenous individuals and communities.[6]
8. I read a news story about a woman who struggled with alcoholism and addiction to prescription painkillers, and spent most of her life on welfare. We should cut welfare programs, since people on welfare are spending it on drugs and alcohol.
9. I taught Johanna to play tennis last summer, and before long she was kicking my butt at it. And even though she just took up squash this year, she is already talking about joining a competitive league. That girl is good at just about any sport!

Evaluate each of the following arguments by analogy, indicating (1) the two things being compared, (2) the conclusion, and (3) whether the argument is strong or weak.

10. "As for one who is choosy about what he learns . . . we shall not call him a lover of learning or a philosopher, just as we shall not say that a man who is difficult about his food is hungry or has an appetite for food. We shall not call him a lover of food but a poor eater. . . . But we shall call a philosopher the man who is easily willing to learn every kind of knowledge, gladly turns to learning things, and is insatiable in this respect." (Socrates)
11. "Recently, several state attorneys general have announced their plans to use the coercive power of their offices to obtain confidential business information from ExxonMobil. The argument goes that Exxon perpetrated a fraud on consumers over the last several decades by misleading them into believing that climate change is false and that emission of greenhouse gases is harmless. The investigation is supposedly justified based on an analogy to the tobacco fraud litigation. . . . The tobacco companies were accused of inducing consumers to purchase cigarettes through misleading characterization of nicotine's risks." (Damien Schiff, *The Hill*, 16 April 2016)

Analyze each of the following causal arguments. Identify the conclusion and whether the argument is weak or strong. If it's weak, explain why with reference to the material in this chapter.

12. Among students in our study, most of the students who went into the exam with a positive attitude got either an A or a B. Most of the students who went in with a negative attitude got either a C or a D. A positive attitude can increase grades on university exams.
13. Why are crime rates so high, the economy so bad, and our children so prone to violence, promiscuity, and vulgarity? These social ills have arisen—as they always have—from the "moral vacuum" created when Canadians turn away from religion. Our current slide into chaos started when kids stopped saying "The Lord's Prayer" before class and families stopped saying grace before dinner. And as God has slowly faded from public life, we have got deeper in the hole.
14. Cancer is mainly caused by TV. Cancer rates have risen substantially since the middle of the twentieth century, when TV first became popular. Today, people even watch TV on their computers and mobile phones. And in rural parts of Japan, where they don't have TV, cancer is seldom reported at all.
15. I love this new magnetic knee brace. I wrapped it tightly around my knee and didn't run for a couple of days. The next thing you know, my knee felt a lot better. The power of magnets to heal is truly amazing!

Integrative Exercises

These exercises pertain to material in Chapters 3 and 6–8.

For each of the following arguments, specify the conclusion and premises, and say whether it is deductive or inductive. If it's deductive, use Venn diagrams or truth tables to determine its validity. If it's inductive, say whether it's an enumerative, analogical, or causal induction and whether it's strong or weak. If necessary, add implicit premises and conclusions.

1. As the Scottish philosopher David Hume put it, "No testimony is sufficient to establish a miracle, unless the testimony be of such a kind, that its falsehood would be more miraculous than the fact which it endeavors to establish." And the falsehood of anyone's testimony is never miraculous. So no one's testimony is enough to prove a miracle has happened!
2. Neighbours heard the dog barking just after 7 p.m.—and Mr Levin was found dead just after 8 p.m. This doesn't prove that the barking of the dog killed him, but it does show that the two events—the dog's barking and the death of Mr Levin—were somehow causally linked.
3. Nurses have substantial scientific knowledge. Anyone who has scientific knowledge knows that homeopathic remedies contain literally no active ingredients. So any nurse who recommends or administers a homeopathic remedy is doing something they know to be useless.
4. If you really cared about people in Haiti, you'd donate money to help efforts to rebuild the country in the wake of that awful earthquake. But you haven't donated a dime, so you must not care about the people of Haiti after all.
5. Dr Gosling says that anyone who has missed two or more doses of medication should be considered a non-compliant patient and can't be a patient in his medical practice anymore. But anyone can miss a pill or two; in some cases, it happens because people just can't afford their medication. Gosling's rules are punishing people for being poor.

6. Whenever Nancy eats something with garlic in it, she gets a stomach ache. She got a stomach ache in the hour after dinner, so the dressing on the salad must have had garlic in it.
7. Because the core values of the Canada Health Act are universality and accessibility, we believe it is crucial that health care in Canada remain a public good, and we reject two-tier health care of any kind.
8. That person argues against fair medical services for transgender individuals. But trans rights are human rights, and our campus should be a warm and welcoming place for people regardless of sexual orientation or gender identity. So that person should not be invited to speak on campus.
9. [Be careful: This one has an unstated conclusion.] The standard of living in Canada ranks among the very highest in the world. Yet that fact glosses over some very uncomfortable facts. Despite its promises and obligations, the Canadian government has done little to improve the lot of its Indigenous peoples, many of whom continue to struggle with poverty, poor health care, and substandard educational opportunities. And many Indigenous communities continue to be plagued by crime and addiction.
10. Most people who are good at math go into engineering. After all, every engineering major I know is really good at math.
11. "The evils of the world are due to moral defects quite as much as to lack of intelligence. But the human race has not hitherto discovered any method of eradicating moral defects. . . . Intelligence, on the contrary, is easily improved by methods known to every competent educator. Therefore, until some method of teaching virtue has been discovered, progress will have to be sought by improvement of intelligence rather than of morals." (Bertrand Russell)
12. Television is destroying morality in this country. As TV violence, sex, and vulgarity have increased, so have violent crimes, sexual assaults, and violations of obscenity laws.
13. "Some people would have us believe that the Supreme Court of Canada, emboldened by the Charter of Rights and Freedoms, has adopted an increasingly 'activist' stance and is now usurping powers that should legitimately be exercised by the legislature. . . . [But] it is highly misleading to speak as though the Supreme Court is taking power away from the legislature when it rules on charter cases. The role of the Supreme Court is to decide whether the legislature has satisfied the conditions required for the creation of legitimate law. Thus the only power that the Supreme Court takes away, when it rules against the legislature, is the power to engage in an illegitimate use of force. And this is not a power that anyone should want the legislature to have." (Joseph Heath, "Why Have a Constitution at All?" *Policy Options*, October 2003)
14. When asked whether or not they recreationally smoked marijuana, 90 per cent of the students at QWE Community College said "yes." A recent scientific study shows that students who smoke marijuana recreationally end up trying harder drugs. Since George will be attending QWE Community College, he will end up trying hard drugs.
15. The expansion of the new airport, on an island near downtown, has created serious traffic congestion. There's always a huge lineup of taxis near the ferry terminal waiting to pick up arriving passengers, and the excess traffic often backs up into neighbouring streets. I've lived here for years and have never seen such serious traffic delays downtown. Now, almost every weekday, traffic is a nightmare.

Writing Assignments

1. In a 250-word essay, use an enumerative inductive argument to argue that your school is (or is not) relatively free of plagiarism. Feel free to invent some plausible data to flesh out your argument.
2. Using either enumerative induction or argument by analogy, write a 500-word rebuttal to Essay 6 ("Raspberry Ketone, Pure Green Coffee Extract, Garcinia Cambogia, Weight Loss, and the Fallacy of Appealing to Authority") in Appendix A.
3. In a short essay (400–500 words), argue for or against one of the following claims. At the end of your essay, indicate in point form what type of argument you have produced (inductive or deductive, analogical, causal, etc.) and what the key strength of your argument is.
   - The people of Canada enjoy the highest levels of freedom on Earth.
   - People are fundamentally selfish.
   - People caught texting while driving—endangering their fellow citizens—should be put in jail.
   - Racial discrimination is not a problem at your school.
   - Aggressive behaviour in business is a bad thing.
   - No topics should be forbidden for discussion on a university campus.

Notes

1. Daniel Goleman, "Pollsters Enlist Psychologists in Quest for Unbiased Results," *New York Times*, 7 September 1993.
2. Tom Fish, "The 12 Most Educated Countries in the World," *Newsweek*, 20 June 2021. https://www.newsweek.com/most-educated-countries-world-1600620.
3. Carly Yoshida-Butryn, "Nearly Half of Canadians Never Learned about Residential Schools as Students: Survey," *CTV News*, 28 August 2020. https://bc.ctvnews.ca/nearly-half-of-canadians-never-learned-about-residential-schools-as-students-survey-1.5083723.
4. "Spurious Correlations." http://tylervigen.com/page?page=7.
5. Derek Lowe, "Get Ready for False Side Effects," *Science*, 4 December 2020. https://www.science.org/content/blog-post/get-ready-false-side-effects?cookieSet=1.
6. "The Plurality Disapprove of Removing Sir John A. MacDonald's Name from Things," The Form Poll, 27 January 2018. http://poll.forumresearch.com/post/2823/sir-john-a-january-2017/.

PART FOUR

Explanations

Inference to the Best Explanation

Chapter Objectives

Explanations and Inference

You will be able to

- define *inference to the best explanation* and understand how it differs from other kinds of induction.
- clarify what an explanation (including theoretical explanation) is and how it differs from an argument.
- appreciate how inference to the best explanation is used in all disciplines and in everyday life.
- demonstrate how to use inference to the best explanation in a range of different situations.

Theories and Consistency

You will be able to

- check an explanation for internal and external consistency.

Theories and Criteria

You will be able to

- understand the importance of using criteria to judge the adequacy of theories.
- list and explain the five criteria of adequacy.

- apply the criteria of adequacy to simple causal theories.
- define and explain an *ad hoc hypothesis*.

Telling Good Theories from Bad

You will be able to

- list and explain the four steps in the TEST formula.
- recognize the importance of considering alternative explanations.
- use the TEST formula to evaluate theories.

Let's take stock of the inductive terrain we've travelled so far. In Chapter 8, we closely examined the nature and uses of inductive reasoning. We were reminded that a deductive argument, unlike an inductive one, is intended to provide logically conclusive support for its conclusion. If it succeeds in providing such support, it is said to be valid; if it does not, it is invalid. If a valid argument has true premises, it is said to be sound. But an inductive argument is intended to supply only probable support for its conclusion. If it manages to provide such support, it is said to be strong; if it does not, we call it weak. The conclusion of an inductively strong argument is simply more likely to be true than not. If a strong argument has true premises, it's said to be cogent.

We also saw that inductive arguments come in several forms. One of them is enumerative induction in which we reason from premises about *some* members of a group to a conclusion, or generalization, about the group *as a whole*. All the banjos you have ever seen have five strings, so you conclude that *all* banjos have five strings. Only twenty per cent of your classmates have a driver's licence, so you conclude that only twenty per cent of people your age, everywhere, have a driver's licence. (Whether these enumerative inductive arguments are strong or cogent is another matter.)

Another kind of inductive argument is argument by analogy (or analogical induction) in which we reason that since two or more things are similar in several known respects, they are likely to be similar in some additional respect. In an analogical induction you might argue, for example, that (1) since humans can move around, solve mathematical equations, win chess games, and feel pain, *and* (2) since robots are like humans in that they, too, can move around, solve mathematical equations, and win chess games, it is therefore probable that robots can also feel pain. Analogical induction, like all inductive reasoning, can establish conclusions only with a degree of probability.

Finally, we saw that causal arguments—inductive arguments whose conclusions contain causal claims—can be enumerative inductions, analogical inductions, or arguments that rely on Mill's methods and similar kinds of inferences. Reasoning well about causal connections means avoiding numerous common errors, including misidentifying or overlooking relevant factors, confusing coincidence with cause, and committing the post hoc fallacy.

Review Notes

A Look Back at the Basics

- *Statement (claim):* An assertion that something is or is not the case.
- *Premise:* A statement given in support of another statement.
- *Conclusion:* A statement that premises are intended to support.
- *Argument:* A group of statements in which some of them (the premises) are intended to support another of them (the conclusion).
- *Indicator words:* Words that are frequently found in arguments and signal that a premise or conclusion is present.
- *Deductive argument:* An argument intended to provide conclusive support for its conclusion.
- *Inductive argument:* An argument intended to provide probable support for its conclusion.

inference to the best explanation
A form of inductive reasoning in which we reason from premises about a state of affairs to an explanation for that state of affairs:

Phenomenon Q.
E provides the best explanation for Q.
Therefore, it is probable that E is true.

We previously noted only in passing that there is another kind of inductive reasoning that is so important that all of Part 4 of this book is devoted to it: **inference to the best explanation**. Well, here we are in Part 4, and so it's time to look closely at this kind of inductive reasoning, perhaps the most commonly used form of inference and arguably the most empowering in daily life.

9.1 Explanations and Inference

Recall from Chapter 1 that an explanation is a statement (or statements) asserting why or how something is the case. For example: I can't use my phone because the battery is dead. She was sad because her pet snake had died. He cracked the egg by hitting it against the edge of the bowl. These explanations and all others are intended to clarify and illuminate and thereby to increase our understanding. Remember also our discussion of the important distinction between an explanation and an argument. Whereas an explanation tells us *why or how something is the case*, an argument gives us reasons for believing *that something is the case*.

As you've probably already guessed, there are also different kinds of explanations (see the box "The Lore of Explanations"). For instance, some explanations are what we might call procedural—they try to explain how something is done or how an action is carried out. ("She opened up the engine, then examined the valves, and then checked the carburetor.") Some are interpretive—they try to explain the meaning of terms or states of affairs. ("This word means 'fancy' or 'showy.'") And some are functional—they try to explain how something functions. ("The heart circulates and oxygenates the blood.")

But the kind of explanation we're concerned with here—and the kind we bump into most often—is what we'll call, for lack of something snappier, a **theoretical explanation**. Such explanations are theories, or hypotheses, that try to explain why something is the way it is, why something is the case, or why something happened. In this category we must include all explanations intended to explain the cause of events—the causal explanations that are so important to both

theoretical explanation
A theory, or hypothesis, that tries to explain why something is the way it is, why something is the case, or why something happened.

science and daily life. Theoretical explanations, of course, are claims. They assert that something is or is not the case.

Don't be scared off by the word *theoretical* here. We're not necessarily talking about science, although the pursuit of theoretical explanations does play a very large role in science. Theoretical explanations, as you'll see below, are very often just common-sense explanations of everyday things. When you assert that "the house is cold because someone left a window open," you're offering a theoretical explanation.

Now, even though an explanation is not an argument, an explanation can be *part* of an argument. It can be the heart of the kind of inductive argument known as *inference to the best explanation*. And in this kind of inference, the explanations we use are theoretical explanations.

In inference to the best explanation, *we reason from premises about a state of affairs to an explanation for that state of affairs*. The premises are statements about observations or other evidence that we want to explain. The explanation is a claim about why the state of affairs is the way it is. The key question that this type of inference tries to answer is "What is the best explanation for the existence or nature of this state of affairs?" The best explanation is the one most likely to be true, even though there is no guarantee of its truth (as there would be if we were using deductive reasoning).

"There is nothing more practical than a good theory."

—Leonid Ilyich Brezhnev

Recall that enumerative induction has this pattern:

> X per cent of the observed members of group A have property P.
> Therefore, X per cent of all members of group A probably have property P.

And recall that analogical induction has this pattern:

> Thing A has properties P_1, P_2, and P_3, plus the property P_4.
> Thing B has properties P_1, P_2, and P_3.
> Therefore, thing B probably has property P_4.

Inference to the best explanation, however, has this pattern:

> I've noticed phenomenon Q.
> E provides the best explanation for Q.
> Therefore, it is probable that E is true.

For example:

> The cancer rate in that town has doubled over the last decade. The best explanation for that fact is that a new factory that was built in town ten years ago is emitting cancer-causing chemicals. So I think that factory is definitely spitting out dangerous stuff!

> The best explanation for Maria's absence today is that she's angry at the boss. Yeah, she's mad at the boss, all right.

> The defendant's fingerprints were all over the crime scene, the police found the victim's blood on his shirt, and he was in possession

> of the murder weapon. The only explanation for all this that makes any sense is that the defendant actually committed the crime. So he must be guilty.

If the explanations in these arguments really are the best, then the arguments are inductively strong. And if the premises are also true, then the arguments are cogent. If they are cogent, we are justified in believing that the explanations provided for these phenomena are in fact correct.

Notice that an inference to the best explanation always goes "beyond the evidence"—it tries to explain facts but does so by positing a theory that is not derived entirely *from* those facts. It tries to understand the known by putting forth—through inference and imagination—a theoretical pattern that encompasses both the known and the unknown. It proposes a plausible pattern that expands our understanding. I don't *know* if there's a bolt loose on the underside of my car, but if there is, *that* would explain the rattling noise I'm hearing!

The fact that there are *best* explanations, of course, implies that not all explanations for a state of affairs are equally good; some are better than others. Just because you've come up with an explanation for something doesn't mean that you're justified in believing that the explanation is the right one. If other explanations are just as good, then your initial explanation is in doubt. If other explanations are better than yours, you are not justified in believing yours simply because it is "an explanation." But much of the time, after further study or thought, you can reasonably conclude that a particular explanation—though maybe not your first guess—really is the best explanation. (We'll see later how to evaluate the quality of an explanation.) In this way, you can come to understand the state of affairs better than you did before.

"Gee, mom, how DID that happen? Maybe we better Google it!"

Chris Wildt/CartoonStock

Causation can be hard to figure out. And no, technology won't always help. How might building a proper causal argument help you to determine which explanation is the best?

Inference to the best explanation probably seems very familiar to you. That's because you use it all the time—and need it all the time. Often, when we try to understand something in the world, we construct explanations for why this something is the way it is, and we try to determine which of these explanations is the best. Devising explanations helps to increase our understanding by fitting our experiences and background knowledge into a coherent pattern. At every turn we are confronted with phenomena that we can only fully understand by explaining them.

Review Notes

The Lore of Explanations

An explanation is a statement (or statements) asserting why or how something is the case. In traditional terminology, the fancy term for the thing that is to be explained in an explanation is *explanandum*, and the term for the thing that does the explaining is *explanans*. Take this explanation: "The dog barked because a prowler was nearby." In this example, the explanandum is "the dog barked," and the explanans is "a prowler was nearby."

You can categorize explanations in many ways, depending on the kind of explanandum you're interested in. Here are a few of the more common categories:

- *Teleological* explanations try to explain the purpose of something, how it functions, or how it fits into a plan. (*Telos* is an old Greek word meaning "end" or "purpose.")

  Example: The wall switch is there so you can turn off the lamp from across the room.
  Example: These flowers are my way of apologizing to you.

- *Interpretive* explanations concern the meaning of terms or states of affairs. These explanations seek to understand not the purpose or cause of something but rather its sense or semantic meaning.

  Example: When Mary smiled and nodded, she was indicating her agreement.
  Example: The verb *to effect* means to accomplish, but the verb *to affect* means to influence.

- *Procedural* explanations try to explain how something is done or how an action is carried out.

  Example: To cool the broccoli and keep it from cooking further, Eric plunged it into ice water.
  Example: They paid their taxes by filling in the online forms and then using their credit card number.

In all cases, remember that an example of an explanation is not always an example of a *good* explanation! Each of the examples above is an explanation, but without knowing more about the situations referred to, we cannot know whether they are the best, or even plausible, explanations.

Sometimes we're barely aware that we're using inference to the best explanation. If we awaken and see that the streets outside are wet, we may immediately posit this explanation: *it's been raining.* Without thinking much about it, we may also quickly consider whether a better explanation is that a street-sweeper machine has wet the street. Just as quickly we may dismiss this explanation because we see that the houses and cars are also wet. After reasoning in this fashion, we may decide to carry an umbrella that day.

Let's consider a more elaborate example. Say you discover that your car won't start in the morning; that's the phenomenon to be explained. You would like to know why it won't start (the explanation for the failure) because you can't take appropriate action unless you know what the problem is. You know that there are several possible explanations or theories:

1. The battery is dead.
2. The fuel tank is empty.
3. The starter has malfunctioned.
4. A vandal has sabotaged the car.
5. All or several of the above.

So you need to try to figure out which theory is the most plausible, that is, most likely to be true. Let's say you see right away that there is snow around the car from yesterday's snowstorm—and there are no footprints (except yours) and no signs of tampering anywhere. So you dismiss theory 4. You remember that you filled up the gas tank yesterday, the fuel gauge says that the tank is full, and you don't see any signs of leakage. So you can safely ignore theory 2. You notice that the lights, heater, and radio work fine and the battery gauge indicates a fully charged battery. So you discard theory 1. When you try to start the car, you hear a clicking sound like the one you heard when the starter had failed previously. Among the theories you started with, then, theory 3 now seems the most plausible. This means that theory 5 also cannot be correct, since it involves two or more of the theories and you've already ruled out all but one.

"A superstition is a premature explanation that overstays its time."

—George Iles

If you wanted to, you could state your argument like this:

1. Your car won't start in the morning.
2. The theory that the starter has malfunctioned is the best explanation for the car's not starting in the morning.
3. Therefore, it's probable that the malfunctioning starter caused the car not to start in the morning.

Food for Thought

shalamov/iStockphoto

The blue-footed booby was one of the many species collected by Charles Darwin in the Galapagos Islands. How can alternate theories lead to accurate theories?

Darwin and the Best Explanation

Charles Darwin (1809–82) offered the theory of evolution by natural selection as the best explanation for a wide variety of natural phenomena. He catalogued an extensive list of facts about nature and showed that his theory explained them well. He argued that the alternative theory of the day, on the other hand—the view that God independently created various species—did not explain them. Darwin declared:

> It can hardly be supposed that a false theory would explain, in so satisfactory a manner as does the theory of natural selection, the several large classes of facts above specified. It has recently been objected that this is an unsafe method of arguing; but it is a method used in judging of the common events of life, and has often been used by the greatest natural philosophers.[1]

Note what you've accomplished here: you've started with a description of a situation, evaluated possible explanations, and reasoned your way to a causal conclusion.

In science, where inference to the best explanation is an essential tool, usually the theories of interest are causal theories in which events are the things to be explained and the proposed causes of the events are the explanations. Just as we do in everyday life, scientists often consider several competing theories for the same

Food for Thought

Sherlock Holmes and Inference to the Best Explanation

AJ Pics/Alamy Stock Photo

The TV show *Sherlock* makes good dramatic use of Holmes's famous powers of inference.

The fictional character Sherlock Holmes owed his great success as a detective primarily to inference to the best explanation. He was, in the stories written by Sir Arthur Conan Doyle, so good at this kind of inference that people (especially his sidekick, Dr Watson) were frequently astonished at his skill. Holmes, however, was guilty of spreading some confusion about his ability. He called his method deduction, though it was clearly inductive. Here is Holmes in action, speaking to Dr Watson shortly after meeting him for the first time:

> I knew you came from Afghanistan. From long habit the train of thoughts ran so swiftly through my mind that I arrived at the conclusion without being conscious of intermediate steps. There were such steps, however. The train of reasoning ran, "Here is a gentleman of medical type, but with the air of a military man. Clearly an army doctor, then. He has just come from the tropics, for his face is dark, and that is not the natural tint of his skin, for his wrists are fair. He has undergone hardship and sickness, as his haggard face says clearly. His left arm has been injured. He holds it in a stiff and unnatural manner. Where in the tropics would an English army doctor have seen much hardship and got his arm wounded? Clearly in Afghanistan."[2]

Here Holmes explains how he knew that a man had "gone about in fear of some personal attack within the last twelve-month":

> "You have a very handsome stick," I answered. "By the inscription I observed that you had not had it more than a year. But you have taken some pains to bore the head of it and pour melted lead into the hole so as to make it a formidable weapon. I argued that you would not take such precautions unless you had some danger to fear."[3]

In each of these cases, Holmes makes an observation and then seeks to arrive at a theory as to what would best explain what he has observed.

event or phenomenon. Then—through scientific testing and careful thinking—they systematically eliminate inadequate theories and eventually arrive at the one that's rightly regarded as the best of the bunch. Using this form of inference, scientists discover planets, viruses, cures, subatomic particles, black holes—as well as many things that can't even be directly observed.

And then there are all those other occupations and professions that rely on inference to the best explanation. Physicians use it to pinpoint the cause of symptoms in patients. Police detectives use it to identify lawbreakers. Judges and juries use it to determine the guilt or innocence of accused persons. And mechanics use it to determine why a car is failing to function properly.

With so many people in so many areas of inquiry using inference to the best explanation, you would expect the world to be filled with countless theories proposed by innumerable people looking to explain all sorts of things.

And so there are. Here's a brief table of notable or interesting proposed theories and the phenomena they are meant to explain:

Theory	to explain . . .
Atomic	behaviour of subatomic particles
Germ	spread of disease
HIV	cause of AIDS
Oedipus complex	behaviour of men and boys
Placebo effect	apparent cure of disease
Bleak winters	why Canadians are funny
Violent video games	violence in children
El Niño	bad weather
El Niña	good weather
Incumbent politicians	a bad economy
Carbon emissions related to human activity	climate change

Of course, it's often easy to make up theories to explain things we don't understand. The harder job is sorting out good theories from bad, a topic we'll explore more fully later in this chapter.

Exercise 9.1

Answers to exercises marked with an asterisk (*) may be found in Appendix B, Answers to Exercises.

1. What is an explanation?
2. What is inference to the best explanation?
3. Is inference to the best explanation a deductive or inductive exercise?
4. What is it that theoretical explanations attempt to explain?*

5. Under what circumstances can an inference to the best explanation be deemed strong? What makes such an inference cogent?
6. What is the basic logical pattern of enumerative induction? Of inference to the best explanation? For analogical induction?
7. What is a teleological explanation? A procedural explanation? An interpretive explanation?
8. What is a causal explanation? Can causal explanations be used in inference to the best explanation?*
9. How does the kind of explanation used in inference to the best explanation differ from a procedural explanation?
10. Give an example of an occupation or profession (not one discussed previously in this chapter) whose members make regular use of inference to the best explanation in their work. Give an example of how they use it.
11. Have you seen someone you know use inference to the best explanation today? If so, how did they use it? (Give an example from people you observed or spoke to today.)

Exercise 9.2

For each of the following explanations, say what state of affairs is being explained and what the explanation is.

1. Applications from foreign students to Canadian universities are up these days because more students are avoiding the United States.
2. We all know that the polar bear is endangered, and the only explanation for that is the thinning of Arctic ice, caused by global warming.*
3. Why is Georgia wearing orange goggles? Because she's a bit eccentric and she likes the way they look.
4. Some Indigenous Canadians mistrust health care professionals because of historical injustices that past health professionals were involved in perpetrating.
5. Yes, I can tell you why the "hot" water from your faucet isn't very hot: your hot-water heater is over 20 years old and just can't keep up with modern water usage patterns.*
6. Many consider the crow to be one of the smartest animals in the world. Crows have been shown to be able to make and use rudimentary tools and can even recognize human faces.
7. Nursing students love Professor Walton's class because she takes dull material and makes it interesting.
8. Oh, man, is my stomach churning! I think that food was too spicy for me.*
9. Salaries for programmers are rising, because the work they do is in demand.
10. It wasn't about greed. Toby fudged the numbers in the monthly sales reports out of loyalty—out of a desire to make the boss look good.

Exercise 9.3

For each of the following, determine whether the type of explanation offered is theoretical (the kind used in inference to the best explanation) or non-theoretical (e.g., teleological, interpretive, procedural). Be careful to note any borderline cases (explanations that could be interpreted as either theoretical or non-theoretical).

1. Dana took the job on Bay Street so that he could pay off his student loans.
2. Homeopathic treatments are controversial because while such treatments have many fans, reputable scientists say they are entirely without scientific merit.
3. Ethics is the critical study of morality.
4. Horatio caught a cold because he stood outside in the cold rain.*
5. There is no peace in the Middle East—and there never will be—because of the stubbornness of all sides in the conflict.
6. A dog that has its ears folded back and is showing its teeth is a dog that is very angry.
7. When you experience memory loss, that can only mean one thing: Alzheimer's disease.*
8. Jimbo knew her username and guessed her password—that's how he hacked into her account.
9. He did well on his essay by starting it early, writing a clear outline, researching the topic, and paying attention to the way he expressed his ideas.
10. He keeps the music box on his desk because it reminds him of his long-lost love.
11. See that player sitting on the bench? She's in her uniform and ready to go, just in case the star player gets hurt.
12. That painting is without vibrancy or cohesion. Just look at the dull colours and mishmash of forms.*
13. J.P. has trouble keeping women employees because he doesn't treat them with respect.
14. Marshall is wearing that helmet because he's a fire dog.
15. Blech! I got food poisoning after eating a bad burger at the campus pub.
16. I misunderstood the instructions because my understanding of Cantonese is not very good.
17. I didn't see that car coming—the sun was in my eyes!

Exercise 9.4

In each of the following examples, a state of affairs is described. Devise two theories to explain each one. Include one theory that you consider plausible and one theory that you think is not plausible.

1. After the new school was built in Timville (a small mining town in a developing nation), managers at the mine started noticing fewer workers missing their shifts.

2. When Akane came home, she noticed the window in the kitchen was broken, there were muddy footprints on the kitchen floor, and some valuable silverware was missing.*
3. At the height of the pandemic, just after spending the weekend at a house party with his friends, Jason had a new cough, shortness of breath, and a fever. He also tested positive for the COVID-19 virus, but he doesn't believe that the pandemic is real.
4. Many Canadians are now avoiding travel to the United States.
5. During the 1980s, the demand for food assistance rose dramatically, and a massive charitable food-assistance system emerged.
6. Alice has been taking vitamin C every day for a year, and during that time she has not had a cold or a sore throat.*
7. Last night, I drank four glasses of red wine and ate a bag of chips. And this morning I woke up with a headache.
8. Small, local coffee shops in my area have all been closing down one by one over the past six months. None of the owners has given any explanation as to why. They've just gone without even saying goodbye. Some of my neighbours pointed out that Starbucks shops have filled those vacant locations, one by one.
9. The most famous act performed by the illusionists Penn and Teller is the one in which they catch bullets in their teeth. The audience sees Penn and Teller fire powerful .357 Magnum handguns at each other, and then each of the pair smiles to reveal a bullet resting safely between his teeth.

Exercise 9.5

Read each of the following passages, and answer these questions:

1. What is the phenomenon being explained?
2. What theory is suggested as a possible explanation for the phenomenon?
3. Is the theory plausible? If not, why not?
4. Is there a plausible theory that the writer has overlooked? If so, what is it?

Passage 1

Students who major in philosophy tend to do very well on the Law School Admissions Test (LSAT) and Medical College Admissions Test (MCAT). This is because studying philosophy gives students a chance to practise the abstract reasoning skills that are the key to success on such tests.

Passage 2

"The number of worldwide unprovoked shark attacks dropped 17.3 per cent in 2016. "The International Shark Attack File (ISAF) analyzed 150 incidents involving shark–human interaction and concluded that 81 of these events were, in fact, unprovoked attacks on humans.

"In 2015, the number shark attacks had hit 98. According to the ISAF, an unprovoked attack is an attack that occurred in the shark's habitat with no human provocation of the predator.

"'These totals are remarkably low given the billions of human-hours spent in the water each year,' explains George H. Burgess, curator of the International Shark Attack File, a project run at the University of Florida.

"The long-term trend in fatality rates has been one of constant reduction over the past eleven-plus decades, reflective of advances in beach safety practices and medical treatment, and increased public awareness of avoiding potentially dangerous situations."[4]

Passage 3

L'École de Choix ("School of Choice") is a private, nonprofit elementary school in Haiti. Haiti is the poorest country in the western hemisphere, with one of the weakest education systems in the world. At L'Ecole de Choix, students receive a high-quality education focused on leadership. After Grade 6, many students go on to various middle schools, and qualifying students receive scholarships to help them do so and continue to attend Choix for after-school programming. Currently, among Choix scholarship students, 41 per cent end up among the top 10 students in their middle-school classes, and 7 per cent end up at the very top of their middle school and high school classes. By the time they reach 9th grade, 100 per cent of Choix scholarship recipients pass their government exams (which only 72 per cent of other students pass). The school's leaders believe that their "holistic approach" to caring for the whole student (including not just education, but also the school's focus on leadership, safety, and nutritional support of students) and ongoing support through middle and high school are responsible for these results.

Passage 4

In Canada, women are wildly underrepresented on corporate boards of directors. Despite making up more than half the population and a growing proportion of business-school graduates, women make up only about 20 per cent of the boards of publicly traded companies. But the reason is clear: women simply don't have business instincts required to be involved in the crucial task of guiding a big company. Besides, women generally don't want to be on boards—it seems like that's just not the kind of role women want. If they did want to play that kind of role, there would be more of them actively seeking board positions.

9.1.1 Abductive Reasoning

abduction (abductive reasoning)
The form of reasoning used when putting forward a hypothesis as to what would explain a particular phenomenon or set of circumstances.

The process involved in making an inference to the best explanation is sometimes referred to by philosophers as **abduction**, or **abductive reasoning**. Abductive reasoning involves looking at a phenomenon, or a set of circumstances, and putting forward a hypothesis as to what would be a good explanation for that phenomenon or those circumstances.

For example, imagine you're at home and you hear a loud bang outside. Your mind immediately generates some possible explanations—some potential sources of such a noise. Maybe it occurs to you that the noise might have been produced by a collision between two cars. You then have the option of looking outside to verify your hypothesis or looking for other evidence that might tend to confirm or disconfirm it. Are there any cars on the street? Do any of them show signs of damage?

Abduction is sometimes half-seriously referred to as a process that involves making a guess. And it's true that abduction involves something like guesswork: if the facts of the case pointed to one, and only one, possible explanation, then we would be dealing with deduction rather than abduction. But although abduction involves taking a leap, it is not a leap into thin air. Our "guesswork" in such cases should be guided by our background knowledge and, where possible, by experience. If we have an upset stomach, our abductive reasoning about its cause will be guided by our knowledge of what sorts of things can and cannot cause an upset stomach. Of course, our background knowledge can sometimes be misleading, and our experience may be insufficient.

We can formalize the process of abduction as follows:

O = an observation (the phenomenon that needs to be explained)
T = a background theory (about how some part of the world works)
E = an explanation (of the observation)

In terms of the example cited above:

O = a bang outside
T = cars sometimes crash into each other, making a bang
E = cars crashed into each other outside your house

The process of abduction involves first asking, "Is E consistent with T?" In other words, does E fit with your background knowledge of what sorts of things make loud bangs? Second, abduction involves asking, "Would O follow from E and T together?" In other words, if in fact cars crashing sometimes make a bang, and if two cars crashed into each other outside your house, is it true that you would then hear a bang? That seems quite likely, so E is a pretty good explanation of O in this case.

But of course, that's just a start. Several possible Es may satisfy these conditions; lots may be consistent with both the initial observation and with your background knowledge. You must therefore use some common sense to weed out all sorts of highly improbable possibilities (e.g., a meteor just landed outside your house). Once you've narrowed it down a bit—and your brain may well do that automatically—you can apply more formal rules, like our criteria of adequacy.

9.2 Theories and Consistency

Very often we may propose a theory as an explanation for a phenomenon, or we may have a theory presented to us for consideration. In either case, we will likely be dealing with an argument in the form of inference to the best explanation.

The conclusion of the argument will always say, in effect, *this* theory is the best explanation of the facts. And we will be responsible for trying to decide if it really is. How do we do that?

The work is not always easy, but there are special criteria we can use to get the job done. Before we apply these criteria, though, we have to make sure that the theory in question meets the minimum requirement of *consistency*. A theory that does not meet this minimum requirement is worthless, so there is no need to use the special criteria to evaluate the theory or to compare it to other available theories. A theory that meets the requirement is at least eligible for further consideration. Here we are concerned with both *internal* and *external* consistency. A theory that is internally consistent is consistent with itself—it's free of contradictions. A theory that is externally consistent is consistent with the data it's supposed to explain—it fully accounts for the observable data.

"Sitting on a bedroom floor crying is something that makes you feel really alone. If someone's singing about that feeling, you feel bonded to that person. That's the only way I can find an explanation for why 55,000 people would want to come see me sing."

—Taylor Swift

If we show that a theory contains an internal contradiction, we have refuted it. A theory that implies that something both is and is not the case cannot possibly be true. By exposing an internal contradiction, Galileo once refuted Aristotle's famous theory of motion, a long-respected hypothesis that had stood tall for centuries. Galileo showed that Aristotle's theory implied two contradictory things—namely, that a large, light object falls both faster *and* slower than a small, heavy one. Those things can't both be true, so there's a fatal internal contradiction in Aristotle's theory.

If a theory is externally inconsistent, we have reason to believe that it's false. Suppose you leave your car parked on the street overnight and the next morning discover that (1) the windshield has a large round hole in it, (2) there's blood on the steering wheel, and (3) there's a brick on the front seat. And let's say that your friend Charlie offers this theory to explain these facts: someone threw a brick through your windshield. What would you think about this theory?

You would probably think that Charlie had not been paying attention. His theory is consistent with the fact that the windshield is broken, and it would also explain why there's a brick on the seat. And it's not inconsistent with the observation of blood, but it doesn't explain it either. But most important, Charlie's theory (that someone threw a brick—a sharp-edged, rectangular object—through your windshield) is inconsistent with the fact that the hole in the windshield is round. Charlie's theory is a good try, but it doesn't work. It's externally inconsistent—inconsistent with the data. You'll need to keep looking for a better answer!

Review Notes

Minimum Requirement: Consistency

- *Internal consistency:* A theory that is internally consistent is free of contradictions.
- *External consistency:* A theory that is externally consistent is consistent with the data it's supposed to explain.

9.3 Theories and Criteria

For a moment let's return to our example, discussed earlier in this chapter, of the car that won't start. Recall that we examined five possible explanations for the non-start phenomenon:

1. The battery is dead.
2. The fuel tank is empty.
3. The starter has malfunctioned.
4. A vandal has sabotaged the car.
5. All or several of the above.

But what if someone suggested that our analysis of this problem was incomplete because we failed to consider several other possible theories that they feel are at least as plausible as these five? Consider these, for example:

6. Each night, you've been sabotaging your own car while you sleepwalk.
7. Your 90-year-old uncle, who lives 1000 kilometres away from you, has secretly been visiting at night and going for joyrides in your car, thus damaging the engine.
8. A poltergeist (a noisy, mischievous ghost) has damaged the car's carburetor.
9. Yesterday, you scrambled the electrical system by accidentally driving the car through a portal to an alternative space–time dimension.

What do you think of these theories? More specifically, are these last four theories *really* at least as plausible as the first five? If you think so, *why*? If you think not, *why not*?

A critical perspective is a good start: we shouldn't accept these theories as plausible just because someone says they are. But next we want to give you some specific tools that you can use to evaluate theories. Remember that the strangeness of a theory is no good reason to discount it. It will not do simply to say that theories 6 to 9 are too weird to be true. In the history of science, plenty of bizarre theories have turned out to be correct. (Quantum theory in physics, for example, is about as weird as you can get.) Earlier we concluded that theory 3 was better (more likely to be true) than theories 1, 2, 4, and 5. But what criteria did we use to arrive at this judgment? And on the basis of what criteria can we say that theory 3 is any better than theories 6 to 9? There must be *some* criteria because it is implausible that every theory is equally correct. Surely there is a difference in quality between a theory that explains rainfall by positing some natural meteorological forces and one that alleges that ghosts and goblins cause weather phenomena.

A simple answer to the problem of theory choice is this: just weigh the evidence for each theory, and the theory with the most evidence wins. As we will soon see, the amount or degree of evidence that a theory has is indeed a crucial factor—but it cannot be the sole criterion by which we assess explanations. Throughout the history of science, major theories—from the heliocentric theory of the solar system to Einstein's general theory of relativity—have never been established by empirical evidence alone.

criteria of adequacy
The standards used to judge the worth of explanatory theories. They include *testability, fruitfulness, scope, simplicity,* and *conservatism.*

Fortunately, there are reasonable criteria and reliable procedures for judging the merits of eligible theories and for arriving at a defensible judgment of which theory is best. The **criteria of adequacy** are the essential tools of science and have been used (sometimes implicitly) by scientists throughout history to uncover the best explanations for all sorts of events and states of affairs. Science, though, doesn't own these criteria. They are as useful—and as used—among non-scientists as they are among men and women of science.

Applying the criteria of adequacy to a set of theories constitutes the ultimate test of a theory's value, for *the best theory is the eligible theory that meets the criteria of adequacy better than any of its competitors*. Here, *eligible* means that the theory has already met the minimum requirement for consistency (discussed earlier).

All of this implies that the evaluation of a particular theory is not complete until alternative, or competing, theories are considered. As we've seen, there is seemingly no limit to the number of theories that could be offered to explain a particular phenomenon or a given set of data. The main challenge is to give a fair assessment of the relevant theories in relation to each other. If you fail to somehow address the alternatives, you may be overlooking or denying relevant evidence, which risks reaching biased conclusions and increasing the likelihood of error. Such failure is probably the most common error in the appraisal of theories.

A theory judged, according to these criteria, to be the best explanation for a certain set of facts should be considered worthy of our belief, and we may legitimately claim to know that such a theory is true. But the theory is not then necessarily or certainly true in the way that the conclusion of a sound deductive argument is necessarily or certainly true. As with other forms of induction, inference to the best explanation cannot guarantee the truth of the best available explanation. That is, it is not truth-preserving. The best theory we happen to have examined so far may actually turn out to be false. Nevertheless, we would have excellent reasons for supposing our best theory to be a true theory.

The criteria of adequacy that we will apply to in order to judge the value of an explanatory theory are *testability*, *fruitfulness*, *scope*, *simplicity*, and *conservatism*. Let's examine each one of those in detail.

9.3.1 Testability

testability
A criterion of adequacy for judging the worth of theories. A testable theory is one in which there is some way to determine whether the theory is true or false—that is, it predicts something other than what it was introduced to explain.

Most of the theories that we encounter every day and all the theories that scientists take seriously are **testable**—*there is some way to determine whether the theories are true or false*, or at least to generate new evidence that points in one direction or the other. If a theory is untestable—if there is no possible procedure for checking its truth—then it is worthless as an explanatory theory. Suppose someone says that an invisible, undetectable spirit is causing your headaches. What possible test could we perform to tell if the spirit actually exists? None. So the spirit theory is

Food for Thought

Inference to the Best Explanation and the External World

In Chapters 10 and 11, we will explore in detail how inference to the best explanation can be used to tackle some big issues. Here we just want to mention one of the "big questions" to which philosophers and other thinkers have applied inference to the best explanation.

A problem that has historically occupied thinkers in the history of philosophy is whether we have any good reasons to believe that there is a world outside our own thoughts. That is, is there an *external world* independent of the way we represent it to ourselves? Some people have denied that we have any such good reasons because we can never look at ourselves "from the outside" to objectively compare our subjective, internal experiences with reality. All we know is the nature of our perceptions—which may or may not be linked to the "real world" in any way.

Many philosophers have applied inference to the best explanation to this puzzle. They argue that we can indeed know that there is an external reality because that belief is the best explanation of the peculiar pattern of our perceptions. In other words, the best explanation—though admittedly not the only *possible* explanation—of why we *seem* to see a tree in front of us is that there *really is a real tree in front of us.* Our senses might fool us on particular occasions, but it's highly unlikely that they are doing so literally all of the time.

entirely empty; it's a wild guess that can never be confirmed or disconfirmed, and we can assign no weight to such a claim.

Here's another way to look at it. Theories are explanations, and explanations are designed to increase our understanding of the world. But an untestable theory does not—and cannot—really explain anything. It is equivalent to saying that an unknown thing with unknown properties acts in an unknown way to cause the thing we're trying to understand—which is the same thing as offering no explanation at all.

We often run into untestable theories in daily life, just as scientists sometimes encounter them in their work. Many practitioners of alternative medicine claim that health problems are caused by an imbalance in people's *chi*, an unmeasurable form of mystical energy that is said to flow through everyone. Some people say that their misfortunes are caused by God or the Devil. Others believe that certain events in their lives happen (and are inevitable) because of fate. And parents may hear their young daughter say that she did not break the lamp but her invisible friend did. None of those theories, unfortunately, is testable.

Many theories throughout history have been untestable. Some of the more influential untestable theories are the theory of witches (some people called witches are controlled by the Devil), the moral fault theory of disease (immoral behaviour causes illness), and the divine-placement theory of fossils (God created geological fossils to give the false impression of an ancient Earth). People have believed these theories, but not for good reasons.

But what does it mean to say that a theory is testable or untestable? A theory is testable *if it predicts something other than what it was introduced to explain.*

Suppose your electric clock stops each time you touch it. One theory to explain this event is that there is an electrical short in the clock's wiring. Another theory is that an invisible, undetectable demon causes the clock to stop. The wiring theory predicts that if the wiring is repaired, the clock will no longer shut off when touched. So it is testable—there is something that the theory predicts other than the obvious fact that the clock will stop when you touch it. But the demon theory makes no predictions about anything *except* the obvious, the very fact that the theory was introduced to explain. It predicts that the clock will stop if you touch it, but we already know this. So our understanding is not increased, and the demon theory is untestable.

Now, if the demon theory says that the demon can be detected with X-rays, then there is something the theory predicts other than the clock's stopping when touched. You can X-ray the clock and examine the film for demon silhouettes. If the theory says the demon can't be seen but can be heard with sensitive sound equipment, then once again you have a prediction, something to look for other than clock stoppage. But you'll note that people who propose such spooky theories are seldom able even to propose a test that could be performed to shed light on the situation.

So, other things being equal, testable theories are superior to untestable ones; they may be able to increase our understanding of a phenomenon. But an untestable theory is just an oddity.

9.3.2 Fruitfulness

Imagine that we have two testable theories, theory 1 and theory 2, that attempt to explain the same phenomenon. Theory 1 and theory 2 seem comparable in most respects when measured against other criteria of adequacy. Theory 1, however, successfully predicts the existence of a previously unknown entity, say, a star in an uncharted part of the sky. What would you conclude about the relative worth of these two theories?

"The weakness of the man who, when his theory works out into a flagrant contradiction of the facts, concludes 'So much the worse for the facts: let them be altered,' instead of 'So much the worse for my theory.'"

—George Bernard Shaw

If you thought carefully about the issue, you would probably conclude that theory 1 is the better theory—and you would be right. Other things being equal, theories that perform this way—that successfully predict previously unknown phenomena—are more credible than those that don't. They are said to be **fruitful**—to yield new insights that can open up whole new areas of research and discovery. This fruitfulness suggests that the theories are more likely to be true.

fruitfulness
A criterion of adequacy for judging the worth of theories. A fruitful theory is one that yields new insights.

If a friend of yours is walking through a forest where she has never been before, yet she seems to be able to predict exactly what's up ahead, you would probably conclude that she possessed some kind of accurate information about the forest, such as a map. Likewise, if a theory successfully predicts some surprising state of affairs, you are likely to think that the predictions are not just lucky guesses but grounded in some underlying truth.

Food for Thought

The Importance (and Fun) of Outrageous Theories

Many theories proposed throughout the history of science have been, well, quirky or even outrageous. That is, they have been unorthodox or heretical, with a shockingly different take on the world. The heliocentric (or sun-centred) theory of our solar system is a prime example. Some of these outrageous theories have turned out to be good theories—they measured up to the criteria of adequacy very well. So an outrageous theory is not necessarily a bad theory. Science as a whole has always been open to offbeat explanations, but they had to be judged to have merit. Most kooky theories in science or on the fringes of science, though, fail the criteria of adequacy miserably. The challenge for scientists and other critical thinkers is to remain open to unorthodox theories but not be afraid to test them through critical reasoning. Besides, offbeat theories are fun. The following theories have been found on the internet:

> "The Rife Machine was developed by an American scientist and inventor, Royal Raymond Rife, in the 1920s. The machine is also called a Rife Frequency Generator. Rife and his supporters say that each disease or condition has its own electromagnetic frequency, and by finding that exact frequency and producing an impulse of the same frequency, it is possible to kill or disable diseased cells.[5] Believers claim that Rife's 'discovery' could cure cancer, and in the 1980s (long after Rife's death) some claimed that it could cure AIDS, too. Modern medical science says 'no!'"

> "It was the mid-1970s and Pyramid Power was a huge topic of interest all over the world. Researchers were creating scale models of the Great Pyramid of Khufu, aligning them to the magnetic poles and experimenting, using pyramids for everything from meditating under them to sharpening razor blades. . . . Over the decades, brilliant minds have spent hundreds of thousands of hours and millions of dollars in research, attempting to discover if there is such a thing as Pyramid Power. They've sought to affirm if there's some sort of mysterious energy, spirituality or doorway to other dimensions contained within. To my knowledge, there haven't been any scientifically recognized, definitive results that prove that Pyramid Power exists. This doesn't mean that it doesn't exist. . . ."[6]

> "It was 20 years ago today, or almost, that Tom Bearden's (et al.) Motionless Electromagnetic Generator (MEG) burst onto the scene, putting out a solid overunity power performance which was replicated by a number of researchers. One buildup was tested to destruction, producing a Coefficient of Performance (COP) over 100. The unit was awarded a patent by the US Patent Office, and Tom incorporated it into a personal briefing that he gave to two Senate technical committees in Washington. For a while, its details and performance were listed on the Department of Energy website, and later removed. . . . After 20 years, this proven technology, whose basis was peer reviewed in a number of scientific journals, should be functioning in the public domain producing free Energy From the Vacuum™. . . . As Tom says, any competent electrical researcher should be able to replicate this machine."[7]

Chris Madden/CartoonStock

Just because an explanation genuinely is the best one, does that mean it's going to be welcomed by everyone? What fallacies might lead people to disregard a better theory?

All empirical theories are testable (they predict something beyond the thing to be explained). But fruitful theories are testable and then go beyond that—they not only predict something, but they also predict something that no one expected. The element of surprise is hard to ignore.

Decades ago, Einstein's theory of relativity gained a great deal of credibility by successfully predicting a phenomenon that was extraordinary and otherwise entirely unexpected. The theory predicts that light travelling close to massive objects (such as stars) will appear to be bent because the space around such objects is curved. The curve in space causes a curve in nearby light rays. At the time, however, the prevailing opinion was that light always travels in straight lines—no bends, no curves, no breaks. In 1919, the physicist Sir Arthur Eddington devised a way to test this prediction. He managed to take two sets of photographs of exactly the same portion of the sky—when the sun was overhead (in daylight) and when it was not (at night). He was able to get a good photo of the sky during daylight because there was a total eclipse of the sun at the time. If light rays really were bent when they passed near massive objects, then stars whose light gets to us via a path that travels near the sun should appear to be shifted slightly from their true position (as seen at night, when the sun isn't a factor). Eddington discovered that stars seen near the sun did indeed appear to have moved relative to their position as seen at night and that the amount of their apparent movement was just what Einstein's theory predicted. This novel observation demonstrated the fruitfulness of Einstein's theory, provided a degree of confirmation for the theory, and opened up new areas of research.

So the moral is that, other things being equal, fruitful theories are superior to those that aren't fruitful. Certainly, many good theories make no really novel predictions but end up being accepted nonetheless. The reason is usually that they excel in other criteria of adequacy.

9.3.3 Scope

Suppose theory 1 and theory 2 are two equally plausible theories to explain phenomenon X. Theory 1 can explain X well, and so can theory 2. But theory 1 can explain or predict *only* X, whereas theory 2 can explain or predict X—as well as phenomena Y and Z. Which is the better theory?

We must conclude that theory 2 is better because it explains more diverse phenomena. That is, it has more **scope** than the other theory. The more a theory explains or predicts, the more it extends our understanding. And the more a theory explains or predicts, the less likely it is to be false because it has more evidence in its favour.

scope
A criterion of adequacy for judging the worth of theories. A theory with scope is one that explains or predicts phenomena other than that which it was introduced to explain.

A major strength of Newton's theory of gravity and motion, for example, was that it explained more than any previous theory. Then came Einstein's theory of relativity: it could explain everything that Newton's theory could explain *plus* many phenomena that Newton's theory could not explain. This increased scope of Einstein's theory helped to convince scientists that it was the better theory.

Here's a more down-to-earth example. For decades psychologists have known about a phenomenon called *constructive perception* (discussed in Chapter 4). In constructive perception, what we perceive (see, hear, feel, etc.) is determined in part by what we expect, know, or believe. Studies have shown that when people expect to perceive a certain stimulus (say, a flashing light, a certain colour or shape, or a shadow), they often *do* end up perceiving it, even if there is no stimulus present. The phenomenon of constructive perception then can be used to explain many instances in which people seem to perceive something when it is not really there or when it is actually very different from the way people think it is.

One kind of case that investigators sometimes explain as an instance of constructive perception is the sighting of UFOs (Unidentified Flying Objects). Many times, people report seeing lights in the night sky that look to them like alien spacecraft, and they explain their perception by saying that the lights were caused by alien spacecraft. So we now have two theories to explain the experience: constructive perception and UFOs from space. If these two theories differ only in the degree of scope provided by each one, then we must conclude that the constructive perception theory is better. (In reality, theories about incredible events usually fail on several criteria.) The constructive perception theory can explain not only UFO sightings but also all kinds of ordinary and extraordinary experiences—hallucinations, feelings of an unknown "presence," misidentification of crime suspects, contradictory reports in car accidents, and more. The UFO theory, however, is (usually) designed to explain just one thing: an experience of seeing strange lights in the sky.

Scope is often a crucial factor in a jury's evaluation of theories put forth by both the prosecution and the defence. The prosecution will have a very powerful case against the defendant if the prosecutor's theory (that the defendant committed the crime in question) explains all the evidence while the defence theory (innocence) does not. The defendant will be in big trouble if the prosecutor's theory explains the blood on the defendant's shirt, the eyewitness accounts, the defendant's fingerprints on the wall, and the sudden change in his usual routine—*and* if the innocence theory leaves these facts downright mysterious.

Other things being equal, then, the best theory is the one with the greatest scope. And if other things aren't equal, a theory with superior scope doesn't necessarily win the day because it may do poorly on the other criteria or another theory might do better.

9.3.4 Simplicity

Let's return one last time to the scenario about the non-starting car. Recall that the last four theories are as follows:

10. Each night, you've been sabotaging your own car while you sleepwalk.
11. Your 90-year-old uncle, who lives 1000 kilometres away from you, has been damaging the engine by secretly visiting and going for joyrides in your car.
12. A poltergeist (a noisy, mischievous ghost) has damaged the car's carburetor.
13. Yesterday, you accidentally drove the car through a portal to an alternative space–time dimension, scrambling the electrical system.

simplicity
A criterion of adequacy for judging the worth of theories. A simple theory is one that makes as few assumptions as possible.

By now you probably suspect that these explanations are somehow unacceptable, and you are right. One important characteristic that they each lack is **simplicity**. Other things being equal, the best theory is the one that is the simplest—that is, the one that makes the fewest assumptions. The theory making the fewest assumptions is less likely to be false because there are fewer ways for it to go wrong. Another way to look at it is that since a simpler theory is based on fewer assumptions, less evidence is required to support it. If the theory makes assumptions, especially strange ones, then to defend that theory, you're going to need to dig up evidence in support of each of those assumptions.

Explanations 8 and 9 lack simplicity because they each must assume the existence of an unknown and unproven entity (poltergeists and another dimension that scrambles electrical circuits). Such assumptions about the existence of unknown objects, forces, and dimensions are common in occult or paranormal theories. Explanations 6 and 7 assume no new entities, but they do assume complex and unlikely chains of events. This alone makes them less plausible than the simple explanation of 3, the starter malfunction.

The criterion of simplicity has often been a major factor in the acceptance or rejection of important theories. For example, simplicity is an important advantage that the theory of evolution has over creationism, the theory that the world was created all at once by a divine being (see Chapter 10). Creationism must assume the existence of a creator and the existence of unknown forces (supernatural forces used by the creator). But evolution does not make either of these assumptions.

Scientists eventually accepted Copernicus's theory of planetary motion (which held that the planets orbit around the sun) over Ptolemy's older theory (Earth-centred orbits) because the former was simpler (see Chapter 10). In order to account for apparent irregularities in the movement of certain planets, Ptolemy's theory had to assume that planets have extremely complex orbits (orbits within orbits). Copernicus's theory, however, had no need for so much extra baggage. His theory could account for the observational data without so many orbits within orbits.

ad hoc hypothesis
A hypothesis, or theory, that cannot be verified independently of the phenomenon it is supposed to explain. Ad hoc hypotheses always make a theory less simple—and therefore less credible.

Sometimes a theory's lack of simplicity is the result of constructing ad hoc hypotheses. An **ad hoc hypothesis** is one that cannot be verified independently of the phenomenon it's supposed to explain. If a theory is in trouble because it is not matching up with the observational data of the phenomenon, you might be able to rescue it by altering it—by dreaming up additional entities or properties that could in principle account for the data. Such tinkering is legitimate (scientists do it all the time) if there is an independent way of confirming the existence of these proposed entities and properties. But if there is no way to verify their existence, the modifications are ad hoc hypotheses. Ad hoc hypotheses always make a theory less simple—and therefore less credible.

Food for Thought

There's No Theory Like a Conspiracy Theory

Conspiracy theories try to explain events by positing the secret participation of numerous conspirators. The terrorist attacks of 9/11 and the COVID-19 pandemic, among many other famous events, have been the subject of countless conspiracy theories, both elaborate and provocative. Even Tim Hortons coffee has been the subject of conspiracy theories! Some conspiracy theories, of course, have been found to be true after all. But most of them are implausible. The main problem with them is that they usually fail to meet the criterion of simplicity. They would have us make numerous assumptions that raise more questions than they answer. How do the conspirators manage to keep their activities secret? How do they control all the people and organizations involved? Where is the evidence that all the parts of the conspiracy have come together just so?

Nonetheless, many conspiracy theories remain quite popular, perhaps because they engage our imaginations. Here's a short list of things that, we are told, are at the centre of a massive conspiracy:

- The terrorist attacks of 9/11
- The causes of autism
- The assassination of Martin Luther King Jr
- The selection of the winner of the Stanley Cup each year
- The death of Princess Diana
- The identity of Justin Trudeau's "real" father
- The death of former Enron CEO Kenneth Lay

And here are a few of the alleged evil-doers that are doing all the dirty deeds:

- The US government
- The Vatican
- The CIA
- The Illuminati, a secret society controlling the government
- Doctors
- The Freemasons
- The pharmaceutical industry

The growth of such conspiracy theories seems to have accelerated in the online world. On the internet, literally anybody—regardless of their knowledge or expertise—can publish their opinion on any topic, and sometimes succeed in gaining a large audience.

9.3.5 Conservatism

What if a trusted friend told you that—believe it or not—some dogs lay eggs just as chickens do? Let's assume that your friend is being perfectly serious and believes what she is saying. Would you accept this claim about egg-laying dogs? Not likely. But why not?

conservatism
A criterion of adequacy for judging the worth of theories. A conservative theory is one that fits with our established beliefs.

Probably your main reason for rejecting such an extraordinary claim would be that it fails the criterion of **conservatism**, though you probably wouldn't state it that way. (Note: the word "conservatism" in this sense of has nothing to do with politics or social values!) This criterion says that, other things being equal, *the best theory is the one that fits best with our established beliefs*. In other words, we want a theory that allows us to *conserve* or keep what we already know. We would reject the canine-egg theory because, among other things, it conflicts with our well-founded beliefs about mammals, evolution, canine anatomy, and much more. Humans have an enormous amount of experience (scientific and otherwise) with dogs, and none of it suggests that dogs can lay eggs. In fact, a great deal of what we know about dogs suggests that they *cannot* lay eggs. To accept the canine-egg theory even though it conflicts with a mountain of solid evidence would be irrational—and destructive of whatever understanding we had on the subject.

Perhaps one day we may be shocked to learn that, contrary to all expectations, dogs do lay eggs. But given that this belief is contrary to a massive amount of credible experience, we must assign a very low probability to it.

We are naturally reluctant to accept explanations that conflict with what we already know, and we should be. Accepting beliefs that fly in the face of our knowledge has several risks:

1. The chances of the new belief being true are not good (because it has no evidence in its favour, while our well-established beliefs have plenty of evidence on their side).
2. The conflict of beliefs undermines our knowledge (because we cannot know something that is in doubt, and the conflict would be cause for doubt).
3. The conflict of beliefs lessens our understanding (because the new beliefs cannot be plausibly integrated into our other beliefs).

So everything considered, the more conservative a theory is, the more plausible it is.[8]

Here's another example. Let's say that someone claims to have built a perpetual motion machine. A perpetual motion machine is a device that is supposed to function without ever stopping and without requiring any energy input from outside the machine; it is designed to continuously supply its own energy.

Now, this is an intriguing idea—but one that we shouldn't take too seriously. The problem is that the notion of a perpetual motion machine is not conservative at all. It conflicts with a very well-established belief, namely, one of the laws of physics—specifically, one of the laws of thermodynamics. The law of conservation of mass-energy states that mass-energy cannot be created or destroyed. A perpetual motion machine, though, would have to create energy out of nothing. Like any law of nature, however, the law of conservation of mass-energy is supported by a vast amount of empirical evidence. We must conclude, then, that it is extremely unlikely that anyone could escape the law of conservation of mass-energy through the use of any machine. (This fact, however, has not stopped countless optimistic inventors from claiming that they've invented such devices. When the devices are put to the test, they invariably fail to perform as advertised.)

Food for Thought

Can a Pandemic Be a Hoax?

In October of 2020, as the rate of deaths due to COVID-19 was accelerating, US President Donald Trump was promoting a dangerous idea, namely that the entire pandemic was nothing but a hoax—that it was, in his words, "fake news." In typical fashion, he claimed that news media were promoting the idea of a pandemic as a way to hurt his chances at being re-elected in the November 4th election.

Trump tweeted:

> "The fake news media is riding COVID, COVID, COVID, all the way to the Election. Losers!"

As case numbers rose, Trump claimed that the numbers were being artificially inflated by what he implied was a foolish program of, well, testing people for COVID-19:

> "Cases up because we TEST, TEST, TEST. A fake news media conspiracy. Many young people who heal very fast. 99.9%. Corrupt media conspiracy at all time high. On November 4th, topic will totally change. VOTE!"[9]

Sadly, Trump wasn't alone in casting doubt on the seriousness and magnitude of the COVID-19 pandemic. Despite the declarations of reputable agencies such as the World Health Organization (WHO), the U.S. Centers for Disease Control and Prevention (CDC), and the Public Health Agency of Canada, stories of doubt kept erupting. Some downplayed the seriousness of the pandemic, comparing COVID-19 to the flu or the common cold. Others suggested that governments, drug companies, and others were conspiring to exaggerate the pandemic in order to instill fear in—and thereby exert control over—a gullible public. Many claimed that, despite the number of hospitalizations and deaths being reported, COVID-19 was really no big deal.

"Anyone who thinks this virus is a hoax needs to wake up and smell the coffee... If they still have a sense of smell."

Sometimes the evidence we need to detect a hoax is right under our noses.

What was truly amazing was that such doubters got any attention at all, given how implausible their

continued

theories were. After all, their theories required the denial of a truly stunning amount of evidence, coming from an enormous and diverse range of sources. Beyond a readiness to believe that things might not be as they seemed, these conspiracy theorists needed their audience to ignore entirely the following factors:

- the warnings of government agencies with long histories of truth-telling;
- the pleas of thousands of doctors and nurses who testified to the fact that intensive care units (ICUs) around the world were overflowing;
- TV images of body bags containing the remains of COVID-19 victims; and
- the fact that, in some cases, their own neighbours and even family members had been hospitalized—and had in some cases died—of this disease they were trying to trivialize.

This is not to say that governments never lie, that health professionals never exaggerate, or that everything you see on TV is true. The point is that, given the evidence available, the *best explanation* was the existence of a terrible and contagious disease.

It's possible, of course, that a new theory that conflicts with what we know could turn out to be right and a more conservative theory could turn out to be wrong. But we would need good reasons to show that the new theory was correct before we would be justified in tossing out the old theory and bringing in the new.

Science looks for conservative theories, but it still sometimes embraces theories that are departures (sometimes *radical* departures) from the well-worn, accepted explanations. When this dramatic change happens, it's frequently because other criteria of adequacy outweigh conservatism. We'll explore the creation and evaluation of scientific theories in the next chapter.

Supernatural or paranormal theories often run afoul of the criterion of conservatism. Take *dowsing*, for instance. Dowsing is the practice of allegedly detecting underground water by using a hand-held Y-shaped wooden stick (known as a divining rod or dowsing rod), a pendulum, or another device. It's a folk tradition that's hundreds of years old. Dowsers claim to be able to detect the presence of underground water by walking over a given terrain and holding the dowsing rod, pendulum, or other device in a prescribed manner. When the device moves in a certain way (e.g., if the point of the rod dips toward the ground or the pendulum swings in a certain direction), that's supposed to indicate that water is beneath the dowser. It seems to the dowser (and sometimes to observers) that the device moves on its own as though under the influence of some hidden force.

One theory to account for the rod or pendulum's movements is that an unknown form of radiation emanating from the underground water pulls on the divining device, causing it to move. (A well-supported alternative theory is that the movement of the device in the dowser's hands is caused by suggestion and unconscious muscular activity in the dowser.) As it stands, the radiation theory is not testable, fruitful, or simple. But its major failing is its lack of conservatism. The claim about the strange, occult radiation conflicts with what scientists know about energy, radiation, and human sensory systems. It is possible that the dowser's radiation exists, but there is no reason to believe that it does and good reason to doubt it.

We will look at many more examples shortly, but before we go any further, you need to fully understand two crucial points about the nature of theory appraisal.

First, there is no strict formula or protocol for applying the criteria of adequacy. In deductive arguments there are rules of inference that are precise and invariable. But inference to the best explanation is a different thing altogether. There are no precise rules for applying the criteria, no way to quantify how a theory measures up according to each criterion, and no way to rank each criterion according to its importance. Sometimes we may assign more weight to the criterion of scope if the theory in question seems similar to other theories on the basis of all the remaining criteria. Other times we may weight simplicity more when considering theories that seem equally conservative or fruitful. The process of theory evaluation is not like solving a math problem—but more like diagnosing an illness or making a judicial decision. It is rational but not formulaic, and it depends on the dynamics of human judgment. The best we can do is follow some guidelines for evaluating theories generally and for applying the criteria of adequacy. Fortunately, this kind of help is usually all we need. (You'll get this kind of guidance in the following pages.)

Second, despite the lack of formula in theory assessment, the process is far from subjective or arbitrary. There are many judgments that we successfully make every day that are not quantifiable or formulaic—but they are still objective. We can agree, for example, on many key features that go into making a car a good one: various safety features, fuel efficiency, cargo space, and so on. We cannot say exactly how to rank those features, but that doesn't stop us from arriving at sound judgments; leaving aside questions of price, a BMW 520i is a better car than a Ford Fiesta. Of course, there are cases that are not so clear-cut that give rise to reasonable disagreement among reasonable people—various luxury sedans may be very similar in quality, with only minor differences. But there are also many instances that are manifestly unambiguous. Pretending that these questions of quality are unclear would be irrational. It would simply be incorrect to believe that a Toyota Yaris is "just as good" a car as an S-Class Mercedes. The same goes for evaluating theories. The criteria that apply are well understood. The fact that there's no formula for applying those criteria does nothing to prevent us from applying them in a sensible manner to tell good theories from bad ones.

Review Notes

Criteria of Adequacy

- *Testability:* Whether there is some way to determine if a theory is true.
- *Fruitfulness:* The number of novel predictions made.
- *Scope:* The number of diverse phenomena explained.
- *Simplicity:* The number of assumptions made.
- *Conservatism:* How well a theory fits with existing knowledge.

Critical Thinking and the Media

Experts and Explanatory Theories

As this book is being revised, in the winter of 2022, the world is reacting to the invasion of Ukraine by Russian forces under the leadership of Vladimir Putin.

One of the issues that has most interested the public and experts alike is this: "What are Putin's motives?" That is, given the obvious costs of such a war, why is Putin doing this?

Experts and commentators of various kinds have expressed opinions. Here are some of the theories currently being voiced:

- Putin is doing this because he wants access to Ukraine's rich natural resources.
- Putin is doing this because Ukraine constitutes a strategically important piece of land from which Russia might want to carry out military operations in future.
- Putin is doing this because he believes that, historically, Ukrainians and Russians are a single population, necessitating re-unification.
- Putin is doing this because he wants to begin rebuilding the former Soviet Union, with himself as leader.
- Putin is doing this because he feels threatened by the possibility that Ukraine might eventually become part of NATO (the North Atlantic Treaty Organization).
- . . . and others!

One or more of those may be true. Two of the skills you've learned in this book can help you evaluate those possibilities.

First, for each theory being offered, we should examine the expertise of the person putting it forward. In particular, we should use the tools from Chapter 4 of this book to ask questions like whether those putting a particular theory forward really have relevant evidence, and whether multiple experts agree with each other on any of those theories.

Second, we can use tools from the present chapter to examine each theory to ask whether it is testable, fruitful, simple, and conservative, as well as how much scope it has. The question of scope is particularly useful here. Putin has been a public figure for more than twenty years, and so we have lots of other behaviours of his to help explain the current situation. Does one of the theories above explain not just his invasion of Ukraine, but also his role in Russia's 1999 war against Chechen separatists, the changes he made to the Russian Constitution in 2020, and his aggressive stance toward Finland in 2022?

Exercise 9.6

Answers to exercises marked with an asterisk (*) may be found in Appendix B, Answers to Exercises.

1. Why is the quantity of evidence available for various theories *not* a sufficient indication of which theory you should accept?
2. In theory evaluation, what is the minimum requirement of consistency?*
3. What does it take to completely evaluate a particular theory? What does this imply about what makes a theory the "best" theory?
4. According to the text, what are the criteria of adequacy?
5. What does it mean for a theory to lack scope? To be testable? To be fruitful?
6. What does it mean to say that a theory is not conservative?*
7. What does it mean when we say that a best explanation is not "truth-preserving"? Why is this important?
8. What role does the concept of simplicity play in determining the best theory? What are the risks involved in accepting a theory that is not simple?

Exercise 9.7

Following are several pairs of theories used to explain various phenomena. For each pair, determine (1) which theory is simpler and (2) which one is more conservative.

1. Phenomenon: You watch a show one evening starring an actor who happens to look a lot like your favourite high school teacher, and the next day you see your old teacher at a coffee shop. Theories: Coincidence; psychic connection between you and your old teacher.
2. Phenomenon: Your cold symptoms end. Theories: Part of the natural cycle of the cold; the result of taking a homeopathic remedy with no measurable active ingredients.*
3. Phenomenon: The morning after an evening of drinking with friends, you have a terrible headache. Theories: a brain tumour; a hangover.
4. Phenomenon: A huge drop in the incidence of measles over the last 100 years. Theories: Mandatory immunization; lower levels of air pollution.*
5. Phenomenon: Your professor has brought candy to class. Theories: Her husband is a dentist, and she wants to make sure he keeps getting lots of business; today is the day students will fill out course evaluations and she wants you all in a good mood.
6. Phenomenon: A woman is limping across campus, wearing a ski jacket with a day-pass for a local ski hill attached to the zipper. Theories: She hurt her leg skiing; she is an international spy who escaped an assassination attempt but was wounded in the leg.

7. Phenomenon: A hurricane hitting Nova Scotia. Theories: A pre-existing tropical storm was amplified by unusually warm ocean currents; radiation from outer space.*
8. Phenomenon: Sales of our smart phone are down this year. Theories: Apple's newest iPhone has more features and more innovations than ours does, at a competitive price; Apple has bribed a huge number of our salespeople to do what they can to make sure our phones don't sell.

9.4 Telling Good Theories from Bad

"For any scientific theory is born into a life of fierce competition, a jungle red in tooth and claw. Only the successful theories survive—the ones which in fact latched onto the actual regularities in nature."

—Bas Van Fraassen

TEST formula

A four-step procedure for evaluating the worth of a theory:

Step 1. State the Theory and check for consistency.
Step 2. Assess the Evidence for the theory.
Step 3. Scrutinize alternative theories.
Step 4. Test the theories with the criteria of adequacy.

Many (perhaps most) explanatory theories that you run into every day are easy to assess. They are clearly the best (or not the best) explanations for the facts at hand. The dog barked because someone was approaching the house. Your friend blushed because he was embarrassed. The mayor resigned because of a scandal. In such cases, you may make inferences to the best explanation (using some or all of the criteria of adequacy) without any deep reflection. But at other times, you may need and want to be more deliberate, to think more carefully about which explanation is really best. In either case, it helps to have a set of guidelines that tells you how your inquiry *should* proceed if you're to make cogent inferences. Here, then, is the **TEST formula**, four steps to finding the best explanation:

Step 1. State the **T**heory and check for consistency.
Step 2. Assess the **E**vidence for the theory.
Step 3. **S**crutinize alternative theories.
Step 4. **T**est the theories with the criteria of adequacy.

(In the next chapter, you will see that this formula is also one way of describing the general approach used in science to evaluate sets of theories.)

Step 1. State the theory and check for consistency. Before you can evaluate an explanatory theory, you must express it in a statement that's as clear and specific as possible. Once you do this, you can check to see if the theory meets the minimum requirement for consistency. If it fails the consistency test, you can have no good grounds for believing that it's correct. And, obviously, if the theory fails step 1, there's no reason to go to step 2.

Step 2. Assess the evidence for the theory. To evaluate any theory critically, you must understand any reasons in its favour—the empirical evidence or logical arguments that may support or undermine it. Essentially, this step involves an honest assessment of the empirical evidence relevant to the truth (or falsity) of the theory. To make this assessment, you must put to use what you already know about the credibility of sources, causal reasoning, and evidence from personal and scientific observations (topics covered in Chapters 4 and 8).

In this step, you may discover that the evidence in favour of a theory is strong, weak, or non-existent. You may find that there is good evidence that seems to count against the theory. Or you may learn that the phenomenon under investigation did not occur at all. Whatever the case, you have to have the courage to face up to reality. You must be ready to admit that your favourite theory has little to recommend it.

Step 3. Scrutinize alternative theories. Inference to the *best* explanation will not help us very much if we stop after examining just one explanation and aren't willing to consider *alternative* ones. Simply examining the evidence relevant to a single eligible theory is not enough.

Theories can often appear stronger than they really are if we don't bother to compare them with others. To take an outrageous example, consider this theory designed to explain the presence of the Canadian superhero Wolverine in the X-Men movies and comic books. The explanation? Wolverine isn't a fictional character at all but a *real Canadian superhero.* The evidence for this explanation is the following: (1) Millions of young children read the comic books or see the movies and believe Wolverine is real. (2) The other characters in the movies and comic books speak to Wolverine as if he's real. (3) It's possible that there really are mutants like Wolverine in the world and that they mostly just remain hidden from the public. (4) It's not *impossible* that the science exists to have coated Wolverine's bones and claws with an indestructible metal known as adamantium. (5) The creators of the comic books and movies have "stolen" Wolverine's life story for use in entertainment because they know it is an exciting story.

Now, you don't believe that Wolverine is real (do you?), even in the face of reasons 1–5. But perhaps you'll admit that the Wolverine theory is at least a tiny bit plausible. And if you never hear any alternative explanations, you might

Everyday Problems and Decisions

Grades, Studying, and the Criteria of Adequacy

Explanations are an important part of everyday life, and inference to the best explanation is at the heart of many important decisions. Consider, for example, the question of what to do in the wake of a poor performance on a test or quiz. Let's say you're a B+ student who gets a D on a particular quiz. Of course, you're disappointed and maybe a little upset. But what should you do about it? What's your plan, as a student? Deciding what to do requires that you first figure out why the bad grade happened. What's the best explanation? So you start listing the possibilities. Maybe you didn't study enough. Maybe the test was unfair. Maybe the material was much harder than usual. Maybe the professor made a grading error. The criteria of adequacy can help you to sort through what the most likely explanation is. And knowing what the most likely explanation is helps you to know what to do next—both regarding this quiz and regarding how to prepare for the next one.

eventually become a true believer. (Anthropologists can plausibly argue that various cultures have come to believe in many very unlikely phenomena and exotic deities in large part because of *a lack of alternative explanations.*)

When you do consider an alternative explanation—for example, that Wolverine is an imaginary character invented to entertain you—the Wolverine-is-real theory looks a little silly. And once you consider the evidence for this alternative theory (e.g., documentation that Wolverine was dreamed up by Roy Thomas and Len Wein at Marvel Comics in the early 1970s), the other explanation looks even sillier.

Step 3 requires us to have an open mind, to think outside the box, to ask if there are other ways to explain the phenomenon in question, and to consider the evidence for those theories. Specifically, in this step we must conscientiously look for competing theories, *then apply both step 1 and step 2 to each one of them.* This process may leave us with many or few eligible theories to examine. In any case, it's sure to tell us something important about the strength or weakness of competing theories.

Many times, the criteria of adequacy can help us to do a preliminary assessment of a theory's plausibility without our surveying alternative theories. For example, a theory may do so poorly regarding a particular criterion that we can conclude that, whatever the merits of alternative explanations, the theory at hand is not very credible. Such a clear lack of credibility is often apparent when a theory is obviously neither simple nor conservative.

Skipping step 3 is an extremely common error in the evaluation of explanations of all kinds. This is a classic example of many types of errors discussed in earlier chapters—overlooking evidence, preferring available evidence, looking only for confirming evidence, and denying the evidence.

Carrying out step 3 does not come naturally. The human tendency is instead to grab hold of a favourite theory—and then to halt any further critical thinking right there.

Our built-in bias is to seize on a theory immediately—because we find it comforting or because we supposedly just "know" it's the right one—and then ignore or resist all other possibilities. The result is a greatly increased likelihood of error and delusion and a significantly decreased opportunity to achieve true understanding.

Failure to consider alternative theories is the classic mistake in inquiries into the paranormal or supernatural (a topic we touch upon in Chapter 10). The usual pattern is this: (1) you come across an extraordinary or impressive phenomenon, (2) you can't think of a natural explanation of the facts, and (3) you conclude that the phenomenon must not be natural but instead paranormal or supernatural. This conclusion, however, would be unwarranted. Just because you can't think of a natural explanation doesn't mean that there isn't one. You may simply be unaware of the correct natural explanation. In the past, scientists have often been confronted with extraordinary phenomena that they couldn't explain—phenomena that were later found to have a natural explanation.

Step 4. Test the theories with the criteria of adequacy. As we've seen, simply adding up the evidence for each of the competing theories and checking to see which one gets the highest score will not do. We need to measure the plausibility of the theories by using the criteria of adequacy. The criteria can help us put any applicable evidence in perspective and allow us to make a judgment about theory plausibility even when there's little or no evidence to consider.

By applying the criteria to all the competing theories, we can often accomplish several important feats. We may be able to eliminate some candidate theories immediately, assign more weight to some than to others, and distinguish between candidate theories that at first glance seem equally strong.

The best way to learn how to do step 4, as well as steps 1–3, is by example. Watch what happens when we assess the plausibility of theories for the following set of events.

9.4.1 A Doomed Flight

On 2 September 1998, Swissair Flight 111 crashed into the Atlantic Ocean not far from Peggy's Cove, Nova Scotia, killing all 229 people on board. The incident, like most airline disasters, prompted a search for explanations for the crash. The ensuing investigation was led by the Canadian Transportation Safety Board (TSB), with the cooperation of the US Federal Aviation Administration (FAA) and the aircraft manufacturers Pratt & Whitney. The investigation relied heavily on criteria of adequacy to sort through competing theories. After an investigation lasting five years, the TSB concluded that faulty wiring in the aircraft's entertainment system had started a fire that eventually brought the plane down.

Using this incident as inspiration and guide, let's devise another story of a mysterious jetliner crash and examine the main theories to explain it. We will assume that all the facts in the case are known, that all relevant reports are honest (no intent to deceive), and that no other information is forthcoming. In other words, this is a very contrived case. But it suits our purposes here just fine. Here we go.

The (made-up) facts of the case are these: at 8:30 p.m., Flight 222, a McDonnell Douglas MD-11, left JFK airport in New York on its way to Oslo, Norway.

Review Notes

Evaluating Theories: The TEST Formula

Step 1: State the Theory and check for consistency.

Step 2: Assess the Evidence for the theory.

Step 3: Scrutinize alternative theories.

Step 4: Test the theories with the criteria of adequacy.

At 9:38 p.m. the crew issued a "Mayday" call, and at 9:42 the plane crashed into the ocean 50 kilometres off the coast of Newfoundland. The crash happened during a time of heightened awareness of possible terrorist attacks on aircraft.

Now let's try steps 1–4 on a supposedly popular theory and some of its leading alternatives. Here's the pop theory in question. Theory 1: *A missile fired by a terrorist brought down the plane.* This meets the requirement for consistency, so our first concern is to assess the evidence for the theory. Those who favour this theory point to several pieces of evidence. Eyewitnesses said that they had seen a bright streak of light or flame speeding toward the plane. A few people said that they thought they were watching a missile intercept the plane. And a journalist reported on the internet that the plane had been shot down by a missile fired from a boat.

There are, however, some problems with this evidence. Eyewitness reports of the movements of bright lights in a dark sky are notoriously unreliable, even when the eyewitnesses are experts. Under such viewing conditions, the actual size of a bright object, its distance from the observer, its speed, and even whether it's moving are extremely difficult to determine accurately by sight. Also, another phenomenon could have easily been mistaken for a speeding missile. It's known that an explosion rupturing a fuel tank on an aircraft's wing can ignite long streams of fuel, which from the ground may look like a missile heading toward the plane. In addition, the Canadian Coast Guard monitors boats and ships in the area in which Flight 222 crashed, and it says that there were none in the immediate area when the crash occurred. Because of the distances involved and other factors, firing a missile from the ground at Flight 222 and hitting it was virtually impossible. Finally, an unsupported allegation—whether from a journalist or anyone else—is not good evidence for anything.

Then we have this explanation. Theory 2: *An alien spacecraft shot the plane down.* For the sake of illustration, we will assume that this explanation meets the consistency requirement. The evidence is this: several people say that they saw a UFO fly near the plane just before the plane exploded. And tapes of radar images show an unknown object flying close to the MD-11.

These eyewitness accounts suffer from the same weakness as those mentioned in theory 1. Observations under the conditions described are not reliable. Thus, many alleged alien craft have turned out to be airplanes, helicopters, blimps, meteors, and even the planet Venus, an extremely bright object in the sky. Radar tapes may show many objects that are "unknown" to untrained observers but are identified precisely by experts. The radar evidence might be more impressive if the flight controllers had not been able to provide an alternative account for an object flying close to Flight 222.

Theory 3: *A bomb on board the plane exploded, bringing the aircraft down.* This explanation is internally and externally consistent. The main evidence for it is the existence of trace amounts of explosive residue on a few of the recovered aircraft parts. Also, the story of the crash of Flight 222 resembles the media account of the crash of another jetliner that's known to have been brought down by an onboard bomb.

This resemblance, though, is only that—it's not evidence that counts in favour of the bomb theory. And the explosive residue is not such clear evidence after all. Investigators determined that the residues were most likely left over from a security training exercise conducted on the plane a week earlier. Moreover, examination of the wreckage and patterns of damage to it suggests that a bomb was not detonated inside the aircraft.

Theory 4: *A mechanical failure involving the fuel tanks caused the explosion that brought the plane down*. This is an eligible theory. It's backed by evidence showing that an explosion occurred in one of the plane's fuel tanks. Experts know that a short circuit in wiring outside a fuel tank can cause excess voltage in wiring that's inside the tank and thus ignite the fuel. Investigators found that there was indeed a short circuit in some of the fuel-tank wiring. In addition, explosions in several other large jets, some smaller planes, and various machine engines have been linked to faulty wiring in fuel tanks.

Theory 5: *A solar flare disrupted electrical circuits in the plane, releasing a spark that made the fuel tanks explode*. This too is an eligible theory. Solar flares are massive electromagnetic explosions on the surface of the sun. They can sometimes disrupt radio communications and even cause radio blackouts. Theory 5 says that a solar flare so dramatically affected electrical circuits in the plane that a spark was emitted that ignited the fuel. The rationale behind this theory is that flying planes, being closer to the sun, are more susceptible to the powerful effects of solar flares. The evidence for this theory, however, is nil. There is no good reason to believe that a solar flare could ever cause a spark in an electrical circuit.

Now let's apply the criteria of adequacy to these explanations. We can see right away that all the theories do equally well in terms of testability and fruitfulness. They're all testable, and none has yielded any surprising predictions. Except for theory 4, they also have equal scope because they explain only the phenomenon they were introduced to explain, the crash of Flight 222 (and perhaps similar airline crashes). Theory 4, however, has a slight edge because it can explain certain airline crashes as well as explosions in other systems that have wired fuel tanks. So if we are to distinguish between the theories, we must rely on the other criteria.

This is bad news for theories 2 and 5 because they fail the criteria of simplicity and conservatism. The evidence in favour of the alien spacecraft theory is extremely weak. Even worse, it conflicts with a great deal of human experience regarding visitors from outer space. We simply have no good evidence that anyone has ever detected any beings or technology from outer space. Moreover, the probability of the Earth being visited by beings from outer space must be considered low (but not zero) in light of what we know about the size of the universe and the physical requirements of space travel. Likewise, the solar flare theory has no evidence to support it, and it too conflicts with what we know. There are no documented cases of solar flares causing sparks in electrical wiring. And neither theory is simple.

Theory 2 assumes an unknown entity (aliens), and theory 5 assumes unknown processes (solar flares causing sparks in wiring). These are excellent grounds for eliminating theories 2 and 5 from the running.

That leaves theories 1, 3, and 4, which we must also sort out by using the criteria of simplicity and conservatism. They fare equally well in terms of simplicity because none assumes any unknown or mysterious entities or processes. Conservatism, though, is a different story. Neither theory 1 nor 3 accords with the evidence. In each case, existing evidence counts *against* the theory. Theory 4, though, accords well with the evidence. It not only doesn't conflict with what we know, but the evidence also supports the theory in important ways. Theory 4, then, is the best explanation for the crash of Flight 222 and the theory most likely to be true. And the explanation we started with, theory 1, is implausible.

"Science is organized common sense where many a beautiful theory was killed by an ugly fact."

—Thomas H. Huxley

Without a detailed formula, without a weighting system, and without quantifying any criteria, we have arrived at a verdict regarding competing theories. Deciding among theories is not always so straightforward, of course. But this lack of clear-cut answers is what gives rise to more research and more critical thinking.

Exercise 9.8

Answers to exercises marked with an asterisk (*) may be found in Appendix B, Answers to Exercises.

Based on what you already know and the criteria of adequacy, determine which theory in each group is most plausible.

1. Phenomenon: Tania is home one day at lunchtime when an Uber Eats delivery shows up. Tania is hungry, but she didn't order anything, and the order is definitely for her address.
   Theories: (1) computer error, (2) someone else in Tania's house ordered lunch, (3) Tania has forgotten entirely that she ordered lunch.
2. Phenomenon: A sudden and dramatic drop in the price of a particular food corporation's shares.
   Theories: (1) rumours of a sex scandal involving the entire senior management team, (2) manipulation of the share price by one powerful shareholder, (3) a hard winter in the prairies raises the price of key ingredients for the company's products.
3. Phenomenon: Extraordinarily large humanlike footprints in the snow on a mountainside.
   Theories: (1) the legendary man-beast known as the Yeti, (2) foot-shaped rocks falling from the sky, (3) a very big human mountain-climber.*
4. Phenomenon: A decrease in the number of subscribers for cable tv.
   Theories: (1) a decrease in the overall population, (2) the increasing popularity of on-demand internet media streaming services such as Disney+ and

Netflix, (3) the younger generation's preference for reading books over watching television.

5. Phenomenon: An increase in reports of sexual harassment in the workplace. Theories: (1) a startling new epidemic of sexual harassment, (2) an increase in the willingness of women to report sexual harassment when it happens because of the #MeToo movement, (3) an increase in the number of women in the workplace.

Exercise 9.9

Evaluate the following theories by using the TEST formula. As part of your evaluation:

a. State the claim to be evaluated.
b. Indicate what phenomenon is being explained.
c. Specify at least one alternative theory.
d. Use the criteria of adequacy to assess the two theories, and determine which one is more plausible.
e. Write a paragraph detailing the reasons for your choice. Use your background knowledge to fill in any information about the theories and how well they do regarding each criterion.

1. A religious sect based in Montreal predicts that the end of the world will occur on 1 January 2017. The world, of course, does not end then. The leader of the sect explains that the prophecy failed to come true because members of the sect did not have enough faith in it.
2. A group of American corporations—advertisers—control who wins the NHL's Stanley Cup. That's why no Canadian team has won since the Montreal Canadiens did in 1993. After all, there are 25 American teams and only 7 Canadian teams, and so American advertisers have a lot more power—so they've been able to conspire with the league and with various coaches to make sure that no Canadian team wins.
3. I'm pretty sure I'm dying. I feel terrible. I threw up several times this morning. Last night, after getting home from the sushi restaurant, I had awful stomach cramps, and so I went straight to bed, but I slept badly. I looked up stomach cancer online, and the article I read listed symptoms just like these. I'm pretty sure I have cancer.
4. My professor doesn't like me very much. I did badly on my first test. I tried to speak to her about it at the start of class, but I was a bit late because I was rushing to class from a meeting of the Choir Club. I thought about talking to her after class but had to go to work. I know I could have talked to her about it during her office hours, but I couldn't make it due to soccer practice, and she said she didn't have any other time that day. She really isn't willing to make time to see me.

5. What difference does footwear make? Well, your feet are connected to your legs, which are connected to your back, and your back includes your spine. And your spinal cord is the conduit for electrical impulses that either control or affect every major organ of your body. So we looked at the shoes people wear. We went out in public and found people wearing soft-soled sneakers and asked them about their health. We also found people wearing hard-soled leather shoes and asked them about their health. We also took both groups' blood pressure. We found that people wearing sneakers tended to be less overweight and had lower blood pressure and had fewer complaints about depression and anxiety. These results demonstrate that the right shoes can have a huge impact on your health.
6. Professor, it's not what it looks like. I know my essay was a lot like Bruce's—the same topic, same overall structure, and even very similar first and last sentences. But I swear it's just a coincidence!

Exercise 9.10

Read the following passages, and answer these questions for each one:

1. What is the phenomenon being explained?
2. What theories are given to explain the phenomenon? (Some theories may be unstated.)
3. Which theory seems the least plausible and why? (Use the criteria of adequacy.)
4. Which theory is the most plausible and why?
5. Regarding the most credible theory, what factors would need to change in order to convince you to regard it as even more plausible?
6. What factors might be different that could persuade you to regard the least credible theory as at least somewhat more plausible?

Passage 1

Unethical behaviour seems quite common in the world of business. Some people blame this on the role that greed plays in human psychology. Others blame it on the capitalist system. Some blame it on the kind of people who are attracted to the world of business and believe that such people are typically ones who were not raised to have good values. But in reality, people in the world of business don't act unethically any more than people do in other aspects of life. The world of business is full of good, honest people. They mostly go about their day, producing goods and services in an entirely ethical way. Sometimes business behaviour that seems unethical really isn't. When a company lays off workers, sometimes that's to ensure the long-term survival of the company and the continued employment of the rest of their workforce. And when companies outsource manufacturing to factories in developing countries, they are providing much-needed jobs and are doing something those countries really need. The amount of truly unethical behaviour in business seems higher than it is because journalists report on business very selectively: they only report the worst behaviours, and so that's all that the public gets to see.

Passage 2
Some people who live near wind turbines—those big "windmills" used to generate electricity—have reported a variety of illnesses and symptoms. They've reported everything from headaches and trouble sleeping to problems with their memories. Some activists have even claimed that living too near wind turbines can cause birth defects and cancer. The cause, according to activists, is the very low-frequency sounds emitted by wind turbines—sounds too low in frequency to be within the range of human hearing. A number of scientific studies, however, have failed to find any concrete evidence of a pattern. While it is, of course, true that some people living near wind turbines do get headaches, and some do develop cancer, that's true of people everywhere. There's no evidence that the kinds of low-frequency sounds generated by wind turbines can cause cancer or have other negative effects on the human body. What *can* have an impact on human well-being? Noises that people can hear. Some turbines make noises that people can hear (depending how close their houses are), and such noises are annoying. People who are seriously annoyed can end up with headaches, disturbed sleep, mood disruptions, and so on, so audible noises—not super-low-frequency sound—are the real culprit here.

Summary

Even though an explanation is not an argument, an explanation can be part of an argument—a powerful kind of inductive argument known as inference to the best explanation. In inference to the best explanation, we reason from premises about a state of affairs to an explanation for that state of affairs. Such explanations are called *theoretical explanations*, or theories.

To be worthy of consideration, a theory must meet the minimum requirement for consistency. We use the criteria of adequacy to judge the plausibility of a theory in relation to competing theories. The best theory is the one that meets the criteria of adequacy better than any of its competitors. The criteria of adequacy are testability (whether there is some way to determine if a theory is true), fruitfulness (the number of novel predictions made), scope (the number of diverse phenomena explained), simplicity (the number of assumptions made), and conservatism (how well a theory fits with existing knowledge).

Judging the worth of a theory involves using a four-step process called the *TEST formula*: (1) stating the theory and checking for consistency, (2) assessing the evidence for the theory, (3) scrutinizing alternative theories, and (4) testing the theories with the criteria of adequacy.

Field Problems

1. Many companies have recently marketed products that are supposed to relieve various ailments (arthritis, low-back pain, migraine headaches, tennis elbow, etc.) through the use of simple magnets. This "magnetic therapy" is said to work because magnetic fields generated by the magnets act on the body's processes or structures. Look online to find a health claim made for one of these products. Then, in a 150-word paragraph, evaluate the claim in light of the criteria of simplicity and conservatism. Check for any relevant scientific research and information at www.quackwatch.com or www.sram.org (The Scientific Review of Alternative Medicine).
2. Using the TEST formula, evaluate the theory that the illness known as COVID-19 is really caused by 5G communications networks. Write a 200-word mini-essay summarizing your findings.
3. Go to the website of a major newspaper (or your own town's main newspaper). Find a story or editorial that presents an explanation for some recent trend—a rise in crime or a drop in crime; visible changes in a particular neighbourhood; a rise in unemployment or a drop in unemployment; something like that. Does the explanation presented pass the tests suggested in this chapter?

Self-Assessment Quiz

1. What is the basic pattern of inference to the best explanation? How does this pattern differ from that of analogical induction? How does it differ from enumerative induction?
2. What are the criteria of adequacy?
3. What is external consistency ?
4. According to the text, what does it mean for a theory to be testable or untestable?

Each of the following theories is offered to explain how Arthur was aware that the mysterious stranger he met on the train was his long-lost twin brother, Arnold, before they had even exchanged names or talked about their childhood. Indicate which theory (a) lacks simplicity, (b) is not conservative, (c) is untestable, and (d) has the least scope. (Some theories may deserve more than one of these designations.)

5. This is an example of the strong "telepathic" bond between twins: their brains respond to each other's presence, even if they are not fully aware of the effect.
6. The fact that Arthur correctly guessed that the stranger was his brother was coincidence. We all feel from time to time that someone else is familiar and perhaps connected to us somehow, and sometimes that feeling is bound to come true.
7. Arthur arrived at the conclusion mathematically: he met the "stranger" on the train on 13 January 2021, and the birthdate he shared with his long-lost twin was 13 January 2001. And of course 2001 subtracted from 2021 is 20. And they were on train number 20!

Indicate which theory in each of the following groups is most plausible.

1. Phenomenon: The Canadian Coast Guard reports that several small ships and boats have disappeared off the coast of Vancouver Island over the last several years.
   Theories: (1) considering the meteorological and atmospheric conditions of the area, it's normal for some craft to be lost from time to time, (2) the

craft have all been hijacked, (3) the waters off Vancouver Island are infested with sea monsters.

2. Phenomenon: You have noticed that your grades have been slowly getting worse over the last two school terms.

   Theories: (1) your professors are working together to destroy your life, (2) a brain tumour is affecting your ability to think clearly, (3) your new part-time job is taking up too much time and preventing you from studying sufficiently.
3. Phenomenon: The rise in popularity of a newly elected prime minister. Theories: (1) the so-called honeymoon effect in which a newly elected politician enjoys popularity until he or she is involved in serious or controversial decisions, (2) the systematic manipulation of all polling organizations by the prime minister's staff, (3) the influence of a powerful secret organization controlling the media.
4. Phenomenon: Public health officials in Manitoba have noticed an unusual number of cases of serious gastrointestinal illness among otherwise healthy people.

   Theories: (1) an unknown criminal has been sneaking into people's homes and poisoning them, (2) they all ate contaminated meat products from the same meat-processing plant, (3) genetically modified foods are making people sick.

Evaluate the following theories using the TEST formula. As part of your evaluation, (1) state the claim to be evaluated, (2) indicate what phenomenon is being explained, (3) specify at least one alternative theory, and (4) use the criteria of adequacy to assess the two theories and determine which one is more plausible.

1. Krista's credit card was declined at the supermarket today. Someone must have stolen her card number and used up all the available credit.
2. People only buy expensive iPhones because they are seduced by Apple's flashy advertising.
3. Horses that are badly behaved are ones that have been abused by humans in the past.
4. The coach selected Jasmin for the team because she performed best during the tryouts.

Integrative Exercises

These exercises refer to lessons in Chapters 3 and 6–9.

1. What is a valid argument?
2. What is an inductive argument?
3. What is the logical pattern of *modus ponens*?

   For each of the following arguments, specify the conclusion and premises, and state whether it is deductive or inductive. If it's deductive, use Venn diagrams or truth tables to determine its validity. If it's inductive, say whether it's an enumerative, analogical, or causal induction and whether it's strong or weak. If necessary, add implicit premises and conclusions.
4. Either you're here to collect the money I owe you or you're here for a friendly visit, and the fact that you've got two big, tough-looking dudes behind you suggests you're not here for a friendly visit, so I'm guessing you're here to collect the money.
5. I've read a lot about the Black Lives Matter movement, and I'm convinced that the issue is an essential one. In the US, a disproportionate number of shootings by police involve Black victims. And juries basically never convict a cop when the person he shot was Black, and in Canada's biggest city, Toronto, police have many times been accused of racism. This has to stop.
6. I think Don has a crush on David. He smiles shyly whenever David enters the room, and he won't look David in the eye.

7. It's essential for businesses to innovate. Businesses that don't believe in this principle will never earn a profit and inevitably go bankrupt. That's why all businesses strive to be innovative.
8. Senior citizens should not drive because they have slower reflexes, and slower reflexes are dangerous on the road. Plus, older people tend to have worse eyesight and worse hearing, both of which make them more dangerous on the road.
9. People will continue to go to buy so-called "natural" health products. The problem is that if people realized just how few of those products actually work, they wouldn't buy them anymore. But people don't realize that yet, and too few people want the truth to be known.
10. Rose is really fortunate. She has a nice house, a wonderful partner, and a career that she seems to really enjoy. How can one person be so lucky?
11. I can tell he's the one who drank the last of the coffee without starting a new batch. I noticed him shifting uneasily in his seat and avoiding eye contact when the boss asked the whole office who had done that. He's also the only one in the room who has a *full* cup of coffee sitting on his desk.

Evaluate each of the following theories and indicate whether it is plausible or implausible.

12. Capricorns—people born between the 21st of December and the 21st of January—are unusually ambitious, and are very hard workers.
13. David Milgaard was sent to prison for raping and murdering a nursing assistant, Gail Miller, and he spent 21 years behind bars for that crime. Three of Milgaard's friends testified against him in court. Milgaard was released in 1997 after DNA evidence supposedly proved he didn't commit the crime. But I'll trust the word of three witnesses over some fancy scientific test any day!
14. People who complain about not being able to find a job are really saying that they can't find a job that they are *willing* to do. There are plenty of positions that need to be filled—the restaurant across the street has a "Dishwasher Wanted" sign in the window, for crying out loud, and Tim Hortons is pretty much always hiring. People are just too lazy and entitled to actually work hard for their money.
15. The availability of government funding (in the form of loans and bursaries) is a key factor in whether young adults between 17 and 22 years of age attend university.

Writing Assignments

1. Think about the last several TV series or movies that you watched and thought were excellent. Write a 250-word essay evaluating at least two theories that explain why *those* ones in particular were so good. Use the TEST formula.
2. In a 300-word essay, evaluate the theory that all major decisions made by the president of your university are motivated by money and have very little to do with the merits of ideas or programs. Use the TEST formula.
3. Write a 500-word paper in which you use the TEST formula to assess two theories for the apparent huge popularity of Justin Bieber in Canada. One theory is the "guerilla advertising" theory (call that Hypothesis 1). According to this theory, Bieber's record company is paying hundreds of millions of dollars to have thousands of people *pretend* to like Bieber's music in order to influence the opinions of others. The other theory (call it Hypothesis 2) is that Bieber is not really so popular after all, but the Government of Canada has issued secret legal orders requiring radio and television networks to play Bieber's music and videos and requiring newspapers to print false stories about how hordes of fans follow Bieber wherever he goes.

Notes

1. Charles Darwin, *The Origin of Species* (New York: Collier, 1962), 476.
2. Arthur Conan Doyle, *A Study in Scarlet* (New York: P.F. Collier and Son, 1906), 29–30.
3. Arthur Conan Doyle, "The 'Gloria Scott,'" *Memoirs of Sherlock Holmes* (London: George Newnes, 1894).
4. "Unprovoked Shark Attacks Declined in 2016," *SurferToday* (27 January 2017). https://www.surfertoday.com/environment/13403-unprovoked-shark-attacks-declined-in-2016.
5. "7 Suppressed Technologies That Could Have Changed the World," *Wake Up World*. https://wakeup-world.com/2017/09/10/7-suppressed-inventions-that-could-have-changed-the-world/.
6. "Pyramid Power: My Search for Truth," *Gaia* (14 March 2016). https://www.gaia.com/article/pyramid-power.
7. "Tom Bearden's Motionless Electromagnetic Generator," *The Fractalier's Web Log* (1 January 2021). https://worldtalkfree.com/2021/01/commentary/tom-beardens-motionless-electromagnetic-generator/.
8. W.V. Quine and J.S. Ullman, *The Web of Belief* (New York: Random House, 1970), 43–4.
9. Quoted in "US Election: Trump Says Reporting on Covid is 'Fake News Conspiracy,'" *Irish Times*, 26 October 2020. https://www.irishtimes.com/news/world/us/us-election-trump-says-reporting-on-covid-is-fake-news-conspiracy-1.4391563.

Judging Scientific Theories

Chapter Objectives

Science and Not Science

You will be able to

- understand why science is not the same thing as technology, ideology, or scientism.

The Scientific Method

You will be able to

- list the five steps of the scientific method.
- understand the logic of scientific testing.
- understand why no scientific hypothesis can be conclusively confirmed or conclusively confuted.

Testing Scientific Theories

You will be able to

- use the steps of the scientific method and be able to explain how a scientist would go about testing a simple hypothesis in medical science.
- understand why scientists use control groups, make studies double-blind, include placebos in testing, and seek replication of their work.

Judging Scientific Theories

You will be able to

- list the five criteria of adequacy and explain what they mean.
- understand how to apply the criteria of adequacy to the theories of evolution and creationism and why the text says that evolution is the better theory.

Science and Weird Theories

You will be able to

- explain why evaluating weird claims might be worthwhile.

Making Weird Mistakes

You will be able to

- understand why it can be so easy to make mistakes when trying to evaluate weird theories.
- explain three major errors that people often make when they are trying to assess extraordinary experiences and theories.
- explain the distinction between logical possibility and physical possibility.

Judging Weird Theories

You will be able to

- use the TEST formula to evaluate extraordinary theories.
- understand why eyewitness testimony is often unreliable.

So people and organizations are constantly making claims in the form of explanations—*theoretical explanations*, to be more precise—about why something is the case or why something happens or happened. An overwhelming number of such theories are offered to explain the cause of events, such as why the window broke, why the water in the ocean looks blue, why Ralph stole the bike, or why the stock market crashed. As critical thinkers, we do the best we can in evaluating the theories that come our way, testing them if possible, looking for alternative theories, and applying the criteria of adequacy. As it turns out, this kind of testing in pursuit of better explanations is exactly what scientists do for a living.

Science seeks to acquire knowledge and an understanding of reality, and it does so through the formulation, testing, and evaluation of theories. When this kind of search for answers is both systematic and careful, science is being done. And when we ourselves search for answers by scrutinizing possible theories—and we do so systematically and carefully—we are searching scientifically.

Let's examine the scientific process more closely.

10.1 Science and Not Science

First, let's explore what science is *not*.

Science is not technology. Science is a way of searching for truth—a way that uses what is often referred to as *the scientific method*. Technology, on the other hand, is not a search for truth; technology is the use of knowledge to do things in the world, and it is often embodied in products—mobile phones, smart watches, laptop computers, robot vacuums, better mousetraps, VR headsets. Technology applies knowledge acquired through science to practical problems that science generally doesn't care about, such as the creation of electronic gadgets. Technology seeks facts to use in producing stuff. Science tries to understand how the world works, not by merely cataloguing specific facts but by discovering general principles that both explain and predict phenomena.

This nice distinction sometimes gets blurry when technologists do scientific research to build a better product or when scientists create new scientific instruments to help them do better scientific research. But in general, there is a difference: science pursues knowledge; technology makes things.

Science is not ideology. Some people say that science is not a way of finding out how the world works but a world view affirming how the world is, just as Catholicism or socialism affirms a view of things. To some, science is not just an ideology but a problematic one—one that posits a universe that is entirely material, mechanistic, and deterministic. On this "scientific view," the world—including us—is nothing more than bits of matter forming a big machine that turns and whirs in ways determined by impersonal laws of physics. This mechanistic notion is thought to reduce the value of humans and human endeavours by reducing us to the role of little pieces in a giant machine.

But, in reality, we can't identify science with a specific world view. At any given time, a particular world view may predominate in the scientific community or some part of it, but this fact doesn't mean that the world view is what science is all about. Predominant world views among scientists have changed over the centuries, but the general nature of science as a way of searching for truth has not. For example, the mechanistic view of the universe, so common among scientists in the seventeenth century, has now given way to other views. Discoveries in quantum mechanics (the study of subatomic particles) have shown that the old mechanistic perspective is incorrect.

"Nothing in life is to be feared, it is only to be understood. Now is the time to understand more, so that we may fear less."

—Marie Curie

Science is not scientism. One definition of *scientism* is the view that science is the only reliable way to acquire knowledge. Put another way, it is the view that science is the only reliable road to truth. But in light of the reliability of our sense experience under standard, unhindered conditions (see Chapter 4), this claim is clearly dubious. We obviously do come to know many things without the aid of scientific tools or methods.

But there is a related point that is not so obviously dubious. Science may not be the only road to truth, but it is an extremely reliable way of acquiring knowledge about complex questions about the empirical world. (Many philosophers of science would go a step further and say that science is our *most reliable* source of knowledge about the world.) Why is science so reliable? Science embodies, to a high degree, what is essential to a reliable knowledge of empirical facts: systematic consideration of alternative solutions or theories, rigorous testing of them, and careful checking and rechecking of the conclusions.

Some would say that science is reliable because it is self-correcting. Science, when done properly, does not grab hold of an explanation and refuse to let go. Instead, it looks at alternative possibilities to explain a phenomenon, tests these

Critical Thinking and the Media

How Science Gets Reported

Most people, on a daily basis, get their understandings of changes in the world of science from the media—specifically, from the science stories that news outlets choose to cover, as explained to you by the experts those outlets choose to interview. And that leaves us somewhat vulnerable. Most of us know relatively little about science and certainly not enough to help us evaluate the work of professional scientists. We may have taken a few classes in high school, but that is likely not enough. Even if you major in physics at university, that's unlikely to give you the tools to evaluate the findings of health researchers. Likewise, majoring in biology is unlikely to prepare you to assess the work of astrophysicists. And so we have to rely on how journalists cover science.

There are numerous worries about the ways in which science gets reported in the mainstream media. For one thing, sometimes science news is reported by journalists without sufficient background in science. And that's not always the journalist's fault: journalists can't be experts on everything, and a reporter at a small outlet might be reporting on a political protest in the morning and interviewing a cancer researcher in the afternoon. Note also an obvious, and to some extent understandable, bias in which science news stories get reported. "Scientists Find Cancer Gene!" is a great headline, and maybe a great story. "Scientists Find Gene Plays No Role in Cancer!" might be extremely interesting and important scientifically, but as a news story in your social media feed it's not likely to grab much attention. So there are sometimes problems with the way science news gets reported.

Of course, there are specialist outlets like *Scientific American* and *Canadian Geographic*, and those outlets have expert journalists who are more likely to know what good science looks like. But most of us are not getting are science news from those sources. We're getting our science news from the CBC, and from CNN, and from the website for our local news.

Luckily, the tools of critical thinking—the tools you're learning through this book—are ones that apply to science, and science reporting, of all kinds.

alternatives, and opens up the conclusions to criticism from scientists everywhere. Eventually, initial conclusions may turn out to be false, and scientists will have to abandon the answers they thought were solid. But usually, after much testing and thinking, scientists hit upon a theory that does hold up under collective scrutiny. They are then justified in believing that the theory is true, even though there is some chance that it is flawed.

10.2 The Scientific Method

The scientific method cannot be identified with any particular set of experimental or observational procedures because there are many different methods for evaluating the worth of a hypothesis. In some sciences, such as physics and biology, hypotheses can be assessed through controlled experimental tests done under laboratory conditions. In other sciences, such as astronomy and geology, hypotheses must usually be tested through predictions and observations of the world outside the lab. For example, an astronomical hypothesis may predict the existence of certain gases in a distant part of the Milky Way, and astronomers can use their telescopes to check whether there are signs that those gases exist as predicted.

The scientific method, however, does involve several standard steps, regardless of the specific procedures involved:

1. Identify the problem or pose a question.
2. Devise a hypothesis to explain the event or phenomenon.
3. Derive a test implication or prediction.
4. Perform the test.
5. Accept or reject the hypothesis.

Scientific inquiry begins with a problem to solve or a question to answer. So in step 1, scientists may ask: What causes X? Why did Y happen? Does hormone therapy cause breast cancer? Does Aspirin lower the risk of stroke? How is it possible for whales to navigate over long distances? How did early hominids communicate with one another? What are things like inside a black hole?

In step 2, scientists formulate a hypothesis that will constitute an answer to their question. In every case, there are facts that need to be explained, and the hypothesis is a *potential* explanation for them. The hypothesis then guides the scientists' research, suggesting what kinds of observations or data would be relevant to the problem at hand. Without a hypothesis, scientists couldn't tell which data are important and which are worthless—they wouldn't know where to begin their research.

Where do hypotheses come from? One notion is that hypotheses are generated through induction—by collecting the data and drawing a generalization from them to get a hypothesis. And sometimes that's true. But this can't be the way that most hypotheses are formulated because they often contain concepts that aren't in the data. (Remember, theories generally reach beyond the known data to posit the existence of things unknown.) The construction of hypotheses is not usually based on any such mechanical procedure. In many ways, they are created just as works of art are created: scientists dream them up. Scientists, however, are guided in the process of hypothesis creation by certain criteria—namely, the criteria of adequacy we examined in the last chapter. With testability, fruitfulness, scope, simplicity, and conservatism as their guides, they devise hypotheses from the raw material of the imagination.

Remember, though, that scientists must consider not just their favourite hypothesis but alternative hypotheses as well. The scientific method calls for consideration of competing explanations and for examining or testing them at some point in the process. Sometimes applying the criteria of adequacy can immediately eliminate some theories from the running, and sometimes theories must be tested along with the original hypothesis.

In step 3, scientists derive implications, or consequences, of the hypothesis to test. As we've seen, sometimes we can test a theory directly, as when we simply check the gas tank of the lawnmower to confirm the theory that it won't run because it's out of gas. But often theories cannot be tested directly. How would we directly test, for example, the hypothesis that chemical X is causing leukemia in menopausal women? We can't.

> *"Science and everyday life cannot and should not be separated."*
>
> —Rosalind Franklin, chemist and X-ray crystallographer

So scientists test *indirectly* by first deriving a test implication from a hypothesis and then putting that implication to the test. Deriving such an observational consequence involves figuring out what a hypothesis implies or predicts. Scientists ask, "If this hypothesis were true, what consequences would follow? What phenomena or events would have to occur?"

Recall that we derived test implications in the problem of the car that wouldn't start in Chapter 9. One hypothesis was that the car wouldn't start because a vandal had sabotaged it. We reasoned that if a vandal had indeed sabotaged the car, there would be tracks in the snow around it. That's an implication of the vandal theory. But there were no tracks, a fact that disconfirms that hypothesis.

The logic of hypothesis testing, then, works like this: when we derive a test implication, we know that if the hypothesis to be tested (*H*) is true, then there is a specific predicted consequence (*C*). If the consequence turns out to be false (that is, if it does not obtain as predicted), then the hypothesis is probably false, and we can reject it. The hypothesis, in other words, is disconfirmed. We can represent this outcome in a conditional, or hypothetical, argument:

If *H*, then *C*.
Not *C*.
Therefore, not *H*.

Food for Thought

Are You Scientifically Literate?

According to a 2021 Ipsos poll, nearly half of Canadians believe in ghosts.[1] This is despite these facts:

- No credible scientific evidence of ghosts has *ever* been produced.
- The existence of ghosts would contradict much of what is known about physics.

A little scientific literacy can help you to avoid unreasonable beliefs!

Test *Your* Scientific Literacy!

True or False?

1. Antibiotics (such as penicillin) are effective against viruses such as the virus that causes COVID-19.
2. Atoms are smaller than electrons.
3. The universe began with a huge explosion, the "Big Bang."
4. The earliest humans lived at the same time as the dinosaurs.
5. Human activity is responsible for global warming.
6. Autism is caused by vaccination.

Answers: 1. False, 2. False, 3. True, 4. False, 5. True, 6. False.

This is, remember, an instance of *modus tollens*, a valid argument form. In this case, *H* would be false even if only one of several of its consequences (test implications) turned out to be false.

On the other hand, we would find ourselves in a very different situation if *C* turned out to be true:

If *H*, then *C*.
C.
Therefore, *H*.

Notice that this is an instance of affirming the consequent, an invalid argument form. So the fact that *C* is true doesn't necessarily mean that *H* is true. If a consequence turns out to be true, that doesn't *prove* that the hypothesis is correct. In such a result, the hypothesis is confirmed, and the test provides at least some evidence that the hypothesis is true. But the hypothesis isn't then established. If other consequences for the hypothesis are tested and all the results are again positive, then there is now additional evidence that the hypothesis is correct. As more and more consequences are tested and they are shown to be true, we can have increasing confidence that the hypothesis is in fact true. As this evidence accumulates, the likelihood that the hypothesis is actually false decreases—and the probability that it's true increases.

In step 4, scientists carry out the testing. Usually this experimentation is not as simple as testing one implication and calling it quits. Scientists may test many consequences of several competing hypotheses. As the testing proceeds, some hypotheses are found unsatisfactory, and they're dropped. If all goes well, eventually one hypothesis remains, with considerable evidence in its favour. Then step 5 can happen as the hypothesis or hypotheses are accepted or rejected.

Because scientists want to quickly eliminate unworthy hypotheses and zero in on the best one, they try to devise the most illuminating tests they can. This means that they are on the lookout for situations they can observe or generate in which competing hypotheses have different test consequences. If hypothesis 1 says that *C* is true and hypothesis 2 says that *C* is false, a test of *C* can then help to eliminate one of the hypotheses from further consideration.

As we've seen, implicit in all this is the fact that no hypothesis can ever be *conclusively* confirmed. It's always possible that we will someday find evidence that undermines or conflicts with the evidence we have now.

Likewise, no hypothesis can ever be *conclusively* proven wrong. When scientists test hypotheses, they never really test a single hypothesis—they test a hypothesis together with a variety of background assumptions and theories. So a hypothesis can always be saved from refutation by making changes in the background claims. (As we detailed in the previous chapter, sometimes these changes are made by constructing ad hoc hypotheses—by postulating unverifiable entities or properties.) In such situations, no amount of evidence logically compels us to conclusively reject a hypothesis.

Review Notes

Steps in the Scientific Method

1. Identify the problem or pose a question.
2. Devise a hypothesis to explain the event or phenomenon.
3. Derive a test implication or prediction.
4. Perform the test.
5. Accept or reject the hypothesis.

But our inability to confirm or deny a hypothesis conclusively at the present time does not mean that all hypotheses are equally acceptable. Maintaining a hypothesis in the face of mounting negative evidence is unreasonable and so is refusing to accept a hypothesis despite accumulating confirming evidence. Through the use of carefully controlled experiments, scientists can often affirm or deny a hypothesis with a high degree of confidence.

10.3 Testing Scientific Theories

Let's see how we might use the five-step procedure to test a fairly simple hypothesis. Suppose you hear reports that some terminal cancer patients have lived longer than expected because they received high doses of vitamin C. And say that the favoured hypothesis among many observers is that the best explanation for the patients surviving longer is that vitamin C is an effective treatment against cancer. So you decide to test the hypothesis that high doses of vitamin C can increase the survival time of people with terminal cancer. (Years ago, this hypothesis was actually proposed and tested in three well-controlled clinical trials.[2]) An obvious alternative hypothesis is that vitamin C actually has no effect on the survival of terminal cancer patients and that any apparent benefits are due mainly to the placebo effect (the tendency for people to feel better temporarily after they're treated, even if the treatment is a fake). The placebo effect could be leading observers mistakenly to believe that people taking vitamin C are being cured of cancer and are thus living longer. Or the placebo effect could be making patients feel better, thereby enabling them to take better care of themselves (by eating right or complying with standard medical treatment, for example) and increasing survival time—regardless of whether the tablet contains vitamin C, a different vitamin, or just sugar.

Now, if your hypothesis about vitamin C (whether vitamin C is effective at treating cancer) is true, what would you expect to happen? That is, what test implication could you derive? If your hypothesis is true, you would expect that terminal cancer patients given high doses of vitamin C would live longer than terminal cancer patients who didn't receive the vitamin (or anything else).

"The grand aim of all science is to cover the greatest number of empirical facts by logical deduction from the smallest number of hypotheses or axioms."

—Albert Einstein

How would you conduct such a test? To begin with, you could prescribe vitamin C to a group of terminal cancer patients (called the *experimental group*) but not to another group of similar cancer patients (called the *control group*) and keep track of their survival times. Then you could compare the survival rates of the two groups. But many people who knowingly receive a treatment will report feeling better—even if the treatment is an inactive placebo. So any positive results you see in the treated group might be due not to vitamin C but to the placebo effect.

To get around this problem, you would need to treat both groups, one with vitamin C and the other with a placebo. That way, if most of the people getting the vitamin C live longer than expected and fewer of those in the placebo group do, you can have slightly better reason for believing that vitamin C works as advertised.

But even this study design is not good enough. It's possible for the people conducting the experiment, the experimenters, to bias the results unknowingly. Through subtle behavioural cues, they can unconsciously inform the test subjects which treatments are real and which ones are placebos—and this, of course, would allow the placebo effect to have full effect. Also, if the experimenters know which treatment is the real one, they can unintentionally misinterpret or skew the study results in line with their own expectations.

This problem can be solved by making the study *double-blind*. In double-blind experiments, neither the subjects nor the experimenters know who receives the real treatment and who the inactive one. A double-blind protocol for your vitamin study would ensure that none of the subjects would know who's getting vitamin C, and neither would the experimenters.

What if you have a double-blind set up but most of the subjects in the vitamin C group were sicker to begin with than those in the placebo control group? Obviously, this would bias the results, making the vitamin C treatment look less effective—even if it *is* effective. To avoid this skewing, you would need to ensure that both groups are as much alike as possible to start—with all subjects being around the same age, having the same physical condition, being at the same stage of cancer, and so on.

Finally, you would need to run some statistical tests to ensure that your results are not a fluke. Even in the most tightly controlled studies, it's possible that the outcome is the result of random factors that cannot be controlled. Statisticians have standard methods for determining when experiment results are likely, or not likely, to be due to chance.

Suppose you design your study well and you conduct it. The results are that the patients receiving the high doses of vitamin C did not live longer than the placebo group. In fact, all the subjects lived about the same length of time. Therefore, your hypothesis is disconfirmed. On the other hand, the alternative hypothesis—that vitamin C has no measurable effect on the survival of terminal cancer patients—is confirmed.

Should you now reject the vitamin C theory? Not yet. Even apparently well-conducted studies can have hidden mistakes in them, or there can be factors that the experimenters failed to take into account. This is why scientists insist on study *replication*—the repeating of an experiment by different groups of scientists. If other scientists replicate the study and the study results hold up, then you can be more confident that the results are solid. In such a case, you could safely reject the vitamin C hypothesis. (This is, in fact, what scientists did in the real-life studies of vitamin C and cancer survival.)

At this point, when evidence has been gathered that can bear on the truth of the hypothesis in question, good scientific judgment is crucial. It's here that consideration of other competing hypotheses and the criteria of adequacy again come into play. At this stage, scientists need to decide whether to reject or accept a hypothesis—or modify it to improve it.

scientific realism
The school of thought that says the goal of science is to bring our understanding of the natural world closer and closer to the truth.

scientific instrumentalism
The school of thought that says the goal of science is to put forward theories that are useful in helping us to predict and control the world around us.

problem of induction
The philosophical question as to whether the process of induction can ever lead to real knowledge.

Food for Thought

The Philosophy of Science

Many of the issues discussed in this and the previous chapter would be considered by philosophers to be part of the study of the philosophy of science. The philosophy of science is concerned with understanding the foundations, methods, and limits of science as a whole.

One of the key questions asked by philosophers of science is "What distinguishes science from non-science?" Certainly we can give *examples* of disciplines that we think of as branches of science, such as physics and biology and chemistry. But what, other than tradition, justifies designating them as sciences but not using that word to describe, for instance, astrology or engineering or needlepoint or the study of law? In this regard, some philosophers of science have focused on the scientific importance of generating knowledge through observation. Others (such as Karl Popper) have focused on the significance of *falsifiability*. In order for a claim or hypothesis to be scientifically meaningful, they argue, it must be possible, at least in principle, for there to be some empirical observation that would prove it false. As we pointed out in Chapter 9, if a theory makes no testable claims, it is of little use to us.

Another important set of debates within the philosophy of science has to do with what the proper goals of science are. Some—adherents of **scientific realism**—argue that the goal of science is to bring our understanding of the natural world closer and closer to the truth. Philosophers who hold this view would say, for example, that from Aristotle to Ptolemy to Copernicus and beyond, science has moved ever closer to a true understanding of planetary motion. Others, however, believe that this way of thinking about science is misguided. Those who hold the position known as **scientific instrumentalism** argue that it makes more sense to think in terms of the usefulness of scientific theories rather than their truth. According to this view, a good theory is one that we find makes useful predictions, ones that help us to predict and control the world around us.

It is also worth noting—after all the time we spent discussing inductive logic in Chapters 8 and 9—that philosophers of science have given considerable thought to what is known as the **problem of induction**. Science is fundamentally about devising theoretical explanations for how the world works and testing those theories through observation. As evidence builds up, scientists reason inductively to an eventual conclusion about

continued

which theory is best. However, as the Scottish philosopher David Hume (1711–76) pointed out, no amount of evidence can ever allow us to generalize with certainty—we could still be missing crucial evidence. And besides, Hume pointed out, how do we even know that inductive reasoning itself is a good way to learn things? The answer, it seems, is that we figured that out inductively, by trial and error. But saying that we've learned inductively that induction works amounts to begging the question! This may not pose much of a problem for working scientists, but it poses a serious intellectual problem for philosophers of science, who are deeply concerned about understanding how, and why, science works.

10.4 Judging Scientific Theories

As you can see, theory testing is part of the broader effort to assess the merits of one theory against a field of alternatives. And as you know by now, this broader effort will always involve, explicitly or implicitly, the application of the criteria of adequacy to the theories in question:

> Testability: Whether there's some way to determine if a theory is true.
> Fruitfulness: The number of novel predictions made.
> Scope: The amount of diverse phenomena explained.
> Simplicity: The number of assumptions made.
> Conservatism: How well a theory fits with existing knowledge.

Let's study two important examples to see how scientists manage this task. The first is a classic case from the history of science; the second, a contemporary tale of what many perceive as a battle between science and religion. Notice that the steps itemized by the TEST formula are implicit in the evaluation process.

10.4.1 Copernicus versus Ptolemy

Consider the historic clash between the geocentric (Earth-centred) and the heliocentric (sun-centred) theories of planetary motion. It's difficult to imagine two rival theories that have more profoundly influenced how humanity views itself and its place in the universe.

In the beginning was the geocentric view. Aristotle got things going by putting forth the theory that a spherical Earth was at the centre of a spherical universe consisting of a series of concentric, transparent spheres. On one celestial sphere, we see the sun, the moon, and the known planets. On the outermost sphere we behold the stars. All the heavenly bodies rotate in perfect circles around the stationary Earth. The heavenly bodies are pure, incorruptible, and unchanging; the Earth, impure, corruptible, and transient.

Then came the great astronomer and mathematician Ptolemy, who lived in Alexandria, in Egypt, and wrote his key works between the years 127 and 148 CE (nearly 1900 years ago). He discovered inconsistencies in the traditional

Food for Thought

Ancient Interest in Stars and Planets

Ptolemy advanced his theory of planetary motion in the second century CE, and Copernicus advanced his theory early in the sixteenth century. But an interest in cosmology—the study of the physical universe—is much older than that. The ancient Greek mathematician, Aristarchus of Samos (310–230 BCE), correctly believed that the Earth and other planets orbit around the sun and correctly thought that the stars are suns that are very far away. But many cultures have had their own theories about the universe. The oldest of them blend beliefs about the physical universe with beliefs about religion. Ancient Hindu cosmology, for instance, held that the physical universe has no beginning and no end but is instead cyclical. According to one version of this view, the stars and sun all revolve around Mount Meru—a mountain that may or may not have been mythical. As early as the eighth century BCE, the ancient Babylonians were trying to work out a systematic understanding of the motion of the planets, and they were involved in cataloguing the stars as early as 1200 BCE. But the oldest mathematical approach to cosmology may be much older still. A bone fragment known as the Lebombo bone, found in the mountains between South Africa and Eswatini, has markings on it suggesting it may have been used to count the phases of the moon. The Lebombo bone is thought to be about 43,000 years old!

geocentric system between the predicted and observed motions of the planets. He found, in other words, that Aristotle's theory was not conservative—a crucial failing! So he fine-tuned the old view, adding little circular motions (called epicycles) along the planet orbits and many other minor adjustments. He also allowed for an odd asymmetry in which the centre of planet orbits was not exactly the centre of Earth—all this so the theory would match up with astronomical observations. By the time Ptolemy finished tinkering, he had posited 80 circles and epicycles—80 different planetary motions—to explain the movements of the sun, moon, and five known planets.

The result was a system far more complex than Aristotle's. But the revised theory worked well enough for the times, and it agreed better than the earlier theory did with observational data. Despite the complications, learned people could use Ptolemy's system to calculate the positions of the planets with enough accuracy to manage calendars and astrological charts. So for 15 centuries, astronomers used Ptolemy's unwieldy, complex theory to predict celestial events and locations. In the West, at least, Earth stood still in the centre of everything as the rest of the universe circled around it.

The chief virtue of the Ptolemaic system, then, was conservatism. It fitted, mostly, with what astronomers knew about celestial goings-on. It was also testable, as any scientific theory should be. Its biggest failing was simplicity—or the lack thereof. The theory was propped up by numerous assumptions for the purpose of making the theory fit the data.

Then along came Nicolaus Copernicus (1473–1543). He was disturbed by the complexity of Ptolemy's system, which was a far cry from the simple theory that Aristotle had bequeathed to the West. Copernicus proposed a heliocentric theory

Scott Masear/CartoonStock

"I think you're right, Bender. <u>We</u> revolve around the bulb."

Even when your everyday experience supports an "obvious" explanation, scientists dedicate themselves to looking for a better one. What steps do scientists take when judging new scientific theories?

in which Earth and the other planets orbit the sun, which he said is the true centre of the universe. In doing so, he greatly simplified both the picture of the heavens and the calculations required to predict the positions of planets.

Copernicus's theory was simpler than Ptolemy's on many counts, but one of the most impressive was retrograde motion, a phenomenon that had stumped astronomers for centuries. From time to time, certain planets seem to reverse their customary direction of travel across the skies—to move backward! Ptolemy had explained this retrograde motion by positing yet more epicycles, asserting that planets orbiting Earth will often orbit around a point on the larger orbital path. Seeing these orbits within orbits from Earth, an observer would naturally see the planets sometimes backing up.

But the Copernican theory could easily explain retrograde motion without all those complicated epicycles. As the outer planets (Mars, Jupiter, and Saturn) orbit the sun, so does Earth, one of the inner planets. The outer planets, though, move much more slowly than Earth does. On its own orbital track, Earth sometimes passes the outer planets as they lumber along on their orbital track, just as a train passes a slower train on a parallel track. When this happens, the planets appear to move backward, just as the slower train seems to reverse course when the faster train overtakes it.

Copernicus's theory, however, was not superior on every count. It explained a great many astronomical observations, but Ptolemy's theory did too, so they were about even in scope. It had no big advantage in fruitfulness over the Ptolemaic system. It made no impressive predictions of unknown phenomena. Much more troubling, it seemed to conflict with some observational data.

One test implication of the Copernican theory is the phenomenon known as *parallax*. Critics of the heliocentric view claimed that if the theory were true, then as Earth moved through its orbit, stars closest to it should seem to shift their position relative to stars farther away. There should, in other words, be parallax. But no one had observed parallax.

Copernicus and his followers responded to this criticism by saying that stars were too far away for parallax to occur. As it turned out, they were right about this, but confirmation didn't come until 1832, when parallax was observed with more powerful telescopes.

Another test implication seemed to conflict with the heliocentric model. Copernicus reasoned that if the planets rotate around the sun, then they should show phases just as the moon shows phases because of the light of the sun falling on it at different times. But in Copernicus's day, no one could see any such planetary phases. Fifty years later, though, Galileo used his new telescope to confirm that Venus had phases.

Ultimately, scientists accepted the Copernican model over Ptolemy's because of its simplicity—despite what seemed at the time like evidence against the theory. As Copernicus said, "I think it is easier to believe this [sun-centred view] than to confuse the issue by assuming a vast number of Spheres, which those who keep the Earth at the center must do."[3]

10.4.2 Evolution versus Creationism

Few scientific theories have been more hotly debated among non-scientists than evolution and its rival, creationism (or creation science). Both theories claim to explain the origin and existence of biological life on Earth, and each claims to be a better explanation than the other. Can science decide this contest? Yes. Despite the complexity of the issues involved and the mixing of religious themes with the non-religious, good science can figure out which theory is best. Remember that the best theory is the one that explains the phenomenon and measures up to the criteria of adequacy better than any of its competitors. There is no reason that the scientific approach cannot provide an answer here—even in this thorniest of thorny issues.

Many have argued that we can reconcile science with religious belief if we think of natural processes as tools of a divine power. Of course, this leaves many questions about the source and nature of that divine power! How are creationism and evolution testable theories?

Neither the term *evolution* nor the overall concept began with Charles Darwin (1809–82), who is nonetheless regarded as the father of evolutionary theory. The word showed up in English as early as 1647. The ancient Greek philosopher Anaximander (c. 611–547 BCE) was actually the first evolutionary theorist, having inferred from some simple observations that humans must have evolved from an animal and that this evolution must have begun in the sea. But in his famous book *The Origin of Species* (1859), Darwin distilled the theory of evolution into its most influential statement.

Scientists have been fine-tuning the theory ever since as new evidence and new insights pour in from many different fields, such as biochemistry and population genetics. But the basic idea has not changed since Darwin: living organisms adapt to their environments through inherited characteristics, which results in changes to successive generations. Specifically, the offspring of organisms are physically very similar to their parents, but they are also different from them in various small but occasionally important ways, and these differences can be passed on genetically to their offspring. If an offspring has an inherited trait (such as sharper vision or a larger brain) that increases its chances of surviving long enough to reproduce, that individual is more likely to survive and pass the trait on to the next generation. Individuals with less-useful traits tend to produce fewer offspring. After several generations, the useful trait, or adaptation, spreads throughout a whole population of individuals and differentiates the population from its ancestors. The name that Darwin gave to this process is *natural selection*.

Through natural selection, species come to be well adapted to their environments. Where flying insects are plentiful, for example, populations of birds develop—over many years and many generations—characteristics that make it easier for them to catch such insects. Where there is tall grass to hide in, predators (such as tigers) develop stripes or other patterns to help them avoid being seen by their prey. In this way, Darwin was able to begin, at least, to explain the vast variety of species occupying the various ecosystems we find around the globe.

"It is a good morning exercise for a research scientist to discard a pet hypothesis every day before breakfast. It keeps him young."

—Konrad Lorenz

Creation science, on the other hand, maintains that (1) the universe and all life was created suddenly, out of nothing, only a few thousand years ago (6000–10,000 is the range usually stated); (2) natural selection could not have produced living things from a single organism; (3) species change very little over time; (4) humans and apes have entirely separate ancestries; and (5) the Earth's geology can be explained by catastrophism, including a worldwide flood.[4]

The first thing we should ask about these two theories is whether they're testable. The answer is yes. Recall that a theory is testable if it predicts or explains something other than what it was introduced to explain. On this criterion, evolution is surely testable. It explains, among other things, why bacteria develop resistance to antibiotics (adapting to their environment!), why there are so many similarities between humans and other primates, why the influenza virus is a bit different each year and requires a different vaccine, why the chromosomes of closely related species are so similar, why the fossil record shows the peculiar progression of fossils that it does, and why the embryos of related species have such similar structure and appearance.

Creationism is also testable. It too explains something other than what it was introduced to explain. It claims that Earth's geology was changed in a worldwide flood, that the universe is only a few thousand years old, that all species were created at the same time, and that species change very little over time.

Innumerable test implications have been derived from evolutionary theory, and innumerable experiments have been conducted confirming the theory. For example, if evolution is true, then we would expect to see a systematic change in the fossil record from simple creatures at the earlier levels to more complex

Food for Thought

Can You See Evolution?

Critics of the theory of evolution often ask, "If evolution occurs, why can't we see it?" Here's how the US National Academy of Sciences responds to this objection, on its website:

> Creationists sometimes argue that the idea of evolution must remain hypothetical because "no one has ever seen evolution occur." This kind of statement also reveals that some creationists misunderstand an important characteristic of scientific reasoning. Scientific conclusions are not limited to direct observation but often depend on inferences that are made by applying reason to observations. . . .
>
> Thus, for many areas of science, scientists have not directly observed the objects (such as genes and atoms) or the phenomena (such as the Earth going around the Sun) that are now well-established facts. Instead, they have confirmed them indirectly by observational and experimental evidence. Evolution is no different. Indeed . . . evolutionary science provides one of the best examples of a deep understanding based on scientific reasoning.
>
> This contention that nobody has seen evolution occurring further ignores the overwhelming evidence that evolution has taken place and is continuing to occur. The annual changes in influenza viruses and the emergence of bacteria resistant to antibiotics are both products of evolutionary forces. Another example of ongoing evolution is the appearance of mosquitoes resistant to various insecticides, which has contributed to a resurgence of malaria in Africa and elsewhere.[5]

individuals at the more recent levels. We would expect not to see a reversal of this configuration. And this sequence is exactly what scientists see time and time again.

Creationism, however, has not fared as well. Its empirical claims have not been borne out by evidence. In fact, they have consistently conflicted with well-established scientific findings.

This latter point means that creationism fails the criterion of conservatism—it conflicts with what we already know. For example, the scientific evidence shows that Earth is not 6,000–10,000 years old—but billions of years old. According to the US National Academy of Sciences:

> There are no valid scientific data or calculations to substantiate the belief that Earth was created just a few thousand years ago. [There is a] vast amount of evidence for the great age of the universe, our galaxy, the Solar system, and Earth from astronomy, astrophysics, nuclear physics, geology, geochemistry, and geophysics. Independent scientific methods consistently give an age for Earth and the Solar system of about 5 billion years, and an age for our galaxy and the universe that is two to three times greater.[6]

Creationism also fails the criterion of conservatism on the issue of a geology-transforming universal flood. Again, the National Academy of Sciences has this to say:

> Nor is there any evidence that the entire geological record, with its orderly succession of fossils, is the product of a single universal flood that occurred a few thousand years ago, lasted a little longer than a year, and covered the highest mountains to a depth of several meters. On the contrary, intertidal and terrestrial deposits demonstrate that at no recorded time in the past has the entire planet been under water. . . . The belief that Earth's sediments, with their fossils, were deposited in an orderly sequence in a year's time defies all geological observations and physical principles concerning sedimentation rates and possible quantities of suspended solid matter.[7]

Has either theory yielded any novel predictions? Evolution has. It has predicted, for example, that new species should still be evolving today; that the fossil record should show a movement from older, simpler organisms to younger, more complex ones; that proteins and chromosomes of related species should be similar; and that organisms should adapt to changing environments. These and many other novel predictions have in fact been confirmed by scientists. Creationism has made some novel claims, as we saw earlier, but none of these have been supported by good evidence. So creationism is not a fruitful theory.

"If we are going to teach creation science as an alternative to evolution, then we should also teach the stork theory as an alternative to biological reproduction."

—Judith Hayes

The criterion of simplicity also draws a sharp contrast between the two theories. Simplicity is a measure of the number of assumptions that a theory makes. Both theories make assumptions, but creationism assumes much more. Creationism assumes the existence of a creator and unknown forces. Proponents of creationism readily admit that we do not know how the creator created or what creative processes were used.

In this contest of theories, the criterion of scope—the number of diverse phenomena explained—is probably more telling than any of the others. Biological evolution explains a vast array of phenomena in many fields of science. In fact, a great deal of the content of numerous scientific fields—genetics, physiology, biochemistry, neurobiology, and more—would be deeply perplexing without the theory of evolution. As the eminent geneticist Theodosius Dobzhansky put it, "Nothing in biology makes sense except in the light of evolution."[8]

Virtually all scientists would agree—and go much further:

> It [evolution] helps to explain the emergence of new infectious diseases, the development of antibiotic resistance in bacteria, the agricultural relationships among wild and domestic plants and animals, the composition of Earth's atmosphere, the molecular

Food for Thought

Gaps in the Fossil Record?

Creationists hold that if evolution were true, then there should be fossil remains of transitional organisms. But, they insist, there are gaps where transitional fossils should be, so evolution didn't happen. But this claim is incorrect. There are transitional fossils:

Ted Daeschler/Academy of Natural Sciences/VIREO

In 2006, scientists discovered this 375-million-year-old fossil of a species that spans the gap between fish and land animals. What errors do creationists make by rejecting evidence of transitional fossils?

> Gaps in the fossil record are not even a critical test of evolution vs. progressive creation, as evolution also predicts gaps. There are some 2 million described species of living animals, but only 200,000 described fossil species. Thus, it is impossible to provide a minutely detailed history for every living species. This is because, first, the fossil record has not been completely explored. It is pretty hard to overlook a dinosaur bone! Yet, though dinosaurs have been excavated for over 150 years, 40 per cent of the known species were found in the last 20 years or so (*Discover*, March 1987, p. 46). It is likely many more dinosaur species remain to be found. Second, sedimentary rocks were formed locally in lakes, oceans, and river deltas, so many upland species were never fossilized. Third, many deposits that were formed have been lost to erosion. Thus, a complete record is impossible.
>
> However, there is a critical test. Evolution predicts that some complete series should be found, while [creationists predict] that none should ever be found. In fact, many excellent series exist. The evolution of the horse is known in exquisite detail from *Hyracotherium (Eohippus)* to the modern horse (G.G. Simpson, *Horses*, 2nd ed., Oxford, 1961). Scientific creationists have been forced to claim that the series is but allowed variation within a created "kind." If so, then rhinoceroses, tapirs, and horses are all the same "kind," as they can be traced to ancestors nearly identical to *Hyracotherium*! All of these fossils lie in the correct order by both stratigraphic and radioisotope dating.
>
> Another critical test is Darwin's prediction that ". . . our early ancestors lived on the African continent. . . ." (*The Descent of Man*, p. 158). An excellent, detailed series of skulls and some nearly complete skeletons now connect modern man to African australopithecines. Some of the extinct australopithecines had brains about the size and shape of those of chimpanzees.[9]

> machinery of the cell, the similarities between human beings and other primates, and countless other features of the biological and physical world.[10]

Creationism, however, can explain none of this. And it provokes, not solves, a great many mysteries. What caused the worldwide flood? Where did all that water come from? Where did it all go? Why does Earth seem so ancient (when it's said to be so young)? How did the creator create the entire universe suddenly—out of nothing? Why does the fossil record seem to suggest evolution and not creation? So many questions are an indication of diminished scope and decreased understanding.

Note that creationism tries to explain biological facts by appealing to something that's incomprehensible—a creator and his means of creating. The creationist view is that something incomprehensible using incomprehensible means created the universe. But appealing to the incomprehensible does not increase our understanding. Creationism, then, explains nothing. Creationism has zero scope.

Good scientists must be prepared to admit this much: if creationism meets the criteria of adequacy as well as evolution does, then creationism must be as good a theory as evolution. But creationism fails to measure up to the criteria of adequacy. On every count it shows itself to be inferior. Scientists then are justified in rejecting creationism in favour of evolution—and this is exactly what they do.

Exercise 10.1

Answers to exercises marked with an asterisk (*) may be found in Appendix B, Answers to Exercises.

1. What is the difference between science and technology?
2. According to the text, why is science not an ideology?
3. According to the text, why is science such a reliable way of knowing things?
4. What is the scientific method?
5. What are the five steps of the scientific method? (State them in order, if you can!)
6. Can hypotheses be generated entirely through induction? Why or why not?
7. What does it mean to derive a test implication from a theory?*
8. What is the conditional argument reflecting the fact that a theory is disconfirmed? Is that argument valid or invalid?*
9. What is the conditional argument reflecting the fact that a theory is confirmed? Is that argument valid or invalid?
10. Why can theories never be conclusively confirmed?
11. Can theories be conclusively disconfirmed? Why or why not?*
12. What is the difference between scientific instrumentalism and scientific realism?
13. What is falsifiability? Why is it important in the consideration of claims and hypotheses?

Exercise 10.2

For each of the following phenomena, devise a hypothesis to explain it, and derive a test implication to test the hypothesis.

Example

Phenomenon: While riding the elevator to her office one day, Rose finds that reception on her mobile phone is very bad.
Hypothesis: The metal walls of the elevator are interfering with the phone signal.
Test Implication: If the walls of the elevator are interfering with the phone signal, the phone signal should improve as soon as Rose steps off the elevator.

1. My mom takes multivitamins every day, and she never gets a cold.
2. Jamal found giant footprints in his backyard and mysterious tufts of brown fur clinging to bushes in the area. Rumours persist that Bigfoot, the giant primate unknown to science, is frequenting the area. Two guys living nearby also claim to be perpetrating a hoax about the existence of the creature.*
3. Practitioners of traditional Chinese medicine believe that the body's energy, or *chi*, circulates through the body along channels called *meridians*.
4. In the months directly following the tragedy of 11 September 2001, there were no major terrorist attacks in the United States or Canada.
5. People who are wealthy tend to have more windows than people who are not wealthy.
6. Weight trainers swear that the supplement creatine dramatically improves their performance.*
7. The number of suicides in our community went up after a major employer, a tire factory, closed.
8. "Whenever I think back to my childhood, all I remember are really great times and really bad times. I guess life was just never dull when I was a kid!"
9. When John got home, he found that the lock on his door had been broken and his high-definition, flat-panel TV was missing.
10. The doctor established that Eilidh had a cough, a fever, and chills, and had refused to be vaccinated against COVID-19.

Exercise 10.3

Using your background knowledge and any other information you may have about the subject, devise an alternative theory to explain each of the following, and then apply the criteria of adequacy to both of them—that is, ascertain how well each theory does in relation to its competitor on the criteria of testability, fruitfulness, scope, simplicity, and conservatism.

1. Phenomenon: A significant number of philosophy majors end up going to law school after they graduate.

Theory: A training in philosophy is not useful, so philosophy majors end up needing to do additional university training in order to get jobs.

2. Phenomenon: Your latest quiz score is unusually low.
   Theory: The professor set an unusually difficult quiz.
3. Phenomenon: Massive chunks of the world's glaciers are unexpectedly melting.
   Theory: Local climate changes are melting glaciers.*
4. Phenomenon: There has been a substantial increase in the number of news stories about sexual harassment in Hollywood.
   Theory: There has been a sudden increase in the number of instances of sexual harassment in Hollywood.
5. Phenomenon: The average Fortune 500 CEO makes a salary that far exceeds that of even the highest-paid doctors.
   Theory: Our society values making a profit over saving lives.
6. Phenomenon: Species of flightless birds on two adjacent islands are genetically closely related.
   Theory: Both populations descended separately from the same flying ancestor.
7. Phenomenon: A lot of crime is committed by people who are in financial need.
   Theory: Poverty fosters crime.*
8. Phenomenon: After an unusually embarrassing loss, the coach of the basketball team yelled at the team for 20 minutes. They did better during their next game.
   Theory: Yelling at basketball players motivates them to try harder.
9. Phenomenon: You invite your brother over to share a dinner you've made—a new fish dish you're trying out—and he hardly eats anything.
   Theory: Your brother doesn't like fish.
10. Phenomenon: Entrance marks required to get into most Canadian universities are at their highest level in years.
    Theory: Increased immigration is resulting in greater competition from new Canadians, which drives up the entrance requirements.

Exercise 10.4

For each of the following theories, derive a test implication, and indicate whether you believe that such a test would likely confirm or disconfirm the theory.

1. Birds evolved from flying mammals, such as bats, rather than from reptiles as is generally believed by scientists.
2. Last year, the city created dedicated bike lanes on two major streets, which resulted in the rate of accidents involving bikes dropping by 28 per cent.*
3. The J-Ray bracelet emits energy that improves athletic performance.
4. All lawyers are driven primarily by the pursuit of money.

5. Elephants cannot climb stairs of any kind.
6. Eating foods high in fat contributes more to being overweight than eating foods high in carbohydrates.*
7. The Mazda CX-9 is more a reliable car than the Dodge Journey.
8. My uncle claims to be able to read people's minds.

Exercise 10.5

Read the passages below, and answer the following questions for each one:

1. What is the phenomenon being explained?
2. What theories are advanced to explain the phenomenon? (Some theories may be unstated.)
3. Which theory seems the most plausible and why? (Use the criteria of adequacy.)
4. Regarding the most credible theory, is a test implication mentioned? If so, what is it? If not, what would be a good test implication for the theory?
5. What test results would persuade you to change your mind about your preferred theory?

Passage 1
Angikuni Lake lies in what is now Nunavut, in Canada's far north. In the early 1900s, a small Inuit village lay on the banks of the lake, consisting of six tents and perhaps two dozen men, women, and children. The village was also frequently visited by fur trappers who were passing through the area. In 1930, a Manitoba newspaper reported that a trapper named Joe Labelle had visited the little village and found it entirely deserted. However, the village was not merely deserted. There were signs that the villagers had left very suddenly: meals were left cooking on the fire, and shirts that some villagers had been sewing were left half-finished, still with needles in them; furthermore, sled dogs were found starved to death, and a grave had been dug up. When Labelle reported the incident to the Northwest Mounted Police, an investigation was carried out, but none of the villagers was ever found. Later reports added observations of "strange lights in the sky," leading some to conclude that the villagers at Angikuni Lake had been abducted by aliens.

Passage 2
Michael Behe, a Lehigh University biochemist, claims that a light-sensitive cell, for example, couldn't have arisen through evolution because it is "irreducibly complex." Unlike the scientific creationists,

however, he doesn't deny that the universe is billions of years old. Nor does he deny that evolution has occurred. He only denies that every biological system arose through natural selection.

Behe's favorite example of an irreducibly complex mechanism is a mouse trap. A mouse trap consists of five parts: (1) a wooden platform, (2) a metal hammer, (3) a spring, (4) a catch, and (5) a metal bar that holds the hammer down when the trap is set. What makes this mechanism irreducibly complex is that if any one of the parts were removed, it would no longer work. Behe claims that many biological systems, such as cilium, vision, and blood clotting, are also irreducibly complex because each of these systems would cease to function if any of their parts were removed.

Irreducibly complex biochemical systems pose a problem for evolutionary theory because it seems that they could not have arisen through natural selection. A trait such as vision can improve an organism's ability to survive only if it works. And it works only if all the parts of the visual system are present. So, Behe concludes, vision couldn't have arisen through slight modifications of a previous system. It must have been created all at once by some intelligent designer. . . .

Most biologists do not believe that Behe's argument is sound, however, because they reject the notion that the parts of an irreducibly complex system could not have evolved independently of that system. As Nobel Prize–winning biologist H.J. Muller noted in 1939, a genetic sequence that is, at first, inessential to a system may later become essential to it. Biologist H. Allen Orr describes the processes as follows: "Some part (A) initially does some job (and not very well, perhaps). Another part (B) later gets added because it helps A. This new part isn't essential, it merely improves things. But later on A (or something else) may change in such a way that B now becomes indispensable." For example, air bladders—primitive lungs—made it possible for certain fish to acquire new sources of food. But the air bladders were not necessary to the survival of the fish. As the fish acquired additional features, however, such as legs and arms, lungs became essential. So, contrary to what Behe would have us believe, the parts of an irreducibly complex system need not have come into existence all at once.[11]

Exercise 10.6

Read the following passage about a study conducted on the use of vitamin C to treat cancer. Identify the hypothesis being tested, the consequences (test implication) used to test it, and whether the hypothesis was confirmed or disconfirmed.

Passage 1

In 1978, the Mayo Clinic embarked on a prospective, controlled, double-blind study designed to test Pauling and Cameron's claims [for the effectiveness of vitamin C in treating cancer]. Each patient in this study had biopsy-proven cancer that was considered incurable and unsuitable for further chemotherapy, surgery, or radiation. The patients were randomized to receive 10 grams of vitamin C per day or a comparably flavored lactose placebo. All patients took a glycerin-coated capsule four times a day.

The patients were carefully selected so that those [in the] vitamin C [and] placebo groups were equally matched. There were 60 patients in the vitamin C group and 63 in the placebo group. The age distributions were similar. There was a slight predominance of males, but the ratio of males to females was virtually identical. Performance status was measured using the Eastern Cooperative Oncology Group Scale, a clinical scale well recognized by cancer researchers. Most study patients had some disability from their disease, but only a small proportion were bedridden. Most patients had advanced gastrointestinal or lung cancer. Almost all had received chemotherapy, and a smaller proportion had undergone radiation therapy.

The results were noteworthy. About 25 per cent of patients in both groups showed some improvement in appetite. Forty-two per cent of the patients on placebo alone experienced enhancement of their level of activity. About 40 per cent of the patients experienced mild nausea and vomiting, but the two groups had no statistically significant differences in the number of episodes. There were no survival differences between patients receiving vitamin C and those receiving the placebo. The median survival time was approximately seven weeks from the onset of therapy. The longest surviving patient in this trial had received the placebo. Overall, the study showed no benefit from vitamin C.[12]

10.5 Science and Weird Theories

What good are science and inference to the best explanation in the realm that seems to lie *beyond* common sense and scientific inquiry—the zone of the extraordinary, the paranormal, and the supernatural? In this land of the weird—the interesting and mysterious domain of UFOs, ESP, ghosts, psychic predictions, tarot-card readings, and the like—exactly what work can science do?

From reading Chapter 9, you probably have already guessed that science and critical thinking can be just as useful in assessing weird claims as they are in sizing up mundane ones. Inference to the best explanation—whether used in science or everyday life—can be successfully applied to extraordinary theories of all kinds. Fortunately for critical thinkers, the TEST formula outlined in Chapter 9 for finding the best theoretical explanation is not afraid of ghosts, zombies, or space aliens. In the next few pages, we will get a good demonstration of these points by examining some extraordinary theories in much greater detail than we have previously.

"I maintain there is much more wonder in science than in pseudoscience. And in addition, to whatever measure this term has any meaning, science has the additional virtue, and it is not an inconsiderable one, of being true."

—Carl Sagan

Science has always been interested in the mysterious, and from time to time it has also ventured into the weird. In the past 150 years, scientists have tested spiritualism, clairvoyance, telepathy, telekinesis, astrology, dowsing, therapeutic touch, faith healing, and more. Among these we should also count some bizarre phenomena that scientists never tire of studying—black holes, alternative dimensions of space, and the micro-world of subatomic particles, where the laws of physics are crazy enough to stretch the imagination of a science fiction writer.

Food for Thought

Critical Thinking and "Magic"

Some of the most well-respected stage magicians and escape artists of all time have dedicated themselves to demonstrating to the public that many weird beliefs—including belief in psychics, telekinesis, and the belief that a stage magician can saw a woman in half—are false.

Harry Houdini was a stage magician and the most famous escape artist of all time. Back in the 1920s, Houdini devoted himself—when he wasn't on stage—to debunking psychics who said they could tell the future and mediums who claimed to speak to the dead. He used his own knowledge of how stage magic works to show the tricks that allowed those who claimed supernatural powers to fool the gullible.

Library of Congress

Harry Houdini was a master at performing illusions so convincing that the audience actually believed he could do magic. Was Houdini's audience guilty of the mistakes outlined in this chapter? If so, which ones?

The heir to Houdini's role as debunker of the paranormal was James Randi, who went by the stage name "The Amazing Randi" when he performed stage magic in the 1960s and '70s. Like Houdini, Randi was an expert stage magician who loved entertaining people, but who thought it unethical to use the tricks of that trade to truly fool people, especially for money. In 1996, he founded the James Randi Educational Foundation, an organization whose mission is to educate the public about the risks of accepting unproven paranormal claims and to subject such claims to controlled scientific investigation. For many years, the foundation also administered a million-dollar prize: they offered to give $1 million to anyone who could prove, under controlled circumstances, that they have any supernatural ability. During the several decades that the foundation offered it, the prize was never successfully claimed, although about a thousand people tried. What does this suggest to you about all those people out there who claim to be psychics?

Today, the illusionist duo Penn and Teller likewise use their skill at stage magic both to entertain and to educate. Some of their best illusions end with the pair demonstrating to the crowd precisely the tricks of the trade, revealing how their "magic" is accomplished.

But why should anyone bother to learn how to evaluate weird claims in the first place? Well, for one thing, some weird claims are widely believed, and they are often difficult to ignore. They are, after all, heavily promoted in countless television programs, movies, books, magazines, and tabloids. And—like claims in politics, medicine, and many other fields—they can dramatically affect people's lives, for better or worse. It's important, then, for anyone confronted with such popular and influential claims to be able to assess them carefully.

In addition, if you really care whether an extraordinary claim is true or false, there is no substitute for the kind of critical evaluation discussed here. Accepting (or rejecting) a weird claim solely because it's weird will not do. A hearty laugh is not an argument, and neither is a sneer. Weird claims often turn out to be false, but as the history of science shows, they sometimes surprise everyone by being true.

10.6 Making Weird Mistakes

So in science and in our own lives, the critical assessment of weird theories is possible, but that doesn't mean the process is without risks. It's easy for a scientist or anyone else to make mistakes when thinking about extraordinary claims. Weird claims and experiences have a way of provoking strong emotions, preconceived attitudes, and long-held biases. In the world of the weird, people (including scientists and other experts) are prone to the kinds of errors in reasoning we discussed in Chapter 4, including resisting contrary evidence, looking for confirming evidence, and preferring available evidence. Those who love to contemplate extraordinary things also seem to be especially susceptible to the following errors.

10.6.1 Leaping to the Weirdest Theory

When people have an extraordinary experience—when something happens to them that is very unusual—they usually try to make sense of it, one way or another. They may have a seemingly prophetic dream, see a ghostly shape in the dark, watch their astrologer's prediction come true, think they've witnessed a miracle, or feel they have somehow lived another life centuries ago. Then they look around for an explanation for such experiences and feelings. And when they cannot think of a natural explanation, they often conclude that the explanation must be paranormal or supernatural. This line of reasoning is common but fallacious. *Just because you can't think of a natural explanation doesn't mean that there isn't one.* The correct explanation simply may not be obvious to you. Throughout history, scientists have often been confronted with astonishing phenomena that they could not explain in natural terms at the time. But they didn't assume that the phenomena had to be paranormal or supernatural. They simply kept investigating—and they eventually found natural explanations. Comets, solar eclipses, meteors, mental illness, infectious diseases, and epilepsy were all once thought to be supernatural or paranormal, but were later found through scientific investigation to have

Bill Whitehead/CartoonStock

Sometimes it takes a cartoon to make us see how silly the idea of a supposed supernatural power is.

perfectly natural explanations. When confronted, then, with a phenomenon that you don't understand, the most reasonable response is to search for a natural explanation.

The fallacious leap to a non-natural explanation is a version of the *appeal to ignorance* discussed in Chapter 5. People think that since a paranormal or supernatural explanation has not been shown to be false, it must be true. This line of reasoning, though logically fallacious, can be very persuasive.

The failure to consider alternative explanations is probably the most common error in assessing paranormal claims. As we've seen, this failure can be wilful. People can refuse to consider seriously a viable alternative. But honest and intelligent people can also simply be unaware of possible natural explanations. Looking for alternative explanations requires imagination and a deliberate attempt to "think outside the box."

10.6.2 Mixing What Seems with What Is

Sometimes people leap prematurely to an extraordinary theory by ignoring this elementary principle: *the fact that something seems real doesn't mean that it is.* Because of the nature of our perceptual equipment and processes, we humans are bound to have many experiences in which something appears to be real but is not. The correction for mistaking the unreal for the real is to apply another important principle that we discussed in Chapter 4: it's reasonable to accept the evidence provided by personal experience *only if there's no good reason to doubt it.* We have reason to doubt personal experience when our perceptual abilities are impaired (when we are under stress, drugged, afraid, excited, etc.), we have strong expectations about a particular experience (when we strongly expect to see a UFO or hear spooky noises, for example), and observations are made under poor conditions (when the stimuli are vague and ambiguous or the environment is too dark, too noisy, too hazy, etc.). Scientists can falter here just as anyone else can, but they are also keenly aware of that fact, and so they try to guard against faltering by using research methods that minimize reasons for doubt.

10.6.3 Misunderstanding the Possibilities

Debates about weird theories often turn on the ideas of possibility and impossibility. Skeptics may dismiss a weird theory by saying, "That's impossible!" Believers may insist that a state of affairs is indeed possible, or they may proclaim, "*Anything* is possible!" Such protestations, however, are often based on misunderstandings.

The experts on the subject of possibility (namely, philosophers) often talk about *logical possibility* and *logical impossibility*. Something is logically impossible if it violates a principle of logic (that is, if it involves a logical contradiction). Something is logically possible if it does not violate a principle of logic (does not involve a logical contradiction). Anything that is logically impossible can't exist. We know, for example, that there are no married bachelors because these things involve logical contradictions (men who are both married and not married). Likewise, we know that there are no square circles because they involve logical contradictions (things that are both circles and not circles). We must conclude from all this that despite what some people sincerely believe, it is not the case that

Everyday Problems and Decisions

Conspiracy and Vaccines

Vaccines against various diseases constitute one of the true wonders of modern science, a scientific discovery that plays an important part in everyday life. In fact, most of us get multiple vaccines in childhood—vaccines that help us live longer and healthier than children often did in past generations. Standard vaccinations for infants include those that protect against diphtheria, tetanus, measles, mumps, rubella, polio, and more. Some of the diseases that these vaccines help to prevent are deadly. Many of them have been virtually eliminated in countries like Canada and the United States, because almost all children are now vaccinated against them. But many of them are still a frequent cause of illness and death in parts of the world where vaccination is unavailable or unaffordable.

Other vaccines are given on a yearly or as-needed basis. Vaccines against the flu (influenza) are given yearly (typically in the fall). The flu vaccine doesn't entirely prevent the flu, but it makes you less likely to catch it, and if you catch it, the vaccine tends to make the illness less severe. Vaccines are also an important tool in fighting pandemics, such as COVID-19. But recent experience shows that not everyone is enthusiastic about being vaccinated. In some cases, they fear the side effects they believe the vaccines to cause. And it is true that all vaccines can have side effects, but most of them are very minor (like a sore arm or a mild fever), and more serious side effects are rare. In other cases, parents may believe that vaccines are simply unnecessary and that their widespread use could injure their child or hinder expected development. Some believe vaccines are the result of an evil scheme, a conspiracy funded by the major pharmaceutical companies that make them. Is that possible? Perhaps, but is it likely? One particular theory even suggested that the COVID-19 vaccine was being used to inject microchips into recipients. Others were quick to point out that injecting microchips along with a vaccine would be inefficient, costly, technically difficult, and without much plausible purpose.

In the end, people who choose not to be vaccinated are ignoring the guidance of the entire medical profession, the conclusions of epidemiologists (scientists who study the spread of disease), and the advice of every single public health agency. Which theory stands up best when subjected to the tests provided in the present and previous chapter?

Review Notes

Common Errors in Evaluating Extraordinary Theories

1. Believing that just because you can't think of a natural explanation, a phenomenon must be paranormal.
2. Thinking that just because something seems real, it is real. (A better principle is that it's reasonable to accept the evidence provided by personal experience only if there's no good reason to doubt it.)
3. Misunderstanding logical possibility and physical possibility. Also, believing that if something is logically possible, it must be actual.

"anything is possible." If a weird phenomenon is logically impossible, we needn't investigate it further because it can't exist. Most alleged paranormal phenomenon, however, are not logically impossible. For example, ESP, UFOs, reincarnation, dowsing, spontaneous human combustion, and out-of-body experiences do not generally involve any logical contradiction.

Philosophers also refer to *physical possibility* and *physical impossibility*. Something is physically impossible if it violates a law of science. Whatever violates a law of science cannot occur. We know that travelling faster than the speed of light is physically impossible because such an occurrence violates a law of science. Perpetual motion machines are physically impossible because they violate the law of science known as the conservation of mass energy. Thus, if an extraordinary phenomenon violates a law of science, we know that it cannot be.

Some things that are logically possible, however, are physically impossible. It's logically possible for my dog to fly to another galaxy in 60 seconds. Such an astounding performance would not violate a principle of logic. But it does violate laws of science pertaining to speed-of-light travel and gravitation; it is therefore physically impossible. The upshot of all this is that, contrary to what some people would have us believe, the fact that something is *logically* possible that doesn't mean it's *physically* possible. That is, if something is logically possible, that doesn't mean it happened or exists—many logically possible things may not be real.

10.7 Judging Weird Theories

Now let's do a detailed evaluation of an extraordinary theory using the TEST formula from Chapter 9. Recall the four steps of the procedure:

Step 1. State the theory and check for consistency.
Step 2. Assess the evidence for the theory.
Step 3. Scrutinize alternative theories.
Step 4. Test the theories with the criteria of adequacy.

Science uses such a procedure to assess all manner of extraordinary explanations, and—by proceeding carefully and systematically—so can you.

10.7.1 Talking with the Dead

Some people claim that they can communicate with the dead, providing impressive and seemingly accurate information about a person's dead loved ones. They are called psychics (a century ago, they were called mediums), and they have gained the respect of many who have come to them in search of messages from the deceased. They appear on television programs, publish books, and offer seminars to thousands. The most famous among these modern-day mediums are psychics Michelle Whitedove (named 'America's # 1 Psychic' by Lifetime TV), and John Edward. Their performances assure many people that their loved ones who "have passed over" are fine and that any unsettled issues of guilt and forgiveness can be resolved.

"The most beautiful thing we can experience is the mysterious. It is the source of all true art and science."

—Albert Einstein

What is the best explanation for these otherworldly performances in which the psychics appear to be in contact with the dead? Several theories have been proposed. One is that the psychics are getting information about the dead and their loved ones ahead of time (before the performances begin). Another is that the psychics are using telepathy to read the minds of the living to discover facts about the dead. But for simplicity's sake, let's narrow the list of theories down to the two leading ones.

Step 1. Here's the psychics' theory.

Theory 1: The psychics are communicating information or messages to and from the disembodied spirits of people who have died. In other words, the psychics are doing exactly what they claim to be doing. They are somehow identifying the appropriate deceased spirit, receiving and decoding transmissions from that spirit, conveying the information to the living, and sending messages back to the dead.

"Don't let anyone rob you of your imagination, your creativity, or your curiosity."

—Mae Jemison, physicist and astronaut

Step 2. The main evidence in support of this theory is the psychics' performance. They usually perform in front of an audience and talk to audience members who have lost loved ones. The psychics appear to know facts about the dead that they could only know if they were actually communicating with the dead. They also seem to inexplicably know things about members of the audience. Often they also provide incorrect information (such as saying that a member of the audience has lost her mother when in fact the mother is very much alive). But their "hits" (times when they produce correct information) occur often enough and seem to be specific enough to impress.

Psychics have rarely been tested scientifically. (See the text box, "Critical Thinking and 'Magic,'" above.) The few experiments conducted to date have been severely criticized for sloppy methodology. And those tests that have been conducted properly have failed to find any evidence at all of psychic ability. So there is no good scientific evidence to support theory 1. Investigators who have seen the psychics' live performances (not just the edited versions of the TV programs) report that the hit rates (the percentage of hits out of the total number of statements or questions) are actually much lower than most people realize. They have found hit rates as low as 5 per cent, with the highest being well under 50 per cent. The low hit rate, though, may not be apparent on TV shows because the misses

"Death is a part of life, and pretending that the dead are gathering in a television studio in New York to talk twaddle with a former ballroom-dance instructor is an insult to the intelligence and humanity of the living."

—Michael Shermer

are often edited out. Psychics tend to explain their misses with ad hoc hypotheses (explanations that cannot be verified).

Step 3. Here's the main alternative to the psychics' theory.

Theory 2: The psychics are doing "cold reading." Cold reading is a very old skill practised by fortune tellers, tarot-card readers, and mentalists (performers who pretend to read minds). When done well, cold reading can astonish and appear to be paranormal—and can be very entertaining! In cold reading, the "psychic" reader surreptitiously acquires information from people (the subjects) by asking them subtle questions, making statements, observing how people behave, and listening to what they say. Good cold readers always make the information they come up with seem truly amazing, and typically give the impression that the information actually comes from some mysterious source, such as the spirits of the departed. But anyone can learn to do cold reading. It doesn't require any exotic skills or special powers—just do a search online, and you'll find quite a few pages dedicated to teaching you how. All that's needed is the practised ability to cleverly manipulate a conversation to elicit information from the subject.

Note that theory 2 does not say that the cold reading is necessarily done to deliberately deceive an audience. Cold reading can be done either consciously or unconsciously. It's possible for someone to do cold reading while believing that they really are getting information via their psychic powers.

To get the relevant information (or appear to have it), a psychic reader can use several cold-reading techniques, including the following:

1. The reader encourages the subject to fill in the blanks.

    READER: I'm sensing something about the face or head or brow.
    SUBJECT: You're right, my father used to have terrible headaches.
    READER: I'm feeling something about money or finances.
    SUBJECT: Yes, my mother always struggled to pay the bills.

2. The reader makes statements with multiple variables so that a hit is very likely.

    READER: I'm feeling that your father was dealing with a lot of frustration, anguish, or anger.
    SUBJECT: Yes, he was always arguing with my brother.

3. The reader makes accurate and obvious inferences from information given by the subject.

    READER: Why was your father in the hospital?
    SUBJECT: He had had a heart attack.
    READER: Yes, he struggled with heart disease for years and had to take heart medication for a long time. You were really worried that he would have another heart attack.

Food for Thought

Eyewitness Testimony and Extraordinary Things

A great deal of the evidence for paranormal phenomena is eyewitness testimony. Unfortunately, research suggests that eyewitness testimony generally can't be trusted—especially when the testimony concerns the paranormal. For example, in some studies people who had participated in a seance (an event aimed at contacting the dead) later gave wildly inaccurate descriptions of what had taken place. Researchers have found that people's beliefs and expectations seem to play a big role in the unreliability of testimony about the paranormal.

> Different people clearly have different beliefs and expectations prior to observing a supposed psychic—skeptics might expect to see some kind of trickery; believers may expect a display of genuine psi [parapsychological phenomena]. Some 70 years ago Eric Dingwall in Britain speculated that such expectations may distort eyewitness testimony: the frame of mind in which a person goes to see magic and to a medium cannot be compared. In one case he goes either purely for amusement or possibly with the idea of discovering "how it was done," whilst in the other he usually goes with the thought that it is possible that he will come into direct contact with the other world.
>
> Recent experimental evidence suggests that Dingwall's speculations are correct.
>
> Wiseman and Morris in Britain carried out two studies investigating the effect that belief in the paranormal has on the observation of conjuring tricks. Individuals taking part in the experiment were first asked several questions concerning their belief in the paranormal. On the basis of their answers they were classified as either believers (labelled "sheep") or skeptics (labelled "goats").
>
> In both experiments individuals were first shown a film containing fake psychic demonstrations. In the first demonstration the "psychic" apparently bent a key by concentrating on it; in the second demonstration he supposedly bent a spoon simply by rubbing it.
>
> After they watched the film, witnesses were asked to rate the "paranormal" content of the demonstrations and complete a set of recall questions. Wiseman and Morris wanted to discover if, as Hodgson and Dingwall had suggested, sheep really did tend to misremember those parts of the demonstrations that were central to solving the tricks. For this reason, half of the questions concerned the methods used to fake the phenomena. For example, the psychic faked the key-bending demonstration by secretly switching the straight key for a pre-bent duplicate by passing the straight key from one hand to the other. During the switch the straight key could not be seen. This was clearly central to the trick's method; and one of the "important" questions asked was whether the straight key had always remained in sight. A second set of "unimportant" questions asked about parts of the demonstration that were not related to the tricks' methods. Overall, the results suggested that sheep rated the demonstrations as more "paranormal" than goats did, and that goats did indeed recall significantly more "important" information than sheep. There was no such difference for the recall of the "unimportant" information.[13]

4. The reader asks many questions and treats answers as though they confirmed the reader's insight.

   READER: Who was the person who got a divorce?
   SUBJECT: That was my daughter. She divorced her husband in 1992.
   READER: Because I feel that the divorce was very painful for her, that she was sad and depressed for a while.

5. The reader makes statements that could apply to almost anyone.

READER: I'm sensing something about a cat or a small animal.
SUBJECT: Yes, my mother owned a poodle.

With such cold-reading techniques a reader can appear to read minds. Theory 2 is bolstered by the fact that the psychics' amazing performances can be duplicated by anyone skilled in the use of cold reading. In fact, stage magicians, mentalists, and other non-psychic entertainers have used cold-reading techniques to give performances that rival those of the top psychics. Regardless of their authenticity, the performances of Whitedove, Edward, and other psychics seem to be indistinguishable from those based on plain old cold reading. The psychics may indeed be communicating with the dead, but it sure looks as if they're using straightforward cold-reading techniques.

Step 4. Now we can apply the criteria of adequacy to these two competing explanations. Both theories are testable, and neither has yielded any novel predictions. So we must judge the theories in terms of scope, simplicity, and conservatism. And on each of these criteria, theory 2 is clearly superior. Theory 1 explains only the psychics' performances as described earlier, but theory 2 explains these performances plus other kinds of seemingly psychic readings, including tarot-card reading, fortune-telling, mentalist acts, and old-fashioned spiritualist seances. Theory 1, of course, fails the criterion of simplicity because it assumes the existence of unknown entities (disembodied spirits with certain abilities) and unknown processes (communication to and from the dead); theory 2 makes no such assumptions. Finally, theory 1 is not conservative. It conflicts with everything we know about death, the mind, and communication. Theory 2, though, fits with existing knowledge just fine.

Here are these judgments in table form:

Criterion	Theory 1	Theory 2
Testable	Yes	Yes
Fruitful	No	No
Scope	No	Yes
Simple	No	Yes
Conservative	No	Yes

We must conclude that theory 1 is a seriously defective theory. It is unlikely to be true. Theory 2, however, is strong. It is not only superior to theory 1, but it is also a better explanation than other competing theories we haven't discussed in that it can explain most or all of the psychics' hits. If the cold-reading theory really is better than all these others, then we have good reasons to believe that Edward, Whitedove, and other psychics perform their amazing feats through simple cold reading.

Food for Thought

Why People Believe Psychic Readings

Ray Hyman is professor emeritus of psychology at the University of Oregon and an expert on the scientific investigation of paranormal claims, including psychic readings. Years of research have led him to be skeptical of the validity of psychic readings, but he used to be a true believer. He explains why he went from believer to skeptic:

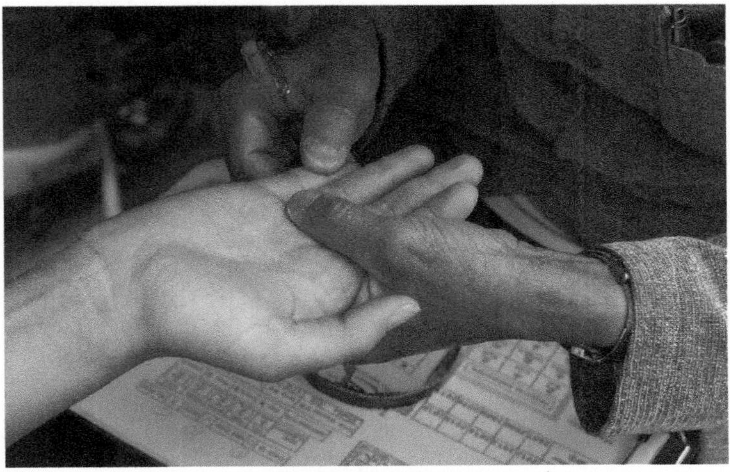

Nimazi/Thinkstock

What is this palm saying? Psychologists think they know. How might the illusion of specificity sway a non-critical thinker?

> Now it so happens that I have devoted more than half a century to the study of psychic and cold readings. I have been especially concerned with why such readings can seem so concrete and compelling, even to skeptics. As a way to earn extra income, I began reading palms when I was in my teens. At first, I was skeptical. I thought that people believed in palmistry and other divination procedures because they could easily fit very general statements to their particular situation. To establish credibility with my clients, I read books on palmistry and gave readings according to the accepted interpretations for the lines, shape of the fingers, mounds, and other indicators. I was astonished by the reactions of my clients. My clients consistently praised me for my accuracy even when I told them very specific things about problems with their health and other personal matters. I even would get phone calls from clients telling me that a prediction that I had made for them had come true. Within months of my entry into palm reading, I became a staunch believer in its validity. My conviction was so strong that I convinced my skeptical high school English teacher by giving him readings and arguing with him. I later also convinced the head of the psychology department where I was an undergraduate.
>
> When I was a sophomore, majoring in journalism, a well-known mentalist and trusted friend persuaded me to try an experiment in which I would deliberately read a client's hand opposite to what the signs in her hand indicated. I was shocked to discover that this client insisted that this was the most accurate reading she had ever experienced. As a result, I carried out more experiments with the same outcome. It dawned on me that something important was going on. Whatever it was, it had nothing to do with the lines in the hand. I changed my major from journalism to psychology so that I could learn why not only other people, but also I, could be so badly led astray. My subsequent career has focused on the reasons why cold readings can appear to be so compelling and seemingly specific.

continued

Psychologists have uncovered a number of factors that can make an ambiguous reading seem highly specific, unique, and uncannily accurate. And once the observer or client has been struck with the apparent accuracy of the reading, it becomes virtually impossible to dislodge the belief in the uniqueness and specificity of the reading. Research from many areas demonstrates this finding. The principles go under such names as the fallacy of personal validation, subjective validation, confirmation bias, belief perseverance, the illusion of invulnerability, compliance, demand characteristics, false uniqueness effect, foot-in-the-door phenomenon, illusory correlation, integrative agreements, self-reference effect, the principle of individuation, and many, many others. Much of this is facilitated by the illusion of specificity that surrounds language. All language is inherently ambiguous and depends much more than we realize upon the context and non-linguistic cues to fix its meaning in a given situation.[14]

Summary

Science seeks knowledge and understanding of reality, and it does so through the formulation, testing, and evaluation of theories. Science is a way of searching for truth. It is not the only way to acquire knowledge, but it is, however, a highly reliable way of acquiring knowledge of empirical facts.

The scientific method cannot be identified with any particular set of experimental or observational procedures. But it does involve several general steps: (1) identifying the problem; (2) devising a hypothesis; (3) deriving a test implication; (4) performing the test; and (5) accepting or rejecting the hypothesis.

This kind of theory testing is part of a broader effort to evaluate a theory against its competitors. This kind of evaluation always involves, implicitly or explicitly, the criteria of adequacy.

Inference to the best explanation can be used to assess weird theories as well as more commonplace explanations in science and everyday life. However, when people try to evaluate extraordinary theories, they often make certain typical mistakes. They may believe that because they can't think of a natural explanation, a paranormal explanation must be correct. They may mistake what seems for what truly is, forgetting that we shouldn't accept the evidence provided by personal experience if we have good reason to doubt it. And they may not fully understand the concepts of logical and physical possibility. In both science and everyday life, the TEST formula enables us to appraise fairly the worth of all sorts of weird theories, including those about communication with the dead, which we examined in this chapter.

Exercise 10.7

Answers to exercises marked with an asterisk (*) may be found in Appendix B, Answers to Exercises.

1. Is it unwise to reject an extraordinary claim solely because of its weirdness? Why or why not?
2. Why is it unreasonable to accept an extraordinary claim solely because of its weirdness?
3. Why is it unreasonable to conclude that a phenomenon is paranormal just because you cannot think of a natural explanation?
4. What logical fallacy is the fallacious leap to a non-natural explanation an example of?*
5. What is the critical thinking principle that can help you to avoid mistaking how something seems for how something is?
6. What is logical impossibility? What is logical possibility?*
7. What is physical possibility? How would changes in our understanding of science affect our use of this term?
8. Is it true that "anything is possible"? If not, why not?
9. Are cows (or cow-like things) that fly physically possible?
10. Are cows (or cow-like things) that fly logically possible?
11. Can something be physically possible but logically impossible? Can it be physically impossible but logically possible?

Exercise 10.8

In each of the following examples, a state of affairs is described. Devise three theories to explain each one. Include two plausible theories that are natural explanations and one competing theory that is paranormal.

1. On Tuesday afternoon, Madame Mavis (a psychic who works out of a storefront on Davie Street) gazed into my eyes and held my hand. "I see troubling things in your future," she said. "You will have very bad luck this week!" The next day, my boss called me into my office to tell me I was fired.
2. Jacques lives in a house built back in the 1940s, and that is now in bad shape. The previous owner died in the house. As Jacques sat reading in the living room, he heard creaking sounds coming from upstairs.*
3. Farida came home to find her room a terrible mess. The window was open, and the papers that had been on her desk were scattered all over the floor.

4. A number of people you know all report the same strange phenomenon: their cats seem to know in advance when company is coming. They always seem to sit in a window facing the street, as if waiting for someone.
5. Want to hear something strange? One time when I was a kid we went camping, and in the middle of the night we heard these eerie sounds, and when we looked out of our tent we saw a bright light flash across the sky. It was definitely nothing we had ever seen before!
6. For her seventeenth birthday, Kerry really wants a car of her own. Her neighbour, Jed, is selling a relatively nice one, but another neighbour warns her that Jed's father had died of a heart attack while driving the car and that "everyone says" his spirit still lives in the car. Ignoring the warning, Kerry buys the car. The next day, she wakes up to find that the car is outside by the curb, even though she distinctly remembers parking it in her garage.
7. Wayne dreamed that his uncle was killed by a bear in Algonquin Provincial Park. When Wayne woke up, he got a call from his mother saying that his uncle had been injured in a car accident near the park: his car had hit a bear!*
8. Reginald had begun acting strangely. Soon after his seventieth birthday, he began speaking incoherently as if in some bizarre foreign language, and he sometimes looked at his family as if he had no idea who they were.

Exercise 10.9

Using your background knowledge and any other information you may have about the subject, devise a competing, naturalistic theory for each paranormal theory that follows, and then apply the criteria of adequacy to both of them—that is, ascertain how well each theory does in relation to its competitor on the criteria of testability, fruitfulness, scope, simplicity, and conservatism.

1. Phenomenon: Yolanda's parrot, "Charlie," talks, and has a vocabulary of about 20 words—words like "hello" and "cracker." Recently Charlie started saying "Cookie" over and over, which happens to be Yolanda's deceased grandmother's nickname for Yolanda.
   Theory: Yolanda's parrot is the reincarnation of her grandmother.
2. Phenomenon: Steve and Kwan are twins. They often seem to know what the other is thinking and can finish each other's sentences. Many times, they report knowing what the other is up to, even when miles apart.
   Theory: The twins share a special psychic connection.
3. Phenomenon: In 1917, in Cottingley, England, three little girls claimed to have taken photos of fairies who played with them in the garden. The photos showed the girls in the garden with what appeared to be tiny fairies dancing around them. (The 1997 movie *Fairy Tale* was about the girls and their story.)
   Theory: Fairies really do exist, and the girls photographed them.*

4. Phenomenon: Ogopogo is alleged to be a large water serpent inhabiting Okanagan Lake in British Columbia. The creature is unknown to science. The serpent was known as N'ha-a-itk by the Interior Salish First Nations tribe, and there have been many reported sightings over the years. There is no hard evidence proving that the monster exists.
   Theory: Ogopogo actually exists.
5. Phenomenon: Margaret wears black at school all the time and keeps to herself. When a bully made fun of her unstylish clothes, Margaret glared at him and said, "You'll be sorry one day." The next day, the bully tripped on the school stairs and broke his leg.
   Theory: Margaret is a witch.

Field Problems

1. Find a controversial health or medical theory on the internet, and design a study to test it. Indicate the makeup and characteristics of any group in the study, whether a placebo group should be used, whether the study is double-blind, and what study results would, in principle, confirm and disconfirm the theory.
2. Find a controversial theory in the social sciences (e.g., anthropology, economics, psychology, political science) on the internet, and design a simple study to test it. Indicate the makeup and characteristics of any group in the study, whether a placebo group is to be used, whether the study should be double-blind, and what kinds of study results would confirm and disconfirm the theory. If the theory is one that you strongly believe, indicate the kind and level of evidence that could convince you to change your mind about it. If there is no imaginable evidence that could convince you to change your mind, explain why.
3. Think of someone you know well, and engage in a bit of scientific reasoning about him or her. In particular, formulate a theory regarding the question "*What does it take to make them smile?*" Then devise a way of testing your theory. (Note: you don't need to carry out your test! Just design it.)

Self-Assessment Quiz

1. What is a test implication?
2. When a test implication is confirmed, what conditional argument type is exemplified?
3. Briefly explain two errors that people frequently make when evaluating extraordinary theories.

For each of the following phenomena, devise a hypothesis to explain it, and derive a test implication to test the hypothesis.

4. There are police on my neighbour's lawn, digging through his rose garden and hedges.
5. You hear a man on the sidewalk exclaim, "This time tomorrow I'll be at the regional jail!"
6. Cory's father comes home one Wednesday afternoon, and exclaims, "Guess what? I'm quitting my job!"

For each of the following phenomena, suggest (1) a possible hypothesis to explain it, (2) a possible competing hypothesis, (3) a test implication for each hypothesis, and (4) what testing results would confirm and disconfirm the hypothesis.

7. Boaters have found dozens of dead fish floating in the waters near the waste outlet of a plastics manufacturing factory.
8. Statisticians have noticed that people who live within 1 km of a bank headquarters make significantly more money than people who live 10 km or more from a bank headquarters.
9. Alyssa loves plants, but has trouble keeping them alive. She loves cacti in particular, but really has a hard time with them. Of the last five she bought, four of them died within a few months, and the fifth is barely alive.

For each of the following hypotheses, specify a test implication, and say what evidence would convince you to accept the hypothesis.

10. Red wine is good for your heart.
11. Most people—regardless of ethnicity—are economically better off now than their parents were 30 years ago.
12. Canada has the most effective health care system in the northern hemisphere.

Each of the theories that follow is offered to explain why an astrological reading by a famous astrologer turned out to be wildly inaccurate. On the basis of a single person's horoscope, he had predicted that the person was a kind and generous person. The person turned out to be Martin Shkreli, the pharmaceutical company CEO who bought the patent for a drug used to treat AIDS patients and immediately raised the price by 5000 per cent. Say which theory (a) lacks simplicity, (b) is not conservative, (c) is untestable, and (d) has the most scope. (Some theories may merit more than one of these designations.)

13. Theory: Astrology—the notion that the position of the stars and planets at your birth controls your destiny—has no basis in fact.
14. Theory: Astrology works, but the astrologer read the horoscope wrong.

Evaluate the following theory using the TEST formula. Say what phenomenon is being explained. Use your background knowledge to assess the evidence. Specify one alternative theory, use the criteria of adequacy to assess the two theories, and determine which one is more plausible.

15. Camila has always been a bit of a loner. She doesn't have any real friends among her co-workers, and she always eats her lunch alone at her desk. Recently, she has seemed even more isolated. She avoids unnecessary conversations with co-workers. She skipped the office's holiday party. And she has been showing up slightly late for work most days. I think she's lost interest in her job and is thinking of quitting.

Integrative Exercises

These exercises pertain to material in Chapters 3–5 and 8–10.

1. What is an enumerative induction?
2. What is an analogical induction?
3. What is a sufficient condition?
4. What is a necessary condition?
5. What is the appeal to ignorance?

For each of the following arguments, specify the conclusion and premises. If necessary, add implicit premises and conclusions.

1. "Conflating opposition to abortion with bigotry is simplistic, and no better than demagoguery. It's possible to be against abortion without malice in your heart toward women. For those who call themselves 'pro-life,' abortion isn't exclusively about women—it is about a woman and a fetus, and whether her right to security of the person outweighs its right to life. They will always argue that it doesn't, regardless of what the Supreme Court says, because, if you choose to believe—either personally or because your faith dictates it—that human life begins at conception, it's impossible to reach another conclusion." (Editorial, "In Canada, Abortion Is a Right. But So Is Criticizing It," *The Globe and Mail*, 22 January 2018)
2. "Privatization is neither an efficient nor an effective response to the shortage of long-term care facilities. Some Regional Health Authorities see [privatization] as an obstacle to the provision of well-coordinated and fiscally responsible care. Centralized administration of public health care provides both lower administrative costs and economies of scale. Indeed, the fact that health care costs so much more in the US than in Canada—13.5 per cent of GDP in the US compared with 9.2 per cent in Canada—is largely the result of higher administrative costs in a system comprised of numerous competitive insurance firms, hospitals, clinics, and so on." (Editorial, Canadian Centre for Policy Alternatives (CCPA), https://policyalternatives.ca)
3. "The current tax burden is massively distorted by land values (since buildings depreciate as they get older) and falls heavily on those in built-up areas where values reflect scarcity, not service costs or incomes. The perverse impact is to push residents and small businesses out of denser areas on the basis of high taxes. That's totally at odds with the city's development plan to encourage inner-city growth. And it is simply wrong and completely backwards for the city to dictate where you can live or where you do business just to maximize taxes on property.

   "Homeowners have some protection under an assessment cap, but this only puts more burden on small business. Instead, we need a new system based on actual service costs and real ability to pay, and that doesn't tax people out of homes and business locations they can otherwise afford and want to remain in." (Editorial, *Halifax Chronicle-Herald*, 25 January 2012)

For each of the following phenomena, suggest (1) a possible hypothesis to explain it, (2) a possible competing hypothesis, and (3) a test implication for each hypothesis.

1. Every year, a number of hikers need to be rescued, due to various injuries and illnesses, from British Columbia's West Coast Trail. After a government ad campaign explaining the dangers of the trail, the yearly number of hikers in need of rescue dipped slightly but significantly.
2. The popularity of Indigenous music has risen in Canada over the last five years.
3. There are several new businesses on the east side of town despite the fact that the new Walmart there resulted in several small stores closing. Indeed, business near the new Walmart seems to be booming!

Evaluate each of the following theories by using the TEST formula. Use your background knowledge to assess the evidence. Specify one alternative theory, use the criteria of adequacy to assess the two theories, and determine which one is more plausible.

1. Canadian universities have seen an increase in applications from international students over the past couple of years because of anti-immigrant sentiment in the US.
2. The key to a happy life-long career is to choose the right company to start your career with.

3. The NDP has never formed a federal government in Canada because influential Americans have worked hard to prevent Canada from becoming "too left-wing."
4. Controlling the supply of illegal firearms in Canada is so hard because the lax gun laws in the United States makes smuggling guns from the US into Canada much easier.

Writing Assignments

1. In a one-page essay, use the TEST formula to evaluate one of the following theories:
   a. Phenomenon: People with the flu report feeling better after drinking chamomile tea.
   Theory 1: Chamomile tea cures the flu.
   Theory 2: The placebo effect.
   b. Phenomenon: A drop in the unemployment rate in northern Alberta occurred during a particularly cold winter in Ontario.
   Theory 1: Higher prices for heating oil in Ontario created demand for oil (and oil-field workers) in northern Alberta.
   Theory 2: Many northern Albertans headed to Ontario to take advantage of new jobs in the snow-removal industry.
   c. Phenomenon: We took six puppies to a nursing home for senior citizens one morning, and nurses reported that the patients generally reported fewer minor health problems during the rest of the day.
   Theory 1: Puppies prevent minor illnesses.
   Theory 2: Puppies improve patients' mood, which results in them complaining less about their health.
2. Read Essay 8 ("Unrepentant Homeopaths") in Appendix A, and write a 500-word essay evaluating homeopathy by comparing the following two theories: (1) homeopathy is an elaborate system of placebos, without any real effect; (2) homeopathy is effective in a way not fully understood today by science. Use the TEST formula.
3. Devise two theories to explain the prevalence of plagiarism among university students, and then write a 500-word essay evaluating the adequacy of the two theories.

Notes

1. "New Canadian Survey Reveals One in 10 Canadians Claim to Have Stayed in a Haunted Hotel; Nearly Half Have Felt the Presence of a Ghost," Blue Ant Media (9 June 2021). https://blueantmedia.com/2021/06/new-canadian-survey-reveals-one-in-10-canadians-claim-to-have-stayed-in-a-haunted-hotel-nearly-half-have-felt-the-presence-of-a-ghost/.
2. See Stephen Barrett et al., *Consumer Health*, 6th ed. (New York: McGraw-Hill, 1993), 239–40.
3. Thomas S. Kuhn, *The Copernican Revolution: Planetary Astronomy in the Development of Western Thought* (Cambridge, MA: Harvard University Press, 1957), 179.
4. Section 4a of Act 590 of the Acts of Arkansas of 1981, "Balanced Treatment for Creation-Science and Evolution-Science Act."
5. National Academy of Sciences, "The Intersection of Science and Religion." https://www.nationalacademies.org/evolution/science-and-religion.
6. National Academy of Sciences, *Science and Creationism* (Washington: National Academy Press, 1998).
7. Ibid.
8. Theodosius Dobzhansky, quoted in National Academy of Sciences, *Science and Creationism*, ix.
9. George S. Bakken, "Creation or Evolution?" *Skeptic Report*, 10 September 2004. www.skepticreport.com/sr/?p=216.
10. National Academy of Sciences, "Preface," in *Science and Creationism*, xi.
11. Schick and Vaughn, *How to Think about Weird Things*, 4th ed., 206.
12. Stephen Barrett, "High Doses of Vitamin C Are Not Effective as a Cancer Treatment," Quackwatch.com, revised 3 October 2011. www.quackwatch.org/01 QuackeryRelatedTopics/Cancer/c.html.
13. Richard Wiseman, Matthew Smith, and Jeff Wiseman, "Eyewitness Testimony and the Paranormal," *Skeptical Inquirer* (November/December 1995). https://skepticalinquirer.org/1995/11/eyewitness-testimony-and-the-paranormal/.
14. Ray Hyman, "How *Not* to Test Mediums," *Skeptical Inquirer* (January/February 2003). www.csicop.org/si/show/how_not_to_test_mediums_critiquing_the_afterlife experiments.

Contexts of Application: Thinking Critically about Health, Law, and Ethics

Chapter Objectives

Thinking Critically about Health and Health Care

You will be able to

- appreciate the risks posed by various causal confusions in reasoning about health.
- understand the importance of critically evaluating all news reports related to health.
- recognize the importance and limits of expert advice related to health.
- avoid the most common fallacies found in reasoning about health.

Thinking Critically about the Law

You will be able to

- appreciate the role of "inference to the best explanation" in legal reasoning.
- understand the way that legal reasoning involves application of categorical logic.
- recognize the significance of key fallacies as they appear in legal reasoning.

Thinking Critically about Ethics

You will be able to

- distinguish between ethical claims and descriptive claims.
- appreciate why critical thinking skills are as relevant to ethical claims as they are to other sorts of claims.
- distinguish among ethical premises that draw upon the three historically important traditions of ethics.

In this chapter, we turn to examining several contexts in which the application of critical thinking skills is especially important. In Chapter 10, we applied our critical thinking skills to the world of science. But there is a sense in which science, rather than being an area of application, is really just a specialized form of critical thinking itself. In the present chapter, we will look at four different areas of decision-making in which the sorts of skills you have learned in the preceding chapters turn out to be especially important.

11.1 Thinking Critically about Health and Health Care

There are few decisions that we make in life that are more important than the decisions we make about our health. When it comes to our health, good decision-making can literally be a matter of life and death. And even when the question at hand is not quite that serious, decisions about our health still matter greatly, not least because good health makes it easier to enjoy the other things we enjoy in life. As we saw during the beginning of the COVID-19 pandemic, making good decisions about health depends on figuring out what we should believe. This is precisely the business of critical thinking.

This textbook began with the observation that all of us are faced with the challenge of figuring out what to believe given the enormous number of possible beliefs vying for space in our brains. This is nowhere more obvious than in the world of health. Every day we are bombarded with news reports detailing medical breakthroughs, friendly advice on how to stay healthy, and half-remembered lessons taught to us by our parents. In addition, we now see both experts and amateurs posting information and perspectives about specific health care issues online. We are faced with claims about what kinds of foods we should eat, how much exercise we should get, what sorts of personal habits will keep us healthy, and what to do when we get sick. It can all be truly bewildering.

11.1.1 Key Skills

In order to make sense of this flood of information, we really do need to apply the full range of critical thinking skills and techniques. But a few skills stand out as being particularly useful in evaluating health information.

The most basic critical thinking skill when it comes to thinking critically about your health is the ability to engage in reasoning about causation. In essence, almost all significant health claims are answers to questions about causation. That is true whether we are interested in the cause of illness or in what will reverse illness and maintain health. With regard to the causes of illness, we need to find good answers to questions like these:

- What sorts of foods lead most readily to obesity?
- Can a sexually transmitted infection like herpes or chlamydia *really* be transmitted by the seat of a public toilet?

- Will lack of sleep make me more likely to "get run down" and catch a cold or the flu? If I get extra sleep later, will that let me "catch up"?
- What are the most likely causes of a headache or a rash or aches and pains?
- Is it risky to shake hands with someone who has HIV/AIDS or COVID-19?

With regard to preserving or restoring health, we need to be able to evaluate causal claims to answer questions such as the following:

- Does drinking red wine reduce our risk of heart disease?
- Will taking an antibiotic cure my cold?
- Will wearing a mask during a pandemic reduce the risk of infection?
- How important is exercise in maintaining a strong immune system?
- Does stretching before running make it less likely that I will pull a muscle?
- Are herbal remedies a safe and effective way to treat various illnesses?

As a starting point, evaluating such claims requires that you recall the lessons learned about causal reasoning in Chapter 8. In many cases, evaluating causal claims related to health will require that you critically examine the arguments behind various causal claims. To begin with, you need to remember that causal reasoning is a branch of inductive logic. As such, causal reasoning can only ever give us conclusions that are probable rather than certain—although in some cases, the weight of available evidence is sufficient to make particular conclusions *highly probable*. For example, the evidence marshalled over the last several decades makes it *highly probable* that smoking cigarettes has a strong tendency to cause cancer. This is not a deductive argument, so it can never guarantee its conclusion. But the evidence in this case is so strong that it would be foolish not to believe this causal claim. Compare this to more recent claims that yoga may be effective in treating depression. A handful of recent studies point in this direction, but this is a very small amount of evidence, relatively speaking. An inductive argument that reasons from this evidence alone to a conclusion about how to treat depression would be a relatively weak one.

As in all situations requiring the evaluation of causal explanations or hypotheses, we must be on guard against various causal confusions. For example, we must be careful not to be misled by coincidence. Imagine you notice that every time you've caught a cold over the last year, it has happened just before a major essay is due at school. Is it really likely that having an essay due is *causing* you to catch a cold? Is that consistent with what you know about the role of viruses in causing colds? As we learned previously, a correlation is not enough to establish causation. Another common causal confusion involves confusing temporal order with causation. As we learned in Chapter 8, if we assume that simply because A is followed by B, then A must have caused B, we commit the fallacy known as *post hoc, ergo propter hoc* ("after that, therefore because of that"). If you take a homeopathic remedy on the fourth day of a bad cold, you may well find that the cold goes away two or three days later. Is that because the homeopathic remedy was effective or because the average cold lasts only about seven days anyway? Likewise, we must be careful not to ignore common causal factors. When A is found to be correlated with B, is that because one of them causes the other, or is it instead because both are caused by some third factor, C? For example, you might have heard that knee trouble is common among people who also have heart disease. But does knee trouble cause heart disease? Does heart disease cause knee trouble? We might be tempted by one of those causal hypotheses until we consider that both of those ailments are known very often to result from a common cause—namely, obesity.

Barbara Smaller/CartoonStock

"The active ingredient is marketing."

Some products really have very little going for them, beyond a fancy marketing campaign.

Of course, in many cases we do not evaluate health-related causal hypotheses ourselves but instead rely—directly or indirectly—on expert opinion. Sometimes expert opinions come to us directly, from our physician or from other health professionals, and sometimes expert opinions are conveyed to us by the news media.

11.1.2 Evaluating Health Claims in the News

Another important skill is the ability to critically evaluate claims in the news. To begin with, we need to adopt a critical attitude to the process by which news—including health news—is reported. As outlined in Chapter 4, not all news is created equal. The quality of reporting varies enormously, especially, perhaps, with regard to health. For example, a 2011 study published in the journal *Public Understanding of Science* examined claims made in news stories about the relationship between various foods and people's health. The authors of the study systematically looked at stories reported in various UK newspapers and examined whether various health claims were justified based on available scientific evidence. They concluded that 72 per cent of health claims made in UK newspapers were supported by levels of evidence *lower* than what would be thought of as "convincing," and 68 per cent were supported by levels of evidence lower than what would be required even to make those claims "probable."[1] This suggests that we cannot take health claims found in the news at face value—they may or may not be true. In part, this may be an indirect result of the very fact that health is so important to us. News outlets are motivated to feature stories that will get our attention, and they know that stories about food and health are likely to do just that. In some cases, that motivation is liable to outweigh news outlets' motivation to report carefully and critically. It is also worth pointing out that, in some cases, reporters themselves may lack the necessary skills to evaluate claims about health science. Most reporters know no more about health and science than you do. Some news outlets do have dedicated health and science reporters, but even they may have taken on such roles more out of interest than out of any special expertise. The result of this lack of expertise can be reporting that exaggerates the significance of new scientific findings or that fails to ask hard questions about just how much evidence there is in favour of particular points of view.

In evaluating novel health claims made in news stories, you should ask yourself the following questions:

- Are the opinions cited in the story the opinions of people with genuine, relevant expertise?
- Does the news story report a range of views, including the opinions of experts who are skeptical (or who would be likely to be skeptical) of those novel claims?
- Does the reporter make an effort to explain the overall body of evidence with regard to the topic at hand, or does he or she merely report narrowly on what is newest and apparently most exciting?
- Is the reporter experienced at reporting on health and science? Is he or she a "health reporter" or just a reporter who happens to be covering a health story?
- Finally, is the media outlet doing the reporting a credible source of information? Major news outlets like the *Globe and Mail* and the *New York Times* have long reputations for high-quality reporting. That doesn't mean they don't make mistakes, but it does tend to make their health reporting more reliable.

It is also important to read beyond the headlines. In many cases, sensationalistic headlines accompany news stories about scientific findings related to health that are actually pretty bland and unexciting. A headline may trumpet a "PROMISING NEW TREATMENT FOR CANCER!" even though the story below it merely describes a relatively small advance in scientific understanding of one aspect of one type of cancer.

11.1.3 Finding and Evaluating Expert Advice

There are many health issues that we are all perfectly capable of thinking through on our own. Most of us don't need expert advice to understand the health dangers of sharp objects or to know that a diet consisting entirely of candy would be bad for us. But in some cases, understanding what will cause health problems or what will prevent or cure them requires the input of experts. As we learned in Chapter 4, an expert is someone who is more knowledgeable in a particular subject area or field than most others are. When experts tell us that some claim (in their area of expertise) is true, they are more likely to be right than we are, and more likely than amateurs posting opinions online are. Experts on health are more likely to be right because (1) they have access to more information on health than we do, and (2) their experience makes them better at judging health information than we are. They tend to have access to vast quantities of data and are specially trained at evaluating such data to arrive at useful conclusions.

"Be careful of reading health books. You may die of a misprint."

—Mark Twain

As we also noted in Chapter 4, the special insight that experts have means that they can help us evaluate novel claims, and that includes claims about health.

> *If a health claim conflicts with the opinion of a health professional, we have good reason to doubt that claim.*

Food for Thought

Critical Thinking and Health Professionals

How does critical thinking fit into the world of health professionals? Obviously, critical thinking plays an essential role in that world; we rely on health professionals precisely because they are able to critically evaluate health information, including the information relevant to diagnosing and treating our own ailments and illnesses.

It may already have occurred to you that health professionals are *experts* in the sense discussed in Chapter 4. That is true, and it has implications for their ability to assess and understand claims about health and health care. As we noted in Chapter 4, experts have an advantage in that they have access to more information on the subject of health than the average consumer does, and they are better at judging that information than the average consumer is. A well-trained doctor, pharmacist, or nurse, for example, knows a lot about how to evaluate the conclusions reached by particular scientific studies—the announcement of a breakthrough in cancer care or the development of a new vaccine, for example. They also know how to assess the cumulative weight of the various pieces of evidence that are relevant to a particular question, such as whether acupuncture is effective at treating back pain.

But health professionals themselves face challenges in deciding what to believe. After all, the amount of relevant information is truly enormous and growing rapidly; it is probably impossible for any health professional to keep up with all the latest findings in anything but a very narrow specialty. A top cardiologist may know practically everything about recent discoveries related to diseases of the heart, and yet—despite being a doctor—know next to nothing about the latest treatments for diseases of the skin. Expertise is always limited in scope. A nurse or pharmacist will generally not know as much about diagnosing illness as a physician does; a physician or nurse will generally not know as much about the interactions of different drugs as a pharmacist does; and a pharmacist or physician will generally not know as much about measuring and recording a patient's vital signs (pulse, blood pressure, etc.) as a nurse does. Outside of his or her own specialty, a health professional may be more knowledgeable than the *average* person but not a true expert. When health professionals are faced with claims on topics that fall partly or entirely outside their field of practice, they must be cautious: they must not only proportion their belief to the evidence but must also temper their degree of belief according to what they know to be the limits of their own ability to judge that evidence. And, ethically speaking, they are obligated not to overstate their degree of certainty with regard to matters that fall outside their special areas of expertise.

But of course, there are plenty of occasions on which experts disagree with each other with regard to health. There is expert disagreement, for example, about the value of various health-screening tests—such as cholesterol testing, Pap smears, prostate cancer–screening, and so on—at least for particular populations or sub-populations. In such situations, we should follow a further principle, modified from one in Chapter 4, regarding expert disagreement:

> *When health experts disagree about a health claim, we have good reason to doubt it.*

However, with regard to our health we often cannot afford simply to throw up our hands when faced with disagreement among experts. We can *doubt* whether a particular claim is true or not, but that doesn't necessarily help us to make a decision. If a particular health issue is of special significance for us such that we need to arrive at a conclusion, we can ask the following questions to help us navigate through expert disagreement:

1. Are the experts involved all true experts, with relevant expertise? (Make sure the apparent disagreement, in other words, is not a disagreement between health researchers on one hand and concerned celebrities on the other!)
2. Does the issue in question deeply divide the population of relevant experts, or are there just a few experts who disagree with a large majority? In such situations, you still have *reason to doubt*, but if you need to make a decision about your health, you should take expert opinions as bits of evidence, and—as we have said previously—*proportion your belief to the evidence.*
3. You should consider whether expert disagreement is rooted in evidence that is specific to the particular segment of the population of which you are part. For example, there might be expert disagreement concerning the value of cholesterol testing for the general population yet wide expert agreement concerning the importance of such testing for people of *your* age group.

Roy Delgado/CartoonStock

Food choices are among the most frequent, and most important, health choices we make. How might an appeal to tradition affect what we eat?

We should also remember that disagreement among experts often pertains to small details, which can sometimes distract us from broad expert agreement on more important issues. They might disagree, for example, about the exact kind and quantity of exercise that is required to keep us healthy—and news reports might make a big deal out of such disagreement—despite fundamental agreement on the importance of maintaining an active lifestyle.

11.1.4 Stumbling Blocks

Deciding what to believe with regard to staying healthy and responding to illness is an effort that is subject to many of the fallacies discussed in Chapter 5. Think, for example, of the prominence of *appeal to tradition* and *appeal to popularity* in the realm of health. For instance, you may have been told that "everyone knows" that you can catch a cold if you go outside in winter without a scarf. But of course, that's pure appeal to popularity—the fact that it is widely believed doesn't mean it's true. Such appeals are particularly worrisome with regard to health. Health is a complex matter, and there are many subtopics on which the general public simply is not well informed.

"It is easier to change a man's religion than to change his diet."

—Margaret Mead, anthropologist

Similarly, your grandmother may tell you that the best cure for a cold is chicken soup or a "mustard plaster" applied to your chest while you rest in bed. Why? Maybe because that's what her mother told her, and what her mother's mother told her, and so on. But of course, that doesn't make it true. That's just an appeal to tradition. Appeal to tradition is particularly problematic in the realm of health because advances in health science have resulted in enormous changes in what we know about how to stay healthy, why we get sick, and what we should do about

Food for Thought

Hey, Doc! Don't Look for Zebras!

One particular critical thinking challenge faced by health professionals has to do with availability error, which we discussed in Chapter 4. Recall that the availability error has to do with the human mind's tendency, when evaluating various risks, to think first of the most exciting and exotic possibilities. We pointed out that most people think of shark attacks as a relatively common source of danger, despite the fact that shark attacks are actually incredibly rare, because when such attacks do happen they are so gruesome and frightening and therefore easily remembered. As a result, it is easy for us to vividly imagine a shark attack when asked to close our eyes and imagine something dangerous.

When this tendency is observed in physicians, it often takes the form of what is known as the "zebra problem." It is the reason that experienced physicians have come up with this diagnostic rule of thumb, often taught to medical students: "When you hear the beat of hooves, think 'horse,' not 'zebra.'" In other words, when diagnosing a patient, don't think *first* of the most exotic possible explanation for the patient's symptoms—begin instead with the most common and likely possibilities. For instance, when a patient has a rash, don't think first of rare and exotic diseases like Legionnaires' disease or the bubonic plague! Work first to rule out simple, commonplace causes like chicken pox and poison ivy. That is also very likely to be good advice for the average individual: your headache at the end of a long and stressful day is probably not an indication that you've got a brain tumour.

it when we do. For centuries, people believed that a healthy diet had to include meat, and plenty of it. Today there is growing evidence that meat should play a relatively small role in our diets, and many experts recommend a vegetarian or even vegan diet. Appealing to tradition, here, does not serve us well! The same goes for treating illness. The fact that a particular treatment—some mixture of herbs, for example—was used "for hundreds of years" within a particular culture doesn't prove that this treatment was effective; it merely proves that it was popular and perhaps that the people using it simply had no alternatives that were superior.

It is also worth noting how evaluating health claims often amounts to a process very much like the one we described in Chapter 10 for judging scientific theories. For example, do Wi-Fi signals (radiation given off by wireless internet) cause health problems? In determining whether that theory is credible, we ought to ask whether that theory is testable and fruitful, whether it is broad in scope, whether it

Critical Thinking and the Media

Pharmaceutical Advertising without Information

As we have emphasized throughout this textbook, good decision-making requires good information. But good information isn't always easy to get.

In the realm of advertising pharmaceuticals, experts and regulators make a distinction between over-the-counter (OTC) drugs and prescription drugs that must be prescribed by a physician in order for you to access them.

That distinction affects the rules about advertising. With regard to prescription pharmaceuticals, experts and regulators also make a distinction between efforts by drug companies to advertise to physicians and efforts to advertise directly to consumers. In Canada, direct-to-consumer advertising of prescription pharmaceuticals is tightly regulated. The thinking is that regular consumers don't have the expertise to evaluate manufacturer claims about prescription pharmaceuticals—that, after all, is precisely why they are prescription pharmaceuticals. Only someone with the relevant expertise can give you access.

You may be able to think of lots of commercials or other ads you've seen for prescription drugs. Quite likely you saw those on American TV shows or on international websites, not on Canadian TV or in Canadian magazines. Under Canada's Food and Drug Act, direct-to-consumer advertising is forbidden with regard to drugs intended "as a treatment, preventative or cure" of most major diseases or symptoms (the full list of which is included in Appendix A of the Act). However, the Food and Drug Act specifically permits direct-to-consumer ads that do not "make any representation other than with respect to the brand name, the proper name, the common name and the price and quantity of the drug."[2]

The net effect is that direct-to-consumer advertising of prescription drugs is in effect permitted as long as no information is given about most of the things you might care about, namely what the drug is for, its side effects, and so on.

What kinds of persuasive strategies are likely to show up in direct-to-consumer drug ads in Canada, given this special permission? What critical thinking skills do you think would be relevant to effectively interpreting such ads?

is simple, and whether it is conservative. Most so-called "alternative medicines" do very badly when evaluated in this way. Some of them fail the test of conservatism because they assume the existence of strange flows of "energy" through the human body, energy of a kind not known to modern physics and not detectable by scientific equipment. Others rest on theories that turn out not to be very broad in scope. Homeopathy, for example, is a form of alternative therapy that assumes that water has a "memory" of every molecule it ever came in contact with, and so medicines diluted beyond the point at which there is any active ingredient left can, supposedly, still have an effect on our bodies. Yet homeopaths assert that this effect only becomes relevant during the manufacturing process for homeopathic remedies: it supposedly has no implications whatsoever for the water we drink! (For more about homeopathy, see essay 8, "The Unrepentant Homeopath," in Appendix A.)

Weird theories of all kinds are especially common with regard to health. And so it is particularly important to avoid the temptation, noted in Chapter 10, to leap to weird theories in the absence of evidence. In the face of unusual experiences, our "background knowledge" may let us down, and we may be tempted to jump to unwarranted conclusions. If you are not accustomed to getting headaches, the sudden onset of a headache may cause you to assume the worst: maybe it's a brain tumour! The fact that you can't happen to think of a more mundane explanation for your headache doesn't imply that no such explanation exists.

11.2 Thinking Critically about the Law

Nowhere is critical thinking more essential than in the application of law. The law represents the strongest rules of behaviour in any society, rules typically enforced by means of the full power and authority of government. When individuals are found to have violated the law, they may be subject to substantial fines or imprisonment. Taking away an individual's freedom is a very serious matter and should be done only in full light of the facts, evaluated according to the strictest possible standards of critical thinking.

Critical thinking is relevant to many aspects of the law. Members of Parliament and their staff must think critically about the need for, and wording of, new legislation if they are to make sure that new laws are both truly necessary and clearly worded. Police officers must use critical thinking skills in applying the law. For example, police officers must apply the law without the kind of bias that results from *hasty generalization* about people in particular racial or socioeconomic categories. Citizens, too, must use their critical thinking skills with regard to the law. If the law forbids "vehicles" in the park, does that include *toy* vehicles? Does it include wheelchairs?

In this section, however, we will focus on the application of critical thinking skills to deliberations in the courtroom. That is, we will focus on the need for critical thinking skills on the part of judges, lawyers, and members of juries in criminal proceedings.

Critical thinking is particularly important in a court of law for a couple of reasons. The first reason has to do with the importance of such proceedings: as noted above, legal proceedings can result in individuals being thrown in jail for long periods, which means losing their freedom along with the ability to have regular contact with friends and family. The second reason has to do with the adversarial nature of our legal system. Under the current system, any time someone is charged with a crime, the court is faced with the challenge of evaluating two competing points of view. On one side is the Crown attorney, representing the government. His or her job is to attempt to convince the court that the accused is guilty and ought to be punished. On the other side are the accused and his or her defence counsel. The defence counsel's job is to attempt to convince the court that the accused is innocent, has been wrongly charged, and ought to be set free. Neither side is responsible for presenting a *balanced* view of the evidence. It is the job of the Crown to argue vigorously for a guilty verdict, just as it is the defence counsel's job to argue zealously for a finding of innocence. And in most cases, the truth of the matter will not be obvious. The court must hear the evidence, weigh it carefully, and reach a verdict. In some circumstances, that task falls to a judge, and in other circumstances it falls to a jury of 12 regular citizens. Either way, it is a task that requires the most serious attention to the demands of critical thinking. The conclusion reached must be supported by the best possible argument.

Everyday Problems and Decisions

Jury Duty

One of the most important decisions any citizen can make, or help to make, is the decision whether to send a fellow citizen to jail. As a member of a jury in a criminal trial, you are part of a group of 12 citizens making just such a decision.

If you serve on a jury in such a case, what factors should you take into consideration? Most generally, a juror's job is to take into consideration all information presented during the trial and to formulate a conclusion about the accused person's guilt or innocence. And, importantly, that is *all* that should influence a juror. It is a juror's duty to do his or her best not to be influenced by other factors, such as prejudices or biases. A juror needs to use good judgment and common sense to evaluate the evidence presented. Of course, jurors are not experts in the law. (In fact, lawyers are not eligible to serve as jurors in Canada.)

The relevant legal expertise is provided by the two lawyers (the Crown prosecutor and defence counsel) and by the judge. It is the task of the prosecutor and defence counsel to present evidence and to explain to the jury what they take to be the key facts of the case and key aspects of the relevant laws. They will naturally do so in a way that is intended to persuade jurors. The prosecutor will try to convince the jury that the defendant is guilty, and the defendant's lawyer will try to convince the jury that the defendant is innocent—or, at least, that the prosecutor has not provided enough evidence to prove guilt. After all evidence is presented, the judge will instruct the jury, in an impartial way, on what the relevant laws say, what the relevant standards of proof are, and what factors they must—and must not—take into consideration.

"My client pleads not guilty on the grounds that Saturn was transiting his natal Pluto at the time of the incident."

How do courts use critical thinking skills to assess whether a particular explanation for the available evidence makes sense or not?

11.2.1 Key Skills

Of all the critical thinking skills needed in a court of law, the most fundamental is a good command of the argument type referred to in Chapter 9 as "inference to the best explanation." Recall that inference to the best explanation is a form of inductive argument in which the arguer gives reason for believing one explanation for a set of facts rather than another. And that, of course, is precisely what goes on in a court of law. In a criminal trial, various kinds of evidence are presented to the court: a body was found; the accused, Mr Levin, was found near the scene with blood on his hands; an eyewitness testifies to having seen Mr Levin arguing with the victim just a few hours earlier; DNA evidence suggests the involvement of some third party; and so on. After such evidence is presented, each lawyer—the Crown attorney and the defence counsel—will provide a story, an account of the events of the day that they will argue constitutes a good explanation for that evidence, taken as a whole. And the court—the judge or the jury—must evaluate those competing explanations to determine which one is best.

Recall from Chapter 9 that all instances of inference to the best explanation follow this pattern:

> Phenomenon Q.
> E provides the best explanation for Q.
> Therefore, it is probable that E is true.

In a criminal trial, "Phenomenon Q" would be evidence related to the crime in question—the murder, the theft, or whatever. "E" would be one or another of the explanations offered by the competing lawyers—either that the defendant committed the crime or she did not. The middle premise, then, would be the claim that E provides the best explanation for the evidence at hand. And the conclusion of the argument would be either that the defendant did commit the crime or that the defendant did not commit the crime.

In most instances of inference to the best explanation, we say that the argument that presents the best explanation is inductively strong. But in a criminal trial, we are looking not just for a *strong* argument regarding whether the accused is guilty or innocent but for a truly *compelling* argument. During criminal proceedings, the burden of proof (a notion discussed in Chapter 5) rests squarely upon the prosecution. The accused, in the words of a phrase you've no doubt heard before, is "innocent until proven guilty" and in order to be punished must be found "guilty beyond a reasonable doubt." The reason for this high standard is clear. First, as noted above, the stakes in criminal trials are often very high. Second, our legal system is rooted in the principle that it is a heinous wrong to convict someone who is in fact innocent and that if errors are to be made, it is much better that they be made in favour of the defendant. As the eighteenth-century English judge William Blackstone famously put it, it is "better that 10 guilty persons escape than that one innocent suffer." Finally, note that the individual accused generally faces significant disadvantages during the legal process. They are, after all, just one person with one lawyer, being prosecuted by a Crown attorney who is backed, in principle, by the very considerable resources of the entire government. The government, it is believed, has so many obvious advantages that the least we can do is ask it (as represented by the Crown prosecutor) to bear the burden of proof.

Finally, it is worth noting that many aspects of legal reasoning involve categorical logic of the kind we studied in Chapter 6. In determining whether a person violated the law, we are essentially determining whether his or her actions fall into a particular category of prohibited behaviours. Look, for example, at the start of Section 221 of the Criminal Code of Canada, the section dealing with homicide:

> *A person commits homicide when, directly or indirectly, by any means, he causes the death of a human being.*

Though it may not look like it, this is a categorical statement—specifically, a universal affirmative statement. If we reword it to make it look more like a categorical statement (while retaining its meaning) it would look like this:

> *All persons who directly or indirectly cause the death of a human being are persons who have committed homicide.*

An argument rooted in that section of the Criminal Code might look like this:

> Mr Levin indirectly caused the death of a human being. According to the Criminal Code, anyone who causes the death of a human being, even indirectly, is guilty of homicide. So Levin must be found guilty of homicide.

Put into standard form, that argument might look like this:

> P1. All persons who are Mr Levin are persons who directly or indirectly caused the death of a human being.
>
> P2. All persons who directly or indirectly cause the death of a human being are persons who have committed homicide.

C. Therefore, all persons who are Mr Levin are persons who committed homicide.

Simplifying, this becomes:

All *S* are *M*.
All *M* are *P*.
Therefore, all *S* are *P*.

And we can easily demonstrate, using a Venn diagram, that this is a valid argument. The key problem for the court to decide, of course, is whether the key premise—premise 1—is in fact true! That is, the court needs to decide whether the argument is *sound*.

The way convicted criminals are sentenced is also a matter of categorical logic. For example, according to Section 47 of the Criminal Code of Canada:

> *Every one who commits high treason is guilty of an indictable offence and shall be sentenced to imprisonment for life.*

This, too, is a categorical claim of the universal affirmative variety, one that would serve as the foundation for a categorical argument regarding the appropriate punishment for a particular individual.

11.2.2 Stumbling Blocks

Most fundamental among the critical thinking challenges faced in modern courts of law is the difficulty implied by the need to evaluate competing theories—the one offered by the Crown and the one offered by the defence—in light of what may be an absolutely overwhelming quantity of evidence. But we can also identify a number of other, more specific, challenges.

Judges and juries must be on guard against the effect of many of the argumentative fallacies discussed in Chapter 5. Prosecutors, for example, may offer juries a *false dilemma*: "You must either convict the accused or let a vicious killer go free!" Prosecutors might also be tempted to make *ad hominem* arguments. If they can make the accused seem like a bad person, or even simply unlikeable, this may make it easier for a jury to believe that they have committed the specific crime of which they are accused. But, strictly speaking, the character of the accused is not relevant. People with histories of wrongdoing are sometimes wrongly accused, and people of good character do, unfortunately, sometimes commit crimes. So character is really beside the point; what matters is whether the facts about the present case support the conclusion that the accused actually committed the crime in question. Jurors may also be tempted to *beg the question* against the accused. If the accused weren't guilty, they might wonder, why would he be accused of this vicious crime? After all, only criminals get arrested, right? But that, of course, is a premise that assumes an answer to the very question we are trying to answer—namely, whether the accused should be considered a criminal or not. The accused,

Food for Thought

Public Law, Private Law, and Burden of Proof

In Chapter 5, we learned that burden of proof is the weight of evidence or argument required of one side in a debate or disagreement. And we said that, typically, the burden of proof rests on the side that makes a positive claim—that is, the person asserting that something exists or is the case rather than the person asserting that something does not exist or is not the case.

Courts of law take a very special approach to the notion of burden of proof, and the way that notion is treated depends in important ways on the kind of court case in question. The Canadian system (and other similar systems) makes a distinction between *public law* (which governs the relationship between individuals and society as a whole) and *private law* (which governs the relationship between particular individuals). Criminal law is an example of public law: when someone is thought to have committed a criminal offence, they are said to have violated *society's* rules, and it is society as a whole—via police and Crown prosecutors—that is expected to take action. Private law (also known as civil law) is about settling disputes between individuals, such as when one person sues another for having harmed their property. In such cases, it is up to the person who claims to have been harmed to hire a lawyer and initiate legal action.

These two branches of law assign the burden of proof quite differently. In a criminal case, the burden of proof lies almost entirely with the prosecution. This is why the accused is considered "innocent until proven guilty," and will be *declared* guilty only if the prosecution proves its case "beyond a reasonable doubt." It is relatively easy to see why it is desirable for the burden of proof to be assigned this way: the possible outcome for the defendant is very severe, and prosecutors have at their disposal the vast resources of the government. In such circumstances, it is reasonable for the court to be extremely careful to give the defendant the benefit of the doubt. Civil cases, on the other hand, are quite different. Civil cases are assumed to be matters of conflict between two individuals, who are assumed for this purpose to be roughly equal in power. In such circumstances, there's no particular reason for the court to give any special consideration to one side. Instead, courts decide such cases based on "the balance of probabilities." This means that, in order to win, one side must convince the court that it is *more likely than not* that their version of the facts is more probable—more likely true—than the other side's version.

for their part, might attempt an *appeal to emotion*: "Please don't convict me because I've got a family to support!" The judge and jury must of course do their best to avoid being influenced by such considerations; their job is strictly to judge the evidence, to believe one theory or the other in proportion to the evidence, and to return the verdict that fits best.

In legal contexts, we must also beware of the risks of faulty conditional reasoning. Look, for instance, at this imaginary (but not unlikely) bit of legal reasoning:

> Ladies and gentlemen of the jury, it is clear what has happened here. If Mr Alkoby committed this crime, we would surely find his fingerprints on the knife that killed Ms Swansburg. And his fingerprints were indeed found on that weapon! So it is clear that Mr Alkoby committed this gruesome crime.

This may sound like a compelling argument! But notice the argument's logical structure: it is a piece of propositional logic—more specifically, a conditional argument of a particular kind, first discussed in Chapter 3. If you look carefully, you'll see that this is an example of *affirming the consequent*, which we know is always invalid. Of course, the fact that the defendant's fingerprints were found on the murder weapon is not irrelevant. At the very least, that is likely to be an important part of a strong inductive argument for the defendant's guilt. But here, even more essentially than in other instances, we must avoid being drawn in by the deductive style of the prosecutor's argument, which tends to suggest to our mind that the argument is much stronger than it actually is. The prosecutor's wording suggests certainty, while all his logic can provide is probability.

Finally, criminal courts must also be wary of the limits of the reliability of eyewitness testimony. An eyewitness is someone who reports, in court, things he or she claims to know from personal experience. In Chapter 4, we learned about the worrisome effect of things like impairment and expectation on the reliability of personal experience. And, according to Toronto defence lawyer Jaki Freeman, Canadian courts have long been aware of these problems:

> For years, Canadian courts have been aware that eyewitness evidence is remarkably frail and fraught with problems. Such evidence has been identified as a major source of wrongful convictions in Canada. A number of factors influence the accuracy of an identification of a suspect by a witness, such as whether the suspect is known or a stranger to the witness, the circumstances surrounding the contact between the suspect and the witness, the individual make-up of the witness, and the nature and methods used during any pre-trial identification of the suspect. There are multiple reasons for this frailty including that the initial contact between witness and suspect is often made under traumatic and unexpected circumstances and when the observation conditions are not ideal. In addition to the factors present at the time of the observations and the personal characteristics of the observing witness, postevent identification procedures can influence the identification of a particular person. Pre-trial identification procedures may be flawed and designed—intentionally or unintentionally—to influence the witness so that a particular suspect is identified.[3]

In other words, courts of law do and should worry—for many of the same reasons discussed in Chapter 4—about relying on personal experience in the form of eyewitness testimony.

The adversarial nature of our legal system presents the opportunity for a very practical application of the tools of critical thinking. As we have learned, in an adversarial legal system, each side is expected to present their case in court. In a criminal case, the Crown prosecutor presents their argument for the conclusion that the accused is guilty and should be punished. And the defence counsel presents their argument for the conclusion that the accused is innocent and should be set free. As the trial proceeds, each side has an opportunity not just to build their own arguments, but to examine and respond to the other side's arguments. In doing so, they have a chance to use many of the critical skills discussed in this textbook. They will likely be asking questions like these:

- Has the other side engaged in any fallacious reasoning, such as *post hoc* reasoning?
- Are they attempting to make use of cognitive biases to sway the judge or jury?
- Does the "expert" witness they put on the stand really have sufficient expertise on the issue at hand?
- Most generally, does their conclusion really follow from the premises they have presented?

11.3 Thinking Critically about Ethics

Finally, we turn to the topic of ethics. Some will be surprised at the very idea of applying critical thinking skills to the realm of ethics. After all, ethics is about what is right and wrong from a moral point of view, and isn't that a personal matter? Don't we all have—and aren't we all entitled to—our own views on that? Shouldn't we respect each other's opinions on ethics rather than adopting a critical attitude?

"In matters of conscience, the law of the majority has no place."

—Mahatma Gandhi

There is, of course, something right in this: we ought to adopt a respectful attitude to other *people* and take their points of view and their values seriously. But this doesn't imply an exception to the general need to think critically. We don't, after all, want to commit to the *subjectivist fallacy* discussed in Chapter 2. Recall that subjective *relativism* is the idea that truth depends on what someone happens to believe—that believing something is enough to make it true. But that view is no more credible with regard to ethics than it is with regard to other sorts of claims. It just doesn't make sense to think, as subjective relativism implies, that none of us is ever wrong about anything related to ethics. We are all fallible—capable of making mistakes—and that's as true with regard to ethics as it is with regard to anything else. Our claims about ethics deserve to be backed up by good arguments. And when confronted with new ethical claims, we need to be able to evaluate critically the arguments offered in support of those claims. If the arguments offered are not good ones, then the ethical claims presented should be doubted.

11.3.1 Key Skills

Ethics is the critical, structured examination of how we ought to behave when our behaviour affects others. The most fundamental critical thinking skill when it comes to ethics is perhaps the very basic ability, learned in Chapter 3 of this book,

ethics
The critical, structured examination of how we ought to behave when our behaviour affects others.

Brigida_Soriano/iStockphoto

With regard to ethics, Socrates (469–399 BCE), in Plato's *Republic*, noted that "We are discussing no small matter, here, but how we ought to live." What fundamental critical thinking skill leads to ethical decision-making?

to identify the fundamental building blocks out of which any argument, including any ethical argument, is constructed. Ethical claims are often put forward with considerable passion, and so a systematic approach can help us to move past emotion to look carefully at the structure of an ethical argument.

As with other sorts of arguments, the basic building blocks of ethical arguments are claims or statements. Ethical claims come in many forms. They may be claims about specific actions by specific people—"It was wrong of Janice to lie to Richard"—or they may be generalizations about entire categories of behaviour—"It is wrong to tell lies." Claims about how we ought to behave may take the form of claims about particular types of actions, the outcomes of our choices, or the kinds of people we should be. Such claims answer questions regarding what kinds of behaviour are right and what kinds are wrong and about what kinds of outcomes and what kinds of character traits are good or bad. Consider the following examples of ethical claims:

- Serena should keep her promise to you.
- It is wrong to treat James so harshly.
- Racism is immoral.
- We ought to protect Liu from the angry mob.
- My father is a good man.

Ethical claims can be differentiated from plain descriptive claims, such as the following:

- Serena did not keep her promise to you.
- James is going to be fired.
- Many people think racism is immoral.
- Liu was protected from the angry mob.
- My father tried to be a good man.

Each of these statements merely describes some element of the (human) world, but doesn't attempt to tell us what we should think or do about it. They express no opinion about right or wrong, good or bad. They simply state what happened, what is happening, or what will happen.

Most ethical arguments in fact feature some combination of ethical and descriptive claims. In one standard kind of ethical argument, the arguer puts forward a general ethical principle of some sort, then describes some behaviour to which that principle applies, and then concludes that the behaviour is either right or wrong. For example:

> Ethical Premise: It is unethical to take other people's belongings without their permission.
> Descriptive Premise: You borrowed my sweater without my permission.
> Ethical Conclusion: You did something unethical.

Note first that this argument has two premises. One is about ethics, and one is merely descriptive—it describes the facts of the case. This is actually an important thing to note about ethical arguments. Every ethical argument, once its premises are made explicit, *must* contain at least one ethical premise and at least one descriptive premise. Without at least one descriptive premise, we don't know the facts of the case under consideration; without an ethical premise, the argument has no ethical or moral foundation at all. As the eighteenth-century philosopher David Hume pointed out, mere facts alone cannot support an ethical conclusion. Or to put it another way, descriptive premises tell you only how the world *is*; an ethical conclusion tells you how the world *should be*. Logic won't take you from the former to the latter without an ethical premise to help.

What does spelling out the premises and conclusions of an ethical argument accomplish? For one thing, we achieve a certain amount of clarity just by putting it all there in black and white. Keep in mind that in real conversation, ethical arguments will often have pieces missing. In many instances, arguers simply leave out ethical premises that they assume are widely shared and that they think are too obvious to state. Why would you bother saying "lying is bad" when pretty much everyone agrees that lying is bad? By making those pieces explicit, however, we can examine them carefully to see if they really are plausible, or whether they might in some circumstances be open to question.

Making the parts of an ethical argument explicit can also help us to see its structure, the way its premises work to attempt to support its conclusion. Notice, for example, that the two premises in the argument above need each other. The fact that I took your sweater wouldn't prove that I had done something wrong, if taking people's stuff were not wrong. And, the fact that taking people's stuff is wrong wouldn't prove *I* had done something wrong, if it weren't for the fact that I took your sweater. Those premises are, in other words, *dependent premises*, something we learned about in Chapter 3. That means that if either premise fails to be acceptable, then the entire argument falls apart.

Notice also that the argument above is made up entirely of categorical claims—or, at least, claims that can be reworded slightly to make them into categorical claims. Put in categorical terms, that argument might look like this:

> All instances in which you took my sweater are instances of taking other people's belongings without their permission.

All instances of taking other people's belongings without their permission are unethical actions.

Therefore, all instances in which you took my sweater are unethical actions.

Putting it this way is somewhat awkward, but it accurately reflects the meaning of the original argument. Further, we can go ahead and put that argument into standard form, as follows:

All *S* are *M*.
All *M* are *P*.
Therefore, all *S* are *P*.

And of course, once we see the argument in this form, we can evaluate it as we would any other categorical syllogism, for example, by constructing a Venn diagram.

Categorical arguments of this sort are very common. In such an argument, the arguer tries to fit a particular action into a category of actions generally acknowledged to be either ethical (e.g., keeping promises) or unethical (e.g., stealing). This also happens to be a kind of syllogism that is a valid argument. (Check for yourself and see!) This means that, if presented with such an argument, you will already know that the logic is solid, and so you can proceed directly to evaluating the premises to determine if they are reasonable. Did the person in question really take the sweater without permission? Is it really true that taking things without the owner's permission is always unethical? Are there exceptions? Do the exceptions apply to this case?

Next, consider the following ethical argument:

Ethical Premise: If Earl was a good man, he would take care of his family.
Descriptive Premise: Earl has not taken care of his family.
Ethical Conclusion: Earl is not a good man.

Notice the structure of this argument. You might begin by noting that the first premise—the ethical premise—is a *conditional* statement, a statement with an "if–then" structure. This suggests that the argument here can be evaluated using the tools of propositional logic, as discussed in Chapter 7. So we could, in principle, construct a truth table to evaluate this argument. But there's no need for that in this particular case. If you look closely, you'll see that the preceding argument is an instance of *denying the consequent*, an argument structure that is always *valid*.

But compare that to this argument:

Ethical Premise: If you're a good person, you keep your promises.
Descriptive Premise: You keep your promises.
Ethical Conclusion: So you're a good person.

Notice that, again, we have a conditional argument, in this case an instance of *affirming the consequent*. And so, again, there's no need for a truth table: you already know that arguments that affirm the consequent are always invalid.

So much for the logical structure of ethical arguments. How can we tell whether the premises of an ethical argument are acceptable? Well, to begin, we noted above that every ethical argument will have at least one descriptive premise, and we can evaluate that just as we would evaluate the claims made in any other kind of argument. (For more on that, see Chapter 4.) But what about ethical premises? The evaluation of ethical claims, and the standards to which ethical claims should be subjected, is a vast topic, one that is the subject of extensive philosophical debates. We cannot delve into those debates in any detail here, but we will provide just a couple of hints at how an assessment of ethical premises might begin.

First, we can apply the ethical component of what we referred to in Chapter 4 as our *background information*—that huge collection of very well-supported beliefs that we all rely on to inform our actions and choices. That background information includes not just descriptions but also ethical rules and standards. The fact that it is generally wrong to lie or to intentionally hurt people is so well established that for most purposes it is unreasonable to doubt it. An argument that starts there is off to a good start.

Another tactic we can apply is to look for certain structural features that experts in ethics generally think ethical claims ought to have. One such feature is universality. An ethical starting point ought to be one that could apply to all persons in the relevant circumstances. For example, "It is wrong to lie" is universal in the relevant sense. It doesn't claim to apply to just one or a few people—by default, it applies to everyone. (In fact, we could reasonably, though awkwardly, reword that claim as a *universal affirmative* categorical statement: "All persons are persons who should not lie.") A claim that singles out a particular individual for special treatment is usually not acceptable as a foundation for an ethical argument. We can, of course, arrive at *conclusions* that are about specific individuals, but those conclusions must be reached as the result of an argument rooted in an ethical premise that is universal in its scope.

Chris Wildt/CartoonStock

"What would my mom say?" might not always be a reliable ethical guide, but if you suspect your mother or father (or someone else you respect) would not approve, then that is at least reason to pause and think it through.

Another key feature to look for in ethical claims is consistency. This means that our ethical judgments should be the same for situations that have the same features. If someone proposes an ethical rule for one situation, it ought to apply also in other, relevantly similar, situations. For example, if an office worker says "taking office supplies home is morally justified," we are justified in asking whether that person thinks that stealing is justified in other situations too. (Note that our skill at evaluating *analogies* is going to come in handy here.) To think that a particular kind of behaviour is permissible in one situation but not in situations that share the relevant characteristics is inconsistent. An ethical premise that demonstrates inconsistency need not be taken very seriously.

Finally, we can gain some confidence in specific ethical premises if they are drawn from one or more of the great traditions of philosophical ethics. The Western philosophical tradition (the tradition in which the authors of this text were trained) stretches back more than 2000 years, and during that time philosophers have proposed and debated an enormous number of ethical theories claiming to sum up everything that needs to be said about the topic. Today, no one theory stands out as having won that grand intellectual struggle. But a few contenders have stood the test of time and continue to be defended by at least a respectable subset of philosophers. We cannot discuss these theories in any detail here, but for our purposes it will be enough to point out that each of these theories represents a tradition of moral thinking that has stood the test of time. Each of them proposes a respectable set of principles or ethical reasons that can serve as premises for ethical arguments.

These three grand traditions of ethics are as follows:

argument from consequences
An ethical argument that takes as a starting point the idea that our most fundamental ethical obligation is to produce certain kinds of outcomes.

- **Argument from consequences**. Arguments rooted in this tradition take as a starting point the idea that our most fundamental ethical obligation is to produce certain kinds of outcomes. In other words, in making ethical choices, it is the expected outcomes or consequences of our behaviour that matters. Arguments rooted in an appeal to consequences will generally point out that certain actions are likely to make people better off, to prevent harm, to make people happy, and so on. In philosophical terms, this tradition is known as *consequentialism*, and the most respected form of consequentialism is known as *utilitarianism*. This tradition is most famously represented by the English philosopher John Stuart Mill (1806–1873).

argument from rights and duties
An ethical argument that begins with the notion that there are certain kinds of actions that we must always do or always avoid doing.

- **Argument from rights and duties**. Arguments grounded in this tradition focus not on outcomes but on performing or avoiding certain kinds of actions. This tradition holds that there are certain actions that we must always avoid doing (like killing innocent persons) and certain actions that it is our duty always to do (such as, perhaps, keeping promises or telling the truth). It is from this tradition that we get the notion of human rights—the idea that humans are to be respected, and that therefore there are certain ways they must be treated. Philosophically, this tradition is referred to as *deontology* and is most famously associated with the work of the German philosopher Immanuel Kant (1724–1804).

- **Argument from character.** Arguments rooted in this tradition start from the assumption that what really matters, ethically, is character. That is, the key is not so much the individual choices we make on particular occasions, but the kinds of people we show ourselves to be through our actions. Arguments of this kind will tend to focus on whether specific behaviours—or more likely, patterns of behaviour—demonstrate one or another of various desirable traits of character, such as honesty, bravery, and compassion, and whether those behaviours avoid such undesirable character traits as greed, dishonesty, and spitefulness. To philosophers, this tradition is known as *virtue theory* and is associated historically with the highly influential work of the ancient Greek philosopher Aristotle (384–322 BCE).

argument from character
An ethical argument that proceeds from the assumption that what really matters ethically is character rather than the nature or outcome of particular actions.

In contrast, there are ethical points of view that have not stood the test of time. These include ethical egoism (the theory that the only important ethical reason is self-interest) and ethical relativism (the theory that all that matters is the moral beliefs of your own society). Any ethical argument that begins with such premises is on very rocky ground.

Finally, it is worth pointing out that premises rooted in these three different ethical traditions sometimes point to quite different conclusions. Arguments from rights and duties, for example, are often seen as providing a counterweight to reasoning that is rooted entirely in argument from consequences. It is easy to imagine a situation in which a police officer, for example, believes she could do some good—achieve some ethically good outcome—by framing an innocent man. Such behaviour would of course violate the innocent man's rights. Unfortunately, when ethical premises from different ethical traditions conflict, there is no formula for settling the debate. We will generally need to apportion our belief according to the available evidence, and the relevant evidence, here, consists not just of facts but of values and principles too.

11.3.2 Stumbling Blocks

We have already noted that the subjectivist fallacy is perhaps the greatest barrier to clear thinking about ethics. If we are even to begin to apply the tools of critical thinking to various ethical claims, we must first get past the unhelpful notion that ethics is all just a matter of personal opinion.

But a number of other fallacies are likewise common in ethical arguments. Among the most common, perhaps, is the appeal to popularity. Appeal to popularity, as we learned in Chapter 5, occurs when we cite the popularity of some idea—the sheer number of people who believe it—as evidence that it must be true. Historically, a kind of appeal to popularity was likely responsible for the perpetuation of injustices against women, minority groups, and members of the LGBTQ community. Prior to 1919, the year when Canadian women were granted the right to vote, it was sometimes argued that "everyone knows" that women have no ability to

Food for Thought

Ought Implies Can

Philosophers are fond of pointing out that "ought implies can." This is a brief way of saying that whenever someone says that they *ought to* do something, this logically implies that they *can* do it. That is, to believe that someone ethically should do something, you must first believe that doing it is physically possible.

This can be explained in terms of propositional logic. The claim that "ought implies can" can be expressed more clearly if we express it as a conditional claim:

"If I ought to do something, then it is possible to do it."

It can then be represented as follows:

$a \rightarrow b$

Since the claim that "ought implies can" is understood as a claim about ethics, it is not essentially a claim about what it is possible to do. That is, the conditional $a \rightarrow b$ is not the starting point for an argument to the effect that a (whatever b stands for) is in fact possible. It is not often that an ethical claim (about what you are obligated to do) is more certain than a factual claim (about what is possible). So it's more useful, in practice, to argue in the other direction and to think of the claim "ought implies can" as a starting point for figuring out which things you are *obligated* to do. It is typically used in arguments that point out that because a certain behaviour is not possible, the individual is not ethically required to do it.

Such an argument will take this form:

$a \rightarrow b$

$\sim b$

$\therefore \sim a$

This is a valid deductive argument. We could easily prove this by constructing a truth table. But it's simpler still to point out that this is an instance of *denying the consequent*, an argument form that is always valid.

In many cases, arguments of this form provide very good, common-sense advice. Imagine that a = "Ms O'Neill ought to refrain from causing any pollution at all" and that b = "Ms O'Neill can refrain from causing any pollution at all." The first premise above ($a \rightarrow b$), plus the second premise, which is the negation of b (namely "It's not the case that Ms O'Neill can refrain from causing any pollution at all"), lead deductively to the conclusion that Ms O'Neill is not obligated to avoid causing any pollution at all. This of course leaves open the possibility that it would be good of her to *reduce* pollution; it merely makes clear that—because ought implies can—it's not true that she ought to avoid causing all pollution altogether.

understand politics and would just vote for whichever candidate was the most handsome! Of course, critical thinkers recognize that the fact that many people "know" (or rather *believe*) something doesn't make it true. It's also worth pointing out that sometimes appeal to popularity is combined with appeal to tradition: an arguer may say that "everyone knows" that Group X isn't worthy of being treated equally, and that "that's the way it has always been." A critical approach to ethics is dedicated to pointing out such fallacies and to questioning their factual and ethical basis.

Another common fallacy found in arguments concerning ethics is the straw man fallacy. Recall that in a straw man, the arguer presents a distorted, weakened, or oversimplified version of someone's position so that it can be more easily attacked or refuted. Occurrences of the straw man fallacy happen very easily when discussing ethics. It is relatively easy to produce cartoonish versions of someone else's subtle ethical claims or arguments. If Mark argues that companies in developing nations might be justified in not purchasing expensive safety equipment, an opponent might express horror at Mark's belief that "workers' lives have no value." And that criticism, of course, would be off-target: Mark may well value such workers' lives very highly, but also believe that trade-offs can reasonably be made between safety and wages. Similarly, if Josephine argues, out of concern for the effects of climate change, that Canada ought to consider reducing industrial greenhouse gas emissions, an opponent might be tempted to make her look foolish by accusing her of wanting to shut down Canada's industrial sector altogether, thereby wrecking our economy—which, of course, is not likely what Josephine is arguing for at all.

Finally, we must also be on guard for instances of the slippery slope fallacy when discussing ethics. Recall that a slippery slope involves arguing, without good reason, that taking some particular step will inevitably lead to some further, highly undesirable step. Such arguments are common in ethics precisely because discussions of ethics are so often focused on what we should or should not do—the steps we should or should not take. Note also that ethics is generally about rules of behaviour, about drawing lines between acceptable and unacceptable actions. So it is often tempting for us to worry that some action that is on *this* side of the line separating right from wrong is going to lead to some other action that is on *the other* side of that line, especially if we don't look carefully at what the relevant differences might be between the two actions. Slippery slope arguments sometimes arise in discussions of medical assistance in dying, for example. Advocates might argue that, under some circumstances, it could be reasonable for an individual with a serious, incurable illness to ask a physician for help in dying, and it could be reasonable for a physician to agree to help. Critics of such a view may suggest that if we allow physicians to help the seriously ill to commit suicide, there's nothing to stop physicians from deciding on their own to start killing patients. "Next thing you know," the critic may conclude, "no one will be safe in a hospital." But of course, that doesn't obviously follow. Supporters of medical assistance in dying typically only argue for the availability of a fully voluntary process. They also often recommend safeguards, such as the participation of an entire committee of physicians and a requirement that the patient's desire to die be documented as persisting over a number of weeks. The slope from physician-assisted suicide to rampant murder by doctors, in other words, is not necessarily so slippery!

As with other kinds of arguments, we must recall that the fact that someone has offered a fallacious argument for a particular ethical point of view doesn't mean that their view is incorrect. All it means is that the argument *as presented* does not work. As critical thinkers, we recognize that we can, and should, do better.

Summary

Health care, law, and ethics are among the most important topics that any of us deals with in our daily lives. Clear thinking about health is among our greatest challenges. Health is universally agreed upon as fundamental to a good life, an essential precondition to the enjoyment of whatever particular projects and pastimes bring us joy. Clear thinking in courts of law is essential to making sure that justice is served—that the guilty are punished and the innocent are not. And clear thinking about ethics is the foundation of a morally good life. The very best—that is, the most reliable—thinking in health care, in law, and in ethics relies heavily on the tools of critical thinking.

Exercise 11.1

Review Questions

Answers to exercises marked with an asterisk (*) may be found in Appendix B, Answers to Exercises.

1. According to the text, what is the most basic critical thinking skill when it comes to thinking about health?*
2. Is causal reasoning treated as part of inductive or deductive logic in this textbook?
3. If the conclusion of an argument is true, does that mean that the argument is logically strong? Why or why not?
4. What is the most reasonable attitude to adopt toward health claims over which experts disagree?
5. According to the study cited in this chapter, roughly what per cent of health claims reported in UK newspapers are supported by good evidence?
6. Name one key question you should ask yourself when you see novel health claims being published in the news.

7. When engaging in "inference to the best explanation" in criminal trials, what constitutes the phenomenon to be explained?
8. How does the concept of "burden of proof" apply to criminal trials?*
9. What role does the fallacy of *appeal to emotion* play in legal reasoning?
10. Why is subjectivism about ethics tempting?
11. Why is subjectivism about ethics a mistake?
12. What is the difference between a descriptive claim and an ethical claim?
13. What constitutes our background information with regard to ethics?
14. Name the three "grand traditions" of ethics discussed in this chapter.*

Exercise 11.2

On the basis of claims you already have good reason to believe, your background information, and your assessment of the apparent credibility of any cited experts, indicate for each of the following statements whether you would accept it, reject it, or proportion your belief to the evidence. Give reasons for your answers. If you decide to proportion your belief to the evidence, state generally what degree of plausibility you would assign to the claim.

1. An apple a day keeps the doctor away!*
2. Cycling is not a good form of exercise because it is hard on your knees.
3. Dr Campagna, my high school physics teacher, says that Wi-Fi radiation is pretty much harmless.*
4. Dr Fabro, who was found guilty of publishing fraudulent research, argues that smoking cigars increases a person's chance of contracting cancers of the mouth.
5. Public possession of cannabis is illegal in Canada.
6. Of course Bartkiw is guilty. It doesn't matter that his plane ticket shows he was in another country at the time—an eyewitness described him almost perfectly as the one who stole the jewels!
7. Mr Abdolmalaki is a Crown attorney, and he says very few people in Canada go to jail for simple possession of marijuana.
8. Just ask my father, and he'll tell you. I'm innocent.
9. Killing innocent people is wrong.*
10. LeBron James says that professional athletes have a moral obligation to speak up on political issues.
11. Torture is never ethically justified.
12. My ethics professor, Professor Li, says that he has studied the debate carefully and there simply are no philosophically sound arguments against allowing same-sex marriage.

Exercise 11.3

For each of the following claims, name the fallacy or fallacies involved, if any.

1. Moms have a "sixth sense" that tells them when their kid is lying. Every mother knows that!
2. I don't believe that a diet with lots of meat in it is bad for you. My family is German, and we've always loved lots of meat products—bratwurst, schnitzel, liverwurst, you name it!*
3. Ladies and gentlemen of the jury, you can't find my client guilty. If she goes to jail, she won't be able to care for her kids!
4. All companies misrepresent their products. So how can this exaggeration in our ad be wrong?
5. Shahram is obviously guilty of this crime. He's a notorious thug with a long history of criminal behaviour.*
6. Wow, that herbal tea my neighbour recommended was awesome. I had a cold for a week, and then I drank a pot of that stuff and the cold was gone the next day!
7. Who do you think you are, telling me I shouldn't hit my kids? I'm entitled to my own morals, and that includes how to raise my own children.*
8. I can't believe you think it's OK to download "pirated" music. I'm amazed that you think it's better for struggling artists to starve rather than being paid fairly for their music!*
9. If you commit first-degree murder, you should go to jail. But my client didn't commit first-degree murder, so he should not go to jail.

Exercise 11.4

For each of the following arguments, construct a Venn diagram to assess for validity. If the argument is valid, briefly outline whether the argument's premises are acceptable. (Hint: you may need to supply a missing premise or conclusion.)

1. Anyone who smokes heavily is sure to get cancer. And you're a heavy smoker!*
2. Fencing is a dangerous sport. After all, Ukrainian fencer Vladimir Smirnov died at the 1982 World Championship when his opponent's broken blade pierced Smirnov's protective mask. Any sport where people have died should be considered dangerous.
3. Some falsehoods are lies, and some lies do great harm. So some falsehoods do great harm.
4. Anyone who takes office supplies home for personal use is a thief. That's exactly what Alison did. So . . . !
5. Killing is wrong. So eating meat is wrong.
6. You must avoid lying. Because you're a moral person and all moral persons must avoid lying.
7. Some people who lie have good reasons. Some people who have good reasons are actually saints. So some people who lie are saints.*

Field Problems

1. Go online and find the Letters to the Editor section of the website for your local newspaper or a national (Canadian) newspaper (such as *The Globe and Mail* or *National Post*). Identify a letter to the editor that makes an ethical argument—an argument about some ethical issue. Does the writer commit any logical fallacies? Overall, is his or her argument a strong one?
2. Think of something you believe to be an obvious myth with regard to staying healthy—some claim either about what helps you to stay healthy or about what would make you get sick. What reasons do you think believers have for believing that claim? Go online and find at least three websites that offer support for that claim. Is the support for it strong or weak? Next, find at least two websites that make the opposite argument. Did any of the arguments convince you? Why or why not?
3. Imagine that you've been charged—falsely!—with a serious crime. What critical thinking tools from this textbook would you most want your lawyer to understand? What critical thinking skills would be most important for your lawyer to help keep you out of jail?

Self-Assessment Quiz

1. When experts seem to disagree over a particular claim about health, what sorts of questions can be asked to try to gain clarity?
2. According to the text, what form of reasoning is most important in reasoning about health?
3. Explain the "zebra" problem in medical diagnosis.
4. According to the text, which weak form of conditional reasoning is often used in courtrooms?
5. Give one reason why the burden of proof should be thought to lie with the prosecution in criminal cases in Canada.
6. What form might an ad hominem argument take in a court of law?
7. Why must all ethical arguments have at least one ethical premise?
8. Name one of the key features of any ethical premise.

For each of the following claims, state whether it is (a) probably true, (b) probably false, (c) almost certainly true, (d) almost certainly false, or (e) quite uncertain.

9. Red wine consumed in moderation is actually good for you.
10. Eating lots of candy is a sure route to obesity.
11. Pomegranate juice prevents cancer.
12. My baby has been crying and has little red bumps. I'm sure she's got skin cancer!
13. Joon was in another country when the crime took place. He cannot be directly responsible.
14. Saying you're sorry when you aren't actually sorry is the same as lying.
15. It's unfair that the company refused to hire Sui because she's Chinese.

Writing Assignments

1. Write a 350-word essay explaining which of the domains discussed in this chapter—health, law, or ethics—should be thought of as requiring the greatest reliance on expertise, and which should be thought of as requiring the least. Explain your point of view.
2. Go online and find a website that encourages belief in at least one health-related myth. Write a 300-word essay explaining why it is a myth, providing one fallacious argument that tends to perpetuate that myth.

Notes

1. Ben Cooper et al., "The Quality of the Evidence for Dietary Advice Given in UK National Newspapers," *Public Understanding of Science* (April 2011), 664–73.
2. "Schedule A and Section 3 to the Food and Drugs Act." https://www.canada.ca/en/health-canada/services/drugs-health-products/drug-products/applications-submissions/guidance-documents/guidance-document-schedule-section-3-food-drugs-act.html. Accessed 6 March 2022.
3. Jaki Freeman, "The Supreme Court of Canada and Eyewitness Identification—*R. v. Bruce*, 2011 S.C.C. 4," *Briefly Speaking* 20, no. 2 (May 2011).

APPENDIX A

Essays for Evaluation

ESSAY 1

Deterrence

by David M. Paciocco

The theory of deterrence has two components. The first, known as "specific" or "individual" deterrence, is that punishment will discourage the offender from committing further offences in the future. The second, known as "general deterrence," is that punishing offenders will discourage other like-minded people from committing offences.

Based on its 1987 study, *Sentencing Reform*, the Canadian Sentencing Commission gave up on specific deterrence. It acknowledged that the claim that punishment is effective in reducing the tendency to reoffend is undermined by rates of recidivism (or repeat offending), the apparent "undeterrability" of certain groups of offenders, and the "acknowledged fact" that most prison inmates have been convicted on prior occasions.[1] Anyone who has the time should sit in provincial court and watch offenders being sentenced. As a prosecutor, I became so accustomed to finding a copy of the criminal record in the file that if there wasn't one, I would look around the floor to see if I had dropped it.

In spite of our failure to intimidate offenders from reoffending by punishing them, we continue to rely on specific deterrence as a justification for punishment. If we are going to send a first offender to jail, our preference is to give a "short, sharp" sentence that will "send a message" to him or her. This practice shares a philosophical kinship with giving a child a sharp smack to the back of the head, and is probably about as effective. It is, however, a lot more expensive.

General deterrence, the theory that punishing offenders will intimidate others into being law-abiding, is even more central to our theories of punishment. For the most hated crimes, those involving sexual assault, violence causing bodily harm, robbery, and drugs, the primary sentencing principle is general deterrence. Trial judges are overruled by appeal courts when they fail to give general deterrence sufficient weight in sentencing offenders. Yet, paradoxically, most of the crimes for which we emphasize this sentencing principle are the kinds of offences that are most resistant to general deterrence.

The official position appears to be that we must accept the general deterrence theory as a matter of faith, but that we cannot put too much faith in it. The Canadian Sentencing Commission asked Professor Cousineau of Simon Fraser University to review the latest literature. He concluded that "there is little or no evidence to sustain an empirically justified belief in the deterrent effect of legal sanctions."[2] In spite of this report, the commission could not bring itself to reject the intuitively appealing notion that if people know there is a heavy cost associated with their conduct, they may, as rational people, opt not to engage in that behaviour.[3] But even the Sentencing Commission was guarded in its assessment. It cautioned that there is no reason to believe that legal sanctions can be used to deter specific crimes, or to believe that making an example out of a particular offender will have any effect on other potential offenders. It therefore concluded its discussion of general deterrence by saying that "deterrence is a general and limited consequence of sentencing."[4]

A moment's reflection will demonstrate why general deterrence is so ineffective. Deterrence is based on theories of rational decision making. It presupposes that actors weigh to a nicety the pros and cons of their acts before action. The most dangerous criminals do not fit that model. They are not people renowned for their good judgment and considered action. At the same time, the most horrendous crimes do not lend themselves to this kind of judgment. Sexual offenders give in to vile urges. Assailants strike out in anger. Homicide, in particular, is primarily a crime of passion. It is only rarely a contract hit or a neatly planned exercise. It is more often the worst result of the free reign of jealousy, rage, vindictiveness, hatred, and anger, the most powerful of human emotions. Even when not spontaneous, it is still most commonly done in the throes of extreme emotion. In 1995, by no means an exceptional year, 9 per cent of killers committed suicide, almost invariably immediately after they had killed.[5] If these people are not afraid to inflict mortal violence on themselves as the price for their crime, what makes us think we can deter them by threatening them with a cell with a television?

Some Canadians believe that the television in the cell is part of the reason that general deterrence does not work; we are not hard enough on criminals. If we ratcheted up the sentences, they believe, and began to treat criminals as criminals, we might just reduce crime. In fact, there is "a great deal of empirical research in the United States and elsewhere [that] has shown that crime rates are not greatly affected by changes to the severity of penalties imposed."[6]

The Canadian Sentencing Commission came to the same conclusion.[7] This result has been effectively demonstrated in Canada with respect to the offence of murder. Murder rates did not rise with the abolition of capital punishment in 1976. They went down and stayed down. One of the great American ironies is that those states with the highest murder rates are the same ones that invoke the death penalty most frequently.

The Ontario Court of Appeal was recently asked to increase the typical sentencing range for men who attempt to murder their female partners. Sentences for that offence range around ten years. The court was right to reject the submission that imposing higher sentences would discourage men from trying.[8] By definition, these men are attempting to succeed in killing their spouses. If they succeeded, they would get life imprisonment, subject to lengthy parole ineligibility. How can anyone think that a man who knows he might get life if he succeeds is going to sit down and say, "OK. If I fail they are going to give me 12 years instead of ten, so I had better not do it." This is simply silly. Even at 20 or 30 or 40 years, there would be no difference. The violent among us are destructive actors, not constructive thinkers.

Cesare Beccaria, sometimes called the father of criminology, was a proponent of general deterrence. He nonetheless sensed that employing brutal punishments would do nothing to reduce crime rates: "The countries and times most notorious for severity of penalties have always been those in which the bloodiest and most inhumane deeds were committed, for the same spirit of ferocity that guided the hand of the legislators also ruled that of the parricide and assassin."[9] Savage punishments reinforce savage attitudes in some people. For the just, savage punishments defeat themselves. They can cause a humane public to rebel against the values demonstrated by the administration of justice, thereby undermining the educational effect of criminal prosecutions. Experience has shown that they can even cause courts to rebel by finding technical ways to prevent imposing the punishment.[10] When felons were executed for minor felonies in England, judges became creative in finding ways not to convict.

Even if the theory of general deterrence is sound, its promise is easily defeated in practice. It is universally accepted that to be effective systematically, general deterrence depends more than anything else on the certainty of punishment. That is why high-profile RIDE programs and high police presence in crime areas can help produce a reduction in crime rates, but an abstract fear of being caught is tremendously less effective. Some commentators have added that the punishment must also be swift for general deterrence to work. For reasons we can do nothing about, punishment in our system is neither certain nor swift. In terms of the certainty of punishment, with the exception of homicide, where detection and conviction rates are high, only a very small percentage of offenders are even sentenced. This is partially because of the chronic underreporting of most offences, and partially because some crimes are simply not solved by the police. There are also incredibly high attrition rates for most offences. Complaints tend not to get to trial, either because there is insufficient evidence, the complainants recant, witnesses disappear, the accused disappears, the matter is judged not serious enough to proceed, or the case otherwise falls through the cracks. Some cases end up in acquittals. A leading English academic, Andrew Ashworth, estimates that, in Britain, only 3 per cent of actual offences end up at the sentencing stage.[11] The John Howard Society of Alberta estimated that the clearance rate by conviction in Canada in 1987 was unlikely to exceed 20 per cent.[12] Even if both these figures are gross underestimates, they demonstrate poignantly that we will never attain certainty of punishment, no matter how much money we throw at the system or how much we tinker with its rules.

All indications are that general deterrence, in the form of creating conditions through the punishment of offenders that will make others decide not to offend, is woefully ineffective for most crimes. It is particularly so for crimes of violence. If the marginal return of general deterrence was the only gain to be made by incarcerating violent offenders, it would not make economic sense to do so. Our continued reliance on it as a reason for the punitive sentencing of such people is therefore misleading and distorting. It creates a public expectation that cannot be satisfied.

Notes

1. Canadian Sentencing Commission, *Sentencing Reform: A Canadian Approach* (Ottawa: Ministry of Supply and Services, 1987), 135. Between 1975 and 1985, 60 per cent of those released on mandatory supervision were readmitted to federal penitentiary, while 49 per cent of those who had been released on parole were readmitted.
2. Ibid., 136.
3. Ibid., 136–137.
4. Ibid., 138.
5. Statistics Canada, Canadian Centre for Justices Statistics, *Homicide in Canada*—1995 16, no. 11 (1996): 5.
6. Julian V. Roberts, "New Data on Sentencing Trends in Provincial Courts" (1994), 34 CR (4th) 181: 194.
7. Canadian Sentencing Commission, *Sentencing Reform*, 137.
8. *R. v. Edwards* (1996), 28 OR (3d) 54 (CA).
9. Daniel J. Curran and Claire M. Renzetti, *Theories of Crime* (Boston: Allyn & Bacon, 1994), 13.
10. H.R.S. Ryan, *The Theory of Punishment* (1970), Study Note, reproduced in Don Stuart and R.J. Delisle, *Learning Canadian Criminal Law*, 5th ed. (Toronto: Carswell, 1995), 139.
11. Andrew Ashworth, *Sentencing and Criminal Justice* (London: Weidenfeld & Nicolson, 1992), 23.
12. Canadian Sentencing Commission, *Sentencing Reform*, 148.

ESSAY 2

The Last Honourable Man

by Andrew Potter

Hours after the beginning of the Russian invasion of his country in late February, Ukraine president Volodymyr Zelensky told a group of European leaders on a Zoom call that this might be the last time they saw him alive.*

*Source: Andrew Potter, "The Last Honourable Man." https://theline.substack.com/p/andrew-potter-the-last-honourable. Used by permission of the author.

He wasn't being dramatic. The Russians had made plain their intention to take Kyiv; it was widely assumed that, if successful, they would shoot Zelensky and install a puppet regime; pretty much everyone believed the Russians would be successful within a matter of days.

And yet Zelensky refused to leave Kyiv, remaining in the Ukrainian capital along with his family. Two days into the invasion, his response to an American offer to help him evacuate was to say: "The fight is here; I need ammunition, not a ride." The line instantly became one of the great tough-guy catch-phrases of our time, fantastically meme-worthy, turning Zelensky overnight into some pop cultural admixture of Churchill and an '80s action hero. It also made him the moral leader of the free world. For six weeks now, the Ukrainians have stubbornly refused to capitulate, while Zelensky demanded the West stand up for the values it purports to believe in and give Ukraine weapons it needs to do the job.

When asked by journalists to explain his refusal to head for safety, Zelensky has made it clear that he has no wish to die, and that he fears for the lives of his loved ones (his wife and kids have since been moved to relative safety.) But, he added: "As for my life: I am the president of the country, and I simply do not have the right to it." Sure, he could flee to preserve his own life. But, he has said, how would he explain his actions to his kids? As Zelensky sees it, he has no choice in the matter. His duty requires that he remain and lead his country in the fight; to do anything less would be dishonourable.

But while his Last Action Hero schtick has proven enormously popular with European and North American audiences, Zelensky's refusal to leave Kyiv, and Ukraine's insistence on fighting off the Russians instead of capitulation, has put our so-called leaders in a bit of a bind.

To begin with, Ukraine's refusal to capitulate to Russian aggression has forced many governments into taking steps they almost certainly would have preferred to avoid—economic and political sanctions against Russia, costly shipments of arms and other aid, diplomatic side-choosing, rethinking of trade agreements, and so on. Ukraine's defence is coming at a pretty high cost, and the final bill is far from being tallied.

But beyond the economic and political price that is being paid to support Ukraine, there is the extraordinary amount of cognitive dissonance Zelensky's behaviour has generated amongst the leadership of the West. Honour? Duty? Sacrifice? What century does he think he's living in?

For centuries, honour reflected the sorts of qualities that gentlemen were expected to possess: dignity, integrity, courage. But it is hard to even talk about honour now with a straight face. It brings to mind 19th-century aristocrats in wigs and hose, demanding satisfaction and challenging one another to a meeting over some best-forgotten offence. The old honour codes couldn't survive the triumph of the values of liberal democracy and the arrival of what Francis Fukuyama famously called the End of History, where the willingness to risk one's life for abstract ideas or principles has been replaced by voting and economic calculation in the public sphere and "the satisfaction of sophisticated consumer demands" in the private.

Today, the old notion of honour survives only in small and isolated precincts of (mostly) male society, places like the military and some sports, places where how you behave in front of your peers matters more than comfort, more than money, more than health, maybe even more than life itself. The rest of us have become versions of what Nietzsche derided as "the last man"—creatures of liberalism who have no pride, take no risks, and desire only comfort and security.

Anyway, what could possibly be worth dying for in the consumerist pleasure cruise of the 21st-century West? Well, as it turns out, history might have ended but someone forgot to tell the Ukrainians, who appear to be very willing to fight and die for the very old 19th-century idea of nationalism. As the historian Adam Tooze put it in a recent essay, "It is the Ukrainians, to the amazement and not inconsiderable embarrassment of the West, who are enacting a drama of national resistance unto death. Under Russian attack, they are bonding together and demanding recognition of their sovereignty."

As Tooze notes, the West doesn't really know how it is supposed to respond. On the one hand, there is no question that Ukraine's courage and resolve in the face of outrageous Russian criminality has captured the imagination of the people of the West. But this has put some governments on the spot, especially those who have spent years cozying up to Russia (Germany), cynically playing both sides (France), or letting Putin-friendly Russian oligarchs and FSB assassins have run of the place (Britain).

To their credit, the Americans appear to have finally grasped the importance of the moment, and there remains enough of an atavistic sense of Churchillian honour in the British psyche that it has stepped up admirably. For all his domestic loucheness, Boris Johnson's trip to Kyiv, where he walked in the open streets with Zelensky, was an act of genuine courage and statesmanship.

Then there's Canada, the Last Man of NATO, which is performing its usual trick of doing the least amount it possibly can while still looking like it is helping. While Justin Trudeau hosts hashtag-friendly Zoom conferences and tweets about "holding the Putin regime to account," the Ukrainians keep insisting that they don't want justice tomorrow, they want victory today. And they are hell bent on shaming the West into giving them all the help they require.

What the Ukrainian fight has revealed is something deeply metaphysical about the concept of freedom: Without honour, freedom is just the temporary or fortuitous absence of tyranny. That is, it is only freedom if you're willing to die for it. But once you get there, you find that you're already free. As a Belarussian volunteer fighting for Ukraine put it: "We are Free Men, we have nothing to fear, and as you can see, victory shall be ours." In some way, they've already won.

The Ukrainians are under vicious attack, with their cities ruined, their populations massacred. The Russian horde is massing in the East. But the men and women fighting for Ukraine are the freest people in the world right now, unshakeably led by Volodymyr Zelensky, the undisputed leader of the free world.

The hour has come. So has the man. So has the people.

Glory to Ukraine.

ESSAY 3

Electronics in the Classroom—Time to Hit the "Escape" Key?

by Shannon Dea

With each new term and each new syllabus, a perennial question emerges: Should I ban laptops in the classroom?*

The motivations for this question are understandable. Research shows that students learn better when they take notes by hand rather than typing them (http://www.scientificamerican.com/article/a-learning-secret-don-t-take-notes-with-a-laptop/). Moreover, laptops (and other electronic devices) in the classroom distract not only the owners of the screens, but also all of the nearby students who can see the screens. A recent study found that not only electronic multi-taskers, but also students seated near them, experience a drop in grades.

On the other hand, for some disabled students, and for ESL students, laptops can be crucial learning tools. While disabled students can get special permission to use laptops in courses in which such devices are banned, their use of the devices thereby "outs" them as having special needs. Violating their privacy in this way is, on my view, unacceptable. (It might also be illegal.)

Moreover, whatever the pedagogical merits of hand-written notes, those of our students who go on post-university to work with words and ideas (a large proportion of Arts alumni, clearly) will likely do so with computers in front of them. Thus, to educate them in a computer-free zone is not only anachronistic, but arguably means missing an opportunity to train our students in the thoughtful, appropriate use of electronic devices.

It's worth noting that university faculty and staff themselves spend a great deal of time multi-tasking on electronic devices. One need only attend a meeting of Senate or a university Town Hall to see university employees using their screens in ways very similar to those that we discourage among our students.

So, what is to be done?

I used to put my laptop users in the last couple of rows of the classroom so that they wouldn't distract anyone behind or beside them. I've come to think better of this. After all, some of these students may have good reasons to sit in other

*Source: Shannon Dea, "Electronics in the Classroom—Time to Hit the "Escape" Key?" *The Chalkboard*, https://uwaterloo.ca/arts/blog/post/electronics-classroom-time-hit-escape-key. Reproduced with permission of the author.

locations in the classroom. Over the years, many of my front row, hands-always-up students have been laptop users. And, of course, a student with limited hearing or vision may need to sit at the front.

Here's my new solution. At the first class meeting, I lay out all of these difficulties for my students. I discuss both the cognitive merits of writing notes by hand, and the distraction attendant upon using a laptop or sitting near someone who does. I discuss the important role that electronic devices can play for disabled students, and the reasons to respect those students' privacy. Then, I instruct students to spend the next couple of classes getting used to the physical learning space, and developing some ideas about the most appropriate "zones" for laptop users. The only stipulations I make are that whatever zones the students develop cannot be exclusively at the back of the class, and must leave some portion(s) of the classroom free from the distraction of nearby laptops. After a couple of classes to get used to the space, the students themselves draw the boundaries of the distraction/no distraction zones in the class.

Is this method perfect? Probably not. But it helps students to make empirically supported decisions about what devices to bring to class; it keeps some spaces distraction free; it models inclusiveness; and it supports students' development of intellectual autonomy and metacognitive skills.

ESSAY 4

What's Wrong with "Body Mass Index"*

by Samantha Brennan

I'd like us to ditch all talk of Body Mass Index (BMI) as a meaningful measure when it comes to individuals. And please don't say it's better than weight because it's just weight + height taken into account. Insofar as weight is a problematic measure and BMI relies on weight, so too is BMI problematic. I've long loved Kate Harding's project "BMI Illustrated" over at *Shapely Prose* (kateharding.net/bmi-illustrated). She describes it this way: "I put together a slideshow to demonstrate just how ridiculous the BMI standards are." This isn't to deny that BMI talk is useful about populations and big picture trends, it's just that I think it's misleading and harmful when it comes to individuals.

Lots of thin people are falsely reassured by their BMI, while lots of people with BMIs in the "overweight/obese" categories might be worrying with no good reason. Fit and fat are linked but not in the ways most people think. I worry that lots of fat people don't exercise because they worry what people will think especially if you exercise and don't get any smaller. Yet fat and fit people can be very healthy. "People can be obese yet physically healthy and fit and at no greater risk of heart disease or cancer than normal weight people," say researchers. The key is being "metabolically fit," meaning no high blood pressure, cholesterol, or raised

*Source: Samantha Brennen, "Fit, Fat, and What's Wrong with BMI," *Fit Is a Feminist Issue*, 9 September 2012, http://fitisafeministissue.com/2012/09/09/fit-fat-and-whats-wrong-with-bmi. Reproduced with permission of the author.

blood sugar, and exercising, according to experts. Looking at data from over 43,000 US people they found that "being overweight per se did not pose a big health risk," reports the BBC (www.bbc.co.uk/news/health-19474239).

I love my family doctor who cheered me up immensely when she looked at my chart and said, "This is the part of the visit when, given your weight, I should warn you about the health problems associated with overweight and obesity. However, given that you've got low to normal blood pressure, no sugar issues, and the best ratio of good to bad cholesterol we've ever seen at this clinic, I can't in good conscience do that. You're extremely healthy. Whatever you're doing, keep doing it."

A few years ago I tried Weight Watchers—for probably the sixth time in my life, will I never learn?—and I was shocked at their weight range for my height. Weights I haven't seen since Grade 6. And to give you some perspective they were also weights I never weighed even when at 5′ 7″ I wore size 8 clothing. The so-called "healthy" or "normal" weight range for me has never seemed plausible.

I had an interesting experience recently. This summer I was measured in the BodPod at the Fowler Kennedy Sports Medicine Clinic which tells you exactly how much of your body is fat and how much is muscle, bone etc. I was happy to see that to weigh what Weight Watchers thought of as my ideal, I'd be allowed a mere 20 lbs of body fat. I won't discuss exact weights today but I will tell you that I'm 122 lbs of not fat. It's my goal as part of my "fittest at fifty" plan to improve my ratio of lean body mass. I plan to both develop my muscles and lose some body fat. I'd also like to lose pounds in absolute numbers too, mostly though to make running easier on my joints and to make it easier to get up hills faster on the bike! Hill climbing on the bike is all about power to weight ratio and so I'll never be a climber but I hate to get dropped on hills on a regular basis. According to BMI, I'll likely always be overweight or obese and I've made my peace with that.

Marc Perry notes in *Get Lean* that according to BMI most American football players count as obese. So too do many Olympic athletes. You can find a list online of all of the gold medal athletes from the 2004 Olympics in Athens who count as overweight or obese according to BMI. We need to change our image of what athletes look like. Usually they don't look like fitness models.

ESSAY 5

How Ontario Ended Up with "Cap and Trade"

by Joseph Heath

Like many people, I was encouraged to see the Government of Ontario finally stepping into the breach and taking action on the climate change issue, but I was very disappointed to see them choosing to go with a cap-and-trade system rather than a carbon tax.* Prior to yesterday, there were two models out there: BC's

*Source: Joseph Heath, "Ontario Chickens out, Chooses Cap-and-Trade," *In Due Course*, 14 April 2015, http://induecourse.ca/ontario-chickens-out-chooses-cap-and-trade. Reproduced with permission of the author.

carbon tax and Quebec's cap-and-trade system. Ontario joining Quebec probably represents a tipping point that will push the country as a whole in the direction of cap and trade, which is, as far as I'm concerned, a second-best outcome.

How did we wind up here? This is all a consequence of what I consider to be the most important political shift to have occurred in Canada in the past two decades, which is the near-total collapse of moderate conservatism. Indeed, it's not a surprise that the major spokespersons of the centre-right in Canada—Andrew Coyne, Tasha Kheiriddin, etc.—were lining up today to criticize the Ontario plan. And yet the problem, ultimately, stems from the failure of the centre-right in Canada to control their own political parties. And if they're looking for someone to blame, they should be pointing the finger at Canadian prime minister Stephen Harper, not Ontario premier Kathleen Wynne.

Right now, the policy space on climate change can be organized in the following way (starting with positions that involve the least government involvement in the economy, moving down to those that involve the most):

1. *The Alberta fantasy.* Under this scenario, we just keep on digging up bitumen and selling synthetic oil, investing in new mines, processing and pipeline infrastructure, subject to absolutely no constraints and a carbon price of zero. And people don't have to pay taxes, because, yay! we're digging money out of the ground.
2. *Carbon tax.* The government puts a price on carbon emissions, which raises the price of fossil-fuel derived energy relative to other forms. The price is adjusted until the desired quantity of emissions is achieved.
3. *Cap and trade.* Firms are issued permits to produce emissions. If their emissions exceed the quantity permitted, they must purchase additional permits on the market. If they are under their emissions quota, they can sell their unused permits.
4. *The "planning and banning" fantasy.* Here the government gets involved in micro-managing the transition, mandating specific technology for emitters, and subsidizing what it considers to be promising technologies.

I think everyone can see why, for people who have a distrust of government, scenario 1 is the best and scenario 4 is by far the worst. But why is 2 (carbon tax) ahead of 3? It's because cap and trade is so much easier for governments to fiddle around with. In particular, it allows the government to play around with the permit allocations, giving specific firms or industries special exemptions, or extra permits. That's why the NDP supports it (keeping in mind that there is significant alignment of interest between the Canadian Auto Workers and the automobile industry—a major beneficiary of these fiddles). It also appeals to some of the worst political instincts of the

Ontario Liberal Party, and of Kathleen Wynne specifically, who is constantly going on about how government needs to be a "partner" in all major economic activity in the province—which basically means subsidizing manufacturing in ways both subtle and gross.

The nice thing about a carbon tax is that it's really hard to fiddle. So while in practice cap and trade and carbon tax come to the same thing, in reality they don't. This is Andrew Coyne's major complaint. And yet he fails to note that if you survey the political landscape in Canada, you find that no major political party (with the exception of the BC Liberals), is willing to champion option 2. In other words, the centre-right in this country is missing in action. Both the Liberals and the NDP are now down into zones 3 and 4 (the Liberals having been pushed there by conservative rhetoric) while the federal Conservative party, not to mention the various provincial Progressive Conservative parties, including Ontario's, remain resolute champions of option 1—the Alberta fantasy.

There are two reasons for this. First, conservative political parties in Canada have largely been captured by ideological extremists. One can see this very clearly with the federal Conservative Party in Canada—up to and including the prime minister—which can best be described as "anti-environmental." There is simply no one there willing to champion market-based approaches to solving environmental problems. One can see the same thing in the Ontario Progressive Conservative Party, where the idea of "promoting a market solution" to a public problem seems to be confused with "doing nothing" or "pretending that there is no problem." The second reason is connected to the first, and it has to do with electoral strategy. Roughly speaking, the reason that ideological extremists have had such success in controlling conservative parties is that their particular brand of "common sense" conservatism produces a set of incredibly powerful electoral strategies (far better than anything the centre-right can come up with). For instance, the "job-killing carbon tax" sound bite is so powerful that it has taken on a life of its own, effectively tying the hands of the federal government on this issue. (One can see it as well in the current contest for the leadership of the Ontario PC party, where both candidates have locked themselves into supporting option 1, because of the power of the anti-tax sound bite.)

In other words, the reason that option 2 winds up being a political orphan is that the people who champion this sort of an approach can't win elections. Indeed, the Liberal Party of Canada started out supporting option 2, and got slaughtered by the Conservatives for it. (Indeed, there are striking similarities between the Conservative treatment of carbon taxes in Canada and the Republican approach to health care reform in the United States, where Mitt Romney wound up disavowing his own health care reform plan, because there was so much mileage to be had from demonizing "Obamacare." As a result, conservatives in both countries have wound up taking positions that put them completely outside the space of reasonable policy disagreement, largely for reasons of electoral strategy.)

The irony is that, by insisting on getting option 1—and by painting themselves into a corner with their rhetoric—what conservatives are winding up with is option 3. In fact, what they're winding up with is even worse: First, they are getting a provincial patchwork rather than a more efficient national system. And second, they are getting cap and trade, a system that is more open to government meddling in the economy. It's almost as though what they need to learn to do is *compromise*, and speak out in favour of option 2. Unfortunately, in order to get option 2 onto the table, someone on the right in this country would need to figure out how to control—or even influence—Stephen Harper, and apparently no one is able to do that.

I understand that it's no fun being a moderate. But seriously, someone on the right in Canada needs to step up to the plate. Is there *any* politician in Ontario—not a journalist, a politician—willing to stand up to the government and say, "we should have a carbon tax instead"? Because so far all I've heard from the opposition has been the same old fantasy, that all taxes are evil, and that we should be doing nothing about climate change.

ESSAY 6

Raspberry Ketone, Pure Green Coffee Extract, Garcinia Cambogia, Weight Loss, and the Fallacy of Appealing to Authority

by Tracy Isaacs

My usually skeptical husband forwarded me an email message late last week with the subject "weight loss."* It contained a short video of Dr Oz endorsing pure green coffee bean extract as a miracle weight loss potion. My husband's question to me: "What do you think?"

The clip I watched showed an enthusiastic Dr Oz with the creator of the product. Oz declared it a weight loss miracle. When I went back to the link a few days later, the link led me to something different. This time, Dr Oz was interviewing someone about a different weight loss miracle: Garcinia Cambogia. Apparently it's also an amazing fat burner! Like pure green coffee bean extract, this product is supposed to result in weight loss without any changes to diet or activity.

Neither the green coffee bean extract page nor the garcinia cambogia page would let me leave them without not one but two pop-ups asking me if I was sure I wanted to leave that page.

*Source: Tracy Isaacs, "Raspberry Ketone, Pure Green Coffee Extract, Garcinia Cambogia, Weight Loss, and the Fallacy of Appealing to Authority," *Fit Is a Feminist Issue*, 24 January 2013, http://fitisafeministissue.com/2013/01/24/raspberry-ketone-pure-green-coffee-extract-garcinia-cambogia-weight-loss-and-the-fallacy-of-appealing-to-authority. Reproduced with permission of the author.

Dr Oz has also spoken highly of "raspberry ketone." Available in pill form (because you'd have to eat NINETY pounds of raspberries to get the appropriate "dose"), raspberry ketone is no less than "a fat-burner in a bottle," according to Dr Oz.

His website states that "research has shown that raspberry ketone can help in your weight-loss efforts, especially when paired with regular exercise and a well-balanced diet of healthy and whole foods." I love the addendum "especially when paired with regular exercise and a well-balanced diet. . . ."

I think I will stick to the regular exercise and healthy whole foods and save myself the $180 for a 90-day supply.

Most reviews of these products that I've read have questioned the research. A *Globe and Mail* article notes that the study on which the main claims about green coffee bean extract were based involved very few participants. Moreover, participants also lost weight during the placebo phase of the trial.

A *Canadian Living* article on raspberry ketone notes that so far mice have been the only research subjects. Both articles quoted credible MDs claiming that, surprise, surprise: There are no magic solutions!

From the *Globe and Mail:* "Usually when studies break the physical laws of the universe, there's usually something wrong with the study itself," said Dr Yoni Freedhoff, medical director of Ottawa's Bariatric Medical Institute, who writes *Weighty Matters*, a popular blog on nutrition issues. (http://www.theglobeandmail.com/life/health-and-fitness/health/green-coffee-bean-extract-does-it-really-help-you-lose-weight/article 6116816)

I haven't linked to Dr Oz's website and I am not going to say a lot more about these products. Both his site and the products are easy to find on the Internet.

What I do want to say is this: there is a well-known fallacy that we learn about in philosophy called "the appeal to authority." Appealing to authority is not a good strategy for those seeking truth claims. Just because some authority like Dr Oz said it's true doesn't mean it's true. Of course we do not need to dismiss the claims of experts. Good science is based on sound studies that have undergone peer review and are based on approved methodologies and ample evidence.

Unfortunately, Dr Oz is not an expert in most of what he goes on about. And yet he is accepted as an authority by countless people. His stamp of approval on some product or health claim is taken as gospel by many people. It boosts sales the way Oprah's endorsement of books used to (perhaps still does) have undue influence in the publishing industry.

This is not to say that everything he says is false. It is only to say that just because he said it doesn't make it true. We need more evidence than that.

But the medical community has long told us that there are no magic pills for weight loss. Dr Oz's claims about these miracle weight loss products are just plain irresponsible, given his level of influence.

I've heard all sorts of claims about this and that miracle food or product. When I was a teenager, people took caffeine pills to lose weight. As an undergraduate, smoking cigarettes was the thing. At one time or another, the special powers of cabbage, grapefruit, and bananas took centre stage in the weight loss culture. Now it's more likely to be raspberry ketone, pure green coffee bean extract, or garcinia cambogia.

And I haven't even touched on fad diets like eating for your blood type (based on totally ungrounded claims), the lemon–cayenne pepper–maple syrup–water detox, or any variant of a low-carb/high-protein plan (my first diet—circa 1980—was the Scarsdale diet, a high-protein, low-carb plan that people loved because you got to eat "plenty of steak" for dinner).

If healthy and sustainable weight loss is what you are seeking, none of these supplements or plans will work. They are not sustainable ways of eating for the rest of your life. And like the claim about raspberry ketone, pair anything with regular exercise and healthy eating and you're good to go.

No magic and no surprises. As *Globe and Mail* reporter Carly Weeks says in her evaluation of raspberry ketone, the bottom line hasn't much changed: "While the promise of the synthetic compound sounds alluring, the best way of losing weight hasn't changed: It's still diet and exercise."

I would only add that "diet" shouldn't be taken to mean "diets," those restricted eating plans designed to lose weight. Diets don't work. In this context we should understand "diet" to mean simply the way we eat on a regular basis. We talk a lot on our blog about why weight loss alone is not a great measure of fitness and why we're not big fans of dieting. . . .

Just to reiterate: "Dr Oz said it" is not a reason on which you can base a strong conclusion. In philosophy we call that an appeal to authority, and it's a fallacy.

ESSAY 7

Nurses, Social Media, and Whistleblowing

by Nancy Walton

In a recent news story out of Prince Albert, Saskatchewan, Carolyn Strom, a nurse, was found guilty of professional misconduct for a post on her personal Facebook page, citing problems in her grandfather's care at a local long term care centre.* In her Facebook post, she praised but mainly criticized the quality of care that her grandfather received. The excerpt of the posting that the CBC and other news media have presented cite her dissatisfaction with the care her grandfather received while he was in palliative care in the facility, in the last week(s) of his life. The more complete version of the posting, as appears in the redacted decision, goes on to state that the problems and dissatisfaction with her grandfather's care were ongoing, and she warned others whose loved ones were in the facility

*Source: Nancy Walton, "Nurses, Social Media, and Whistleblowing," *The Nursing Ethics Blog*, 4 December 2016, https://nursingethicsblog.com/2016/12/04/nurses-social-media-and-whistleblowing/. Reproduced with permission of the author.

to "keep an eye on things and report back anything you Do Not Like!" The post suggested that she had tried to take other steps to address what she calls "subpar" care for her grandfather, and that "not much else seems to be working."

A disciplinary committee for her provincial regulatory body found her guilty of professional misconduct for posting what she did, and in the manner that she did so. Many argue that this is a "silencing" of discussion over inadequate and poor-quality health care for seniors and those at the end of life. Others counter this argument by suggesting that her posting was unprofessional, and inappropriate.

Nurses—and all health care professionals—have a complicated relationship with social media. Is my "personal" Facebook page separate from my identity as a regulated health care professional, with particular obligations and responsibilities? Can I separate out the professional from the personal cleanly and easily? No, it's not easy nor straightforward. In this case, the personal and professional are clearly enmeshed—Strom is making clear accusations of very poor quality of care, and stating that problems related to care were ongoing. As a nurse, she has particular knowledge of how to work within the system to have her voice heard and a clear idea of what "good quality" care might have looked like. As a family member, she obviously has an emotional reaction to what she viewed as poor care for her loved one, and her post reflects a deep entanglement of these perspectives—which can be, and was, seen as problematic, at least by the provincial regulatory body. Be clear: social media platforms very much want you to mix the personal and the professional. They have a strong desire for you to have a bigger social media reach, offering us more "suggested friends" and "connections" every day. But as health care professionals, with particular and unique obligations—such as maintaining confidentiality—that *extend beyond formal working hours*, we must use social media more judiciously than many others, and with awareness of those obligations that continue even when we walk out the hospital doors at the end of our shift.

The nurse in this case used her personal Facebook page to engage in a form of professional whistleblowing. One can pick up on her obvious frustration, sadness, and anger at the care of her grandfather, in the posting. But was this the most appropriate and effective way to address the problem? Whistleblowing can be effective as it calls attention to what is usually a serious problem, but in most cases, it should only be used as a last-ditch effort and with full knowledge of the potential fallout that can ensue for the person bringing light to a particular problem. When all other avenues of possibility have been exhausted, then whistleblowing may seem like a timely and often desperate plea for change or action. It requires moral courage and stoicism and, sometimes, personal sacrifice. Whistleblowing was discussed in great public detail as the instigating force behind the investigation into the deaths of 12 children, (between the ages of 4 months and 2 years, who died while in hospital for cardiac surgery in Winnipeg) and the subsequent Manitoba Paediatric Cardiac Surgery Inquest, led by Justice Murray Sinclair.

There's a lot in Strom's posting when you read through it. There's a list of accusations and claims beyond her grandfather's palliative care. There are accusations of poor-quality care, of ongoing and unresolved practice issues, of particular staff providing subpar care, of lack of education of staff, of efforts to address these problems without resolution, accusations of complete lack of compassion and care, of treating patients in a way that fails to respect their dignity and a charge to others to be vigilant about the care of their loved ones—inherently suggesting that the problems cited are systemic, rather than tied to individuals. It's also not clear if she really did exhaust all possible avenues of seeking better quality care for her grandfather. Did she voice complaints to the staff, the manager, the institution, the Board or health region, the regulatory body, the Ministry? Did she report particular nurses, as is our professional obligation, if the situation demands such? Her complaints cite a specific need for education into palliative care, quality care and compassion for some of the nurses in that unit and a demand for them to "step back"—but don't clearly state what particular professional problems or inappropriate practices she may have witnessed that would underpin that comment. And if these problems are as she has described, the provincial regulatory body should have been involved. There are clear avenues to bring practice problems to the attention of the regulatory body, which is required to take these types of claims very seriously.

As nurses, we often may not be in positions of "enough" power to have our voices heard in the way we would like, but that does not mean we should abandon the avenues that we do have. We must still persevere, in professional and ethically responsible ways, to be heard and to voice our valuable and needed perspectives in ways that can help enact change. As a family member and an RN, Strom had a clear and deeply emotional stake in the care of her grandfather and was able to see where his care could—and should—have been better. We can all imagine—and some may have well experienced—how it feels when you have knowledge about what constitutes high quality care and you see that the care of your loved one is not up to the standards you would expect. It would be, without a doubt, deeply morally distressing. But the question remains, should she have pressed the "post" button on her personal Facebook page to voice her professional views on her grandfather's care? And if the answer is no, she should not have done so, the subsequent question for many is—does this then shut down discussion of quality health care and problems within our systems and institutions? No, I don't think it does, and many might argue Strom may had other options to engage in such a discussion more professionally and effectively, even publicly.

There are ways to make whistleblowing ethically permissible as long as other avenues are explored first and you have reasonable evidence that whistleblowing might work. It's a high-risk avenue of action, and without being clear that it might effect change and ensuring that the message is crafted in a way to be most effective, some might claim it is then potentially ethically problematic. It's not clear here if this posting has resulted in any kind of change or attention to the alleged problems in the named long term care facility—as was Strom's intention—or if the case has simply just raised more discussion on how nurses should use social media.

A Facebook posting, "rant," or "vent" is an easily accessible mechanism that absolutely any person with a device can utilize as a tool. There's nothing particularly professional or effective about a Facebook "rant" and due to their ubiquity, and the fact that many are written "off the cuff" or in passing emotionally driven moments, they're seen as very weak or, at best, very limited forms of advocacy. Strom posted a deeply emotional Facebook posting on a very personal experience, and used her unique knowledge and professional position to inform her posting and to underpin her claims of poor care and lack of compassion. As a nurse, she has far more sophisticated tools at her disposal, with knowledge of how to advocate personally and professionally, knowing systems and how to maneuver through them (even problematic systems, as she suggests in her post). It's not clear if she was driven to this, exhausted by lack of action through these other avenues—but this case will continue to raise questions about how we, as health care professionals, manage the personal and professional intermingling that social media involves. The message from the Saskatchewan Registered Nurses' Association is clear: Don't mix them up. Use social media with care.

As health care professionals, sitting in front of a screen when we are upset, angry, or disheartened by the systems in which we work can result in problems—and for many of us, that may be the time for us to close our browser window, step back, and return later, or look to other avenues to have our voices heard.

ESSAY 8

Unrepentant Homeopaths

by Scott Gavura

Alternative medicine is ascendant in Canada.* From the dubious remedies that are now stocked by nearly every pharmacy, to the questionable "integrative medicine" at universities, there's a serious move to embrace treatments and practices that are not backed by credible evidence. Canada's support for alternative medicine, and for its "integration" into conventional health care, is arguably worse than many other countries. Canada's drugs regulator, Health Canada, has approved hundreds of varieties of sugar pills and declared them to be "safe and effective" homeopathic remedies. Some provinces are even moving to regulate homeopaths as health professionals, just like physicians, nurses, and pharmacists. Given the regulatory and legislative "veneer of legitimacy" that homeopathy is being granted, you can see

*Source: Scott Gavura, "Unrepentant Homeopaths Still Selling Sugar Pills to Prevent Infectious Disease," *Science-Based Pharmacy*, 7 December 2014, https://sciencebasedpharmacy.wordpress.com/2014/12/07/unrepentant-homeopaths-still-selling-sugar-pills-to-prevent-infectious-disease. Reproduced with permission of the author.

how consumers might be led to believe that homeopathic remedies are effective, or that homeopaths are capable of providing a form of health care. The reality is far uglier, and the consequences may be tragic. Canadian homeopaths are putting the most vulnerable in society at risk by selling sugar pills to consumers, while telling them that they're getting protection from communicable diseases.

CBC Marketplace, a consumer affairs show, recently used hidden cameras to record reporters asking homeopaths about vaccines. The show sent young mothers (with their babies) to speak with homeopaths about immunizations and vaccines in Toronto and Vancouver.

Of the five homeopaths filmed, four warned the mothers against vaccines, and advised them to avoid giving basic vaccinations like MMR (measles, mumps, and rubella). Only brief clips are shown in the episode, but the standard anti-vaccination tropes and misinformation are all there, such as saying that vaccines "overwhelm" the immune system, or blaming autism on vaccines. After the fear is created, then the sales pitch comes. Homeopaths just happen to have a substitute for real medicine and its toxic vaccines. The solution is sugar pills. The homeopaths pull out their homeopathic "nosodes" and offer them as "risk-free" substitutes, claiming that they have effectiveness rates of "93–95 per cent." It's appalling and frightening. As I watched the sales pitch, I wondered how many times homeopaths have counselled parents against vaccines—and how many parents actually knew that they'd been sold an expensive placebo, with zero ability to protect their children from infectious disease.

How did it ever come to this?

If you're new to the world of alternative medicine, you might think of homeopathy as a variation of herbalism. The marketing and labelling of homeopathic "remedies" encourages you to think this, describing it as a "gentle" and "natural" system of healing, and putting cryptic "30C" codes beside long Latin names. But with herbalism, at least you're getting some herb. Homeopathy's remedies contain no medicine at all—herbal, natural, or otherwise. They are inert. Homeopathy is the air guitar of alternative medicine, going through the motions of medicine, without actually providing medicine. How water and sugar pills are thought to heal is based on nonsensical, prescientific ideas about biology, biochemistry, and medicine itself. Homeopathy is based on the idea that "like cures like" (which is simply a form of magical thinking) and then performing successive dilutions of substances in water. Each dilution is believed to *increase*, not decrease, the "potency" of the final product. And these are serious dilutions. Think of putting one drop of a substance into a container of water. Only that container is 131 light-years in diameter. That's the "30C" dilution you'll see on packages. Homeopaths believe that the water molecules retain a "memory" of the original substance (while somehow forgetting all the other products it has come in contact with). The final remedy is diluted so completely that most "remedies" *don't contain a single molecule* of the original substance you started with. The CBC used a great image to illustrate the absurdity—a tablet *the size of the Earth* might contain a single molecule of the original substance. The rest is sugar.

You might wonder how homeopathy could ever be approved as "safe and effective" by a drug regulator. It comes down to how you define "effective." In the case of homeopathy, regulators diluted the standards just like homeopaths dilute their remedies. Health Canada was required to collect and evaluate some sort of evidence of effectiveness for each product it was responsible for regulating. But it realized that homeopathy could never meet conventional scientific standards of evidence. Consequently it allows citations about homeopathy from texts that date back to the 1800s as "evidence" that homeopathy is effective. To put this in perspective, this means that homeopaths can cite "evidence" that precedes germ theory. Forget about randomized controlled trials—this is anecdote-based medicine.

Through this process, Health Canada approved 82 homeopathic "nosodes" for sale over the years. A "nosode" is a remedy that starts with infectious material, like polio, measles, or smallpox, and then it's diluted sequentially until mathematically, there's nothing left but water. Those appear to be the remedies the CBC caught the homeopaths selling as vaccine substitutes. Last year the advocacy group Bad Science Watch (www.badsciencewatch.ca) launched a public campaign against nosodes, and succeeded in getting Health Canada's agreement to force commercial manufacturers to place a label on their products stating "This product is not intended to be an alternative to vaccination." This was the warning *CBC Marketplace* was looking for on the packages sold on camera. The warning wasn't there—because Health Canada apparently doesn't require the warning when the remedy is produced by the homeopaths themselves, only when the products are commercially prepared. Rather than reflecting on CBC's question and Health Canada's intent, homeopaths are instead gloating about their supposed "victory" over a requirement to give consumers a fair warning. No regulator is going to stop Canada's homeopaths from selling fake vaccines to Canadians, it seems.

This isn't the first time *CBC Marketplace* has scrutinized homeopathy. A 2011 episode asked if homeopathy was a "Cure or Con" and came to the expected conclusion. This episode had a similar reaction, with homeopaths outraged over the "bias" from CBC. (For LOLs, check out the Homeopathy and CBC Marketplace Facebook page, at www.facebook.com/HomeopathyandCBC.) CBC notes that not one of the five homeopaths filmed on camera was willing to go back on camera to defend their actions. Nor was any homeopathy spokesperson from the various homeopathy organizations that exist in Canada. But now that the show has been broadcast, several homeopaths are defending themselves in print. Their own words are further evidence that homeopaths do not appear to comprehend the risks they are taking with the health of children.

While these homeopaths may genuinely believe their homeopathic "remedies" are effective, their customers are not receiving full disclosure of the scientific facts. This is where homeopathy can harm. Choosing homeopathy over a vaccine is a *decision to forsake immunization*, something a homeopath's customers may not even realize—and seemingly something homeopaths have no intention of disclosing, even when they know the product should be labelled this way. Frustratingly, regulation has given homeopaths an opportunity, and now they're exploiting it, suggesting that homeopathy may offer something valuable. It does not. Regulating homeopathy and its providers makes as much sense as regulating magic carpets and their vendors.

Why is all this so important? Because vaccines work. And we need high vaccination rates to control or eradicate disease. Vaccines are one of the most remarkable health interventions ever developed. This fact has been written about countless times in this blog, so I won't rehash that evidence.

Millions of lives saved by an inexpensive and safe medical intervention. The potential that we'll be able to eradicate a disease from the earth, like we did with smallpox. That's what vaccines are doing. And that's why the actions of homeopaths are so frustrating. With vaccine rates dropping in some areas (some Toronto public schools have up to 40 per cent of students with "exemptions" from the vaccination schedule), health professionals and public health advocates need to be prepared to recognize and address the antagonism against vaccines that's fostered by homeopaths.

Another image that really hit home for me recently was a photo series from Anne Geddes, whom you probably associate with photos of cute children. She recently did a photo session with the victims of meningococcal disease, an illness that can steal limbs and even kill within 24 hours. The photos are beautiful but heartbreaking, and speak to the catastrophic harm that this infectious disease can cause. Amazingly, this infection is now vaccine preventable. But you need to be vaccinated with medicine—not sugar pills.

Anti-vaccine sentiment is ugly, and it's even uglier when there's a profit motive behind it. I commend *CBC Marketplace* for yet again taking a hard look at homeopathy from a consumer protection perspective, as it's something that regulators like Health Canada seem to show little interest in. The evidence is unequivocal—homeopathy has nothing to contribute to immunization or public health issues. One thing that you can do to counter-balance the harms of Canadian homeopaths is to contribute to vaccine programs directly, like those coordinated by Bill Gates or by other organizations. I've just contributed to UNICEF's program and bought vaccines (https://shop.unicef.ca/vaccine-pack) which should prevent measles, tetanus, and polio in 139 children. The costs are modest, the risks are low, and the vaccines will save lives. If only this type of health care was supported by homeopaths.

ESSAY 9

What If You Could Save 250 Lives by Feeling a Little Disgusted?

by Peter Jaworski

Picture having to eat a mealworm. Mealworms are the slimy, crawling larvae of the mealworm beetle.* They are perfectly safe to eat. But you and I would probably not eat them here or there, we would not eat them anywhere. Not on a canape, and not with a fox. Not in a house, nor in a box.

Reflect for a moment on the feeling you get in your stomach at the thought of eating something so disgusting. That's uncomfortable.

Now suppose a large number of Canadians will suffer from that very same stomach-turning feeling for the next 24 hours. Let's say a million of us will suffer from that feeling. That's a lot of people feeling a great deal of repugnance. But imagine we could alleviate that stomach-turning feeling. All we have to do is let 256 people die. If we let 256 people die, a million of us will not have to feel repulsed or disgusted.

Would you trade the lives of 256 people in order to ensure one million people won't feel disgusted?

In Canada, that's what we do every year. Every year, we decide that we'd rather let about 250 people die than have to put up with feeling repulsed.

There are about 4,500 people waiting for organs in Canada. Most of those waiting—nearly 80 per cent—are waiting for a kidney transplant. In 2012, 256 people died on the waiting list. In the U.S., there are now 120,990 people on a waiting list for organs. 99,201 are waiting on kidneys. Last year, 3,381 people died waiting on a kidney transplant.

We have tried increasing altruistic donations. We have tried to get people to sign their organ donor card. But every year only about 2,000 transplants get performed, a number that has remained steady since 2006. In the U.S., about 16,500 people donate organs altruistically.

We could fix this. But it would mean allowing a market in organs. It would mean letting people sell one of their kidneys, like they do in Iran. Iran still has a waiting list. But no one waits for organs. Instead, there is a waiting list of people who want to sell an organ. We already know that a market in kidneys would work.

I know, I know: Gross! Repugnant! Repulsive! Disgusting! And so on.

But this really is the choice. 250 lives in exchange for your not feeling disgusted.

For every other concern, there is a simple fix.

*Source: Peter Jaworski, "What If You Could Save 250 Lives by Feeling a Little Disgusted?" *HuffPost*, 5 May 2014, http://www.huffingtonpost.ca/peter-jaworski/organ-trade_b_5267905.html. Reproduced with permission of the author.

Some of you might be worried about economic exploitation. Very well, we can restrict the market to all and only those people who make a certain amount of money per year. We can prohibit the poor from selling their organs.

If you're concerned about exploiting those who don't know enough, those who might regret their decision later, we can institute a waiting period of six to 12 months, coupled with a mandatory course. We can test how much people know about what they are getting into. If you pass the test, you get to sell a kidney, if not, then not.

That waiting period and test could also be designed in such a way that any worries about coercion or insufficiently informed consent gets taken care of as well.

If you're worried that only the rich will be able to afford organs, no problem: We distribute the organs according to the current standard, or based on need. We have a third party, like the government, or a charity, pay for the kidneys. So no one on the waiting list would have to pay for the kidneys at all. Whether or not you get a kidney would not depend on how thick your wallet is.

And if you're concerned about the meaning of money, or the symbolism of the whole thing, we can change how people get paid. Instead of a cheque, we could pay with a tax credit, or a tuition voucher. We could also insist that people can only use the tuition voucher, for example, on someone other than themselves. That would preserve the altruistic component—you're not selling the kidney to benefit yourself financially, you would be exchanging a gift of life for a gift of education for someone else.

We can keep going like this for any worry you might raise, but I trust that you have enough imagination to figure out how to come up with a way to design the market to alleviate whatever concerns you can come up with.

All that's left is that uncomfortable feeling in the pit of your stomach. Would you really trade the lives of 256 people to avoid having to feel a bit uncomfortable?

If a market in kidneys disgusts you, so much the worse for your dinner plans. Get over it.

ESSAY 10

Christmas Is a Secular Holiday

by Mark Mercer

People who would ban Christmas decorations and celebrations from public places are moved by the thought that to celebrate Christmas publicly is to privilege one tradition and the constellation of values around it over all the other traditions and constellations of values current in Canadian society.* Celebrating Christmas, they

*Source: Mark Mercer, "Christmas Is a Secular Holiday," *Ottawa Citizen*, 24 December 2008. Reproduced with permission of the author.

think, disparages other holidays or traditions of celebration, and that, in turn, marginalizes or excludes everyone outside the Christian tradition.

One point we must keep in mind here, though, is that Christmas is not an exclusively Christian holiday. For at least a couple generations, Christmas has been evolving into a secular holiday, a holiday that for many of us has no religious significance at all. Christmas is a celebration of good will, generosity, and peace among nations. It is a time to appreciate and enjoy the company of family and friends. Children are central to Christmas—partly because it is to them that the future belongs, mainly because they are strange and clever people of whom we are fond.

Now for the Christians among us, Christmas marks the birth of Jesus and, so, is also an occasion for worship. But it isn't any such occasion for the rest of us. And while the activities and symbols through which we honour and celebrate good will, generosity, peace, family, friends, and children derive from Christian traditions, they now have a life of their own independent of those traditions. They don't put us in mind of any values or doctrines specifically Christian.

Christmas, that is, is for many who celebrate it an entirely secular holiday. So if public displays of Christmas trees or greetings of "Merry Christmas!" privilege or exclude, it is not in virtue of their privileging Christianity or excluding non-Christians. What we honour and celebrate at Christmas and through such things as Christmas trees, gift giving, and greetings of "Merry Christmas!"—good will, generosity, peace, family, friends, children—are important in many, if not all, traditions and ways of life current in Canada.

Still, though a secular holiday that honours values to which almost all of us subscribe, Christmas is *someone's* particular celebration of these values and, so, maybe not someone else's. And that fact brings us to the question what sort of multicultural society we would like ours to be.

In one sort of multicultural society, no celebrations or holidays are public celebrations or holidays. There are, perhaps, statutory holidays, or maybe each of us just gets a certain number of days off work each year to take when she chooses. Each of us congregates with others of her group when according to her traditions or authorities it's time to honour something, and we do with members of our group whatever our traditions or authorities would have us do. Some of us might invite outsiders to be with us on our celebration day; perhaps we have a fair that anyone can attend. Others of us might instead just have one of our elders write an article for the paper about who we are and what we are honouring. We might make use of public money or public facilities in conducting our event. But in this sort of society, no celebration is by everyone for everyone.

In another sort of multicultural society, some celebrations or holidays *are* public events—events funded and organized by or through civil authorities acting on mandates from the federal government. These holidays would, of course, have to honour values important to most people in the country and to honour them in ways the people find congenial, or else they would attract few participants. In this second sort of multicultural society, a few holidays, maybe only two or three a year, belong to *all* the people. They are times when everyone gets together to enjoy themselves and to enjoy each other.

The second sort of multicultural society is much more attractive than the first sort. The people in it enjoy whatever group identities they have and they are free and welcome to honour them. But they also see themselves as citizens of a country and view their neighbours as fellow citizens. In the first sort of multicultural society, though, people see themselves merely as residing among their neighbours, not as connected to them through projects of citizenship.

What might be a holiday that all of us can celebrate together simply as Canadians, a holiday whose values touch us all? An obvious candidate is the secular holiday known as Christmas. If we want to have a few holidays that belong to all of us and that all of us can enjoy, I say we make Christmas one of them.

Christmas has been evolving into a secular holiday for decades. Sadly, not everyone has received the news. Some people would have us say "Season's greetings" rather than "Merry Christmas" and not have us put Christmas trees in public areas, wrongly thinking that Christmas in Canada is a Christian affair. They would undo the good work people have been doing over the decades to transform Christmas into a celebration that's moving and fun for everyone. They would return Christmas to the Christians. Willingly or not, these people are helping to make all celebrations in our country small, sectarian, private affairs. I say we instead take up the noble task of continuing to offer Christmas to all as a delightful secular holiday that we enjoy together and at which we honour values we all cherish.

So let us say "Merry Christmas" to each other and decorate Christmas trees in public places. And let us explain to anyone who worries that our behaviour will offend or exclude someone that while Christmas does have its origins in Christian traditions, the Christmas we celebrate is not at all a Christian or a religious holiday. Christmas now belongs to all of us, it privileges no particular religious or other tradition, and no one is excluded from it.

APPENDIX B

Answers to Exercises

CHAPTER 1

Exercise 1.1

1. Critical thinking is the systematic evaluation or formulation of beliefs, or statements, by rational standards.
4. The *critical* in critical thinking refers to the exercising of careful judgment and judicious evaluation.
5. Critical thinking operates according to rational standards in that beliefs are judged by how well they are supported by reasons.
8. A statement is an assertion that something is or is not the case.
11. An argument is a group of statements in which some of them (the premises) are intended to support another of them (the conclusion).
13. In an argument, a conclusion is a statement that premises are intended to support.
17. False.
19. Indicator words are words that frequently accompany arguments and signal that a premise or conclusion is present.
23. Look for the conclusion first.

Exercise 1.2

1. Statement
4. Not a statement
7. Not a statement
10. Statement

Exercise 1.3

1. Argument
   Conclusion: Nachos are the perfect study food.
7. Not an argument
11. Argument
    Conclusion: You should hire Kaitlin.
15. Argument
    Conclusion: Canada should pursue its trade negotiations with the United States on the assumption that Mr Trump is aiming for another grand, empty gesture.

Exercise 1.4

1. No argument
4. Argument
   Conclusion: The flu epidemic on the east coast is real.
   Premise: Government health officials say so.
   Premise: I personally have read at least a dozen news stories that characterize the situation as a "flu epidemic."
7. Not an argument
10. Argument
    Conclusion: Raising the price of our shoes is sure to hurt sales.
    Premise: It's a law of economics that if prices go up, demand will fall.

Exercise 1.5

3. Premise 1: Freedom to seek out food to sustain oneself and one's family is a basic moral right.
   Premise 2: Treaties signed by the Canadian government state that Indigenous Canadians will always be able to hunt and fish.
6. Premise 1: MacDonald has admitted that he knows nothing about animals.
   Premise 2: The Society for the Prevention of Cruelty to Animals has declared MacDonald a dummy when it comes to animals.
9. Premise 1: The internet has led to the capture of more terrorists than anything else.
   Premise 2: The attorney general of Canada has asserted that the internet is the best friend that anti-terrorist teams have.
12. Premise 1: Dress codes promote uniformity over creativity.
    Premise 2: Dress codes discriminate against people whose religions prescribe particular kinds of clothes.

Exercise 1.6

2. Conclusion: We can expect that most elderly Canadians in long-term care facilities will be safe from COVID-19.

4. Conclusion: You are likely happier than people who aren't married.
8. Conclusion: Canada doesn't care about its children.

Exercise 1.7

1. Argument
   Conclusion: Advertising isn't manipulative.
   Premise: The main thing advertising does is provide information about products.
   Premise: Ads that don't seem to provide much information are really just trying to entertain us, not manipulate us.
3. Argument
   Conclusion: It is important to ensure that the high number of users does not lead to an abusive exploitation of data power.
   Premise: WhatsApp is now used by almost 60 million people in Germany.
   Premise: WhatsApp is the most widely used social media app in Germany.

CHAPTER 2

Exercise 2.1

1. The two main categories of barriers are those that arise because of *how* we think and those that occur because of *what* we think.
5. We take things too far when we accept claims for no reason.
7. You are most likely to let your self-interest get in the way of clear thinking when you have a significant personal stake in the conclusions you reach.
11. Group pressure can affect your attempts to think critically by allowing your need to be part of a group or your identification with a group to undermine critical thinking.
14. A world view is a set of fundamental ideas that helps us to make sense of a wide range of issues in life.
17. Critical thinking is concerned with objective truth claims.
21. Reasonable doubt, not certainty, is central to acquiring knowledge.

Exercise 2.2

1. Group pressure
4. Face-saving
7. Group pressure
10. None of the above (but possibly group pressure is involved)

Exercise 2.3

1. a. The charge comes from a single source who is a known liar.
   c. Important evidence that would exonerate Father Miller was not mentioned in the newspaper account.

3. d. Janette has a degree in criminology.
6. No good reasons listed.

Exercise 2.4

1. Better-than-others group pressure. Possible negative consequence: failure to consider other points of view; discrimination against people who disagree with Marie-Eve.
4. It's not entirely clear what the group's motivations are. This passage could easily be an example of better-than-others group pressure.
7. Appeal to popularity. Possible negative consequence: failure to pay attention to other environmental issues that *might* be even more important than recycling.

Exercise 2.5

1. Face-saving. Possible negative consequences: continued poor performance due to misidentifying problems; alienation of workers.
2. Self-interest. Possible negative consequences: wasting taxpayers' money; being thrown out of office for misconduct.

CHAPTER 3

Exercise 3.1

4. Deductive
8. Sound
12. No

Exercise 3.2

1. Step 1: Conclusion: She is a very good athlete.
   Premises: Ethel played hockey for Saint Mary's University. If she played hockey for Saint Mary's, she's probably a very good athlete.
   Step 2: Not deductively valid.
   Step 3: Inductively strong.
   Step 4: Does not apply.
6. Step 1: Conclusion: Thus, every mechanic has a university degree.
   Premises: Every mechanic has had special training, and everyone with special training has a university degree.
   Step 2: Deductively valid.
   Step 3: Does not apply.
   Step 4: Does not apply.
9. Step 1: Conclusion: Some immigrants from India also have degrees in engineering.
   Premises: Some immigrants are from India, and some immigrants have degrees in engineering.

Step 2: Not deductively valid.
Step 3: Not inductively strong.
Step 4: Intended to be deductive.

15. Step 1: Conclusion: So it's impossible for androids to have minds.
    Premises: If minds are identical to brains—that is, if one's mind is nothing but a brain—androids could never have minds because they wouldn't have brains. Clearly, a mind is nothing but a brain.
    Step 2: Deductively valid.
    Step 3: Does not apply.
    Step 4: Does not apply.

Exercise 3.3

3. Valid
8. Valid
14. Valid
18. Valid
21. Invalid

Exercise 3.4

I.

1. The honourable member from Algoma-Manitoulin-Kapuskasing was caught misusing campaign funds.
5. She's not incompetent.
10. Only someone who is pro-American would fail to criticize US military action in the Gulf War or in the war in Afghanistan.

II.

3. Sixty per cent of the teenagers in several scientific surveys love rap music.
6. Assad's fingerprints are on the vase.
9. Add a premise to the effect that the murder rates in almost all cities in central Canada are very low too.

Exercise 3.5

1. Valid; *modus tollens*
6. Valid; *modus tollens*
9. Valid; *modus ponens*

Exercise 3.6

2. If Lino is telling the truth, he will admit to all charges.
   Lino is telling the truth.
   So he will admit to all charges.
   If Lino is telling the truth, he will admit to all charges.
   He will not admit to all charges.
   So he is not telling the truth.

5. If religious conflict in Nigeria continues, thousands more will die.
   The religious conflict in Nigeria will continue.
   Therefore, thousands more will die.
   If religious conflict in Nigeria continues, thousands more will die.
   Thousands more will not die.
   Therefore, the religious conflict in Nigeria will not continue.
9. If solar power can supply six megawatts of power in Vancouver (which is certainly not the sunniest place in the world), then solar power can transform the energy systems in sunnier places like Edmonton and Calgary.
   Solar power can supply six megawatts of power in Vancouver.
   So solar power can transform the energy systems in sunnier places like Edmonton and Calgary.
   If solar power can supply six megawatts of power in Vancouver (which is certainly not the sunniest place in the world), then solar power can transform the energy systems in sunnier places like Edmonton and Calgary.
   But solar power cannot transform the energy systems in sunnier places like Edmonton and Calgary.
   So solar power cannot supply six megawatts of power in Vancouver.

Exercise 3.7

The sample answers below are some possible solutions. Remember, you've been asked to use the counterexample method, which means there are lots of possible answers that are correct (but also lots that are incorrect).

4. One possible counterexample: If Stephen Harper was the prime minister of Canada in 1970, then he would be a Canadian.
   Stephen Harper was not prime minister of Canada in 1970. Therefore, he is not a Canadian.
   If *a*, then *b*.
   Not *a*.
   Therefore, not *b*. (That's denying the antecedent, an invalid argument form.)
5. Not possible to construct a counterexample. This is a valid argument (denying the consequent).
   If ~*a*, then *b*.
   ~*b*.
   Therefore, *a*.
7. One possible counterexample: If Vaughn is a dog, he is a mammal.
   He is a mammal.
   Therefore, he is a dog.
   If *a*, then *b*.
   b.
   Therefore, *a*. (That's affirming the consequent, an invalid argument form.)

8. One possible counterexample: If ducks are sea turtles, then they are at home in the water.
   Ducks are not sea turtles.
   Therefore, ducks are not at home in the water.
   If *a*, then *b*.
   Not *a*.
   Therefore, not *b*. (That's denying the antecedent, an invalid argument form.)
11. One possible counterexample: If Victoria is the capital of British Columbia, then Victoria is in British Columbia.
   Victoria is in British Columbia.
   Therefore, Victoria is the capital of British Columbia.
   If *a*, then *b*.
   b.
   Therefore, *a*. (That's affirming the consequent, an invalid argument form.)

Exercise 3.8

1. Any argument that provides three separate, stand-alone reasons supporting a single conclusion will do. For example:
   (1) The stores are closed. (2) We have no money. (3) And we have no way of travelling to any place of business. (4) Therefore, we are just not going to be able to go shopping right now.

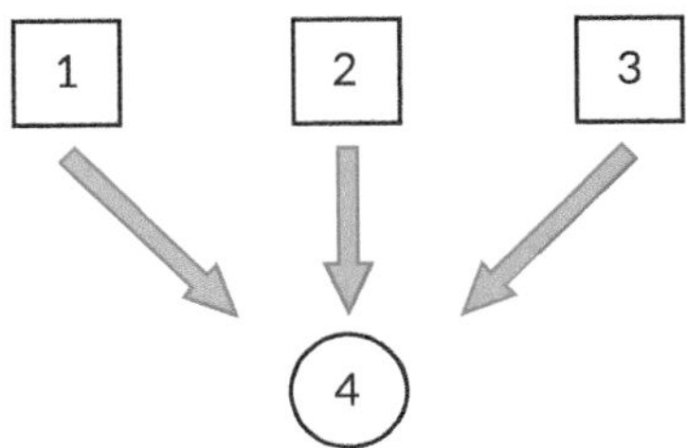

4. (1) If the pipes have burst, there will be no running water. (2) The pipes have burst. (3) And if all the water is rusty, we won't be able to use it anyway, (4) and all the water is rusty. (5) So we have no usable water at this point.

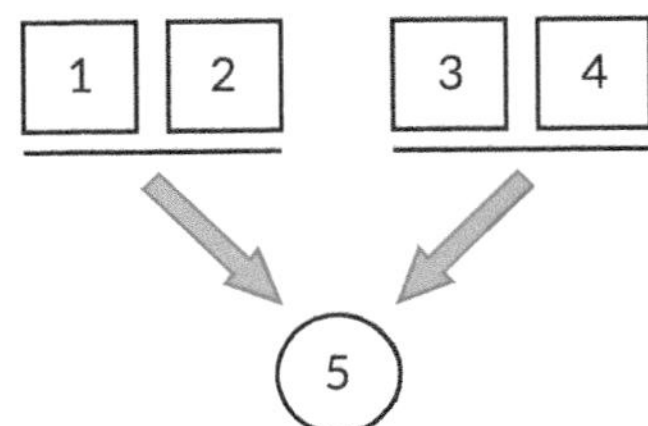

Exercise 3.9

6. (1) If Marla buys the house in the suburbs, she will be happier and healthier. (2) She is buying the house in the suburbs. (3) So she will be happier and healthier.

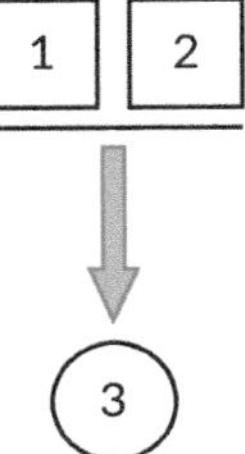

10. (1) The existence of planets outside our solar system is a myth. (2) There is no reliable empirical evidence at all showing that planets exist outside our solar system.

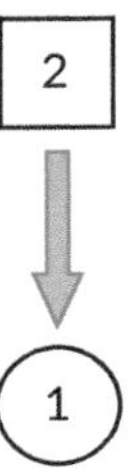

17. ~~(1) There are at least two main views regarding the morality of war. (2) Pacifism is the view that no war is ever justified because it involves the taking of human life. (3) Just-war theory is the view that some wars are justified for various reasons—mostly because they help prevent great evils (such as massacres, "ethnic cleansing," or world domination by a madman like Hitler) or because they are a means of self-defence.~~ (4) I think that our own moral sense tells us that sometimes (in the case of the World War II, for example) violence is occasionally morally justified. (5) It would be hard for anyone to deny that a war to prevent something like the Holocaust is morally right. [Implied conclusion] (6) Just-war theory is correct.

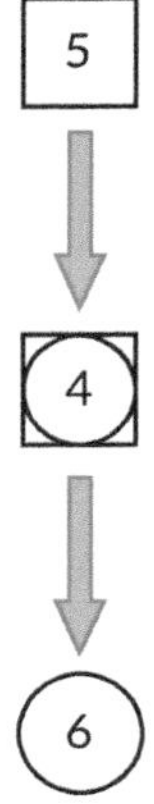

20. (1) The picnic will probably be spoiled because (2) there is a 90 per cent probability of rain.

Exercise 3.10

1. Conclusion: (9) You should skip the supplements.
   Premises: (2) There's no persuasive evidence yet to suggest that collagen supplements help with joint pain. (3) Collagen is a specific thing (something unstated). (4) Collagen is absorbed in a certain (unstated) way. (5) Collagen is synthesized in the body in a certain (unstated) way. (6) It's implausible that a small supplement of amino acids consumed daily will have any meaningful therapeutic effects. (8) Genacol, like other collagen supplements, appears to be little more than an expensive protein supplement.

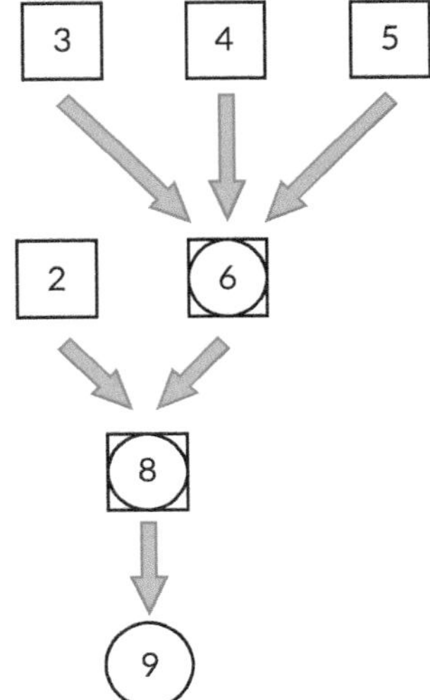

CHAPTER 4

Exercise 4.1

4. We should proportion our belief to the evidence.
10. Two additional indicators are reputation among peers and professional accomplishments.
17. By making a conscious effort to consider not only information that supports what we believe but also the information that conflicts with it.

Exercise 4.2

4. Proportion belief to the evidence; the claim is not dubious enough to dismiss out of hand and not worthy of complete acceptance. Low plausibility.
6. Proportion belief to the evidence; a physics professor is not an expert on public policy, but might have insight into how promising solar energy is technologically.
10. Proportion belief to the evidence; the claim is not dubious enough to dismiss out of hand and not worthy of complete acceptance. Moderate plausibility.
14. Reject it; it conflicts with a great deal of background information.
17. Reject it; it conflicts with a great deal of background information.

Exercise 4.3

3. Do not agree. Persuasive evidence would include the body of an alien or the alien craft itself, both scientifically documented as being of extraterrestrial origin.
8. Do not agree. Persuasive evidence would include several double-blind, controlled trials demonstrating that meditation and controlled breathing shrink tumours.

CHAPTER 5

Exercise 5.1

4. The fallacy of division involves arguing that what is true of the whole must also be true of the parts. The fallacy of composition does the opposite: it involves arguing that what is true of the parts must be true of the whole.
10. They are fallacious because they assume that a proposition is true merely because a great number of people believe it, but as far as the truth of a claim is concerned, what many people believe is irrelevant.
15. Yes.
19. A false dilemma may assert that there are only two alternatives to consider when there are actually more than two or assert that there are two distinct alternatives that may in fact not be mutually exclusive. People are often taken in by false dilemmas because they don't think beyond the alternatives laid before them.

Exercise 5.2

1. Composition
5. Genetic fallacy
10. Appeal to the person
14. Equivocation (the word *desirable* is used as if it means "capable of being desired" and also as if it means "worthy of being desired"). Alternatively: faulty analogy.
20. Appeal to the person

Exercise 5.3

4. False dilemma
6. Hasty generalization
10. False dilemma

Exercise 5.4

3. Jones says that Mrs Anan deserves the Nobel Prize. But he's a real jerk. Clearly, then, Mrs Anan does not deserve the Nobel Prize.
6. In light of ethical considerations, Scouts Canada should allow gay kids to be members. The reason is that banning LGBTQ kids from the organization would conflict with basic moral principles.
11. Newfoundland's fisheries are a mess because the Department of Fisheries and Oceans—a federal department—has too much power over them. Nobody likes intrusive governments!

CHAPTER 6

Exercise 6.1

1. *S* = dogs, *P* = things that like mushrooms; particular negative; O.
5. *S* = theologians who have studied arguments for the existence of God, *P* = scholars with serious misgivings about the traditional notion of omnipotence; universal affirmative; A.
8. *S* = people who play the stock market, *P* = millionaires; particular negative; O.
12. *S* = Loch Ness Monster, *P* = things that are fictional; universal affirmative; A.
16. *S* = new Canadians, *P* = immigration reform supporters; universal negative; E.

Exercise 6.2

1. All Montreal Canadiens fans are loyal to their team (or, are people who are loyal to their team). A.
5. All good investments in cellphone companies are investments in cellphone companies that keep up with the latest technology. A.
9. All intelligent thoughts are thoughts that have already happened. A.
13. Some things are things meant to be forgotten. I.

Exercise 6.3

1. All people who test the depth of the water with both feet are fools. A.
4. All digital assistants like Apple's Siri are non-persons. A.
5. No things that satisfy the heart are material things. E.
8. Some treatments said to be part of "alternative medicine" are unproven treatments. I.
12. All days that give her any joy are Fridays. A.

15. All pictures identical with the one hanging on the wall are things that are crooked. A.
20. All great achievements are things that require time. A.

Exercise 6.4

1. No persons are persons exempt from federal income tax.
   S = persons; P = persons exempt from federal income tax.

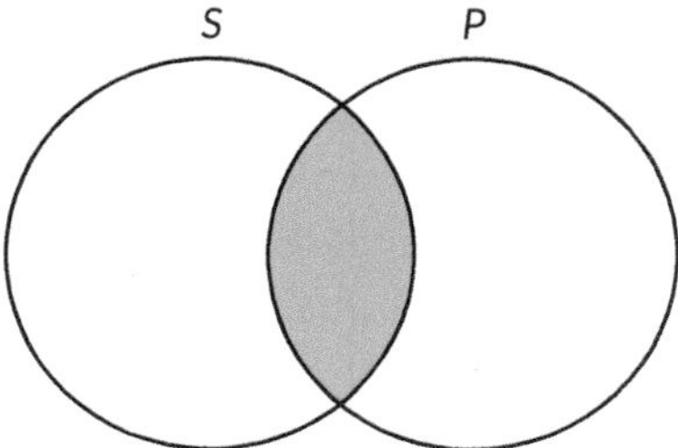

5. No things are things more useless in a developing nation's economy than a gun.
   S = things; P = things more useless in a developing nation's economy than a gun.

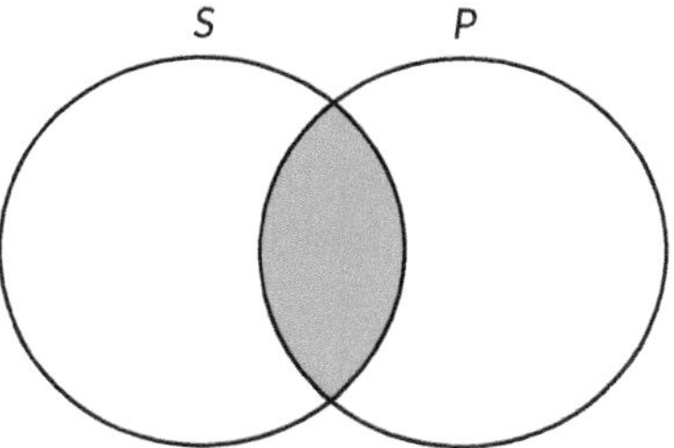

8. Some news stories are stories written by computers.
   S = news stories; P = stories written by computers.

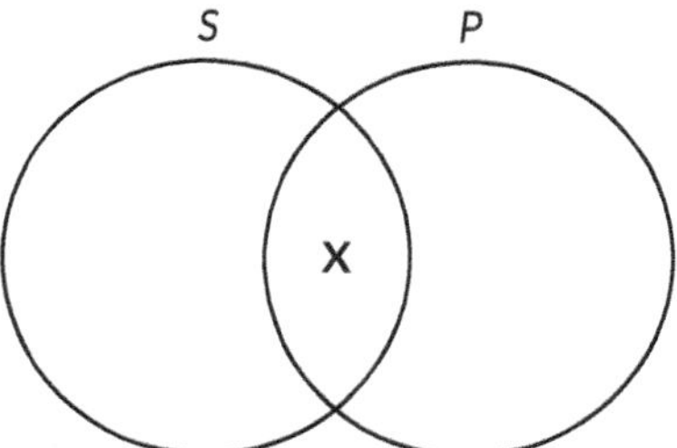

12. All corporations are corporations with social obligations.
 S = corporations; *P* = corporations with social obligations.

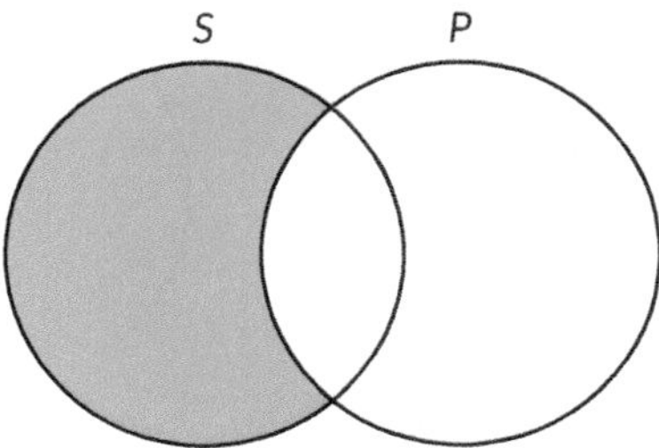

Exercise 6.5

1. No *S* are *P*; No *P* are *S*.

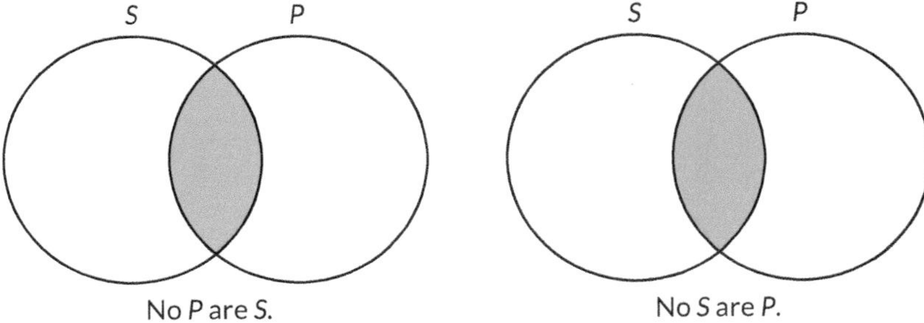

 Equivalent.

3. All *S* are *P*; All *P* are *S*.

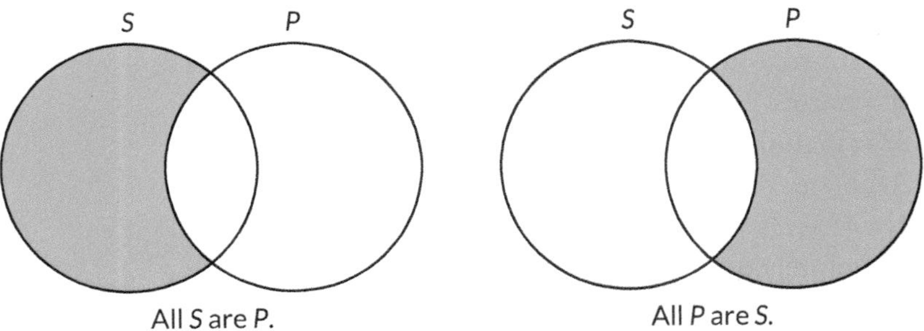

 Not equivalent.

6. All S are non-P; All P are non-S.

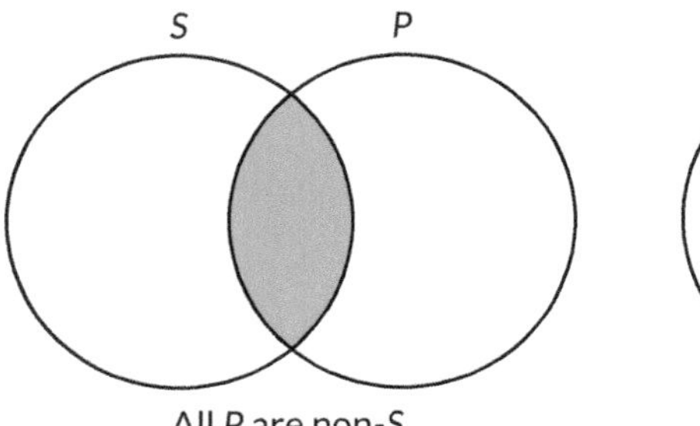

All P are non-S.

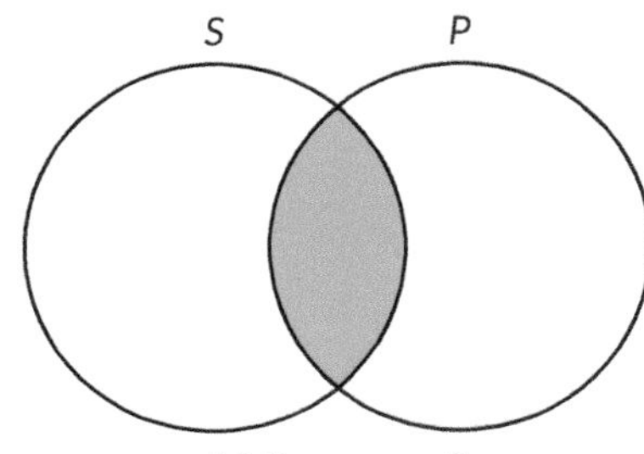

All S are non-P.

Equivalent.

9. Some S are not P; Some P are not S.

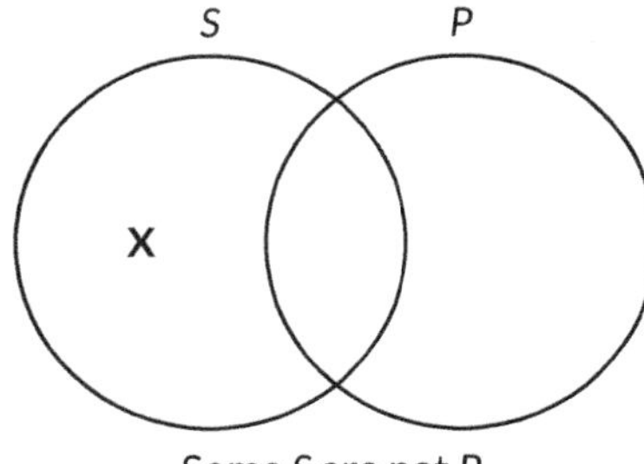

Some S are not P.

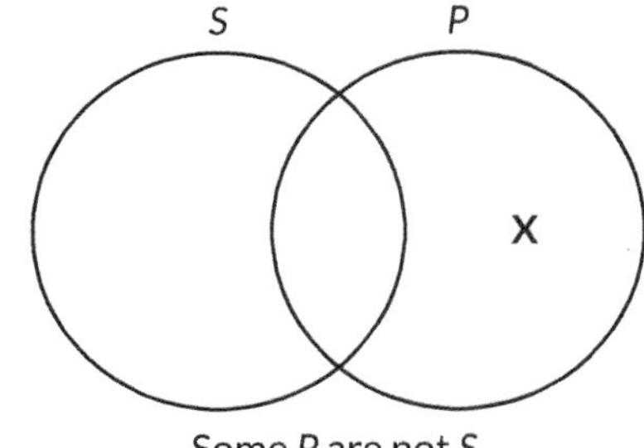

Some P are not S.

Not equivalent.

Exercise 6.6

2. All horses are mammals, and no mammals are lizards. Therefore, no lizards are horses.
   S = lizards
   P = horses
   M = mammals
   All P are M.
   No M are S.
   Therefore, no S are P.
6. Some DVDs are not film classics, but all black-and-white movies are film classics. Therefore, some black-and-white movies are not DVDs.
   S = black-and-white movies
   P = DVDs
   M = film classics
   Some P are not M.
   All S are M.
   Therefore, some S are not P.

9. No elm trees are cacti. Some tall plants are elm trees. So some tall plants are not cacti.
   S = tall plants
   P = cacti
   M = elm trees
   No *M* are *P*.
   Some *S* are *M*.
   Therefore, some *S* are not *P*.

Exercise 6.7

2. All *P* are *M*.
   No *M* are *S*.
   Therefore, no *S* are *P*.

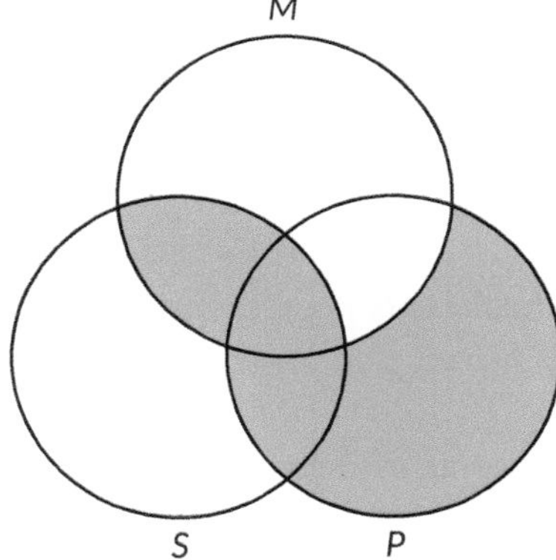

   Valid.

6. Some *P* are not *M*.
   All *S* are *M*.
   Therefore, some *S* are not *P*.

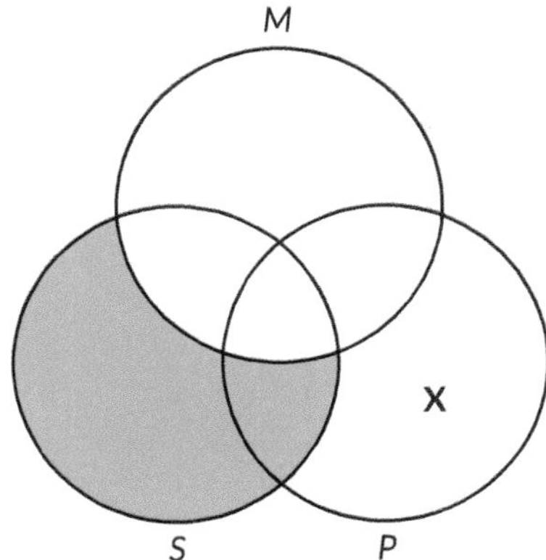

   Invalid.

9. No M are P.
   Some S are M.
   Therefore, some S are not P.

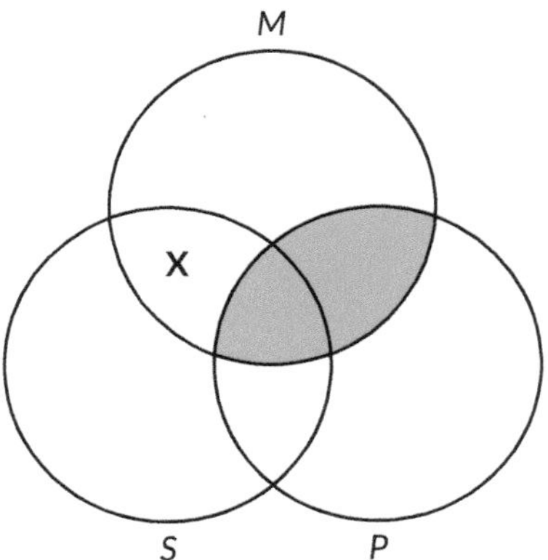

Valid.

Exercise 6.8

1. Some "alternative" healers are people who claim to cure cancer, for all herbalists are "alternative" healers and some herbalists are people who claim to cure cancer.
   Some herbalists are people who claim to cure cancer.
   All herbalists are "alternative" healers.
   Therefore, some "alternative" healers are people who claim to cure cancer.
   Some M are P.
   All M are S.
   Therefore, some S are P.

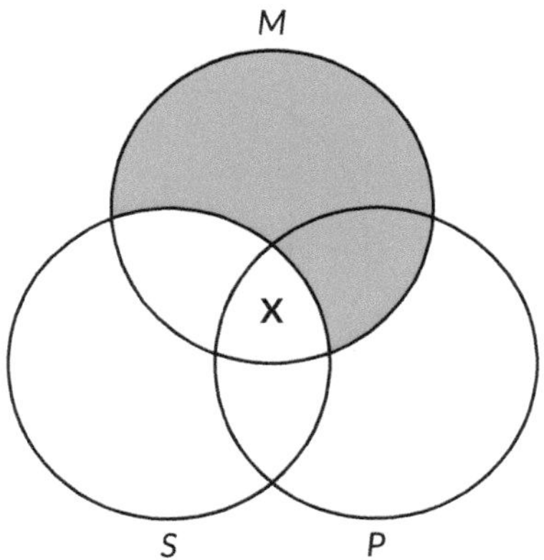

Valid.

3. All SUVs are evil vehicles because all SUVs are gas guzzlers and all gas guzzlers are evil vehicles.
   All gas guzzlers are evil.
   All SUVs are gas guzzlers.
   Therefore, all SUVs are evil vehicles.
   All *M* are *P*.
   All *S* are *M*.
   Therefore, all *S* are *P*.

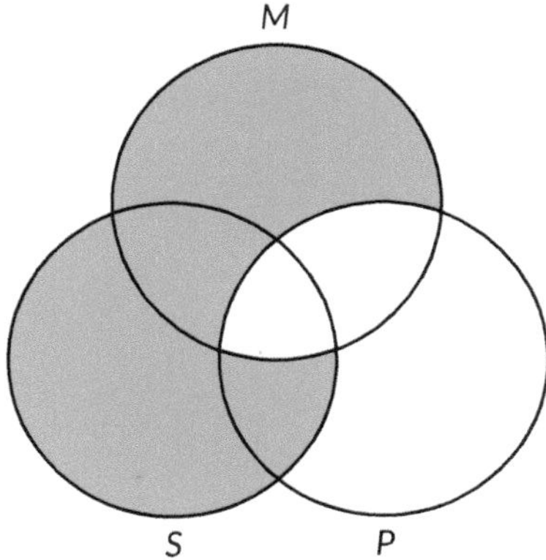

   Valid.
8. No wimps are social activists because no wimps are people of honest and strong conviction. And all social activists are people of honest and strong conviction.
   All social activists are people of honest and strong convictions.
   No wimps are people of honest and strong convictions.
   Therefore, no wimps are social activists.
   All *P* are *M*.
   No *S* are *M*.
   Therefore, no *S* are *P*.

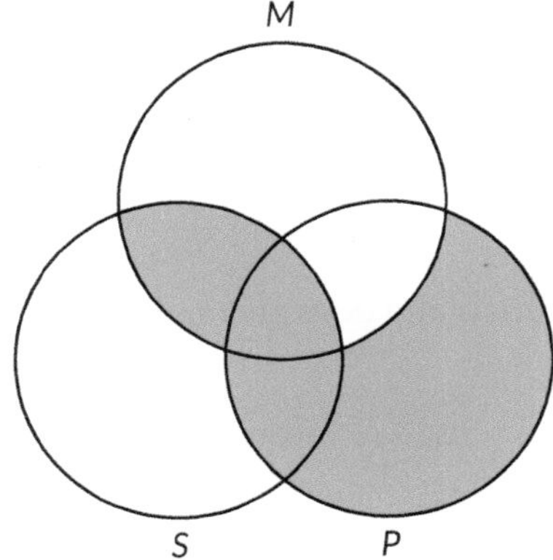

   Valid.

CHAPTER 7

Exercise 7.1

1. Conjunction. Components: The Liberals raised taxes, The Conservatives cut programs; &
5. Conditional. Components: Taslima can read your mind, You're in trouble; →
7. Conditional. Components: God is all-powerful, He can prevent evil in the world; →

Exercise 7.2

1. $p \vee q$
4. $e \,\&\, f$
8. $\sim g \,\&\, \sim h$
14. $\sim\sim p$

Exercise 7.3

2. False
6. True
8. False

Exercise 7.4

2. False
5. True
9. False

Exercise 7.5

2. Either John is not home or Mary is not home.
5. If the sun is shining, then we will go outside.
9. If the day goes well, then we will not regret our efforts.

Exercise 7.6

2. $p \vee q$
5. $\sim a \rightarrow \sim b$
9. $p \rightarrow q$

Exercise 7.7

2. Alligators are mammals and dogs are mammals.

a	*d*	*a* & *d*
T	T	T
T	F	F
F	T	F
F	F	F

6. Either dogs are not mammals or snakes are reptiles. [Hint: To avoid confusion, you can *add* columns after the guide columns, such as the one for ~*d* in this truth table. This extra column reminds you that the truth values for ~*d* are the flip side of those for *d*.]

d	*s*	~*d*	~*d* ∨ *s*
T	T	F	T
T	F	F	F
F	T	T	T
F	F	T	T

8. Dogs are not reptiles, and alligators have fur.

d	*a*	~*d*	~*d* & *a*
T	T	F	F
T	F	F	F
F	T	T	T
F	F	T	F

Exercise 7.8

1. Valid

$p \rightarrow q$
p
$\therefore q$

p	*q*	*p* → *q*	*p*	*q*
T	T	T	T	T
T	F	F	T	F
F	T	T	F	T
F	F	T	F	F

7. Valid

$p \rightarrow q$
$\sim q \,\&\, r$
$\therefore r$

p	*q*	*r*	~*q*	*p* → *q*	~*q* & *r*	*r*
T	T	T	F	T	F	T
T	T	F	F	T	F	F
T	F	T	T	F	T	T
T	F	F	T	F	F	F
F	T	T	F	T	F	T
F	T	F	F	T	F	F
F	F	T	T	T	T	T
F	F	F	T	T	F	F

14. Valid
$p \rightarrow q$
$\sim(q \vee r)$
$\therefore \sim p$

p	q	r	$\sim p$	$p \rightarrow q$	$\sim(q \vee r)$	$\sim p$
T	T	T	F	T	F	F
T	T	F	F	T	F	F
T	F	T	F	F	F	F
T	F	F	F	F	T	F
F	T	T	T	T	F	T
F	T	F	T	T	F	T
F	F	T	T	T	F	T
F	F	F	T	T	T	T

Exercise 7.9

3. This is either olive oil or canola oil. And it's not olive oil, so it must be canola oil.
$o \vee c$
$\sim o$
$\therefore c$

o	c	$o \vee c$	$\sim o$	c
T	T	T	F	T
T	F	T	F	F
F	T	T	T	T
F	F	F	T	F

Valid

11. Either the herbal remedy alleviated the symptoms or the placebo effect alleviated the symptoms. If the placebo effect is responsible for easing the symptoms, then the herbal remedy is worthless. The herbal remedy alleviated the symptoms. So the herbal remedy is not worthless.
$h \vee p$
$p \rightarrow w$
h
$\therefore \sim w$

h	p	w	$h \vee p$	$p \rightarrow w$	h	$\sim w$
T	T	T	T	T	T	F
T	T	F	T	F	T	T
T	F	T	T	T	T	F
T	F	F	T	T	T	T
F	T	T	T	T	F	F

h	p	w	$h \vee p$	$p \rightarrow w$	h	$\sim w$
F	T	F	T	F	F	T
F	F	T	F	T	F	F
F	F	F	F	T	F	T

Invalid

Exercise 7.10

2. $p \vee q$
   q
   $\therefore \sim p$

   T T F

   $p \vee q$ $\quad q$ $\quad \sim p$
   T T T T

   Invalid

9. $p \rightarrow q$
   $\therefore p \rightarrow (p \,\&\, q)$

   F F

   $p \rightarrow q$ $\quad p \rightarrow (p \,\&\, q)$
   T F T T F

   Valid

15. $(d \vee e) \rightarrow (d \,\&\, e)$
    $\sim(d \vee e)$
    $\therefore \sim(d \,\&\, e)$

    T F F

    $(d \vee e) \rightarrow (d \,\&\, e)$ $\quad \sim(d \vee e) \sim (d \,\&\, e)$
    T T T T T T T T

    Valid

CHAPTER 8

Exercise 8.1

1. Target group: Canadian adults; sample: several thousand horse owners; relevant property: being in favour of banning horse meat. The argument is weak because the sample is not representative.
4. Target group: Decembers in Vancouver; sample: many years of Decembers in Vancouver; relevant property: receiving over 150 millimetres of rain. The argument is strong.

8. Target group: dentists; sample: dentists who suggest that their patients chew gum; relevant property: recommending Brand X gum. The argument is weak because the sample is not representative.
12. Target group: Canadians; sample: adults with an annual income of $48,000–$60,000; relevant property: being happy and satisfied with one's job. The argument is weak because the sample is not representative. (Middle-income workers are likely to have attitudes toward job satisfaction that are different from those of workers in other income brackets, especially lower ones.)

Exercise 8.2

1. Weak. To ensure a strong argument, draw the sample randomly from the entire Canadian population, not just from horse owners.
4. Strong. To make this into a weak argument, rely on a much smaller sample, such as "the last few Decembers."
8. Weak. To ensure a strong argument, draw the sample randomly from the set of all dentists, not just the dentists who recommend gum.
12. Weak. To ensure a strong argument, draw the sample randomly from the set of all Canadian workers, including respondents representative of all income groups.

Exercise 8.3

1. Does not offer strong support for the conclusion. The problem is non-random—and therefore non-representative—sampling.

Exercise 8.4

1. a, b

Exercise 8.5

1. More likely to be true.

Exercise 8.6

1. Individual: Barb; group: people who ride their bikes to work; characteristic: riding recklessly; proportion: almost all.
4. Individual: next meal eaten at the Poolhouse Café; group: meals eaten at the Poolhouse Café; characteristic: being wonderful; proportion: almost every.
5. Individual: your car; group: Fords; characteristic: work poorly; proportion: most.

Exercise 8.7

1. Statistical weakness (given weak anecdotal evidence).
2. Non-typical individual (being a professor makes Professor Norman unusual; professors are more likely than most people to have read Plato).
4. Statistically weak (53 per cent might technically be "most," but just barely).

Exercise 8.8

2. Literary analogy.
5. Argument by analogy. Two things being compared; relevant similarity: working with numbers; conclusion: "he'll be a whiz at algebra;" weak argument.
7. Argument by analogy; four things being compared; relevant similarity: being beef; conclusion: "I will like tongue;" weak argument.
11. Argument by analogy; two things being compared; relevant similarity: being foundations; conclusions: "no lasting reputation worthy of respect can be built on a weak character;" weak argument.

Exercise 8.9

1. Instances being compared: the economic joining of newlyweds, on one hand, and the countries of Europe on the other; relevant similarities: linked economic fate; optimism; seeing benefits; likelihood of tough times together; diversity among cases not a significant factor; conclusion: the countries of Europe may regret linking their economies; weak argument (because of several unmentioned dissimilarities—including very different reasons for joining together and different degrees of linkage).
5. Instances being compared: having terminal cancer and being threatened by an assailant; relevant similarities: being threatened with death or great pain; diversity among cases not a significant factor; conclusion: "suicide must sometimes be morally justified when it is an act of self-defence against a terminal disease that threatens death or great pain." This is a strong argument—*if* all the relevant similarities and dissimilarities have indeed been taken into account. A critic could argue, though, that killing oneself in self-defence is just not relevantly similar to killing another human in self-defence. The critic, then, would have to specify what the significant difference is.

Exercise 8.10

2. Conclusion: "Research suggests that eating lots of fruits and vegetables may provide some protection against several types of cancer." Correlation. The argument is strong. The conclusion is a limited claim ("*may* provide some protection . . ."), which the stated correlation could easily support.
7. Conclusion: "Education increases people's earning power." Correlation. The argument is strong.
13. Conclusion: "Tune-ups can improve the performance of lawnmowers." Correlation. The argument is strong.
16. Conclusion: [Implied] "Having a major war somewhere in the world causes the price of oil to hit $40 a barrel." Method of agreement. The argument is strong if all relevant factors have been taken into account, which may not be the case.

19. Conclusion: Police presence has caused the reduction in crime. Method of difference. The argument is relatively strong. More information is needed in order to rule out other possible causes.

Exercise 8.11

2. a, d (It may be that a diagnosis of cancer leads people to start eating healthier!)
7. a
13. a
16. a, b, d
19. a, b, d

Exercise 8.12

1. a
4. b
9. a

CHAPTER 9

Exercise 9.1

4. A theoretical explanation is an explanation that serves as a theory, or hypothesis, used to explain why something is the way it is, why something is the case, or why something happened.
8. A causal explanation is a kind of theoretical explanation. Like all theoretical explanations, causal explanations can be used in inference to the best explanation.

Exercise 9.2

2. The state of affairs being explained is the endangered status of the polar bear. The explanation is the thinning of Arctic ice, caused by global warming.
5. The state of affairs being explained is the "hot" water from your faucet not being very hot. The explanation is that your hot-water heater is old and can't keep up.
8. The state of affairs being explained is the fact that your stomach is churning. The explanation is that the food you've eaten is too spicy.

Exercise 9.3

4. Theoretical
7. Theoretical
12. Interpretive

Exercise 9.4

2. Theory 1: Akane's house was burglarized.
   Theory 2: Akane's dog went on a rampage.

6. Theory 1: Alice was not exposed to any germs.
   Theory 2: Vitamin C supercharged Alice's immune system.

Exercise 9.6

2. The minimum requirement of consistency is the criterion that any theory worth considering must have both internal and external consistency—that is, be free of contradictions and be consistent with the data the theory is supposed to explain.
6. A theory that is not conservative is one that fails to fit with our established beliefs.

Exercise 9.7

2. The first theory is both simpler and more conservative.
4. The first theory is both simpler and more conservative.
7. The first theory is both simpler and more conservative.

Exercise 9.8

3. Theory 3

CHAPTER 10

Exercise 10.1

7. It means to ask yourself, "If this theory were true, what testable consequences would follow from it?"
8. Denying the consequent. Valid.
11. No. Hypotheses are tested together with other hypotheses. A hypothesis can always be saved from refutation by making changes in one of the accompanying hypotheses.

Exercise 10.2

2. Hypothesis: Two guys are perpetrating a Bigfoot hoax. Test implication: If the two guys are perpetrating a hoax, then monitoring their behaviour day and night should yield evidence of hoaxing activity.
6. Hypothesis: Creatine dramatically increases the performance of weight trainers. Test implication: If creatine increases performance, then giving creatine to weight trainers in a controlled way (in a double-blind controlled trial) should increase various measures of performance in the trainers compared to weight trainers who get a placebo (inactive substance).

Exercise 10.3

3. Theory: Local climate changes are melting glaciers.
   Competing theory: Heat from volcanic activity around the planet is melting the glaciers.

Both theories are about equal in terms of testability, fruitfulness, and scope. The volcanic theory, however, is neither simple nor conservative. It's not simple because it assumes an unknown process. It's not conservative because it is not consistent with what is known about the effects of heat from volcanoes.

7. Theory: Poverty fosters crime.
   Competing theory: People commit crimes because they lack basic human values.
   Both theories are about equal in terms of testability, fruitfulness, scope, and simplicity. The values theory, though, is not conservative. It conflicts with what we know about those who commit crimes. Some crimes are indeed committed by people who lack basic human values (for example, sociopaths), but that is not true for *most* crime.

Exercise 10.4

2. Test implication: If the creation of bike lanes is responsible for the drop in accidents involving bikes, then creation of additional bike lanes on other large streets should result in a further (perhaps smaller) reduction in accidents involving bikes. The test would likely confirm the theory.
6. Test implication: If eating foods high in fat contributes more to being overweight than eating foods high in carbohydrates, then over time people should gain more weight when they are eating X number of grams of fat per day than when they are eating the same number of grams of carbohydrates per day.

Exercise 10.7

4. The appeal to ignorance.
6. Something is logically possible if it does not violate a principle of logic; something is logically impossible if it violates a principle of logic.

Exercise 10.8

2. Theory 1: The aging of the building materials in the house caused creaking.
   Theory 2: The wind blowing against the house caused the creaking.
   Theory 3: The ghost of the former owner caused the creaking.
7. Theory 1: A coincidental matching between the dream and real events made the dream seem prophetic.
   Theory 2: Wayne had the same dream every night because he was concerned about his uncle, so there was a good chance that the dream would match something in reality.
   Theory 3: The dream was a genuine prophetic dream.

Exercise 10.9

3. Alternative theory: As a prank, the little girls cut drawings of fairies out of a book, posed them in the garden, and took photos of themselves with the

cut-outs. Then they claimed that the photos showed actual fairies. Both theories seem to be about equal in testability and fruitfulness. The prank theory has more scope because faked photos can explain many other phenomena, including many different kinds of paranormal hoaxes. The fairy theory is neither simple nor conservative. Fairies are unknown to science, and claims about their existence conflict with many things that we know.

CHAPTER 11

Exercise 11.1

1. The ability to carefully reason about causation.
8. The burden of proof is always on the prosecution, which means that the defendant is considered innocent until proven guilty.
14. Argument from consequences, argument from rights and duties, argument from character.

Exercise 11.2

1. If taken literally, reject it. The idea that eating apples literally prevents the need to see a doctor conflicts with a great deal of background knowledge.
3. Proportion belief to the evidence. The expert cited likely has relevant expertise. But the study of the effects of Wi-Fi radiation is relatively new, and new technologies may change existing estimates of risk. High plausibility.
9. Accept it. Although we might be able to think of exceptions, the idea that killing innocent people is unethical is widely agreed upon and is an essential rule for a stable society.

Exercise 11.3

2. Appeal to tradition
5. Ad hominem
7. Subjectivist fallacy
8. False dilemma; appeal to emotion

Exercise 11.4

1. Anyone who smokes heavily is sure to get cancer. And you're a heavy smoker!
   All smokers are people who will get cancer.
   All people who are identical with you are smokers.
   Therefore, all people who are identical with you will get cancer. [hidden conclusion]
   All *M* are *P*.
   All *S* are *M*.
   Therefore, all *S* are *P*.

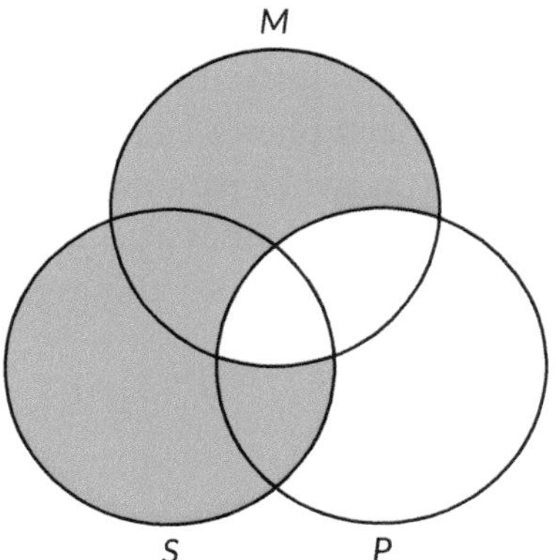

Valid.

The first premise is not acceptable. Many people who smoke get cancer, but not all of them do.

7. Some people who lie have good reasons. Some people who have good reasons are actually saints. So some people who lie are saints.
   Some people who lie are people who have good reasons (to lie).
   Some people who have good reasons (to lie) are saints.
   Some people who lie are saints.
   Some *S* are *M*.
   Some *M* are *P*.
   Some *S* are *P*.

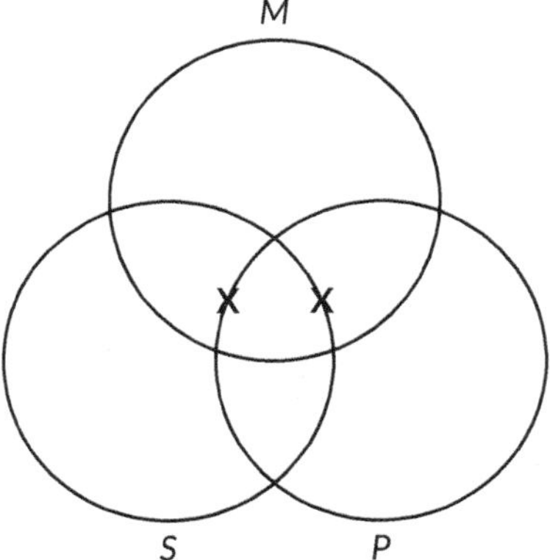

Invalid.

Glossary

abduction (abductive reasoning) The form of reasoning used when putting forward a hypothesis as to what would explain a particular phenomenon or set of circumstances.

ad hoc hypothesis A hypothesis, or theory, that cannot be verified independently of the phenomenon it is supposed to explain. Ad hoc hypotheses always make a theory less simple—and therefore less credible.

ad hominem *See* **appeal to the person.**

affirming the antecedent *See* ***modus ponens***.

affirming the consequent An invalid argument form:

> If *p*, then *q*.
> *q*.
> Therefore, *p*.

analogical induction *See* **argument by analogy**.

analogy A comparison of two or more things alike in specific respects.

antecedent The first part of a conditional statement (If *p*, then *q*), the component that begins with the word *if*. *See* **conditional statement**.

appeal to authority The fallacy of relying on the opinion of someone deemed to be an expert who in fact is *not* an expert.

appeal to common practice The fallacy of accepting or rejecting a claim solely on the basis of what groups of people generally do or how they behave (when the action or behaviour is irrelevant to the truth of the claim).

appeal to emotion The fallacy of using emotions in place of relevant reasons as premises in an argument.

appeal to ignorance The fallacy of arguing that a lack of evidence proves something. In one type of this fallacy, the problem arises from thinking that a claim must be true because it hasn't been shown to be false. In another type, the breakdown in logic comes when you argue that a claim must be false because it hasn't been proven to be true.

appeal to popularity (or **to the masses**) The fallacy of arguing that a claim must be true merely because a substantial number of people believe it.

appeal to the person (or **ad hominem**) The fallacy of rejecting a claim by criticizing the person who makes it rather than the claim itself. *Ad hominem* means "to the man."

appeal to tradition The fallacy of arguing that a claim must be true just because it's part of a tradition.

argument A group of statements in which some of them (the premises) are intended to support another of them (the conclusion).

argument by analogy (analogical induction) An argument that makes use of analogy by reasoning that because two or more things are similar in several respects, they must be similar in some further respect.

argument from character An ethical argument that proceeds from the assumption that what really matters ethically is character rather than the nature or outcome of particular actions.

argument from consequences An ethical argument that takes as a starting point the idea that our most fundamental ethical obligation is to produce certain kinds of outcomes.

arguments from rights and duties An ethical argument that begins with the notion that there are certain kinds of actions that we must always do or always avoid doing.

availability error The cognitive bias that makes people tend to rely on evidence not because it is trustworthy but because it is memorable or striking.

background information The large collection of very well-supported beliefs that we all rely on to inform our actions and choices. It consists of basic facts about everyday things, beliefs based on very good evidence (including our own personal observations and excellent authority), and justified claims that we would regard as "common sense" or "common knowledge."

begging the question The fallacy of attempting to establish the conclusion of an argument by using that conclusion as a premise. Also called arguing in a circle.

biased sample A sample that does not properly represent the target group. *See also* **representative sample**.

burden of proof The weight of evidence or argument required by one side in a debate or disagreement.

categorical logic A form of logic whose focus is categorical statements, which make assertions about categories, or classes, of things.

categorical statement A statement or claim that makes a simple assertion about categories, or classes, of things.

categorical syllogism A deductive argument consisting of three categorical statements.

causal argument An inductive argument whose conclusion contains a causal claim.

causal claim A statement about the causes of things.

claim A statement; an assertion that something is or is not the case.

cogent argument A strong inductive argument with all true premises.

composition The fallacy of arguing that what is true of the parts must be true of the whole. The error is to think that the characteristics of the parts are somehow transferred to the whole, something that is not always the case.

compound statement A statement composed of at least two constituent, or simple, statements.

conclusion In an argument, the statement that the premises are intended to support.

conditional statement An "if–then" statement; it consists of the antecedent (the part introduced by the word *if*) and the consequent (the part introduced by the word *then*).

confidence level In statistical theory, the probability that the sample will accurately represent the target group within the margin of error.

confirmation bias The psychological tendency to seek out and remember information that confirms what we already believe.

conjunct One of two simple statements joined by a connective to form a compound statement.

conjunction Two simple statements joined by a connective to form a compound statement.

consequent The part of a conditional statement (If *p*, then *q*) introduced by the word *then*.

conservatism A criterion of adequacy for judging the worth of theories. A conservative theory is one that fits with our established beliefs.

copula One of four components of a standard-form categorical statement; a linking verb—either *are* or *are not*—that joins the subject term and the predicate term.

criteria of adequacy The standards used to judge the worth of explanatory theories. They include *testability*, *fruitfulness*, *scope*, *simplicity*, and *conservatism*.

critical thinking The systematic evaluation or formulation of beliefs or statements by rational standards.

deductive argument An argument intended to provide logically conclusive support for its conclusion.

denying the antecedent An invalid argument form:

> If *p*, then *q*.
> Not *p*.
> Therefore, not *q*.

denying the consequent *See* ***modus tollens***.

dependent premise A premise that depends on at least one other premise to provide joint support to a conclusion. If a dependent premise is removed, the support that its linked dependent premises supply to the conclusion is undermined or completely cancelled out.

disjunct A simple statement that is a component of a disjunction.

disjunction A compound statement of the form "Either *p* or *q*." A disjunction is true even if only one disjunct is true and false only if both disjuncts are false.

disjunctive syllogism A valid argument form:

> Either *p* or *q*.
> Not *p*.
> Therefore, *q*.

In the second premise of a syllogism, either disjunct (either of the parts separated by "or") can be denied.

division The fallacy of arguing that what is true of the whole must be true of the parts. The error is thinking that characteristics of the whole must transfer to the parts or that traits of the group must be the same as traits of individuals in the group.

enumerative induction An inductive argument pattern in which we reason from premises about individual members of a group to conclusions about the group as a whole.

equivocation The fallacy of using a word in two different senses in an argument.

ethics The critical, structured examination of how we ought to behave when our behaviour affects others.

expert Someone who is more knowledgeable in a particular subject area or field than most others are.

explanation A statement or statements intended to tell why or how something is the case.

fallacy An argument form that is both common and defective; a recurring mistake in reasoning.

false dilemma The fallacy of asserting that there are only two alternatives to consider when there are actually more than two.

faulty analogy A defective argument by analogy.

fruitfulness A criterion of adequacy for judging the worth of theories. A fruitful theory yields new insights.

gambler's fallacy The error of thinking that previous events can affect the probabilities in the random event at hand.

genetic fallacy The fallacy of arguing that a claim is true or false solely because of its origin.

hasty generalization The fallacy of drawing a conclusion about a target group on the basis of a sample that is too small.

hypothetical syllogism A valid argument made up of three hypothetical, or conditional, statements:

> If *p*, then *q*.
> If *q*, then *r*.
> Therefore, if *p*, then *r*.

independent premise A premise that does not depend on other premises to provide support to a conclusion. If an independent premise is removed, the support that other premises supply to the conclusion is not affected.

indicator words Words that are frequently found in arguments and signal that a premise or conclusion is present.

inductive argument An argument in which the premises are intended to provide probable, not conclusive, support for its conclusion.

inference The process of reasoning from a premise or premises to a conclusion based on those premises.

inference to the best explanation A form of inductive reasoning in which we reason from premises about a state of affairs to an explanation for that state of affairs:

Phenomenon Q.
E provides the best explanation for Q.
Therefore, it is probable that E is true.

invalid argument A deductive argument that fails to provide conclusive support for its conclusion.

logic The study of good reasoning, or inference, and the rules that govern it.

margin of error The variation between the values derived from a sample and the true values of the whole target group.

mixed argument An argument that includes both inductive and deductive elements.

***modus ponens* (affirming the antecedent)** A valid argument form:

If *p*, then *q*.
p.
Therefore, *q*.

***modus tollens* (denying the consequent)** A valid argument form:

If *p*, then *q*.
Not *q*.
Therefore, not *p*.

necessary condition A condition for the occurrence of an event without which the event cannot occur.

peer pressure Group pressure to accept or reject a claim solely on the basis of what one's peers think or do.

philosophical skepticism The view that we know much less than we think we do or that we know nothing at all.

philosophical skeptics Those who embrace philosophical skepticism.

***post hoc, ergo propter hoc* ("after that, therefore because of that")** The fallacy of reasoning that just because B followed A, A must have caused B.

predicate term The second class, or group, named in a standard-form categorical statement.

premise In an argument, a statement or reason given in support of the conclusion.

principle of charity The interpretive principle that says that whenever we find someone's meaning unclear, we should attempt to interpret it in a such a way as to make them make sense, rather than interpreting them as saying something silly or confused.

problem of induction The philosophical question as to whether the process of induction can ever lead to real knowledge.

property in question *See* **relevant property.**

propositional logic The branch of deductive reasoning that deals with the logical relationships among statements.

quality A characteristic of a categorical statement, determined by whether the statement affirms or denies that a class is entirely or partly included in another class. A categorical statement that affirms is said to be affirmative in quality; one that denies is said to be negative in quality.

quantifier In categorical statements, a word used to indicate the number of things with specified characteristics. The acceptable quantifiers are *all*, *no*, or *some*. The quantifiers *all* and *no* in front of a categorical statement tell us that it's *universal*—it applies to every member of a class. The quantifier *some* at the beginning of a categorical statement says that the statement is *particular*—it applies to some but not all members of a class.

quantity In categorical statements, the attribute of number, specified by the words *all*, *no*, or *some*.

random sample A sample that is selected randomly from a target group in such a way as to ensure that the sample is representative. In a simple random selection, every member of the target group has an equal chance of being selected for the sample.

red herring The fallacy of deliberately raising an irrelevant issue during an argument. The basic pattern is to put forth a claim and then couple it with additional claims that may seem to support it but that, in fact, are mere distractions.

relevant property (property in question) In enumerative induction, a property, or characteristic, that is of interest in the target group.

representative sample In enumerative induction, a sample that resembles the target group in all relevant ways. *See also* **biased sample.**

sample (sample member) In enumerative induction, the observed members of the target group.

scientific instrumentalism The school of thought that says the goal of science is to put forward theories that are useful in helping us to predict and control the world around us.

scientific realism The school of thought that says the goal of science is to bring our understanding of the natural world closer and closer to the truth.

scope A criterion of adequacy for judging the worth of theories. A theory with scope is one that explains or predicts phenomena other than that which it was introduced to explain.

simple statement A statement that doesn't contain any other statements as constituents.

simplicity A criterion of adequacy for judging the worth of theories. A simple theory is one that makes as few assumptions as possible.

singular statements In categorical logic, statements that assert something about a single person or thing, including objects, places, and times.

slippery slope The fallacy of arguing, without good reasons, that taking a particular step will inevitably lead to further, undesirable steps.

social relativism The view that truth is relative to societies.

sound argument A deductively valid argument that has true premises.

standard-form categorical statement In categorical logic, a categorical statement that takes one of these four forms:

1. All *S* are *P*. (All bears are omnivores.)
2. No *S* are *P*. (No bears are omnivores.)
3. Some *S* are *P*. (Some bears are omnivores.)
4. Some *S* are not *P*. (Some bears are not omnivores.)

statement (claim) An assertion that something is or is not the case.

stereotyping Drawing conclusions about people based merely on their membership in some group.

straw man The fallacy of distorting, weakening, or oversimplifying someone's position so it can be more easily attacked or refuted.

strong argument An inductive argument that succeeds in providing probable—but not conclusive—support for its conclusion.

subject term The first class, or group, named in a standard-form categorical statement.

subjective relativism The idea that truth depends on what someone believes.

subjectivist fallacy Accepting the notion of subjective relativism or using it to try to support a claim.

sufficient condition A condition for the occurrence of an event that guarantees that the event occurs.

syllogism A deductive argument made up of three statements—two premises and a conclusion. *See* ***modus ponens*** and ***modus tollens***.

symbolic logic Modern deductive logic that uses symbolic language to do its work.

target group (target population) In enumerative induction, the whole collection of individuals under study.

testability A criterion of adequacy for judging the worth of theories. A testable theory is one in which there is some way to determine whether the theory is true or false—that is, it predicts something other than what it was introduced to explain.

TEST formula A four-step procedure for evaluating the worth of a theory:

Step 1. State the **T**heory and check for consistency.
Step 2. Assess the **E**vidence for the theory.
Step 3. **S**crutinize alternative theories.
Step 4. **T**est the theories with the criteria of adequacy.

theoretical explanation A theory, or hypothesis, that tries to explain why something is the way it is, why something is the case, or why something happened.

truth-preserving A characteristic of a valid deductive argument in which the logical structure guarantees the truth of the conclusion if the premises are true.

truth table A table that specifies the truth values for claim variables and combinations of claim variables in symbolized statements or arguments.

tu quoque **("you're another")** A type of ad hominem fallacy that argues that a claim must be true (or false) just because the claimant is hypocritical.

valid argument A deductive argument that succeeds in providing conclusive support for its conclusion.

variables In modern logic, the symbols, or letters, used to express a statement.

Venn diagrams Diagrams consisting of overlapping circles that graphically represent the relationships between subject and predicate terms in categorical statements.

weak argument An inductive argument that fails to provide strong support for its conclusion.

world view A philosophy of life; a set of fundamental ideas that helps us to make sense of a wide range of important issues in life. A world view defines for us what exists, what should be, and what we can know.

Index